The Complete Guide to
Your
Emotions
& Your
# Health

The Complete Guide to
Your
Emotions
& Your
Health

New Dimensions in Mind/Body Healing

by Emrika Padus
and the Editors of *Prevention*® Magazine

Rodale Press, Emmaus, Pennsylvania

Printed in the United States of America on recycled paper
containing a high percentage of de-inked fiber.

Book design by Philadelphia Design Company

Library of Congress Cataloging in Publication Data

Padus, Emrika.
    The complete guide to your emotions and your health.

    On t.p. the circled registered trade mark symbol "R" is
superscript following "Prevention" in the statement of
responsibility.
    Includes index.
    1. Health.   2. Holistic medicine.   3. Mind and body.
4. Nutrition.   I. Prevention.   II. Title.
RA776.5.P225   1986   613   85-19360
ISBN 0-87857-589-8   hardcover

            8   10   9   hardcover

List of Contributors

Book Editors: Emrika Padus, William Gottlieb,
    Mark Bricklin

Contributions by: Joe Adcock, Stefan Bechtel,
    Dominick Bosco, Susan Brandell, Mark Bricklin,
    Martha Capwell, Peggy Jo Donahue, Bill Ehrhart,
    Sharon Faelten, Bruce Fellman, John Feltman,
    Denise Foley, William Gottlieb, Marcia Holman,
    Allan Klein, Jody Kolodzey, Michael Lafavore,
    Gale Maleskey, Eileen Mazer, Penny Mesic, Emrika
    Padus, Kerry Pechter, Cathy Perlmutter, Heidi
    Rodale, Linda Shaw, Porter Shimer, Erica Stein,
    Debora Tkac, Jonathan Uhlaner, Lewis Vaughn,
    Tom Voss, Ed Weiner, John Yates, Susan Zarrow

Copy Editor: Peg Chagnon

Copy Coordinator: Joann Williams

Research Coordinator: Carole Rapp

Associate Research Chief, Prevention Health Books:
    Susan Nastasee

Assistant Research Chief, Prevention Health Books:
    Holly Clemson

Research Associates: Pam Boyer, Jan Eickmeier, Amy
    Jordan, Jill Polk, Martin Wood

Office Personnel: Susan Lagler, Roberta Mulliner

NOTICE

The information and ideas in this book are meant to supplement the care and guidance of your physician, not to replace it. The editor cautions you not to attempt diagnosis or embark upon self-treatment of serious illness without competent professional assistance. An increasing number of physicians are ready to cooperate with clients who want to improve their diet and lifestyle; if you are under professional care or taking medication, we suggest discussing this possibility with your doctor.

Contents

**Part I:
Super Nutrition
for the Mind**

How vitamin and mineral deficiencies (even
when slight) can disrupt brain function and create such common problems as fatigue, insomnia, irritability, anxiety, premenstrual tension,
and depression . . . analyzing your personal
nutritional/emotional balance . . . suggested
"brain foods" for optimal emotional health.

How to avoid "nutritional burnout" . . . supplements to boost your stress resistance . . . an
unsuspected nutritional link to Type A behavior.

**Part II:
Building Emotional
Hardiness**

"hardy" attitudes and resistance to stress-related diseases . . . rate the major stressors in your life . . . test your hardiness quotient . . . three techniques to help you become happier, healthier, and hardier . . . how to accept change by learning the art of letting go.

The importance of a support community and social bonding in maintaining emotional and physical health . . . why all diseases are "social diseases" . . . how to effectively guard against the ill effects of bachelorhood . . . which friends are best for your health . . . the importance of intimacy.

Running, swimming, and the endorphin phenomenon . . . how aerobic exercise can relieve tension, boost self-esteem, heighten our sense of well-being, and even reduce depression better than psychotherapy . . . how to get started in a running program . . . seven techniques to motivate and maximize the mind/body rewards of an aerobics program . . . the effect of music on the runner's psyche.

**Part III:
Tuning In to Optimism**

Test your positive thinking . . . how to shed negative thinking through a simple technique called "cognitive therapy" . . . learn to identify automatic self-critical thoughts . . . reprogram your mind with effective affirmations.

Learning to love yourself first, then opening yourself to loving others . . . the art of giving unconditional love.

**Part IV:
Shedding Negative
Emotions**

Self-help for phobics . . . how to ease out of a
panic attack . . . developing a positive and challenging attitude toward fear . . . learning how
to "float" instead of fight your way through
tension.

Separating the lonely from those who live alone
. . . finding peace and happiness through solitude . . . learning to look at time alone as an
opportunity for self-discovery . . . the importance of maintaining a pattern of caring . . .
how pets and people can help relieve loneliness.

A course of treatment that includes relaxation,
desensitization, and practice, practice, practice
. . . mastering the art of making contact with
others . . . visualizing yourself as the calm,
outgoing person you can become.

Recognizing that boredom is a universal experience . . . why eating is a common response to
boredom . . . the greatest antidote to boredom.

**Part V:
Minimizing Key
Stressors**

Why worrying over life's uncertainties produces
a particularly devastating kind of stress response
. . . when stress leads to depression . . . effective techniques for coping with the unknown
. . . how to take optimal control—knowing
when to act on worries and when to let go of them.

The five qualities of a happy family . . . how
grandchildren help bridge the generation gap
. . . building a mutual support group within
the family . . . learning the art of giving and
receiving praise through a technique called
"strength bombardment" . . . opening the
lines of communication.

Coping with the anger, depression, and anxiety
that accompanies financial concerns . . . how
to resolve family conflicts that arise over money
. . . taking control of spending . . . tips for
getting the most from your dollar.

Rate your job stress . . . some surprising facts
about high-stress jobs (the middle-manager may
be worse off than the chairman of the board)
. . . the mixed blessing of VDTs . . . the
deadly impact of monotonous tasks . . . how
to get the privacy you need from the space you
don't have . . . beating the Sunday night blues
. . . easing friction in office relationships.

Finding opportunities in unemployment . . .
guarding against the stress-related illnesses that
can follow loss of a job . . . evaluating your
skills and interests . . . setting your sights on
a better job . . . psychological help for the survivors of a major layoff.

Rate your lifestyle on 15 potential sources of
hassle . . . how to gear yourself toward hassle-
free living.

A conversation with Dennis Jaffe, Ph.D., author of *Healing from Within; From Burnout to Balance; Body, Mind and Health* . . . how we create our own stress . . . identifying Type A and other self-destructive behaviors . . . what's behind the phenomenon known as the "self-fulfilling prophesy" . . . learning how to take control of our happiness and health.

How the "relaxation response" counters the effects of the body's stress response . . . the mind/body benefits of a regular relaxation program . . . some proven benefits of Transcendental Meditation . . . a practical guide to the best techniques for deep relaxation: Dr. Herbert Benson's Meditation-Relaxation technique, Progressive Relaxation, Autogenic Training, Deep Breathing, and Visualization or Guided Imagery . . . fine-tuning your relaxation with biofeedback.

Are you burning out? . . . a three-part burnout recovery program . . . getting in touch with your stress reactions . . . taking a good, hard look inside . . . a visualization exercise to help you discharge tension and explore alternative solutions for dealing with stress . . . determining your optimal stress level . . . assessing your personal values and goals as a key element in stress mastery . . . time-saving tips from a time-management consultant . . . how to use stress to achieve peak performance.

**Part VI:
Healthful Living
in a Stressful World**

members of the clergy, friends, health educators, lifestyle counselors, and social workers have to offer . . . where to get a second opinion.

Part VIII:
Taking the Reins

What an alcoholism and drug addiction counsel-
or can tell us about workaholism, perfectionism,
procrastination, sugar, coffee, and cigarette addictions, even addictions to unhealthy relationships
. . . why eliminating the addictive element (be
it sugar, coffee, or cigarettes) is but a prerequisite
to the actual treatment . . . characterizing the
addiction-prone personality . . . why overcoming any compulsion involves a process of self-
discovery . . . how to relax and get in touch
with our inner feelings . . . a technique to ease
withdrawal pains.

How to overcome inertia and get started on a
self-improvement program . . . five rules to
maintain your motivation until you've achieved
your goals.

How to adjust your palate to desire less sugar—
even no sugar at all . . . 13 trade secrets from
medical people who deal with sugar addictions
every day.

Do you have what it takes to quit? . . . the four
types of smokers . . . why quitting "cold turkey" may be the least painful method . . . how
a stop-smoking clinic can help . . . what you
can do to keep from backsliding . . . how to
use a "slip" as a learning experience rather than
as justification for taking up the old habit again.

**Part IX:
Heightening
Self-Awareness**

**Part X:
Getting Better
at Everything You Do**

imagery to help you achieve any skill . . . how
to overcome the fear of difficulty and failure
. . . relaxation techniques and tape recordings
that enhance learning potential . . . strategies
for remembering.

Three techniques—Creative daydreaming, EPS
(Effective Problem Solving), and Focusing—to
give you the leverage you need to solve troublesome problems and make sound decisions . . .
a how-to guide.

How to develop effective communication skills
. . . learning to be a good listener . . . why
it's so important to "keep your head" while
"speaking your mind" . . . interpreting the
subtle meaning in body language . . . what
your clothes and sleeping patterns communicate.

Banishing negative thought patterns that stand
in the way of a slimmer you . . . identifying
the underlying purpose of your overeating . . .
why psychologists stress the importance of building self-esteem and learning to love yourself
before starting any weight loss program . . .
psychological "tricks" to keep you motivated.

Tuning out the demanding, competitive, critical
self and turning on our "automatic pilot" . . .
how deep relaxation sets us up for high performance . . . mental training techniques . . .
an "Inner Tennis" workshop with Tim Gallwey.

**Part XI:
Using Emotions
to Heal**

. . . what's behind the medical miracle called "spontaneous remission" . . . why the best medical treatment is only as effective as the unconscious mind allows . . . how a combination of stress reduction, conflict resolution, and positive reinforcement (in the form of guided imagery and positive emotions such as hope and love) can stimulate the immune system and heal the body of cancer.

A conversation with Kenneth Pelletier, Ph.D., longevity expert and author of numerous books, including *Mind as Healer, Mind as Slayer* . . . defining the "will to live" . . . what emotions, attitudes, and behaviors feed this flame of inner strength . . . how we keep it burning bright or rekindle it once it begins to flicker and die.

Mind/body techniques that relieve pain without drugs or side effects . . . why the cause of chronic pain is often emotional . . . how to stimulate endorphins, the body's natural painkillers.

How a healthy love or marital relationship can improve a person's chances for recovery . . . when holding on to an illness could be a way of avoiding intimacy in a relationship . . . the importance of cooperation, understanding, and sharing feelings and emotions . . . how a relationship can grow stronger through convalescence.

The link between humor and longevity . . .
how joy and laughter can ease anxiety and depression, relieve pain, and block the panic that
can jeopardize the recovery of a heart attack victim . . . how former *Saturday Review* editor
Norman Cousins laughed himself back to health
from an "incurable" illness . . . distinguishing
healthy laughter.

What happens to our immune system when we
feel love toward another . . . how love acts as a
stress reliever.

Musical "prescriptions" for pain relief, stress
release—even for the treatment of high blood
pressure, migraine headaches, and ulcers . . .
how singing can tap and release hidden emotions.

Why people with pets have an edge on survival
. . . petting and the relaxation response . . .
the use of pet therapy in the treatment of depression and other emotional ills . . . weighing the
pros and cons of pet ownership . . . choosing
your pet pal.

Why good, honest, noncompetitive, let-down-
your-hair fun is essential for total health . . .
the value of play in lifting the spirits of cancer
patients . . . learning to balance love, work,
and play.

How poetry is helping the stressed to relax, the
stricken to recover, and the psychotic to relate

Tables

Boxes

Preface

Thoughts and emotions are the nutrition of the mind.

Just as we need a certain balance of vitamins, protein, and other nutrients to help our bodies reach maximum health and energy levels, each of us needs a specific balance of mental "nutrients" for a happy, tranquil, and creative mind.

Many people—perhaps most—don't appreciate this. They believe that happiness is a result of circumstances, of good luck. If the sun is shining, your stocks are up, and your weight down, you're happy. Flip-flop, you're miserable.

Only it isn't like that. Not at all.

The new holistic psychology says that how we feel is within our power to change. More, it's our *responsibility* to create the good, positive feelings that make life worth living. *And the new holistic psychology teaches us how to do this.*

The new mind mentors also tell us—and prove it through countless studies—that our mental attitude is a powerful influence on our physical health. As you will read in this book, our attitudes and emotions can either act as a mighty shield against illness of all kinds—from headaches to cancer—or, conversely, can bring on all manner of aches and pains—all the way up to the pain of a heart attack.

Our power to control and reshape our attitudes and emotions, then, serves a double purpose: happiness *and* health.

I personally believe we are now in a kind of breakthrough stage where we are learning that certain thoughts, feelings, and experiences are the vitamins A, B, and C of this happiness/health connection. There are, in fact, already specific prescriptions—"mental diets," if you will—of thought and behavior that can rejuvenate body/mind health. David Breslow, Ph.D., was recommending "ten hugs a day" as a kind of Recommended Daily Allowance a decade ago, when I first met him at the University of California at Los Angeles. At the time, I thought this was a bit on the fanciful side. Today I see it as a pioneering observation—equivalent, perhaps, to one made more than a hundred years ago, that a fresh lime eaten every day would prevent scurvy, the terrible vitamin C deficiency disease.

Now, perhaps you're thinking that a feeling of alienation or loneliness that can be prevented by hugging (and the warmth and love thereby engendered) is nothing compared to a physical disease like scurvy that destroys blood vessels and makes your teeth fall out. But don't be too sure.

If you follow nutrition, you may know that the Japanese have a very low rate of heart disease. When Japanese emigrate to Hawaii, however, and begin to eat more Western foods, higher in fat than their traditional diet of vegetables, rice, and fish, their heart attack rate goes up. And when Japanese have lived in California for a number of years, and accepted a totally Western diet, their heart attack rate goes higher still. But scientists looking at the data from these research projects have found that some Japanese living in California seem to be relatively immune to this new plague of heart problems. The difference between this group and the others, they discovered, probably has nothing to do with diet. It has nothing to do with serum cholesterol, smoking, or other risk factors for heart attack. The only difference they could identify was that the heart-healthy group was more deeply immersed in traditional Japanese culture. They were exposed to more of it as children, and clung to it in adulthood. Although they lived in mainland America, they were in touch with the spirit of "the old country." There, group welfare is emphasized, and individual competitiveness downplayed. The most "traditional" group of Japanese in America had an incidence of heart disease no higher than men in Japan, even though they'd given up the Japanese diet believed to be so protective.

There is more than one way, evidently, to get your daily requirement of "hugs."

Studies of Americans born here tell the same story. People who have close ties to others, who share time and thoughts and worries and laughter with kindred souls, reap profound health benefits. You don't have to be Japanese, in other words, to soothe heart and soul with the tonics of togetherness and tranquility.

This book will open your mind to enormous possibilities of better health and fuller enjoyment of life. They may be just a moment away.

Executive Editor, **Prevention**® Magazine

Acknowledgments

To the many physicians, psychologists, researchers, and other health professionals who contributed their knowledge and insight to the preparation of this book, I'd like to offer my sincere appreciation. In particular, my thanks go out to the following people who devoted a considerable amount of time meeting with me to discuss their views on mind/body health: Diane Cirincione, Patricia Garfield, Ph.D., Steven Halpern, Ph.D., Dennis Jaffe, Ph.D., Gerald Jampolsky, M.D., Emmett Miller, M.D., Naomi Remen, M.D., Bernard Siegel, M.D., Jacqueline Small, and George Solomon, M.D.

Special thanks, too, to Takla Gardey and Nan Crocker for their West Coast research assistance.

Also, to Tom, my very supportive "friend and lover," and to Charlotte, Emily, and Percy, three four-legged companions who filled my otherwise solitary workdays with much contentment and humor.

PART **I**

Super Nutrition for the Mind

1. The Well-Nourished Mind: A Stronghold against Fatigue, Irritability, Depression
2. Break Out of the Stress Cycle
3. Energy Balancing: Diet Strategies for Peak Performance and Sound Sleep
4. Mood-Altering Food Allergies
5. Boost Your Brainpower with Super Nutrition
6. Nutritional Help for Tough Emotional Problems

The Well-Nourished Mind: A Stronghold against Fatigue, Irritability, Depression

Devouring a good book is one way to nourish the mind. Taking in the opera is another. In fact, any intellectually stimulating experience or juicy morsel of prose is considered good food for thought. Sort of the equivalent to a bran muffin for the body.

But what would you say if we told you that *real* food—with all its vitamins and minerals—is just as important to healthy minds as to healthy bodies?

You might think that's pretty obvious. But it wasn't always so. Until recently, the scientific community believed that the brain was invulnerable to nutritional fluctuations. If nutrients circulating in the blood fell to dangerous levels, they insisted, the brain was the last organ to feel the effects. Short of a crisis, the brain was stable as a rock.

Today we know that's just not true. A number of new studies have demonstrated that nearly a dozen specific nutrients can alter the biochemistry and function of the brain. A deficiency of any one of them—even slight—can result in such common emotional problems as fatigue, irritability, and depression.

The brain is not immune to nutritional deficits.

Key among these brain nutrients are the B vitamins. The role of B vitamins is extensive and complex. They are coenzymes, or catalysts, in many of the body's most basic functions, including the process of oxidation (the body's burning of food to provide fuel). What this means is that they're needed to supply the brain with its energy source, glucose. Without enough glucose, the brain begins to perform poorly. Fatigue, depression, even hallucinations can

B vitamins help supply the brain with its energy source, glucose.

be symptoms of a low glucose level in the brain. B_6 and niacin are the B vitamins most involved in this process.

But the B vitamins play a second crucial role in our mental health. Several are known to be involved in the production of neurotransmitters, biochemicals that allow the brain cells to pass messages along their nerve pathways.

"B_6 is needed for the production of serotonin, a major neurotransmitter in many body functions," says Eric Braverman, M.D., of the Princeton Brain Bio Center in Skillman, New Jersey. "Folate helps produce catecholamines, which control many body functions. B_{12} is needed to produce acetylcholine, another neurotransmitter. In other words, all the chemicals produced by the brain cells depend on nutrients taken into the body, and in many cases, they seem to depend on certain B vitamins."

What happens when they're not there?

Without enough B vitamins—"a whole host of psychiatric symptoms."

"We know that people who aren't getting enough of these nutrients get a whole host of psychiatric and neurological symptoms, like depression, confusion, fatigue, and psychosis," says Charles Tkacz, M.D., medical director of the North Nassau Mental Health Center in Manhasset, New York.

"We take blood samples for special nutritional testing, then initially put most patients on therapeutic doses of many nutrients, including 40 to 50 milligrams a day of all the B vitamins," Dr. Tkacz says. When nutritional tests have been evaluated, the patient may be given more of a specific vitamin, mineral, or amino acid that's been found to be lacking in the body.

Many depressed patients are low in B_6.

"We've found that many depressed patients are low in B_6," Dr. Tkacz says. "A certain number are helped to recover from their depression by taking B_6 under medical supervision."

Other studies confirm this finding.

B_6 AND DEPRESSION

In Britain, for example, a team of psychiatrists found a specific correlation between depression and a deficiency of vitamin B_6 or pyridoxine, as it is also called. In a study of 154 malnourished psychiatric patients, they found that 9 of 16 patients who lacked adequate B_6 were also depressed. No other mental disease matched a single deficiency that well. Vitamin B_6 has already been used to treat depression

caused by use of oral contraceptives, the researchers noted
(British Journal of Psychiatry).

Another study, although on a somewhat smaller scale, indicates that extra doses of vitamin B_6 just may help fight another form of the blues known as premenstrual depression. The rationale here is that if extra vitamin B_6 is helpful in combating the depression that can be caused by using oral contraceptives, it may also be helpful in other sex-hormone-related depressions.

Extra B_6 may help fight the premenstrual blues.

Jeffrey A. Mattes, M.D., decided to test this theory when a woman colleague told him that pyridoxine helped her beat her premenstrual mood. Over the next eight months, the woman was given either a placebo or a B_6 supplement for 10 days prior to the onset of her period. Although she didn't know which she was taking in any given month, she reported reduced premenstrual depression and irritability on the months she took the supplements *(Human Nutrition: Applied Nutrition)*.

"This subject's premenstrual depression, which was rather typical of the premenstrual depression and irritability reported by many women, was significantly helped by pyridoxine," write the researchers.

"This small study cannot estimate the percentage of premenstrual depressions which would be helped by pyridoxine," says Dr. Mattes. "However, it does appear that for some women pyridoxine can be significantly helpful."

The depression associated with hormone swings of pregnancy and menopause may also be related to lowered levels of vitamin B_6.

The link between low B_6 and menopausal depression.

A study of 15 depressed pregnant women showed that those with the deepest depression had the lowest blood levels of vitamin B_6 *(Acta Obstetricia et Gynecologica Scandinavica)*.

Researchers discovered that postmenopausal women with depression have a disturbance in their tryptophan metabolism very similar to that found in patients hospitalized for depression *(British Medical Journal)*.

Why is B_6 effective in all these conditions?

Because of that all-important neurotransmitter, serotonin. Some scientists theorize that low levels of serotonin cause depression. But to have enough serotonin, you need enough tryptophan, the amino acid that is essential in its formation. And to have enough tryptophan, you need

Why B_6 works.

enough B_6, without which tryptophan can't be formed. B_6, tryptophan, serotonin: The chemical chain reaction that forms this neurotransmitter is more complex, but these links are crucial.

Estrogen can break them.

Estrogen, a female hormone, can block the activity of B_6, forcing it out of the body. And estrogen can speed up the metabolism of tryptophan, making less of it available to form serotonin. That doesn't happen every day. But if estrogen levels are high—if you're pregnant, taking the Pill, or about to have your period—then you can have a shortage of tryptophan, or B_6.

NIACIN: ANOTHER B FOR BAD MOODS

The B vitamin niacin is also necessary to ensure that tryptophan won't get side-tracked from serotonin production. When niacin is in short supply, tryptophan is converted to this vitamin to meet body needs. As a result, serotonin production suffers and so do your moods.

Symptoms of a niacin deficiency include anger and worry.

"The first noticeable symptoms of niacin deficiency are entirely psychological," Michael Lesser, M.D., a California psychiatrist, states in his book *Nutrition and Vitamin Therapy* (Grove Press). "Victims may feel fearful, apprehensive, suspicious, and worry excessively with a gloomy, downcast, angry, and depressed outlook. They may experience headaches, insomnia, loss of strength, and burning sensations all over the body. Their depression may range from 'blue Mondays' to the wish to end it all. . . ."

Of course, pyridoxine and niacin aren't the only two B vitamins involved in emotional health.

Derrick Lonsdale, M.D., a Cleveland physician with a special interest in biochemistry and nutrition, found that one of the first signs of a thiamine deficiency was changes in behavior—neurotic symptoms like depression, insomnia, chest pain, and chronic fatigue. All 20 of the patients he studied improved with additional thiamine.

Beriberi from junk food.

Apparently, those people were consuming large quantities of carbohydrates, often in the form of "junk food," without maintaining enough thiamine to metabolize or "burn" it. Dr. Lonsdale theorizes that the body experiences this kind of imbalance as a thiamine shortage, and shows nervous symptoms characteristic of beriberi, the classic thiamine deficiency disease. All 20 patients improved after thiamine supplementation *(American Journal of Clinical Nutrition)*.

Nowadays, too, more and more physicians are looking into folate (also called folic acid) deficiency as a cause of depression. A recent study at McGill University, Montreal, examined the folate levels of three different groups of patients: those who were depressed, those who were psychiatrically ill but not depressed, and those who were medically ill. Six of the patients were men, 42 were women, and their ages ranged from 20 to 91 years. All were hospitalized for one week and were put on standard, identical diets with no drugs or supplemental vitamins. Low folate levels were found in the depressed patients. In fact, the psychiatric patients had almost twice as much serum folate as the depressed patients. Not only did the low-folate patients show signs of depression, they also displayed reduced work productivity, lack of interest, psychic anxiety, and loss of sex drive *(Psychosomatics)*.

Low folate, no sex drive.

Would folate therapy help clear up depression?

A. Missagh Ghadirian, M.D., of the Royal Victoria Hospital, Montreal, was the head researcher in the study. "Based on my clinical observations, it seems that people whose depressions are purely due to folate deficiency do get better with folate therapy," Dr. Ghadirian says. "To make absolutely sure, we will have to wait for the results of the second phase of our study in which folate therapy is used."

Such positive findings for folate therapy may explain the remarkable case of a young woman with "baby blues," or postpartum depression. Her pregnancy and the delivery of her baby were uncomplicated. However, several weeks after delivery, she became progressively withdrawn and emotionally unstable.

Soon she became disoriented, panicky, and had hallucinations about large, ugly figures that intended harm to her and her new baby.

Hospitalized in two different psychiatric facilities for a period of 19 months, she received shock treatments and various tranquilizers. She also tried to commit suicide three times.

According to the physician who saw her as a result of her third suicide attempt, "She was an attractive but very distressed-appearing young woman who was extremely frightened, whining, and literally withdrawn into the corner of her hospital room." Three blood tests for folate levels were performed on her, one of which was reported as very low, and two of which were reported as "none detectable,"

Shock treatment and tranquilizers failed, but folate succeeded.

The doctor's report continues: "She was treated for anemia with 5 milligrams of folic acid twice a day . . . for ten days [a large therapeutic dose that should be taken only under a doctor's supervision]. On the seventh day of folic acid treatment, an improvement in the mental status was noted; by the tenth day a complete remission had occurred. The patient was discharged on 1 milligram of oral folic acid daily.

"She was followed for the next 2½ years without evidence of any psychiatric disturbance. She became an active student in nursing school and did very well academically" (*American Journal of Obstetrics and Gynecology*).

It's worth noting that folate supplementation has been used with some success in the treatment of mental fatigue and some forms of hypoglycemia.

VITAMIN B₁₂: MORE THAN AN ENERGIZER

A case history: psychosis from low levels of B₁₂.

Vitamin B_{12} has gotten quite a reputation as an energizer. But new evidence suggests that its stake in our mental health goes far beyond that. Take the following case study as an example.

According to her family, the patient had been in her usual state of good health when suddenly, for no apparent reason, she became extremely irritable and began to criticize and threaten them and throw objects around the house.

Naturally, her husband was alarmed and sought help from a doctor, who proceeded to prescribe antipsychotic drugs to calm the woman down. However, after taking the drugs for one day, she not only refused to take them again but also refused all food as well. Frightened at this turn of events, the family brought her to the local emergency room for help.

When she was first brought in, her doctors report, she was agitated and uncooperative, and didn't know where she was. Her mind wandered and she was experiencing visual illusions. The doctors immediately checked out her physical condition and tested her blood for abnormalities. Nothing seriously wrong showed up—except for a very low vitamin B_{12} level.

Replacement therapy was started right away along with an antipsychotic drug. But after only one week, the woman's mental state improved so dramatically that the drug was discontinued. Nine months after the treatment, the patient had had no return of her bizarre symptoms and only her monthly B_{12} replacement shots reminded her of the close brush she had with insanity.

"A wide range of psychiatric symptoms has been associated with pernicious anemia [a disorder that results in a B_{12} deficiency]," say the doctors who treated this patient. But it turned out that the woman didn't even have pernicious anemia.

In spite of their efforts, the doctors never did find out why their patient had a low B_{12} level. She didn't have any of the typical symptoms of a deficiency. And her blood cells appeared normal. If it hadn't been for the test to determine the B_{12} level in her blood, the doctors may never have uncovered the problem.

Fact is, psychiatric problems may be the *first* symptom of vitamin B_{12} deficiency, even before an anemia shows up. That's all the more reason for extra-careful screening of psychiatric patients, say the doctors who treated the woman. "We recommend consideration of B_{12} deficiency and serum [blood] B_{12} determinations in all patients with [severe] psychiatric symptoms" *(American Journal of Psychiatry)*.

Psychiatric problems—possibly the first symptom of B deficiency.

A RARE CASE OF BIOTIN DEFICIENCY

In another case, a doctor inadvertently created a problem of severe depression in one of his patients. The man, who was only 34 years old, had had complications from an ulcer and was placed on total intravenous (I.V.) feedings while his insides healed. These I.V. feedings contained every nutrient needed by the human body for survival—except biotin, a B vitamin.

"Because biotin is so plentiful in foods and produced by intestinal bacteria," explains James L. Levenson, M.D., of the Medical College of Virginia in Richmond, "it has been thought that spontaneous biotin deficiency occurs

(continued on page 10)

BOX 1: ANALYZING YOUR NUTRITIONAL/
EMOTIONAL BALANCE

Putting together a personal nutrition plan for optimal emotional health is a delicate balancing act. One way to start is by taking stock of your nutritional and emotional status—paying particular attention to habits and situations that can drain you of essential nutrients and becoming sensitive to those emotional symptoms that may be caused or aggravated by resulting deficiencies.

Here, then, is a two-part check list to help you determine where you may be coming up short.

Part 1

If you are:	You may have increased needs for:
Under emotional stress	B vitamins, C, calcium
Physically active	B vitamins, C, E, iron
On a reducing diet	All nutrients, depending on the diet
Exposed to pollution	Vitamins A, C, E, calcium, iron, zinc
Taking diuretics	Folate, magnesium, potassium, zinc, phosphorus
Taking oral contraceptives	Thiamine, riboflavin, B_6, folate, B_{12}, C, zinc
Pregnant	B vitamins (especially folate, B_6), calcium, iron
Breast feeding	Calcium
A coffee drinker	Thiamine, C, all minerals
An alcohol drinker	Thiamine, B_{12}, C, copper, calcium, zinc, potassium, magnesium
A vegetarian	Riboflavin, vitamin B_{12}, folate, iron
A smoker	Vitamins B_{12}, B_6, C, E, calcium
Recovering from illness or injury	Vitamin A, thiamine, pantothenate, folate, C, E, iron, zinc, calcium

Part 2

If you suffer from:	You may benefit from a higher intake of:
Fatigue	Thiamine, riboflavin, B_6, B_{12}, folate, pantothenate, potassium, magnesium, iron
Irritability, nervousness	Thiamine, riboflavin, B_6, B_{12}, folate, pantothenate, potassium, magnesium, iron
Insomnia	Thiamine, riboflavin, B_6, B_{12}, folate, pantothenate, potassium, magnesium, iron
Lack of concentration	Folate, B_{12}, iron
Forgetfulness	Choline (lecithin), thiamine, iron
Depression	Thiamine, riboflavin, B_6, B_{12}, folate, pantothenate
Premenstrual tension	B_6, calcium, magnesium

BOX 2: GOING TO THE SOURCE

Thiamine *(RDA: 1–1.1 mg)*
Brewer's yeast/1 tbsp = 1.3 mg; sunflower seeds/¼ cup = 0.7 mg; kidney beans, dried/¼ cup = 0.2 mg.

Niacin *(RDA: 13–14 mg)*
Beef liver/3 oz. cooked = 14 mg; white meat chicken/3 oz. = 10.6 mg; peanuts, chopped/¼ cup = 6.2 mg.

Pyridoxine *(RDA: 2 mg)*
Salmon/1 steak (3 oz.) = 0.6 mg; beef or chicken liver/3 oz. = 0.5 mg; banana/1 medium = 0.9 mg.

Biotin *(RDA: has not been established)*
Chicken liver/3 oz. = 146 mcg; calves liver/3 oz. = 45 mcg; oats, rolled, uncooked/½ cup = 16 mcg; egg, hard cooked/1 large = 12 mcg.

Folate *(RDA: 400 mcg)*
Orange juice/1 cup = 136 mcg; brewer's yeast/1 tbsp. = 313 mcg; beef liver/3 oz. = 123 mcg.

Vitamin B$_{12}$ *(RDA: 3 mcg)*
Beef liver/3 oz. = 94 mcg; beef/3 oz. = 2.0 mcg; tuna drained/3 oz. = 1.8 mcg.

Pantothenate *(RDA: 4–7 mg)*
Beef liver/3 oz. = 4.8 mg; chicken liver/3 oz. = 4.6 mg; broccoli, raw/1 medium stalk = 1.0 mg; turkey, dark meat/3 oz. = 1.1 mg.

Choline *(RDA: has not been established)*
Pure soybean lecithin/1 tsp. = 1450 mg; beef liver/3 oz. = 578 mg; egg/1 large = 412 mg; fish/3 oz. = 100 mg.

Vitamin C *(RDA: 60 mg)*
Orange juice/1 cup = 124 mg; papaya/½ medium = 94 mg; grapefruit juice/1 cup = 94 mg.

Calcium *(RDA: 800 mg)*
Swiss cheese/2 oz. = 544 mg; yogurt/1 cup skim = 452 mg; sardines/3 oz. = 371 mg.

Magnesium *(RDA: 300–350 mg)*
Soybeans/¼ cup dried = 138 mg; almonds/¼ cup = 96 mg; tofu/3 oz. = 95 mg.

Iron *(RDA: 18 mg)*
Beef liver/3 oz. = 7.5 mg; blackstrap molasses/1 tbsp. = 3.2 mg; roast beef/3 oz. = 3.1 mg.

Suicide by I.V.

Biotin to the rescue.

Only 3 of 12 hospitals supplied biotin.

only if a biotin antagonist, like avidin [a substance found in raw egg whites], is present in the diet."

Dr. Levenson soon learned what would happen if biotin were not in the diet. After about a month on the I.V. feedings, the patient developed a depression that continued to worsen during the next few months. He began to withdraw socially, was irritable, had feelings of hopelessness, severe insomnia, and suicidal thoughts. When he threatened to jump off the roof of the hospital, a psychiatrist was brought in. He recommended suicide precautions be taken (including constant observation) and prescribed daily psychotherapy visits.

Dr. Levenson reviewed the patient's I.V. feeding formula and realized that no biotin had been given for five months. A deficiency was suspected and supplementation began immediately. After one week the patient was no longer suicidal. "He regained his ability to joke with the nurses," says Dr. Levenson. In fact, almost all of his symptoms disappeared over the first week of supplementation, and he has had no episodes of major depression since that time.

Although this was an isolated case, there may be a larger number of patients at risk for developing biotin deficiency than has been previously thought. "A survey of 12 hospitals in Westchester County, New York, revealed that only 3 institutions routinely added biotin to hyperalimentation solutions [I.V. feedings], and 6 never did so," says Dr. Levenson. Yet, "this is a problem that is easily treated and can be prevented. . . . If biotin deficiency is present and unrecognized for a significant period of time, the [deficiency] syndrome can become dangerously severe, as evidenced by our patient's suicidal ideation" *(Journal of Parenteral and Enteral Nutrition)*.

Minerals are essential to healthy moods, too. Case in point: iron.

HOW IRON FIGHTS FATIGUE

Iron-poor blood? Is it the energy drain the TV ads and magazine articles lead us to believe?

Michael Colgan, Ph.D., nutritional counselor and author of *Your Personal Vitamin Profile* (William Morrow & Co.), says quite a few of the tired people he sees have an iron deficiency. "They very often show what we call poor red blood status," he says. "That is, their hematocrit, hemoglobin, and red blood cell count may not be in the anemic range, but they are low.

"Unfortunately, what is considered a medically sufficient iron level is not sufficient for optimal health. Iron levels (in micrograms percent) may vary between 45 and 200 and still be considered medically sufficient, but we have found that almost anyone with an iron level under 100 is not in good shape."

Sufficient for health, no.

Iron helps to form hemoglobin, the substance in our red blood cells that carries oxygen from the lungs to the rest of the body. When you don't have enough hemoglobin, the oxygen supply to your tissues is reduced, causing apathy, tiredness, pallor, shortness of breath, and irritability— "that run-down feeling," as the TV commercials so often remind us.

How iron works to stop fatigue.

One study shows just how slowly you go compared to someone who's not iron deficient. Researchers at the University of California who studied the physical-work capacity of 75 women, some anemic, some not, found that the most severely anemic women could stay on a treadmill an average of eight minutes less than the nonanemic group. None of those severely anemic women could perform under the highest workload conditions, while all of the nonanemic group could. During a work test, the heartbeat of those with the severest anemia rose to an average of 176 per minute; for nonanemics, the heartbeat rose to just 130. Levels of lactate, a chemical in the muscles that is linked to fatigue, were almost twice as high in the most severely anemic group *(American Journal of Clinical Nutrition)*.

If you think you have an iron deficiency, see your doctor. Therapeutic doses to correct anemia or a pre-anemic state can be quite high initially, compared to a typical maintenance dose of 10 to 30 milligrams daily.

GROUCHY DISPOSITION?

"Ninety-nine percent of our body calcium is present in the bones and teeth," writes Dr. Michael Lesser in *Nutrition and Vitamin Therapy.* "It is the other 1 percent, present in the soft tissues and blood, which crucially affects the nerves. . . . Calcium shortage may result in a grouchy, irritable, tense disposition, with depression, impairment of

The crucial 1 percent.

memory, insomnia, and cramping in the calves."

Dr. Lesser admits that extreme calcium deficiencies are rare. But, he says, perhaps 30 percent of the adult U.S. population suffers from a deficiency severe enough to cause the above symptoms.

Moderate deficiencies can also trigger symptoms that resemble an anxiety attack, Dr. Lesser reports. And, to compound the problem, anxious people frequently hyperventilate—which has the peculiar physiological effect of lowering blood calcium levels even further.

A NATURAL SEDATIVE

Magnesium is also known for its calming effects and some doctors frequently recommend it for anxiety, insomnia, and depression.

In one study, depressed patients had "significantly lower" blood levels of magnesium than healthy people *(Journal of Nervous and Mental Disease)*.

In a second, depressed patients who took the drug lithium and improved had a rise in their magnesium levels, while the magnesium levels of those who took lithium and didn't improve stayed much the same *(Lancet)*.

A doctor who prescribes magnesium.

August F. Daro, M.D., a Chicago obstetrician and gynecologist, routinely gives all his depressed patients calcium and magnesium.

"Many depressed men and women are short on calcium and magnesium," he said in an interview. "I put them on a combination of 400 milligrams calcium and 200 milligrams magnesium a day. These minerals sedate the nervous system, and most of the depressed patients feel much better while taking them. Calcium and magnesium especially take care of premenstrual depression."

BOX 3: THE QUESTION OF SAFETY

Are vitamins and minerals safe to take without a doctor's supervision?

Probably.

Notice, we didn't say yes. That's because nothing is *perfectly* safe, not even water. Anything can be harmful if it's taken in large enough quantities. And that goes for nutritional supplements. Of course, millions of people take them every day, and the only "side effect" is better health. B$_6$ is a good example. Doctors have used it to counter premenstrual tension syndrome, to combat depression caused by the Pill, to control asthma, to cure infertility. But a few people looked at those results and decided that if a little is *good,* a lot must be *great*. For example, a woman who took B$_6$ at a thousand times the level of the Recommended Dietary Allowance (RDA) developed severe neurological problems. We want to emphasize that this type of case is very rare (like winning the lottery jackpot, but in reverse). But it shows us that it's always good to be cautious. So we urge you to consult a nutrition-oriented physician before you take supplements in amounts greater than the RDA. He or she can help guide you in developing a program suited to your personal needs.

2

Break Out of the
Stress Cycle

From depression to exhaustion to deeper depression.

The divorce was hard on Tim, but he was determined to pick up and go on with his life. Instead, though, he began feeling so emotionally and physically exhausted he found it hard to do his job, much less look after himself. Instead of slowly getting better, Tim was slowly getting worse and worse. Could the stress be catching up with him?

Nutrition-oriented doctors see this kind of case again and again. They call it the "stress cycle," and nutritional factors play a key role.

Emotional stress (anxiety, grief, anger, even irrational fears) can deplete the body of certain nutrients—many of them critical to healthy brain function. Unless they are replaced quickly—and adequately—coping mechanisms will break down, emotional problems will worsen, and the pattern is likely to repeat itself, dragging you in a downward spiral.

People under stress may be too busy or nervous to eat.

"Take someone who's just a little depressed or a little stressed because of things going on in his life. That person might find himself eating poorly. And that could lead to nutritional deficiencies that push him over the brink, into true depression or mental problems," says Charles Tkacz, M.D., medical director of the North Nassau Mental Health Center in Manhasset, New York, which specializes in nutritionally related psychiatric problems.

Beyond a depleted intake, there's also the problem of nutrient loss. Laraine C. Abbey, R.N., a nurse practitioner who holds a master's degree in clinical nutrition, explains:

"When you're under stress, hormones are released, and they in turn increase the speed of many functions and systems of the body. With this faster rate, a large amount of nutrients are pushed into the bloodstream and excreted. The body loses nutrients all the time, of course. But when you're pressured, you lose *more*."

If the stress drives you to drink—alcohol or coffee—or smoke, you can count on even greater losses. Alcohol, coffee, and smoking destroy B vitamins. And, to make matters worse, coffee acts as a diuretic, flushing the water-soluble vitamins—the Bs and C—and essential minerals out of your system.

The net result: nutritional burnout.

There's also the problem of nutrient loss.

NUTRITIONAL BURNOUT

"I've run into this kind of situation too many times to count," says Robert Picker, M.D., a Walnut Creek, California, psychiatrist. "The body's nutritional needs are increased during times of stress. What may normally be adequate suddenly becomes a deficiency. And that deficiency could begin a vicious circle of mental symptoms that the person just doesn't seem to be able to shake. In fact, as a psychiatrist, I am painfully aware that many of these people are in psychotherapy for long periods of time without ever realizing that the correction of a nutritional deficiency could have significantly helped or possibly cured their problem, or perhaps have prevented it in the first place."

Overall nutrition is essential, but doctors should take a special look at the B complex vitamins, especially B_6, B_{12}, thiamine, niacin, folate, and pantothenate. They've more than earned their reputation as the "antistress" nutrients.

The B vitamins have earned their reputation as "antistress" nutrients.

Pantothenate, for example, has helped both rats and humans adjust physically to stressful situations. In one study, an extra-rich diet of the vitamin helped rodents swim twice as long as those fed only an "adequate" amount. And in another study, men made to swim for eight minutes in 48° water had less of a drop in white blood cells and excreted less uric acid (both signs of lower stress) when they took pantothenate supplements than when they did not.

Vitamin C has also been labeled an antistress vitamin. And for good reason. "Stress is just one factor that steps up your vitamin C requirements," says Robert Haskell, M.D.,

Vitamin C helps battle the effects of stress.

of San Francisco. "If anything helps you battle the effects of stress, it's extra vitamin C."

How does vitamin C work to counter stress? Writing in the British medical journal *Lancet,* one physician suggested that vitamin C is necessary for the conversion of dopamine to norepinephrine or noradrenaline, an antistress hormone (also called a catecholamine). Scientists at the Wellcome Research Laboratories, in Research Triangle Park, North Carolina, also believe that C helps in the production of norepinephrine and adrenaline—another hormone critical to our overall response to stress.

C-supplemented persons exposed to stress excreted more adrenaline.

A study conducted in Stockholm, Sweden, seems to add credence to the vitamin C-catecholamine link. In it, researchers found that C-supplemented persons exposed to stress excreted higher levels of adrenaline, noradrenaline, and dopamine than nonsupplemented persons. The researchers, however, caution that there are two ways to interpret these findings. "These results would at first imply that persons on a high intake of ascorbate [vitamin C] react more to a given stress since the excretion rate of catecholamines is related to the degree of perceived stress," they explain. "It could, however, be argued that an increased excretion of adrenaline is of benefit . . . and that therefore a high intake of ascorbate would lead to a better-prepared individual" *(Human Nutrition: Clinical Nutrition).*

MAGNESIUM, STRESS, AND HEART DISEASE

Behind the cardiovascular vulnerability of a "Type A" lies a magnesium deficiency.

French researchers, studying the human stress response, have come up with another very interesting hypothesis. Somewhere between the hard-driving behavior and the heart disease vulnerability of a Type A, they say, lies a magnesium deficiency.

Magnesium levels in the urine rose in response to stress.

Several studies have already established a link between magnesium deficiency and an increase in heart disease. And a U.S. study demonstrated that excessive catecholamine release—which occurs during the stress response in some persons—accelerates magnesium depletion. Now, the French researchers have found that persons who exhibit the classic hard-driving behavior characterized as "Type A" release much higher levels of catecholamines—and excrete more magnesium—during stress than the more easy-going Type

Bs. That, say the researchers, may explain why Type A people are coronary prone.

In their study, involving 42 healthy young Type As and 37 Type Bs, exposure to a stress-provoking situation resulted in significantly higher urine levels of catecholamines and magnesium in the A group. At the same time, magnesium levels in the red blood cells dropped in more of the Type A persons; 80 percent of the A group experienced a decrease compared to just 44 percent of the B group.

While more studies are needed before any conclusions can be drawn from this, it does appear that *the way* we respond to stress can influence the rate at which nutrients—and especially magnesium—is depleted from the system.

The researchers theorize how this may happen: During stress, magnesium may be released from the cells into the bloodstream, they suggest. But in the presence of excessive catecholamine levels, magnesium is chased out of the bloodstream and into the urine, where it is excreted. This, then, may eventually lead to a magnesium deficiency which, in turn, can have a profound effect on our physical health.

Researchers speculate that magnesium may be chased out of the bloodstream.

Whatever the mechanism involved, other studies confirm the end result: Stress does deplete the body's magnesium levels.

And of all the stress the twentieth century has accustomed us to, what could be more common, or more irritating, than noise?

To test what effect prolonged noise stress might have on magnesium levels, German scientists at the federal health office in Berlin subjected five groups of rats to varying amounts of racket, up to levels that would drive any human buggy: Several groups had to listen to tape-recorded traffic noise during 12 night hours for 12 weeks! Meanwhile, in their food and drinking water, the rats were fed levels of magnesium that were deficient to varying degrees.

At the end of the experiment, measurements showed that for all groups, "noise stress leads to a decrease of the cellular Mg [magnesium] content and an increase of the Ca [calcium] content." And the longer and louder the noise, the greater the decrease in magnesium levels. One group, subjected to traffic noise alternated with semiquiet periods, showed a 4 percent decrease in cellular magnesium. But the luckless bunch that was forced to listen to continuous noise, without any break at all, registered magnesium losses of 14 percent *(Artery)*.

Continuous noise caused magnesium losses of 14 percent.

Similar results were found in human test subjects. After one working day with and one without loud traffic noise (85 decibels, or roughly the level of noise made by a kitchen garbage-disposal unit), the scientists found "statistically significant alterations" in cellular magnesium levels.

On the other hand, even small increases in dietary magnesium seem to protect against noise-induced stress. Two groups of rats, for example, were kept on identical diets and exposed to the same amount of noise. The only difference was in their drinking water: One group was given magnesium-free distilled water, and the other was given water containing about the same amount of magnesium that occurs in hard water. Measurements taken after the experiment demonstrated that "under a Mg-deficient diet an increase of the Mg content of the drinking water will reduce stress effects."

Catch 22: Low magnesium greatly *increased* the stressful effects of noise.

The researchers tied the experiment together with an intriguing observation. They had noticed that a magnesium-deficient diet *alone* could cause stress effects. And when magnesium deficiency was combined with noise, "the stress effects were amplified remarkably"; low magnesium greatly *increased* the stressful effects of noise.

In short, they concluded, there is a "feedback mechanism" at work, with noise stress lowering magnesium levels, and low magnesium levels in turn heightening the effects of stress, and so on. What it all boils down to, they noted, is that "the feedback interaction between noise stress and decrease of cellular Mg demonstrated may cause an increasing risk of cardiovascular diseases."

3

ENERGY BALANCING: DIET STRATEGIES FOR PEAK PERFORMANCE AND SOUND SLEEP

The fifties had their four basic food groups. But in the three decades since, the well-balanced diet has undergone radical redefinition. Talk of the "big four" is definitely out. Today's nutritional buzz words are fiber, complex carbohydrates, polyunsaturated fats, and amino acids, to name a few. We've also learned that there is more than one way to structure a diet based on your personal needs and the desired results. Sure, you can still get by on the old "well-balanced" diet. But if you want to feel really great—buoyant, productive, relaxed, and full of energy—you'll need more.

The latest nutritional breakthroughs and research on brain biochemistry suggest new diet strategies designed to keep you alert, active, and high on energy during the day while promoting sound, restful sleep at night. We call it "energy balancing." It's not just what we eat, but *when* we eat it that makes the difference.

PROTEIN IN THE MORNING

According to the new school of nutrition, the healthiest diet is one that concentrates on whole-grain breads, cereals, pastas, beans, and fresh fruits and vegetables—the so-called complex carbohydrates—because they are low in fat and sodium (salt) and high in important vitamins and minerals and fiber. The general consensus is that Americans get plenty of protein—in most cases, more than the necessary 30 to 40 grams a day. The problem is, we may not

The healthiest diet concentrates on complex carbohydrates.

be eating enough protein at the time when the brain needs it the most: in the morning.

There are two reasons for this. The first has to do with blood sugar. After a hard night's sleep, your blood sugar level drops. And, ironical as it may sound, it takes protein—not sugar—to build it up again.

Refined carbohydrates send your blood sugar—and energy levels—on a rollercoaster ride.

The problem with refined sugars and refined carbohydrates (such as you'll find in syrup-smothered pancakes or overly processed and presweetened cereals) is that they dump too much sugar into the system too quickly. You get an initial rush as blood sugar levels soar. But then your pancreas tries to make up for the sugar overdose by releasing extra insulin, a hormone that withdraws sugar from the blood. The end result: a sudden, stultifying *dip* in blood sugar.

But protein is a different story. Your body turns it into sugar at a slow, steady rate. You feel better longer because the pancreas isn't triggered to dampen the effect.

Blood sugar is glucose—the fuel your body runs on.

What happens when blood sugar is on a downswing? To put it simply, blood sugar is glucose—the fuel your body runs on—and when it runs low, every part of you begins to sputter and slow down. Muscles can ache. Vision can blur. Digestion can clog. But these are *physical* problems.

The mind is powered by the brain, and the brain—more than the muscles, more than any other organ—*demands* glucose.

The brain is a glucose addict.

Some parts of the body store glucose, and burn reserves if the supply drops below normal, or in a pinch use substances other than glucose for fuel. But the brain is a glucose addict. It has to have glucose, and it has to have it *now*—a steady, second-to-second flow. You could say the brain breathes glucose, and chokes without it. That's why low blood sugar can cause *any* mental problem. Fatigue, nervousness, anxiety, irritability, depression, forgetfulness, confusion, indecisiveness, poor concentration, nightmares, suicidal tendencies—all these and more have been linked to low blood sugar.

Too little sugar reaching the brain and you've got problems: nervousness, anxiety, depression.

Too little sugar reaching the brain is one reason lowered blood sugar levels can cause emotional symptoms. But there's another mechanism involved too. Just as insulin is released when blood sugar levels get too high, adrenaline is released when blood sugar levels drop too low, as happens in the rebound effect of a high sugar intake. When this occurs, symptoms mimic an anxiety reaction—racing pulse, sweaty palms, labored breathing, dry mouth. It's as if you've come face to face with your worst enemy. And, in a way, maybe you have.

ANYONE YOU KNOW?

Michael Lesser, M.D., a California psychiatrist and author of *Nutrition and Vitamin Therapy* (Grove Press), describes a typical case:

"Alan tells me he is happily married, with two small children and a thriving [dental] practice. He would seem to have few problems, but clearly he is worried. . . . 'It's just that here I am, at the height of my powers, making good money, my wife is fine, my kids are great, and I should be happy. But I'm not. Instead, I dread going to work. I feel tired and exhausted. I get angry at the drop of a hat. Sometimes I cry for no reason and just don't know what's wrong."

"I should be happy. But I'm not."

Dr. Lesser sent Alan for a five-hour glucose tolerance test to determine how his body handles sugar. Blood is drawn first on an empty stomach (to get a fasting blood sugar reading) and then at hourly intervals following the ingestion of a sugary drink. Physical and emotional symptoms are also noted.

Test results showed that Alan's blood sugar was 90 mg% (per 100 milliliters of blood) at his fasting level, which is normal, and peaked at 150 mg% about an hour after his sweet drink. Alan felt fine. But then, Dr. Lesser reports, "his blood sugar plummeted to 40 mg% by the third hour, and simultaneously he felt 'terrible, irritable, and depressed.'

The results of a five-hour glucose tolerance test.

"This sudden reactive drop in blood sugar coupled with symptoms at the time of the drop is called low blood sugar or hypoglycemia," Dr. Lesser explains.

The literally stupefying effect of hypoglycemia is documented in the book *Body, Mind and Sugar* (Avon) by E. M. Abrahamson, M.D. Dr. Abrahamson describes two studies which show that many so-called "neurotics" should call their doctors on the carpet for having made the wrong diagnosis.

Many so-called "neurotics" are in fact hypoglycemics.

In the first study, Dr. Abrahamson gave a glucose tolerance test to 220 neurotic patients with obvious physical symptoms of low blood sugar, such as fatigue. *The test showed that 205 had hypoglycemia.* When these 205 depressed, anxious, and fear-ridden people were put on a corrective diet, their physical *and* psychological problems began to clear up.

A man who for 6 years had blasted at his family with daily temper tantrums was even-tempered and reasonable after a few weeks. A claustrophobic woman who for 20 years had refused to enter an elevator, car, or subway was confidently traveling on her own after six months. A woman obsessed by thoughts of suicide was free of them in a week.

Claustrophobia may be a symptom of hypoglycemia.

Not surprisingly, Dr. Abrahamson was intrigued. So intrigued that he gave a glucose tolerance test to 700 mildly neurotic people who had *no* physical symptoms of low blood sugar. This time, the test showed that 600 had hypoglycemia. When put on a corrective diet, they regained mental health.

But a psychiatrist's office isn't the only place where you're likely to find a hypoglycemic. A principal's office is another.

Learning disorders in children have also been linked to low blood sugar.

Studies show that millions of American children have a "learning disability," a problem that includes erratic behavior, short attention span, emotional instability, and poor memory. Paul J. Dunn, M.D., a pediatrician from Oak Park, Illinois, gave a glucose tolerance test to 144 children with learning disability and found that 78 percent had hypoglycemia *(New Dynamics of Preventive Medicine)*.

In a similar study, Sydney Walker III, M.D., a neuropsychiatrist from La Jolla, California, found that 44 of 48 children with learning disability, depression, temper tantrums, or poor concentration had, among other problems, a blood sugar disorder. Dr. Walker said in an interview that once these children were put on a sugar-free diet rich in vegetables, fruit, and high-protein foods, almost all of them had improved behavior.

Low blood sugar may affect all of us to some degree.

That's not to say that everyone suffering from this vague collection of symptoms is hypoglycemic. Truth is, hypoglycemia is a very controversial issue in medical circles. Many physicians contend that hypoglycemia is a rare problem—hardly the epidemic the above studies would lead you to believe. Others, however, cautiously point out that while extreme cases are perhaps uncommon, low blood sugar may affect all of us to some degree. In the words of one physician, "Hypoglycemia is not like rabies, where you either have it or you do not . . . everybody has some, it is just a matter of how much."

That may be why so many people find they feel better—physically and especially emotionally—when they switch from a diet of sugar-laden, overly processed foods to one that emphasizes complex carbohydrates with low-fat sources of protein.

Doctors also recommend that to avoid blood sugar problems, you eat several smaller meals instead of the usual three big meals a day or moderate the traditional meal plan by eating smaller portions at the table and high-protein or complex carbohydrate snacks between meals.

Eat several smaller meals a day.

Of course, the key to any high energy nutrition plan is the high-protein breakfast. And by high we mean higher than what you're eating now. One scientific study indicates that 15 grams for breakfast is the minimum for most people to keep their energy level high all morning. That's more than two large eggs (13 grams) or an average bowl of whole-grain cereal (7 grams including the milk). For tips and recipes that boost your breakfast protein see Box 4.

A WAKE-UP CALL FROM THE BRAIN

There's a second reason why protein may be your best bet in the morning. And it has nothing to do with blood sugar. It involves neurotransmitters, those chemical sparks that jump between neurons and nerve endings conveying important messages in the brain.

A second reason why protein makes the best breakfast fare.

According to a new series of studies, protein contains an amino acid called tyrosine that converts in the brain to three neurotransmitters: dopamine, norepinephrine, and epinephrine (sometimes called adrenaline). These brain sparks are referred to collectively as the catecholamines—and each one of them is associated with wakefulness.

As evidence of the mind-wakening ability of the catecholamines, French researchers have shown that the chemical L-dopa—which, together with tyrosine, forms dopamine—"suppressed sleep episodes during both day and night" when administered to a patient who had been suffering from daytime sleep attacks (New England Journal of Medicine).

Catecholamines produced sleepless nights.

Richard Wurtman, M.D., a neuroendocrinologist and

(continued on page 27)

BOX 4: HIGH-ENERGY BREAKFASTS

Skip it, and you may have just missed the most important meal of the day. But downing a donut, coffee, or glass of OJ on the run won't give you an edge either.

When it comes to breakfast fare that delivers energy and mental alertness, you've got to think protein, with a capital P—15 to 25 grams' worth. Here's how:

Concentrate on Low-Fat, High-Protein Foods

The typical American bacon-and-eggs breakfast has lots of protein. But it also hits you with an unhealthy wallop of fat and sodium—not to mention sugar, if eaten with a side order of jelly toast, orange juice, or sweetened coffee. Opt instead for an energizing, health-enhancing meal that emphasizes the kinds of protein listed in Table 1. For low-fat eggs, poach or scramble them in a pan lightly coated with liquid lecithin.

TABLE 1: Low-Fat, High-Protein Foods

Food	Protein (grams)
Cottage cheese (large curd, 1 cup)	31
Milk (skim, 1 cup)	8.3
Yogurt (part skim, 8 ounces)	13
Egg (1 large)	6
Brewer's yeast (1 tablespoon)	3.1
Peanuts (shelled, 1 tablespoon)	2.4
Wheat germ (toasted, 1 tablespoon)	1.8

Choose a High-Protein Cereal and Supplement It with Foods from Table 1

Most breakfast cereals—even *with* milk—can't supply the protein you need for maximum energy. Use Table 2 to figure out exactly how much protein your breakfast cereal *does* supply, and then check our list of protein-rich foods in Table 1 to select additions to your breakfast to bring your protein total *up*.

To use Table 2: Add the protein value of your cereal (in the second column) to the protein value of milk. (Values for skim and whole milk are along the bottom row.) You may have to estimate more or fewer grams of protein if your portions are normally larger or smaller than the ones given here. But unless you're eating double portions, the cereal and milk alone won't add up to 15 grams.

Table 2 also shows you how much fiber, sugar, and sodium and how many calories you're getting in cereal and milk.

TABLE 2: High-Protein Cereals

Cereal	Protein (grams)	Dietary Fiber (grams)	Fat (grams)	Sugar (grams)	Sodium (grams)	Calories (grams)
Kellog's Special K (1 cup)	6	0.2	.1	1.6	199	83
Wheatena (1/4 cup uncooked)	4.6	.6	1	0	4	122
Old-Fashioned Quaker Oats (1/3 cup uncooked)	4.3	1.5	1.7	0	1	104
Kellogg's Bran Buds (1/3 cup)	3.9	7.8	.66	7	172	72
Kellogg's Nutri-Grain* Wheat and Raisins (2/3 cup)	3	2	0	8	165	140
Post Fruit & Fibre* Apples & Cinnamon (1/2 cup)	3	3	1	7	195	90
Post Fruit & Fibre* Date, Raisin, & Walnut (1/2 cup)	3	3	1	6	170	90
Quaker 100% Natural Cereal (1/4 cup)	3	.95	5.6	6	11.25	122
Nabisco Shredded Wheat (1 biscuit)	2.05	1.75	.25	0	.50	66.5
Skim milk (1/2 cup)	4.2	0	.22	6.25	63	43
Whole milk (1/2 cup)	4	0	4.1	5.7	60	75

*Manufacturer provided nutritional information

When Time Permits, Try These Recipes

Creamy Eggs*

Protein	Fiber	Calories
15.6 g	—	178

Serve with fresh fruit and whole wheat toast.

Serves 1

2 eggs, beaten
2 tablespoons cottage cheese

1. Spray a small skillet with nonstick lecithin coating, and place over low to medium heat. Pour in the eggs, and stir gently.

2. When eggs are about half set, stir in the cottage cheese, distributing it evenly. Cook another minute or two, until eggs are cooked through but still moist.

*Adapted from *The 20-Minute Natural Foods Cookbook* by Sharon Claessens (Rodale Press, 1982).

(continued next page)

BOX 4— *Continued*

Yogurt Melon Basket

Protein   Fiber   Calories
15.6 g   3.72 g   503

For vitamin C and fiber, this fast breakfast can't be beat. Serve with skim milk
to raise protein value over 15 grams.

Serves 1

½ small cantaloupe
½ cup vanilla or plain yogurt
¼ cup high-protein whole-grain
       cereal
1 tablespoon wheat germ
3 tablespoons grated coconut
3 tablespoons raisins

1. Remove seeds from cantaloupe.
Fill cavity with yogurt.

2. Mix cereal and wheat germ.
Spoon onto yogurt. Top with coconut
and raisins.

Note: You can vary the ingredients
to suit your personal preference and avail-
ability of ingredients. Try peaches or
bananas in place of the raisins, or use
sunflower seeds or nuts in place of coconut. Keep the yogurt, though, for that
all-important protein!

Egg-Cheese Toast

Protein   Fiber   Calories
20.6 g   2.6 g   305

Serve with apple slices, lightly sautéed
in butter and sprinkled with cinnamon.

Serves 1

2 eggs
2 tablespoons water
⅛ teaspoon cayenne
1 tablespoon minced parsley
2 teaspoons snipped chives
1 slice whole-grain bread
¼ cup shredded mozzarella cheese

1. Spray a small skillet with nonstick
lecithin coating, and place over medium-
low heat.

2. In a small bowl beat eggs, water,
and cayenne until blended. Add eggs to
pan. As they set, gently draw a spoon
across center to scramble them. When
eggs are almost set, add parsley and chives.

3. While eggs are cooking, lightly
toast bread. Top with cheese and place
under broiler to melt and brown cheese.
Serve topped with eggs.

Banana–Yogurt Drink

Protein   Fiber   Calories
18.2 g   401 g   291

Serves 1

½ cup plain yogurt
½ cup skim milk
1 small banana
2 tablespoons wheat germ
1 tablespoon good-tasting nutritional
       yeast
1 teaspoon lecithin

1. Place ingredients in blender container. Process until smooth.

professor at the Massachusetts Institute of Technology, and associate John D. Fernstrom, Ph.D., further demonstrated that eating protein will result in a rise in the brain levels of catecholamines. In their study, laboratory animals were fed a single meal composed of 40 percent protein. The result? Tyrosine went up and so did catecholamines. "These observations," say Drs. Wurtman and Fernstrom, "suggest that . . . catecholamine-containing brain neurons are normally under specific dietary control" *(American Journal of Clinical Nutrition)*.

Dr. Wurtman has spent even more time investigating another mind-altering amino acid, tryptophan. Tryptophan is converted to serotonin, another neurotransmitter—this one involved in the regulation of sleep, appetite, aggression, and pain sensitivity.

Tryptophan converts to serotonin, the neurotransmitter associated with sleep.

THE AMINO ACID THAT QUIETS THE MIND

Tryptophan's effect on sleep is perhaps the easiest to document. According to a study by Dr. Wurtman, a single dose of tryptophan brought on feelings of fatigue and inertia in a group of young healthy men. Confirmation that the tryptophan was the responsible factor came when placebo pills, given to the same men, failed to produce drowsiness.

Dr. Wurtman isn't the only one who's noted this effect. According to Ernest Hartmann, M.D., professor of psychiatry and renowned sleep researcher at Tufts University School of Medicine in Boston, 1 gram of tryptophan is enough to shorten sleep latency (time needed to fall asleep) by 30 to 50 percent in the normal subjects and mild insomniacs that he's tested—even those who have trouble falling asleep in a strange place.

One gram of tryptophan can help you fall asleep 30 to 50 percent faster.

Does it take you several sleepless nights before you acclimate yourself to a new environment? Dr. Hartmann studied 42 people who had this common complaint. Each person spent one night in the sleep laboratory with electrodes attached to his or her head (increasing the strangeness of the place). Before bedtime, 14 were given 1 gram of tryptophan, 14 others were given 3 grams, and the remainder were given a placebo. Even in this strange situation, says Dr. Hartmann, who is the author of *The Sleeping Pill* (Yale University Press), tryptophan reduced sleep latency

Unlike many sleeping pills, tryptophan is safe and nonaddictive.

Carbohydrates—not protein— hold the key to higher brain levels of tryptophan.

without producing any distortion of the various stages of sleep. Furthermore, the effects of the 1-gram dose and the 3-gram dose were almost identical.

Best of all, tryptophan is safe—unlike the hypnotic drugs often prescribed for sleep problems. "Tryptophan is rapidly metabolized and cleared by the body . . . ," writes Dr. Hartmann. "Indeed, our sleep recordings show that the effects on sleep EEGs [electroencephalograms] seem to last only a few hours: Sleep latency is almost always shortened in our studies, and waking time is significantly reduced in the early portions of the night. Waking time in the last hours of sleep is not altered. This leads to the hope that tolerance to tryptophan would not be built up by the body on a long-term basis."

So, if you have difficulty falling asleep, you may do well to increase your intake of tryptophan. But this is not as simple or straightforward as one might guess. Contrary to the logic that to increase the level of tryptophan in the brain one must eat high-protein (tryptophan-containing) foods, Dr. Hartmann found that eating carbohydrates about 40 to 60 minutes before bedtime brings on the desired effect.

THE CARBOHYDRATE CONNECTION

It's true that protein delivers tryptophan to the blood. But it also brings tyrosine and about five other amino acids—all of them competing with tryptophan for "carrier molecules" to transport them from the blood capillaries to the brain neurons, writes Dr. Wurtman in *Scientific American.* The only way to give tryptophan the competitive edge is to increase its level in the blood *without* increasing the level of the other amino acids. Eating protein won't do that. But eating carbohydrates will.

When you eat a high-carbohydrate meal insulin is released, says Dr. Wurtman. Insulin reduces the blood levels of the competing amino acids without disturbing the tryptophan, which is somehow immune to its effect. The result is less competition for tryptophan so that more of it can reach brain neurons, where it is converted to serotonin— the brain's sleeping potion.

Sleep therapist Alice Kuhn Schwartz, Ph.D., offers some healthful practical advice based on this new data.

"If you've been eating high-protein [high-tryptophan

BOX 5: THE SNACK BAR
FOR INSOMNIACS

Next time you raid the refrigerator for a late
night snack, think about falling asleep, not just filling your stomach. Keep in mind that some high-
protein foods contain tryptophan, the sleep-inducing
amino acid, but carbohydrates contain the "releasing
agent" that allows tryptophan to work.

To maximize the effect, combine any high-protein,
high-tryptophan food (or foods) from list A with any
carbohydrate from list B. The possibilities are practically endless: cream cheese on a bran muffin, carrot
cake and a glass of milk, a bowl of granola and milk
topped with a banana, or cheddar cheese and apple
slices. Or, choose a snack from list C—a ready mix of
protein and carbohydrate.

Remember, too, timing is all important. Plan
your raid about two to four hours before turning it.

A [**high-protein foods**]: milk, cheese, yogurt,
cottage cheese, cream cheese, eggs, beef, chicken,
tuna, nuts

B [**high-carbohydrate foods**]: dates, bananas,
apples, watermelon, fruit juice, carob brownies, oat-
meal, granola, carrot cake, bran muffin, bread

C [**protein/carbohydrate combination foods**]:
rice pudding, fruit yogurt, cheese and crackers, tortel-
lini salad, turkey sandwich

and high-tyrosine] foods during the day, and you want to
fall asleep at night, then it may help to eat some bread, have
a banana, drink some grape or apple juice, have some figs or
dates—all of those high-carbohydrate foods and many others will help activate tryptophan."

Dr. Schwartz explains further that it's important to
eat your carbohydrate food two to four hours before bedtime so that the food will reach its peak effect when you are
ready to retire. On the other hand, if your problem is
frequent awakenings during the night—quite a common

**Best bets for bedtime snacks:
a banana, apple juice,
popcorn.**

complaint after the age of 40—or short sleep periods, or light sleep, you should eat your carbohydrate immediately before "lights out." Since falling asleep in the first place is not your problem, you will want your carbohydrates to operate at top efficiency after you have been asleep for a few hours.

Drowsy during the day? Reduce your carbohydrate intake until late-afternoon.

"In any case," concludes Dr. Schwartz, "if you tend to fall asleep during the day or early evening, you must try to eliminate carbohydrates during the day. If you usually eat dessert after your evening meal, you should defer your dessert until the time appropriate to your particular sleep problem."

Mood-Altering Food Allergies

Some people eat in response to anxiety and depression. Now we're discovering many people get anxious and depressed in response to eating—a direct result of brain sensitivity to certain foods.

According to the pioneering work of a small but growing number of doctors, unsuspected food allergies can masquerade as many emotional ills. Violent outbursts and suicidal tendencies erupt in the worst cases. But typically, symptoms surface in feelings of fatigue, irritability, anxiety, depression, inability to concentrate, and lack of motivation—exactly the kind of complaints that can wind up in the diagnostic wastebasket marked "stress" or "emotional tension." To add to the diagnostic confusion, food allergies can also trigger such "stress-related" physical symptoms as headaches and digestive disturbances.

Surprised? Don't be.

"It's well known that allergies may cause such symptoms as hay fever, asthma, and hives," says Bernard Rimland, Ph.D. "And since it is so widely recognized that the nasal membranes, the lungs, and the skin can be affected by food or other substances to which some individuals are intolerant, [it's not surprising that] the brain, the most intricate and biochemically complicated organ in the body, could also be affected by allergies."

Body allergies and brain allergies often go hand in hand. Barbara Solomon, M.D., a specialist in food allergy, relates one such case:

"A 17-year-old boy had been going to a psychiatrist for

Food sensitivity: a cause of
"aggressive personality."

six years, and had been labeled an 'aggressive personality.'
He came into my office with many of the signs of a chronic
food allergy: blotchy skin, swollen eyes, red nose. I tested
him for 200 foods, and found that he was allergic to 70.
Well, after he stopped eating the foods he was allergic to, he
simply lost that 'aggressive personality' and was discharged
by his psychiatrist."

So, if a person breaks out whenever he gets near a
tomato or wheezes his way through the ragweed season,
there's a good chance that any corresponding bouts with
irritability or depression are at least partially related to
allergies.

An allergy-free body is no
guarantee of an allergy-clean
slate psychologically.

On the other hand, a seemingly allergy-free body is no
guarantee of an allergy-clean slate psychologically. In a
study at the University of Massachusetts, several patients
exposed to allergens reported such psychological problems
as anxiety, depression, and difficulty concentrating.

Sometimes, too, the body reacts in such subtle ways
that food allergies are never suspected. Such was the case of
one patient in the above study who felt drugged, unable to
concentrate, and sapped of all motivation after being exposed
to a particular allergen. He had but one vague physical
complaint: gas.

Mood-altering food allergies
are tough to diagnose.

Clearly, mood-altering food allergies are tough to
diagnose, but for many who suffer from unexplained emotional swings, it may provide the missing piece to some
long-standing psychological puzzles.

Case in point: A 33-year-old woman with no known
allergies lived for years with depression, irritability, and
migraine headaches. She also reported a history of learning
disabilities (as a child she was diagnosed as "hyperactive")
and a lifelong struggle with weight problems (no matter
what weight loss method she tried—diets, behavior
modification, self-control techniques—she couldn't keep
off the weight).

Allergy tests offer insight into
a puzzling case.

Eventually, and fortunately, she found her way to North
Texas State University where food allergies were under
investigation. There, extensive allergy tests revealed that
she was sensitive to a wide variety of foods including corn,
beef, milk, wheat, eggs, sugar, coffee, citrus fruits, pork,
lamb, carrots, nuts, watermelon, and pineapple. The foods
deemed safe for her to consume—her so-called "nonreactive"
foods—included fish, chicken, most green and yellow

vegetables, bananas, cantaloupe, pears, apples, strawberries, and blueberries.

To verify these food sensitivities, researchers then examined her physical and psychological reactions during six consecutive six-day periods on either a good diet (consisting of only her safe foods) or a bad diet (defined as the good diet with the addition of some forbidden foods). Not surprisingly, whenever she ate the wrong foods, she became increasingly depressed and irritable. Her coordination, memory, and learning abilities also suffered. And during two consecutive "bad diet" phases (12 days) she gained 13 pounds — presumably the result of water retention since calorie intake remained constant throughout the good and bad diet phases.

Within four days of resuming a good diet (the time it takes for all residue of the bad diet to work its way out of the system), her moods brightened and her learning ability and coordination improved. By the end of the week, her weight had dropped significantly. Three months later, a follow-up visit revealed a happy and contented lady who was continuing to lose weight on her carefully orchestrated allergy-free diet.

Without citing hundreds more of these cases, here are several physicians' comments confirming the mind-altering effect of foods:

• In persons with known allergies who suffer from depression of unknown origin, "treatment of the allergy will, in most cases, cure the depression. I have seen this in several hundred patients," writes Abram Hoffer, M.D., Ph.D., a psychiatrist in Victoria, British Columbia (*Journal of Orthomolecular Psychiatry*).

• Allergy should be considered in every patient who for no obvious reason is subject to hyperactivity, or irritability, along with fatigue. This is especially true if other causes have been ruled out. "Certainly no patient should be classified as [neurotic] until allergy has been ruled out," says Frederick Speer, M.D., author of *Allergy of the Nervous System* (Charles C Thomas).

• "In my experience, allergy is the commonest cause of otherwise unexplained fatigue in children. I've been thrilled by the number of pale, drowsy, tired, listless children whose entire outlook on life has changed when hidden food allergens were removed from the diet," says William

Whenever she ate the wrong foods she became depressed and irritable.

Within four days of resuming a good "nonreactive" diet, her moods brightened.

Depression in an allergic person usually lifts with allergy treatment.

Allergy is the commonest cause of unexplained fatigue in children.

G. Crook, M.D., a clinical allergist in preventive medicine in Jackson, Tennessee.

• "Allergies affect different areas of the brain in different children. For example, we've seen reading ability plummet from eighth- to fifth-grade level because of an allergic challenge," explains Doris J. Rapp, M.D., pediatrician and allergist in Buffalo, New York.

Aggression is a common allergic response.

• "Aggression as an allergic response is a well-documented phenomenon that has been known to researchers since early in this century," writes Kenneth E. Moyer, Ph.D., in an article entitled "The Physiology of Violence, Allergy and Aggression" published in *Psychology Today.*

That food allergies can upset emotional equilibrium is a medical fact. Exactly how the reactive mechanism works in these cases remains somewhat of a mystery.

Allergens may trigger neurotransmitters in the brain.

One theory maintains that allergens trigger an increase or reduction in the amount of neurotransmitters in the brain. These neurotransmitters are the chemicals responsible for determining most behavior. A second theory suggests that allergens cause localized swelling in the brain tissues. The type of behavior change that occurs, then, depends on which area of the brain is affected. Other theories are emerging as more and more research is being conducted in the field.

"Just recently researchers have discovered that the immune mechanism may be involved," explains Michael B. Schachter, M.D., a practicing psychiatrist and author of *Food, Mind and Mood* (Warner). "Apparently, in sensitive persons, certain foods stimulate the body's production of antibodies which can clump together in large molecules. If these molecules collect in the blood vessels of the brain, they can interfere with the oxygenation process and cause the wide variety of emotional symptoms we're seeing."

HOW TO IDENTIFY FOOD ALLERGIES

The worst offenders are foods we eat every day.

Food allergies wouldn't be a problem if they were limited to foods like shrimp, chocolate, or peanuts—foods we could probably give up without crimping our lifestyles too much. But reactions to seldom-eaten, easily incriminated foods like shrimp account for only 5 to 10 percent of all food allergies. The vast majority of food allergies are nagging symptoms produced by foods (and food ingredients)

TABLE 3: The Common and Not-So-Common Culprits in Food Allergies

While anyone can become allergic to any food, some
foods are more apt to cause allergies than others.

Most Commonly Cause Allergies	Often Cause Allergies	Sometimes Cause Allergies	Seldom Cause Allergies
Chocolate (cola)	Alcohol (in adults)	Bananas	Apples
Corn	Berries	Beef	Apricots and juice
Egg whites	Buckwheat	Celery	Bacon
Fish	Cane sugar	Cherries	Barley
Milk	Coconut	Chicken (in women)	Beets
Mustard	Coffee (in adults)	Coloring agents	Carrots
Nuts	Orange or other citrus	Cottonseed	Chicken (in men)
Wheat	Peanut butter	Garlic	Cranberries and juice
	Peas	Melons	Grapes and juice
	Pork	Mushrooms	Honey
	Potatoes	Onions	Lamb
	Soy (in adults)	Plums	Lettuce
	Tomatoes	Prunes	Lobster
	Yeast	Spices	Oats
		Spinach	Peaches and juice
		Vitamins	Pineapples and juice
		Water—tap, chlorinated, and softened	Raisins
			Rice
			Rye
			Salmon
			Salt
			Soy (in children)
			Squash
			Sweet potatoes
			Tapioca
			Vanilla extract
			Vinegar (apple cider)

SOURCE: Adapted from *Basics of Food Allergy,* Second Edition, by James C. Breneman, M.D. (Charles C Thomas, 1984).

that most people eat *every day*—milk, wheat, eggs, corn, citrus, fruits, yeast.

Think about it. It's not just corn on the cob that you may be allergic to but also corn syrup, cornstarch, corn oil.

Skin tests are little help.

You may not feel the reaction for hours—or a day—after eating.

You can still be allergic, even if you don't react every time.

You may be able to get away with one or two strawberries.

It's not just those sunny-side ups but also the eggs in almost every baked good on the market. We don't want to kid you: Pinpointing a food allergy and keeping the offender out of your diet can be tough.

Skin tests are little help. Physicians say they're far less reliable for food than for inhalants like dust or pollen. And symptoms don't usually fall into simple, easily observed patterns because of the complex (and not fully understood) way that foods trigger allergy.

A few people can feel their lips, mouths, and throats begin to swell or itch even before the food in question reaches their stomachs. More often than not, though, trouble erupts farther along as food is processed by the digestive system. Since food takes about four or five days to journey from entrance to exit, allergic symptoms can take time to develop—a few hours, maybe. Or a day or so. Because of that time lag, you may have difficulty linking what you ate to how you feel. In other words, you may blame your symptoms on the cheese you ate at lunch, when the real cause is the eggs you had for breakfast. Or the melon you ate yesterday.

Here's another variable. Do you seem to tolerate a food sometimes but not others? You still can be allergic to a food even if you don't react every time you eat it. The problem food may very well be eaten for quite a while with no symptoms. Then, as antibodies accumulate to a certain threshold, the attack occurs. One doctor compares this "allergic threshold" to water filling a rain barrel. All's well until the water level reaches the brim. Then a tiny drop causes an overflow. By "rotating" foods—eating troublesome food only at widely spaced intervals—you can keep most food allergies from reaching that critical point.

How close you come to going over the edge also depends on how much you eat and when. Perhaps you're only mildly allergic—you may be able to get away with one or two strawberries, but eating a pintful is a full-scale disaster. Or, since cooking breaks down food to a degree, you may discover that you can eat celery cooked, for instance, but not raw. Or your symptoms may appear only if two or more allergenic foods are eaten at the same meal. That's particularly true for closely related foods like beef and milk, or mushrooms and yeast.

By the same token, you may react to a food only during

pollen season or when suffering from other airborne particles. Or when you have a cold. Or when drinking alcohol. Or when eating the food on an empty stomach.

No wonder food allergy can be a hard case to crack!

To completely unravel a food-allergy problem, you'll have to sort out not only your symptoms but also exactly what's in your diet.

You'll have to sort out your symptoms and your diet.

STEP #1: KEEP A FOOD DIARY

A record of what you eat, how much you eat, and how you feel afterward can signal what you're allergic to—especially if your symptoms come and go unpredictably. Your diary will be most helpful if you keep a few basic rules in mind.

1. List all ingredients of mixed dishes and combination foods. If you eat a ham sandwich, for instance, note the kind of bread and mayonnaise or mustard.

List all ingredients of mixed dishes.

2. Weigh yourself every morning. A sudden weight gain plus increased thirst, decreased urine output, tighter shoes, or a tight ring are all signs of edema, or fluid retention—a common food reaction.

3. Note any foods you crave.

Make note of food cravings.

4. Keep track of how you're feeling throughout the day. James C. Breneman, M.D., chairman of the Food Allergy Committee of the American College of Allergists and author of *Basics of Food Allergy* (Charles C Thomas), has noticed that food-allergy symptoms often fall into certain patterns. They include: hives, runny nose, asthma, heartburn, sleepiness, or drowsiness that can occur within 1 hour; abdominal cramps, gas pains, or headaches that may occur within 2 to 4 hours; delayed hives that may appear 6 to 12 hours later; a weight gain or water retention that can occur within 12 to 15 hours; confusion, forgetfulness, depression, inability to concentrate, or other mental symptoms that may appear within 12 to 24 hours; canker (cold) sores or aching joints, muscles, or back that can occur after three to five days.

After you've kept a diary for a week or two, you can use it to help recognize problem foods. Dr. Rapp suggests that you make a list of all foods eaten on a day you felt well. Compare that list with a list of foods eaten on a day you felt terrible. Cross out all foods that appear on both lists. The foods left on the second list are your prime suspects.

Keep a food diary for two weeks.

STEP #2: ELIMINATE THE SUSPECTED CULPRITS—ONE AT A TIME

An elimination diet is a self-test.

Basically, an elimination diet is simply a self-test. You avoid a prime suspect, such as milk or wheat, in *all forms* for up to three weeks and see how you feel. Then you eat the food again—preferably in generous portions at several meals. Meanwhile, continue to observe your symptoms.

Going off the offending food can cause withdrawal symptoms.

The first four or five days on an elimination diet can be pretty rough if you're on the right track. For one thing, foods like milk, wheat, and eggs—so often the glue and mortar of baked goods and other dietary staples—aren't easy to avoid. And even if you eliminate every trace, you may feel worse instead of better at first; withdrawal symptoms, more or less. Don't let all that discourage you, though. By the fifth day or so you'll feel much better.

After two or three weeks on an elimination diet, try the excluded food. Choose a day on which you feel free of symptoms until lunchtime. Then eat the food in various forms for three consecutive meals. If the food provokes symptoms, you've identified the culprit.

BOX 6: MASTERMINDING YOUR OWN ALLERGY-FREE DIET

If all goes according to plan, elimination diets will leave you with a list of foods responsible for your allergies. Those foods, of course, should be avoided for several months.

Notice we didn't say "avoided *forever*." Allergies change. After a year or more, you lose your sensitivity to a food to which you are now allergic. After not eating the food for several months, test it once more. If symptoms reappear, you will have to continue to avoid it indefinitely. If nothing happens, however, you can add that food to your diet, at intervals of four days or longer.

In fact, Herbert J. Rinkel, M.D., a

pioneer in allergy treatment, proposes that some people can build up their tolerance to foods—and prevent new food allergies from developing—by following a four-day "rotary diet." First, you avoid the problem food or foods completely for up to six months, to give your body an allergy rest period. Then you reintroduce the food to your diet—but no more than once every four days. This four-day rotation allows antibody levels to subside before you once again encounter the food in question. Eventually, rotation increases your tolerance to certain foods simply by exposing you to them less often. Best of all, perhaps, a rotary diet allows you to

BOX 6 — *Continued*

eat at least some of the foods you really love without suffering.

"The key to overcoming food allergy is rotation," emphasizes Robert W. Boxer, M.D., an allergist in Chicago and one of the few-but-growing number of allergists in this country who now prescribe the rotary diet.

In fact, following a rotary diet is all some people need to do to control their food allergies, Dr. Boxer says. "If you took all the people who are allergic to foods and did nothing more than rotate their foods, you would probably diminish their symptoms by 80 percent."

It's a very effective technique. "And it's something people could try on their own, even before they go to a doctor. You may feel so well on a rotary diet that you really don't need any professional help," Dr. Boxer adds. If you're severely allergic, you will need more help. But it still couldn't hurt to rotate foods.

All you need to start your own rotary diet is a list of foods to which you are not allergic, plus others to which you are only mildly allergic. Then follow these basic rules:

1. For the first few weeks, try your best to avoid all foods to which you know you are even moderately allergic, giving yourself an allergy "rest period." You can start a rotary diet without this initial rest period, but you'll probably experience some symptoms for the first few cycles.

2. Stick to primary foods—fish, meat, poultry, fruits, and vegetables—in as close to their natural state as possible. Avoid secondary or combination foods, such as mixes, sauces, blends, packaged foods.

3. Similarly, rotate only wholesome, nutrient-packed food, not cupcakes, soda, and the like. "I tell my patients to rotate *and* stay off junk food," says Dr. Boxer. And stay away from alcohol, coffee, and tobacco.

4. Select a minimum number of foods for each meal, and fill up on them, rather than choosing a potpourri of multiple foods. For instance, an eight-ounce portion of broiled fish, a half plate of steamed broccoli, and a large potato would comprise a typical rotary-diet meal.

5. Whenever possible, avoid eating the same food more than once a day.

6. Don't forget to rotate spices, cooking oils, and beverages. Soybean, safflower, and sunflower oils, for instance, are derived from different plants. Among herb teas, lemongrass, mint, sassafras, verbena, hibiscus, and rose hips are unrelated to each other.

7. Write down everything you eat. Otherwise, it's practically impossible to keep foods straight.

8. If you go off the diet, don't give up. Kendall Gerdes, M.D., an allergist in Denver, Colorado, told us that some people are able to return to their customary eating habits as long as they periodically return to a rotary diet long enough to build up their resistance to troublesome foods.

BOX 7: FOOD ADDITIVES: ANOTHER CAUSE
FOR CONCERN

If you're not allergic to a food itself, you may be allergic to an additive in it: a coloring, flavoring, stabilizer, emulsifier, or preservative. Benjamin Feingold, M.D., author of *Why Your Child Is Hyperactive* (Random House), was one of the first to uncover the curious link between food additives and hyperactivity in children. Today we know about a whole host of allergic reactions that stem from chemicals in our foods.

One doctor tells of a member of her family who experienced sudden weakness, extreme fatigue, and a swollen throat whenever she ate cornflakes or instant potatoes. The problem was neither corn nor potatoes, however, but BHA and BHT, two common preservatives.

All told, the Food and Drug Administration estimates that 50,000 to 100,000 people, many of them children, are allergic to tartrazine (better known as Yellow No. 5), which is present in thousands of foods, beverages, cosmetics, and drugs.

Sulfur additives are another problem item. Used to preserve foods, beverages, and drugs, sulfur is equally liable to trigger asthma, flushing, or even shock in allergic people.

Monosodium glutamate (MSG) is perhaps the most famous instigator of "restaurant allergies." Have you ever gone out to eat Chinese food only to come home feeling headachy and nauseated?

For years, MSG reactions were dismissed by doctors as merely imaginary, or at most a slight irritation of the esophagus.

There are few reliable tests for food allergy; there are *none* for additive allergy. The only way to test for allergy to an additive is to eliminate it just as you eliminate milk or wheat. To avoid additives, though, your label-reading skills have to be doubly sharp.

Boost Your Brainpower
with Super Nutrition

We all have days when our thinking is fuzzy, our logic defies reason, when we can't for the life of us remember some name or fact that was so familiar just the day before. On days like those you might want to trade in your gray matter for a new, improved model with rechargeable batteries and a software system that lets you discover the unknown secrets of the universe in one easy lesson.

Unfortunately, we have to make do with what Mother Nature has given us. Luckily, that's usually more than adequate. And with better nutrition, we can make better use of the brainpower we do have—and even stave off the mental deterioration we know as senility.

Cloudy thinking, forgetful, illogical? Brain foods can help.

IRON-POOR INTELLECT

The brain needs large amounts of oxygen to function effectively, and the only way it can get it is through iron-packed red blood cells, says Don M. Tucker, Ph.D., associate professor of psychology at the University of Oregon at Eugene.

Oxygen clears the mind, keeps all circuits functioning.

Some studies show that children with iron-deficiency anemia have short attention spans and trouble learning new material. They also know that boosting iron intake reverses these problems.

And Dr. Tucker's research shows that adults can suffer from related problems with alertness and memory when their iron levels are in the "low but normal" range.

Alertness and memory can suffer with "low but normal" iron levels.

Iron influences brain chemicals and pathways.

In one study, for instance, the higher the blood iron levels, the greater the word fluency. (Volunteers were asked to come up with as many words as they could that begin with "Q" and end with "L.") In another, in adults over age 60, blood iron levels were one of the more important measures in determining whether or not the person had normal brainwave patterns.

"Getting enough oxygen to the brain is certainly part of its function, but we think iron also influences brain chemicals and pathways," Dr. Tucker says. "We know now that iron is heavily concentrated in a part of the reticular activating system. This area of the brain turns the brain on, so to speak. It maintains alertness. So we can't help but think that iron plays an important role in awareness and alertness."

"B" SMART

The brain seems to have a special need for the B vitamins. Memory loss, disorientation, hallucination, depression, lack of coordination, and personality changes can occur with B-complex deficiencies.

Short-term memory is sometimes impaired in alcoholics who develop thiamine deficiencies.

Alcoholics, for instance, who sometimes develop thiamine (B₁) deficiencies, have problems with short-term memory. They may remember in detail that little café in Paris 20 years ago, but not what they had for supper that previous night.

Thiamine linked to confusion.

Thiamine may also keep the brain thinking straighter and younger. An orthopedic surgeon in England thinks that thiamine deficiency can cause confusion and that confusion can lead to stumbles and broken bones.

The surgeon, M. W. J. Older, M.D., had noticed that people who came to him for hip and thighbone surgery all experienced a dip in their thiamine levels as a result of the stress of the operation. He also noticed that until the thiamine shortage passed, the patients suffered a bout of confusion.

Digging a little deeper, Dr. Older found that patients who came in for *elective* hip surgery—planned in advance, that is—weren't thiamine deficient before the operation, and their postsurgical thiamine deficiency didn't last as long. But the patients with *emergency* fractures, he discovered, were deficient before, during, and after their operations. That raised the possibility that preoperative thiamine-related confusion may even have helped cause the emergencies.

"Mental confusion in the elderly awaits further study," Dr. Older notes, "but our data support the concept that thiamine deficiency may be a contributory factor to postoperative confusion. We . . . suggest that the causation of the fracture itself may be attributable to thiamine deficiency, with confusion precipitating the fall" *(Age and Aging)*.

Confusion, attributable to thiamine deficiency, may precipitate falling in the elderly.

But if there were a contest for the most promising anti-senility nutrients, the prize might be awarded to vitamin B_6 and copper. Two University of Texas nutritionists have reported the remarkable news that a deficiency of B_6 or copper in young rats causes some of the same kind of brain cell abnormalities as those seen in senile humans. The results implied that those two nutrients might prevent mental decline.

Science, of course, is never that simple. But the evidence seems striking. The researchers found, among other things, that in rats and humans, the dendrites—delicate, branching roots that carry electrical impulses from one brain cell to another—tend to shrivel up and die when deprived of B_6 or copper. Without the all-important dendrites, brain circuitry breaks down *(American Journal of Clinical Nutrition)*.

Though the rats were fed a diet skimpier in the two nutrients than any human diet would be, the researchers said that a mild deficiency of those nutrients over the years could have the same devastating effect. The Texas researchers, Elizabeth Root, Ph.D., and John Longenecker, Ph.D., recommended getting adequate amounts of B_6, copper, and other nutrients into the diet as soon as possible for the sake of prevention. (Liver is a fine source of both.)

"If you catch these changes early, then you might prevent some of the neurological damage from occurring," Dr. Root told us. "But it's not just B_6 and copper. People who have a poor diet in general are the most likely to get in trouble. We're starting some more experiments on the possible effects of deficiencies in magnesium and folate, two nutrients that also come up low in most diet surveys."

For best results, catch the deficiencies early.

KEEPING A KEEN MIND

Actually, there's evidence that physically healthy people over age 60 can be measurably keener of mind than their peers if they maintain sufficient dietary levels of

Even mild deficiencies of B_{12}, C, folate, and riboflavin can impede brain function.

vitamins B_{12}, C, folate, and riboflavin. Even mild, virtually unnoticeable deficiencies of those nutrients can mean less-than-optimal brain function.

At the University of New Mexico, senility experts Jean M. Goodwin, M.D., and her husband, James S. Goodwin, M.D., and others placed advertisements in newspapers and on TV and radio in the Albuquerque area asking for volunteers for an experiment. Each volunteer had to be at least 60 years old, free of all serious diseases, and not on medication. After a screening process, the Goodwins chose 260 men and women between the ages of 60 and 94 from various social and income levels.

All the volunteers gave a sample of their blood and filled out a three-day food diary stating exactly what they ate during that period. Taken together, the blood test and diet survey showed the researchers almost exactly what each person's levels of most vitamins and minerals were.

Memory and problem-solving tests administered to 260 people yielded definite nutritional links.

After the process, the volunteers underwent two mental-performance tests. In the first one, a researcher read a one-paragraph story to each person and asked him to repeat it as quickly and accurately as possible. A half hour later, the volunteers had to recite the paragraph from memory, with no cues. The second test measured each person's ability to solve nonverbal problems and to think abstractly.

The researchers fed all the test scores and nutritional profiles into a computer and waited to see if good nutrition would correlate with quicker thinking. It turned out that the volunteers with the lowest B_{12} and C levels scored worst on the memory test. Those with the lowest levels of B_{12}, C, folate, and riboflavin did worst on the problem-solving test *(Journal of the American Medical Association)*.

"We showed that in a population of healthy older people, those people who had a deficient intake and low blood levels of certain vitamins scored significantly worse on the tests," Dr. Jean Goodwin told us. "Our recommendation is that everyone maintain an adequate intake of those nutrients."

THE PROMISE OF CHOLINE

Thiamine and B_{12} are also needed to produce and use one of the brain's major chemical messengers, acetylcholine.

But the real star in acetylcholine production is another B vitamin, choline. Many of the foods touted as "brain foods" —fish, for instance, and liver and eggs—contain choline, a substance researchers are finding really can help preserve the brain's ability to reason, learn, and remember.

Choline: the active component of "brain foods" like fish, liver, and eggs.

For instance, researchers at Ohio State University recently found that mice fed a diet heavy in choline-rich lecithin, or one of lecithin's "brain active" ingredients, phosphatidylcholine, had much better memory retention than mice on regular diets. They took much longer to go into a back room in their cages where they had received a mild electric shock, meaning they hadn't forgotten their unpleasant experience.

What's more, their brain cells, examined under a microscope, showed fewer of the expected signs of aging, says Ronald Mervis, Ph.D., of Ohio State University's Brain Aging and Neuronal Plasticity Research Group.

Brain cells of mice fed choline showed fewer signs of aging.

"Normally, as the brain ages, its cell membranes become more rigid with fatty deposits and lose their ability to take in and release brain chemicals and to relay messages," Dr. Mervis says. This can cause memory loss and confused thinking.

But a lecithin-rich diet seems to repress or delay this membrane hardening.

As part of the deterioration process, aging brain cells also tend to lose dendritic spines, the chemical receptor areas that are vitally important in passing along information. Having too few dendritic spines is like having a bad phone connection. Messages get distorted and lost. But lecithin-fed older mice had the same number of dendritic spines as much younger mice.

A lecithin-rich diet seems to keep nerve channels open to send and receive messages.

"Despite the differences between mice and people there are, nevertheless, remarkable similarities in the structure of their nerve cells," says Dr. Mervis. "I believe lecithin could help to repress or delay similar problems in people, although we have yet to verify that."

LINK TO ALZHEIMER'S DISEASE

Acetylcholine deficits have also been associated with Alzheimer's disease, an insidious debilitating illness that strikes in midlife, causing memory loss, confusion, and

Research is under way to determine if choline can help victims of Alzheimer's disease.

senility. To date there is no treatment or cure. Scientists are seeking a link with lecithin, but so far the results are, at best, mixed.

In severe cases of Alzheimer's disease, the neurons that make acetylcholine may already be disintegrating in the brain, suggesting that lecithin's ability to produce more has already been lost.

One patient showed a 50 percent improvement in recall.

One group of researchers administered high concentrations of lecithin to patients with a wide range of symptom severity for eight weeks. They found little or no improvement in memory—with one exception. A patient whose memory impairment was considered mild had greater than 50 percent improvement in recall *(Journal of Clinical Psychopharmacology)*.

"If it turns out that lecithin in the diet improves short-term or long-term memory function in patients with Alzheimer's disease, or if it makes them more efficient on other cognitive tasks or in motor performance, the benefits to such patients in their day-to-day activities and to their families would be significant," Massachusetts Institute of Technology researcher Suzanne Corkin, Ph.D., told the Symposium of the Foundation for Life Sciences in February 1981.

Can lecithin boost mind power in normal, healthy people?

Lecithin also shows some promise in boosting the mind power of normal, healthy persons.

"Our studies show that choline has a weak to moderate memory enhancement effect," N. Sitaram, M.D., professor of psychiatry at Wayne State University in Detroit, said in an interview. "It's not a robust effect, but it can be measured."

Dr. Sitaram, who was associated with the Biological Psychiatry Branch of the National Institute of Mental Health (NIMH), and his colleagues Herbert Weingartner, Ph.D., and Christian Gillin, M.D., wanted to find out if choline could improve memory in young, healthy persons.

Using choline and a placebo, researchers tested recall in healthy subjects.

On two separate days they gave ten healthy volunteers, ranging in age from 21 to 29, either a supplement of 10 grams of choline chloride or an identical-appearing but worthless substitute. Then after an hour and a half, the people were given a memory test.

In a serial learning test, subjects had to memorize *in proper order* a sequence of ten unrelated words. The list was read to each person and repeated as often as necessary until perfect recall was achieved and could be repeated twice in a row.

"Choline significantly enhanced serial recall of unrelated words as measured by the number of trials required . . . ," the researchers reported. "Furthermore, the enhancement was more pronounced in 'slower' subjects . . . than in subjects who performed well" *(Life Sciences)*.

Indeed, choline enhanced memory—particularly in people who were forgetful.

In other words, the people most in need of help had their memories prodded the most when they took choline. One individual who normally needed six trial readings to master a ten-word list cut that to four after taking choline. Another dropped from seven to five attempts with the choline supplement.

One person who normally required ten trials to master a list of difficult words reduced that to five (a 50 percent improvement!) after taking choline.

And unlike certain drugs which also raise acetylcholine levels in the brain, the authors point out that choline is a natural food component which is safe even in large amounts. The doses of choline given in these tests were at least ten times as great as the 900 milligrams or less supplied by a typical diet.

Safer than certain drugs, choline is a natural food component.

As promising as Dr. Sitaram's results were, however, he was quick to point out that many questions still remain. For example, these tests measured memory 90 minutes after a single dose of choline. We still don't know how long the effects last or whether they would continue over several weeks or months if extra choline were consumed daily.

Long-term effects of choline supplementation are still unknown.

And the trials involved only younger, healthy volunteers with a normal range of remembering ability.

More recent choline research, however, has been directed at elderly people with serious memory impairments brought on by the brain deterioration of senility. Writing in *Scientific American* magazine, Richard Wurtman, M.D., explains why so much attention is being devoted to this aspect of choline research—and why researchers are so optimistic about the findings.

The diseases currently generating the most interest as candidates for lecithin therapy are the memory disorders associated with old age. Aging brings with it a loss of neurons in the brain, and cholinergic (choline-receptive) neurons seem to be particularly vulnerable. The hippocampus, a region of the brain known to be essential for the formation of new memories, has a particularly large number of cholinergic neurons. The administration to young people of drugs such as scopolamine, which block cholinergic transmission, causes short-term memory impairments similar to those observed in the aged. For these reasons it seems possible that treatments calculated to increase brain acetylcholine may be effective in some patients with memory disorders.

Nutritional Help for Tough Emotional Problems

Sarah never left her home. She couldn't, because she spent 12 hours each day grooming and washing her body. Mostly she washed her hands. From the elbows down, the skin was raw, chapped, and at times even ulcerated. She used incredible quantities of creams and ointments, but it didn't do much good.

A woman who never left home.

Sarah underwent ten years of psychoanalysis. She took every antidepressant available as well as every major and minor tranquilizer on the market in an effort to break out of her destructive behavior. She even underwent six series of electroshock treatments and was hospitalized for three of them. And still the washing continued.

Yet today Sarah is free of her obsessive-compulsive disorder and leads a normal, productive life.

What made the difference?

In Sarah's case, says Jose A. Yaryura-Tobias, M.D., it was doses of the amino acid tryptophan, niacin, and pyridoxine (vitamin B_6). Dr. Yaryura-Tobias, a native of Argentina and medical director of Bio-Behavioral Psychiatry in Great Neck, New York, says the therapy increases the blood level of serotonin, an agent responsible for promoting nerve impulses which, in the brain, dictate much of our behavior. Tryptophan is a precursor of serotonin and is also a source of niacin, a vitamin. When niacinamide is given with the tryptophan, less tryptophan will be converted into the vitamin, and more of it will be used to make serotonin. Vitamin B_6 is essential to that conversion.

Three nutrients that led to a normal life.

"But there's more to it than that," says Dr. Yaryura-

Tobias. And he should know. For over 20 years he's been doing research while practicing medicine, first as an internist and then as a psychiatrist with a strong background in psychopharmacology (drug therapy). "I realized early in my practice," says Dr. Yaryura-Tobias, "that psychoanalysis and drugs were not enough.

"Why not a diet for the brain?"

"In medical school in Argentina we had to take one year of nutrition. We could not practice medicine if we didn't study nutrition first. When we examined a patient, we not only had to make a diagnosis at the bedside, we also had to prescribe an appropriate diet. After all, if you have a gallbladder problem, you must follow a certain diet. If you have diarrhea, you need a certain diet. As a psychiatrist I reasoned, why not a diet for the brain? That's as much a part of the body as the gallbladder or intestines."

Still, psychological problems are as varied and complex as the people afflicted. Faulty nutrition may play an important role in the development of symptoms, but so do childhood trauma, genetics, society, and environment. The solutions to those problems must therefore involve numerous therapies in order to gain the maximum chance of recovery. No one method covers it all. Rather, a mixing and blending of philosophies is the best bet.

"An integrated approach to psychiatry."

"And that's what we practice here," says Dr. Yaryura-Tobias. "I call it an integrated approach to psychiatry. We have 15 people on our staff, including two psychiatrists, six psychologists, one neuropsychologist, a nutritionist, two research assistants, an art therapist, a psychiatric social worker, and an EEG-EKG technologist. We each contribute our special area of expertise to the diagnosis and treatment of our patients so they get the benefit of the various disciplines. By working together we find the best approach for each particular case. Because people are different, what works best for one may not work for another.

"Take the case of Sarah, for example. For her, diet alone was enough. For others, a combination of diet and medication may be necessary. But even if a drug is used, adding the appropriate nutrients allows us to cut the dose of the drug by about half, eliminating annoying or damaging side effects."

Calming down "aggressives."

This approach has also done wonders with people suffering from severe aggression associated with hypoglycemia. Of course, not all people with low blood sugar have a violent nature. But the ones who do often have an abnormal EEG (brain wave test), too. Just giving them an anticonvulsant to straighten out the EEG (which is what most doctors do) won't bring results.

"What we did," says Fugen A. Neziroglu, Ph.D., a clinical director of Bio-Behaviorial Psychiatry, "was to divide 45 patients with this disorder into four groups. One group was placed on a special diet to alleviate the hypoglycemia; another group got an anticonvulsant for their abnormal EEG; the third group got traditional tranquilizers; and the fourth got a combination of the diet, vitamin B_6, and an anticonvulsant. The only group that improved statistically was group four, the one receiving the combination.

"We believe that about 33 percent of all aggressives can be helped by the combination of diet, B_6, and an anticonvulsant," she adds.

A NUTRITIONAL FACTOR IN AGORAPHOBIA

Nutritional therapy also plays a role in the treatment of agoraphobia (literally, a fear of open spaces), a paralyzing fear of the "outside world" in which people are unable to leave their homes without suffering a panic attack.

Agoraphobia: a paralyzing fear of the outside world.

A common thread has been found among agoraphobics, who suffer from psycho-physiological problems like anxiety, depression, hyperactivity, and learning disabilities. The link is B vitamins. It's not an unlikely mesh, for B vitamins have long been known to play a big role in managing moods.

Taking the lead in the nutritional approach to agoraphobia is Laraine C. Abbey, R.N., director of Health Extension Services, a clinical nutrition center in East Windsor, New Jersey. And her results to date have been promising.

What Abbey has found in many cases goes beyond a simple vitamin B *deficiency.* She has found that a big problem for a lot of agoraphobics is that they have difficulty *assimilating* their Bs. It's much like having the nutrients swim around in the bloodstream without a dock (the cell) to latch onto.

She cites the cases of 23 clients, all of whom displayed classic signs of agoraphobia and vitamin B abnormality. Disturbed thiamine (B_1) metabolism was the most frequent, followed by niacinamide, B_{12}, folate, and riboflavin. All

B vitamins improved 83 percent of all cases.

were put on large individualized doses of B complex supplements. The result: an 83 percent success rate!

Seven totally recovered, experiencing neither panic nor anxiety attacks nor any of the other symptoms that had inhibited them from moving about in the real world. Twelve were classified as markedly improved, with panic episodes significantly reduced. Slight improvement was observed in the remaining four.

44 of 48 symptoms vanished.

One severely obsessive-compulsive agoraphobic who at certain times wouldn't get up from a chair "was completely recovered when in three months 44 of her 48 symptoms vanished," reports Abbey *(Journal of Orthomolecular Psychiatry)*.

"The massive doses of the B vitamins helped boost cell utilization," Abbey said in an interview. "Some of these people were eating a good supply of B vitamins in their food each day. They just weren't assimilating it."

For some, she says, the problem is genetic. "In one family, grandma, daughter, and granddaughter all had agoraphobia. In another, mother and daughter suffered." In others, enzyme disturbance was caused by poor nutrition. "Many of the agoraphobics I see get up to three-fourths of their calories from processed foods—usually junk carbohydrates," she says. Overprocessed foods, in particular sugar and white flour, can deplete micronutrients.

"Nutrition therapy alone is not the answer for all agoraphobics," says Abbey. "For some the problem is more complex than that. But nutritional treatment is opening the doors for a number of people. It's just the beginning."

TREATING BEHAVIOR PROBLEMS IN CHILDREN

While vitamin B therapy with agoraphobics is still in its infancy, a great track record is being established by the esteemed Canadian physician Abram Hoffer, M.D., Ph.D., in treating children with learning and behavior disorders. And, as was the case with some of the agoraphobics described above, Dr. Hoffer has found the need for large doses of B vitamins a result of diets largely dependent on junk foods.

The children Dr. Hoffer treats display the classic symptoms of hyperactive syndrome—disruption in school, short attention span, restlessness, cheating, lying, temper tantrums, and a basic inability to learn.

B vitamins aren't the cure-all for all hyperactives but they are the solution for 50 percent of the patients Dr. Hoffer sees.

Over the past six years he has successfully treated some 400 children by getting them off their poor diets and putting them on B vitamins.

A doctor who successfully treated 400 hyperactive children with B vitamins.

"Most of the children have recovered," says Dr. Hoffer. "This was assessed by their school record, by their behavior at home, and by the absence of symptoms. I consider a child well when he is free of symptoms, is normal at home, gets on well at school, and has no difficulty in the community."

An even more severe behavior problem, characterized by wild excitability and excessive activity, has also been linked to a B vitamin deficiency. In this case, to one B in particular: vitamin B_{12}.

B_{12} FOR MANIC BEHAVIOR

The patient's behavior changed quite suddenly and became increasingly bizarre. He was irritable and agitated. He was hardly sleeping at all and was hyperactive. And he had delusions that he was of great importance. In fact, he was convinced that his hometown was planning a day of celebration in his honor, and that several Hollywood celebrities would attend. When he was finally admitted to a hospital, it took six men to restrain him. And the patient was 81 years old!

His doctors performed all of the proper physical and neurological tests, but the results were normal. And all of his blood tests were normal too. Except for one. The test for vitamin B_{12} showed that he had an abnormally low level of the vitamin in his blood.

Abnormal behavior—and an abnormally low level of B_{12}.

The doctor prescribed daily B_{12} intravenously, and by the end of one week, the patient's mental status returned to normal. He continued to receive weekly B_{12} by injection and six months later was still completely normal.

"That particular syndrome, called mania, has never before been traced to B_{12} deficiency, so most general physicians may not be aware of that possibility," says Frederick Goggans, M.D., the doctor who treated that patient. "But what makes the case even more unusual is that the patient's mental problems appeared before any other signs of B_{12} deficiency."

A healthy nervous system needs B_{12}.

Usually, a B_{12} deficiency is easy to spot, because even though it's needed only in tiny amounts (the Recommended Dietary Allowance, or RDA, is 3 *micro*grams), B_{12} works for us in a big way. It's needed for the production of healthy red blood cells and for proper functioning of the nervous system.

When there's not enough B_{12} to go around, the nerves and spinal cord are affected, leading to numbness and tingling in the hands and feet and an unsteady gait. The red blood cells become enlarged and misshapen, and are unable to carry oxygen properly (which is their main job). The condition is called pernicious anemia, and other symptoms are pallor, weakness, fatigue, and diarrhea. Mental problems can eventually occur, but not until much later. Or that's what doctors used to think. New reports are proving that's not always true.

At the University of North Carolina, doctors recently described the cases of two patients with psychoses (severe mental disorders) caused by vitamin B_{12} deficiencies. Both of the patients had no other symptoms of B_{12} deficiency, and both returned to normal after receiving B_{12} injections.

The first symptoms of B_{12} deficiency may be psychiatric.

The doctors warn that "psychiatric manifestations may be the first symptoms of vitamin B_{12} deficiency," and they recommend that all patients with psychoses caused by brain-tissue dysfunction be checked for B_{12} deficiency *(American Journal of Psychiatry)*.

"Even though most doctors are aware that B_{12} deficiency can lead to psychiatric symptoms, they may not be aware that it can happen before any signs of anemia," says Lorrin Koran, M.D., associate professor of psychiatry at Stanford University Medical Center.

Choline for manic-depressives.

Choline, a vitamin-like substance usually classified as part of the B vitamins, is also being used with great success by manic-depressives.

Take the case of a euphoric, bug-eyed young man who came sailing into the psychiatric unit at Belmont (Massachusetts) Hospital. Although he hadn't slept in several days, he was running in high gear.

"He had typical symptoms of mania," says one of the doctors who treated the case, "confusion, delusion, paranoia.

He was not sleepy and was overly sexual. He thought he was an extraordinarily important businessman and that someone was out to get him." Lecithin, a natural food source of choline, brought him back to earth.

The doctors at Belmont and at Harvard Medical School had found earlier that patients taking lithium or other antipsychotic medications responded better to treatment when high doses of lecithin were also taken. And subsequent studies showed that lecithin *alone* was also effective.

Lecithin boosts the effectiveness of antipsychotic drugs.

For two weeks, patients were given either approximately 50 percent or 90 percent pure lecithin mixed with ice cream or peanut butter. All those on the low-dose lecithin suffered side effects and only one of four showed measurable improvement. However, no side effects and marked improvement were found in all the patients on the high-dose lecithin. They also were well enough to go home after 3½ weeks, compared to the 8 weeks normally spent hospitalized for standard treatment *(American Journal of Psychiatry)*.

The exciting news in all this is that lecithin could someday replace the dependence on lithium by mania patients.

Lecithin could replace lithium, a drug for mania patients.

"Lithium has been used as the drug to treat mania and it has been effective in 80 percent of the cases," says one of the researchers. "The problem is it's only a treatment and not a cure. So, we're looking for a cure. And that's why we're looking at lecithin."

Another disease of the mind in which lecithin has played a winning role is tardive dyskinesia (TD), a disorder resulting from the use of some psychiatric drugs.

Lecithin relieves symptoms of a drug-caused disease.

TD is a disfiguring ailment characterized by uncontrollable twitches of facial and other muscles. Previously, choline was found effective in relieving some of the embarrassing symptoms of the disease.

But this treatment has its drawbacks—mainly the fishy odor that results when choline is ingested and goes into action. So, lecithin was put to the test. Not only was it effective, it was found to work better than choline.

In, one study, a group of TD sufferers were given daily doses of lecithin for 14 days and another group was given placebos, or dummy pills. Involuntary movement and twitching was recorded daily by videotape. All those on lecithin showed progressive, daily improvement over the other group *(American Journal of Psychiatry)*.

SCHIZOPHRENIA RESPONDS TO NUTRITION

But perhaps the most interesting work to date is in the area of nutritional therapy for schizophrenia.

"Fear was the overwhelming feeling: fear jerking my stomach to a yammering, screaming cloud of butterflies," recalled a man diagnosed as a paranoid schizophrenic, describing his last breakdown. "People in the streets, shopkeepers, faces on television . . . all looked angry and threatening. The flat upstairs seemed to have been divested of its usual occupants for others who were spying on me with bugging devices. I wouldn't eat meat because I thought it was taken from the morgue; the food was poisoned; the tablets were LSD. . . . For the first four weeks I did not sleep, and spent my days and nights in terror of madness."

Schizophrenia—a word describing this and dozens of other kinds of secret agony—is a disorder that's been estimated to afflict 1 in every 100 people. Yet the cause and proper treatment of schizophrenia remain a matter of heated debate among psychiatrists and researchers.

"Is schizophrenia a disease of the mind, brought about by psychological interactions and producing some secondary physical changes? Or is it a disease of the body which happens to affect the brain? This is the most bitterly contested issue in psychiatry," says David Horrobin, M.D., Ph.D., of Efamol Research, Inc., Kentville, Nova Scotia. A growing number of doctors have come to believe that many kinds of mental illness are caused by "an elaborately disordered metabolism," as one put it—particularly mix-ups in the complex interplay of brain chemicals. In other words, the sick mind may best be reached by healing the sick body.

In fact, the widespread use of major tranquilizers and other drugs has shown that altering the body's biochemistry can have a dramatic effect on mental states. But drugs take their toll. "My personality has been so stifled that sometimes I think that the richness of my preinjection days—even with brief outbursts of madness—is preferable to the numbed cabbage that I have become," one schizophrenic said of the tranquilizers he might take for life.

BALANCING AN UNBALANCED BODY

Isn't there a better way? Psychiatrists practicing what's come to be known as orthomolecular medicine believe

---

Sidenotes (left margin):

"Days and nights of madness."

A disease of mind or body?

Tranquilizers created a "numbed cabbage."

Restoring natural balance through nutrition.

there is. They, too, believe schizophrenia can be treated by altering the body's chemistry. But to them, it's a matter of restoring the natural balances in a wildly unbalanced body, through good nutrition and the use of specific vitamins, minerals, amino acids, and other substances that occur naturally in the human body.

The word orthomolecular, in fact, simply means "correct molecule"; orthomolecular psychiatry, as Linus Pauling, Ph.D., once defined it, means "the treatment of mental disease by the provision of the optimum molecular environment for the mind."

"Optimum molecular environment for the mind."

"Back in the late sixties I was practicing traditional psychotherapy, but I came to feel this new approach might have something to offer," recalls Moke Williams, M.D., founder and director of the Coral Ridge Institute, in Fort Lauderdale, Florida. He went to work with Dr. Abram Hoffer and Humphrey Osmond, M.D., the Canadian psychiatrists whose pioneering work using massive doses of the B vitamin niacin to treat schizophrenia opened the era of orthomolecular psychiatry. The experience "completely reorganized my philosophy" about psychiatry, Dr. Williams says. Today his practice combines the use of specific nutrients, psychotherapy, and patient education.

"The orthomolecular approach is more efficient, less expensive, and less time-consuming than traditional approaches," Dr. Williams says. "We still use some drugs, but we've found that with good nutrition, we can greatly reduce the dosages of drugs patients have to take."

Nutrition reduces the drug dosage.

Getting patients off drugs can have other benefits as well. It now appears that the long-term use of antipsychotic drugs is one of the primary causes of the mysterious disorder TD. David Hawkins, M.D., and Charles Tkacz, M.D., directors of the North Nassau Mental Health Center in Manhasset, New York, have reported that among some 11,000 patients treated with vitamin therapy over a period of ten years, not one developed TD. Yet among drug-treated patients, they say, the disorder develops with alarming frequency.

"Since you're working with substances that are normally present in the body, the orthomolecular approach is relatively free of risk," adds Michael Lesser, M.D., a California psychiatrist and author of *Nutrition and Vitamin Therapy* (Grove Press). And there's something else: "There's no proof psychotherapy or drugs actually cure

"Relatively free of risk."

mental illness, though they often help suppress the symptoms," Dr. Lesser says.

"But vitamin deficiencies have been shown to cause mental illness," continues Dr. Lesser. And vitamin supplementation has been found to reverse the problem.

Niacin for schizophrenia.

Dr. Hoffer was a pioneer in the nutritional treatment of schizophrenia. In 1952, he and a colleague gave niacin to eight schizophrenic patients. They immediately improved. Continuing the study, the doctors checked their patients' progress for the next 15 years. All were well 15 years later —and all were still taking niacin (*Orthomolecular Psychiatry*).

Schizophrenia can last a lifetime, or a few weeks. Many patients walk out of state hospitals only to return. To see if niacin could keep schizophrenics permanently out of hospitals, Dr. Hoffer gave 73 hospitalized schizophrenics niacin and compared them to 98 who were not taking niacin. During the next three years, only 7 of the niacin patients had to be readmitted to a hospital, while 47 of the non-niacin patients were readmitted (*Lancet*).

A "vitamin dependency."

The patients Dr. Hoffer treated did *not* have pellagra, the scientific term for a niacin deficiency. They had what he calls a "vitamin dependency."

A vitamin dependency, Dr. Hoffer explains, is the need for a larger amount of a vitamin than most people require. If you don't get that amount, you can suffer from a variety of physical and mental ills. Schizophrenia is one of them.

The dependency could be inherited. Or, if you were deprived of the nutrient over a long period of time, you might need more of it to function normally. Many of the mental patients with pellagra, for instance, had to take 600 milligrams of niacin every day for the rest of their lives. (No one should take that much, of course, unless they're under the supervision of a doctor.) Most people need only around 15 milligrams.

Niacin isn't the only nutrient involved, however. Vitamin C is another.

Schizophrenics need up to 8 times more vitamin C.

When normal people are given 5 grams of vitamin C, their tissues are saturated—they can't absorb any more. But studies show that it takes about *20 to 40 grams* of vitamin C to saturate the tissues of schizophrenics. They don't need that much to get better, though. A doctor gave 1 gram of vitamin C a day to 40 schizophrenics, all of whom had had the disease for years. Many of them showed significant improvement.

B VITAMINS: THE MIND HEALERS

But when it comes to schizophrenia, the B vitamins are still the focus of attention.

In a study of the thiamine levels of 154 psychiatric patients, researchers found more thiamine deficiencies among those patients with severe disorders (such as schizophrenia) than among those with milder illnesses *(British Journal of Psychiatry)*.

One of the more recent examples of schizophrenia related to a B vitamin deficiency is found in a case report from doctors at Arlington Hospital in Arlington, Virginia.

"An 18-year-old male entered the emergency room and was diagnosed as having acute catatonic schizophrenia," says Lawrence D'Angelo, M.D., one of the investigating doctors. "He showed signs of restlessness, insomnia, mental confusion, anorexia, hallucinations, psychomotor retardation, and other symptoms. But we could find no evidence of organic brain damage, drug toxicity, or any other specific cause for his condition—even after about three weeks of intensive medical investigation."

The doctors tried antipsychotic drugs on the patient, discontinued them because of severe side effects, tested the patient some more, then considered B_6. "We knew about other psychiatric case reports involving B_6," says Dr. D'Angelo. "So we started the patient on a daily B_6 regimen."

The dosage was 150 milligrams three times a day, then 500 milligrams per day—a therapeutic intake far above normal levels. The RDA is 1.8 to 2.2 milligrams. (Because evidence suggests very large doses can be dangerous, you should never exceed 50 milligrams daily unless advised to do so by a knowledgeable physician.) Within 48 hours after the dose was increased, the patient started to improve—and kept improving as long as he stayed on the nutrient therapy.

48 hours after B_6 therapy: improvement.

"Over a period of seven months, most of the patient's symptoms went away," Dr. D'Angelo says. "He thought more logically and clearly and didn't demonstrate any of the abnormal behavior he had when he first came to the hospital."

But when he reduced his B_6 intake . . . relapse. He was virtually back where he started. And only the high

No more B_6: relapse.

therapeutic dose of the nutrient could bring him back toward normal.

Do the investigators understand why B_6 has such a profound effect? Not yet, but they do know that B_6's power could not be due to a single biological action. Vitamin B_6, they say, causes a whole spectrum of biochemical actions in the brain, and such multiplicity is required to affect the bundles of symptoms known as schizophrenia *(Biological Psychiatry).*

Richard Kunin, M.D., past president of the Orthomolecular Medical Society and author of *Mega-Nutrition for Women* (McGraw-Hill), has one theory.

A key to schizophrenia: essential fatty acids.

"The past ten years has been a really exciting decade of progress," he says, explaining that one of the most promising new developments is an increased understanding of the importance of essential-fatty-acid metabolism—potentially a key to unlocking the lonely prison of schizophrenia. Ever since niacin deficiency (pellagra) was shown to produce bona-fide neuroses and psychoses, the B vitamins have been recognized as playing a role in mental illness, Dr. Kunin explains. As a result, the B vitamins have become the "old standby" of orthomolecular psychiatry—though precisely how they work has remained something of a mystery.

But in a paper in *Medical Hypotheses,* molecular biologist Donald Rudin, Ph.D., argues that the B vitamins merely help to convert a type of fatty acid called omega-3 into prostaglandins, "the most diverse regulatory system in the body." The prostaglandins, some psychiatrists now believe, may be the key to schizophrenia. Yet because modern food-processing techniques deplete the omega-3 fatty acids in common foods by as much as 90 percent, Dr. Rudin believes deficiencies of these substances are widespread.

"Striking" results with linseed oil.

Using common linseed oil, Dr. Rudin reported "striking" results in 32 cases of pellagralike diseases, including schizophrenia and neurosis. The linseed-oil supplements, he says, led "the families of severe psychotics to conclude, after decades of disruptive behavior, that there had been startling improvement."

From a practical point of view, says Dr. Kunin, "it's all still very new, but so far I've had some exciting success with fatty acids. Patients I couldn't get off tranquilizers before I've now been able to." (The omega-3 fatty acids are also present in some fish oils.)

There's been a great deal of interest recently in amino acids, such as tryptophan and methionine, Dr. Kunin says, "but it's all quite complicated and we probably won't really feel the impact of this research for another five years."

Metal poisoning is another problem that's received a great deal of attention. "Hair-tissue analysis frequently shows a significant amount of toxic metals," Dr. Lesser says. Vitamin supplements or certain foods can be used to bind with these metals and draw them out of the body, he explains. Aluminum, for example, can be scoured out of the body with magnesium supplements. "Minerals, unlike the B vitamins, have the potential to cause harm if taken inappropriately and should only be used therapeutically under a physician's supervision," he says. Dr. Lesser also uses foods naturally rich in sulfur to draw out dangerous metals—foods like onions, chives, garlic, and asparagus.

Metal poisoning and the brain.

Essential minerals like copper, zinc, manganese, calcium, and chromium are also becoming more widely appreciated for their role in mental health, says Dr. Williams. "Copper and zinc levels can give us an idea what kind of mental illness we're dealing with," he explains. "In hyperactivity, very often we find high copper and low zinc levels. That gives us an idea of what combinations of nutrients to put together, what nutritional direction we're going to take." Vitamin B_6 in combination with magnesium can be effective in soothing the hyperactive, he says.

Does copper cause hyperactivity?

Carl Pfeiffer, M.D., Ph.D., director of the Brain Bio Center in Skillman, New Jersey, has found calcium useful in the treatment of some cases of schizophrenia.

Sixty percent of schizophrenics suffer from a histamine disorder, according to Dr. Pfeiffer. Histamine, as any hay fever victim who takes antihistamines can tell you, is involved in allergic reactions. But that's not all it's involved in. "It would take a half hour to explain all of histamine's functions in the body," says Dr. Pfeiffer. And one of those functions is as a neurotransmitter. When histamine levels rise too high or dip too low, the brain can relay the wrong information and cause schizophrenia.

Using calcium to treat schizophrenia.

For patients with low histamine, large doses of niacin and vitamin C are usually effective, he explains. But for schizophrenics with high histamine, Dr. Pfeiffer prescribes calcium, which lowers histamine levels and relieves the constant or frequent headaches that accompany the disorder. Along with calcium, he gives the minerals zinc and manganese.

THE ULTIMATE TEST

The value of nutrition in mental problems, however, is really put to the test in the treatment of the mentally retarded.

Treating retardation with nutrition.

Ruth F. Harrell, Ph.D., research professor at Old Dominion University in Norfolk, Virginia, and her colleagues examined the intriguing possibility that retardation might be the result of nutritional deficiencies and therefore could be "amenable to treatment" with supplementary vitamins and minerals.

Their report, published in the *Proceedings of the National Academy of Sciences,* is cautiously optimistic.

In the introduction to her study, Dr. Harrell relates the case of G. S., a severely retarded seven-year-old who, before being treated, was in diapers, could not speak, and had an estimated I.Q. of 25 to 30.

After the boy's tissues and blood were analyzed, an appropriate nutritional supplement was devised. It took several weeks of trial and error to get the ingredients just right, but once Dr. Harrell had the correct dosage of vitamins and minerals, the boy's progress was remarkable.

A boy's I.Q. went from 30 to 90.

"In a few days, he was talking a little. In a few weeks, he was learning to read and write and he began to act like a normal child. When G. S. was nine years old, he read and wrote on the elementary school level, was moderately advanced in arithmetic and, according to his teacher, was mischievous and active. He rode a bicycle and skateboard, played ball, played a flute, and had an I.Q. of about 90," she writes.

A study of 16 retarded children.

With that heartening result (and earlier successes) in mind, Dr. Harrell enlisted the help of a team of biochemists and psychologists and recruited a group of 16 retarded children (including four with Down's syndrome, or "mongolism") whose I.Q.'s ranged from 17 to 70 to participate in an eight-month study.

For the first four months, 11 children took a useless placebo while 5 received a six-tablet daily regimen of 11 vitamins and 8 minerals. The supplements included the B-complex vitamins (including folate and pantothenate), and vitamins A, C, D, and E, along with calcium, zinc, manganese, copper, iron, and other minerals.

In determining the strength of most of the nutrients, "we went far beyond the RDA," Dr. Harrell told us. "It was 'mega' in size and went up and up and up until we got a mental response."

To give you an idea of just how "mega" the dosage was, the 15,000 international units of vitamin A represents approximately four times the RDA. The B-complex supplements were over 100 times the RDA, while there was in excess of 25 times what is thought to be the body's normal requirement of C and E.

Most of the minerals, however, were closer to RDA levels.

High levels of vitamins, individually adjusted.

Following the initial segment of the study, all of the children took the supplements for an additional four months. And when all the data was collected and analyzed, and the progress of the children could be examined, "the results were such that I was afraid to believe them," Dr. Harrell admits.

"During the first four-month period . . . the 5 children who received supplements increased their average I.Q. from 5.0 to 9.6 points, depending on the investigator, whereas the 11 subjects given placebos showed negligible change. The difference between these groups is statistically significant. During the second period, the subjects who had been given placebos in the first study received supplements; they showed an average I.Q. increase of at least 10.2, a highly significant gain," she writes.

"Several children improved greatly in school achievement. For example, J. B. (age five to six), who said only single words such as 'Mama' or 'bye-bye' initially, could recite without prompting the Pledge of Allegiance after eight months of supplementation and could read the first-grade primer. Two (T. C. and R. S.) have been transferred from programs for the mentally retarded to regular schools and grades, on the teacher's recommendations.

From single words to reading at the first-grade level.

"They're not blockbusters — not superior, mind you — but I hope they can fend for themselves in an average sort of way," she notes.

"All of our subjects who cooperated in taking the supplements showed improvement, sometimes dramatic and surprising to the teachers and other professionals who dealt with them."

What is perhaps startling is that "everyone posted

"New hope for the mentally retarded."

Nutrients reduced retardation by 25 percent.

some kind of gain" across the entire spectrum of retardation, even those with Down's syndrome.

"If our findings are confirmed by more extensive experiments, they bring new hope for improving the quality of life for the mentally retarded 3.2 percent of our population."

In essence, nutritional supplements were instrumental in reducing the mentally retarded portion of the study group by one-fourth. Translate that into the millions of members of the human family considered "slow"—I.Q.'s below 75—and the billions of dollars going into their special, and often custodial, care, and it's easy to see the far-reaching implications of Dr. Harrell's study.

If supplements are the key to unlocking the retarded mind—if they enable many of those so afflicted "to make their own way, to become hewers of wood and drawers of water," to use Dr. Harrell's words—we're clearly onto something major.

PART II

Building Emotional Hardiness

Commitment, Control, and Challenge: The Winning Combination for a Long and Happy Life

*O*nly the strong sur-
vive. So it's been said and few would dispute. But what does
it take to be *strong*? A heart that won't quit? A long lineage
of "die-hards"? A strong constitution?

What does it take to survive?

Certainly, those factors can help. But in these days of
relentless emotional and psychological pressures—when
stress is blamed for every malady from chronic depression
to cancer, ulcers to heart disease—there emerges some new
strength factors. According to studies at the University of
Chicago by psychologist Suzanne Ouellette Kobasa, Ph.D.,
and associates, survivors share three specific personality
traits that appear to afford them a high degree of stress
resistance: they are *committed* to what they do; they feel in
control of their lives; and they see change as a *challenge*
rather than a threat.

Survivors share three specific
personality traits.

"It helps explain why one executive gets severe headaches or pains in his chest, while his office neighbor weath-
ers the same pressures in perfect health," Dr. Kobasa says.

What follows is Dr. Kobasa's own account of her
remarkable new research—what prompted it and what it
means to you.

The fatalistic view of stress dates from the 1950s,
when many researchers began to look for links between it
and illness. For two decades, they explored the pessimistic
notion that the more frequent and serious the stress in your
life, the greater your chance of getting sick.

A 1950s notion: The more
stress in your life, the greater
your chance of illness.

In one typical study, researchers interviewed a group

of hospital patients, in treatment for everything from depression to heart attack, and asked them about stressful experiences in the past three years. These hospitalized people had, it turned out, been under more stress than a comparable group of healthy people.

In another, better-designed study, medical researchers gave people a questionnaire to fill out while they were still healthy. They asked about stressful events in the previous six months, then waited to see whether those who'd had a difficult half year would develop more symptoms.

They did. People who scored in the upper third of the stress scale had nearly 90 percent more illnesses in the first month of the follow-up period than did those scoring in the lowest third of the scale. And the high-stress group stayed physically sicker over the next five months of the study.

These two studies and the many others like them used a simple way of thinking about and measuring stress. In the 1960s, medical researchers Thomas Holmes and Richard Rahe developed a popular scale, which you may have seen, that was a checklist of stressful events. They appreciated the tricky point that *any* major change can be stressful. Negative events like "serious illness of a family member" and "trouble with boss" were high on the list, but so were some positive life-changing events, like marriage. You might want to take the Holmes–Rahe test to find out how much pressure you're under [see Table 4]. But remember that the score does not reflect how you deal with stress—it only shows how much you have to deal with. And we now know that the way you handle these events dramatically affects your chances of staying healthy.

By the early 1970s, hundreds of similar studies had followed Holmes and Rahe. And millions of Americans who work and live under stress worried over the reports. Somehow, the research got boiled down to a memorable message. Women's magazines ran headlines like "Stress causes illness!" If you want to stay physically and mentally healthy, the articles said, avoid stressful events.

But such simplistic advice is impossible to follow. Even if stressful events are dangerous, many—like the death of a loved one—are impossible to avoid. Moreover, any warning to avoid *all* stressful events is a prescription for staying away from opportunities as well as trouble. Since any change can be stressful, a person who wanted to be

How many stressful events have you experienced in the last six months?

Any major change—from marriage to divorce—can be stressful.

Message boiled down to: Avoid stress and stay healthy.

TABLE 4: Stress Rating Scale

Event	Value	Event	Value
Death of spouse	100	Son or daughter leaving home	29
Divorce	73	Trouble with in-laws	29
Marital separation	65	Outstanding personal achievement	28
Jail term	63	Spouse begins or stops work	26
Death of close family member	63	Starting or finishing school	26
Personal injury or illness	53	Change in living conditions	25
Marriage	50	Revision of personal habits	24
Fired from work	47	Trouble with boss	23
Marital reconciliation	45	Change in work hours, conditions	20
Retirement	45	Change in residence	20
Change in family member's health	44	Change in schools	20
Pregnancy	40	Change in recreational habits	19
Sex difficulties	39	Change in church activities	19
Addition to family	39	Change in social activities	18
Business readjustment	39	Mortgage or loan under $10,000	17
Change in financial status	38	Change in sleeping habits	16
Death of close friend	37	Change in number of family gatherings	15
Change to different line of work	36	Change in eating habits	15
Change in number of marital arguments	36	Vacation	13
Mortgage or loan over $10,000	31	Christmas season	12
Foreclosure of mortgage or loan	30	Minor violation of the law	11
Change in work responsibilities	29		

Researchers at the University of Washington School of Medicine developed this scale for ranking stressful events in a person's life. The higher the total score accumulated in the preceding year, the more likely there will be a serious illness in the immediate future.

Reprinted with permission from *Journal of Psychosomatic Research*, Volume 11, T. H. Holmes and R. H. Rahe, "The Social Readjustment Rating Scale," 1967, Pergamon Press, Ltd.

completely free of stress would never marry, have a child, take a new job, or move.

Life without change or challenge can become boring.

The notion that all stress makes you sick also ignores a lot of what we know about people. It assumes we're all vulnerable and passive in the face of adversity. But what about human resilience, initiative, and creativity? Many come through periods of stress with more physical and mental vigor than they had before. We also know that a long time without change or challenge can lead to boredom, and physical and mental strain.

In 1975 I became interested in people who stay healthy under stress. My colleagues and I decided to look first at high-powered business executives—widely viewed as the walking wounded of the stress war. We found a group of telephone executives whose life experiences, on the standard scale, would have put them at high risk for illness—but who were still in good health. So we asked the question: What was special about them?

THE HARDINESS NOTION

How does stress damage the body?

The first question, really, was how does stress damage the body? The prevailing theory, developed by Dr. Hans Selye, is that stress hurts you by sounding the alarm to mobilize for fight or flight. When you feel you're in danger, your heart rate speeds up, the fats, cholesterol, and sugar in your bloodstream increases, your stomach secretes more acid, your immune system slows down. All of these changes are a colossal strain. And the strain is greatest if the stresses you face are numerous, severe, and persistent.

Over time, the strain leads to symptoms like gastrointestinal distress, high blood cholesterol, insomnia, and low back pain. It also leaves you vulnerable to disease agents. Depending upon their biological make-up and exposure, one person may eventually develop heart disease, another a peptic ulcer, and a third a severe depression.

Is it possible to cope with stress without becoming anxious?

We thought some people might be able to handle stress without becoming anxious and aroused in the first place—and without starting the spiral that leads to illness. So we checked out three major personality traits that seemed most likely to help:

1. Commitment to self, work, family, and other important values.

2. A sense of personal control over one's life.

3. The ability to see change in one's life as a challenge
to master.

We saw these three "Cs"—commitment, control, and
challenge—as the ingredients of what we called psychological hardiness. Hardy people should be able to face change
with confidence and self-determination, and the eagerness
of seeing change as opportunity. In contrast, a less hardy
person could feel alienated, threatened, or helpless in the
face of any major challenge to the status quo.

We had an ideal chance to put our hypothesis to the
test. We studied executives in an operating company of one
of the world's largest corporations—AT&T—as it moved
into some of the biggest changes of its hundred-year history.

With the support of Illinois Bell's medical director,
Dr. Robert Hilker, we recruited hundreds of middle- and
upper-level executives. As we followed these people over
the next eight years, we saw how they handled various work
and home pressures, including the AT&T divestiture—one
of the biggest corporate earthquakes ever. As we saw who
stayed healthy and who got sick, the importance of being
hardy was clear from the beginning.

Nearly 700 executives filled out two questionnaires: a
version of the Holmes-Rahe stress inventory modified to
include the specific stresses of Illinois Bell, and a checklist
of symptoms and illnesses. Some did report that they'd been
under unusual stress and had taken ill. But an equal number had stayed healthy under stress. And some had gotten
sick even though nothing unusual had been happening in
their lives.

We took 200 executives who'd scored high on the
stress scale—100 who stayed healthy under stress, and 100
who got sick. Then we tried to see what made the difference
between them. We asked them about their jobs, age,
educational background, income—and personality questions,
similar to those on our quiz here [see Box 8], that were
designed to measure hardiness.

When the computer analysis was done, it turned out
that the healthy executives were not younger, wealthier,
higher on the career ladder, or better-educated than their
colleagues who became sick under stress. But one difference clearly counted: They were hardier.

The stressed but healthy executives were more

Hardy people see change as an opportunity.

Dr. Kobasa followed AT&T executives for eight years.

100 stayed healthy; 100 got sick.

The stressed but healthy executives were more committed, felt in control.

committed, felt more in control, and had bigger appetites for challenge. In fact, on some indicators the healthy executives showed twice as much hardiness.

These personality traits were their most potent protection against stress.

To strengthen the result, Salvatore Maddi, a colleague at the University of Chicago, and I retested the executives twice in the next two years. We wanted to make sure that people stayed healthy because they were hardy—and that they had not simply felt hardy on the first test because they had come through recent stresses unscathed. But the connection held up over time. When hardy executives came under serious stress, they were only half as likely to get sick as were less hardy people with the same stress level.

Hardiness protects all kinds of people from stress.

Though the telephone executives were a homogeneous lot—mostly male, middle-class, middle-aged, married, and Protestant—we've since found that hardiness protects all kinds of people from stress.

We've found it, for example, in a continuing study of women. A few years ago, we distributed hardiness questionnaires to hundreds of women in their gynecologists' offices.

Those who were more helpless developed more illnesses— mental and physical.

We've found that those who were more helpless than hardy have developed more illnesses, both mental and physical.

We've also seen the hardiness effect in lawyers. Two large groups of general practice lawyers from the U.S. and Canada completed questionnaires like those we gave the telephone executives. If anything, a hardy personality type protected the lawyers even more than it had the executives. Other groups that demonstrate the stress-buffering power

---

BOX 8: HOW HARDY ARE YOU?

On the next page are 12 items similar to those that appear in the hardiness questionnaire. Evaluating someone's hardiness requires more than this quick test. But this simple exercise should give you some idea of how hardy you are.

Write down how much you agree or

disagree with the following statements, using this scale:

0 = strongly disagree,
1 = mildly disagree,
2 = mildly agree,
3 = strongly agree.

BOX 8 — *Continued*

A. Trying my best at work makes a difference.

B. Trusting to fate is sometimes all I can do in a relationship.

C. I often wake up eager to start on the day's projects.

D. Thinking of myself as a free person leads to great frustration and difficulty.

E. I would be willing to sacrifice financial security in my work if something really challenging came along.

F. It bothers me when I have to deviate from the routine or schedule I've set for myself.

G. An average citizen can have an impact on politics.

H. Without the right breaks, it is hard to be successful in my field.

I. I know why I am doing what I'm doing at work.

J. Getting close to people puts me at risk of being obligated to them.

K. Encountering new situations is an important priority in my life.

L. I really don't mind when I have nothing to do.

To Score Yourself: These questions measure control, commitment, and challenge. For half the questions, a high score (like 3, "strongly agree") indicates hardiness; for the other half, a low score (disagreement) does.

To get your scores on control, commitment, and challenge, first write in the number of your answers—0, 1, 2, 3—above the letter of each question on the score sheet. Then add and subtract as shown. (To get your score on "control," for example, add your answers to questions A and G; add your answers to B and H; and then subtract the second number from the first.)

Add your scores on commitment, control, and challenge together to get a score for total hardiness.

A total score of 10-18 shows a hardy personality. 0-9: moderate hardiness. Below 0: low hardiness.

$$\underline{\quad}_{A} + \underline{\quad}_{G} = \underline{\quad}$$
$$-$$
$$\underline{\quad}_{B} + \underline{\quad}_{H} = \underline{\quad} = \underline{\quad}\text{Control Score}$$
$$\underline{\quad}_{C} + \underline{\quad}_{I} = \underline{\quad}$$
$$-$$
$$\underline{\quad}_{D} + \underline{\quad}_{J} = \underline{\quad} = \underline{\quad}\text{Commitment Score}$$
$$\underline{\quad}_{E} + \underline{\quad}_{K} = \underline{\quad}$$
$$-$$
$$\underline{\quad}_{F} + \underline{\quad}_{L} = \underline{\quad} = \underline{\quad}\text{Challenge Score}$$
$$\underline{\quad}_{Control} + \underline{\quad}_{Commitment} + \underline{\quad}_{Challenge} = \underline{\quad}\text{Total Hardiness Score}$$

Reprinted by permission of the publisher from "How Much Stress Can You Survive?" by Suzanne Ouellette Kobasa, Ph.D., in *American Health,* September 1984, pp. 64-77.

of character include men and women at the "craft" level with the telephone company (e.g., foremen and operator supervisors), U.S. Army officers, and college students.

Social support and exercise can also help fight stress.

Important as hardiness is, it's not the only way people fight stress. Social support, exercise, and a strong constitution can all help. But hardiness, or a lack of it, can change the way people use these other resources.

The kind of body you're born with, for example, certainly affects your chances of getting sick. We reviewed the family histories of the telephone executives, and classified them as being at high or low genetic risk for illnesses like coronary heart disease. Not surprisingly, when the going got rough, those with a high risk were more prone to illness.

Hardiness is more important than a healthy family history.

But biology is not destiny. A hardy personality, we found, was more important than a strong constitution. Hardy people from sickly families did better under stress, on average, than those from healthy families but with fewer inner resources.

Vigorous exercise is a good anti-stress tool. Under high stress, we have found, executives who work out stay healthier than those who don't. Those who are hardy personalities *and* exercisers are healthier than those who are only one or the other. . . .

Hardy people use support systems well.

Besides handling conflict better, hardy people also accept support from their families and coworkers, and use that support well. . . .

LEARNING TO BE A SURVIVOR

Hardiness is clearly a good thing. But all these studies left one crucial question unanswered. Can you actually *learn* to be hardy? Or is this aspect of personality fixed early in life?

Hardiness can be developed through self-reflection.

I think it's possible to become hardier: more committed, in control, and open to challenge. The change can come through self-reflection. Or, as we are learning, through teaching.

Salvatore Maddi and I took 16 executives from Illinois Bell, men under high stress and starting to show such signs of strain as psychological problems and high blood pressure. Half the men participated in weekly group meetings, led by Sal Maddi, where they studied techniques designed to make them hardier [see Box 9]. After eight weeks, they scored higher on the hardiness scale and had less psychological distress than before. Even more striking, their blood pressure—a clear measure of health—dropped. Three months later, the benefits still held. The other 8 men who served as controls—they just kept a stress journal and met only at the beginning and end of the eight-week period—showed no such changes.

We plan to test group training with more people, including women and non-executives. We would also like

People who worked at becoming hardy experienced a drop in blood pressure.

BOX 9: THREE PATHS TO HARDINESS

In working with groups of executives, we have found three techniques help them become happier, healthier, and hardier. Though the techniques may work best in a group, you can try them on your own.

Focusing. A technique developed by psychologist Eugene Gendlin, focusing is a way of recognizing signals from the body that something is wrong. Many executives are so used to pressure in the temples, neck tightness, or stomach knots that they stop noticing they have these problems, and that they worsen under stress. We've found that it helps them to take a strain inventory once a day, to check out where things are not feeling quite right. Then they mentally review the situations that might be stressful (we encourage group members to ask themselves questions like: "What's keeping me from feeling terrific today?"). This focusing increases your sense of control over stress, and puts you psychologically in a better position to change.

Reconstructing stressful situations. Think about a recent episode of distress, then write down three ways it could have gone better and three ways it could have gone worse. If you have trouble thinking of what you could have done differently, focus on someone you know who handles stress well and what he or she would have done. It's important to realize that things did not go as badly as they could have—and even more important to realize that you can think of ways to cope better.

Compensating through self-improvement. Sometimes you come face to face with stress, like illness or impending divorce, that you cannot avoid. It's important to distinguish between what you can and cannot control. But when life feels out of control, you can regain your grip by taking on a new challenge. Choosing a new task to master, like learning how to swim or tutoring a foreign student in English, can reassure you that you still can cope.

Reprinted by permission of the publisher from "How Much Stress Can You Survive?" by Suzanne Ouellette Kobasa, Ph.D., in *American Health,* September 1984, pp. 64-77.

BOX 10: ACCEPTING CHANGE, LETTING GO

Life's changes, as we've seen, can be major stumbling blocks on the road to health. But they don't have to be. First step: Put them in a healthy perspective.

Every Exit Is an Entrance Somewhere Else

Any change, positive or negative, marks the end of a page in your life. But, like a college commencement, it also signals the beginning of another chapter—and one that has the potential to be richer and more exciting than the last because you have grown through your past experiences.

Know, too, that change is one of the few constants in life. Look around you. Every living thing is in the process of changing and growing. To stop changing is to cease living. That helps explain why the ability to change is such an important factor in longevity.

Learning the Art of Letting Go

Granted, a divorce, job separation, or other radical change in your life can be followed by a difficult period of adjustment. And, psychologists explain, it's important to give your emotions enough time to heal (see Chapter 17, Good Grief: Healing and Growing through Loss).

"Stay as long as you need to," says Emmett Miller, M.D., author of *Feeling Good: How to Stay Healthy* (Prentice-Hall). "But know that, in time, you must let go of the past and move forward."

Dr. Miller, whose soothing voice is known the world over through his series of relaxation and self-healing tapes, has produced a tape specifically for people confronting change. The tape (entitled, appropriately enough, *Accepting Change—Moving On*) combines techniques for deep relaxation with guided imagery.

One exercise uses progressive relaxation, a technique that involves the systematic tensing and release of individual muscle groups beginning with the toes and working upward through the muscles of the legs, pelvis, arms, shoulders, neck, and face (see Chapter 29, The Best of the Relaxation Techniques). Dr. Miller suggests that as we make a fist, for example, we think of the motion symbolically as "holding on." How does it feel? Are you straining? How long can you hold on comfortably? Then, as we release our muscles, we imagine ourselves letting go of whatever it is that we're clinging to in real life. Think about how it feels to let go. Does it feel easy, natural? *How much* are you willing to let go? Repeat the exercise with each muscle group.

Similarly, we can combine deep breathing, another excellent relaxation technique, with imagery. Sitting in a comfortable position with your eyes closed, gradually clear your mind of thoughts and clutter and focus on your breathing. Notice how effortlessly the air breathes you. There's no beginning, no end; it's a cycle like waves lapping the shore. Now, imagine each exhalation as "letting go." Breathe out all unnecessary thoughts and pressures. Become aware of the brief pause between exhalation and inhalation. Feel the silence, the calm, the peace of this pause. Think of it as this period in

---

BOX 10 — *Continued*

your life, just as you've let go of the past and before you move on to the future. At the end of this pause, notice the burst of energy you feel as the air fills your lungs again. Your whole body expands. It is a symbol of awakening and renewal.

EDITOR'S NOTE: The tape *Accepting Change — Moving On* by Emmett Miller is available through "Source," Post Office Box W, Stanford, CA 94305, (415) 328-7171, and in major bookstores nationwide as part of Dr. Miller's Software for the Mind series.

---

to compare our methods with meditation, relaxation training and other forms of stress management. But so far, we believe that three specific techniques, described in [Box 9], are especially useful.

Anyone can learn how to be hardy instead of helpless.

If techniques like these really work, we have an important tool for improving health. The key will not be to make our lives stress-free; that's impossible. But it may be possible for anyone to defuse stress by learning to be hardy instead of helpless.

Reprinted by permission of the publisher from "How Much Stress Can You Survive?" by Suzanne Ouellette Kobasa, Ph.D., in *American Health*, September 1984, pp. 64-77.

Friends and Lovers:
Guardians of Good Health

T

Sociability of any kind is worth cultivating.

o some people, happiness is a social calendar packed with parties. To others, it's having lots of free time to spend with a one and only. Whatever your preference, psychologists and medical doctors agree: Sociability of any kind is worth cultivating. According to mounting evidence, people who belong to a network of community, friends, and relatives are happier and healthier, better able to cope with stress, and remarkably resistant to emotional and physical ills.

We have only to look to residents of Roseto, Pennsylvania, for confirmation. There, in the early sixties, researchers found a close-knit Italian-American community with a startlingly healthy reputation. Roseto boasted one of the nation's lowest fatality rates for heart disease. Only 1 in 1,000 men died of heart attacks (compared to the national average of 3.5 per 1,000); female residents fared even better with a rate of 0.6 per 1,000 (well below the average 2.09 per 1,000 women nationally). Rosetans also emerged from the study with a better-than-average "resistance" to peptic ulcers and senility. All this, despite risk factors that rivaled any other American community.

Cigarettes, stress, and a high-fat diet didn't matter. They still lived longer.

Rosetans smoked as much and exercised as little as their friends in neighboring towns. They faced the same stressful situations. They met the national average for obesity and high blood pressure. Plus, they ate *more* meat and fat than the "average American." Still, they lived longer.

The researchers were understandably puzzled. They turned the town inside out looking for the missing clue and even traced relatives of several Rosetan families to Philadelphia and New Jersey hoping to uncover a genetic or ethnic link. But they needn't have searched so hard; the answer was as big as the town and all the people in it. What gave Rosetans such a healthy edge, the researchers finally concluded, was their strong sense of community and camaraderie.

THE COMMUNITY: A PROTECTIVE ENVELOPE

"More than any other town we studied, Roseto's social structure reflected old-world values and traditions," says Stewart Wolf, M.D., professor of medicine at Temple University School of Medicine in Philadelphia, author of *The Roseto Story: An Anatomy of Health* (University of Oklahoma Press), and director of the Roseto study. "There was a remarkable cohesiveness and sense of unconditional support within the community. Family ties were very strong. And what impressed us most was the attitude toward the elderly. In Roseto, the older residents weren't put on a shelf; they were promoted to 'supreme court.' No one was ever abandoned."

Strong family ties and a cohesive community gave them the edge.

Unfortunately, the expanding ideals of a younger generation changed all that. As the younger Rosetans moved away from the community core—marrying outside the clan, trading their traditional wooden homes for sprawling suburban "ranchers," and generally severing the emotional and physical ties to the old neighborhood—the town's healthy statistics began to deteriorate. By the mid seventies, Dr. Wolf reports, mortality rates had climbed as high as neighboring communities.

"The experience clearly demonstrates that the most important factors in health are the intangibles—things like trust, honesty, loyalty, team spirit," Dr. Wolf says. "In terms of preventing heart disease, it's just possible that morale is more important than jogging or not eating butter."

Morale may be more important than jogging.

Dennis T. Jaffe, Ph.D., co-director of the Health Studies Program at Saybrook Institute in San Francisco and author of *Healing from Within* (Alfred A. Knopf, Inc.), agrees. "A close-knit community can act as a protective envelope against the stresses of the environment," he noted at a recent conference on humanistic psychology in New York City. "As in cases such as Roseto, evidence is mount-

Overinvolvement with oneself can create psychological—and ultimately physical—problems.

ing that overinvolvement with oneself, at the expense of the community, leads to psychological dislocation that results not only in anxiety, but in various psychological ailments as well."

Roseto isn't the only community that bears this out. Scientists know that several tradition-oriented cultures characterized by close social ties, including Japan, Italy, Greece, and Yugoslavia, enjoy low rates of heart disease. Japanese-Americans living a Westernized life have a much higher rate of heart disease than Japanese. Usually that is explained solely in terms of diet or health habits.

The autonomous American life style: a major risk factor for heart disease.

But a recent study of Japanese-Americans in California revealed that, even when factors like diet, blood pressure, and smoking were taken into account, people who clung to traditional Japanese culture emphasizing strong community ties had lower levels of heart disease than those who adopted the more autonomous American way of life *(American Journal of Epidemiology).*

CHURCH AND STATE OF MIND

For some Americans, becoming an active member of a religious congregation can provide the tradition and social support lacking in their community. And, at least for members of the Mormon and Seventh-day Adventist sects, church affiliation has yielded health benefits similar to those seen among Rosetans and tradition-bound Japanese-Americans.

Mormon men have half the cancer risk as the average American male.

According to studies on select groups of Mormon men, researchers found about half the cancer risk and 35 percent the heart attack risk as the average American male. This translated into a more favorable life expectancy: at 35, the average American male can expect to live 37 more years; by comparison, a Mormon can look forward to another 44 years.

The vital statistics for Adventists are just as impressive. In California, Adventist men were found to have a risk for cancer estimated as only 53 percent of the average risk, and only 18 percent for lung cancer. Surprisingly, nonsmoking Adventists develop fatal lung cancer only half as often as non-Adventist nonsmokers *(American Journal of Epidemiology).* Devout Adventists also suffer less from cardiovascular disease.

As with the statistics for long-living Japanese-Americans,

lifestyle is cited as the responsible factor. It's true, both religious groups practice under strict guidelines for diet and lifestyle. Among Adventists this includes about eight hours of sleep per night, regular exercise, and avoidance of pepper, fried foods, and pork (about 44 percent of Adventists are vegetarian). The Mormon lifestyle is much the same, without the ban on meat. This no doubt contributes to their healthy reputation. But now many social scientists suggest that various social and psychological aspects of religion may foster the kind of positive attitudes that increase longevity.

Diet may contribute to these statistics.

"Adventists seem to have a sense of personal worth reinforced by belonging to an accepting and caring community," reports an Australian research group. As evidence of this phenomenon, Adventists have been found to use tranquilizers less often than control groups and they report fewer problems with "mental illness, suicidal thoughts . . . anxiety and tension and difficulty with interpersonal relationships" *(Medical Journal of Australia).*

Adventists are healthier emotionally.

Church membership was just one source of social support examined in perhaps the largest, most impressive study on this topic to date. The study, conducted by public health researchers Lisa F. Berkman, Ph.D., of Yale University and S. Leonard Syme, Ph.D., of the University of California, Berkeley, took nine years to complete and involved nearly 7,000 residents of Alameda County, California. The objective: to systematically assess four specific sources of social support—marriage, contacts with close friends and relatives, church membership, and informal and formal group associations.

Church membership is a source of social support.

Results confirmed that people with social ties—no matter what the source—lived longer than isolated people. This held true regardless of cigarette smoking, alcohol consumption, obesity, sleeping and eating habits, and medical care.

THE REWARDS OF INTIMATE RELATIONSHIPS

Not surprisingly, too, the more intimate ties of marriage and contacts with friends and relatives offered greater protection from illness than church or group affiliation. "People who have a close-knit network of intimate personal

Marriage provides more protection from illness than group affiliation.

ties with other people seem to be able to avoid disease, maintain higher levels of health, and in general, to deal more successfully with life's difficulties . . . ," says Dr. Syme.

Of particular interest is the apparent cumulative effect of various contacts. According to the researchers, "People with many social contacts had the lowest mortality rates and people with the fewest contacts had the highest rates." This may not seem so startling but it is good news for the single set.

Single, divorced, and widowed people have higher rates of many diseases. Consequently, they don't live as long. Studies have shown, for example, that widows, particularly in the first year after their husband's death, have many more symptoms of physical and mental disease, as well as death rates four times higher than average.

Close friends can guard against the ill effects of bachelorhood.

Based on the Alameda study, however, it appears that one can guard against the ill effects of bachelorhood through a solid network of friends and associates. Indeed, Drs. Berkman and Syme point out, an unmarried person with close friends faces no greater health risks than the married person who is otherwise socially isolated *(American Journal of Epidemiology)*.

How do social supports prevent disease?

Drs. Berkman and Syme offer several theories. The socially isolated may be more likely to adopt self-destructive health habits, they suggest, or they may get depressed because of their isolation and become suicide- or accident-prone. The researchers are quick to point out, however, that these theories do not explain why, with health habits and emotional outlook taken into account, isolated people are still more susceptible to a wide variety of illnesses including heart disease and cancer as well as arthritis, gastrointestinal upsets, skin problems, headaches, and complications of pregnancy.

All diseases are "social diseases."

"All diseases are 'social diseases,' " says Dr. Dennis Jaffe. "It's as though a breakdown in the social support structure precipitates a breakdown in the body's immune system."

The Alameda researchers agree that the absence or presence of a social network appears to produce physiological changes that determine one's susceptibility or resistance to disease. These effects, they say, resemble the body's stress response. People who lack outlets for stress release are susceptible to a long list of "stress-related" illnesses not unlike the ones mentioned above. On the other hand, people who can cope with stress are generally healthier and more resistant to disease. From that standpoint, it may be that one way social support protects our health is by buffering the impact of stress. The evidence that this is so is mounting.

FRIENDS AGAINST STRESS

You may recall the famous Social Readjustment Rating Scale devised a number of years ago by psychiatrists Thomas H. Holmes, M.D., and Richard H. Rahe, M.D., of the University of Washington School of Medicine in Seattle. Holmes and Rahe proposed that major stressful events (e.g., death of a spouse, divorce, loss of a job, etc.) foreshadowed serious illness. Several new studies, however, suggest that your score on a social support scale is far more predictive of future illness than your grade on the Holmes-Rahe stress test.

Social support buffers the impact of stress.

Take death of a spouse and loss of a job as two examples. On the Holmes–Rahe scale, they practically add up to a death warrant. But, based on two separate studies, the harmful consequences of these highly stressful events can be significantly reduced through an active network of friends and relatives. High levels of stress are also related to emotional problems, but, again, social support can reverse this effect *(Journal of Health and Social Behavior)*.

Psychologists further tell us that people who have a number of close friends and confidants, who have "a high capacity for intimacy," and who are able to openly discuss their deepest feelings are better able to cope with stress in general. Instead of being overwhelmed and exhausted by crises, they appear to be stimulated and challenged by them.

People who confide in others are more stress-resistant.

Jenny Steinmetz, Ph.D., a psychologist at the Kaiser Permanente Medical Center in Hayward, California, explains: "Having one or two close friends that you feel free to say anything to is invaluable," she says. "Often when you are overwhelmed, you don't trust your own judgment enough to realize that you're OK. But an objective view from a friend helps validate your opinion."

This kind of social support can be expanded to the workplace, too, says C. David Jenkins, Ph.D., professor of

Social support can help in the workplace, too.

preventive medicine and community health at the University of Texas medical branch in Galveston. To illustrate this point, he recalled a hospital that provided the opportunity for its intensive-care nurses to hold weekly group sessions with a very warm and nurturing psychiatrist. The nurses gained support from each other and from the psychiatrist and were able to surmount their crises with less emotional drain.

James S. House, Ph.D., knows how important social support is, too. He's the author of *Work Stress and Social Support* (Addison-Wesley) and research scientist at the Institute for Social Research, University of Michigan at Ann Arbor.

It's true that there's a certain amount of irreducible stress associated with any work organization—deadlines, production pressures, he says. Social support apparently helps to buffer these stresses and makes them more tolerable.

Good friends are essential to good health.

Writing in the *American Journal of Medicine*, Leon Eisenberg, M.D., has perhaps summed up the people-who-need-people situation most eloquently. "There are, of course, no pharmacies available to fill a prescription for 'spouses, confidants, and friends, p.r.n. [as needed],'" says Dr. Eisenberg, but "the point remains that social isolation is in itself a pathogenic factor in disease production. Mechanisms of social bonding are as ancient as the evolution of our species; their disruption has devastating impact. Good friends are an essential ingredient for good health."

Head Strong: Emotional Conditioning through Aerobic Exercise

It's no secret that exercise builds healthy bodies. But now there's more than a little bit of evidence that physical exercise—particularly running, swimming, or other aerobic activity—can strengthen our emotional well-being, tone our mental capabilities, even work out such serious psychological dilemmas as depression.

Exercise strengthens our emotional well-being.

"Exercise is emotional aerobics," says Bob Conroy, M.D., a psychiatrist at the Menninger Clinic in Topeka, Kansas, where he organized a cardiovascular fitness program that boosts sagging spirits. "You don't have to run marathons, either. Any good aerobic routine [that speeds up heart and breathing rates] carried on a minimum of three times a week for 30 minutes each session pays big dividends."

Indeed, new studies and clinical evidence suggest that such an aerobic program can build emotional hardiness at least nine ways by:

Aerobic exercise builds emotional hardiness at least nine ways.

- Energizing
- Relieving tension and anxiety
- Strengthening the body's stress-coping mechanism
- Counteracting hostile, Type A behavior
- Clearing the mind, improving concentration and memory
- Encouraging a more positive self-image and improving self-confidence
- Contributing to feelings of exhilaration and physical well-being
- Improving sleep
- Alleviating depression

AN ENERGY INVESTMENT WITH HIGH RETURNS

The energizing effect is the result of improved body efficiency.

Some of the effects can be explained quite simply. The energizing effect, for example, is the result of improved body efficiency, says Kenneth Cooper, M.D., M.P.H., in his book *The Aerobics Program for Total Well-Being* (Evans). Like a well-tuned engine that uses less oil and gasoline, a well-tuned body uses less energy to perform daily functions.

Toned muscles make every movement—from lifting a pencil to walking up a flight of stairs—relatively effortless. And a conditioned heart—which pumps more blood with each stroke—doesn't have to work as hard, circulating the same volume of blood with fewer strokes.

Lowering your resting heart rate is key.

The lower resting heart rate is a key benefit to aerobic conditioning. And the effect is usually noticeable after just a few weeks of regular workouts. In one study of middle-aged men, Dr. Cooper reports, heart rates dropped from an average of 72 to 55 beats per minute after a three-month training program. This not only provides the exerciser with increased stamina but, as Dr. Cooper explains, it offers a form of stress resistance.

"Better cardiovascular fitness tends to put a 'governor' on the effect that the adrenal gland's secretions can have on the heart. In response to intense emotions, anxiety, or fear, the resting heart rate increases to some extent. This is the result of the outpouring of adrenaline into the body. The adrenal gland stimulates the heart to beat faster and thus prepares us for 'fight or flight,' " he says.

A fit person is better able to withstand stress.

A fit person subject to stress will still experience a rise in heart rate, but not nearly to the extent that a sedentary person would. Again Dr. Cooper cites two related studies to demonstrate this point. One study measured the heart rate of a sedentary elementary school teacher at rest (75 beats per minute) and in action, teaching before her class (95 beats per minute). Another study made similar measurements on a very fit male college instructor. By comparison, his resting heart rate was 65 beats per minute and his teaching rate rose to just 67 beats per minute. Even in the throes of a heated argument with a student, he was clocked at just 70 beats per minute.

How does this translate into benefits?

Emotionally taxing ordeals can be deadly.

"A lower heart rate during stress means you tend to stay calmer and more in control of your emotions. But there are even more important consequences: To put it bluntly, a well-conditioned heart may save a person's life," says Dr. Cooper, citing several cases in which unfit people succumbed to sudden heart attacks following emotionally taxing ordeals. "Chances are, if [they] had been in good aerobic condition, [they] could have tolerated that stress and would still be alive today."

IMMEDIATE STRESS RELEASE

Of course, you don't have to wait for a crisis to feel the effects of your effort. Every time you work out hard, you're helping to release pent-up tension. Immediately afterward, you'll feel relaxed, refreshed, and energized. As evidence of this, a study on 15 men demonstrated that a 15-minute aerobic workout was sufficient to reduce anxiety below pre-exercise levels. Not only did tests show the men to be more relaxed immediately following their workout, but they remained that way 20 minutes later.

A 15-minute workout can reduce anxiety below pre-exercise levels.

To get the most stress-reducing benefits from your fitness program, Dr. Cooper advises that you schedule your workouts after work and before dinner. At that time, exercise helps release tensions that have accumulated during the day. As a bonus, he says, exercising at this time is a sort of appetite depressant—good news to all you weight watchers.

The calming power of exercise is really put to test in the treatment of phobias, one of the most anxiety-provoking problems we know. But, not surprisingly, this unlikely therapy passes with high grades. According to several reports, running reduces the anxiety associated with irrational fears ranging from agoraphobia (fear of open spaces) to claustrophobia (fear of closed spaces). Exercise therapy is particularly effective when combined with visualizations of pleasant fantasies, it is noted. In fact, one study demonstrates that running and fantasizing is as effective as standard desensitization tapes.

Running reduces the anxiety associated with phobias.

BUILDING CONFIDENCE WITH SWEAT

While exercise is reducing anxiety levels to new lows, it's raising confidence quotients to all-time highs.

"One case that comes to mind involves a woman who was a classic introvert," says Dr. Cooper. "For example, she always stayed in the background in conversations and social gatherings and was so self-conscious that she would never have been seen on a track running in shorts. But then she became involved in our programs at the Aerobics Center, and immediately her attitude changed. She began to run regularly, performed exceedingly well on the treadmill stress tests, and completely reversed her personality traits. . . .

Expect a transformation to an outgoing, self-confident person.

"One of the things that can be most easily documented about people's responses to our exercise programs is an improvement in the self-image," he adds. "And along with an improved self-image, I have come to expect a transformation of the person into an outgoing, self-confident personality."

The elderly feel better about themselves.

Studies on the attitudes of elderly people likewise show that those who exercise feel better about themselves than those who don't. On a psychological test designed to measure a person's self-image, people who exercised least felt that they didn't live up to their ideal image of themselves. Those who exercised the most showed a good body image, close to their desired image of themselves (*Medicine and Science in Sports*).

A chief factor in this, says John H. Greist, M.D., a psychiatrist and professor at the University of Wisconsin, is what he calls *capacity for change.* "Runners learn, often dramatically, that they can change themselves for the better. Running improves physical health, appearance, and body image, and also increases self-acceptance."

A fitness program builds strong character traits.

In addition, he says, a regular fitness program builds strong character traits in at least three other areas:

• **Mastery.** "Individuals who become independent runners develop a sense of success and mastery of what they perceive as a difficult skill."

• **Patience.** "To become an independent runner takes time, and one learns the necessity of patience and making regular efforts until running becomes a habit."

• **Positive habit.** "Some patients recognize running as a positive activity and consciously substitute it for more negative and neurotic defenses and habits such as smoking, drinking, overeating, and nonproductive arguing."

Running takes negative energy and turns it around.

"Depressed people feel better about themselves after becoming runners," says Austin Gontang, director of the San Diego Marathon Clinic. "Initially, a person might feel 'I can't do anything' or 'I can't go on.' Running takes that negative energy and turns it around—the person *can* go on. Maybe for five more miles!"

Psychiatrist Thaddeus Kostrubala, M.D., author of *The Joy of Running* (Lippincott), agrees. "Running works because it changes the personality patterns," he says. "People develop a greater sense of their own value. They feel better about themselves. They feel an increased sense of personal strength."

"We know now that personality in adults is a dynamic thing, not a static thing," says A. H. Ismail, M.D., professor of physical education at Purdue University (and former Olympic basketball player). "There can be changes and the changes that are produced through a fitness regimen are in a positive direction." For over 20 years, Dr. Ismail has been conducting fitness programs involving hundreds of participants and has found that those who scored low on emotional stability tests before exercising showed marked improvement after completing a fitness program.

Low scores on emotional stability tests reversed with exercise.

The results of a Duke University study seem to bear this out. According to researcher James Blumenthal, Ph.D., and associates, participation in a regular exercise program can modify one of the toughest—and most self-destructive—personality patterns known: the hard-driving coronary-prone Type A behavior *(Psychosomatic Medicine).*

It's hard to say why exercise has such a marked effect on personality, Dr. Blumenthal admits, but "the decision to exercise could be related to an overall reevaluation in lifestyle behaviors and a change in values. It's difficult to document whether or not the pervasive 'I feel so much better' is a function of exercise, the group setting, or time. But people doing something they know is good for them—and they can tell that quickly just by walking up two flights of stairs without being so winded—experience a positive feeling of accomplishment."

A regular fitness program can modify Type A behavior.

BOOSTING BRAIN POWER

If all this is beginning to sound a bit incredible, consider this: Growing evidence suggests that people who are aerobically fit may also have an edge intellectually. Researchers in this area are convinced that exercise can help improve concentration, creativity, problem-solving abilities. How?

Improve your creativity, concentration.

"Twenty percent of the blood flow from the heart goes to the brain," says Dr. Kostrubala. "During running, when the heart is pumping hard, that blood flow is increased and that changes the biochemistry of the brain. There's an increase in oxygen."

It stands to reason that good oxygen levels in the blood can boost brain power. Working with that logical hunch, Claude Fell Merzbacher, Ph.D., of the department of natural science at San Diego State University, gathered together a group of 31 volunteers to test the effect of diet and exercise on their mental skills. The volunteers were part of a group enrolled in a diet, exercise, and education program at the Longevity Research Institute of Santa Monica. The average age of the group was 60 years, and every member suffered from cardiovascular or some other degenerative disease such as diabetes, claudication, or arthritis—diseases that at an advanced age are especially trying and distracting. For 26 days, the volunteers followed the Institute's exercise program, consisting mostly of daily walks.

Daily walks and a high-fiber diet improved intellectual efficiency.

At the same time, the group ate a wholesome high-fiber diet containing vegetables, fruits, very small amounts of meat, minimal cholesterol, no fats or oils (except those in grains), no simple carbohydrates (especially refined sugar, honey, and molasses), and no added salt.

Both before and after the completion of this regimen, the group was given various tests. On one test, which measured specialization, self-control, tolerance, achievement, and intellectual efficiency, volunteers who took it showed higher scores after the regimen. This meant improved verbal fluency, quick, clear thinking, intellectual efficiency, and perceptiveness.

Results were noticeable in less than a month.

On another test, which measured changes in mental sharpness, the group again scored higher after the combined diet and exercise regimen. And all this in the remarkably short time of less than a month *(Perceptual and Motor Skills)*.

JOGGING YOUR MEMORY

Two other studies have examined the relationship between exercise and brain functions like memory.

Exercisers beat sedentary people on a memory test.

In the first study, adults in their 40s took part in a walking/jogging program for ten weeks. A similar group remained sedentary. Then the researchers tested both groups' reaction time, which is one of the skills scientists use to measure how well we recall things. The exercisers beat the group of sedentary people hands down in the time it took them to respond on a test of numbers both groups had been asked to remember.

A second study showed that elderly people, who often complain of memory lapses, also bounce back with exercise. The researchers put older, out-of-shape people on a four-month brisk-walking program. When compared with a similar group who remained sedentary, the exercisers improved in six out of eight mental-ability tests, including reaction time and short-term memory. The sedentary people showed no improvement.

Whether these effects are due to increased oxygen levels in the brain is not known. But psychologist-neurologist Ronald Lawrence, M.D., Ph.D., believes that these improvements in mental sharpness are at least partially the result of the meditative trance that many regular exercisers, particularly runners, are lulled into. "Rhythmic exercise allows the mind to wander, fantasize, and enter a tranquil state of clarity and uncluttered thinking," he says.

Rhythmic exercise allows the mind to enter a tranquil state of clarity.

FEELING GOOD ALL OVER

Ask any runner why he runs and chances are he won't rave about improvements in intellectual acumen. Pure and simple, he does it for the feeling. And what a feeling it is! Exhilarating. Euphoric. A natural high. In fact, it's called "runner's high" (or, its counterpart among other aerobic activities: "bicyclist's bliss" "swimmer's joy," "hiker's happiness").

That—coupled with the fact that people who quit their fitness program have been known to suffer from such "withdrawal" symptoms as irritability, sleeping difficulties, and chronic fatigue—would lead you to believe the effects were drug-related. To a certain extent, they may be.

Regular exercise is associated with an emotional "high."

In recent years, researchers have discovered that aerobic exercise dramatically alters the biochemistry of the brain. Most notable among these changes is the powerful release of endorphins from the pituitary gland. Endorphins are chemically akin to the addictive pain reliever morphine, but about 200 times more potent. That may explain why muscle soreness and joint stiffness seem to vanish once exercise is under way and why, in a few extraordinary cases, people have run marathons and danced ballets with serious injuries.

Studies on exercise-induced endorphin release have

Vigorous exercise can increase endorphin levels fivefold.

found that vigorous workouts can increase endorphin levels by as much as fivefold. In one such study, eight male athletes were tested before, during, and at 15- and 30-minute intervals following an exhausting treadmill run. Pre-exercise endorphin levels averaged 320, rising to 1,620 at 100% maximal effort. Fifteen minutes after the completion of the run, endorphin levels were still 1,080. Measurements taken 30 minutes after the exercise session showed levels dropped to 420, which was still higher than starting-line levels *(Experientia)*.

Whether this endorphin release is responsible for alleviating the agony and creating the feeling of ecstasy among long-distance runners is not known for sure. We do know that euphoria and altered states of consciousness have been reported by many athletes—especially marathon runners.

Endorphins may be behind the euphoria experienced by some runners.

Dr. Kenneth Cooper explains: "According to individual accounts we have received from people who work out at our Aerobics Center, it seems that most runners who run for about three miles at a rate of 7½ to 9 minutes per mile get at least a transient feeling of euphoria during and after the experience."

THE AEROBIC ANTIDOTE TO DEPRESSION

If you're down, exercise can bring you up.

It's no wonder, then, that exercise can be so effective in fending off the blue moods that all of us have from time to time. If you're down, exercise can bring you up—and if you're up, well, it can help your spirits soar.

But what about those people who are really down, people who feel tired, sad, or apathetic *all the time*—can exercise help them? You bet.

Unlike antidepressant drugs, running has beneficial physical side effects.

"Running seems a sensible treatment for many depressed people, since it's not expensive and, unlike some other treatments, it has beneficial physical side effects," write Dr. John Greist and his associates in a paper entitled "Running Out of Depression" *(Physician and Sportsmedicine)*.

"Depression is a painful experience, and many people who have been depressed dread a recurrence more than severe physical illness," says Dr. Greist. So depressed people often do seek treatment, and they usually end up in some form of psychotherapy. But, as Dr. Greist points out, all those therapies are "marginally effective."

"Moderate depression," he adds, "is a health problem for which no single uniquely effective treatment has yet been developed."

Enter running. Dr. Greist is a runner himself, and he decided to try it on his patients after he noticed that, if he felt irritable or low when he started to jog, by the end of the run he usually felt great.

As a scientist, Dr. Greist had to *prove* that running was at least as good as psychotherapy before recommending it to his patients. So he divided depressed patients—15 women and 13 men, aged 18 to 30—into three groups. One group ran. One group had "time-limited" psychotherapy (which means that the date the treatment ends is specified ahead of time). One group had time-unlimited psychotherapy. Depression levels on a scale of one to four were measured before, during, and at the end of the study (one meant a little depressed; two, moderately; three, quite a bit; four, extremely).

The final results? The patients who had time-limited psychotherapy scored an average of just below one on the depression scale. The patients in time-unlimited therapy averaged just below two. The patients who ran, however, averaged just above zero—not at all depressed.

Dr. Greist isn't the only one who has conducted studies like this. Robert Brown, M.D., Ph.D., a psychiatrist and professor at the University of Virginia, studied 101 depressed college students. He divided them into two groups: one that exercised regularly and one that didn't.

"Jogging five days a week for a ten-week period was associated with significant reductions in depression scores," says Dr. Brown. "Similar patterns were exhibited by those who jogged only three days a week for the same period. The subjects who did not exercise during the same interval had virtually unchanged scores."

Dr. Brown also gave the depressed students "adjective checklists" that described their emotional states. "Among the depressed subjects who jogged," he says, "negative states of anger/hostility, fatigue/inertia, and tense/anxious decreased. Positive states of cheerfulness and energy increased."

However, Dr. Brown doesn't think that physical activity *cures* depression. He thinks that a lack of exercise *causes* it—and that running puts something back into life that should have been there in the first place.

Moderate depression is difficult to treat.

A test to pit running against psychotherapy.

The runners overcame their depression.

Jogging five days a week for ten weeks brought measurable benefits.

Running doesn't *cure* depression. Lack of exercise *causes* it.

BOX 11: GETTING A RUNNING START

You may have done it with free abandon as a child. But as an adult, running takes on a whole new set of rules. You can't spring into a sprint cold. You shouldn't run in cheap sneaks. And you can't keep at it like there's no tomorrow. If you do, there may not be. We don't mean to overstate the risk. It is miniscule—especially compared to the tremendous mind/body benefits. But the point is, if you haven't charged across a playground in years, play it safe and keep the following in mind:

Consult a physician before beginning any vigorous exercise program like running. In addition to working muscles, aerobic exercise puts stress on the lungs, heart, and circulatory system. That is, after all, what makes it such a healthy pursuit. By exerting ourselves repeatedly and for short periods at a time, the body—and especially the heart—becomes conditioned and much stronger in the long run. However, if you have an existing health problem or history of heart troubles, such exertion could aggravate the condition. So see a doctor first. No matter how old you are, it can't hurt.

Invest in a good pair of running shoes. Sneaks are neat. But if you're 12 or over—and serious about running—it's best to buy *running* shoes, engineered to reduce injury an make running easier and therefore more enjoyable. What to look for: a securely fitted, lightweight, well-cushioned shoe with a wide and slightly elevated heel. Yes, there are probably hundreds that fit that description. To narrow your options, go to a specialty store, preferably one where the sales staff are athletes. They will help you analyze, examine, and choose *your* best shoe. Some tips to a good fit: The shoes should fit snugly (but not tightly) at the heel and allow for all-around toe room, in addition to the thumb's width up front. Make sure your foot flexes easily and comfortably. Never swallow the old "break-in period" sales pitch. Running shoes should feel great from day one or you'll be sorry by day five.

Warm up to your run. To get the heart and muscles primed for action, you've got to raise body temperature, or as they say, "warm-up." The most popular way to do this is by *gently* stretching the muscles slated for exercise. This increases the blood supply to these areas, warming them, and thereby helping to prevent muscle stiffness and injury. Unfortunately, this technique doesn't do much for your heart. And, since aerobics taxes the heart as much as the leg muscles, it's important to prepare it, too. For that reason a good warm-up includes a slow-motion rehearsal of the upcoming exercise. In other words, walk before you run. What's an adequate warm-up? Exercise physiologists say 10 to 15 minutes, or until you just begin to sweat, which is a signal that your body temperature is on the rise.

Take it slow. The most common mistake beginning runners make is that they run too fast. But speed does little to enhance the beneficial effects of running. It's more important to conserve your energy and go for distance—you'll feel better, physically and mentally. So pace yourself. If you can carry on a conversation while running, that's fine; if you can't, put on the brakes.

But don't stop cold. Keep moving. Walk until you regain your wind.

If you have pain, stop. Athletes are frequently advised to "run through the pain." While it's true that the anesthetizing effect of endorphins—those morphinelike chemicals that are released by the brain during exercise—can help you forget you have sore muscles, it can also camouflage the pain that may be signaling serious damage. By "working through the pain," then, you may be adding insult to injury. Exercising to relieve mild aches and stiffness shouldn't be a problem. But if the relief you get is only temporary and the pain returns with a greater vengeance, take it easy for a few days. And if rest doesn't relieve the pain, see a doctor.

Cool down after the run. Gear down from a run in the same way you gear up for it: walk. Exercise physiologists have warned us for some time that because exercise draws blood out to the muscles in your arms and legs—and away from the heart and brain—stopping suddenly can cause faintness. But now, researchers have discovered another important reason why the cool-down is critical.

The researchers, principally from Harvard Medical School, asked ten healthy young men to work out on exercise bicycles. They made sure the men did *not* perform a proper cool-down after they stopped riding.

The researchers watched what happened to two important body functions when the men didn't adequately cool down. Blood pressure, which normally rises during exercise, dropped back to normal too fast. Catecholamines—hormones, including norepinephrine and epinephrine (sometimes called adrenaline)—skyrocketed.

The researchers theorize that the body misinterprets the quick drop in blood pressure and thinks it's going into shock. So it releases catecholamines to stabilize blood pressure. The trouble is, it releases too many. And overly high doses of catecholamines in the blood can trigger irregular heartbeats. "That's particularly dangerous for people who already have arrhythmias or heart disease," says Joel Dimsdale, M.D., the principal researcher on the study.

Dr. Dimsdale speculates that this catecholamine reaction may be the culprit behind sudden-death incidents that have been reported after exercise, though he has no specific evidence yet to back up his speculation. He says a proper cool-down would soft-pedal the drop in blood pressure so the body doesn't release too many catecholamines (*Journal of the American Medical Association*).

Don't work out every day. Whether or not pain interferes with your program, it's best to give yourself an occasional break. Some people schedule their workouts every other day. Others like to work out for two days and skip the third. Again, let your body be your guide. Just remember, your brain, hooked on the feeling, may push you ever onward. But your body may need a day to repair imperceivable tears and bruises in the muscles and joints. A general rule of thumb is to take a rest at least every two days. But don't overdo these layoff periods, either. For optimal benefits, you shouldn't let more than two days lapse between workouts.

BOX 12: RUNNING THROUGH YOUR MIND

Though the mind may reap the benefits, we tend to think of running as a purely physical act. Not so. The legs may move us, the arms propel us, the lungs sustain us. But it's the mind that gets us out there in the first place—and keeps us in the running come bad weather and barking dogs. That's no easy job. Fortunately, we can help. By employing the following mind-pleasing techniques, we can boost our motivation level and maximize our mind-body rewards.

Do it at the time of day that feels most natural. People who jog at dawn swear that morning is the best time of day to kick up the heels. The air is crisp and clean then, and the body's refreshed. But if you're not a morning person, don't force it. You might feel more alert and inclined to run after work. And there's something to be said for that, too. According to Dr. Kenneth Cooper, a pre-dinner run releases tensions from the day and curbs the appetite somewhat. So take your pick. Any time of day will do—just do it.

Pick a beautiful place. Some people run inside on a crowded track. Others pound the pavement along busy streets. Unfortunately, these environs do little for the psyche. Choose instead a grassy field or woodland path—peaceful and inspirational surroundings where your mind can converge with nature. Your feet will thank you too for the soft flooring.

Don't be competitive; have fun. The nice thing about sports like running is that they are noncompetitive. You don't have to race against anyone else. There's no keeping score. It's something you can do for the sheer enjoyment of it—no pressure, no risk of failure. This is particularly important to people who may be suffering from depression or low self-esteem, says Dr. John Greist. "We have had a 10 percent dropout rate (as compared with most programs' 30 to 70 percent) with depressed beginning runners when we've used an approach that emphasizes the pleasures of satisfactions in each day's run rather than point tallies [based on time and distance] or other, more distant goals, such as completing a marathon."

Run with a friend. For support and encouragement, two heads are better than one. And for additional strength, look to numbers. Join a group—perhaps at your local YM/WCA or health club—and align yourself with people who share the same goals. Or make a pact with a friend. But, says Dr. Greist, choose your friends carefully. If the friend is a competitor, he may discourage rather than encourage your fitness program. What you need is a fellow runner—not a racer.

Warm up your mind before each run. Most runners know the importance of a physical warm-up—gently stretching the muscles, readying them for exercise. But few consciously prepare the mind for the task ahead. And that can make a big difference. "Setting the mood and tone of your feeling state before training takes only a few minutes . . . [but] may be as important as the run itself," says Dyveke Spino, Ph.D., a world class jogging coach and author of *New Age Train-*

BOX 12—*Continued*

ing for Fitness and Health (Grove Press). "When I get my runners doing this, their whole Type A compulsive driving behavior balances to an inner calm. . . ." Dr. Spino recommends lying quietly on the ground, eyes closed, and taking a few deep cleansing breaths. Gently quiet the mind. Then let the mind go inside your body and feel the position of each part— from the head and shoulders to the ankles and toes. Take your time. When you feel calm and relaxed you're ready to begin the physical part of your warm-up.

Use visualization to reinforce the sense of relaxation as you run. The key to motivation and avoiding injury during exercise is to keep the mind and body as relaxed as possible. That's where visualization techniques can help. "I have seen people overcome inertia, eliminate repeated injuries to a muscle or limb, or, in the case of a nationally ranked athlete, surpass his wildest ambition [through the use of visualization]," Dr. Spino says. Here is a sampling of some of the visual-

ization exercises she describes in her book:

Waterfall. Visualize a stream of water flowing down your back and streaming off your shoulders.

Air puffs. Imagine each foot coming down on a soft air puff.

Giant hand. When running up a hill, visualize a giant hand pushing you along so that you are propelled by a source of energy not your own.

Soft eyes. Run with your eyes partially closed. This allows your intuitive sense to open. Don't drop your head to look at the ground, as this puts your body out of alignment. Allow your feet to find their own way.

Run only if you enjoy it. If you can't get enthused about running, don't despair. There are plenty of other aerobic activities to choose from: swimming, dancing, bicycling, walking. Remember, having fun is the whole point of this exercise. Without it, all the other promises of emotional rewards are meaningless.

Depression is in many cases a result of a life style of physical immobility. "Confinement and physical inactivity have been used as punishment for thousands of years," says Dr. Brown. "It may be that some people have happened upon inactivity as a form of self-punishment."

Dr. Greist believes that *distraction* is another factor. "Patients who run notice new and real bodily sensations that distract them from preoccupations with minor but annoying physical symptoms of depression."

Distraction is another factor.

"In running you have to think about breathing, you have to notice the sky and the sun and the wind. You have to let go of your thoughts," says Dr. Austin Gontang. "It's like pinching yourself, bringing yourself back into the present.

Bad posture can cause depression.

Another key reaction: the release of the hormone norepinephrine.

"By the end of the run I feel whole. My mind and body are one."

Most depressed people are busy worrying about the future or ruminating on the past."

Dr. Gontang goes so far as to say that a bad *posture* can cause depression. "When people are depressed they assume a depressed posture—a slouching, tense, contracted pose. But this type of posture can also be a cue that causes depression. A person with chronically poor posture gets tired, starts having negative thoughts, and *then* gets depressed."

"There's no way to separate the mind from the body," says Dr. Gontang. "The body's condition has a big effect on what you feel and think, and negative thoughts and feelings are two of the main components of depression."

Dr. Thaddeus Kostrubala further points out some biochemical changes that may also play a role. We've already discussed the effect of increased levels of endorphins on mood. But, says Dr. Kostrubala, another key reaction to aerobic exercise is the release of the hormone norepinephrine.

"A current theory of depression says that it's caused by a deficiency of norepinephrine in the synapses of the brain, the spaces between nerve cells across which messages are relayed. Norepinephrine increases during a run, and there's a surge right afterward. So just as doctors treat diseased organs with drugs, you could think of running as a self-induced pharmacological treatment of the brain, which is the organ of behavior."

Whether or not you're running away from depression, however, you should be aware of what an uplifting, emotionally balanced feeling you get from exercise. Speaking to Dr. Kenneth Cooper, one running convert describes the sensation: "Many days when I run several miles, I have a much greater awareness of my body than I ever had before. Sometimes, at the end of a good run, my body seems to be working like a well-oiled machine. I may start the run in a fragmented emotional state, with many concerns and worries about various things, but by the end of such a run, I feel whole. My mind and my body become one."

BOX 13: RUNNING TO MUSIC: A PSYCHOLOGICAL ADVANTAGE?

Used to be, nature serenaded the runner. Today, it's just as likely to be Vivaldi or Michael Jackson. Next to Nike, Sony is the hottest name in running gear. But do stereo tape players contribute as much to our psyche as a good pair of shoes do to our feet?

Eric Miller, a graduate student in exercise physiology, and Gopi A. Tejwani, Ph.D., an assistant professor of pharmacology, both at Ohio State University in Columbus, decided to find out. They measured the effects of a 30-minute treadmill run—with and without a musical accompanyment from a stereo headset—on ten experienced runners. At the end of two weeks of daily testing, they compiled their results.

On first glance, the music didn't appear to make any difference physiologically. Heart rates and lactate levels (a reflection of how hard the muscles are working during exercise) were the same with and without the headset. Psychologically, there was a difference, however. All the runners said the run *felt* easier when they donned the earphones.

Before you turn up the volume, we should warn you that this effect can produce a slight biochemical whiplash. According to the study, when perceived exertion was lower, so too was the body's production of endorphins, those mysterious chemicals believed responsible for the euphoria associated with the so-called "runner's high."

Dr. Tejwani explains: "Music makes running less stressful. But endorphin release is dependent on a certain amount of stress. And what we've found is that the psychological perception of stress is at least as important to endorphin production as the actual physical stress you're subject to."

What does all this mean?

It means that if you're having trouble making that extra mile, portable music could keep you in the running. But if you're in the running to lift your spirits and get as much psychological benefit as you can from your workout, you might be better off tuning into the sound of the wind and the whippoorwill.

PART III

Tuning In to Optimism

Are You a
Positive Person?

Y ou submit a brilli-
ant proposal at work for which you are highly commended.
Do you feel (A) proud and deserving of the praise, confident that continued efforts could lead to a promotion or (B)
awkward and unworthy of such acclaim, certain that this
bright idea was just "dumb luck"—you'll never have another.

Do you take praise well?

A tree limb falls crashing to the ground just a few
inches from where you stand. Do you feel (A) relieved and
grateful that it missed you or (B) shaken and distraught by
your near clash with catastrophy?

You visit a friend in the hospital. When you enter his
room, the first thing you notice is the monitoring device
next to his bed. Do you feel (A) reassured by its presence, an
indication to you that your friend is getting state-of-the-art
medical care or (B) disturbed by its presence, an inescap-
able reminder of your friend's fragile state of health?

**Do you think of hospitals as a
place for sickness or healing?**

Whether you choose the positive A answers or the
more negative B answers, these three examples illustrate a
point: Situations don't change your moods—your *perception*
of them does. Or, as David D. Burns, M.D., explains in his
book, *Feeling Good: The New Mood Therapy* (New American Library), you feel the way you think.

You feel the way you think.

How you think, then, can have a profound effect on
our physical and emotional health. People who constantly
see themselves and life in a negative light work themselves
into a state of low self-esteem and depression. They also
burden their bodies with unrelenting stress.

Every time you think the worst, your body reacts as if it

BOX 14: TEST YOUR POSITIVE THINKING

To find out how positive you are, answer these 15 questions as honestly as possible, using this scoring system: Give yourself a 5 if your answer is Always or Almost Always; 4 if it's Usually; 3 for Sometimes; 2 for Rarely; 1 for Never.

1. When the unexpected forces you to change your plans, are you quick to spot a hidden advantage in this new situation?

1 2 3 4 5

2. When you catch a stranger staring at you, do you conclude it's because he or she finds you attractive?

1 2 3 4 5

3. Do you like most of the people you meet?

1 2 3 4 5

4. When you think about next year, do you tend to think you'll be better off then than you are now?

1 2 3 4 5

5. Do you often stop to admire things of beauty?

1 2 3 4 5

6. When someone finds fault with you or something you've done, can you tell the difference between useful criticism and "sour grapes," which is better off ignored?

1 2 3 4 5

7. Do you praise your spouse/best friend/lover more often than you criticize him or her?

1 2 3 4 5

8. Do you believe the human race will survive into the twenty-first century?

1 2 3 4 5

9. Are you surprised when a friend lets you down?

1 2 3 4 5

10. Do you think of yourself as happy?

1 2 3 4 5

11. If a policeman stopped you for speeding when you were quite certain you *weren't*, would you firmly argue your case and even take it to court to prove you were right?

1 2 3 4 5

12. Do you feel comfortable making yourself the butt of your own jokes?

1 2 3 4 5

13. Do you believe that, overall, your state of mind has had a positive effect on your physical health?

1 2 3 4 5

14. If you made a list of your ten favorite people, would you be on it?

1 2 3 4 5

15. When you think back over the past few months, do you tend to remember your little successes before your setbacks and failures?

1 2 3 4 5

Scoring

If you scored 65 or over, consider yourself a "superstar"—someone whose optimism is a powerful, healing force.

60-65: Excellent—you're a genuine positive thinker.

55-60: Good—you're a positive thinker—sometimes.

50-55: Fair—your positive side and your negative side are about evenly matched.

50 and below: Do you see any consistent negative patterns? Where could you improve?

were actually in the throes of a tension-filled situation. Your fight-or-flight instincts are called into action. Adrenaline flows. Your pulse quickens. And if you dwell on these thoughts, you'll soon exhaust yourself. Not surprisingly, negative thinkers frequently suffer from stress-related physical ailments such as headaches, gastrointestinal problems, and high blood pressure.

Contrary to popular belief, negative or positive thinkers aren't born that way. These thinking patterns grow out of our experiences. Psychologists tell us that how we perceive any situation is, to a large extent, an automatic thought response. "Automatic" in the same way we tie our shoes, or a smoker lights up a cigarette. It's a *learned* response, a kind of habit we develop over years of absorbing the attitudes of those around us—parents, teachers, peers, even TV idols.

Negative thinking grows out of our experiences.

You don't even know it's happening. But day after day, week after week, messages are being encoded in your mind. Then something happens and you automatically "know" what it means. A friend doesn't return your call and you "know" you must have done something to offend him or he's done something behind your back and is embarrassed to talk to you or, more realistically, he's just bogged down at work.

This kind of automatic thinking goes on continually over the course of a day. Silently, in your head, you are carrying on a conversation with yourself, interpreting situations, casting judgements on people. Depending on the nature of your experiences, this self-talk can be a barrage of self-doubt and self-criticism ("I'll never be able to finish this project on time"; "I know I'll say the wrong thing"; "No one can be trusted") or a continual reinforcement of positive messages ("Things will work out"; "I can handle it"; "He likes me").

You are continually carrying on conversations with yourself.

HOW TO SHED NEGATIVE THINKING

Fortunately, there's a relatively simple and effective technique called "cognitive therapy" that can turn the most incorrigible grouch or melancholiac into a positve thinker. Originally developed in the 1950s by University of Pennsylvania psychiatrist Aaron T. Beck, M.D., cognitive therapy was found to be more effective than antidepressant drugs in the treatment of severe depression. A recent study at Washington University School of Medicine in St. Louis confirms

Cognitive therapy: a technique that's as effective as antidepressant drugs.

that it is *at least as effective* as drugs for patients with moderate to severe depression. And its effects may be longer lasting than drug therapy.

But cognitive therapy isn't only for the 40-fathom blues. It helps everyone who has to fight an "internal critic"—that nagging, shrill inner voice that can berate and bully you into a low-grade depression every time you face a challenging situation or, heaven forbid, make a mistake.

Your negative thoughts almost always contain gross distortions.

What cognitive therapists have also discovered, however, is that your negative thoughts almost always contain gross distortions. You may think you are dealing in reality, but you're not.

Cognitive therapy teaches you to first recognize your distorted thought processes and then to work on methods that will help you eliminate them. Doing this is a proven mood lifter.

SIX COMMON DISTORTIONS

What are some characteristic cognitive distortions? Typically, they run along these lines:

Do you wildly overestimate the size of your problems?

Exaggerating: "I just can't get myself to do any work around the house—my whole marriage is falling apart." You wildly overestimate the size of your problems at the same time you underestimate your ability to deal with them. You jump to conclusions without any evidence, and erroneously believe your conclusions are correct.

Ignoring the positive: "Sure the dinner party went all right, but I burned the toast." You tend to be impressed by and remember only negative events, or view completely positive events in a negative way, often as a way of "proving" the correctness of your negative self-image.

Do you think everything revolves around you?

Personalizing: "Everybody at the meeting kept looking at me because I'm gaining weight." You tend to think everything revolves around you—a major distortion of the facts.

Either/or thinking: "Either I get elected head of this committee or I'm a complete failure."

Overgeneralizing: "*Nobody* likes me . . . I'm losing *all* my friends . . . *Nothing* ever turns out right . . . "

"She's ignoring me. I must have done something wrong."

Jumping to conclusions: Actually, there are two parts to this distortion. Mind Reading: "She's ignoring me. I must have done something wrong." And Fortune Telling: "The doctor hasn't called me yet with my test results. I must be really sick."

TABLE 5: Talking Back to the Internal Critic

Once you've learned to recognize distorted thinking, you also have to learn how to push it out of your mind.

Here's an example of a three-column chart approach. Say you suddenly realize you're late for an important meeting. Your heart sinks and you're gripped with panic. This is what your chart might look like.

Automatic Self-Critical Thought	Cognitive Distortion	Rational Response
1. I never do anything right.	1. Overgeneralizing	1. Nonsense! I do a lot of things right.
2. I'm always late.	2. Overgeneralizing	2. I'm not always late. That's ridiculous. Think of all the times I've been on time. If I'm late more often than I'd like, I'll work on this problem and develop a method for being more punctual.
3. Everyone will look down on me.	3. Overgeneralizing, Either/Or Thinking, Fortune Telling	3. Someone may be disappointed that I'm late, but it's not the end of the world. Maybe the meeting won't even start on time.
4. I'll make a fool of myself.	4. Fortune Telling	4. Come on, now, I'm not a fool. I may appear foolish if I come in late, but this doesn't make me a fool. Everyone is late sometimes.

Reprinted by permission of the publisher from *Feeling Good: The New Mood Therapy,* David D. Burns, M.D. (New York: New American Library, 1980), p. 67.

As you can see, negative thoughts begin to sound monotonously alike after a while. That's because they *are* very much alike, says Gary Emery, Ph.D., a former student of Dr. Beck's and author of *A New Beginning* (Touchstone). For one thing, "the chief characteristic of negative thoughts is that they're generally wrong." They're a distortion or an exaggeration of the truth. That's at least partly because they tend to be automatic. That is, they simply leap into your mind unbidden; they're not conclusions you've reached through reason and logic. In fact, in a sense they're not "thinking" at all.

How do "thought therapists" go about reshaping these negative, self-defeating, soul-saddening thought patterns?

Put your life and problems in a realistic perspective.

The point is to put your life and your problems in a *realistic* perspective. Like a reporter, a scientist, or a detective, you're looking to find the true facts of the case, to apply the principles of hard science to your own thought processes.

The plan of attack is in three phases, Dr. Emery says: awareness, answering, and action.

FIRST PHASE: AWARENESS

Become aware of your thoughts and feelings.

Vague, unfocused negative thoughts that lurk just below the surface of consciousness cause more harm than those that are dragged out into the open. So the first step out of the rut of depression is to become aware of what you're actually thinking and feeling.

Sometimes that's more difficult than it sounds, since these thoughts tend to be well disguised. Dr. Emery suggests using a sort of "instant replay" technique, thinking back to what crossed your mind just before a mood change or a physical sensation like fatigue, heaviness, or butterflies in the stomach. Sometimes there is no preceding thought — you only later attribute a certain thought ("I'm worthless") to a certain feeling (sadness), says Arthur Freeman, Ed.D., a therapist at the Center for Cognitive Therapy at the University of Pennsylvania. "But whichever comes first, the thought or the feeling, we still find cognitive intervention effective," Dr. Freeman says.

A gimmick that works: Count your negative thoughts.

Another way to become more aware of your negative thoughts is simply to count them. You can use a plastic grocery-store price counter, or a small stitch counter (sold in knitting shops) or just transfer coins (a penny is one thought, a dime ten thoughts) from one pocket to another. "These gimmicks remind you to become aware of your thinking," Dr. Emery says. "You discover that you have the same thoughts over and over again."

"It's important to 'concretize' vague, negative thoughts," agrees Dr. Freeman. "One of the simplest ways is to write them down. We try to help patients separate thoughts into three distinct aspects: what the situation is, what you're feeling about it, and what you're saying to yourself (your thoughts)."

Strip away everything except the plain, simple facts.

Most of us don't consider situations objectively; instead we load them up with all kinds of projections and judgments, Dr. Freeman says. You may think, for instance, "I'm waiting for my girlfriend to call me but she probably won't because she knows I'm a loser." The first step is to strip away everything except the plain, simple facts: "I'm waiting for my girlfriend to call." Period. Next, you sift your experience in search of your true feelings. "The first thing you come up with may be, 'I feel like a loser,' but I submit that's not a feeling, that's a thought," Dr. Freeman says. "Then it's, 'I feel as if she'll never call'—again, not a feeling, a thought. Finally you get to, 'I feel sad.' OK—that's the feeling."

Then you've got to tune in to your self-talk concerning the situation. Why have you concluded your girlfriend isn't going to call? If she's late, has it ever happened before? What other reasonable explanations are there to account for the fact that she's late calling? In short, Dr. Freeman says, you've got to *examine the evidence*. You've got to drag your negative thoughts into court, put them on the witness stand, and confront them with the facts. Usually, they'll wilt under the pressure.

Tune in to your self-talk.

Dr. Emery, when counseling a woman who was depressed because she believed no man would ever want to marry a divorcee with two children, told her to go to the library and look up the statistics. She found that women with children were actually *more* likely to find new mates than childless single women of the same age.

Is there any truth to your negative thoughts?

SECOND PHASE: ANSWERING NEGATIVE THOUGHTS

Once you've identified and clarified the thought patterns that are making you feel bad, you've got to answer them back. One of the best ways to pry open the closed circle of negative thoughts is to learn to ask yourself good questions. Become a hard-nosed prosecutor and drill your negative thoughts but good. What's the evidence that I'm such a worthless person? Am I confusing a mere thought with a fact? Am I overlooking my strengths? Exactly what is the distortion in my thinking? Am I exaggerating or over-generalizing? And so on.

A good way to clarify this process for yourself, Dr. Beck suggests, is to divide a piece of paper into two columns and write out a more balanced, fact-based, realistic answer beside each recurrent negative thought. A gloomy, lonesome housewife may think, "I'm neglected because nobody wants to be around me." But in the opposite column, if she

A comparison test: negative thought versus rational thought.

gave it a little thought, she could answer, "Mary hasn't called because she's in the hospital, Judy is out of town, and Helen really *did* call but I forgot about that."

Occasionally, Dr. Emery says, you may be so upset that no reasonable answer comes immediately to mind. So postpone answering—wait an hour or two, or set aside a certain time each day to write out your answers. One of his patients, expanding on this idea, created a "Wednesday Box" in which she deposited all the thoughts and ideas that bothered her during the week. On Wednesdays, she opened the box, tore up the thoughts that were no longer a problem, and tried to constructively answer those that still were.

THIRD PHASE: TAKING ACTION

Acting out your self-defeating thoughts is a way of "reality testing."

It's not enough to simply answer your negative thoughts—you have to act on your new thoughts and beliefs. In a way, Dr. Emery points out, acting out your written answers to negative, self-defeating thoughts is a way of "reality testing" them to see if they're really true. How do you know for sure that you "can't" speak in public unless you try it? Or that you'll be rejected if you introduce yourself to someone you're attracted to? (It's possible you really can't speak in public, and you really will be rejected—but you'll never know until you try.)

Rate the pleasure or sense of accomplishment you get out of each daily task.

For people mired in the deep mud of depression, Dr. Beck suggests working up an activity schedule, or weekly calendar with each day divided into hour-long boxes. The idea is to schedule something throughout the day, and keep a record of how well you did with each task—perhaps by rating the amount of pleasure or sense of accomplishment it gave you on a scale of one through five.

This simple little calendar can help in many ways. It gives you the true facts about what you actually do during the day—demonstrating to many depressed people that their lives aren't as bleak or empty as they had imagined. It helps you retake control of your life by breaking the rut of inactivity. And it helps you see clearly what gives you pleasure and satisfaction.

A SKILL, NOT A CURE

By becoming *aware* of your negative thoughts, *answering* them with a more realistic, constructive, and adaptive view, and taking *action* to break out of your self-imposed trap, you can get control of depression and anxiety. But can you ever be cured? "Cognitive therapy is a skill-building process— we're not talking about cures," Dr. Freeman says. "Some patients call back in a year or so and ask to come in again for a kind of 'booster' session. But they've learned skills to help them cope, and their relapses tend to be fewer and shorter."

Do you need a therapist at all? "Thirty-five or 40 years ago, when the first psychological self-help books came out, there was a hysterical cry from the public and the profession alike that, 'You can't do it that way! You can't help yourself!'" says Robert Reitman, Ph.D., a psychotherapist who doubles as president of PSYCOMP, a California computer software company that's producing cognitive-therapy computer programs to treat problems ranging from stress to sexual dysfunction. "But now we know that people have a great capacity to help themselves with psychological problems. And cognitive therapy, because it deals with thoughts, is especially suited to books, articles, tapes, and computer programs. This is not therapy, mind you, but these things can really help, if people choose to help themselves."

Now, cognitive-therapy computer software is available.

AFFIRMATIVE ACTION

In their book *From Burnout to Balance* (McGraw-Hill), Dennis T. Jaffee, Ph.D., and Cynthia D. Scott, Ph.D., suggest another technique to counter negative thinking. "When you find yourself being self-critical, write down a list of positive things about yourself, and things that you would like to happen," they say. "Place the list where you can read it often, on the refrigerator or bathroom mirror perhaps, and try to repeat these affirmative messages to yourself several times a day."

Affirmations—defined by Drs. Jaffe and Scott as "positive personal statements that modify negative personal beliefs and expectations, and motivate and influence us in new directions"—are the core of such popular books as Dale Carnegie's *How to Win Friends and Influence People* (Simon & Schuster, Inc.) and Norman Vincent Peale's *Power of Positive Thinking* (Fleming H. Revell Co.). According to these authors, Drs. Jaffe and Scott point out, "people who begin consciously to modify their inner conversations and assumptions report an almost immedi-

Make a list of your positive qualities and read it often.

By repeating criticisms over and over to yourself, they become your reality.

ate improvement in their performance. Their energy increases and things seem to go better. . . .

"We live in a world where it is commonplace to blame others for our shortcomings, where negative messages about our own powers and worth are common," Drs. Jaffe and Scott continue. "The unintended messages we often get from our parents, our teachers, and our employers are that we are not competent or not good. We take these messages into ourselves and repeat them until they become reality for us. We become powerless, incompetent, and incapable of responding to things, thereby giving up our sense of power."

Affirmations are a way to reprogram the mind for more positive results. When practiced properly and often, they too can become "our internal reality."

Create a few of your own. Think of short positive statements to counter some of the negative (self-critical)

BOX 15: EIGHT RULES OF EFFECTIVE AFFIRMATION

1. Place yourself in a receptive state of mind. Enter a deep state of relaxation (see Chapter 29, The Best of the Relaxation Techniques), or simply take a few moments to get your body and psyche ready to receive new information. Before you begin, you need to tell yourself you are ready.

2. Make your affirmations short, clear, unambiguous, and specific. Break down complex desires and changes into smaller, simpler directives.

3. Phrase affirmations in the present tense. You are creating them as a psychic reality that will exist from the moment you state them to yourself.

4. Phrase them positively, as what you want to do. Avoid negative words like "stop," "not," or "don't." State what

you actually want to think, feel, and do instead.

5. When you repeat your intentions, try to suspend your doubts, and inhibit a tendency to make a negative or doubting commentary. Do not undercut or undermine your affirmations. If you begin to think negatively, say "no" or "stop" to yourself, and continue the affirmation.

6. You should feel positive, expansive, and supportive as you say them.

7. Write down your sets of affirmations and place the list where you will see it repeatedly during the day. You need to keep reminding yourself of them to make them concrete and real for you.

8. Make affirmations a continuing, ongoing part of your life.

Reprinted with permission of the publisher from *From Burnout to Balance*, Dennis T. Jaffe, Ph.D., and Cynthia D. Scott, Ph.D. (New York: McGraw-Hill, 1985), p. 60.

thoughts you have such as "I am strong and competent," "I am happy with my work," "I am a giving and loving person." Or you might want to concentrate in other areas that are important to your life such as "I am healthy and full of energy."

"Spend a few moments several times a day slowly repeating your affirmations to yourself," Drs. Jaffe and Scott explain. "As you repeat them, try to imagine how that affirmation is—or can be—true in your life; you might imagine the affirmation as it comes to be part of your life. Actually see yourself changing."

Program yourself with positive statements—"I am competent and healthy."

Imagine the affirmation coming true; see yourself changing.

11

To Love
and Be Loved

When you fall in love, you are out of your mind—your *conscious* mind.

By definition, falling in love seems to imply that circumstances are out of our control. Not true, according to psychiatrist Morris Sklansky, M.D., of Michael Reese Hospital and Medical Center in Chicago. Once you clap eyes on the right person, his or her body attitude and facial expression will activate an automatic response mechanism in you that will set off bells in your heart—and mind.

"Everyone has an unconscious internal program that helps determine to whom he or she is attracted," Dr. Sklansky says, explaining that what seems to be an irrational reaction is actually a complicated, intellectual split-second sequence of events. That initial eye contact is doing more than sending chills up and down your spine. In fact, sensors are checking against that internal program before you realize what's going on. "When we say, 'I love her, but I don't know why,' we're being honest. In fact, the subconscious has done the screening for us," adds Dr. Sklansky.

Once Mr. or Ms. Right clears with the internal program, however, the subsequent effort must be conscious.

Love takes a conscious effort to maintain.

Ari Kiev, M.D., a psychiatrist from New York City and author of *Active Loving* (Crowell), explains how the marvelous spontaneity of love turns into the drudgery of a relationship full of expectations and demands.

The minute we try to hold on, we lose it.

"When we first begin to love someone, everything is new and sparkling. Our tendency is to try to hold on to that sparkle, to structure it, because we're afraid of losing it. But the minute we try to hold on, we destroy the relationship," he says.

To understand why that is we must first learn what love really is.

"Love is the total acceptance of another person," says Gerald Jampolsky, M.D., founder of the Center for Attitudinal Healing in Tiburon, California.

"Love is a relationship without shoulds or shouldn'ts. When we are in love, we accept," says Dr. Kiev.

A relationship without shoulds or shouldn'ts.

"In a loving relationship we feel safe and accepted no matter what we do; we feel safe to be ourselves. When someone loves us freely, they have no expectations or demands," says David Viscott, M.D.

Love, these psychiatrists say, is acceptance. And the opposite of acceptance is expectation. Not simply, "I love you," but "I'll love you *if* . . . " And many of us complete that sentence with: "I'll love you if you love me back."

I'll love you if . . .

GIVE WITHOUT DEMANDS

"We all have a tendency to want to make deals with other people rather than to give without demands," says Harmon Bro, Ph.D., psychotherapist and former professor at Syracuse University.

"It is this manipulative type of loving that blocks the full expression of love in our life," he says.

"Loving with expectations is love that is conditional love," Dr. Viscott, a California psychiatrist and author of *How to Live with Another Person* (Priam), says. "If you need the other person's love to feel good about yourself, you look up to him out of desperation. And you give love out of fear, constantly worried that he might stop loving you. This isn't love, it's dependency, with little joy or happiness in it.

Dependency brings little joy or happiness.

"We tend to hide our normal actions because we want to impress the other person to maintain that sparkle or magic feeling. We become afraid of showing our true feelings, of being open and vulnerable, because we think the person will stop loving us if we have imperfections. And since we don't allow the other person to see our imperfections, we usually don't allow them to show us theirs. We put shoulds and shouldn'ts on them that are impossible to meet.

"When we strive for this certainty, we shut off love.

A fulfilling relationship is sharing, giving, and accepting without expectations.

A relationship, which to be fulfilling must be sharing, giving, and accepting, becomes full of pressures and expectations caused by the fear of losing it. That fear destroys the relationship."

SHARE YOUR FEELINGS

"The only way fear—or any other negative emotion—can destroy a relationship is if we don't let the other person know what we're feeling," says Peter Hansen, a therapist consultant who has conducted hundreds of workshops on love and relationships.

You probably won't get a negative response when you verbalize feelings.

"It's very important to verbalize feelings," agrees Dr. Kiev. "You may think you'll get a negative response, but you probably won't. Everyone really wants to be honest, and it feels so good to just open up and share with someone what you're feeling. They'll appreciate your openness, because it allows them to be open too and to share vulnerabilities.

"However, don't say, 'You hurt me,' or 'You made me angry.' Just talk about *yourself*: 'I feel hurt when you act that way,' or 'I feel angry when you do that.'

Communicating without accusing or berating the other.

"When you express your feelings in this way, you don't attack or accuse or berate the other person, you just communicate. I find that even a bad sexual situation will usually clear up if the communication in a relationship improves."

"What destroys a relationship is dishonesty and a lack of open communication," adds Dr. Viscott. "Dishonesty is one of the two things that block love. The other is not loving yourself.

First, love yourself.

"You can't receive love from another person unless you love yourself. If you don't love yourself, and a person says, 'I love you,' you think, 'I don't deserve it.' You resist the love because you can't think of yourself as worthy, because you can't value their positive estimation of yourself."

"Only if we love ourselves can be give love to others," says Carol Lentz, former director of the Cornucopia Institute, where she taught a self-improvement program called the Living Love Way to Happiness.

Demanding love destroys the process.

"When you don't love yourself, you want the other person to love you," she says. "This demand destroys your ability to accept the other person unconditionally, to love them."

"The love you have for yourself is the nucleus of all motivation," Perry W. Buffington, Ph.D., adds. "If you love yourself, you feel worthy. If you feel worthy, you feel competent. If you feel competent, you're ready to love." How do you set off the chain reaction?

"With my patients I start with physical appearance," Dr. Buffington says. "It's probably the most important factor in most people's self-esteem. I ask them what they don't like about the way they look, then let them change it for the better. Such simple modifications are the fastest routes to increased self-worth."

Physical appearance: the most important factor in self-esteem.

The next step, explains Dr. Buffington, is to wage war on negative thinking. "Most people's thoughts about themselves are negative," he says. "And people tend to accept the negative notions uncritically and act as though they were true. I try to get my patients to find out how accurate their negative thoughts really are. I get them to monitor what they're thinking and ask themselves if it's really true. By the time they finish this process, they're ready to address only the lifestyle changes that truly merit change."

Are your negative thoughts about yourself really true?

"All the negative emotions—anger, fear, grief—stem from lack of self-love," says Peter Hansen. "When you love yourself, you feel complete and zestful. To see the zestful person in yourself and in others is the essence of loving."

PART OF NATURAL LIVING

"Love," he continues, "is simply the most creative use of our own energy, and there are many ways to channel that energy. Eating natural foods, getting aerobic exercise, spending time in unmolested nature, praying, meditating—but most importantly, giving someone 100 percent of your attention when you relate to them—are all effective ways to increase loving."

Give 100 percent of your attention.

"There are many creative disciplines to enrich our ability to love," agrees Dr. Bro. "Meditation or equivalent methods of quieting the mind such as listening to music or spending time with nature can free us of our hang-ups and mobilize our creative energy to pay full attention to others and love.

"Another discipline is to recognize when you are coming from a bad place, when you are rejecting others, manipulating others, or feeling sorry for yourself. Notice your voice, your choice of words, your manner, and if they're negative or destructive, change them.

Learn to recognize negative or destructive behavior.

A flexible and natural process.

"Also, when someone relates to us in an aggressive or defensive or shy way, try to realize the hurt and fear and need of love behind that behavior. We should see someone else's bad behavior as an opportunity to give love, not as a personal affront.

"Yet even with these disciplines, we should realize that love is essentially playful. It is spontaneous, fully present, unguarded, and able to be surprised. It is not a heavy-handed kind of virtue, but a flexible and natural process."

And becoming more loving—more natural—has another benefit: better health.

Emotional defensiveness can express itself physically.

"People who have never developed the capacity for loving find their lovelessness reflected in their body," says Dr. Bro. "That emotional guardedness and defensiveness can express itself physically as muscular tension, shallow breathing, lack of normal sexual function, and an uninflected voice."

"When people hold in their feelings," says Peter Hansen, "they begin to feel hopeless and powerless, they give up. That giving up is expressed in the body as sickness. Cancer, for instance, shows up mostly in personality types who have held back anger all their lives.

Love and health go hand in hand.

"But people who are loving—who completely accept themselves and others—are usually full of energy and joy. Love and health go hand in hand."

GIVE:
The Four-Letter Word
That Spells Health

Looking out for number one may be the fashion, but lending a helping hand never went out of style. Maybe that's because altruism has always had a lot going for it—like a tendency to make people happy and healthy.

Vince Ward will be the first to agree. High blood pressure can be one of the unwelcome perks of his high-tension job. Ward, who is in his 50s, is advertising and public-relations director—"flak-catcher"—for one of the nation's largest telecommunications firms. But Ward says his blood pressure is fine. In fact, everything is fine. He's fit, doesn't lose sleep worrying, "and, my kids like me."

In his spare time, Ward works with parolees from Kansas State Penitentiary, raises money for a children's home, and has donated more than 14 gallons of blood to the Community Blood Bank of Greater Kansas City. All in all, he says, "I'm a pretty happy guy."

When she was a child, they called her "Dummy." And Kay Arnold grew up believing they were right. But the 48-year-old homemaker knew she had musical talent and she knew she wanted to help people. Several years ago, she joined a troupe of entertainers called SENSE, in Newington, Connecticut, that performs for the disabled and elderly. Today, Kay Arnold has a different opinion of herself.

"This gives me a sense of worth I never had before," she says. "It's like therapy that works both ways." And she has noticed something even more remarkable. "I have

Altruism makes people happy and healthy.

Community volunteer work balances a high-tension job.

It's therapy that works both ways.

arthritis," she explains, "and when I perform, it seems to make the pain go away."

Vince Ward and Kay Arnold are more than just a couple of do-gooders. Their lives—full and healthy—illustrate a little-known corollary to the Golden Rule: Doing unto others can do wonderful things unto you.

Generosity may be nature's way of keeping us well.

Though there weren't stress tests and EKGs in the days of St. Luke, he was medically accurate when he wrote, "It is more blessed to give than to receive." We've always known that people with generous spirits tend to be happier, but now doctors are saying they're healthier and live longer, too. Generosity comes naturally to us, they say. In fact, it may be nature's way of keeping us well.

Some prominent scientists believe that giving of yourself to others is an effective antidote to stress.

Like stress, love has a cumulative effect.

One of them, the late Hans Selye, M.D., who was responsible for the early studies tying stress to illness, called the concept "altruistic egoism." Biblical scholars might call it the "As ye sow, so shall ye reap" syndrome. It seems generosity has some valuable paybacks: the love and gratitude we inspire in those we help. Like stress, love has a cumulative effect, Dr. Selye said. We can weather the storms of life if we have hoarded good feelings for bad times, in much the same way squirrels hoard food for the winter. Those feelings are perpetual reminders that although everything else might be bad, we aren't. Knowing that can make life easier.

Psychiatrist George Vaillant, M.D., director of a 40-year study of Harvard graduates, identified altruism as one of the qualities that helped even the most poorly adjusted men of the study group deal successfully with the stresses of life (*Adaptation to Life,* Little, Brown & Co.).

People who say "I" and "me" most often were at highest risk for heart disease.

Does all this mean selfishness could make you ill? Larry Scherwitz, Ph.D., thinks it might. A social psychologist at the Medical Research Institute of San Francisco, Dr. Scherwitz turned up a startling fact in a major study for risk factors in coronary heart disease: The people who referred to themselves using the pronouns I, me, and my most often in an interview were more likely to develop coronary heart disease, even when other health-threatening behaviors were controlled. "The more self-centered people were much more likely to die of heart attack than the less self-centered," says Dr. Scherwitz.

The reason for that may be quite simple, suggests Dean Ornish, M.D., author of *Stress, Diet and Your Heart* (Holt, Rinehart, Winston). "This exaggerated focus on the self may further reinforce the sense of isolation and separateness," he says. In other words, looking out for number one isn't enlightened self-interest at all. It's just lonely. And loneliness kills.

Looking out for yourself is lonely. And loneliness kills.

THE BIOLOGY OF CARING

So says James Lynch, Ph.D., a leading specialist in psychosomatic medicine from the University of Maryland School of Medicine. Dr. Lynch documented the connection between loneliness and heart disease in his book, *The Broken Heart: The Medical Consequences of Loneliness* (Basic Books). "The mandate to 'Love your neighbor as you love yourself' is not just a moral mandate. It's a physiological mandate. Caring is biological," Dr. Lynch says. "One thing you get from caring for others is you're not lonely. And the more connected you are to life, the healthier you are."

An elderly volunteer worker in suburban Baltimore puts it another way: "Involvement makes you keep well so you can keep giving. It makes you take care of your health. It's a blessing to ward off old age."

Alfred N. Larsen sees evidence of that firsthand. Larsen is national director of the federal Retired Senior Volunteer Program (RSVP), which recently placed over a quarter million elderly people in community volunteer jobs. He says he's convinced of the value of volunteer work for the elderly, who lose family, friends, and often a purpose for life as they grow older. "Doctors always tell us that elderly people who engage in volunteer work are a lot better off, visit the doctor less often, and have fewer complaints," he says.

Elderly people who do volunteer work have fewer health complaints.

It keeps you young. It keeps you healthy. The experts are saying that caring for others keeps you alive. And researcher Linda Nilson, Ph.D., a sociologist at the University of California in Los Angeles, goes so far as to say altruism may be a part of our survival instinct.

While poring over data on 100 natural disasters, Dr. Nilson began to discern a strong pattern of altruism among disaster victims. Even when their own lives were disrupted, victims almost invariably lent helping hands to their

During disasters, helping others is part of the recovery process.

neighbors. It seems to be part of the recovery process. In a disaster, she says, "we go back to a sense of tribal cohesiveness, having to reconstruct the society around us under tremendous survival pressure. We realize our survival depends not only on our own happiness but on the survival and happiness of others."

The community that evolves out of a disaster is called "a therapeutic community," says Dr. Nilson, and it is so nurturing it wards off psychological problems later on. In fact, disaster survivors report an exhilarating sense of well-being and feel better not only about themselves but about their neighbors.

HELP ME, HELP YOU

Alcoholics Anonymous offers the solace of mutual aid.

These therapeutic communities are, in essence, makeshift self-help groups. But self-help, with its implications of individual effort, is a misnomer. What self-help groups like Alcoholics Anonymous offer is the solace of mutual aid. "Their members get help from helping," says Frank Riessman, director of the National Self-Help Clearinghouse, City University of New York.

It's no simple idea. Self-help group members give one another a special kind of human companionship. "There's a strong sense of connectedness with people who really understand you because they share your problem," says Reissman. For those with health problems, there's a bonus. Self-help groups literally can be a form of health care. Reissman says this is nowhere more apparent than among victims of high blood pressure, who reinforce their own good health habits— sticking to a low-salt diet and exercising—by giving the same advice to others.

By helping others, we feel more in control of our own lives.

Like Dr. Nilson's disaster victims, people helping others in the proverbial same boat are practicing a survival skill. Lending a helping hand makes the vulnerable feel less vulnerable, says Reissman. "They feel they have some control over their lives."

That measure of control may be the difference between sickness and health, according to a recent study by Colorado researchers. They subjected rats to identical electrical shocks, but allowed one set of animals to control the jolts. When they examined them, they discovered the animals that couldn't escape the shocks showed a reduced disease-fighting ability in their white blood cells. Having control over stress, postulates one of the researchers, Steven F. Maier, Ph.D., can prevent the suppression of the body's immune system, which might otherwise leave you vulnerable to everything from bacteria to cancer cells.

And being a helper can really puff up your ego, says Lowell Levin, Ed.D., professor of public health at Yale University and an expert on the health benefits of mutual aid. "When you're a helper, your self-concept improves. You are somebody. You are worthwhile. And there's nothing more exhilarating than that," he says. "That can influence your health."

When you're a helper, your self-concept improves.

That's exactly what the California Department of Mental Health learned five years ago when it surveyed 1,000 Californians. Those who cared most for themselves and others regarded themselves as being much healthier, both mentally and physically, than those with little concern for themselves and the next guy.

One reason for that, suggests Dr. James Lynch, is that people with high self-esteem take better care of themselves. "Really caring for yourself includes caring for your body," he says. "And that becomes the foundation of caring for others."

People with higher self-esteem take better care of themselves.

Other people also help us establish our own identities, he says. "When you say 'I,' 'I' has no meaning until you look into my eyes and see 'you.' The people who give to others generally find themselves in eyes brimming with gratitude and love, and there's no greater ego boost than that."

So, you want to be happy, healthy, and live a long life. Does that mean you should march right out like Vince Ward and give a pint of blood or belt out a song in a nursing home as Kay Arnold does? No, not if you're only giving to get something in return. The only way a giver can really reap the benefits of giving is if the urge comes from the goodness, not the need, in his heart. Says Dr. Larry Scherwitz, "If you're altruistic because of the goodies you get out of it, you're not altruistic. If the person you've helped doesn't thank you and you get angry, you're not altruistic. You've become too attached to the fruits of your labor."

To reap the benefits of giving, the motivation must be totally unselfish.

13

Courting Romance—
Every Day

Imagine yourself walking
along a deserted beach.

Y ou're walking with a friend along a deserted strand of beach. The sky blazes with a fiery sunset, and the evening fog looks like a fuzzy pink blanket rolling over the ocean. A flock of gulls glides down overhead.

Suddenly you're held fast by a sense of great beauty. Your skin tingles, and your whole body glows inside. You have to stop walking for a minute to let the feeling wash over you.

But your companion is concerned with the tide and the darkness—and tries to get you to move on.

Another day, you're strolling with the same friend down a city street. A gust of wind sends leaves swirling down from the trees. Some nearby children are dancing in circles, unwittingly imitating the spiraling leaves. You are struck by the beauty of the crisp, bright, late fall day. And when the children's laughter reaches you, you feel all aglow and happy to be alive.

You sigh and tell your friend that the world is so beautiful you want to walk slower and enjoy more of it before rushing home.

But your friend is in a hurry and only grunts and walks on, mumbling that you're an incurable romantic.

You should be proud of yourself. Whatever it is you've got, your friend could use a big dose of it. So could we all. Thanks to your "incurable romanticism," you're not only getting more out of that twilight walk on the beach and the

A blazing sunset, a flock of gulls—the beauty overtakes you.

Are you an incurable romantic?

crisp fall day—you're probably leading a healthier, happier life, too.

Why is romance good for us? How can we get more of it into our lives?

What, exactly, is romance?

"Romance is a passionate commitment to the happiness that life can offer," Nathaniel Branden, Ph.D., says. Dr. Branden has helped many people put more romance into their lives and their relationships through his private practice, and in the pages of such best-selling books as *The Psychology of Romantic Love* and, with E. Devers Branden, *The Romantic Love Question and Answer Book* (both published by J. P. Tarcher, Inc.).

Romance: a passionate commitment to the happiness that life can offer.

SEE THE FRESHNESS IN LIFE

"Many people live automatically," Dr. Branden explains. "Life loses its freshness. Enthusiasm dies. Passion dies. And I'm not referring only to romantic *love*. The question is not only must romantic love die, but must *all* enthusiasm and excitement die?"

The answer Dr. Branden (and all the other professionals we talked to) gave to that question was a resounding *no*!

"Beauty and excitement!" was the answer editor Carolyn Nichols gave when we asked her to define romance. As senior editor heading up Bantam Books' romance fiction projects, she devotes her professional talents to helping writers and readers discover more romance in their lives—and in their books.

"To be romantic is to see your life in beautiful, expanded terms," Nichols says. "You ought to talk to some of the best-selling writers who create romance in their books. Their sense are tuned to what is truly romantic in life."

Tom Curtis, who writes in tandem with wife Sharon, defines romance as "the creation of a transcendent moment in time that acts as a prism to break trivialities into the brilliant colors of true meaning."

Sharon Curtis explains, "Romance is the part of you that looks with a child's eye on things—to keep the wonder in your life."

Making a distinction between romance and sentimentality, she says, "Sentimentality makes you feel depressed

When people live automatically, life loses its freshness.

See your life in beautiful, expanded terms.

Look with a child's eye—keep the wonder in your life.

and confused. But romance is very vivid. Romance makes you feel peaceful and excited at the same time."

"Romance is the sensual awareness of things around you," says Helen Mittermeyer, author (under the pen name Ann Cristy) of *From the Torrid Past* (Jove Publications, Inc.). "Romance is an awareness of self and a sense of self-worth. When you hear a bird sing, do you hear the actual notes? Do you hear the melody of the song the bird has written just for you?"

When you hear a bird sing, do you hear a melody created just for you?

The other experts interviewed were unanimous in agreeing that romance strengthens our sense of self-worth. In his private practice, Dr. Branden has found that a lack of this important "emotional nutrient" can be at the heart of serious psychological problems. "When I began the practice of psychotherapy, more than 20 years ago, I was struck by the fact that regardless of the problems for which people sought my help, they all suffered from a deficiency of self-esteem," he says.

Romance: the best "nutrient" to fight emotional deficiencies.

Romance is the best "nutrient" to fight that deficiency, too.

"Romantic love passionately celebrates the person. Romantic love rejects the view of human beings as interchangeable units," continues Dr. Branden. "The romantic attitude says: 'I am important; my life is important; what I do with my life is important; my choices and values are important.'"

Children are taught to stifle their passions and excitements.

This dangerous, illness-producing lack of self-esteem begins very early in life, according to Dr. Branden. "From the day we are born," he says, "we are encouraged to be cool, to put a real chill on our response to life by stifling our passions and excitements. When a child bursts into a room, for example, an adult tells him to be quiet. 'Why do you make such noise?' the adult asks. 'What's wrong with you?'

"The child learns that certain of his feelings and emotions are unacceptable. So the child solves the problem by repressing emotions. But not only does he stop expressing things, he stops *feeling* them, too. The solution the child creates is unconsciousness."

Repression of feelings is deadly to romance.

Unconsciousness, deadening of the senses, repression of feelings and sensations are all deadly to romance, our experts agreed.

"Lots of people close themselves off," says Helen Mittermeyer, "because they don't want to be hurt. But without romance, you might as well be dead. You're only surviving. Romance is good for you. It lifts your spirits. If you allow yourself to be sensitive, it comes right through your pores. You hear a bird sing and . . . you feel better!"

"Romance makes life worth living," agrees Carolyn Nichols. "Along with daydreaming, which is one part of romance, it's one of the essentials of a happy life."

Along with daydreaming, it's an essential of a happy life.

Romance can have a healing, as well as preventive, effect, say Sharon and Tom Curtis. "Romance has to do with being able to heal yourself emotionally," says Sharon. "If I had no concept of romance, I don't know what I'd do. A sense of romance is as necessary as a sense of humor."

Romance can have a healing—and preventive—effect.

GETTING ROMANCE IN YOUR LIFE

How can we start to get more romance into our lives—especially since, as Sharon Curtis says, "Life seems to strip it away"?

"It's a choice we make," she says. "We choose to believe that romantic, happy things are at least as much a real part of life as less pleasant things. You have to hold on to romance. You don't need to work on it. Just remember to increase your romantic awareness."

"Consciousness is the lifeblood of romance," says Dr. Branden. "Consciousness of life, joy, excitement, thoughts, and fantasies—the full range of our mental and emotional world.

Become conscious of life, joy, excitement, thoughts, and fantasies.

"To be more romantic," he says, "we must develop the ability to see life afresh every day; perceive the unexpected as a gift; don't be afraid to leap into the unfamiliar. This is the attitude that is necessary in order to keep passion alive."

"Develop the art of paying attention," says Carolyn Nichols. "We can't allow ourselves to ignore everyday experiences. If we do, we ignore many opportunities for romance. You can transform everyday experiences into romantic and extraordinary ones. Simply pay attention. For example, outside my office building, right on the sidewalk, there's a small chamber orchestra made up of musicians from the Juilliard School of Music. During the lunch hour they give free concerts. Now, that's too wonderful a romantic opportunity to pass by. And the everyday world is filled with such opportunities, if we pay attention."

Master the art of paying attention.

"One of the most romantic—and *healthy*—feelings

I've experienced occurred on a walk in the woods with a friend, listening to the birds," recalls Sharon Curtis. "I became aware that I was tuned in to the birds, to my companion, and to the forest around us. I felt close to myself, close to my friend, close to nature. It was wonderful.

Tune in to nature and feel that you're a part of it.

"Anyone can do this, can walk alone or with a friend in a place where there is access to natural things—a farm, a forest, a park. Become aware of the natural things around you, aware that you are part of nature, too.

"You can say to yourself: I am part of this. This is my home.

Stargazing gets us in touch with our own innocence.

"You can experience this in the city, too, just by watching a sunset. You don't have to be in the wilderness. You can look up at the night sky no matter where you are. When we stargaze, we get in touch with our own innocence."

"To be romantic is to be healthy."

"Romantics do what's good for them," says Helen Mittermeyer, "so it makes sense that if you start at the other end—by taking better care of yourself—your mind will become sharper, you'll feel better about yourself and your life. You'll become a romantic. To be romantic is to be healthy."

Beware of Taking Yourself Too Seriously

Maybe you still feel a little guilty about a faux pas you made at a party two weeks ago. Maybe you finished next to last at a "fun run" on Saturday. Maybe your new hairstylist scrambled your hair and now you have to live with a weird perm for a month. Maybe all those things happened—but so what if they did?

Whoever you are and whatever you do, you probably take yourself and your setbacks too seriously. You could stand to lighten up, laugh at your mistakes, smile more and let people see that beautiful face of yours.

There's a lot to be gained by brightening your outlook. If you can laugh at yourself, you'll probably cope with obstacles more effectively and rebound faster from disappointments. You'll be able to let off steam better, your self-esteem will rise, and people may even like you more.

But if you insist on taking yourself too seriously, you're bound to get steamrollered by Life, with a capital L.

No one is immune to taking him- or herself too seriously, not even Lawrence Mintz, Ph.D., professor of American studies at the University of Maryland and secretary-treasurer of the American Humor Studies Association, a society of scholars interested in humor.

"I have a mirror on my office wall," Dr. Mintz says, "that I use to comb my hair in before I go to class. Underneath the mirror there's a little sign that says, 'This person is not to be taken too seriously.'

"I'm a normal, narcissistic, egotistical person with

"What I'm doing may not be the most important thing in the world."

all sorts of vanities. I'm very happy with myself and I'm glad to be me, but I have a definite tendency to take myself too seriously. I take my teaching and running involvement in politics seriously. But sometimes I have to admit that what I'm doing might not be the most important thing in the world."

For Dr. Mintz, who puts out a publication of his own called the *American Humor and Interdisciplinary Newsletter,* there just isn't enough time to take everything seriously. "People use humor to separate the truly threatening from what's not truly threatening. You learn to laugh at the day-to-day things and reserve seriousness for what is really tragic. We tend to blow things out of proportion."

Humor and threat, strangely enough, go together.

But humor and threat, strangely enough, usually go together, Dr. Mintz says, and sometimes our worst troubles become the material for the best jokes. "All humor requires an element of threat," he said in an interview. "It's the terrible things that become funny when we share our fears about them with other people. We can either let things get to us or we can laugh at them."

And laughing at ourselves is the best way anyone's found to deal with human frailty since Adam took the apple from Eve. "Humor," says Dr. Mintz, "is the way we cope with living in an imperfect world with imperfect selves. When we can't win, the best thing to do is to laugh about it."

Amusement with oneself provides an escape valve from life's pressures.

Harvey Mindess, Ph.D., a professor at Antioch University in California and a counselor who specializes in the use of humor as a tool in psychotherapy, agrees with Dr. Mintz that amusement with oneself provides an effective escape valve from life's pressures.

"I believe, and so do a number of other psychologists, that humor is a great coping mechanism," Dr. Mindess says. "When a client of mine is very anxious about something, I try to get him to break out of his anger or fear by laughing at himself.

"In one case, an 18-year-old girl came to see me. She'd never been to a psychologist before and she told me, 'I know I'm mixed up. But I've heard of people being destroyed by therapy.' I just told her, 'You're in luck. I already destroyed my quota for this week.' I convinced her that all this talk about destroying was foolish and we both laughed about it."

A SENSE OF SELF-WORTH

Dr. Mindess thinks that people who can take a joke have a stronger sense of self-worth than those who can't. "Being able to laugh at yourself means that you have a good kind of self-esteem," he says. "Good self-esteem means that you can feel OK about yourself without deluding yourself that you have no faults.

"When we expand the limits of our laughter to include laughter at ourselves and everything we stand for, we become more perceptive, more candid, and more fully self-accepting than when we take ourselves completely seriously.

By laughing at ourselves, we become more candid and self-accepting.

"The advantage of humor," he adds, "is that you can release safely a lot of repressed thoughts that you wouldn't ordinarily have a chance to express. And the danger of being too serious is that you will be overwhelmed by problems that, later seen in perspective, weren't so terrible."

Like Dr. Mindess, Western Illinois University psychotherapist Frank Prerost, Ph.D., has found a link between self-esteem and humor. His patients seem to gain maturity and self-esteem when they progress through what he calls the "three stages" of humor.

The link between humor and self-esteem.

In the first and least mature stage, the patients or clients usually ridicule their own inadequacies, often weeping as much as laughing. In the second stage, they typically direct hostile laughter at others. In the third stage, they laugh at their own shortcomings, doing it in a confident, nonthreatened way. Dr. Prerost notes that people who attained stage three "soon terminated treatment and reported effective control over their lives.

"In the third stage," he says, "they can look at their own failings in a humorous fashion and they no longer blame other people for their problems. It works two ways. Laughing at themselves means taking responsibility for their own lives, and when they feel in control of their lives, they are able to laugh at themselves more.

When we feel in control of our lives, we can laugh at ourselves more.

"When people have this ability, they start to develop a different attitude. They stop believing that life owes them certain things. They know that they have to work for what they get. They become more effective in life. It's a kind of paradox. Until they can really accept their shortcomings, they can't go out and do what they are capable of doing."

Turning hostility toward others into laughter at themselves.

Dr. Prerost described two of his clients who became healthier and happier when they turned hostility toward others into laughter at themselves. The first one was a woman in her late 40s who mysteriously began to develop a cluster of ailments—headaches, fatigue, and insomnia. She also lost her usual good humor. She criticized her children and acted cruelly to her husband. She also experienced phobialike panic attacks.

It turned out that the woman was very frightened of growing old, Dr. Prerost said. Eventually she learned to laugh at her panic attacks and her exaggerated fears. Her new attitude was: "I may be getting older, but I'm getting better."

"What a klutz I am. But so what?"

In another case, a young woman ridiculed her husband to compensate for her own submissiveness and social clumsiness. She made fun of his extroverted nature and called him "superficial" and "a gladfly." She gradually came to recognize her own inhibitions and self-consciousness. The next time she spilled a drink at party she was able to say: "What a klutz I am. But so what?"

"In my own life," Dr. Prerost says, "I tend to joke about setbacks and disappointments. I try to find the humor in a bad situation. I say to myself, OK, it's a letdown, but next time it won't be. I deal with disappointment by making light of it.

The link between humor and honesty.

"Sometimes when I'm teaching a course, I take the material too seriously. I probably do that when I'm not as familiar with it as I should be. So I use seriousness to hide that fact. It's a kind of cover-up." He stresses the link between humor and honesty. "As one's honesty with oneself increases, the healthy kind of humor starts to increase," he says.

"NATURAL HIGH THERAPY"

Walter "Buzz" O'Connell, Ph.D., a clinical psychologist at the Veterans Administration Medical Center in Houston, uses humor in therapy and pokes fun at his patients as soon as he feels they can handle it comfortably. For Dr. O'Connell, the founder of what he calls "Natural High Therapy," both guilt and unrealistic expectations prevent many people from taking themselves more lightly.

"To feel guilty is to take yourself very seriously," Dr.

O'Connell says. "You're saying to yourself, 'I did this and therefore I'm no good forever.' And you think you have to be perfect. You can't have a sense of humor when you're trying to be perfect.

"Instead of hanging on to what they're supposed to be, people should let go," he adds, "let go of the idea that they must make more money or be the world's greatest lover.

"People should take their *selves* seriously," he says, "but they shouldn't take their *egos* so seriously. The need to feel worthwhile, to feel a sense of belonging, is never ridiculous. But the puny little ego—that drop of water in the ocean—should never be taken very seriously at all."

To feel guilty is to take yourself very seriously.

Take your *self* seriously. But don't take your *ego* so seriously.

Part of Dr. O'Connell's work in Houston involves treating Vietnam War veterans who feel guilty about their role in the war and discouraged by their failures in civilian life. One of the veterans was a huge man named Bill who was angry and hostile and threatened to disrupt group therapy sessions. Dr. O'Connell "shocked Bill with humor" by naming him the "Buddha of Constant Discouragement." He thanked Bill for giving the rest of the group an opportunity to practice not being overwhelmed by outside hostility. "Bill was profoundly aghast," Dr. O'Connell said. If he remained hostile, he would find himself cooperating with the therapist. And if he dropped his hostility and laughed at himself, he would be taking an important step toward mental health. Eventually Bill chose the latter step.

Ultimately, humor is economical. "Someone with a good sense of humor doesn't waste energy pretending to be perfect or hiding their anger or feeling guilty," Dr. O'Connell explains. "He doesn't waste energy trying to suppress his thoughts. A sense of humor means you can roll with the punches and be productive at the same time."

Roll with the punches and be productive at the same time.

People who presently take themselves with extreme gravity might have the best opportunity, strangely enough, to get a large laugh out of their predicament. That is the opinion of Jane Littmann, Ph.D., a clinical psychologist at the William S. Hall Psychiatric Institute in Columbia, South Carolina.

Dr. Littmann wrote her doctoral thesis on individual differences in sense of humor, and she came to the conclusion that "the more serious the subject—such as politics, religion, or sex—the more potential it has to be funny, and the bigger the explosion of laughter if we joke about it.

The more serious the subject, the more potential it has to be funny.

"The more involved someone is in a subject, or the more seriously they take it, the more they will enjoy jokes about it—that is, if they can see humor in it at all," Dr. Littmann says. Surgeons and emergency-room nurses, for example, sometimes release tension by indulging in black humor. "A surgeon takes his job seriously, but if he takes it too seriously," she says, "he might be paralyzed by the responsibility. To an outsider, his kind of humor might look like a horrible thing."

Not taking something too seriously, Dr. Littmann points out, doesn't mean not taking it seriously at all.

Be serious, but see humor at the same time.

"You want to be serious and see the humor at the same time," she says. "You should have a kind of dual vision."

"The person who can keep his sense of humor can deal with a broader range of problems," she adds. "Instead of getting so beaten down that he or she gives up, a person with a sense of humor will bounce back and give it a second try."

TIPS FROM THE EXPERTS

The question comes up, how do you put more lightness in your life? Here are a half-dozen ideas from people dedicated to spreading laughter in this country: Joel Goodman, Ed.D., a public speaker and writer who directs the HUMOR Project, a program at the nonprofit Saratoga Institute in Saratoga Springs, New York; former comedian and now talent agent Marty Ingels of Los Angeles; and H. J. Cummings, president of the Workshop Library on World Humour, an international humor information clearinghouse in Washington, D.C.

"When life hands me lemons, I'll make lemonade."

• Select a humorous saying to repeat to yourself whenever you're disappointed. You could say, "When life hands me lemons, I'll make lemonade." It'll help you recover from the loss or setback.

• Pick a signal (like playfully putting your thumb to your chin and wiggling your fingers) to use when you feel a family or interpersonal conflict brewing. It helps break the tension and put things in perspective.

Plumber's inside joke: "A flush beats a full house."

• To put some humor into your job, be like the plumber whose truck bears a sign saying, "A flush beats a full house," or the sales manager who calls himself the sales "mangler."

• Remember that humor works better than anger. If someone's chronically late, say something like, "I'm glad you're not running an ambulance service," instead of shouting profanities.

   • Remember that very few things are sacred or absolute, and that none of your teachers or elders knew "The Answer." As Ingels puts it, "Even Ann Landers got a divorce."

Even Ann Landers got a divorce.

   • Remember to surround yourself with friends who aren't afraid to laugh in your face. Better yet, as Ingels suggests, "Marry someone, if you can, who thinks everything you say is funny. I married Shirley Jones, who laughs at everything I say."

PART **IV**

Shedding Negative Emotions

Crying and Groaning: Nature's Safety Valves

I t's not easy to cry on cue. To do so, one must mentally re-create a painful experience and conjure up all the associated bad feelings. Once these feelings are firmly entrenched, the tears flow freely, naturally, instinctively. In fact, it's such instinctive outpourings of emotion as crying and groaning that some researchers now say may act as natural safety mechanisms to protect our bodies from overdosing on emotional "downers."

William Fry, Jr., Ph.D., a biochemist in the psychiatry department at the St. Paul-Ramsey Medical Center in St. Paul, Minnesota, was the first to suggest this theory. Dr. Fry believes that emotional distress produces toxic substances in the body and that crying helps remove them from the system.

Crying removes toxic substances.

"This may be why someone who is sad feels better after having a good cry," he says.

To test his theory, Dr. Fry organized a study to determine whether emotional tears are chemically different from tears induced by an irritant. Volunteers were asked to watch a Hollywood tearjerker and, if they were moved to weep, to catch their tears in a test tube. A few days later, the same people were exposed to fresh-cut onions and again collected their tears.

Tears in a test tube.

On analysis, Dr. Fry reported, the tears wept in sorrow had a different chemical composition from those cried over onions. His finding confirmed research published in 1957 which demonstrated that emotional tears contain more protein. But with today's better understanding of the role of chemicals in emotion and more sensitive equipment to measure these chemicals, Dr. Fry hopes to pinpoint some of the finer differences.

Are "emotional" tears different than "irritant" tears?

"What we are now looking for in emotional tears are certain chemicals released during emotional stress. Among these chemicals are endorphin, a pain reliever, various hormones, and the catecholamines, one of which is adrenaline. Measuring the levels of those chemicals in tears is a very complex and difficult procedure, and my research is far from complete. But I have found that emotional tears contain catecholamines, and if there is a higher concentration of catecholamines in emotional tears than in irritant-induced tears, then my theory may be correct."

TENSION IS DISCHARGED

Many psychiatrists and psychologists—even without any biochemical proof—also believe that crying is beneficial.

"Crying discharges tension, the accumulation of feeling associated with whatever problem is causing the crying," says Frederic Flach, M.D., associate clinical professor of psychiatry at Cornell University Medical College in New York City and author of *Choices* (Bantam).

Crying restores balance.

"Stress causes imbalance and crying restores balance," Dr. Flach says. "It relieves the central nervous system of tension. If we don't cry, that tension doesn't go away."

Dr. Flach also believes that crying is a form of communication.

Crying communicates.

"If a couple is arguing and, for instance, the wife starts to cry, the argument will usually lose most of its viciousness. That's because she has communicated to her husband that she is hurt: Her crying is not an act of submission or humiliation, but a manifestation of her pain. And unless her husband is unduly cruel, he will respond by trying to soothe that pain."

A CALL FOR HELP

Research psychologist Robert Plutchik, Ph.D., professor of psychiatry and psychology at Albert Einstein College of Medicine in New York City and author of *Emotion: A Psychoevolutionary Synthesis* (Harper & Row), agrees with Dr. Flach—crying is communication.

"Crying is a directed call for help or an indication of

a need for help," he says. "It is a type of signal that informs other people, particularly those who have a close relationship to the one who is crying, that there is a need for assistance."

And, Dr. Plutchik believes, those who call for help with their tears are usually heard.

"Crying is effective, though of course not equally effective in every case," he says. "Just as when someone is robbed, some people ignore it and some make an effort to do something, so when someone cries, some will help and others won't. But the tendency to respond to another person's sign of injury or loss is something that we all have."

Crying is effective.

And since crying is a healthy, natural form of communication, learning *not* to cry makes us unhealthy—and, in terms of human evolution, less fit to survive.

Don't suppress crying.

"Emotions developed over the course of evolution as a way to communicate, a way for a person to have his intentions understood and to insure his survival," says Dr. Plutchik. "The supression of crying, which is often learned in this society, leads the individual to inhibit all the other emotions he feels when he is hurt, such as fear, anxiety, and anger. This inhibits the individual's effectiveness and decreases the likelihood that humans will survive.

"It's very important to communicate feelings during times of distress."

LETTING THE TEARS FLOW FREELY

What should someone do who has difficulty crying?

"A person should be aware of having the need to cry," says Dr. Plutchik, "and he should feel free to talk about his urge to cry. Yes, cry if you want, but also discuss the feeling of loss that is making you cry."

Discuss the feeling of loss.

Dr. Flach also believes that people should feel free to cry. "Not to cry denies the option of an important form of emotional release and communication," he says.

"Paradoxically, people trapped in depression often can't cry. Depression happens when you react inappropriately to your emotions, to loss, and to grief. And one of the early things that happens to depressed people when they begin to manage their depression is that they cry, they begin to experience and communicate the feelings associated with their grief."

Relearn your ability to cry.

Psychologist Gay Gaer Luce, Ph.D., believes that people who have been taught by society not to cry actually need to relearn their ability to cry.

"This is not a joke," Dr. Luce says. "Men as well as women need this release."

A crying technique.

And so she has developed a "crying technique," which she includes in her book *Your Second Life* (Delacorte).

"Make certain you will not be interrupted by phones or people," she writes. "Sit comfortably."

Allow yourself to make the sound of sobbing.

"Now place your hand on your upper chest, over the collarbone. Begin to breathe only as deeply as your hand, no deeper. Breathe rapidly and make a sound. Listen to the feeling in your voice as you pant and begin to make the sound of a baby crying. Listen to it. Allow yourself to feel its sadness. Allow yourself to make the sound of sobbing. Think of the things that are causing you sadness and grief. Allow yourself to make the sounds that go with those griefs. As you do this, give yourself permission to be human. You should have no trouble releasing. Stay with the exercise if it is difficult at first. Do this if you feel the beginning of a headache in the temples. This is often a sign that you have been controlling crying and have accumulated such tension and eye pain that your head aches. If you feel a little tension at the temples, take time out, and do your crying exercise. When you can work up enough self-pity to sob for a few minutes, you will release that tension. You will feel, as others have: 'What a relief!' That relief is relaxation."

GROAN AWAY PAIN

Groaning is instinctive.

While you're practicing crying, you may want to polish up your groaning technique as well. According to Louis Savary, Ph.D., people have instinctively groaned to relieve physical and emotional pain since the beginning of time.

In hospitals, for example, patients emerging from anesthesia after surgery will spontaneously begin to groan. Likewise, persons in extreme pain may groan to help alleviate their suffering. Unfortunately, says Dr. Savary, who teaches groaning in a stress workshop, doctors and nurses generally discourage this healthful practice, viewing it as negative and disturbing.

A healthful process.

"Once, at a workshop with many nurses participating, I talked about the therapeutic qualities of groaning. I explained how, despite the fact that our culture discourages groaning within anyone's range of hearing, it is a healthful process. Some participants showed signs of disbelief, so I decided to introduce them to groaning."

DON'T BE EMBARRASSED

"I explained I would like them to lie on their backs on the carpeted floor and give out with deep, full-bodied groans. I then gave a sample groan. Watching and hearing me groan, they could picture themselves doing the same thing, and they laughed in embarrassment.

"With a bit more encouragement, the participants each found a place on the floor. When I invited them to begin groaning, I heard instead giggles and laughter: a sign of embarrassment, of course, but also a sign of tension. I let them get the laughter and tension out of their systems. After a few minutes of giggling, everyone settled down and began to groan, with jazz music playing in the background."

After 15 minutes of deep groaning, Dr. Savary asked participants to describe how they felt. Here are some of their comments: "I feel relaxed for the first time this week." "Tenseness gone." "No more tension headache." "My body feels limp and relaxed, inside and out." "My insides have settled down." "I have a whole new excitement about the workshop." "Maybe there *is* a way to get relief from stress and pressures."

"I feel relaxed for the first time this week."

Dr. Savary reminded them they had brought about this temporary relief of tension, exhaustion, and their other emotional pain simply by groaning. They had not used any chemicals or drugs; they hadn't even needed any structured physical movements such as yoga or calisthenics. "I wanted to show that the basic formula for getting some relief from certain kinds of physical and emotional stress is very simple," says Dr. Savary. "*Lie down and groan deeply for at least ten minutes.* If the situation doesn't permit lying down, then groan sitting or standing. That seems to work just about as well."

Physically, groaning helps you relax. One dominant desire of people under severe pressure is to be able to relax. Groaning facilitates relaxation by involving your entire body in gentle, rhythmic activity. First of all, because groaning requires deep, regulated diaphragmatic breathing, maxi-

Groaning involves your entire body.

mum oxygen gets supplied to all parts of your body. Groaning also produces strong vibrations within your body, which effects a kind of inner massage. As you continue to groan deeply and become more and more relaxed, you can begin to feel your groaning creating vibrations, not only in your throat but also in your stomach and chest, and sometimes even in your sinuses. Usually, physical relaxation is the state in which the body can best begin to heal itself. Tension hardly ever helps healing and hardly ever relieves pain.

Exhale and release frustration and fear.

Psychologically, groaning is healthy, too, for when it is consciously done it creates a focus of attention for your mind. Dr. Savary usually suggests that groaners imaginatively picture their anger, hurt, fear or frustration. When they exhale, he asks them to visualize the sources of their tension being released out of their body and mind. In that way, their psychological system is involved in the groaning. The destructive or exhaustive emotions are acknowledged and consciously let go.

A strong groan begins with a deep breath that distends and seems to fill the lower intestines. The pressure, felt there and then pushed out, meets momentary resistance in the throat, where the sound of the groan begins. When the throat is fully opened, the contained air rushes out and, as it passes the voice box, creates the sound we usually associate with groaning.

More forceful than a sigh.

A groan is generally much stronger, louder, and more forceful than a sigh. A groan's objective is also different from that of a sigh. Usually a sigh symbolically acknowledges relief: "I'm glad that's over." You sigh with relief when, for example, the difficult exam is finished, the long report is turned in, the crucial meeting is over, the critical medical report says "nonmalignant." In each of these cases, a sigh would be an appropriate sign that the body and mind feel relief and gratitude.

In contrast, the groan is most appropriate not when the pressure is taken off, but *while it is still on.* The groan acts like a valve that releases a strong overflow of pressure or pain while it is still building up. No matter how distasteful or disapproved the pressured feeling may be, let it come out of you. Otherwise, just as garbage when kept inside indefinitely develops a repulsive odor that eventually fills every part of the house, so if emotions and pains fit for disposal are kept blocked inside they eventually overwhelm your entire self.

Moaning, a gentler form of groaning, usually begins when the strong overflow of pressure of pain lessens. Although the pressure or pain is still present, it no longer has the intensity that tends to produce a groan. Moaning signals a continuous but not quite intolerable level of pain or pressure. Moaning has a self-comforting quality and can generate the soothing effects of a continually voiced chant. Moaning also helps release anxiety.

Moaning has a self-comforting quality.

It is a tradition at Oberlin College that during the week of final examinations, students gather near the social center at scheduled times for "primal moans." In an effort to release almost overwhelming tension, always at a high point during final exams, students in groups use moaning, groaning, shouting, stomping, and shaking to release their anxieties and fears.

ROLL UP YOUR CAR WINDOWS

Groaning may be used regularly, at set times, with great effectiveness. A supervisor in charge of a department used to build up much frustration at work each day. When he got home, he often took out his frustration on his wife, his children, and their pets. Dr. Savary suggested groaning on the way home from work. "Keep your windows rolled up," he advised, "and no one will hear your groaning. Groan away your daily overflow of pressure." The man discovered on days when he spent part of his half-hour drive home groaning, he pulled into his garage much more relaxed than usual and did not need to take out his frustrations from work on his wife and children. So he decided to make groaning a regular part of his journey home every workday.

Groaning on the way home from work.

Groaning is a valuable pressure releaser for people in jobs and relationships where they have no options or alternatives. For example, superiors, administrators, management personnel, nurses, teachers, and parents usually cannot avoid situations that generate pressure, conflict, and frustration daily, almost hourly. Groaning does not eradicate the source of the pressure—nothing can do that as long as the person remains in that type of job or

One caution about groaning.

relationship—but it can help deal with the overflow of pressure as it builds up.

One caution about groaning. It is rather noisy and should be carried out where it will not disturb others—for example, in an automobile with the windows closed. Or, if others must hear your groaning, give them advance warning that the groaning they are about to hear is not a call to them for help.

The Healthful Art
of Diffusing Anger

To vent or not to vent; that is the question.

Are angry feelings best released in an explosive outburst or quietly suppressed using grit-your-teeth tactics? The debate rages on, even within psychological circles, fueled in part by a controversial book, *Anger: The Misunderstood Emotion* by social psychologist Carol Tavris, Ph.D., (Simon & Schuster).

Dr. Tavris challenges popular beliefs that suppressed anger is dangerous to health. Blowing your top can be far more damaging than keeping your cool, she says. For example, men who are at high risk from heart disease—the so-called Type A personalities—usually *over*express their anger.

To support this theory, Dr. Tavris cites an enormous research project, the Western Collaborative Group Study, which followed 3,154 California men aged 39 to 59 for several years to gather information on heart attack-prone behavior.

"Two aspects of Type A, competitive drive and impatience, were associated with the eventual occurrence of heart disease," Dr. Tavris reports. "The men risking illness were also more likely than healthier men to direct their anger outward and to become angry more than once a week."

Another study, this one conducted at the University of Michigan School of Public Health, measured the effects of anger expression, suppression, and "cool reflection" on

Are angry feelings best released or suppressed?

Type A personalities usually overexpress their anger.

Men who kept their cool had lower blood pressure.

blood pressure. Results, again, pointed thumbs down on hot heads. According to Ernest Harburg, Ph.D., chief investigator, the men who kept their cool—who acknowledged their anger but were not openly hostile, verbally or physically—had lower blood pressure than men who either bottled up their anger or became openly hostile.

Dr. Harburg further described the "cool reflective" approach as one in which the provoker and the provoked calm down first, then discuss the conflict reasonably with their goal firmly set on resolution. In other words, if you can get at the problem, you can solve the conflict.

EXPRESSION ESCALATES ANGER

Dr. Carol Tavris would second that strategy.

You'll feel better if you let yourself simmer down first.

"The psychological rationale for ventilating anger does not stand up under experimental scrutiny," she says. "Expressing anger makes you angrier, solidifies an angry attitude, and establishes a hostile habit. If you keep quiet about momentary irritations and distract yourself with pleasant activity until your fury simmers down, chances are that you will feel better, and feel better faster, than if you let yourself go in a shouting match."

Of course, sometimes it just feels good to get it off your chest—even Dr. Tavris admits that, although she reserves these cathartic expressions for situations of social injustice.

Sometimes, telling someone off can be especially satisfying, however.

"Telling off someone who you believe has mistreated you is especially satisfying," she says. "Publishing the true story of how you were victimized by the bigwigs makes you feel vindicated."

Psychologists who favor venting, however, believe there's a physiological basis for the feel-better feeling that follows emotional release. After all, angry feelings are associated with the release of epinephrine and norepinephrine, the same hormones that are produced in the "fight or flight" response to stress. These hormones quicken the pulse, increase blood pressure and blood sugar levels, and constrict blood vessels to the digestive tract.

To vent or not to vent: The controversy continues.

Whether (as Dr. Tavris maintains) this altered state naturally returns to normal with no residual health effects or (as the ventilationists believe) this arousal state continues to escalate and, without an emotional outlet, will give rise to psychosomatic illnesses remains at the core of the continuing controversy.

In his book *Anger: How to Recognize and Cope with It* (Charles Scribner's Sons), Philadelphia psychoanalyst Leo Madow, M.D., writes: "Anger can affect us adversely both physically and mentally. If we think of it as a form of energy which if repressed must come out somewhere, we must recognize that it can harm almost any part of our body or influence our emotions and eventually our minds if a sufficient amount is accumulated."

Dr. Madow, however, does distinguish between "suppressed" and "repressed" anger. The difference has to do with the conscious mind. If you *consciously* hold back your anger because you don't want to start a fight, for example, that's "suppression." If, on the other hand, you have *unconsciously* harbored angry feelings toward your father since you were six years old, that's "repression." Of the two, says Dr. Madow, repression—not recognizing that you feel anger—has the potential to cause greater damage. Research suggests that repressed anger contributes to gastrointestinal, respiratory, circulatory, and skin disorders. Some scientists even believe that this emotion may be linked to cancer.

Consciously holding back is less damaging than *unconsciously* harbouring angry feelings.

Conscious suppression may have its pitfalls, too. Kenneth R. Pelletier, Ph.D., author of *Mind as Healer, Mind as Slayer* (Delacorte), cites a number of studies regarding anger suppression. One researcher, examining the histories of more than 5,000 patients with rheumatoid arthritis, discovered that many of them shared certain personality traits, among them the inability to express anger. Another scientist discovered that patients with ulcerative colitis produced strikingly comparable data to that of the rheumatoid arthritics, reports Dr. Pelletier.

Conscious suppression may have its pitfalls, too.

Marjorie Brooks, Ph.D., research director for the Center for Autistic Children and an assistant professor at Jefferson Medical College in Philadelphia, relates another study: "In the 1950s, two researchers looked at the life history patterns of about 400 cancer patients," Dr. Brooks explains. "They found the patients had some very interesting similarities. Many of them seemed unable to express anger or hostility in defense of themselves. The patients *could* get angry in the defense of others or in the defense of a cause. But when it came to self-defense, they didn't follow through.

Many cancer patients have trouble expressing anger.

"Suppressed hostility was another significant factor appearing in some of the other patients. They seemed to lack the discharge mechanism needed to allow anger to surface, so they kept *all* of their anger inside."

DON'T BLOW YOUR TOP

Lashing out isn't an antidote for holding back.

Dr. Brooks, like Drs. Tavris and Harburg, however, doesn't advocate lashing out as an antidote for holding back.

Other research, she says, which focused on English women undergoing breast biopsies, "indicated that women who were very, very seldom angry and women who were highly volatile were more likely to have malignant tumors than women who had an appropriate expression of anger."

Dr. Brooks's own research bears this out. She recently surveyed 1,100 women who did not have breast cancer and compared the results to those of 15 women with benign tumors and 15 women with malignancies.

Women with breast cancer felt angrier in the year before their illness.

"A significantly higher proportion of both benign and malignant patients stated they had experienced much more anger during the previous year than the 1,100 respondents who did not have disease," Dr. Brooks says. "A larger percentage of women having malignancies had felt angry more often than the women having benign tumors. And a larger percentage of women with benign tumors had felt angrier the previous year than women in normal health."

The *ways* in which the women expressed anger also were different. Women with malignant breast cancer were more likely to apologize for their anger, even when they were right, says Dr. Brooks. So whenever they *did* express their hostility, they often took it back.

Women with benign tumors tended to get angry and stay angry. Their anger often became an unresolved internal conflict.

Healthy women tend to get angry, then forget about it.

Women in normal health were more likely to get angry and then forget about it, says Dr. Brooks. They redirected their attention and energies to more pleasant things.

As a result of those findings, Dr. Brooks suggests that if angry energy can be redirected, patients may feel less stress, and quite likely their physical condition will be positively affected.

There must be a genuine resolution of conflict.

It is not enough just to express anger—there has to be a genuine resolution of conflict or else the tension continues to operate, she says. Some people may suppress angry feelings for a long time, then suddenly explode over something, whether it warrants the rage or not.

A low-grade depression may occur in people who do not face up to their anger, and turn it inward instead. "Low-grade depression is found more often in women than in men," says Dr. Brooks. "Some women may feel powerless at times, but instead of getting mad, they get depressed. As a result, they may constantly feel tired or have a chronic 'headachy' feeling."

Some women don't get mad; they get depressed.

Dr. Brooks believes people must retrain themselves to accept anger as a normal emotion and deal with it accordingly.

"Expressing anger is necessary for good health," she says, "but it doesn't mean a brick over the head. That action only brings retaliation and guilt. Anger is a normal emotion that is a result of our genetics, upbringing, and cultural patterns. The biggest problem we face is learning how to discharge it in a manner that is both acceptable in society and healthy for the self."

Expressing anger is necessary for good health.

Frederic Flach, M.D., associate clinical professor of psychiatry at Cornell University Medical College in New York, believes that parents must have an open attitude toward their children's anger.

"If your six-year-old gets mad and you say, 'If you do that again, you're really going to get it,' that only compounds the problem," says Dr. Flach. "Instead you might say, 'You're mad. OK. Just get over it.' Or 'You're mad. Why are you angry?'"

You're mad. Why are you angry?

TELL ME WHY

Understanding *why* they feel a certain way about a particular act and, perhaps even more importantly, *why* the act was committed in the first place helps to resolve the anger at its deepest level.

Understanding why helps resolve the anger at its deepest level.

Dr. Carol Tavris tells of an interesting study on third-grade children who were given one of three methods for dealing with personal frustration caused by an action of another child. Some were permitted to talk out their feelings, others were allowed to play with guns as a way of acting out their anger, and still others were offered reasonable explanations for the action that caused their anger.

Which method offered the most emotional relief?

BOX 16: SEVEN STEPS TO HEALTHY ANGER RELEASE

1. Recognize the anger you're feeling. That may sound simple enough, but in all too many cases it's the biggest obstacle we face. "Anger may be denied because we feel too guilty about it, or afraid of it," says Dr. Leo Madow. As a result, the feeling is turned inside where it festers.

2. Decide what made you angry. Ask yourself the very important question: Is this worth getting angry over? If it's a small annoyance that's ticked you off—as it is in the majority of angry episodes— forget it. If you can't forget it, then perhaps the source of your anger goes beyond this simple incident. Ferret out the underlying cause of your hostility. Bring your feelings to the surface and deal with them.

3. Give the "provoker" the benefit of the doubt. Instead of inflaming your anger by feeding yourself such thoughts as, "Who does he think he is for treating me in this underhanded way!" suggest to yourself that perhaps this person is having a bad day. Come up with a reasonable justification for the behavior— something that you can understand and relate to.

4. Count to ten. Or practice some form of mental relaxation. Most psychologists agree, there's nothing to be gained by an explosive outburst aimed at retaliation. Calm down first, then discuss the conflict rationally.

5. Make your grievance known without attacking the other person. This calls for tact and some good communication skills (see Chapter 54, How to Say What You Really Mean). One important tip: Register your complaint using "I" instead of "you." For example, instead of saying, "*You're* acting unfairly and *you're* wrong," it's far more effective to say, "*I* feel hurt. What you're doing doesn't take *my* needs into account."

6. Listen. Another tough technique to master. But really try. Listen hard. And above all, understand. This is the key step in resolving the conflict. And resolving the conflict is, after all, the key to safely diffusing your anger.

7. Forgive. "When you forgive someone (and this includes yourself), many clearly positive psychological and physiological changes take place," writes Rick Ingrasci, M.D., in *New Age Journal.* "You feel warm and more relaxed, you sigh and breathe more easily, your heart feels warm and melty, your blood pressure and heart rate drop, you may even cry. But most importantly, through forgiveness you once again experience the love that is the essence of your relationship. You remember that you *care* about this person—which may be why their behavior hurt so much in the first place."

Talking out an emotion doesn't reduce it.

"Not talking about it. . . . Talking out an emotion doesn't reduce it, it rehearses it," says Dr. Tavris. "Not playing with guns; that made them more hostile, and aggressive as well. The most successful way of dispelling their anger was to understand why their classmate had behaved as she did: She was sleepy, upset, not feeling well."

Of course, this lesson is as valuable for adults as children. Once we understand the motive behind an aggressive action, we can better come to terms with our feelings. But in order to get to that point, we must first be willing to confront our true feelings and discuss them openly in a manner that's likely to bring about a satisfying resolution.

"The purpose of anger is to make a grievance known," Dr. Tavris explains, "and if the grievance is not confronted, it will not matter whether the anger is kept in, let out, or wrapped in red ribbons and dropped in the Erie Canal."

The purpose of anger is to make a grievance known.

17

Good Grief:
Healing and Growing
through Loss

Profound emotional pain, potentially serious immunological consequence.

Grief: It's the most profound emotional pain we'll ever experience. It can strike suddenly and with devastating intensity. It grips like a vise for months, even years. And, to make matters worse, medical studies have shown that it can wreak havoc with our immune system, leaving us vulnerable to a variety of physical ailments including cancer and arthritis.

Yet, for all the "grief" it gives us, experts like Elisabeth Kübler-Ross, M.D.—the lady who brought us to terms with death and dying—continue to assure us that this is a natural emotion, even a healthy one.

Grieving: as natural as the formation of a scab.

"Grief is the process of healing from the pain of loss," says Donald Tubesing, Ph.D., a psychologist, minister, and author of *Kicking Your Stress Habits* (Whole Person Associates, Inc.). "[The process is] as natural and predictable as the formation of a scab on a cut and the subsequent itching that signals healing."

Then why is this healing emotion often thought of as harmful?

Fear, not grief, is the culprit.

Apparently, much hinges on our perspective and our preparedness to deal with loss. Fear, not grief, is the culprit here. Fear of death (our own, as well as the loss of those we love) can immobilize us to the point that we deny our grief. It is this denial or suppression, then, that can give rise to serious consequences.

Unfortunately, too, supportive efforts often discourage full expression of our emotions. Well-meaning relatives may tell us to "be strong," "think positive," "don't cry." The clergy may paint a reassuring picture of life after death, explaining that "there's no reason to mourn" since the deceased is in a better place. Doctors may prescribe tranquilizers and antidepressant drugs long after the initial shock period—whether or not they are necessary. These are all common solacing techniques that, in effect, block the natural grieving process. And, in so doing, do more harm than good.

HONOR YOUR FEELINGS

"If we don't grieve, we become chronically disoriented," says Glen Davidson, Ph.D., professor of psychiatry and chief of thanatology (the branch of medicine involved with the care of the terminally ill) at Southern Illinois University School of Medicine. "To fully recover and move forward past the immediate loss, we must affirm and acknowledge our feelings."

To fully recover, we must acknowledge our feelings.

According to Dr. Davidson, who's also author of *Living with Dying* and *Understanding Mourning* (both published by Augsburg Press), sorrow, guilt, anger, depression, loneliness, fear, anxiety, and shame are all normal emotions associated with bereavement that need to be voiced openly and honestly. "Don't think of yourself as a burden—that nobody is willing to listen to you," he says. "Only through telling our story over and over again do we clarify in our own minds what has happened and how we really feel about it. Through that, we come to accept the reality of the loss so we can go on living."

Crying can also provide a healthy outlet, he tells us. "Tears carry away toxins that are produced during emotional shock," Dr. Davidson explains. They may be why we feel genuinely better afterward (see Chapter 15, Crying and Groaning: Nature's Safety Valves).

Crying removes toxins that are produced by emotional shock.

It's important, too, to allow enough time for the grieving—and healing—process. How much time is, of course, different for each person and set of circumstances. Dr. Davidson's own research on 1,200 mourners showed an average recovery time of from 18 to 24 months.

Average recovery time: 18 to 24 months.

But, he warns, with today's emphasis on doing everything faster—whether it's cooking, working, or healing—taking it easy can be tough. "Tradition holds that when a person is bereaved, he is relieved of responsibility. That is how the ritual of taking food to the mourning family originated," Dr. Davidson says. "But as our notion of work changed so did our notion of worth. If a person is non-productive or less productive for a time, society makes him feel worthless."

As a society, then, we need to be more understanding, Dr. Davidson says. As individuals, we need to be more patient. Grieving takes time. There's no way to shorten its duration, he says. But, if you take care of yourself, you may be able to reduce its intensity.

You can't shorten its duration. You *can* reduce its intensity.

THE FIVE FACTORS OF SUCCESSFUL GRIEVING

Dr. Davidson's research points to the following five factors that separate healthy grief experiences from those that are complicated by serious emotional or physical problems. (Keep in mind that only about 25 percent of all mourners run into any difficulty—most emerge stronger from the experience.)

Women recover faster than men because they feel free to discuss feelings.

1. **A nurturing social network.** Mourners who had the support of family and friends fared better than those who did not. Further, it's been suggested that the reason women tend to overcome loss better than men may be due to their close social ties and ability to openly discuss their problems and feelings with others.

2. **A balanced diet.** Dr. Davidson found that mourners whose eating patterns remained stable, and who daily chose nutritious foods from each of the four food groups, stayed healthy throughout the ordeal. Also, the outcome of this study suggests that a 15-pound-plus weight loss (or gain) should be considered a red flag to impending difficulty.

Non-caffeine beverages should be taken in adequate amounts.

3. **Healthy fluid intake.** Dr. Davidson observed that mourners who fared poorly tended to override their thirst. While he can offer no explanation for this, he says that the behavior was apparent in hot weather as well as in cool. Those who did poorly tended to favor beverages containing caffeine and alcohol. Since caffeine and alcohol act as diuretics, this further contributed to their state of dehydration and electrolyte imbalance.

4. **Regular exercise.** Healthy mourners engaged in some form of regular exercise—especially stretching exercises—whereas the unsuccessful group tended to be more sedentary.

5. Regular ritual of rest. Those who rested when they felt the urge and who maintained normal sleeping patterns in the evening were more effective than those who pushed themselves—who tried to keep busy and preoccupied at all times. Grief isn't something we can run away from. Rest and solitude are regenerative, says Dr. Davidson.

Rest and solitude are regenerative.

TOWARD A HEALTHY MINDSET

Of course, at least as important as all of the above is attitude—what Dr. Donald Tubesing describes as "the courage to let go, the faith that they will heal, and the willingness to rejoin life fully."

The courage to let go, the will to go on living.

Experts agree that the best way to achieve this healthy mindset is by developing adaptation skills *before* you face a major loss. By looking to life as an opportunity to practice grieving skills on a daily basis, we can better prepare ourselves for the more serious setbacks.

The remainder of this chapter addresses this aspect of loss—the emotional preparation. It was written by Allen Klein, a teacher throughout the California college system and lecturer at hospices and hospitals.

Every one of us has a 100 percent chance of dying, but for many of us death is taboo and we don't want to talk about it. Sex and death have been two topics that people have felt uncomfortable discussing. In the past decade, however, the abundance of "how to" sex books has, I think, not only opened the door for that subject but somehow made it OK for its co-taboo subject to also come out of the closet (or is it coffin?).

Everyone has a 100 percent chance of dying.

It is, of course, no surprise that death has earned a reputation as a dirty five-letter word. From our very early upbringing, this word has been a source of confusion to us. We hear about Daddy's battery dying in the car, and the next day the car is going again; we see a cowboy shot dead on one TV show suddenly appearing alive on another channel an hour later.

Death: the dirty Five-Letter Word.

Even as we grow older, we continue to be bewildered about death. The TV that confused us about real and fake death now emphasizes everlasting youth in every commercial. All the while our terminally ill are shipped off to hospitals to die, and our aging are in convalescent homes as we kid ourselves by using the name "convalescent." Our dead are

Our exit from life is as important as our entrance.

Each cell is in the birth/ growth/death cycle.

Most of our daily deaths are minor.

touched only by funeral directors, while we the living show how much the dead meant to us by paying a florist to send flowers in our name.

Even the term "life insurance" is denial; as hard as we try, we cannot insure life. Life insurance money is payable upon death; shouldn't we therefore call it "death insurance"?

Thanks to Dr. Elisabeth Kübler-Ross, we have begun to look at death and realize that our exit from life is as important as our entrance into it.

I think we haven't yet realized that every moment of our life is preparation for our death.

Our entire aging process, for example, is a continuing loss of our youth and our physical self. Aging does not suddenly appear. From the moment of our conception, each cell in our body is in the birth/growth/death process. We are part of a continuing, ongoing event. We gradually become aware of our normal body changes around middle age. We might notice that our physical stamina is not what it was in earlier years, our skin may start to show wrinkles, or we might feel a stiffness in our joints.

In middle age we are gradually starting to slow down in preparation for old age and, eventually, our death. Perhaps nature is even forcing us to move at a slower pace to give us an opportunity to notice things that we may have overlooked before.

A BIG LESSON IN SMALL LOSSES

Just as we are given this long-term aging process to prepare us for our future death, so we are also given numerous daily losses for this purpose. Most of our daily deaths are minor; some are major. Our world is filled with cars not starting, broken relationships, incomplete tasks, misplaced objects, financial setbacks, and loss of independence. All of these are preparing us for our ultimate death whether we know it or not, each one putting us through a minute version of our own death.

The way in which we handle the anger, the rage, the guilt, the impatience, and the acceptance of these "daily deaths" is a preview of the way we will handle the final days of our physical existence.

In her book *On Death and Dying* (Macmillan), Dr.

Kübler-Ross talks about the now-famous five stages of dying—denial, anger, bargaining, depression, and acceptance. They are also the five stages of living.

The five stages of dying are the same five stages of living.

The person who stands us up for a date, for example, puts us through the same stages we will encounter as we approach our demise. We might get *angry* at being stood up by other people. We might *bargain* and tell ourselves that if we had only called that person last night to remind her, this wouldn't have happened. We might even totally *deny* (for the time being) that this has happened and pretend that the appointment was on a different day. Or we might become *depressed* and allow this incident to ruin the rest of our day. We can hold on to the situation and wallow in the loss, in the anger, or we can *let go*.

Each "mini-death" can help us to grow. We can accept the fact that we have been stood up and learn from it. Perhaps the lesson might be not to make another date with that person and admit that we knew that she was unreliable. We might notice that we too often break our appointments but that we get angry when the tables are turned. Perhaps we are even more angry with ourselves than with the other person for either making the date in the first place, or not calling beforehand and confirming it.

Each "mini-death" can help us to grow.

Other things we can possibly learn from this incident might be that we go through life denying things have actually happened and that we never resolve situations. Or we might see how our life is full of "if onlys"—"if only I had called previously"; "if only I hadn't made the date"; "if only . . . "

The fact of life is that we have been stood up. We never get things exactly the way we want them. We can get stuck in any of the first four dying stages—denial, anger, bargaining, depression—or we can proceed with our life. We have been given an opportunity. How we use the opportunity is up to us. We can see where we are, acknowledge the need for change, let our old ways die, and move on.

We can get stuck in any of the dying stages—or proceed with life.

We can reach the acceptance stage and look at each loss, each death, as an opportunity for something new. We can look forward to this new growth and birth that inevitably come after death.

We can look at patterns in our life and make mental notes so that we can alter them next time and then proceed

Look at the patterns of your life—and learn.

to look at the new situation as another opportunity for growth. Having been stood up, we can either call someone else to go with us, go alone, or do something else that perhaps we have been putting off.

Even a financial setback, though it may not seem so immediately, can be preparation for our death. First, a diminishing of our funds forces us to cut down on our external desires. We must consider buying and having fewer possessions. It gives us an opportunity to focus inward, rather than on the material world, in a way that perhaps we have never done before.

A financial setback can bring us closer to living—and dying.

Secondly, as we approach our death, we become less concerned about our physical surroundings. Having less money might even be a way of preparing us for the change of consciousness that we will soon be facing. Admittedly a financial setback can appear to be a major burden, but again, it can also bring us closer to our living and our dying.

There is no such thing as a problem without a gift.

Whenever I encounter a difficult situation in my life, I can't help but think of a quote from *Illusions,* written by Richard Bach, who also authored *Jonathan Livingston Seagull.* He says that "there is no such thing as a problem without a gift for you in its hands. You seek problems because you need their gifts." All of our "daily deaths" are gifts which give us the chance to explore our everyday patterns as well as the overall trends in our lives.

Each change in our aging body, though often not noticed immediately, is a loss for us. We may feel a loss, for example, when we can't walk as far or as fast as we once did or when our sexual prowess is not all that it used to be. Once we acknowledge the reality of these facts, we can then be open to new ways of doing and seeing things.

Walking more slowly makes it easier to notice details.

Our walk around the block, rather than being limited, might actually open new vistas for us now as we learn to identify every flower, tree, and herb that we pass on our walk, or even enable us to become expert on the history and architecture of the neighborhood. Even our diminished sexual drive might open up delightfully new areas for us to be affectionate with our partners in a nonsexual way.

The important thing for us to notice is that every time we lose something, we are presented with an opportunity to acquire something new. With each death in our life there is a golden opportunity for a new beginning.

The death of someone close to us or the loss of a

relationship also provides this opportunity. Once we start to work through our grief process and our own anger, depression, denial, and bargaining stages, we can begin to fill the vacuum that was created by this loss with an even fuller sense of life.

ONE MAN'S LESSON FROM DEATH

My wife's death, a few years ago, gave me a golden opportunity to examine the priorities in my life. The vacation that I wanted to take with my daughter was not put off; the chance to return to school was not viewed as something that I was too old for but as something I needed for my own growth and development. My wife's death gave me a chance to look inward to see my own finitude, my own beauty, and the beauty in others. It was true that her death brought a great loss in my life. Once I started to accept it, however, my life opened up and became fuller and richer. Material things had less meaning for me, and my spiritual and inner growth became more important to me. Her death allowed me to see things that I hadn't noticed before. My "walk around the block" now had new meaning.

Life is full of thousands of experiences preparing us for death and rebirth. The job we did not get, the relationship that just ended, or the bus we just missed are all golden opportunities to stop and notice where we are and where we are going. Each experience tests us to see if we are ready for the next step. Each one is preparing us and helping us grow toward our own death. Perhaps this is the day to start noticing how you died and how you responded to it.

Each experience tests us to see if we're ready for the next step.

Are you still angry over the loss of your once-curly head of hair or have you already moved into "bald is beautiful"? Are you depressed over not seeing as clearly as you used to or are you finding a new sight by feeling objects in a way you never did before? Are you grieving over the loss of your former self while missing the beauty of who you are today? Or are you in the growth phase?

Are you still grieving or have you moved on to the next growth stage?

There is a story about two celibate monks walking near a stream and coming across a young woman wanting to cross it. One of the monks, to the dismay of the other, picked up the woman and carried her across the stream. About a mile later the monk who was aghast at the other's action asked how he could pick up a woman when they were supposed to be celibate. The monk replied that he had put the woman down a mile back; why was the other still carrying her around?

How often we continue to carry death and loss around with us and allow it to pale our whole existence! When will we learn what a beautiful experience death, big or small, can be for us to learn, to grow, to be reborn?

The oyster takes an irritating piece of sand within its body and creates a glowing, radiant pearl. We can take the irritant of death within our lives every day and turn it into a jewel. The first step is to be conscious of the process and to be aware of how many times we die each day.

Conquering
Nth-Degree Fears

There was a famous opera star whose stage fright was so intense that she became convulsed with stomach pain before each performance. She didn't complain. Fear, she claimed, added emotional wallop to her voice.

Most people who suffer from such fears—whether it's belting out an aria on stage or white-knuckling it across the Atlantic on board a 747—would be hard pressed to notice a silver lining. Phobias represent the ultimate panic attack. Once triggered, the heart races, the head spins, palms sweat, knees buckle, and breathing becomes labored. Some who are particularly hard hit say it feels as if you're going to have a heart attack.

Phobias represent the ultimate panic attack.

Paradoxically, phobics admit that their fears are irrational. They know there's no logical reason to be fearful—which is why people who will climb ten flights of stairs before taking an elevator don't give a second thought to their children using a lift. Likewise, some people who are deathly afraid of being a passenger on a commercial airline can pilot their own plane. To insist there is a basis for an irrational fear is paranoid, not phobic behavior.

Unfortunately for phobics, knowing the fears are unfounded doesn't lessen the panic. The messages from brain to body are the same whether you're teetering on the edge of a cliff, about to fall, or standing safely at the foot of a mountain, fearful of climbing to the top. The good news is that these panic attacks are self-limiting. That is, the body cannot sustain this aroused level of anxiety indefinitely.

Knowing the fears are unfounded does not lessen the panic.

Gradually, it simmers down to a prestress level—at least until the next real or imagined encounter.

But again, there's good news. Phobias, though among the world's most emotionally crippling complaints, are today among the easiest to treat.

Phobias yield to a combination of group therapy, relaxation, diet changes, and desensitization.

The study of phobias is fairly new. Just in mid-1981, a Phobia Society of America was founded by experts in the field. Within only the last five or six years, physicians, universities, and even the National Institute of Health have opened clinics for sufferers of phobias and other anxiety disorders. Many people report that a clinic program enabled them to control the anxiety that controlled them for years. For those men and women, a combination of group therapy, relaxation techniques, diet changes, family support, and gradual exposure to fear-provoking situations (desensitization techniques) has been very good medicine.

One of those people is Wanda Falci, a 51-year-old woman who lives in Potomac, Maryland. She was frightened by churches since childhood and by restaurants since her 20s.

"When we went to church," she recalls, "I always picked an aisle seat as close to the door as possible so that I could escape if I had to. Usually I would just sweat. I always left the church mentally and physically drained. It ruined every Sunday.

"Restaurants were the same way. When we went out I always made a lot of trips to the bathroom because I thought I might get sick or pass out, which I never did. Passing out is what a lot of phobics are afraid of, but it never happens," she says.

FRIGHTENING SYMPTOMS

Symptoms can mimic serious illness.

Since Wanda Falci had the usual frightening symptoms of phobia—dizziness and light-headedness, rubbery legs, difficulty breathing, and fears of impending death or insanity—she assumed that she had a serious ailment. So, like many phobics, she had her head examined two ways—with a test for a brain tumor and ten months of psychotherapy. But there was no tumor, and the therapy didn't seem to help.

Then she enrolled in the Phobia Program of Washington, a clinic that was opened in 1978 by Robert L. DuPont,

M.D. The 16-week program, which costs about $1,000, includes three steps. The first step is an interview with a psychiatrist.

The second step consists of weekly 90-minute meetings with six to ten other phobics, a therapist, and perhaps a family member. The third step is a weekly one-hour expedition into the real world, where a phobic and a therapist try to face the feared object together in a process called "supported exposure." Since Wanda Falci was working on her restaurant phobia, that meant starting with a quick visit to a fast-food hamburger shop and working up to a comfortable meal at a formal, expensive restaurant.

"Supported exposure": facing the feared object with a therapist's support.

A therapist at the Phobia Program, psychologist Jerilyn Ross, explains how a phobia differs from a normal fear. "This is more than a strong fear," she says. "It is unlike any feeling you've ever experienced if you never had a phobia. It's irrational, involuntary, and inappropriate to the situation. To explain it would be like trying to describe color to a blind person. These people react with the intensity that a two-year-old feels when he loses his mother in a department store."

Jerilyn Ross taught Wanda Falci several antidotes for her fears. One was relaxation. Mrs. Falci practiced relaxation techniques for 20 minutes a day until she became so adept at them that she could compose herself at the first sign of a panic attack. She also learned the concept of "paradoxical intent." Whenever she felt impending anxiety, she said to herself, "OK, phobia, come and get me," and the panic would pass. "It's when you say 'don't come, don't come,' that the panic takes over," she says.

Accept, don't deny, feelings of panic.

TERRIFIED BY BRIDGES

Ross describes a few of the other phobics she has treated. In one case, a professional auctioneer in his late 30s was terrified by bridges—a fear that is technically called gephyrophobia. Because of his work, however, he often had to cross a 5-mile-long, 185-foot-high bridge across the Chesapeake Bay between the eastern and western shores of Maryland. To avoid the bridge meant adding 40 to 50 miles to the trip.

As a solution, he first had his wife drive him across the bridge. But he was still afraid he might panic and jump out

Irrational fears drive people to take drastic coping measures.

of the car, so he handcuffed himself to the steering wheel while she drove. That didn't work either, and before he finally sought effective help, he resorted to having his wife lock him in the trunk of the car.

(The toll facility police who look after that bridge have for more than 25 years accommodated other gephyrophobes by driving them across. During the busy months of July, August, and September, the police make approximately 400 trips for phobics.)

In another case, a woman was so terrified at the thought of roaches in her house that she would not keep food there. Fearing that food would attract the insects, she ate all her meals out and wouldn't entertain guests for fear they might be carrying stray cumbs from their last meal. Her treatment involved gradually bringing food home with the ultimate goal of giving a dinner party.

Washington lawyer Burt Rubin was another patient at the Phobia Program. He'd had a fear of public speaking since he muffed his lines in a school play at age eight. His program of supported exposure started when, accompanied by Jerilyn Ross, he began reading to a blind woman. He has since become active in Toastmasters International, a service group devoted to the art of public speaking.

Ross herself was once phobic about heights. She avoided going up more than ten floors in any building. Unfortunately, she lived in New York City, the home of skyscrapers. The phobia struck for no apparent reason when she was 25 and she was afraid to tell anyone about it for two years. "The phobia literally ran my life," she said.

Like many former phobics, including Wanda Falci, she became a phobia therapist.

THERAPIES THAT DON'T WORK

Supported exposure is only one of many proposed treatments for phobias. Some have a better track record than others. Most of the people we talked with said that couch-style psychoanalysis didn't work for them. At the Phobia Program, Ross says that her patients had made an average of 220 visits to psychiatrists and other mental-health professionals and spent thousands of dollars before coming to the clinic.

For some phobics, it's consoling to learn the root

A service group devoted to the art of public speaking.

Psychoanalysis may not be as successful as other phobia treatments.

causes of their phobia, but the knowledge of its source doesn't necessarily put an end to their panic attacks. A survey of more than 100 phobics at Massachusetts General Hospital in Boston showed that they had averaged 3.8 years of psychiatric care but were still "severely disabled" by their symptoms.

Tranquilizers apparently aren't effective either. Of the patients in the Boston survey, 98 percent found no relief in them. Fifty-seven patients had consumed about 660,000 minor tranquilizer tablets, but they all continued to have panic attacks. The study also found that "no reliable evidence supports the use of antipsychotic drugs (so-called major tranquilizers) although they are prescribed for nearly half of all persons afflicted with agoraphobia [the most general and common phobia, characterized by a fear of public places]" *(Harvard Medical School Health Letter).*

Nearly half of all people with agoraphobia take tranquilizers.

Also, members of a phobia self-help group in England surveyed themselves. As reported in *The Female Patient,* they found that "their previously unsuccessful treatment had included psychoanalysis, narcoanalysis [using barbiturates to release repressed thoughts], hypnosis, behavior therapy, psychotherapy, modified leukotomy [prefrontal lobotomy], LSD, group therapy, occupational therapy, insulin therapy, and, in the words of many, 'drugs and more drugs.' "

So much for therapy that involves doctors and drugs and costs a lot of money.

But is there anything that fearful or phobic people can do for themselves short of going to a phobia clinic? Change their diet for one thing, get some support from spouses and children, and learn a few simple behavior modification techniques.

Self-help starts with diet, family support, and behavior modification.

Phobia experts and former phobics say that symptoms of a panic attack, coincidentally or not, are very similar to those of hypoglycemia (low blood sugar). In both cases, blood rushes from the victim's brain to the limbs, causing light-headedness.

"The typical diet of someone who comes to see us includes eight to ten cups of coffee a day, lots of sweets, and very few slow-release high-protein foods," says Alan Goldstein, Ph.D., director of the Temple University Medical School Agoraphobia and Anxiety Center in Philadelphia.

"They might have coffee and a doughnut for breakfast, more coffee at midmorning, a white-bread sandwich at

Coffee and sugary snacks can contribute to anxiety.

lunch and maybe a good supper. Then something sweet before they go to bed. If I ate like that, I'd be anxious too," he says.

CHANGE OF DIET MAY WORK

In some but not all cases, a change of diet has worked. One woman in Dr. Goldstein's clinic stopped drinking coffee and ate many small meals rather than three large ones and her anxiety levels dropped by half.

Phobics often mistake hypoglycemia for a phobia attack.

Philip Bate, Ph.D., psychologist and former director of the Maitland Psychological Clinic in Maitland, Florida, also links hypoglycemia and phobias. He says that phobics often mistake a hypoglycemia attack for a phobia attack.

What they should do he says, is carry a bag of nuts, seeds, and raisins and munch on them to bring up their blood sugar levels. Treating the hypoglycemia will often stop the anxiety, he believes.

Dr. Bate thinks he knows why many phobics say they're afraid to leave the safety of their own homes. They stay home, he says, because going out would separate them from their refrigerators and the sweets they're addicted to. "The most important thing is to get them away from sugar and white flour," he says.

FACING THE PROBLEM

A four-part recovery program.

Another home remedy for phobias comes from therapist Claire Weekes, D.Sc., of the Rachel Foster Hospital in Sydney, Australia. Her suggested treatment for agoraphobia has four parts: *facing, accepting, floating,* and *letting time pass.*

She believes that many phobics try to withdraw from their fears and turn to any handy activity that will distract them. "This is running away, not facing," she says *(The Female Patient).*

Phobics also cope with panic attacks by tensing themselves—clutching something so hard that their knuckles turn white and digging their fingernails into their palms. "This is fighting, not accepting. . . . Fighting brings more tension, more sensitization, and further illness," Dr. Weekes says.

Float, don't fight.

Floating is the next step. "The simple words 'float, don't fight' have cured some people," she says. "If, instead of trying to fight her way forward as she instinctively does, the patient were to imagine she was floating, she would release enough tension to encourage movement." The last step involves patience. "Since impatience creates further stress, it is important to be willing to let more time pass.

"[A phobic in a frightening situation] should take a deep breath, let it out slowly, let her body slump in her chair, and accept the flash of panic as willingly as she can. If she faces panic this way, it will not mount."

Dr. Weekes and other therapists seem to agree that a phobia binds its victims with not one but two fears. First comes the fear of restaurants or bridges or roaches. Then comes the second fear, "the fear of the first fear," the fear that the phobic will lose control and do something embarrassing or dangerous in public. Dividing these fears and conquering each one separately might be the best way to cure a phobia.

Phobia victims have two fears.

Another factor is family. Ross states plainly that "the amount of progress phobics make during treatment is often dependent on the degree of support they received from their spouses or other family members" *(Learning Theory Approaches to Psychiatry).*

Two former phobics were asked what single best piece of advice they would have for other phobics.

Both recommend turning candidly to friends and family rather than hiding the problem. Wanda Falci says, "Let people know about it. Don't be embarrassed to tell someone. I told my husband, 'As long as I know you won't get upset with me, I'll go out with you in spite of my fears.'"

Share your fears with friends and family.

Linda Spivak, a Falls Church, Virginia, woman who used to fear airplanes, says, "Having a phobia is a very lonely feeling. You must believe that there is hope and you are not alone."

HOW PHOBIAS WORK

There are lots of theories about what causes phobias. Researchers believe that animal phobias have their roots in childhood, often a result of one very frightening episode. Other phobias commonly develop in our 20s and 30s. Phobics themselves often know what triggered their problem—a physical illness, domestic stress, loss of a loved one, stress at work, a domineering parent. The phobia often starts with an inexplicable panic attack. If the attack occurs in a crowded store, stores might become fearful

Phobias commonly develop in our 20s and 30s.

reminders of it. From that point, as one psychologist puts it, "The phobia takes on a life of its own."

The National Institute of Mental Health (NIMH) has focused some attention on the source of phobias. Thomas Uhde, M.D., director of anxiety research at NIMH, is investigating biological factors in phobia. Preliminary evidence suggests that some people with agoraphobia are very sensitive to issues of separation and loss.

Also, there appears to be a high incidence of alcoholism in the families of patients with agoraphobia, particularly those who also have panic attacks.

Women in their 20s are likely candidates for agoraphobia.

Women in their late teens or 20s are the most likely candidates for agoraphobia. Anxiety about leaving the family nest or the stress of an unhappy marriage are among the causes that can initiate the disorder. Perfectionists and people who have an "all or nothing" attitude toward life are also at risk.

Phobia therapists tend not to speak in terms of a "cure" for their patients. "A cure does not necessarily mean the elimination of anxiety," says Jerilyn Ross, and her colleague, Dr. Robert DuPont, states, "We emphasize to the patients that they need to learn techniques to live with anxiety and that as they learn to fear their fears less, the fears will diminish—although probably not disappear."

Practice is an essential part of recovery.

Practice is an essential part of recovery. "The most obvious lesson clinically is that those people who are best able to practice dealing with their fears on a daily basis are the ones who do the best," Dr. DuPont adds. Graduates of his program can stay in mental shape by attending informal monthly self-help sessions.

Sometimes, oddly, it's helpful for phobics to look forward to their next panic attack.

Dr. Claire Weekes says that this is the only route to permanent relief. The phobic, she writes, "should try to view [a panic attack] as an opportunity to practice going through the fearful episode the right way until it no longer upsets her."

Develop a positive and challenging attitude toward fear.

"A more realistic goal," concludes Jerilyn Ross, "is to teach phobics how to lead a normal life by confronting, rather than avoiding, feared objects or situations by developing a positive and challenging attitude toward the fear."

Alone But Not Lonely

Loneliness may be hazardous to your health in a very concrete way.

Blood samples collected from a group of medical students at the Ohio State University College of Medicine revealed important differences between those who scored high on a loneliness assessment test and those who did not. Lonely students were more likely to have reduced levels of natural killer (NK) cell activity, an indicator of immune response. "These cells have been shown to be of vital importance in preventing tumor development and spread," the Ohio researchers point out *(Psychosomatic Medicine)*.

Loneliness appears to impede immune function.

But if living alone doesn't depress you, there's no reason this news should, either. As social psychology researchers Carin Rubenstein, Ph.D., a former associate editor of *Psychology Today,* and Phillip Shaver, Ph.D., of the University of Denver, have observed: Being alone is not synonymous with loneliness. If people feel lonely, it has nothing to do with the number of people around them, but rather with their expectations of life and reactions to their environment. And those are risk factors you can do something about.

Being alone is not synonymous with loneliness.

Drs. Rubenstein and Shaver conducted their research by placing a questionnaire about loneliness in five U.S. newspapers, ranging from the New York *Daily News* to the Billings, Montana, *Gazette*. Twenty-two thousand people over the age of 18 responded.

THE MYTH OF LONELINESS

Social isolation is associated with greater health risks.

Interestingly, these respondents, who appeared to be typical of American adults, did not fit the mold of loneliness. Over the years, health statistics have pointed out that single people are more likely to suffer premature death. That led psychologists, including James J. Lynch, Ph.D., author of *The Broken Heart: The Medical Consequences of Loneliness* (Basic Books), to theorize that people who live alone are socially isolated and because of that, are not as happy or healthy as married folks.

That's not necessarily so, say Drs. Rubenstein and Shaver. While their survey does confirm that feeling lonely—regardless of living arrangement—is associated with greater health risks (people who said they were lonely were more likely to suffer from some 19 health problems listed, including such psychological symptoms as anxiety, depression, crying spells, and feeling worthless), results do not support the view that loneliness is a consequence of living alone.

Single people had more friends than those who lived with other people.

Nearly one-quarter of the people who lived alone fell into Drs. Rubenstein and Shaver's "least lonely" category. Single people had more friends on the average than people who lived with other people and they were less frequently troubled by headaches, anger, and irritability.

By comparison, people who lived with their parents were the loneliest lot of all.

"Young people who live with their parents after high school or college graduation tend to be lonelier than older people who live alone," Dr. Rubenstein explains. "A young person in this situation has different expectations. If there's no boyfriend or girlfriend in the picture, they face a social-psychological conflict. For young adults, in particular, being alone—especially on a Saturday night—can be a stigma. This makes them feel rejected and lonely."

POSITIVE REACTIONS

Two common responses to loneliness.

Through their research, Drs. Rubenstein and Shaver also discovered that when people feel lonely, they generally react in one of two ways. In a "sad passivity" reaction, the person spends much of the time sleeping, eating, and crying. In a "creative solitude" reaction, the person overcomes loneliness through reading, listening to music, working on a hobby, studying, writing, or playing a musical instrument.

"Loneliness is often a synonym for boredom," Dr. Rubenstein says. "People who spend their time creatively when alone are learning to deal with solitude. In the process, they begin to feel more calm, creative, and happy."

Maturity, too, brings new perspectives on solitude. Older people in their 60s and 70s adjust much better to being alone than younger people, says Dr. Rubenstein. One reason may be that they've grown more secure in knowing who they are.

You must be secure with yourself before you can find contentment in solitude. The trouble is, we often grow up in the constant company of others and come to depend on them for our happiness. It isn't until we're forced into "solitary confinement," often under grievous circumstances such as death or divorce, that our self-confidence comes to test.

Finding contentment in solitude requires self-confidence.

"My own experience was typical," says David A. Chiriboga, Ph.D., associate professor of psychology and the director of a study on mental health and divorce at the University of California at San Francisco. "I grew up in a large family, always had roommates at school, and got married as soon as I graduated. After my divorce, I found I wasn't used to being alone. It was devastating, frightening. For a long time, I would play the radio all day just so the house wouldn't feel so empty.

"Time passed and I started getting more comfortable with my life. Realizing that I could enjoy being alone was a major discovery for me."

Now Dr. Chiriboga helps others ease through the transition to singleness. His advice: "When you find yourself alone, see it as an opportunity to discover yourself. Take it as a challenge. Find out what you want to be, where you want to go, and what gives you pleasure," he says. "Anyone can be an interesting person. All you have to do is look inside yourself."

When you find yourself alone, see it as an opportunity to discover yourself.

Of course, when we look inward, the opportunity is there not only to understand ourselves better but to better understand those around us.

"Everyone has an inner and an outer self," explains psychiatrist and psychoanalyst Peter Martin, M.D., of Bloomfield Hills, Michigan. "The outer self deals with family, friends, culture, and all the other aspects of civilization. We modify and compromise the outer self to deal with the people around us. But the inner self is the true self. People

People in touch with their inner selves have a true sense of identity.

in touch with their inner selves have a true sense of identity. They have a feeling of security in knowing who they really are. And by knowing their true selves, they can teach their outer selves how to better interact with others."

After all, mastering the art of being alone does not mean turning into a misanthropic recluse. People who are loving—who completely accept themselves and others—can be happy and content whether in a crowd of people or quietly at home by themselves. Trouble is, too many people who are suddenly faced with the prospect of being alone turn within *at the expense of those outside.* As a result, they may be depriving themselves of the love and affection they need to grow.

"Depression, loneliness, and boredom are all symptoms of affection deprivation," says Allan Dye, Ph.D., associate professor of mental health counseling and personnel services and director of the counseling and guidance center at Purdue University. "And the first sign that someone's heading in the wrong direction is self-preoccupation. People who dwell too much on themselves, even if they don't think of themselves as lonely or bored, are probably not having enough good contact with others.

"Healthful, enriching, mutual experience with others is the best counterweight to self-preoccupation," Dr. Dye continues. "You've got to get that focus off yourself. If you're feeling deprived of affection, turn your attention to other people. Get in contact, pay attention, listen, and be aware. You become more attractive to others when you pay attention to them, and that leads to more affection directed at you."

Moreover, he adds, "if you want to receive affection, you've got to become consciously aware of people *you* feel affection for, and take steps to *show* that affection. People often *feel* affection without ever conveying it in any way. If you make the effort to demonstrate your affection for others, you'll probably receive more affection in return."

Psychiatrist J. Ingram Walker, M.D., author of *Everybody's Guide to Emotional Well-Being* (Harbor), agrees.

"Altruistic people lose themselves in others," Dr. Walker says. "The process can block out depression, make us less aware of our own inadequacies, and help us surmount our personal problems."

"Altruism is what we call prosocial behavior," says

Depression, loneliness, and boredom are symptoms of affection deprivation.

Atlanta psychologist Perry W. Buffington, Ph.D. "It's a way of putting others before your own ego, of reaching out to the people around you. And that can only increase well-being because without some connection with others, life doesn't have much meaning."

"When you focus attention on someone else, you feel better about yourself," Dr. Buffington adds. "So when I get patients who have no caring relationships, I usually recommend they get involved in some small group that has a definite purpose. Probably no more than four people. It could be church related, hobby related, civic—it doesn't matter. Chances are, while they devote themselves to the group's goal, they'll get the attention they need and establish those necessary social bonds" (see Chapter 11, To Love and Be Loved).

When you focus on others, you feel better about yourself.

There's growing evidence that pets can also help satisfy our need to give and receive affection. Not that pets should be considered a substitute for people, but according to Aaron Katcher, M.D., coauthor of *Between Pets and People* (Putnam), for those who really enjoy the company of pets, they can provide a strong supplement to human relationships and in fact help to improve one's rapport with people. In this way they are a significant aid to loneliness (see Chapter 71, Pets).

An important key, then, to warding off loneliness is care. Caring for yourself and what you really feel. Caring for others. Caring for life and everything around you.

Caring: antidote to loneliness.

"When you maintain a pattern of caring, whether for a house, a garden, pets, or other people, you are protecting yourself against despair," says Dr. Katcher. And in the process, you'll live a more happy and healthy existence—whether alone or in the company of others.

20

Breaking the Bonds
of Shyness

Hands sweating, throat dry, short of breath.

Shy people can experience severe anxiety at a Saturday night party.

Shyness may be the most widespread psychological problem today.

Treatment is fairly straightforward.

The feelings took Bob right back to the jungles of Southeast Asia. His hands were sweating. His throat was dry. His breath was coming in little gasps. His stomach was knotted.

But Bob wasn't back in Vietnam. He was at a Saturday night party.

"The feelings are identical for a truly shy person," says John Owen, an instructor at Temple University in Philadelphia. "Bob enrolled in one of my shyness workshops. He does hotel work, and now he's always with people, so it looks as if he's learned to cope."

Like many mental health professionals in universities and medical centers throughout the country, Owen is finding that shyness drives an increasing number of people to seek help. "The world really does feel like a threatening jungle for some people," he says.

In his book *Making Contact: A Guide to Overcoming Shyness* (Fawcett Popular Library), Arthur Wassmer, Ph.D., writes, "Shyness may be at once the most widespread and the least noticed psychological problem of Americans today."

As a result of shyness, many people feel isolated, lonely, frustrated, ineffective, and anxious. The voice of their inner agony says, "If only I could make contact with my fellow human beings and not be shy!"

"But shyness isn't difficult to treat," says John Owen. "It means hard, very hard, work for the shy person. But the treatment itself is fairly straightforward."

Whatever the therapist's orientation, the actual course

of treatment for shyness is pretty much the same: relaxation. Desensitization. And, then, practice, practice, practice.

"If you're not shy, you can't imagine how unrelaxed a truly shy person can be," says Owen. "The anguish. The terror."

If you're not shy, you can't imagine the anguish.

Over the past 2½ years, Owen has worked with hundreds of shy people. In workshops, which cost about $75 for ten sessions, he first teaches clients to relax.

Relaxation exercises can include lying down and focusing on a particular muscle, tensing it, then releasing it. A fantasy of being in a beautiful, comfortable place can also be effective.

Progressive relaxation or guided imagery can help.

Then Owen asks his clients to imagine a shyness-provoking situation while relaxed. This is the desensitization part. "It's like desensitizing an allergy," he says. "Each week a little more bee toxin until finally, bee toxin doesn't send you into convulsions anymore. The thing about anxiety, you can't feel it when you're relaxed. So the relaxation, once you've learned it, is your inner tube for safety as you push into deeper and deeper waters."

Next come simulated life situations. People play roles, making a crucial phone call or asking for a raise or inviting a special person to lunch. Members of Owen's groups take roles and give one another simulated experiences.

Simulate the real-life experience.

Then, the real world! But Owen eases that transition. He might take his workshop members to a church social with assignments like, "Meet five new people," or "Carry on a five-minute conversation with a new person." After that, it's time to use contact-making skills on their own.

FIRST YOU SMILE

Dr. Wassmer cheerily announces in *Making Contact,* "There is good news for shy people." He condenses part of that good news into an acronym, SOFTEN: S, smile; O, open posture (no arm or leg crossing, please); F, forward lean (that is, lean your body, or at least incline your head, toward the person you are trying to contact); T, touch (literally touch people from time to time); E, eye contact (look people in the eye); and N, nod (give the person who is talking to you an understanding response).

"The roots of shyness," according to Dr. Wassmer, "are negative thoughts that people hold about themselves."

Shyness has its roots in negative thoughts.

Picture yourself as you'd like to be.

Start picturing yourself as you would like to be, he suggests, maybe modeling yourself on someone you admire. He argues that just this exercise in imagination can change behavior. "After two weeks of practicing at least once a day, reserve a normal practice period to contemplate changes that have occurred in you," he says. "Generally, you notice that you are a little more relaxed in your 'panic' situations."

Like many counselors, Dr. Wassmer urges shy people to direct their attention outward. Shy people, according to researchers, can be so obsessed with how they look, how they feel, what they're going to say, and so on, that they completely neglect the world around them. Dr. Wassmer prescribes "active listening" as a means of redirecting attention. At the same time it redirects attention, listening also helps shy people become involved with others.

BECOMING LESS ISOLATED

Tell someone a joke.

Next comes self-disclosure. Dr. Wassmer's self-disclosure exercises include telling how you feel about your job, telling about a trip you made, and telling a joke.

Tell someone that you love him or her.

The obvious objection here is "Whom do I tell? I'm shy! I don't know people to whom I can listen actively, let alone disclose myself!" Shyness counselors, however, point out that in daily life—at work, on committees, in clubs, in cafeterias, at churches and synagogues—shy people are exposed to others. They isolate themselves, however, by their own behavior. The social calisthenics recommended by counselors are intended to cultivate new, less isolating behavior. As Dr. Wassmer's students become more and more outgoing, they are finally challenged "to tell someone that you like (care for, love) him or her."

Most students of shyness refer to the work of Stanford University psychologist Phillip G. Zimbardo, Ph.D. Dr. Zimbardo is the author of numerous books and articles, and he is a frequent television and radio talk-show guest.

Forty percent of most populations consider themselves shy.

"I've studied 10,000 shy people over the past ten years, Dr. Zimbardo says. "We've done a cross-cultural survey covering eight societies. On the average, you'll find that 40 percent of most populations, including the United States as a whole, consider themselves shy."

Dr. Zimbardo discovered considerable concern about

shyness among the students at Stanford, where he teaches. As a result he established a Shyness Clinic.

The Shyness Clinic technique is outlined in detail, with self-help exercises, in Dr. Zimbardo's book *Shyness: What It Is and What to Do about It* (Jove/HBJ).

"We have had a 100 percent success rate at the Shyness Clinic in the sense that every client has noted change for the better," Dr. Zimbardo says. "When they begin, clients list three things that they want to do that their shyness prevents. By the end of the 20 sessions, everyone has accomplished at least one of those three things."

List three things your shyness prevents.

Dr. Zimbardo's system is similar to the self-analysis, relaxation, desensitization, and "practice, practice, practice" approaches already described.

His contact-making exercises include "Call the library and ask the reference librarian what the population of the United States is," for starters. They advance to "See how many different stories you can tell other people in the next week . . . your septic tank back-up story might not be compelling for some listeners."

How many different stories can you tell other people?

FREE FROM EXPECTATIONS

Dr. Zimbardo is sensitive to the environment component of shyness. "We're not just talking about the shy individual," he says. "We're talking about the people around him or her. When you make a move—like going to a new school, settling in a new town, changing jobs—that's a good time to give up shyness. Your present contacts treat you as shy, and it's hard to change their attitudes. But new people, what do they know about you? It's easier to be outgoing with them because neither you nor they have any expectations."

Gerald M. Phillips, Ph.D., professor of speech and communications at Pennsylvania State University, has been working with shy people for almost 20 years. "I'd say we're 85 percent effective," he says. "The person who wants to be less reticent identifies a goal. And then we work on it."

First, identify a goal. Then, work on it.

Some researchers have found that women may have special complications when it comes to overcoming shyness. Clorinda Margolis, Ph.D., is a clinical professor of psychiatry at Thomas Jefferson University School of Medicine in

Philadelphia, where a feminist therapy collective specializes in the concerns of women. "Little girls sometimes find they are rewarded for shyness," Dr. Margolis explains. "The teacher likes shy girls. Mommy likes a shy little girl. They are praised for being sweet, shy little things."

Most depressed women are also shy and unassertive.

Michel Hersen, Ph.D., a clinical psychologist at the University of Pittsburgh School of Medicine's Western Psychiatric Institute and Clinic, recently completed a four-year federally funded study of depression in 150 depressed women. Dr. Hersen found that most depressed women are also shy and unassertive. He set out to find if losing their shyness helped their depression. He compared therapy based on social-skill exercises (of the sort already described) with drug therapy and conventional psychotherapy. "I found about 70 percent improved substantially with the social-skills training," Dr. Hersen says. "That compares with 50 percent improvement with the antidepressant medication Elavil, and 46 percent in short-term analytically oriented psychotherapy."

What's important is that people can change.

What's important is that people can change. "That's all I'm looking for," says Temple University's John Owen. "My clients are never going to be gladhanding extroverts. But with some work they can make the most of their natural talents without letting shyness get in the way."

Escaping the Grip of Boredom

You're on the phone, half listening, and filling the message pad with circles and squares. You're at a movie that's as dull and stale as the popcorn under the seats, your head propped up in your hand. You drum a finger on the table or restlessly tap your foot, but you're not listenting to the music, you're facing it—the irritating whine of *boredom.*

How do you shut it off?

Sometimes, it seems, by shutting someone up. Someone we all know. The self-absorbed talker who goes on forever, switching topics and crowding out his listeners. The person who talks to stimulate himself and seems to forget there are other people around. In short, the bore. But if someone is boring you, the way out isn't to mask your discomfort with politeness while planning a quick exit. The way out is to tell the person what you feel—not that *he's* boring you, but that *you're* bored.

"When we want to do something about our experience of boredom in a conversation, we often make the mistake of telling the other person that he or she is a bore," says Gerald Goodman, Ph.D., a psychology professor at UCLA and an authority on communication. "We classify that person, we formulate that person as if he or she were a fixed thing. We tell people what they are, as if we had the ability to diagnose them as human beings. But that ability—to diagnose and classify—is not ours. There is too much room for error—we are simply not experts at interpreting other people.

But what we *are* expert in is our *own* experience.

The restless tapping of feet, drumming of fingers: How do you shut it off?

Instead of interpreting someone else, we can *disclose* our own immediate experience. We can say, "I'm feeling bored." Or, "I'm feeling uninterested." "I'm feeling as if I heard this before." "I'm feeling talked down to." Making any one of those types of disclosures—talking about your own here-and-now experience—is more easily accepted by the other person than telling that person what he or she is. And you end up safer, more caring and, best of all, more effective in remedying the boredom.

Telling someone you feel bored isn't being cruel.

"Telling someone you feel bored isn't being cruel," Dr. Goodman says. "It's not cruel or destructive to tell someone you're feeling lonely or uninterested when he or she talks to you. It may hurt the other person, but in this case causing pain is a form of respect and is much more caring than being placating or condescending. What *is* destructive is feeling put off and bored, not saying anything about it, and then staying away from the person who makes you feel that way."

Dr. Goodman says that telling a person how his or her conversation is making you feel is a form of what psychologists call "meta-communication"—talking about talking. And, he points out, meta-communication not only works to stop someone from boring you but makes *any* conversation more fascinating.

Talking about the way we talk can enhance close relationships.

"We can make our close relationships more exciting by overcoming the discomfort attached to talking about the way we talk. Telling someone what his or her talk just did to you, or telling why you just said something, is the heart of meta-communication. And talking about ourselves with this kind of intimacy—without censorship or strategy—is so uncommon that when we do it our listeners are fascinated."

Dr. Goodman emphasizes that meta-communication is not the same as the musings of a bore. "Boring conversations are usually not from people talking *about* themselves," he says. "The boredom comes when people just go on talking *to* themselves."

EDITOR'S NOTE: Dr. Goodman and his colleagues have recorded a series of audiotapes to teach meta-communication. They are available through BMA Audio Cassettes, 200 Park Avenue South, New York, NY 10003; (212) 674-1900.

LIFE CAN BE BORING

How do you escape a boring situation?

Sometimes, though, "the bore" in your life is life itself. What do you do when it's not a person who's boring you,

but a situation? Well, to really beat boredom—permanently—
you have to know just what it is.

"We have to recognize first of all that boredom is a
nearly universal experience," says Robert Plutchik, Ph.D.,
professor of psychiatry and psychology at Albert Einstein
College of Medicine in New York City and author of *Emotion:
A Psychoevolutionary Synthesis* (Harper & Row). "Everybody
has experienced boredom because it represents an expression of what I call a 'basic emotion'—a type of emotion that
has a very important role."

Basic emotions, says Dr. Plutchik, are the result of
evolution. They are the feelings our primitive ancestors
needed to solve "survival problems." One of those problems was poisonous food, and the feeling associated with
the process of regurgitating unpalatable food was disgust.
But where does boredom come in?

Basic emotions are the result of evolution.

"Disgust has different levels of intensity," Dr. Plutchik
says. "Boredom is associated with a *mild* experience of
disgust, of taking in something unpleasant which one wants
to get rid of.

"The bored person feels a sensation of irritability or
rejection in the digestive system—that's why when a person
feels totally bored and restless he may feel as if something is
being 'shoved down my throat.' And that's why many people deal with boredom by eating. They try to substitute
pleasurable food for an irritation."

Eating is a reflex to alleviate boredom—the feeling that something's being "shoved down my throat."

But the bored person doesn't solve the problem by
eating. Eating to alleviate boredom, Dr. Plutchik points
out, is just a reflex, a throwback to caveman days. What the
modern person needs is a new *interest.*

And, says Dr. Plutchik, you should seek an interest in
something relevant to your own life. "For instance, many
people start out indifferent to nutritional issues," he says.
"Then, when they have an illness, they develop an intense
interest—because they see the relevance of nutrition to
their own life."

INVOLVEMENT COMES FIRST

But New York City psychoanalyst Theodore Rubin,
M.D., believes we have to get our feet wet before we can
enjoy the swim. "In the attempt to mitigate boredom I find
it of great value to remember that *involvement precedes
interest*," he says. "We must risk at least a minimum degree

Involvement precedes interest.

of involvement in any activity or enterprise before interest can be generated. Waiting for an interest to strike us before we take steps to become involved may well keep us in a state of relative boredom for a lifetime."

Learning—with its newness and promise of mastery—is the greatest antidote to boredom.

What activity should you pick? "Learning, with its implication of newness, open-endedness, self-achievement, and pride—with its promise of mastery—is the greatest antidote to boredom," says Willard Gaylin, M.D., a psychiatrist from New York.

Dr. Rubin agrees. "It is just about never too late to go back to books, to take courses, to attend lectures, to develop a latent interest. Boredom simply cannot exist when we are actively engaged in the process of continuing growth through recognition and development of real resources in ourselves."

PART V

Minimizing Key Stressors

Uncertainty:
Public Stressor
Number One

*...W**hat are some of
the things people worry about these days? Well—they're
afraid the world will be blown up; crime on the streets and
in their homes; overpopulation; gray hairs; wrinkles; traffic congestion; parking tickets; marriage; divorce;
houseguests; medical bills; inflation; flying saucers; too
much salt, too much sugar; too much chlorine in the water,
not enough chlorine in the water . . . I could go on and
on. . . .*

*My attitude is, if something is beyond your control—if
you can't do anything about it—there's no point worrying
about it. And if you can do something about it, then there's
still nothing to worry about. I feel that way when the plane
I'm on is bouncing around in turbulence. It's not my problem.
The pilot gets paid a lot of money to fly that plane; let him
worry about it. . . .*

*I can honestly say I was not even uptight about my
heart bypass several years ago. I don't mean to minimize
that operation—I would have preferred to have had my
cuticles cut—but once again, what could I do about it? It
was beyond my control. It was the doctor's business; that's
what he does for a living. Me, I'm a country singer. Besides,
the surgeon had trained for years in medical school, he'd
done this operation many times . . . and he had long,
strong fingers. I had such confidence in him that I didn't
give it a second thought.*

*When I came out of anesthetic I heard the surgeon say,
"George, you did great, you're just fine."*

I said, "Doctor, I wasn't the least bit concerned."
"Really?" he said. "I was a nervous wreck."
Even that didn't bother me. Then he handed me his
bill and I passed out.

"What-ifs" and "If-onlys" can make us sick with worry.

But seriously, George Burns makes a very important point here which, whether he knows it or not, is finding much support among longevity researchers. Mounting evidence suggests that worry over life's uncertainties—those future *what-ifs* and past *if-onlys* that can drive us crazy with speculation—creates a particularly devastating kind of stress response. In other words, it's what we don't know (and can't do anything about) that can really hurt us. For example:

• According to a report by the British Health Service, peptic ulcers increased by 50 percent among people living in the center of London during World War II, where bombings were regular. But in the city's outskirts, where bombings were unpredictable, stomach ulcers increased by more than six times that much.

Shocks given without warning produced ulcers in rats.

• In an experiment reported on by two psychologists from Stockton College in New Jersey, rats given electrical shocks without warning developed gastric complications at a significantly greater rate than rats forewarned of the shocks.

• College students surveyed by a psychologist from the State University of New York at Albany reported being sick most often following events in their lives that, in addition to being undesirable, left the students *uncertain* as to the amount of control they had over them.

The moral of these stories?

That stress, of course, is difficult to swallow—but it's even harder going down when tainted with uncertainty.

And why should uncertainty be so stressful?

The body is in a constant state of semiarousal.

Because, says Jerry Suls, Ph.D. (the psychologist in charge of the above-mentioned survey of college students), it keeps us in a constant state of semiarousal, thus putting "an extreme burden" on the body's "adaptive resources and resistance systems."

The human body, in other words, seems to be a little

*Reprinted by permission of the Putnam Publishing Group from *How to Live to Be 100 or More* by George Burns. Copyright © 1983 by George Burns.

like the team on defense in a football game: It performs best when given some idea of what to expect. When it's kept perpetually guessing, it can never settle down to an optimally effective strategy for survival.

Which is why those rats fared so poorly when given shocks without warning. They couldn't come up with a game plan. The group that was always forewarned of its shocks, on the other hand, could. They learned to live in relative peace—and hence health—during their moments of known comfort.

"Predictable pain is less stressful because . . . the subject is capable of learning when it is safe to 'lower its guard' and relax," Israel Posner, Ph.D., remarked regarding the experiment.

Predictable pain is less stressful.

Stress has been under scientific scrutiny for a long time, but only recently has the importance of this "uncertainty factor" emerged. And it has psychologists fascinated because what it suggests is that we may be able to reduce the amount of trauma caused by stressful events in our lives simply by determining when we do—and *do not*—need to feel responsible for them. The day we can stop feeling angry and/or guilty for missing an appointment because of a traffic jam, for example, is the day we do our health a big favor. In the words of Dr. Jerry Suls, "The inability to distinguish undesirable events that one can do nothing about may be more debilitating than the undesirability of the events themselves."

SOMETHING TO WORRY ABOUT

"Depressed individuals," says Dr. Suls, may, in fact, "be characterized by the inability to discriminate between controllable and uncontrollable situations, feeling helpless (i.e., they are not responsible for their fate) while simultaneously feeling guilty (i.e., they *are* responsible for their fate)." This pinch, Dr. Suls notes, could be viewed "as exacerbating and perhaps even creating the depressive state."

Know when you are—and are not—responsible.

Clinical psychologist and stress management consultant Dennis T. Jaffe, Ph.D., agrees. The people who automatically assume that their efforts won't make the difference, and so won't act even when the situation is within their power to change, come to feel helpless, victimized, and depressed, he says. At the other extreme, there are the people who believe that *nothing* is beyond their control and

There are physical consequences of feeling helpless.

take on every problem as their own. These people constantly worry about problems they can never solve—a self-destructive type of behavior characteristic of Type As that can lead to frustration and burnout.

There are physical consequences, too. Extended periods of feeling helpless and gloomy can depress the immune system and increase our vulnerability to diseases such as rheumatoid arthritis, allergies, cancer, and even AIDS (Autoimmune Deficiency Syndrome). Type A behavior, on the other hand, has been linked to heart disease as well as high blood pressure and ulcers—anything related to the cardiovascular and gastric systems.

For that reason, Dr. Jaffe says, it's important that we first determine which worries are within and which beyond our control, then decide whether or not to take action. In doing this you'll quickly discover that the majority of worries are not worth worrying about.

BOX 17: TAKING OPTIMAL CONTROL

A healthy person, says California psychologist Dennis T. Jaffe, Ph.D., is one who practices *optimal control*—who acts on problems that are within his power to resolve and doesn't waste time worrying about those that aren't. To do otherwise, says Dr. Jaffe, is self-destructive.

As Table 6 illustrates, Type A behavior (which has been linked to heart disease, high blood pressure, and ulcers) is char-acterized by *overcontrol*—acting on problems beyond your control and worrying about events you can't change. The behavior pattern associated with immune-deficiency diseases such as cancer and arthritis is just the opposite. It is characterized by *undercontrol*—neglecting to act on problems within your control and brooding over the consequences.

TABLE 6: Taking Control

	Situation Is Within Your Control	Situation Is Beyond Your Control
Act	Mastery	Type A Behavior (Prone to illnesses of the cardiovascular and gastric systems)
Don't Act	Helpless/Hopeless Syndrome (Prone to illnesses related to immune deficiency)	Acceptance, Letting Go

"Most worries are anticipatory worries," says Barry Lubetkin, Ph.D., a psychologist at the Institute for Behavior Therapy in New York City. "We're afraid of what *might* happen. We're looking negatively and fearfully into the future.

Most worries are anticipatory worries.

TECHNIQUES TO TRY

Dr. Lubetkin explains several techniques he uses to help anxious and worried people at the Institute for Behavior Therapy.

One is called *coping desensitization.* If you are worried about a problem in the future, imagine yourself in the fearful situation. Then imagine that you are coping with it, or even enjoying it. The man who fears airplanes might replace his terror with positive images, such as the view from the window or a pleasant in-flight meal.

Imagine yourself coping with the fearful situation.

Another technique is called *cognitive tracking* or *reality testing.* Ask yourself if your worries are supported by the facts. In similar situations in the past, were you unable to cope? The man afraid of failing to satisfy his wife should ask himself if he failed before. If not, he can stop worrying. This method works well if you set aside 15 or 20 minutes a day to relax and think the problem through, says Dr. Lubetkin.

What's the worst possible consequence?

Then there's the "worst case" method. If the future looks bleak, try imagining the worst possible outcomes. For an accident at home, imagine cuts, poisoning, broken bones. For a long auto trip, imagine flat tires and running out of gas. Ask yourself if the worst would really be all that bad, and imagine yourself coping with it.

For someone who suffers from nameless dread, Dr. Lubetkin suggests a *time sampling.* In this method, you devote the last ten minutes of every hour to writing down in a journal the things your mind is "dwelling on." This helps isolate and identify the "themes of worry."

ADD SOME CERTAINTY

"Periods of psychological safety seem to insulate subjects from the harmful effects of stress," says Dr. Israel Posner.

We should keep that in mind as life's woes begin to burden or confuse us. Because by learning to enjoy regular "periods of psychological safety" (whether by exercising, taking in a movie, or pursuing a hobby), we add some

Exercise adds *predictable* comfort to our lives.

measure of *predictable* comfort, and hence certainty (and health) to our lives.

Exercise and talking to your friends are two proven remedies for allaying mild worries. Leo Hawkins, Ed.D., a human development specialist at North Carolina State University, says, "When I start worrying, I put it aside temporarily and take some physical exercise. Afterward I try to look the problem square in the face. Then I talk things over with someone. If we tell someone what's troubling us, it gets our problems out in the open. We can examine them better. We'll be able to see solutions better."

Step back and get a better perspective.

"Get involved in jogging or sports until you are totally perspiring and almost worn out," agrees Los Angeles therapist Sidney Walter. "Dig up your backyard and plant a vegetable garden. Polish your car."

Keep in mind, too, that worry can be a valuable tool for someone who knows how to turn it to his advantage. Worry keeps us "focused and vigilant" during crises, says Dr. Lubetkin. "Constructive worrying" leads us to solutions instead of away from them, says Dr. Hawkins. At its best, the discomfort of worrying forces us to act. Worry is "a precious opportunity to start talking straight to yourself," says one self-help expert, and another urges us to "recruit it as a spur to necessary action."

But what about those worries that are best forgotten, and not acted on?

Dr. Suls's advice, quite simply, is that we take to heart the words of religious philosopher Reinhold Niebuhr, whose following statement was used by the USO to inspire troops during World War II, and more recently by Alcoholics Anonymous to strengthen fledgling members:

"Give us the grace to accept with serenity the things that cannot be changed, the courage to change the things that should be changed, and the wisdom to know the difference."

23

Family Disharmony: How to Orchestrate Better Relations

Modern living puts a strain on family harmony, but there are things we can do to keep the home fires burning brightly. Experts point to at least five qualities that happy families have:

The five qualities that happy families have.

- love;
- appreciation for each other;
- open communication;
- a willingness to spend time together;
- strong leadership.

Most specialists say that a loving family starts with a loving marriage. It's the flame that lights the stove that warms the house. "The family is a by-product of the relationship between husband and wife," says Daniel Araoz, Ed.D., past president of the Academy of Psychologists in Marital Sex and Family Therapy, a division of the American Psychological Association.

A loving family starts with a loving marriage.

"The family will stay strong only if the couple keeps the original motivation that brought them together," he says. "They need to feel they are happier together than they are alone, and that they accept each other as they accept themselves. If a couple has those feelings, they'll be passed along to the children."

Love between grandparents and grandchildren also can keep a family together. Children may rebel against their parents, grow up, and move away, but when grandchildren come into the world, families seem to be reunited.

Grandchildren seem to reunite families.

In a survey at Wesleyan University in Middletown,

Connecticut, dozens of elderly couples told psychology professor James J. Conley, Ph.D., that they often disagreed with their children on moral and political issues and felt a distinct "generation gap." But love for their grandchildren managed to bridge that gap.

Of the couples surveyed, 90 percent rated their relationships with their grandchildren as good to excellent. They called this new source of love a "solidifying factor" in their families and said it brought about substantial "wound healing."

MUTUAL ADMIRATION

Families who appreciate each other fare better.

One way to express love is to start a miniature "mutual admiration society" in the home. According to Nick Stinnett, Ph.D., a family specialist at the University of Nebraska (Lincoln), families who appreciate each other fare better than those who don't. A lot of people don't express compliments because they don't want to sound insincere, Dr. Stinnet says, but it's important to overcome those inhibitions.

For Alice Honig, Ph.D., of Syracuse University's College for Human Development, family members can either tear each other down or build each other up. Family life can proceed in a "vicious cycle" (tearing down), or in a "virtuous cycle" (building up), she says.

Unhappy families exploit each member's weaknesses.

"In unhappy families," Dr. Honig explains, "everyone provides constant alarms to make each other tense and upset and distressed. Each child and each adult knows the others' weak spots and they know how to shame or embarrass each other.

"In happy families, the same principle works in reverse. Whether it's remembering to write an anniversary card or striving for good marks in school, each person can figure out what they can do to make the others pleased and happy. They learn to accommodate each other and to make each other comfortable."

"Strength bombardment": a process to build strong relationships.

Some psychologists say that a technique called "strength bombardment" can help some families learn how to praise each other. In this gamelike method, each person takes a turn at enumerating his or her own good qualities and then listens to more praise from each of the others. Dr. Nick Stinnett explains the process:

"The entire family comes together. There may be a

group leader or counselor or some member of the family can act as a leader. One person in the family is designated as the target person. For example, the mother may begin as target person. She is asked to list the strengths that she feels she has as a person. If she lists only two or three because she's modest, the leader can urge her to list others. After she has finished the list, her husband is asked to add to her list of strengths. Or he may elaborate on the strengths that she has already listed. When he has finished, each of the children is asked to add to their mother's list of strengths. When this process is finished, the husband becomes the target person. The same procedure is repeated for him. Then each of the children becomes the target person.

"The 'strength bombardment' technique is very simple, but the results have been amazing," Dr. Stinnett adds. Family members "get into a pattern of looking for each other's good qualities and they also get into a habit of expressing appreciation to one another."

Looking for the good qualities first.

COMMUNICATE AND DO THINGS TOGETHER

Open, honest communication lines and a habit of doing things together are two more hallmarks of a happy family, and they go hand in hand. One seldom works without the other. "Often families are so fragmented, so busy, and spend such little time together," says one therapist, "that they communicate with each other through rumor." It's important, however, that the family avoid a "smothering" togetherness or a "false" togetherness, such as being glued to the television together.

Sometimes families find themselves "spread too thin" and short of time for each other. When this happens, Dr. Stinnett recommends scheduling a family conference. During this meeting, each person should make a list of all of his or her activities. By weeding out activities that aren't rewarding or important, they might find more time for each other.

Drifting apart? Schedule a family conference.

The importance of good communication can't be overemphasized. Unexpressed anger (or even unexpressed love) may destroy a family. "Mutual trust is basic," says Eleanor Siegl, Ph.D., director of the Little School, a small private school in Bellevue, Washington. "You've got to express whatever it is that's on your mind. If you don't talk about your doubts and fears and pleasures, they'll become a wedge between you." Dr. Stinnett adds that happy families "get mad at each other, but they get the conflict out in the open and they are able to talk it over. . . . "

Poor communication about "bedroom rights" can cause friction.

Poor communication about "bedroom rights" can cause friction between parents and young adults, Dr. Daniel Araoz says. Young adults sometimes come home unannounced, expecting to return to their old bedroom. But trouble starts when they find the bedroom converted to a sewing room. Dr. Araoz suggests that the families talk about how the rules change after children grow up and leave home.

For families who have difficulty communicating over great distances, Dr. Araoz recommends a frequent exchange of letters with photos or phone calls or even tape recordings. "Those are nice ways of keeping a family close in spirit," he says. "With all the different holidays, there are plenty of opportunities to send greeting cards, which only take a minute to write."

CLEAR CHAIN OF COMMAND

In the absence of parents, an elder child should take charge.

When the parents are no longer living, he suggests that one of the elder children take charge and maintain a central clearinghouse for news and gossip, and organize reunions.

Someone definitely has to take charge before a family can start pulling itself up by the bootstraps. For Jody Schor, Ed.D., formerly at the Philadelphia Child Guidance Center, a happy family must have an organized chain of command, from the adults down to the smallest child.

The role of each family member should be clear.

"Families work when the rules are explicit and said out loud. The role of each family member should be clear, and the children should be differentiated from each other. They shouldn't be lumped together as 'the kids.' "

Not that the family should be a dictatorship. Adults should be willing to apologize when they are wrong—but they should do it with dignity. And someone has to keep an eye on the light at the end of the tunnel—happy families deal with crises by managing, "even in the darkest of situations . . . to see some positive element, no matter how tiny, and to focus on it," Dr. Stinnett says.

Happy families make an effort to become happy.

All the experts we spoke with noticed that happy families share one quality: They make an effort to become happy.

"For relationships to survive, you have to make an effort," Dr. Araoz emphasizes. "It's like a plant. If you don't water it and give it light, it won't grow." Dr. Honig adds, "It's not easy. It's a real challenge to find a way to live so that none of us are being browbeaten. It takes goodwill, thinking, problem solving, and ingenuity."

Happy families are "on the offensive," Dr. Stinnett has found. The strong families he studied "didn't just react, they made things happen. We may have talked too much about families . . . being at the mercy of their environment. In fact there is a great deal that families can do to make life more enjoyable. These strong families exercised that ability."

They don't just react, they take action.

24

Money Worries:
How to Stop
the Budget Blues

**Money worries: another
source of anxiety, Insomnia,
depression.**

**Money represents security,
control, and power.**

**It's a sign that you've
"made it."**

Family therapists have begun to find that money worries can contribute to a whole host of psychological stresses in families—anxiety, tension, insomnia, and depression, to name a few. And those in turn can promote physical ailments such as arthritis, high blood pressure, ulcers, and heart attacks.

In a survey done by *Psychology Today,* respondents were asked which emotions they remember associating with money. Seventy-one percent recalled anxiety; 52 percent, depression; and another 52 percent, anger.

That's because there's so much tied up in our capacity to earn a living. For many of us, money represents security—a way of being in charge of our lives. For others, money means control or power.

"There's an unspoken myth among families," says Craig Everett, Ph.D., associate professor and director of Family Therapy Training at Florida State University, "that whoever controls the money controls the family. In other words, the person who pays the bills has the power."

For still others money represents prestige—the sign that they've "made it."

So it's easy to see that when those values (right or wrong, real or imagined) are taken away—through either the eroding dollar or, worse yet, the loss of a job—a person's self-esteem may be badly damaged. Worry and self-recrimination skyrocket, while confidence in the future and in one's self plummet. In extreme cases, hope and ambition, the characteristics that make people work harder, are destroyed.

"The important factor today," says Herbert C. Modlin, M.D., senior psychiatrist at the Menninger Clinic in Topeka, Kansas, "is being able to cope in order to alleviate family anxiety. We have to recognize the reality of money problems without becoming angry at each other."

Recognize the reality of money problems but don't become angry.

"That can be pretty difficult," says Philip Nastasee, a clinical psychologist at the Center for Psychological Consultation in Allentown, Pennsylvania, "especially if the couple's values surrounding money are totally divergent."

Milo Benningfield, Ph.D., agrees. "Each partner has his or her own style of dealing with money," says Dr. Benningfield, a practicing psychologist in Dallas. "It's kind of like a blueprint that each one has etched in their own minds, which stems from the way their own parents handled money. When a couple hits a financial crisis, they automatically reach back to their own blueprint to deal with the situation. What they sometimes discover is that they have very different blueprints and hence the conflicts begin."

Conflicts erupt over divergent values surrounding money.

A BLUEPRINT FOR TEAMWORK

"First I teach them to communicate what their differences are. And we look at what they learned about finances from their parents. Then we develop a *third* blueprint: one that's all their own. Neither feels that the other is getting his or her own way, because together they have their joint blueprint," Dr. Benningfield says. "If a couple learns to negotiate, compromise, and communicate (in other words, work as a team), there are very few things they can't tackle."

That's especially important for couples hit with unemployment, the ultimate money problem.

Unemployment: the ultimate money problem.

"People going through stressful life experiences tend to draw in," says Marion P. Willis, Ed.D., a psychologist at Temple University's Counseling Center in Philadelphia. "They suppress their fears. They look around and see other people who don't appear to be sharing their nervousness and worry about being hungry and out of work. As a result, they tend to think that they are the only ones with problems. This only makes them more depressed and more stressed. In the long run, you must recognize that you are your own best agent of change."

To begin with, you need to build strong support systems with other people, says Dr. Willis. "We need intimacy on various levels with various people to survive. Humans

Build strong support systems with other people.

don't operate well alone. We need to risk trusting others in interpersonal relationships. We do that by learning to listen to others and ourselves. This is a way to find that others are in similar (although slightly different) situations, but with similar problems, and that knowledge makes us feel not so alone in being stressed."

"Developing a sense of solidarity—perhaps by forming a democratic family counsel—is one way to do that," adds Dr. Modlin.

People need to be reassured that they are still worthwhile.

In fact, the social support level of the family, particularly of the spouse, can be a major buffer against the effects of stress, according to James House, Ph.D., research scientist with the Institute for Social Research at the University of Michigan in Ann Arbor. "People need to be reassured that they are still worthwhile and that the problems they have are not entirely their fault. It's important for them to recognize that they, personally, did not fail but that they are, in many respects, victims of environmental events.

"Even among the long-term unemployed, we found that those who had that kind of strong emotional support had much lower levels of stress," Dr. House says.

Look at the situation as a challenge—a chance to grow.

"People who do the best recognize money worries as a chance to be creative," says Dr. Benningfield. "They look at the total situation and approach it as a challenge—a chance to grow. They experiment with different ideas and then develop the ones that work best for them. There's a certain positive attitude that shines through in couples who want to work together as a unit."

TAKING CONTROL

"Money limitations don't have to mean money worries," adds Dr. Modlin. "Stop and take inventory, then do something—anything—no matter how simple or seemingly insignificant. Doing something is better than doing nothing because any action you take makes you feel less helpless and more in control of your life."

No income will ever be large enough.

"Start from the premise that no income you will earn will ever be large enough to cover *all* your wants," says Sylvia Porter, author of *Sylvia Porter's Money Book* (Doubleday & Co.). "Accept the theory that the more income you have, the greater will be your desires. Make up your mind that if you want something bad enough you will sacrifice other things for it."

In the meantime, examine your yearly income and outgo. If your income appears too small to go around, it could be that you forgot to take into account the "nibblers" —those little items that nibble away at your income until there's nothing left, explains Porter. Or perhaps you ignored the "bouncers," the big expenses that crop up a few times a year that make giant dents in your income—insurance premiums for house, health, or car, for example. Or maybe you missed the "sluggers"—the unexpected expenses such as major auto or household repairs.

Look out for the "nibblers," "bouncers," and "sluggers."

It's important to plan for those a small piece at a time. A separate account that you feed monthly will ease the burden when the yearly bills come due.

Speaking of yearly events, don't let Uncle Sam get the better of you at tax time. Have a few more dollars withheld from each paycheck (would you miss three dollars a week?), and then look forward to a tax refund, not a tax bill.

Learn what's worth sweating over and what isn't. According to Harry Browne, author of *How I Found Freedom in an Unfree World* (Avon Books), it isn't worth worrying and fretting over small expenditures—say, under $10 or $15. "I see people who will spend hours (if not weeks) pondering a $15 expenditure," writes Browne. "They feel they have to because of their limited means. Such choices are subjective, of course. Some people love to shop. I'd much rather spend my time listening to a Puccini opera or making love than trying to choose between a $6 item and an $8 item."

Don't sweat the $10 expenditures.

However, the other extreme is no better. That is, spending indiscriminately with the use of credit cards. "I've seen couples who were $30,000 in debt," says H. Don Morris of the American Association of Credit Counselors in Waukegan, Illinois. "They'd have 16 or 17 credit cards that they were using all at once to spread out their available credit. That is a blatant overuse of the system. These people use credit cards to supplement their income and then find themselves in over their heads. It's frightening to be that much in debt."

"PLASTIC SURGERY"

"Our first recommendation is to cut up the credit cards." Plastic surgery, so to speak. "Besides," continues Morris, "the interest on credit cards really adds up. You

If you can't pay your monthly credit card bill in full, you're overspending.

could make much better use of that money. That's not to say that credit cards are necessarily the villains. Clearly, it's how you handle them that counts. As long as the item you're buying is already included in your budget, it's OK to charge it. When the bill comes, pay the whole thing in full—not just the minimum due. If you can't afford to pay the full amount, you're overspending."

To get the full impact of your buying habits, try paying all your bills in cash. You won't be nearly so eager to part with the green stuff as you are when you're using that piece of plastic.

Don't spend more than you have to on medical care.

As long as you're conserving, don't spend more than you have to on medical care. If you're a senior citizen, learn what legal programs you're entitled to (such as Medicare) and then take advantage of them. "Don't be afraid to appeal a Medicare payment if you don't think it's fair," suggests Barbara Quaintance, senior program specialist in the Health Advocacy Service of the American Association of Retired Persons (AARP) in Washington, D.C. "Only three percent of the claims filed are actually ever questioned, but of those that are, half get increased reimbursement. Sometimes older people are afraid to complain. They worry that they'll wind up with less reimbursement than they started with." But that won't happen, Quaintance assures us.

Senior citizens may be entitled to certain special auto insurance and other discounts, too. In fact, AARP offers a 50-page booklet that gives practical advice on getting full tax benefits. It's called *Your Retirement Federal Income Tax Guide,* and you can get one free by writing to Tax-Aide Program, AARP, 1909 K Street, N.W., Washington, DC 20049.

THE MOST FOR YOUR MONEY

Thrift shops increase your purchasing power.

The idea, of course, is to get the most for your dollar. A unique way of doing that is to take advantage of thrift shops. Not just to shop there, but as a source of income, too. That's what Freda Tucker does. She's a senior citizen from Willow Grove, Pennsylvania, and she's found that she can sell her used clothing (including shoes and handbags) to the local thrift shop and split the profits with the owner 50-50. "Some thrift shops offer you 60 percent while they keep 40 percent of whatever the clothing is sold for," explains Mrs. Tucker. "It depends on the store's policy."

Shopping at thrift shops has come into vogue, too. "Just the other day I overheard a customer tell the owner that she was going on a Caribbean cruise," recalls Freda Tucker. "The customer wanted to know if there was anything in stock that would be appropriate for her trip. Was there! That woman walked out with a bundle of quality clothing and it only cost her about one-quarter of the original price."

When money is limited (or even when it's not), you can lower your anxieties and worries about it if you know you've spent it wisely.

It's reassuring to know you've spent it wisely.

"When you spend," says Sylvia Porter, "you buy more than material things such as bread and shoes; you make decisions that determine your whole way of life. Your decisions bring you closer to—or perhaps send you further away from—your ambitions, your aspirations, the things and nonthings that are really most worthwhile to you.

"Take the trouble to think out your own philosophy of living and your ambitions for the future. Develop a plan of control over your spending. Then you will make progress toward the kind of living that means the most to you."

Think about your priorities, then develop a plan of control over spending.

25

Job Stress:
Resolving the Most
Common Conflicts

What's bugging you?

Franz Kafka was wrong. People don't wake up one morning to discover that suddenly they've turned into bugs. What really happens is people wake up and go to the office and realize—not suddenly, but finally, after months or years—that something is bugging them. The trouble is, they can't quite put their finger on what it is.

Job stress is the most complex and insidious of the key stressors. That's because it involves so many different kinds of stress—environmental, physical, people-related, plus all the usual pressures of decisions, deadlines, and quotas. And contrary to what you may think, it's the subtle factors that pose the most danger.

Watch a secretary at work.

The next time you're in a busy office, take a close look at the secretaries. Watch them as they make photocopies, answer phones, run errands for executives. Watch them as they peck away at new daisywheel electronic typewriters and computer terminals. You won't see them lifting any heavy boxes or pondering any weighty decisions. You'll find their work stations air conditioned, modern, and carpeted. There may even be cheerful, piped-in music.

Sounds like a comfortable job, doesn't it? But if you look at some of the health statistics that show which employees take home ulcers and heart problems along with their paychecks, you'll find secretaries and other clerical workers near the top of the list.

All too often, we assume that the most hazardous or stressful jobs are those that involve toxic chemicals, hard

BOX 18: RATE YOUR JOB STRESS

For each of the following questions, rate your job on a scale of 1 (bothers me a little) to 5 (bothers me a lot). If the question does not apply, give it a 0.

1. Deadlines are a daily part of my job.

2. After leaving the job, I generally complete work I have not had time for during the day (if yes, mark 5).

3. I find it difficult to work with some of my co-workers.

4. I continue to allow myself to accept new job responsibilities without letting go of others.

5. There is little variety or challenge in my job.

6. I often feel overwhelmed with the demands of my job.

7. When I am under pressure I tend to lose my temper.

8. I have a problem completing work assignments because of the many interruptions.

9. I am concerned with the goal of being a perfect employee, spouse, and parent at the same time.

10. My job is at home. I cannot walk out and leave it at night (if yes, mark 5).

Scoring:

Total your score for work stress.

If your score is below 12, you are probably dealing effectively with the pressures of work.

If your score is between 12 and 30, you may be experiencing some physical or mental signs of distress.

If your score is over 30, work stress is signaling danger ahead. "Stress buffers" are needed immediately.

Adapted from *Stressmap: Finding Your Pressure Points* by C. Michele Haney, Ph.D., and Edmond W. Boenisch, Jr., Ph.D. (Impact Publishers).

---

physical labor, or difficult, upper-level management decisions. Those jobs undoubtedly carry their share of pressure and risks. But there are subtler factors that can turn the most innocuous jobs into strenuous ordeals for millions of people.

If your job forces you to keep pace with an electronic or mechanical device, for instance, you probably feel stressed. The same may be true if your work is repetitive and dull. Or if your work is meaningful, but requires lots of responsibility and little recognition, you can feel stressed. If your boss keeps looking over your shoulder, if you sit or stand all day, if you work nights—all that can be stressful. You may be a file clerk, but under the right—or rather, wrong—conditions your job could be riskier than washing windows on the World Trade Center.

Subtle factors can turn an innocuous job into a strenuous ordeal.

Pink-collar workers face hidden stress.

Good examples of employees under hidden stress are the nation's pink-collar workers. This group includes secretaries, clerks, data processors, telephone operators, and others. There are an estimated 18 million of them in the United States (80 percent of whom are women), and together they constitute the country's largest occupational group.

Pink-collar workers have a surprisingly high rate of coronary heart disease, the National Institute of Occupational Safety and Health (NIOSH) discovered. Doctors are seeing a disturbing number of women under 30 who already have angina or heart pain. One survey, in fact, has shown that female clerical workers who have children and are married to blue-collar workers have about one chance in five of developing heart disease. That figure is three times the rate for the average women and 50 percent higher than the average man's risk (American Journal of Public Health).

Heart disease is contagious: Bosses give it to their secretaries.

No one really knows why the deck is stacked against these working women, but researcher Suzanne G. Haynes, Ph.D., of the National Center for Health Statistics, has some theories. "Women in jobs in which they felt they couldn't leave, or who had unsupportive bosses, were all at higher risk of CHD [coronary heart disease]," she says. "Another finding was that working women with the highest rates were those who worked for men with the highest CHD rates."

Secretaries themselves say they resent having to do the same chores over and over and dislike being kept in the dark on decisions that affect their work, according to surveys conducted by Nine-to-Five, a 12,000-member working-woman's association.

"Although the physical hazards of working as a secretary or keypunch operator can't be compared to the hazards of working in a steel mill or iron foundry," says Judith Gregory, a research associate with the Department for the Professional Employees of the AFL-CIO, "they are significant problems and they affect millions of people."

Anger and frustration are common sources of stress.

Bottled-up anger and frustration are often sources of their stress. Since clerical workers are usually nonunionized, they often have no way to file a grievance or express their dissatisfaction, Gregory explains. Complaints about back-wrenching chairs, annoying fluorescent lights, and poor ventilation tend to fall on deaf ears. And hiring freezes during recessionary periods automatically translate into more work per secretary.

VDTs: A MIXED BLESSING?

The magic of computer technology, ironically, seems to make pink-collar work not less but more stressful. Lightning-quick communications and access to vast data bases may streamline and simplify the operations of a major bank or insurance company, it's true. But new studies conducted by NIOSH show that clerical workers who use video display terminals (VDTs) experience more stress, in terms of boredom, fatigue, and reduced self-esteem, than clerical workers performing the same jobs on conventional type-writers *(Human Factors)*.

In fact, a NIOSH study conducted in San Francisco found that "clerical VDT operators showed higher stress ratings than any other group of workers NIOSH has ever studied, including air-traffic controllers," says Nine-to-Five.

The video screens, for one thing, are sites for sore eyes. Screen users suffer from eyestrain, burning and irritated eyes, and blurred vision much more often than typewriter users who do the same work. VDT operators also complain that the visual side effects don't wear off quickly after work and sometimes carry over into the next day.

Computer operators often feel compelled to maintain an impossible pace that can only lead to burnout. "The computer has sent these women back into the 1950s," says Michael J. Smith, Ph.D., formerly a NIOSH psychologist, now with the University of Wisconsin. "They're feeling the same kind of alienation we used to see in blue-collar workers 25 years ago." As Gregory puts it, "computerization can create the electronic equivalent of an assembly line."

Take, for instance, a woman who processes insurance claims on a VDT. She's sitting in front of the screen, and four claim forms appear on it at once. She fills in the appropriate blank spaces on each form and upon completion four fresh claim forms appear instantaneously, without room for a breather. "We interviewed a woman who had a hallucinatory experience from the stress," Gregory says. "She was very relieved to find out that she wasn't alone in having severe problems with VDT work."

Typewriters vs. video display terminals (VDTs).

Taking your eyestrain home with you.

VDT work led to hallucinations.

The same kind of hectic pace applies to some telephone operators. A computerized "automatic call distributor" puts a new call on the operator's headphones as soon as she finishes the last one.

The machine that behaves like "Big Brother."

There's more. Many VDT clerical workers live in fear that their terminal may "fink" on them. NIOSH investigators have found that "clerical VDT operators were monitored closely by the computer systems, which provided up-to-the-minute performance reports to supervisors on the rate of production and error levels. This produced feelings in the clerical VDT operators that they were being constantly watched by the computer and controlled by the supervisor."

Bad as all this makes VDTs sound, they aren't necessarily malicious. One NIOSH study showed that most newspaper editors and reporters are as happy as clams about computers. Unlike clerical jobs, the journalists' jobs were varied and challenging. Most important, the editors weren't tied to their VDTs "for any set time period and could set their own work pace within deadline limits."

You need to be in control of your work pace.

The health consequences of not being at least partially in control of one's own work pace are significant indeed. They can be seen among the government employees who inspect America's chickens. At various plants throughout the country, these inspectors often stand for eight hours or more in white aprons and watch hundreds of chickens pass by them on hooks at the rate of 16 to 23 per minute. In the three seconds or so that inspectors can spend on each chicken, they must check for 20 different health conditions and decide whether to pass or reject the bird. In many cases, they can't stop or even slow down the inspection line.

Frustration, boredom, and anger cause the inspectors to suffer from several psychosomatic illnesses. Acid indigestion, eyestrain and itchy eyes, sore shoulders, stiffness, and difficulty standing are common among full-time chicken inspectors. They also take a lot of aspirin and frequently call in sick *(Scandinavian Journal of Work, Environment and Health)*.

The plight of the chicken inspectors also demonstrates that people are stressed when they feel they're using less than all of their skills. They also suffer when their tasks are fragmented into meaningless specialization and when they're forced to turn in bad work.

"The inspectors said it was very nerve racking to have

one chicken slip by," says Barbara Wilkes, formerly a psychologist at NIOSH. "And if the line was moving too fast they found themselves reaching down the line as it passed. They said that being forced to do less than their best contributed to nervous conditions such as shakiness."

How chicken inspectors become bird-brains.

Worst of all, Wilkes says, the monotony of a job like inspecting chickens can spill over into a worker's private life. The inspectors she talked to seemed to spend a lot of time trying to unwind after work. The time spent recovering interfered with opportunities to make their private lives more interesting. The same kind of dilemma victimizes auto workers and sawmill employees, Wilkes says.

DECISIONS CAN BE HEALTHY

Heart disease may also be a side effect of machine-paced work. The reason, according to researchers in Sweden and at Columbia University in New York, is that those jobs have a "low decision latitude." The researchers disagree with the conventional wisdom that says an overload of decision making promotes heart trouble among high-level executives. Instead, they contend that making too few decisions at work can increase the risk of heart attack. According to Robert Karasek, Ph.D., of the University of Southern California at Los Angeles, making too few decisions can be as bad for the heart as smoking cigarettes or having a high cholesterol level *(New Scientist)*.

Decision makers are healthier.

If you're wondering how your or your spouse's job ranks on the stress scale, you might be interested in a report issued by NIOSH. A group of government researchers went to Tennessee and studied the health records of 22,000 workers in 130 different occupations. Their mission was to find out which kinds of jobs generated the most stress-related illness, such as heart disease, high blood pressure, ulcers, and nervous disorders. They came up with a surprising and controversial list.

The 12 jobs associated with the most stress-related illness were in this order: laborer, secretary, inspector (such as chicken inspector), lab technician, office manager, foreman, administrator, waiter and waitress, machine operator, farm owner, mine worker, and house painter.

The top 12 high-stress jobs.

An additional 28 occupations tied for 13th place: health technologist, licensed practical nurse, nurse's aide, registered nurse, dental assistant, social worker, health aide, computer programmer, bank teller, teacher's aide, telephone operator, sales manager, sales representative, public relations person, police officer, fire fighter, electrician, plumber, machinist, mechanic, structural metal craftsman,

---

BOX 19: HOW TO GET THE PRIVACY YOU NEED FROM THE "SPACE" YOU DON'T HAVE

Anyone who has to think for a living nowadays has got their hands full . . . or, more accurately, their ears full. Noise and cramped space is the order of the day. Is our work suffering because of it? Are there things we can do to procure the kind of intellectual solitude we need?

Those questions were looked into by a team of experts commissioned by an Ohio-based business firm, and the answer in both cases turned out to be yes: Yes, privacy is important; and yes, we can get more of it.

"When our personal space has been invaded, we are likely to react with discomfort, anxiety, irritation . . . even anger and aggression," says one of the study's consultants, Paul Insel, Ph.D., coauthor of *Core Concepts in Health* (Mayfield Publishing Co.). Perhaps even more important, however, privacy is necessary for "permitting us to carry out self-understanding and self-identity," he adds.

Put these two ideas about privacy together and what you have is a picture of modern-day office life capable of leaving us both hostile and confused.

The situation, however, is not as hopeless as it may appear. The attainment of maximum personal privacy, these experts say, is simply a matter of:

1. evaluating the ways in which your present situation (whether it be at work or at home) is annoying you; and then

2. mustering the personal fortitude to do something about it. Not belligerently, of course, but rather with an appropriate mix of honesty and tact.

For example: To discourage the office motormouth from making you his favorite target, try keeping all the seats in the vicinity of where you work covered with whatever you think it might take to keep him from sitting down. And if he sits on your lunch anyway, that's when you politely announce, "Gosh, I'd love to hear how that Achilles tendon is doing, Joe, but I really am under deadline today." Three consecutive mornings of being under deadline *should* have Joe taking his woesome tale elsewhere.

What follows are some questions and some suggestions for helping you evaluate *and then act upon* your current conditions. Good luck. And may you never have to eat another crushed tuna sandwich again.

BOX 19 — *Continued*

• Does your work area have a door? If so, don't be afraid to use it.

• Is your desk arranged so that you face others? If so, don't be afraid to turn it around.

• Have you thought to personalize your work area with memorabilia from your private life? It's amazing how family photos can make passersby feel like trespassers.

• Do you find it necessary to come to work early and stay late? A definite sign that you're being bothered.

• Do you ever find yourself making off to the restroom for moments of solitude? An even more definite sign that you're being bothered.

• Do you feel obligated to be accessible to your coworkers at all times? If so, you might do better, for all concerned, to make yourself a little harder to come by.

• Do you announce to your coworkers that there are times when you would prefer not to be disturbed? It'll only hurt the first couple of times.

• Does it bother you to have people stop and read things over your shoulder? If so, forget what your parents told you about elbows on the table.

• Do you tend to look up when people pass by? Better to keep focused on your work. Many times eye contact is all a traveling troubadour needs to sit right down and sing a song of woe.

• Is the noise level of your work situation distracting? Earplugs, cotton, or a radio with a headset can help tune it out.

• Are you interrupted in the middle of writing, reading, or making a phone call? Keep pencil, book, or telephone receiver well in hand as a visual reminder to your intruder that you *were*, after all, in the middle of something.

Those are suggestions for the workplace. Now, the home.

• Do you have your own separate room where you can get away and shut the door? If not, you might think about sacrificing a spare bedroom or area in the basement or attic. Your sanity will thank you.

• Are there predictable times during the day or evening when no other family members are home? If so, don't waste them.

• Are you always accessible to those who share your residence? If so, it might not be a bad idea to exact a policy as drastic as "Not to be disturbed unless the sky is falling." You may even find that it improves times that you *are* accessible, as absence has, after all, been shown to make hearts grow fonder.

• Does your house have definite rules governing respect for privacy? If not, try making some . . . and not just with regard to the bathroom.

• Do you ever feel *guilty* for wanting privacy? Don't. As one consulting expert to the privacy study said: Family life often boils down to "trying to maintain a relationship with other people and still maintain yourself." Your need for privacy is a statement about *you*, not your affection for your family. Accept that fact — and express it honestly — and home can be sweet after all.

BOX 20: EASING FRICTION IN OFFICE RELATIONSHIPS

Your relationship with your manager, or with the people you manage, is a vital factor when evaluating your job. If either is rocky, you're probably under a lot of stress.

Sometimes a bad relationship is unmendable. If so, it might just be better to end it. But before taking such a drastic step, why not try to improve the situation? "The average individual has more capability to influence a situation than he gives himself credit for," says Jere Yates, Ph.D., author of *Managing Stress: A Businessperson's Guide* (AMACOM).

To get on the same wavelength with an associate, experts recommend the following five actions:

1. Stop and listen. When we listen to someone talking, we often miss what they're saying because we're already rehearsing our defense. You can misunderstand, and that can make you emotional and angry.

2. Ask for feedback. Make the distinction between an evaluation and feedback. An evaluation is judgmental. Feedback simply means asking for another person's perceptions of what you are doing.

3. Initiate communication. Feuds and misunderstandings last so long because both people are trying to save face and neither will take the first step. Managers respect open and effective communicators.

4. Communicate at an appropriate time and place. Do it in private at an appointed time. If you embarrass the person you're trying to reach, forget it.

5. Learn to negotiate. You've got to ask for or provide a clear statement of job role and performance expectations. Both the manager and employee must reach an agreement on what those roles and expectations are.

If you're feeling stymied by a situation and are not sure how to broach the subject with the other person, you might try putting your grievance down on paper first—not necessarily in the form of a letter to him or her but rather a script in which you create a dialogue between the two of you.

It sounds crazy, but dialogues can be a terrific tool for figuring out what's going on in a relationship. Besides, they give you an opportunity to rehearse before a serious discussion. When it's only a rehearsal, you tend to be more open and honest. And in trying to anticipate what your colleague might say back to your comments, you might gain some real insight as to how you view that person—or what your part in the problem might be.

A great way to start a dialogue is just to say whatever comes into your head, without consciously or deliberately trying to guide it. The same goes for the words you put into the mouth of your colleague. Here's an example:

Me: What's wrong with you? I used to be able to count on you for great ideas. Now in meetings, you stare off in space.

Him: I'm bored.

Me: What is so boring? There are a million challenges a day you could run with.

BOX 20 — *Continued*

Him: You think so?

Me: Why are you so hostile?

Him: Did you ever stop to think that I'm returning what I get?

Me: You think I'm hostile?

Him: Just listen to yourself. Don't be so defensive.

Me: Is it me? Am I your problem?

Him: You're too busy to be a motivator anymore. You just tell me what I do wrong.

Me: So it is me? Why don't you be a little more honest?

Him: Because you really don't want to hear it. You just want me to stop being bored.

Me: I want you to stop being bored because I'm worried about you.

Though the Me character opened the dialogue with a lot of hostility, the subsequent discussion caused him to change his tone completely by the end. Maybe now, when he actually has that big talk with his bored colleague, he'll drop the hostility.

---

railroad switch operator, warehouse worker, clergy member, musician, hairdresser, guard, and watchman.

Of the 28 runner-up jobs, 6 involved health care. Those jobs were stressful because the workers had "a great deal of responsibility for the welfare of their patients without the authority to have complete control over that welfare," the researchers concluded. Also, the necessity of dealing with the sick seemed to leave these workers "emotionally drained."

Health care jobs can be bad news for your health.

Workers in the public sector also made the top 40. These were police officers, fire fighters, and clergy members. Such people perform the nitty-gritty jobs that have to be done, but they receive little recognition or financial reward for it. That could be stress provoking, the researchers suggested.

Conspicuously absent from the list were physicians, lawyers, and executives. Clearly, it's not that these people have "low stress" jobs. It's just that they are in positions where, to a large extent, they can control the stress factors (see Chapter 28, You, Your Own Worst Enemy, and Chapter 30, Mastering Stress: How to Beat Burnout and Enjoy Life). Stressful jobs, Dr. Michael Smith says, are characteristically those where the hours are long, the pay is short,

Doctors, lawyers, and executives can control their stress factors.

BOX 21: BEATING THE SUNDAY NIGHT BLUES

The Sunday night blues: They're also known as the Monday morning blahs. We all experience them from time to time, even those of us who enjoy our work.

But if end-of-the-weekend blues plague you on a regular basis, it's time to reexamine both your work and your leisure habits. You may be overdoing it on both fronts.

That's the advice of Ronald Pies, M.D., a Pennsylvania State University psychiatrist and author of *Inside Psychotherapy: The Patient's Handbook* (George F. Stickley Co.).

Dr. Pies says too many people compartmentalize their lives, working exhaustively through the week and escaping on the weekend into a fantasyland of too many parties and activities.

Then Sunday night arrives and reality hits with a vengeance. Besides being exhausted by their frenetic weekends, they're emotionally unprepared to face the overly stressful workweek ahead.

So how do you keep the spectre of Monday from haunting your Sunday-night sleep?

The central problem may be your job. What have you been escaping from all weekend? "What exactly is it that you don't want to go back to Monday morning?" asks Dr. Pies. "Is there a mismatch between your abilities and the demands made on you? Is there too much stimulation on the job? Do you have control over your time and schedule? Are your goals realistic?"

Once you uncover the problem, work out solutions that give you some breathing space during the week. Arrange priorities better and learn to say no to excessive demands. If you can't alter your situation, you might want to consider looking for a better job.

Look next at your attitudes toward leisure. "I think it's important to have some degree of weekend fun *during* the week," says Dr. Pies. "Don't make such sharp divisions between workdays and pleasure days. If you've had a lousy Monday and Tuesday—go out for dinner Tuesday night. Why wait until Saturday?"

Dr. Pies also recommends exercise, hobbies, and seeing friends through the week—not for a wild bash, but just for a few hours to play cards or talk. "If you integrate small pleasures through the week, you'll be less likely to save it up for weekend binges.

"When the weekend does come, it's merely an elaboration of the things that give you pleasure through the week. Your afterwork leisure pursuits should have as much meaning as your weekend fun."

Finally, says Dr. Pies, work on that sense of humor when you find yourself getting obsessive about work and refusing to take time off through the week. He thinks watching old "M*A*S*H" reruns is a good place to start.

"Those characters can laugh at themselves, their jobs, and the absurdity of their situations. And so should we."

and the pace of the work is dictated by a machine or a superior. Control is absent.

Stress would shrink, researchers say, if the workers were emancipated from assembly or inspection lines and given a variety of tasks to perform every day. Most important, researchers who have studied secretaries, assembly-line workers, and mail sorters almost unanimously agree that much of the stress could be relieved by allowing workers to participate in decisions that affect their work, especially the pace of their work.

Unemployment: On Making It a Positive Experience

J ust a few short years ago, we had an epidemic, one so insidious and widespread that it led the medical journal *Lancet* to wonder if it might not be "the new great plague." One psychiatrist was quoted as calling it "one of the great public-health menaces of all times."

One of the great public-health menaces of all time.

It's called unemployment. It makes people sick.

We all know the hardships a layoff can cause—in money, in self-esteem, and in real fear for the future. Some statistics appearing in print show the jobless/illness quotient to be terribly high, and they may be showing only the tip of that proverbial, always ominous iceberg. According to one source, the 1.4 percent rise in unemployment from 1970 through 1975, of and by itself, may have been responsible for almost 1,000 suicides, nearly 500 cirrhosis of the liver fatalities, and well over 20,000 heart and kidney disease deaths *(Medical World News)*.

Here are some suggestions to help you turn unemployment into a positive experience.

SEE THE OPPORTUNITIES

Unemployment is a stress— and an opportunity.

There's no question, unemployment is a stress. But it can be an opportunity, too. Try to think of it as a chance to reassess your life, find new directions, or just to take a much-needed breather. The key to making it a positive experience: Be good to yourself.

"This can be an enriching experience if you use the

time to focus on your goals, pleasures, or unfinished business," says Nancy Stevenson, an Ohio clinical psychologist who counsels unemployed adults. Don't spend every waking minute job hunting. Put aside some time each day to take a long walk, listen to your favorite music, meditate. "Hobbies, activities you enjoy, and experiences you've put off for a rainy day can also turn a negative experience into a positive one and can leave you fresher, more relaxed for those all-important job interviews."

FACE YOUR FINANCES

Financial pressure can be serious when you're not working, but it may not be quite as bad as you fear. Many people panic when they're unemployed and feel they should take the first job that comes along, which can be a mistake.

Give yourself time by doing a realistic assessment of your finances. "People often have more resources than they realize," says John May, author of the *RIF Survival Handbook: How to Manage Your Money If You're Unemployed* (Tilden Press). Figure out how much money you have, how much money you need to get by each week, and how long your money will last. "By inventorying your resources," says May, "you'll realize that you have, say, five months and two weeks before you have to sell your car." This assessment will give you some time and mental space to get on with the more important priorities of unemployment—relaxation and a rewarding job search.

Inventory your resources. Then get on with relaxation and job hunting.

BE KIND TO YOUR BODY

Taking care of your body is as important as taking care of your mind when you're unemployed. "When times are lean," says Celeste Billhartz, author of *The Complete Book of Job Hunting, Finding, Changing* (Rainbow Collection), "think lean, and be lean."

So keep up a vigorous exercise program and eat wholesome foods. Good nutrition and exercise won't guarantee you a job, but they will help you look and feel your best. When you're home alone all day, it's tempting to start an affair with the fridge—so make sure it's stocked with fresh fruits and vegetables. Avoid starches and sugars that can make you feel and look dragged out and depressed. Add protein to your diet.

Protein—the crucial nutrient for the jobless.

APPRECIATE YOURSELF

Identifying your valuable qualities helps self-esteem and job hunting.

Without work, many people feel like they've lost their identity. Now that you have the time, take a good look at all your valuable qualities. This is important for your job search as well as for your self-esteem.

So even before you look at the marketplace and what jobs are out there, take inventory of your valuable, marketable qualities. You have more than you may think. And when you're aware of them, you'll open up worlds of new possibilities.

Look beyond—and within—whatever job you have now or have had in the past: "The degree to which you identify with your job title is the degree to which you're stuck," says Tom Jackson, author of *How to Get the Job You Want in 28 Days* (E. P. Dutton) and *Guerrilla Tactics in the Job Market* (Bantam) and head of the Career Development Team, Inc., in New York City. "You're not a laid-off social worker; you're a human being with skills and abilities. As a social worker, you're in trouble. As a human being, you have opportunities."

Think of all your skills, expertise, talents, interests, aptitudes, and preferences. You're using just a few of them in your current job. You use different ones at home and in volunteer activities, hobbies, and social settings. Some are just potentials.

What do I have? What do I enjoy?

A job hunt should start with an inventory of your strong points and interests. There are two key questions you must ask yourself, says renowned career expert John Crystal, head of The John C. Crystal Center, a career-development organization in New York City, and coauthor with Richard Bolles of *Where Do I Go from Here with My Life?* (Ten Speed Press). They are: "What do I have?" and "What do I enjoy?" "After all," Crystal says, "to quote the beer commercial, you only go around once in life. You might as well enjoy what you're doing. The most successful people are those who whistle while they work."

WHAT ARE YOUR SKILLS?

Put your skills in for a transfer.

No matter what jobs you've had, the skills you've used can be transferred to other fields, but it's not always easy for us to see ourselves and our work clearly enough to separate skills from the particular job that we do. Here's how one woman's ability to identify her skills helped her find a new career.

Roberta Bryant had a glamour job. As coordinator of artist development for a major record company, she toured the country with rock 'n' roll groups like Chicago and Santana. Her job was high-paced and enormously challenging: handling artists' business affairs, arranging myriad concert details.

And then the recession hit the music industry. When record sales dropped, her department was the first to be cut.

She quickly found another job in the music industry, but seven weeks later that company moved its operations to Europe.

It wasn't until she looked outside the music industry that things clicked. She was hired to be an assistant to the construction developer of a Fifth Avenue skyscraper. What she—and the woman who hired her—saw was that even without any expertise in construction, Bryant's ability to organize people and details was of immense value.

Look outside the industry.

The way Bryant describes her job now you'd almost think she was back on tour with Santana—there's not only challenge and excitement but the substance of what she does. "Like in music, things are never firm in construction. You have to be able to deal with many people of different backgrounds. I work with architects, engineers, construction workers, photographers, the press. Construction is dynamic, growing, and changing."

What you don't know, you can learn.

The fact that she didn't know anything about construction when she took the job didn't turn out to be much of an obstacle—she's making up for lost time now, taking courses for a certificate in construction technology.

Roberta Bryant was able to identify her skills and abilities that can be useful in any field—in her case, organizing and managing skills. There are many such skills.

If you need help assessing your marketable, transferable skills, try this exercise from Celeste Billhartz:

"Get yourself alone with several legal pads. Write down every job you've ever held. Under the job, write every detail of what you did—it's all significant. Include those times you've trained someone, every time you've contributed a new idea, anything cost-saving. Repeat this for every job you've ever had."

Write down every job you've ever held.

Now do the same thing for volunteer activities and

**Translate your accomplish-
ments into action verbs.**

hobbies you've been involved in. If you recruited for the neighborhood association, raised funds for a cause, directed a theater group, those use important skills, too.

Now go over your lists, translating your accomplishments into action verbs like designed, sold, researched, trained, supervised, improved, analyzed, wrote, arranged, negotiated.

Then go back over the list and circle the things you did most often as well as the things you enjoyed most. "Soon you'll begin to see a definite pattern emerging," says Billhartz. That pattern will point you in job directions you might enjoy.

WHAT ARE YOUR INTERESTS, TALENTS, AND HOBBIES?

When you can turn an interest or hobby into a job, you'll truly have a labor of love.

Mimi Brace did it. She was a volunteer for a Ralph Nader's Public Citizen organization in 1974, helping to prepare a study of the nuclear-waste issue. "Information about solar energy kept popping up," she recalls. "I got interested." So she did some more research into solar energy. And she decided she wanted a job installing home solar systems. The research she'd done as a Nader volunteer, plus home carpentry experience, landed her a training position with a company that installed solar-heating systems into homes.

Today, Mimi Brace is Solar Energy Lady, Inc., a one-woman company that installs solar-energy systems. She enjoys the education aspect of her job—teaching people about solar—so much that she's thinking about her next possible career move into politics or education, to spread the word on solar.

**Think about hobbies that
lend themselves to careers.**

Think about ways you could turn your hobbies and interests into full-time jobs. Amateur cooks become professional caterers, pet lovers become animal breeders. Let your imagination go, and write down some of the ideas.

WHAT ARE YOUR AREAS OF EXPERTISE?

Your expertise can help get you a better job—or it can hold you back. There are times when you may have to abandon a specialty to get a better job, especially if your expertise is in a field with dwindling opportunities. But you have many areas of expertise, if you really think about it, and even if one can't get you a better job, another might.

Sue Buske taught music in Illinois high schools. Then she decided to return to school herself for a master's degree in music. When she'd finished her degree and started job hunting again, she found there weren't any music teaching jobs at all.

She started looking around in other fields. She interviewed with an education agency that was making a cable television program about her city's school system. Because of her insider's knowledge of the school system, Sue Buske was hired for the job. That led to more involvement in the world of cable TV. Today, she heads an organization that provides services to individuals and groups interested in the community use of cable.

Think about your fields of expertise. You probably know more than you think you know offhand. Buske, a music teacher, knew more than music. She also knew how the school system operates.

You probably know more than you think.

Jot down some of the different fields, areas, and processes in which you have some expertise.

If you really have no idea what you'd like to do or don't have much work experience, an aptitude test can give you a sense of what you might be good at (check with a career-counseling center or book). You should also think about questions of value and preference, like: Do you prefer working with people or objects? In a business setting or a social service setting? How important is prestige or money? These questions can help set a career direction.

KEEP ON GROWING

This is a time to nurture yourself, says Billhartz. Look into free or inexpensive adult classes at high schools or community colleges to learn a new skill for a job or just for the fun of it. You can also develop new skills through internship programs. You'll help others and get out of the house. You may even acquire contacts that can lead to job opportunities.

Nurture your mind—learn something new.

Remember, you can always learn. "Forget the old wives' tale that old dogs can't learn new tricks," says K. Warner

Schaie, Ph.D., former director of the Gerontology Research Institute at the University of Southern California. Some aspects of intelligence—critical judgment, for example—are actually likely to increase in later years, he says. "People with the least decline in intellectual function are generally the ones who are in good health and lead active lives."

The human ability to learn doesn't decline with age.

J. Michael Warren, Ph.D., agrees, based on what he's found in studies with mice. "If old mice are like old people, human ability to learn new things doesn't necessarily decline with age," says Dr. Warren, who is a professor of psychology at Pennsylvania State University. In his experiment, Dr. Warren tested the ability of mice who were raised in a stimulating enriched learning environment against those who were kept alone in "unfurnished" cages. When both groups of mice had reached 750 days of age (equivalent to 62-year-old people), Dr. Warren set up a large box with an exit at one corner leading to water. Both groups of mice were placed briefly in the box several times when they weren't thirsty. Later, when the same animals *were* thirsty, the procedure was repeated. The "enriched" mice were better able to orient themselves in the big space than the other groups, quickly finding the water they had seen before when they didn't need a drink.

Good health ensures brain power.

"The animals exposed to an enriched environment developed a special, specific set of skills—rather than overall superior intelligence. With humans, of course, it's much more complicated," Dr. Warren says. "But the fact that there are so many people who preserve excellent capacity suggests that as long as you're reasonably healthy, there should be no serious decline in brain power with age. Sure, reaction time gets slower. But the quality of performance, which is the critical thing, does not necessarily deteriorate."

"I encourage people to go back to school, whenever appropriate," Jean Davis, a private career counselor in Evanston, Illinois, says. "Sometimes that's just what's needed. But it's true that people are often resistant to the idea, because they assume tough competition with younger students. From my experience, however, older students who return are quite successful in academic settings."

Adult internships are becoming more popular too. Write for information to: National Society for Internships and Experiential Education, 122 St. Mary's Street, Raleigh, NC 27605 or call (919) 934-7536.

KEEP YOUR EYES AND EARS OPEN

You probably won't get enough ideas fom just brainstorming at your office desk or your living-room couch. Make a resolution to become more aware of what's happening around you—in your business, community, state, and the world.

Read magazines and newspapers—not just the want ads, but the financial and local sections, too—with an eye to job opportunities being created by the changes that you're reading about.

Read the financial and local sections—not just want ads.

As you hear about developments in your area—a new industry in town, a political campaign, a problem—keep your mind open to the possibilities.

For example, if you read about a scientific-instrument company in your town, don't assume they only employ scientists. They also need public-relations experts, technical and advertising copywriters, personnel experts, sales executives—a whole range of different skills and expertises that you may have. Your local Yellow Pages can also tell you what's around.

There are plenty of good career books that describe job options in different fields. The U.S. Department of Labor's *Occupational Outlook Handbook,* for example, describes requirements and projects the economy's needs for hundreds of different professions. Another excellent resource that you'll find in any library is the *Encyclopedia of Associations,* which describes thousands of professional and voluntary organizations. You can call or write many of these associations for career material.

Among the best sources of job information are trade magazines—publications for professionals in the field. They can tell you what's really happening in the field and supply contact names. (Many even carry help-wanted ads.)

Trade magazines: great source of job info.

One of the most powerful research techniques of all is the process of "informational interviewing." This is different from a job interview. "At this point, you're not hunting for a job; you're still gathering information," says John Crystal. Write or call a courteous request to a professional in the field or company that interests you. Explain your background, why the field interests you, that you only need around 15 minutes of his or her time. An informational interview can yield valuable information, if you don't abuse the ground rules. "If you approach people from a research point of view and don't ask them for a job, and if they're truly enthusiastic about what they do, they'll be delighted to talk your arm off," says Crystal. You'll find out if the field is really right for you.

RESEARCH PLUS INITIATIVE

There are literally millions of job hunters out there mailing resumés to box numbers in the help-wanted ads.

So your odds of finding a job that way aren't great. And when you add the fact that most good jobs aren't even advertised in the want ads—well, there must be a better way.

Career experts have developed techniques for finding—even creating—a job for yourself.

There is. Career experts have developed powerful techniques for finding—even creating—a job for yourself. Organizations need skilled and talented people just as much as people need jobs.

"There are all kinds of needs that, if you can meet them, you've got a job," says John Crystal. Usually, people to meet those needs are located through personal contacts, and many needs go unmet. But by taking the initiative yourself, you can discover the needs and make the kind of contact that gets you hired.

The key to success: thorough research, plus plenty of personal initiative.

Research will tell you exactly what the needs are. Once you have a list of organizations where you'd like to work, use trade journals, annual reports, company publications, and informational interviews to find out everything you can about the particular company—its strengths and weaknesses, its plans for the future, and especially the specific skills and qualities required for the job you want.

"One by one match what you can contribute to those particular needs," says Tom Jackson. If there are skills you lack, find out how you can learn them quickly, with a short adult-education course or even by having a friend teach you.

Matching your skills to the company's needs.

Once you know exactly how you can meet their needs, it's time to approach them—whether they have advertised vacancies or not. Here's where the resumé, cover letter, and phone campaign begin. John Crystal says it's helpful to think of this process as making a "business proposal—a proposal tailor-made by you that matches your skills to the company's needs."

Forget your own fears and needs, and focus on "I can." Crystal describes the experience of a laid-off auto-industry accountant who used the business-proposal technique successfully: "He was fascinated by the art world. He had also noticed that few art institutions worked with the efficiency he'd brought to his company. So he went to the museum officers with a business proposal. He said, 'I'm familiar with the art world, and I can bring you red-hot administrative efficiency.' They hired him."

Forget your own fears. Focus on "I can."

Avoid personnel departments completely (unless you want to work in one), Crystal adds. The person you should talk to is someone "who has the authority to accept or reject a business proposal from an outside source."

Avoid personnel departments completely.

Another hint: Asking questions during the interview will give you information you can act on right there. Andrew Sherwood, president of The Goodrich & Sherwood Company, a human-resources and career-consulting firm, calls this "setting up targets." Questions like, "What in my letter was of particular interest to you?" and "What do you see as the organization's weaknesses and strengths?" will give you a sense of what they need—and then you can tell them about the relevant parts of your experiences. "The more targets you can set up—and hit—this way, the more successful you'll be," says Sherwood.

Most job-hunt campaigns look like this, says Tom Jackson: "No, No, No, No, No, No, Yes." Every "No" brings you closer to a "Yes." Keep that in mind when you need motivation—even a rejection can be a step in the direction of a new job.

HELP FROM YOUR FRIENDS

Whether you're employed or not, a job-hunting support group can double your effectiveness, says career expert Tom Jackson. Using a good step-by-step job-search strategy book—like Jackson's *Guerrilla Tactics in the Job Market* or Richard Bolles's *What Color Is Your Parachute?* (Ten Speed Press)—the group can work together and plan what each member should do each week. With enough members you may even be able to hire your own career counselor to come in for a few sessions.

KNOW WHEN YOU NEED MORE HELP

Career counselors won't find a job for you, but they can help you assess your talents. They can suggest job-hunting strategies or rehearse interviewing with you. Check with your local universities for a reputable counselor or write to Catalyst, 14 E. 60th Street, New York, NY 10022 (212) 759-9700, for a list of resource centers that can give you more information. Beware of counselors charging exorbitant fees; the service shouldn't cost more than $200.

BOX 22: STILL STANDING AFTER THE AX FALLS? HERE'S HELP FOR SURVIVORS

It's no secret that losing your job is tough. What most people don't know is the fact that keeping your job, while all around you others are losing theirs, can be just as tough.

"What we need to look at are those who aren't unemployed, but who are subjected to spillover effects by virtue of the fact that they are spared in a layoff—they survive," says psychologist Marilyn Machlowitz, Ph.D.

"Survivor guilt" is the official name of the malady, says Dr. Machlowitz, and it's not something new. In fact, the term and the idea came from the psychological aftershocks experienced by survivors of the Holocaust and Hiroshima. Certainly, unemployment and recession haven't the scope of those two events, but the emotional, social, and eventually physiological side effects on the "why-me-and-not-them" survivors have a good deal in common.

"The employer or the union may think that these people are grateful, glad, relieved—but they're not always that

way," explains Dr. Machlowitz. "The psychological employment contract, if not the actual employment contract, has been violated. In a certain way, there's a betrayal."

"There's a sense that the other shoe could drop at any minute: 'I could be next.' There's also the practical difficulty and guilt that ensues when soon-to-be-laid-off colleagues want to gripe and groan and bitch and moan. You want to listen to them—you feel you owe them something—but you can't get anything done.

"There's also a complicated avoidance of each other that goes on. We've all seen how sometimes people who have jobs regard individuals who've been singled out in a firing as if termination were contagious. And there is probably great antagonism among the survivors—survival of the fittest, jockeying for position.

"The gossip mill escalates, and productivity declines."

You become tense because your friends are leaving but you're staying; you feel stress because you fall behind

BOX 22 — *Continued*

schedule. You get nervous for fear that, unless you can do a better-than-great job, you're the next to go. A wave of anxiety washes over you, and the undertow threatens to pull you away from security and both mental and physical health.

"The survivors," says Dr. Machlowitz, "are often likely to leave their jobs even though they don't have to. They're often so scared, they're often so mad, that they wind up being the people who leave, or who are more apt to take another opportunity if it presents itself, although they were the very ones the company struggled to save."

If you are one of the survivors, or could be, there are some very important things to know to help you over the guilt (and associated illnesses) hump.

1. "A new fact of working life," says Dr. Machlowitz, "is not to expect job security. Expect insecurity. There used to be this kind of trade-off where organizations could expect and extract loyalty, and an individual in exchange could expect lifetime employment. Neither of those components really exists anymore, and it's self-defeating to look for them. So, as with any other stressor, knowing that it can happen minimizes tension rather than heightens it."

2. "Be a human being. Extend yourself to the people who've been laid off— they may feel funny about approaching you. It's sort of trite, but apply the Golden Rule: Do unto others as you would want them to do unto you in the same circumstances."

3. "Seek as much information as you can. Is this the last layoff? What's going to happen next? Look around and get the whole picture. You may be scared of the knowledge, but being an ostrich doesn't pay."

4. "Keep working. If necessary, this may mean shutting your door or working at home for a little while, just to stay clear of the people cleaning out their desks, yelling on the phone, even crying.

"Most of all," advises Dr. Machlowitz, "be prepared for this. Know that it exists. That will really lessen its wallop."

27
Everyday Hassles: Choosing the Road of Highest Stress Resistance

H ow do you spell success? Until recently, most people would have answered M-O-N-E-Y, along with all the goodies it could buy—big houses, fancy cars, furs, jewels. But not anymore, according to a Gallup poll published in *Success* magazine. Today's symbols of material wealth ranked lowest on a list of personal success factors. Participants instead cited the things money *can't* buy—enjoyable job, happy family, peace of mind, good friends, and above all, good health.

It may be that people are beginning to realize that the "good life"—replete with exotic car (that you can't get serviced), country home (that's an hour-plus commute from your workplace), and swimming pool (that's a maintenance migraine)—may not be conducive to good health.

The bottom line is this: Does your lifestyle bring you happiness or just hassles? Your answer says more about your standard of living than the size of your house or number of cars you can fit in your garage. After all, if your upper-income-bracket is earning you an ulcer, angina, a drinking problem, and another divorce, then what good is it?

"Income isn't everything," says Richard N. Farmer, Ph.D., a professor at the Indiana University School of Business. "A living standard also depends on such factors as good health, quality schools, freedom from pollution, and other amenities." In a word, happiness.

"Considerations of this sort lead me to propose the Hassle Factor as a microsocial measure for standards of living," says Dr. Farmer. He has organized this Hassle

Money can't buy the important things in life.

The "good life" may be fraught with hassles.

A happy life is really the "good life."

Factor in the form of a test, which anyone can take as a way of determining just how enviable his lot in life really is. Here's how the test works. (It's a little complicated, but that's why it's good.)

Dr. Farmer has identified 15 aspects of daily living that he feels are potential sources of hassle. By grading each (on a scale of 0 to 10), first in terms of its importance to you and then in terms of its quality, you come up with a numerical assessment of just how hassling each is to your life. For example:

Rate your lifestyle on these 15 potential sources of hassle.

If it's very important to you that you live in an area with good schools because you've got children, rate schools a 10 in terms of importance. Now rate the quality of your schools.

If your schools stack up to only about a 2, the difference between what you would like (a 10×10 situation) and what you've got (a 10×2 situation) is a great one (100 minus 20). It is this degree of discrepancy that Dr. Farmer's scoring system ingeniously takes into account. For indeed, the degree to which any of us are bothered by our environment is directly proportional to the degree to which we care. Dr. Farmer's categories are as follows. (We'll walk you through the first category to get you started.)

Bureaucracies. If you don't mind gross incompetence on the part of the people responsible for instrumenting the legalities in your life, you're lucky. Give the bureaucracies in your area a 5 or less in terms of their importance to you. But if administrative ineptitude drives you nuts, chalk up a 6 or above in the importance department.

If administrative ineptitude drives you nuts, don't fight city hall.

Now decide just how bumbling the bureaucrats in your area really are. If you had to wait a month to get a permit just to put up a fence around your garden (and lost your lettuce in the interim), rate the buffoons responsible for that early harvest accordingly.

Have the idea? Two scores: One for importance, the other for quality. When you arrive at these ratings for each category, enter them on the score sheet on page 235. Dr. Farmer's other categories are as follows. (Kindly accept our exaggerations as representing "0" situations.)

Two scores: one for importance, the other for quality.

Shopping facilities. If securing a quart of milk requires the use of a gallon of gasoline, you're being hassled.

Crime. If an evening stroll in your neighborhood is looked upon as a form of suicide, you're being hassled.

Medical care. If there's only one doctor in a 50-mile

radius, and he also sees dogs, cats, pigs, and goats, that's a hassle.

Commuting. If getting to work takes more out of you than being there, that qualifies as a hassle.

Repairmen. If the last time you called a plumber about a clogged toilet the reply was, "Sure, bring it in," that, too, constitutes a hassle.

Neighbors. If you live next to a teenager who's practicing late into the night to become a rock star, there's a strong chance you're being hassled.

Utilities. If your telephone company staffs only one repairman (who also works another job), again, odds are you're being hassled.

Pollution. City living has its advantages, but black lung is not one of them. Daily "stay inside" air-quality ratings are definitely a hassle.

Recreation. If getting to the nearest opera would involve plane fare, you're being hassled.

Education. If school strikes have your 16-year-old still unsure of the multiplication tables, you are *both* being hassled.

Climate. A three-bedroom Cape in Death Valley, for whatever price, is a hassle.

Health. If as much as you love your high-powered job and hyperactive lifestyle, you're not too happy about what it's doing to your body, you're being hassled. If your job is killing you, give it a 3 or less. But if it's giving you a kick in the rear to *improve* your health, give it a 7 or above.

Wealth. It's important to feel you're being paid what you think you're worth. If you're happy with your salary, give it a 7 or above. But if you're displeased with it, give it a 5 or less.

Happiness. It's what Dr. Farmer's Hassle Index is all about. A 10 if your life is immensely gratifying; a 0 if you have trouble facing it every morning.

By having some fun with Dr. Farmer's Hassle Index, we have not meant to diminish its importance. Because what are hassles if not insidious forms of stress?

So what do we do about the hassles in our lives?

We do our best to eliminate or at least minimize them.

Why do you live and work as you do?

Must you live and work as you do?

These are, of course questions that only you can an-

Sidenotes:

If getting to work is more trouble than being there, that's a hassle.

If traffic jams and pollution have you down, city life is a hassle.

If your job is killing you, give it a 3 or less.

Hassles are insidious forms of stress.

BOX 23: HASSLE INDEX SCORE SHEET

Category	The Importance of It	The Quality of It	Combined Score (Importance × Quality)
Bureaucracies			
Shopping facilities			
Crime			
Medical care			
Commuting			
Repairmen			
Neighbors			
Utilities			
Pollution			
Recreation			
Education			
Climate			
Health			
Wealth			
Happiness			

Total Score _____

To determine your overall Hassle Index (the higher the better) divide your total score by your highest possible score (determined by multiplying the sum total of your importance scores by 10).

For example: If your total score comes to 600, and the sum of your importance scores comes to 100, divide 600 by 100 times 10 (1,000). Your Hassle Index, in this case, would be .600. Got that?

$$\frac{\text{Total Score}}{\text{Highest Possible Score}} = \text{Your Hassle Index}$$

The closer your total score comes to equaling your highest possible score, the less hassle there is in your life—so a score of 1.0 (100 percent) would be utopia. But Dr. Farmer says that any score of 80 percent or above means you are living a life that is commendably hassle-free.

Reprinted by permission of the publisher from "The Standard of Living and the Hassle Factor" by Richard N. Farmer, Ph.D., in *Business Horizons,* December 1980, pp. 7-10.

swer—but you can't do that until you've at least asked them. Indeed, at the root of many of the hassles in our lives is the simple fact that we do not take the time to analyze them.

They're tough questions, but ones that life is too short not to answer.

Section referring to Dr. Farmer reprinted by permission of the publisher from "The Standard of Living and the Hassle Factor" by Richard N. Farmer, Ph.D., in *Business Horizons,* December 1980, pp. 7-10.

IV

PART **VI**

Healthful Living in a Stressful World

You, Your Own Worst Enemy

Tricia and Jan grew up in the same neighborhood. Same high school. Same universe of friends. Same dreams of family and career. But now, their differences are black and white. Tricia, who has "everything going for her"—a secure home life, two healthy kids, an emotionally fulfilling and financially rewarding job—is unhappy, depressed, and undergoing therapy. Jan, who's going through a particularly trying period—her husband's been in and out of the hospital with a difficult diabetic condition, she's had two miscarriages, and her once-promising career has stalled—is forever optimistic, even jovial.

Unhappiness is not necessarily the result of environment or situations.

Frank and Jerry work side by side in the same office. Same nagging boss. Same impossible deadlines. Same cramped and noisy office quarters. Same meager salary (with the same basic financial obligations). Frank develops an ulcer; Jerry doesn't.

What accounts for the difference between happiness and misery, health and illness?

Obviously, this is a question with no simple answer. There are a million factors that affect our attitudes and vulnerability to illness—not the least of which, we'd like to think, include heredity and the hand of fate. But many researchers who are studying this phenomenon are convinced that the deciding factor is firmly in our control. Happiness or misery, health or illness, they say, are choices each of us makes.

Happiness or misery is a choice we make.

That misfortune is not misfortune at all, but our own

doing, is not the easiest concept to accept, says psychologist Dennis T. Jaffe, Ph.D., co-director of the Center for Health Studies at Saybrook Institute, San Francisco. If you have trouble swallowing that notion, don't worry. How you got to your present state of emotional and physical health isn't so important, Dr. Jaffe explains. What is important is knowing that you can take control of the situation now—that achieving happiness and health is totally within your power. It's your decision.

How we set ourselves up for misery.

To do this, however, it's necessary to understand how we set ourselves up for misery in the first place; how we unconsciously—and sometimes, consciously—undermine our own well-being; in short, how we sabotage our best chances for happiness and the good health that comes with it.

No one is more qualified to speak on this than Dr. Dennis Jaffe. A Yale-trained clinical psychologist, Dr. Jaffe has helped thousands of people suffering from depression, burnout, and a whole host of physical ailments recognize and reverse their own self-destructive attitudes. He has also authored, edited, and contributed to numerous books related to the power of the mind over the body, including *Healing from Within* (Alfred A. Knopf, Inc.), *Mind, Body and Health* (Human Sciences Press), and *From Burnout to Balance* (McGraw-Hill).

Here, then, our conversation with Dennis Jaffe.

Question: If, as psychologists tell us, happiness is a choice we make, why would anyone choose to be miserable?

Dennis Jaffe, Ph.D.: Usually it's an unconscious choice based on negative thought patterns developed while growing up. If you continually feel frustrated by negative events you may eventually develop patterns of thinking such as "I'll never get what I want" or "I know it won't work; it never does." This leads to a deeply ingrained belief that happiness is unattainable. The rest becomes a self-fulfilling prophesy.

Question: Is it possible to deprogram negative thought patterns?

Changing our belief structure.

Dr. Jaffe: Yes, it is. But you have to keep in mind that if we spend a long time learning these negative things, it's going to take a long time to unlearn them. Changing our belief structure is not a short term process. It involves re-education, positive imagery, and psychotherapy.

CHOOSING HAPPINESS

Question: What's the most difficult thing for most people to re-learn?

Dr. Jaffe: That you can't go around blaming the world for your unhappiness. If you're unhappy, it's your choice.

I do a lot of stress management workshops and people come in all the time complaining that they've been victimized, that their environment is driving them crazy, that they're collapsing under the weight of stress. They see their problem as being external. The actual fact is, stress has to do with the interaction between a changing environment and you. You see, it's not the stress that drives you crazy. It's your own response to that stress that's causing the problem. In other words, a high-stress job won't make you sick. But if you don't pay attention to your body and know your own limits and needs in relating to this job, that could conceivably make you ill.

A high-stress job won't make you ill.

Question: We're all aware of the type of people who seem to superimpose stress on their lives, setting unrealistic goals, working against the clock, rejecting anything less than perfect, delegating few tasks because "no one can do it like I can." Social scientists have labeled this collection of traits the Type A personality. But by referring to this pattern of behavior as a "personality," they suggest to us that it is something inherent to our character, that we are "by nature" driven to behave that way. Not surprisingly, too, people so possessed—the workaholics, perfectionists, worriers— often resign themselves to an I-can't-help-myself-I-just-am state of mind. How much control do we really have over a self-destructive personality?

Dr. Jaffe: That depends on your motivation to change.

First let me say that Type A is not a personality. That is a misconception that's perpetuated by many people in my field. When you call something a personality, you make it seem unnecessarily rigid. Unchangeable. But when you think of Type A as a series of behavior patterns, you see that each one of those patterns is nothing more than a bad habit. You can work on changing a habit. It's difficult and it takes time, but you can do it. You can change.

Type A is a series of behavior patterns—each one a bad habit.

HELPLESSNESS, HOPELESSNESS

Question: Are there other behavior patterns that can increase our susceptibility to, say, cancer or other illnesses?

If you give up, your immune system may, too.

Dr. Jaffe: The cancer pattern is well-established in the literature. It's characterized by feelings of helplessness and hopelessness—the sense that you've been victimized by factors beyond your control and that you have no power to change that.

In recent years we've discovered that this same pattern of behavior is connected to other illnesses. Rheumatoid arthritis. Allergies. Any immune-related diseases—including Autoimmune Deficiency Syndrome (AIDS). It's as if your immune system is acting analogously with your behavior. You're not trying to change your life or take care of yourself—in essence, you've just given up—and your immune system says, well if you've given up, so will I. The result is that the immune system becomes depressed and you are susceptible to a whole host of illnesses.

Question: Has the Type A behavior likewise been linked to other illnesses beyond heart disease?

Dr. Jaffe: Oh yes. Type A activity—being super-charged—can burn out your circulatory system and gastric system. So, in addition to heart attack, you find that people who behave this way very often suffer from hypertension, chronic headaches, ulcers, colitis.

Over-control and under-control.

I have a theory that there are essentially two different types of destructive behavior patterns: One has to do with over-control—the Type A. The other has to do with under-control—the helplessness/hopelessness syndrome. Both relate to stress-coping styles. And the key word here is "control."

Now there are all types of coping styles that fall between these two extreme poles of under- or over-control. The optimal behavior falls right in the middle—the point of balance. I call it optimal control. The person who practices optimal control—the healthy person—seems to actively take care of the things that need to be taken care of and has the capacity to say no, that's not my problem, I'm not going to waste my energy worrying about things beyond my control. He's got a realistic sense of personal power—not overpowered or underpowered.

TUNING IN

Question: How do you keep yourself in check then, monitoring your stress responses to ensure that you're maintaining "optimal control"?

Dr. Jaffe: The key to the process is self-awareness. If you look at burned-out executives, people with health problems people who have difficulty coping with stress, you'll find that they all have a common characteristic: They do not tune in to their bodies. They're not aware, until things really go awry, that stress is in fact taking its toll daily and needs to be countered somehow with a healthful, enriching activity.

Self-awareness: the key to optimal control.

For example, if you begin to become aware of the effect of your work patterns on your body, you might realize that you need to do something to balance your rhythms. For instance, if you're sitting at a desk typing for eight hours straight, even taking your lunch at your desk, you may experiment by going to a health club at noon and then eating a carrot and bowl of soup or some yogurt. Or maybe what you need is to take a walk in the park after work. Then monitor yourself to see if that makes a difference in your energy level. People don't understand that they need to listen to their bodies and exert control over their lives so that they are able to respond. That's where time management and planning come in.

Question: Most people would characterize your lifestyle as high stress. You lecture all over the country, shuttle between offices in San Francisco and Los Angeles every week, work with five different institutions, conduct workshops, write books, see clients, and teach. Can you give us some specific examples of how you minimize the effect this lifestyle has on your outlook and health?

Counteracting a high-stress lifestyle.

Dr. Jaffe: I don't have a routine—I can't because my days are so varied. But I maintain total control. I can cancel anything and I frequently do. Last week, for example, I felt overloaded so I canceled my plans to attend a conference. I'm also devastatingly well organized and I know how to set priorities. I never sweat the small stuff. But I tackle the important things according to their order of priority. I also schedule a lot of breaks, including fitness breaks.

NATURAL PROTECTION

Question: Are all people who handle stress well good organizers and time managers, or are some people just naturally stress-resistant?

Born to be stress-resistant.

Dr. Jaffe: Some people have the natural advantage of

being physiologically tougher than others. It's the same way with athletics: Some people are just better tennis players than others.

But that doesn't mean that those of us who get frazzled by minor hassles were born to burn out on stress. We just have to learn how to relate differently to ourselves. Suppose, for example, you feel hassled by an impolite sales clerk. You can choose to either shrug it off and say to yourself, "She must be having a bad day," or take the affront personally and ask yourself, "Why does this always happen to me?!" Choosing the latter will cause your anger to escalate—a self-defeating response. You see, the clerk isn't really important. What's important is your response, which very often is based on your own self-esteem.

Anger is as bad as smoking.

It's a terrible health habit to get angry and hassled all the time. It's as bad as smoking.

Question: Do you believe there's an accident-prone behavior pattern?

Dr. Jaffe: Yes. In fact, it too can be related to a stress response. Let's say you're walking down the street and you're so tense and preoccupied with problems that you're not paying attention. So you trip on a curb and break your arm. That's obviously related to your inability to deal with stress. When you haven't learned how to defuse your reactions to stress, you become uptight, exhausted, distracted. Of course, you're going to be more susceptible to accidents.

SELF-FULFILLING PROPHESY

Question: We occasionally read about a person who's fallen ill with cancer or dies on an anniversary date of a parent's illness or death. How much of this is the result of heredity and how much the result of emotional/psychological factors?

Genes are not timed release capsules.

Dr. Jaffe: Genes are not timed release capsules. Anniversary reactions are related to emotional processes. If you have a heart attack on the anniversary of your father's death, it's not genetically predisposed. It's caused by your own identification with your father and your expectation that you'll be like him. In a way, it's an exaggerated form of family loyalty. Subconsciously, you feel that it would be disloyal to your father's memory to live longer than he lived.

Question: Can you recall such a case?

Dr. Jaffe: I had a client in his late 40s who suddenly began having anxiety attacks, really debilitating panic episodes that would come on any time of the day—but especially when he was driving in a car.

As we talked he filled me in on his medical history and family health history. It came out that both his parents died in a car accident when he was 13 years old. They were in their late 40s. Obviously, he was remembering this experience and wondering whether it was going to happen to him—which is what brought on the panic attack in cars. But the interesting thing is, he never made the connection between his parents' death and his own fears. I pointed it out. You see, he's not consciously afraid of following his parents' fate. This is something that is happening at an unconscious level.

Unconscious fears become a negative form of wishful thinking.

Question: How can we deprogram these thoughts?

Dr. Jaffe: One thing I taught this client was relaxation. Whenever he felt an anxiety attack coming on, I suggested that he pull over to the side of the road, turn off the car and just sit quietly for awhile breathing deeply and meditating to calm him down.

The second part of the therapy involved awareness. Once you explore your fears and become aware of any connections between past experiences and present difficulties, then you can come to realize that this is not something beyond your control. You can choose not to be affected. Affirmations help. For example, while you're meditating, you can tell yourself that it's OK to live longer than your parents.

You can choose not to be affected.

YOUR OWN BEST FRIEND

Question: We've talked a lot about how we can undo negative patterns that we've developed while we were growing up. What advice can you give to today's parents on how to prevent this negative patterning in the first place? How can we teach our children how to be their own best friends instead of their own worst enemies?

Dr. Jaffe: The most important thing anyone can teach their children is how to tune in to themselves. Children should be encouraged to become aware of their feelings and to express them. That's not to say that you have little

Encourage children to express their feelings.

monsters running around screaming out of control. It means that your children feel comfortable sharing their feelings with you and that you're there to listen.

It's also important to build children's self-esteem, giving them a real positive sense of themselves. That comes with a lot of positive praise and reinforcement. But praise for the right reasons. It's not enough to tell kids they're great for doing nothing. You should be complimenting them on their accomplishments.

How challenges help build self-esteem.

New studies have underlined the importance of challenge in building children's self-esteem. By offering your children a series of challenges, their own sense of accomplishment becomes enhanced. Initially, the external support (you telling them how well they performed) is very important. But as they grow up, their own internal self-esteem becomes most important. By the time they're 8, 9, or 10 years old, the external support isn't important to them. What's important is mastery. It's more powerful for children to feel that they can hit a home run or ride a two-wheeler than to have their parents coddling them with meaningless compliments.

The Best of the
Relaxation Techniques

Y ou breathe 11 times per minute, not the usual 16 to 20. And each breath takes in about 5 percent less oxygen, each exhale contains less carbon dioxide. Your heart rate slows by about three beats per minute and blood pressure decreases. Your skin resistance—the same measurment that's taken during a lie detector test—is some 300 times higher than normal, a sign that anxiety is at an absolute minimum. Blood flow to the brain increases by 25 percent. Even the electrical activity of your brain changes. The "brain waves" that usually flow at random become a synchronized and even field. And the alpha waves, which are associated with a feeling of relaxation and well-being, increase in frequency. But you're not trying to do any of it. It's all happening naturally, easily.

You're simply practicing a meditation-relaxation technique that activates your body's own relaxation response.

First described by Herbert Benson, M.D., a cardiologist and associate professor of medicine at Harvard Medical School, the relaxation response is our protective mechanism against overreaction to stress.

Physiologist Mary Asterita, Ph.D., of the Indiana University School of Medicine, explains:

"In the stress response you escalate the sympathetic nervous system. In the relaxation response, you de-escalate the sympathetic nervous system. In the stress response your pupils dilate, your hearing becomes more acute, your blood pressure increases, your heart rate increases, respiration rate increases, circulation changes and moves away

Activating your body's own relaxation response.

A natural reaction to counter overreaction to stress.

TABLE 7: Proof Positive That TM Produces Deep Relaxation

This graph, from a 1973 British study, illustrates the profound effect Transcendental Meditation (TM) has on skin resistance, the same measurement that's taken during a lie detector test to determine the body's level of anxiety or relaxation. As you can see, skin resistance rose signifcantly (an indication of deep relaxation) in persons practicing TM. By comparison, people in the control group showed relatively small fluctuations in skin resistance.

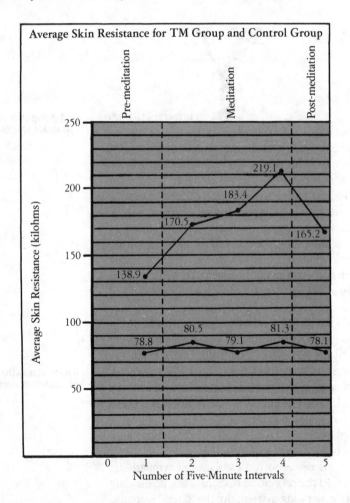

Adapted from "An Investigation into the Changes in Skin Resistance during the Transcendental Meditation Technique" by Gina Laurie in *Scientific Research on the Transcendental Meditation Program*. Maharishi European Research University Press, p. 219.

from the periphery (into the muscles and vital organs) and you become pale. These are just some of the physiological responses that may occur. The relaxation response is the exact opposite."

It's no wonder, then, that people who regularly practice a relaxation technique, like meditation, are less anxious and tense and better able to resist stress. They also report feeling happier—more optimistic, self-confident, energetic, and productive. Research, too, has demonstrated that the relaxation response can counter the cumulative impact of stress on your health.

Feel more energetic, optimistic, and confident.

A few years ago, for example, over 150 employees of the New York Telephone Company learned to evoke the relaxation response. Five months later, they had less anxiety, high blood pressure, and insomnia. They also found it easier to quit smoking, cut down on heavy drinking, or lose weight. And they felt more assertive and happier.

Numerous studies confirm the profound effect meditation has on lowering blood pressure—and recently, on lowering cholesterol levels—which makes it particularly beneficial to heart health. But deep relaxation remains its key benefit.

Lowering blood pressure and cholesterol for better heart health.

HOW THE RELAXATION RESPONSE WORKS

Unfortunately, the stress response occurs automatically but, as Dr. Benson points out, the relaxation response must be "consciously and purposefully evoked." And lounging about on a La-Z-Boy recliner won't do it. To elicit the relaxation response you've got to get yourself into an altered state of consciousness.

Entering a healing state of relaxation.

That may sound mystical but, as Dr. Benson explains, an "altered state" merely refers to a level of consciousness that we don't ordinarily experience. If you've ever slipped into a trancelike state of wakefulness while gazing out a window or driving on a monotonous stretch of highway, you've already experienced altered consciousness. The relaxation response is evoked at another level, one that doesn't usually occur spontaneously and which is described by researchers as a state of profound rest and heightened awareness.

Transcendental Meditation (TM) is one of the Western world's oldest and most scientifically documented tech-

Meditation and other proven techniques to beat stress.

TABLE 8: Personality Plus: The Psychological
Benefits of TM

In a comparison study of 49 meditators and a group of nonmeditators matched
by age and sex, West German researchers
found significant personality differences.

(The chart below shows how meditators
increased positive traits and decreased
negative ones. The nonmeditators showed
little change.)

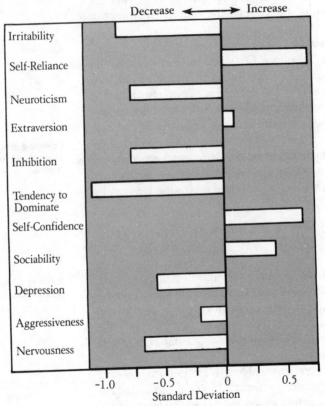

Decrease ◄——► Increase

Irritability

Self-Reliance

Neuroticism

Extraversion

Inhibition

Tendency to
Dominate

Self-Confidence

Sociability

Depression

Aggressiveness

Nervousness

-1.0   -0.5   0   0.5
Standard Deviation

Adapted from "Study of Personality Changes Resulting from the Transcendental Meditation Program:
Freiburger Personality Inventory" by T. Fehr, U. Nerstheimer, and S. Torber in *Scientific Research on
the Transcendental Meditation Program.* Maharishi European Research University Press, p. 421.

niques known to elicit this response. A revised and simpli-
fied form of Yoga, it is the method on which most other
meditation techniques are patterned. Unfortunately, TM is
cloaked in a somewhat ritualistic $400+ program. But for

the cost of a book you can learn everything you need to know to practice a demystified version of TM—or one of several other effective relaxation techniques including progressive relaxation, autogenic training, and deep breathing and visualization. Although all these techniques are quite different in process, research tells us that they produce similar physiological changes (see Table 9).

Here, then, is what to expect from TM and its alternatives plus some practical advice to get you started on five of the best relaxation techniques.

TRANSCENDENTAL MEDITATION

TM has been around for more than 25 years, and as the granddaddy of relaxation techniques, it's the one most celebrated *and* criticized. Dr. Benson first discovered the relaxation response while studying people who practiced TM. And based on the number of TM-related research projects still under way, it appears the scientific fascination with this meditation method has not worn off. According to TM spokesperson Sam Katz, from the Maharishi International University in Washington, D.C. (headquarters in Fairfield, Iowa), there are to date "over 350 scientific studies that show TM is beneficial." No other technique has anywhere near the same amount of scientific support.

TM: a simple technique with profound results.

Still, TM is a remarkably simple technique. Dr. Benson describes the process:

"A trained instructor gives you a secret word or sound or phrase, a mantra, which you promise not to divulge. This sound is allegedly chosen to suit the individual and is to be silently 'perceived.' The meditator receives the mantra from his teacher and then repeats it mentally over and over again while sitting in a comfortable position. . . . Meditators are told to assume a passive attitude and if other thoughts come into mind to disregard them, going back to the mantra. Practitioners are advised to meditate 20 minutes in the morning, usually before breakfast, and 20 minutes in the evening, usually before dinner."

Learning the technique at any one of the 450 TM centers in the United States costs around $400 for a seven-lesson course. So for this one, you have to weigh that cost against the benefits: standard instruction by a qualified teacher and a huge body of scientific research that says TM works.

Learning to relax in seven easy lessons.

DR. BENSON'S MEDITATION-RELAXATION TECHNIQUE

Credit Dr. Herbert Benson with validating the benefits of meditation and removing some of the mystique.
Thanks to him, and his bestselling book *The Relaxation
Response* (William Morrow & Co.), millions—from Main
Street to Wall Street—now practice TM or a variation
thereof. One of the most popular TM takeoffs is Benson's
own method, which focuses on the very essence of meditation.

**For best results, don't
fall asleep.**

Like TM, Benson's technique for eliciting the relaxation response is best performed twice a day for 10 to 20
minutes, preferably before meals when you are less likely to
fall asleep (dozing off may signal the onset of relaxation but
it curtails the full benefit of the relaxation response, Benson
says). However, Benson's technique allows for more individual flexibility. Whereas TM trainers would insist that two
20-minute meditation sessions each day are absolutely necessary for the success of the program, Dr. Benson suggests

TABLE 9: Physiological Changes during Relaxation
Response: How Various Techniques Measure Up

Technique	Physiologic Measurement	
	Oxygen Consumption	Respiratory Rate
Transcendental Meditation	Decreases	Decreases
Zen and Yoga	Decreases	Decreases
Autogenic Training	Not measured	Decreases
Progressive Relaxation	Not measured	Not measured
Hypnosis with Suggested Deep Relaxation	Decreases	Decreases

Reprinted by permission of the publisher from *The Relaxation Response*, Herbert
Benson, M.D. (New York: William Morrow & Co., Inc.), pp. 70-71.

that, while that's the optimum, practicing the technique once a day for 20 minutes will have a favorable effect as well. Adherence to an inconvenient relaxation routine can create more tension that it helps to alleviate, he cautions. Now, for his technique:

SEVEN STEPS TO RELAXATION

1. Find a quiet environment free of distractions. A private room—away from telephones, street noise, and other interruptions—is your best bet. If you need any bit of paraphernalia to perform meditation, it may be a do-not-disturb sign.

2. Choose a word or phrase—a mantra—to focus on. Dr. Benson recommends the word "one." But you may prefer something else, like "love" or "peace." It's nice if the word has special meaning to you but it can be nonsensical too, perhaps a sound or series of sounds that have a sooth-ing tone (see Box 24). Once you pick your word, however,

Word associations that signal peace of mind.

Heart Rate	Alpha Waves	Blood Pressure	Muscle Tension
Decreases	Increases	Decreases*	Not measured
Decreases	Increases	Decreases*	Not measured
Decreases	Increases	Inconclusive results	Decreases
Not measured	Not measured	Inconclusive results	Decreases
Decreases	Not measured	Inconclusive results	Not measured

*In patients with elevated blood pressure.

BOX 24: PASSWORDS TO DEEPER RELAXATION

Here's an interesting little experiment for you to try.

In a place where you're likely to enjoy an undisturbed minute of quiet, close your eyes and slowly repeat out loud a word like calm, ocean, or home. Don't think about what the word means, just concentrate on the sound—especially the nasal, droning ending.

Feel more relaxed? Less angry and harried? Well, don't be surprised. Scientists, too, are discovering the soul-soothing properties of words.

"There is a magic to words—they have potent healing properties," says Lawrence Furst, Ph.D., professor of behavioral science at Temple University in Philadelphia.

Dr. Furst and colleague Donald R. Morse, D.D.S., are trying to unravel just how a batch of sounds can work miracles.

They've looked at the way words can serve as passports to a calm state of mind, which they see as an antidote to our society's anxiety epidemic. They've published their conclusions in several papers as well as in a book, *Stress for Success* (Van Nostrand Reinhold).

Sounds, Drs. Furst and Morse have discovered, are nature's tranquilizers. And, interestingly, the word doesn't have to have any meaning at all. The key to inducing the therapeutic calm of meditation is the final sound left behind to resonate through the mind and set up what might be dubbed physiological "good vibrations."

The end letters m and n, with their almost hypnotic drone, carry the most meditative weight in this regard—as in the words calm, ocean, and home.

"These vibrating sounds create a synchrony of brain waves, and this translates into a calm we can readily see," notes Dr. Furst.

"Heart and pulse rates slow, blood pressure decreases, oxygen consumption goes down," explains Dr. Morse.

This may be the reason why the Sanskrit word "om," which has no meaning but does have a beautiful droning sound, is the chosen word for many Western meditators.

stick with it, says Dr. Benson. In time, then, you will come to associate that word with the calming effects of the relaxation response.

3. Sit upright in a comfortable position, with your hands resting naturally on your lap.

4. Let your eyes close gently and take a few moments to relax your muscles and quiet your mind. (Sometimes a few deep breaths help to prepare you for meditation.)

5. Now, breathing normally, become aware of each breath. Working with the slow, natural rhythm of your breathing, repeat your focus word or sound silently on every exhale.

6. Disregard distractions; they're not important. "A passive attitude appears to be the most essential factor in eliciting the relaxation response," Dr. Benson points out. "Thoughts, imagery, and feelings may drift into one's awareness. One should not concentrate on these perceptions but allow them to pass on."

7. Continue the exercise for 10 to 20 minutes. Use your judgment or sneak an occasional peek at a wristwatch to gauge your time. Don't use a timer or alarm clock as the noise can be too disturbing. When your time is up, remain quiet, with your eyes closed for a few minutes, to allow your thoughts to readjust to full wakefulness.

Don't fight intrusive thoughts. Just let them gently drift out of your consciousness.

PROGRESSIVE RELAXATION

About 70 years ago, a young graduate student from Harvard had a profound insight. When we're under mental stress, we tense our muscles; and by tensing our muscles, we cause ourselves physical discomfort that tends to make our mental stress even worse. His name was Edmund Jacobson, and he went on to become a renowned psychiatrist who gradually perfected a technique for breaking this tense-mind, tense-muscle cycle. He called it progressive relaxation.

Mental stress causes tense muscles—and tense muscles make mental stress even worse.

Well, the technique has been enjoying something of a resurgence lately. Psychologists and psychiatrists have been having luck treating such stress-related disorders as headaches, ulcers, high blood pressure, and colitis with the technique (or adaptations of it).

How does it work? By forcing us to focus in on how it actually *feels* to be physically relaxed.

Thomas D. Borkovec, Ph.D., a psychologist at Pennsylvania State University who teaches relaxation courses, explains the process:

"We have the person start with the muscles of one hand, making a fist, holding it for seven seconds, and then relaxing it," says Dr. Borkovec. "Individuals soon learn to identify what both tension and relaxation feel like, so that they will be able to detect tension throughout their bodies. After sufficient practice, most people are able to deeply relax themselves within five minutes."

Learning to identify what tension and relaxation feel like.

His students gradually learn to relax 16 of the body's muscle groups, Dr. Borkovec says. They also inhale when they tense their muscles, then exhale and relax very slowly (for about 45 seconds). That is good therapy for people who also have trouble falling asleep, and its effect improves with practice, Dr. Borkovec says.

MASTERING THE PROCESS

To try the technique yourself, take a comfortable position either sitting in a chair with your hands resting in your lap, or lying down on your back with your feet against a wall or heavy piece of furniture. Close your eyes.

Tense your muscles for five seconds. Then release and feel the tension drain.

Make a tight fist with your right hand, tensing the muscles in your wrist and forearm as you do. Hold tight for about five seconds, feeling the tension. Then unclench your fist, letting the tension drain from your forearm, wrist, and fingers. Note the difference between how your arm feels now and how it felt when it was tense. Repeat.

Now allow your right forearm and hand to remain relaxed while you clench your left fist and tense your left forearm. Note the difference between how your left arm feels and your relaxed arm feels. Now let your left arm relax, feeling the tension slowly drain out through your fingertips.

Next, tense your upper arms and shoulders. Hold a few seconds, then relax, again noting the difference between how your muscles feel when tense and how they feel when relaxed.

The neck: a primary seat of tension.

Now tense your neck. (It's probably the tensest part of your body.) Hold for a few seconds, then relax. At this point, your entire upper body should feel considerably more at ease than before you started.

Now make a frown, scowling as hard as you can. Relax. Try to feel the tension drain out of your eyes, cheeks, and lips.

Raise up on your toes or push against the wall if lying down to create some tension in your legs. Hold for a few seconds, then relax. Again, try to notice the tension drain away. Now your entire body should feel more at peace.

Your breathing all the while should be normal and rhythmic. Upon conclusion, though, take a deep breath, feeling the tension in your chest. Exhale, breathe in again, hold, and let out, saying to yourself as you do, "I'm calm."

Repeat once or twice. Concentrate on how calm you

are. Relish the sense of well-being throughout your entire body.

To conclude the exercise, slowly count to four. At one, you will begin to discard some of the deeper feelings of relaxation. At two, you are slightly more alert. At three, you will soon be ready to think and be fully alert. And at four, you may open your eyes.

AUTOGENIC TRAINING

Autogenic training is another natural and potent relaxation aid. This technique acts on the premise that your mind can compel your body to relax by concentrating on feelings of heaviness and warmth. Through mental suggestion, the "heavy" muscles actually do relax, and the "warm" flesh receives better circulation, resulting in "a state of low physiological arousal," says Richard R. Bootzin, Ph.D., professor of psychology at Northwestern University.

Focusing on heaviness and warmth for relaxation you can feel.

In an experiment in 1968, researchers taught 16 college-student insomniacs to focus their attention on warmth and heaviness. At the end of the experiment, the students became so relaxed they were able to cut their average time needed to fall asleep down from 52 to 22 minutes. These results matched the findings made by Dr. Bootzin in the Chicago area in 1974: "Daily practice of either progressive relaxation or autogenic training produced 50 percent improvement in time to fall asleep by the end of the one-month treatment period."

A Raggedy Ann doll, says psychologist Beata Jencks, Ph.D., is one image that can facilitate autogenic training. To feel heavy, she says, "make yourself comfortable and allow your eyes to close. Then lift one arm a little and let it drop. Let it drop heavily, as if it were the arm of one of those floppy dolls or animals. Choose one in your imagination. Choose a doll, an old, beloved, soft teddy bear." Once the mind fixes on the doll's image, Dr. Jencks says, lifting and dropping the arm in your imagination works as well as really letting it drop.

Lift your arm, then let it drop like the arm of a floppy doll.

To invoke feelings of warmth, Dr. Jencks adds, "Imagine that you put your rag doll into the sun. Let it be warmed by the sun. . . . You are the giant rag doll, and you are lying in the sun; all your limbs are nice and warm, but your head is lying in the shade and is comfortably cool."

DEEP BREATHING

Proper breathing, just by itself, is another way to reassure the autonomic nervous system that it can settle down and relax. That may sound simple enough except for the fact that most of us have forgotten *how* to breathe properly.

Have you ever watched a baby breathe?

Watch a baby breathe and learn an important rule of relaxation.

In and out, deep and even, slow and easy. As you watch, you can see how the baby's torso rises and falls with every breath. And if you look more closely, you will notice that it isn't the baby's chest that is going in and out, it's the tummy—or, more precisely, the diaphragm, the muscle between the chest and abdominal cavity, without which we couldn't breathe.

If you compare this to your own way of breathing, chances are you'll find it differs. If you're like most people, your upper chest expands as you inhale and contracts as you exhale. Over the years, you have learned to hold your stomach in.

This shift in breathing isn't a natural feature of growing older; many experts believe it is simply a bad habit. They also believe that by breaking the habit, and returning to a style of breathing like that of the infant, we can help rid ourselves of chronic complaints such as headaches and fatigue. Not only that: By adopting proper breathing techniques, we may be able to ward off stress, lower our blood pressure, strengthen our hearts, and more.

The way you breathe affects the way you feel.

"The way we breathe has a profound effect on the way we feel," says psychologist Phil Nuernberger, Ph.D., author of *Freedom from Stress* (Himalayan International Institute). "Many stress-related complaints—whether physical, mental, or emotional—are caused by improper breathing. But fortunately, many of these complaints can be reversed simply by learning to breathe properly."

In a series of studies conducted with more than 1,000 people in the last five years, James J. Lynch, Ph.D., of the Center for the Study of Human Psychophysiology at the University of Maryland School of Medicine in Baltimore, has found that you can help control your blood pressure with relaxation techniques, including proper breathing methods *(Psychosomatic Medicine)*.

Dr. Lynch notes that many people tend to forget that one of the primary reasons our blood flows is in order to carry oxygen to our brain and vital organs. "If we don't take in enough oxygen by breathing, our blood has to circulate more rapidly to compensate, and carry the same amount of oxygen. This can result in an increase in blood pressure, because our blood has to move faster to maintain the oxygen supply."

Our blood receives oxygen during a process called "gas exchange," which takes place in our lungs. During gas exchange, oxygen is taken in by the blood, while waste products, in the form of carbon dioxide, are released back into the lungs and exhaled.

"If you're breathing properly with the diaphragm, most of this gas exchange takes place in the lower part of the lungs," notes Alan Hymes, M.D., a cardiovascular surgeon and a member of the clinical faculty at the University of Minnesota School of Medicine in Minneapolis. Dr. Hymes is coauthor of the book *Science of Breath* (Himalayan International Institute). "Chest breathing will not reach the blood in the lower part of the lungs. It won't carry out this process as efficiently as diaphragmatic deep breathing will," he explains.

Studies conducted by Drs. Hymes and Nuernberger suggest that chest breathers may be more prone to heart attacks as well. In a survey of 153 heart attack patients at Methodist Hospital in Minneapolis, they found that all were primarily chest breathers *(Research Bulletin)*.

Chest breathers are more prone to heart attacks.

DEEP BREATHING DECREASES STRESS

One reason chest breathers may be more prone to heart attacks is that their bodies are under constant stress.

"Chest-type breathing may be directly related to activation of the flight-or-fight arousal system," explains Dr. Hymes. "In times of danger, when we need a burst of energy or strength in order to save our lives, this mechanism may be very helpful as it comes into play.

"However, when there is no need for this level of arousal, it may cause stress."

In his practice, Dr. Hymes has found that one way to alleviate this stress response is simply by consciously switching to a pattern of slow, deep, diaphragmatic breathing. "Try it the next time you find yourself becoming upset or angry," he suggests. "You'll be surprised at the change it makes in your perspective, and how calm your thinking becomes."

A technique based on slow, deep, diaphragmatic breathing.

Diaphragmatic breathing also increases the production of endorphins, which are our bodies' own natural morphinelike painkilling substances. That's one reason why Donald Pentecost, M.D., a general practitioner in Fort Worth, Texas, prefers that his patients learn proper diaphragmatic breathing techniques.

Deep breathing relaxes in minutes, lower blood pressure and heart rate.

"I have taught many of my patients how to breathe diaphragmatically," he says. "I have found it can be particularly helpful when patients are very uptight or disturbed. It works in a matter of minutes, helping to lower their blood pressure and heart rate, and calming them down so they can talk more easily about what's bothering them."

Dr. Pentecost likes to teach his patients how to breathe diphragmatically before they undergo surgery. "Afterward, they are in too much pain and not as receptive. Yet I have found that if they learn the technique in advance, and start breathing that way in the recovery room, they usually require less medication because they are in less pain postoperatively. They also experience fewer complications, such as pneumonia or splitting of sutures in gallbladder patients."

The technique is easy. Wearing loose clothes that do not restrict your midsection, assume a comfortable position either sitting in chair or lying down. Keep your back as straight as possible.

Rest your fingertips on your abdomen to monitor the depth of your breaths.

Begin by breathing in slowly and evenly through your nostrils. In the first few sessions, keep your fingertips lightly on your abdomen and see how deep down into the abdomen you can breathe. Feel how your abdomen expands, then your rib cage, then your entire lungs.

To exhale, simply reverse the process, again breathing through your nostrils slowly and evenly. Finish the breath by gently contracting the abdomen and expelling the last of the stale air.

Inhale and exhale in a smooth, continuous motion.

Don't strain. Never breathe beyond your capacity, trying to force air into your lungs. Just breathe rhythmically and easily, initially keeping your inhalation and exhalation the same length. Do this by using a slow mental count to three for the length of your inhale and exhale. As your breathing capacity improves, you can work slowly up to a higher count.

Pretend you're blowing up a balloon with your stomach.

To make sure you're breathing diaphragmatically, Dr. Nuernberger suggests pretending that you are trying to blow up a balloon in your stomach. John Diamond, M.D., of Valley Cottage, New York, suggests that your mouth remain closed and your tongue positioned on the roof of your mouth. "But don't clench your jaw," he warns.

Then exhale slowly. Most experts agree that it sometimes helps to exhale more slowly than we inhale. Dr. Nuernberger calls this "two-to-one" breathing, where the exhalation is twice as long as the inhalation. This type of breathing is a proven way of lowering stress in a hurry.

"BREATHE THROUGH YOUR FINGERTIPS"

The fine points of breathing have been described by Dr. Jencks in her book, *Your Body: Biofeedback at Its Best* (Nelson-Hall).

"Imagine inhaling through your fingertips," Dr. Jencks writes, "up the arms, into the shoulders, and then exhaling down the trunk into the abdomen and legs, and leisurely out at the toes. Repeat, and feel how this slow, deep breathing affects the whole body, the abdomen, the flanks, and the chest. Do not move the shoulders."

Now imagine that you are inhaling through your fingertips.

To inhale deeply, Dr. Jencks advises, pretend to inhale the fragrance of the first flower in spring, or imagine that your breathing rises and falls like ocean waves, or that the surface area of your lungs—if laid out flat—would cover a tennis court. That's how much air you can feel yourself breathing in.

RELIEF IN A PINCH

Next time you're overwrought, notice how you're breathing. Chances are, if your juices are really flowing, then your breathing is probably rapid and shallow, too. Slowing down your breathing is one of the quickest ways to reverse the effects of overstress, according to Jenny Steinmetz, Ph.D., a psychologist at the Kaiser Permanente Medical Center in Hayward, California.

Slowing your breathing is a quick way to keep your cool.

"I tell my clients to slow their breathing to a seven-second inhale and an eight-second exhale," says Dr. Steinmetz, who is coauthor of *Managing Stress Before It Manages You* (Bull Publishing). "Do four of those per minute for a total of two minutes and that discharges the stress immediately."

Using the second hand of a watch or clock is the easiest way to count the seconds, but if you don't have one nearby, Dr. Steinmetz has devised a clever alternative.

BOX 25: BIOFEEDBACK: FINE-TUNING YOUR RELAXATION

Suppose you had to explain to someone how to raise his right arm over his head. Try it. It's impossible. At best, you could tell him to tense the muscles of his arms, but this would only result in his arm going into a state of spasm. Yet, everyone knows how to raise his arm over his head.

It seems that at some early point in our lives, we all spontaneously and without any particular reason raised our arms over our heads. At *that* point, we became aware that our arms were over our heads, and we "knew" what we did to get them up there. We made a . . . feeling.

Another example. How could you "explain" to someone how to ride a bicycle? Again, impossible. But when the person gets on the bike and begins riding it, she can probably learn how to keep her balance very nicely in half hour or so. What's happened is that she has learned how to control innumerable muscles involved in maintaining balance. But this learning experience is not something you could put down on paper or verbally explain to someone else. Somehow, certain pathways and reflexes that the rider never knew she had become available to accomplish a certain task.

Now that you appreciate the importance of nonverbal learning, biofeedback training will not seem quite so peculiar. There are a number of techniques that can be used, but the most basic one is to attach a galvanic skin response (GSR) device to the person's fingertips. This measures the GSR, or minute amounts of perspiration on the skin. The more

tense you are, the more perspiration there is on your skin. As you become calm, there is less and less.

The electrodes are attached to a machine that converts the electrical information into an easily observable form, such as a light or a buzzing noise. The machine can be adjusted so that the buzzing sound is moderately audible at the beginning of the session. As the device picks up more perspiration, meaning more tension, the noise gets louder. If the person becomes calmer and there is less perspiration, the noise becomes lower and is finally extinguished.

Rather than giving complicated instructions, the usual course is simply to hook a person up to a biofeedback machine and tell him to extinguish the buzz or the light. Naturally, he has no idea at all how to go about doing this, so what he does is simply experiment with himself. If he tenses his muscles, for example, he will find that the noise is getting louder. Then, maybe he figures that if he relaxes, the buzz will go softer. So he relaxes, and the buzz does get softer. But it is not extinguished.

Here's where it gets interesting. What usually happens next is that the person begins to put himself in various frames of mind that he believes will do the trick. There is a delay of several seconds between the feeling and the buzz because it takes that long for the perspiration to appear on the skin, but he will soon enough find out if the machine is doing what he wants it to do. He tries other frames of mind. He imagines different scenes, dif-

BOX 25 — *Continued*

ferent people, maybe different colors. Then, quite suddenly, he discovers that the sound is no longer there. What was he doing? He recalls it and keeps it up.

The next step would typically be to readjust the machine so that it has greater sensitivity. In other words, the buzz is going to sound when smaller amounts of perspiration are detected. In another session or two, the person would probably learn how to counter this, and the process is continued until a satisfactory degree of relaxation is obtained.

The same technique would be used to teach someone how to warm his hands. But instead of measuring perspiration, skin temperature would be measured. The person would imagine whatever he found necessary to do the trick. And, incredibly, it's not only possible for some people to boost the temperature of one hand over the other, but to make *one part* of their palm warmer than the adjacent part! Further, researchers have found that when devices that measure very fine degrees of muscular activity are attached to a hand, it seems that unlike the reflexes involved in balancing a bicycle, this particular trick is not done with muscles at all. How it *is* being done, no one seems to know yet.

In any case, once a person has learned to become deeply relaxed, it becomes possible for him to elicit the same state of mind that he uses in the biofeedback laboratory when he is at home or at work. He simply relaxes and tries to recall precisely how he felt when he was keeping the buzzer or the light continuously extinguished.

"All you have to do is say a number and then a three-syllable word to equal one second. For example, one-*el-e-phant,* two-*el-e-phant,* etc. I'll have people tell me that they've just had a 'ten-elephant' phone call or a 'six elephant' lecture.

"The best thing about this method is that it can be done anywhere, any time, and you don't have to stop any other activity to do it. With enough practice it can actually become an 'automatic' type of response to stressful situations."

VISUALIZATION OR GUIDED IMAGERY

If all else fails, use your imagination. That's the advice of physiologist Dr. Mary Asterita, who reminds us that stress, after all, isn't produced when certain events take place—it's the thinking and feeling, the imagining, about those events taking place that give you that gnawing, head-

Imagine yourself relaxed and it will be so.

in-a-vise feeling. So, it stand to reason that if our imaginations can work *against* us, they can also be put to work *for* us, leading us to believe in the happiest outcome and eliciting the physiological relaxation response in the process.

Referred to as visualization or guided imagery, it involves, simply, playing out positive images in your mind. Visualize as many details—sights, sounds, smells, and feelings—as you need to create a scene so real, your body becomes convinced it's happening.

Touch, feel, smell—play out every last detail in your mind.

The first thing you need to do, according to Dr. Asterita, is to learn how to breathe deeply. Once you've got the hang of that, try this: "Right within yourself," says Dr. Asterita softly and slowly, "focus now on a rose. Now you're going to use all the senses. See the rose unfolding its soft petals. As you see it, notice the color; touch the rose and, in your mind's eye, feel the velvet texture. And as you feel it, enjoy the aromatic scent of this beautiful, unfolding rose. You see one color, but within that one color you see many shades. You are not only seeing the rose, but you are *perceiving* it. You are *experiencing* it. Enjoy it for a few moments. And then, slowly, open your eyes." (You might actually want to tape-record yourself or someone with a soothing voice saying these instructions and those that follow, to be played back whenever you need to take a relaxation break. An instructive guiding voice is always a help.)

Sometimes it helps to visualize a stressful situation and then resolve it.

Sometimes, in your imaginings, or visualizations, it helps to create a pressure atmosphere, a taut and tense and even unbearable situation . . . and then resolve it. By doing so in your mind, sometimes you can do the same in your real-life environment. For example, Dr. Asterita creates this scenario, which you should imagine with your eyes closed: "You're in a room and most of the people are smoking. The windows are closed, and it is so stuffy. You're sitting there and you cannot move. You're far away from the door. And you are breathing in this smoke. See yourself there. Feel what it would be like if your were actually there. See the smoke. Experience it. See the people, everybody smoking and talking and anxious. A tense situation. And now, all of a sudden someone opens a window, and slowly you see the smoke leave, and fresh air enters the room. And now you can breathe clean fresh air. You take a nice deep breath, breathing in this vibrant, clean air. And now you become very comfortable and very relaxed."

Or, perhaps, you might want to try this one: "Imagine you're out camping in the woods and you're walking—but you have an overloaded backpack. It's heavy, and you really are feeling the weight. You don't want to carry this weight and you can't walk carrying so much weight. As you're feeling this and thinking it . . . all of a sudden someone comes up next to you and begins to remove objects from the pack. Slowly, one by one, as they're removed, you're able to move freely and now breathe more deeply. And now you enjoy taking some nice deep breaths, breathing in deeply as you feel a sense of weight being lifted."

Or create your own tense situations, and then provide the welcome relief or the knight in shining armor come to the rescue. Search your psyche for the dreads hiding there, and for the devices that will remove them. If you work it right, it should make you feel a whole lot better—without drugs, without added expense, without setting up housekeeping in a Tahitian thatched hut. After all, those painters probably have their worries, too. And probably not half as much imagination as you do.

30

Mastering Stress:
How to Beat Burnout
and Enjoy Life

People who are too busy to learn about stress management need it most.

Who goes to stress management programs?

"Usually the person who's already doing a pretty good job of handling stress," says Dennis T. Jaffe, Ph.D., a California psychologist and stress management consultant. "Part of what we do in stress management workshops is teach people how to get organized, budget their time, set their priorities, and use all available resources. But, to a large extent, registering to take a workshop requires that the person is already utilizing these skills. People who are good stress managers recognize the value in stress management programs and are well organized, so they make time to attend. People who feel overwhelmed with 'more important things' and who say they'd like to come but just can't spare the time, are the ones who need it the most."

In analyzing stress-coping styles, Dr. Jaffe categorizes people three ways: people who handle stress well—who actually thrive in high-pressure situations; people who don't handle stress well—who get uptight and are unable to function under pressure; and people who think they are great stress managers but aren't—who, on the surface, appear cool and calm while, internally, they seethe like a volcano on the verge of eruption.

A daily workout: tension release or added pressure?

"Those in the third category have actually adapted to stress by going numb. In effect, they're unconscious," Dr. Jaffe explained in an interview. "They're oblivious to the tension building. They say they don't feel the effects.

They're not aware what they're on a self-destructive path. For example, they may think that a daily workout at the gym satisfies their need for tension release when in fact it may represent just another challenge to add to a long list of accomplishments.

"These are closet Type As," says Dr. Jaffe. "These are the people who say, 'I smoke because it relaxes me.' "

Unfortunately, too, these people are setting themselves up for burnout.

WHAT IS BURNOUT?

Burnout. It sounds reminiscently like a Jan and Dean song of the sixties: "Wipe Out." And, in fact, that might not be a bad way to describe it. Herbert J. Freudenberger, Ph.D., who first identified the syndrome among social workers and coined the word, defines burnout as a state of depletion and of physical and mental exhaustion caused by overcommitment to a job, cause, relationship, a way of life.

The overcommitment that causes physical and mental exhaustion.

Sufferers complain initially of feeling "overwhelmed," "frustrated," "blocked by insurmountable circumstances," or "unable to cope." Eventually, they feel "drained of energy," "used up," "having nothing more to give." This, in turn, gives rise to a callous cynicism—a "don't-knock-yourself-out-for-anyone" attitude and, finally, to a sense of personal powerlessness—that the situation is beyond their control—which tends to become a self-fulfilling prophesy.

At highest risk are the high achievers—goal-oriented people with great expectations. These are the people who "want their marriages to be the best, their work records to be outstanding, their children to shine, their community to be better," Dr. Freudenberger writes in *Burn Out: The High Cost of High Achievement* (Doubleday & Co.).

"All their lives, they have undertaken tough jobs and prided themselves on their ability to master situations. . . . Now, however, no matter how great their efforts, the only result seems to be frustration."

At highest risk, the high achievers.

What pushes them over the edge of high achievement to a chasm of low energy and self-esteem?

Dr. Freudenberger says it occurs when commitment becomes *over*commitment. Commitment, he says, is a very positive life force. "A person who feels a true devotion to a

When commitment becomes overcommitment.

BOX 26: ARE YOU BURNING OUT?

Look back over the past six months. Have you been noticing changes in yourself or in the world around you? Think of the office . . . the family . . . social situations. Allow about 30 seconds for each answer to the questions below. Then assign it a number from 1 (for no or little change) to 5 (for a great deal of change) to designate the degree of change you perceive.

1. Do you tire more easily? Feel fatigued rather than energetic?

2. Are people annoying you by telling you, "You don't look so good lately"?

3. Are you working harder and harder and accomplishing less and less?

4. Are you increasingly cynical and disenchanted?

5. Are you often invaded by a sadness you can't explain?

6. Are you forgetting? (appointments, deadlines, personal possessions)

7. Are you increasingly irritable? More short-tempered? More disappointed in the people around you?

8. Are you seeing close friends and family members less frequently?

9. Are you too busy to do even routine things like make phone calls or read reports or send out your Christmas cards?

10. Are you suffering from physical complaints? (aches, pains, headaches, a lingering cold)

11. Do you feel disoriented when the activity of the day comes to a halt?

12. Is joy elusive?

13. Are you unable to laugh at a joke about yourself?

14. Does sex seem like more trouble than it's worth?

15. Do you have very little to say to people?

Very roughly, now, place yourself on the Burnout Scale. Keep in mind that this is merely an approximation of where you are, useful as a guide on your way to a more satisfying life. Don't let a high total alarm you, but pay attention to it. Burnout is reversible, no matter how far along it is. If you have a higher number, you should start being kinder to yourself—the sooner the better.

The Burnout Scale

0-25   You're doing fine.

26-35   There are things you should be watching.

36-50   You're a candidate.

51-65   You are burning out.

over 65   You're in a dangerous place, threatening to your physical and mental well-being.

Acknowledgment: "Are You Burning Out?" from *Burn Out: The High Cost of High Achievement* by H. J. Freudenberger, Ph.D., and G. Richelson. Copyright © 1980 by Herbert J. Freudenberger, Ph.D., and Geraldine Richelson. Reprinted by permission of Doubleday & Company, Inc.

situation or person, usually feels good. He or she goes about his or her activities with a sense of purpose and well-being. His or her energy level is high, and so is the accompanying sense of accomplishment."

Overcommitment, on the other hand, robs us of energy, enthusiasm, and fulfillment. It obliterates our true purpose and goals in life. It threatens our physical and emotional well-being.

FALLING OFF BALANCE

Dr. Jaffe describes the turning point as one of imbalance— when you're giving more than receiving. "When you are in balance, you have a sense that your efforts are being rewarded. You feel satisfaction. You cope well with stress. Your energy is continually renewed. You have the ability to rebound from emotionally or physically taxing situations."

It's not always better to give than receive.

When we fall off balance, the blame tends to fall on external factors—the job, spouse, kids, whatever. But rather than looking outside for fault, Dr. Jaffe suggests we look inside for answers.

" . . . Burnout is not something that lies outside yourself, in the nature of your job and life; it is an effect of inadequate responses to these factors," he says. " . . . Your response to pressure makes the difference between burnout or peak performance."

External factors may contribute, but internal factors ultimately cause burnout.

The bad news, according to Dr. Jaffe, is that burnout looms ominously on the horizon of everyone's stress response scale. The good news is that it is preventable and completely resolvable—no matter how far down the path of self-destruction, you can turn back on the road of health and high performance.

THREE STEPS TO RECOVERY

But getting yourself back on track—and keeping yourself there—requires more than a few good-intentioned resolutions. Burnout is the body's call for "code blue." Nothing short of drastic attitude and lifestyle changes will reverse its course. Healing, says Dr. Jaffe, hinges on a three-tiered process involving self-awareness, self-management, and self-renewal.

Burnout is the body's call for "code blue."

BOX 27: FROM BREAKDOWN TO PEAK PERFORMANCE:
THE FIVE STATES OF HUMAN PERFORMANCE

Our physical/emotional state—how we feel and perform—is directly related to our internal system of dealing with daily stress and pressure, says Dennis T. Jaffe, Ph.D., who has categorized these states in the following five ways:

1. Breakdown. The body literally breaks down. It stops functioning emotionally. You're disabled and hospitalized. You need extensive healing.

2. Burnout. You're barely functioning. Your batteries are running low, like a clock that's losing time. You can't concentrate anymore. You're apathetic. You're exhausted at the beginning of each day. You're about to break down—and you will, if you don't do something about it.

3. Strain. You're managing, but it really takes a lot out of you. You're wiped out at the end of the day and it's getting more and more difficult to bounce back the next day.

4. Balance. You're doing OK, coping well. You may feel tired at the end of the day but you're able to rebound without any difficulty.

5. Peak performance. You feel energized, not drained, at the end of the day. You're enthusiastic and full of energy. You feel nurtured and turned on by what you're doing.

The majority of time, we tend to vacillate between the balance and strain states, says Dr. Jaffe. To get to any of the other states—burnout, breakdown, or peak performance—is a difficult and slow process.

SELF-AWARENESS

"People are not machines that can be pushed to high performance," Dr. Jaffe and coauthor Cynthia D. Scott, Ph.D., explain in their book *From Burnout to Balance* (McGraw-Hill). "When we push ourselves to accomplish something and we experience resistance, we need to ask ourselves why are we doing this, why is it important to us. Burnout and distress are sometimes messages from our bodies that we need to explore these basic questions. The symptoms signal not an inability to manage the outside world, but a disconnection within ourselves."

The more you know about yourself, the better.

To reconnect, then, we must first tune in to our thoughts and feelings. "You have to be willing to look honestly and deeply and to incur some pain. . . . The more you know about yourself, the better," says Dr. Freudenberger.

BOX 28: DETERMINING YOUR OPTIMAL STRESS LEVEL

In the right dose, stress is healthy. Too little stimulation and you are bored; too much, and you burn out. But, as the following performance curve demonstrates, stress at the optimal level can spur us on to our highest achievements.

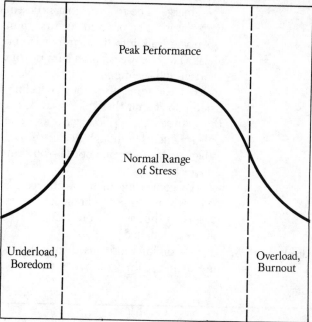

Peak Performance

Normal Range
of Stress

Underload,
Boredom

Overload,
Burnout

Finding the optimal stress level for peak performance is an individual thing. What one person considers a challenge, another may find an unnecessary burden. What some think of as exciting, others find frightening. In every case, however, it's a fine line that we walk between underload and overload. And it takes a good bit of self-knowledge and stress mastery to reach our highest potential.

The following exercise, developed by Dennis T. Jaffe, Ph.D., and Cynthia D. Scott, Ph.D., can help you determine your own optimal level:

"Remember some times when you were working at your best, when you were involved, challenged, and excited. Summon as much detail as possible. Now write down some of the qualities that stimulate you to maximum performance. What are the qualities of your environment? What sorts of pressures or deadlines spur you to action? What tasks energize you and which ones bore you? Do you work best alone or with others? What sort of help or guidance do you need?"

Listen to your inner voice.

"First, think about your image, that competent *you* others have come to expect so much of. Think about your schedule, the tasks you perform, your family's expectations, your own expectations of yourself. Get a pad and write a short vignette of the 'you' the world sees and hears every day. Then put your pad aside and close your eyes. Let that other *you* emerge. The real you that's tucked away beneath all those layers. The one you see first thing in the morning when you walk into the bathroom to prepare for the day ahead. The one you get brief glimpses of when you're all by yourself and feeling kind of beat. Now let that real you speak. Hear some of his or her feelings. And, for once, listen. Don't shut that voice away. It may have important things to say. . . . [Now] write a second vignette. Even if only fragments of thoughts came through, jot them down. Whatever feelings you noticed—no matter how fleeting— include them."

By comparing these two images, Dr. Freudenberger believes you can get to know large parts of yourself that have been shut away—something that's essential to burnout treatment and prevention.

Have you checked in with your body today?

Becoming conscious of your physicality (Do you have any aches, pains, or pent-up tension that has gone

---

BOX 29: TAKING A GOOD, HARD LOOK INSIDE

Being out of touch with yourself— your true feelings and commitments—is a key contributor to burnout, which is why self-reflection is essential. To facilitate the process, Dennis T. Jaffe, Ph.D., and Cynthia D. Scott, Ph.D., offer the following 19 questions to ponder. Jot down a few thoughts on as many of them as you can and don't worry if your answers are incomplete. As Drs. Jaffe and Scott point out in their book *From Burnout to Balance* (McGraw-Hill), "The purpose is to make your feelings about your life more explicit and to define some areas

and dimensions of life that need renewed energy or redefined commitment."

1. What are my current concerns and worries?

2. What are the greatest pressures on me right now? When do I feel it? What must I do about it?

3. What is changing my life?

4. What are the major values or goals that I would like to achieve in my life?

5. What are the most important payoffs or rewards that I am looking for in my life?

BOX 29—*Continued*

6. What intense, gratifying, and deeply meaningful experiences have I had in my life? What sorts of peak experiences would I like to have in the future?

7. What are the major constraints or limits that I experience in my life right now that make it difficult to achieve the rewards, goals, and experiences I seek?

8. What are the major obstacles to getting what I want out of life? (Divide them into obstacles that lie inside you and those which are external. Think of some of the ways you can change or diminish the force of these obstacles.)

9. What are the things I do well? List them.

10. What are the things that I do poorly? Would I like to improve my ability in these areas or stop doing these things?

11. What would I like to stop doing?

12. What would I like to start doing or learn to do?

13. What are the central goals in my life right now? What were my goals five years ago? What do I project will be my goals five years from now?

14. Which of the things that I do regularly do I expect to do less often in the following years? What new things do I expect to have to do, or want to do?

15. What is the most important change or crisis that I expect to face in the next decade?

16. What is the most important choice I will have to make in the next few years?

17. Which domain of my life (work, family, friends, self) is the central one right now? In the next five years which domains do I expect to become more and less important in my life?

18. What ideal futures can I anticipate? (Imagine what you would like to experience, what you would like to be doing, and who or what kind of people you would like to be doing things with.)

19. Imagine at some time in the future you have just died. Write an obituary as the person in your life closest to you might write it. What do you expect you will be remembered for? What sort of achievements do you expect to have?

Reprinted by permission of the authors from *From Burnout to Balance,* Dennis T. Jaffe, Ph.D., and Cynthia D. Scott, Ph.D. (New York: McGraw-Hill, 1985), pp. 147–48.

unrecognized?) and changes in behavior patterns (Are you drinking more alcohol or coffee lately? Eating or sleeping more or less? Watching more TV?) can also help you get in touch with your feelings. Sometimes we hurt physically or drift unconsciously into bad habits when our stress-coping mechanisms aren't working properly, Dr. Jaffe says. Becoming aware of such things—and making an effort to resolve

them—can help bring you in touch with underlying problems that need your immediate attention.

In connection with that, Drs. Jaffe and Scott suggest
that you explore your reaction to stressors. All of us develop
coping methods—some of them more effective than others,
they say. Very often, however, the ineffectiveness of a coping method is not noticeable until a real crisis arises or we
become inundated with multiple stressors. Then, the method
that carries us satisfactorily through mild to moderately
stressful situations suddenly fails us. Drs. Jaffe and Scott
remind us of four such methods: *withdrawal* (postponing
action and/or refusing to face the problem), *internalizing*
(stewing over the problem without resolution or reaching
out for help), *emotional outbursts* (the long-term outcome
of internalizing—reaching the boiling point), and *overcon-
trolling* (trying to resolve every problem, including those
that don't warrant our attention and even those that haven't
yet been encountered).

Take action on only those problems that you can control.

Generally, those who confront stressors head on—who
take action to resolve only those problems that are within
their power to control and seek support or help from others
when they encounter difficulty in coping—are good stress
managers, say Drs. Jaffe and Scott. They have mastered
effective stress-coping skills.

But don't take their word for it. What's important here
is not so much what the experts say—or even what works
for most people. It's what works for *you*.

By looking closely at how you cope with each stressful
situation—and, most importantly, how you respond emotionally and physiologically to your stress response— you
begin to get a clear picture of which methods work for you
and which work against you. A personal stress log can be
extremely useful, says Dr. Jaffe. Note the action you take in
response to specific stressors as well as your subsequent
feelings (relief, frustration, helplessness, exhaustion). Within
a week or two, you'll begin to notice the definite patterns.

What's the worst possible consequence if you don't do it?

One very important aspect of this is in assessing the
importance of each stressful situation and determining
how much energy you want to expend on resolving it.
Sometimes we have no choice: An emergency situation
presents itself and we must act on it immediately. All other
priorities suddenly slip down a notch. But how many times
have you worked yourself into a frenzy over something that

BOX 30: PLAY IT AGAIN . . .

Tensions build. Unresolved problems snowball. Before you know it, you're caught in a downward stress spiral headed for burnout. One way to break your fall is by practicing this simple visualization exercise, which helps discharge tensions at day's end while helping you to explore alternative solutions for dealing with stress:

Sit comfortably in a quiet space. Close your eyes. Become aware of your body. Take a few deep breaths.

Now, imagine that you are sitting in a private film screening room. You're the only one there, seated in a soft overstuffed chair. The film projector is voice activated. That is, you can stop and start the film, back up, fast forward, and run it in slow motion with verbal commands.

The film that's about to be shown stars you. The story is yours. You can start the action anywhere you wish: last year, last week, last night—any scene that represents some unresolved conflict in your life.

Now roll it. Watch yourself in action.

See how the situation unfolds. Take note of the other people involved. What are they saying? How are they responding to you? How are you responding to them? Don't be judgmental, just see the event as it happened.

When you've seen enough, rewind the film, and play it again—this time, with a different ending. The situation is the same. The characters haven't changed. But the actions and interactions between the characters are noticeably different. *This is how it could have been.* Your perception of the situation is somehow better. You respond differently to what the other people are saying, and they to you. The situation is resolved.

The lights come on in the viewing room. Take a few minutes to reflect on your performance. Specifically, what did you do differently in the second sequence that changed the outcome so dramatically? Were these actions "out of character" for you or did they make more sense? Did you learn anything about yourself that you can apply to future conflicts?

was of very little value or consequence? Think about this the next time your adrenaline spurs you into action. Before you start pumping energy into the situation, ask yourself how important is it to you personally, can you really make a difference, and what's the worst possible consequence if you don't get involved.

"Don't waste your stress energy," says Donald A. Tubesing, Ph.D., author of *Kicking Your Stress Habits* (Whole Person Associates, Inc.). " . . . It is possible to spend ten dollars' worth of energy on a ten-cent problem.

"Have you ever fought stubbornly for your point of

It's possible to spend $10 worth of energy on a 10¢ problem.

view when you knew that what you said wouldn't make any difference, that no one cared and even if they had, the point wasn't worth all the trouble? Have you ever kept trying to please someone when it was obvious that nothing could really satisfy him or her? Have you ever felt furious when someone cut into line ahead of you?

"If so, you know what it's like to overspend your stress energy.

"On the other hand," Dr. Tubesing continues, "it's possible to underspend.

On the other hand, have you ever allowed an important relationship to disintegrate?

"Have you ever allowed a relationship to disintegrate, admitting only after it ended how important it was to you? Have you ever ignored signs of trouble with your children until the problems were nearly too big to handle? Have you ever closed your eyes to injustice on your doorstep, in your own church, club, or community, because it was easier not to speak up?

"If so," he says, "you know what it means to spend ten cents' worth of adrenaline on a ten-dollar problem."

Goals give purpose to life.

That's why stress management consultants all agree that a key element in stress mastery is assessing your personal values and goals.

"Goals are motivators," Dr. Tubesing explains. "They give purpose to life and help you select the actions you're willing to take to fulfill them—and yourself. Your values define what is important in your life—your top priorities. Values work under the surface, propelling you to act, to make choices, and to move toward your goals."

"If you don't know what your goals are, you may move from one meaningless task to another or make sloppy decisions by default," he adds. "The vague uneasiness you may feel is a symptom of your aimlessness."

Start today. Determine what's important to you.

So start today. "Determine what's important to you," says Dr. Tubesing. "List the things you like to do, the things you don't like to do, what you wish you could do. Write down the qualities you most admire in your heroes and the attributes you dislike in people around you. Name the ways you would like to be like your parents and the ways you would rather be different.

"Then look at your day. Do you see any conflict between your values and the way you spend your time?"

Alan Lakein, a time management consultant whose advice has gone a long way to prevent corporate burnout at such fiercely competitive firms as AT&T and IBM, offers his technique of self-reflection. He poses three questions: What are your life goals? How would you like to spend the next three to five years? And, if you had just six months to live, how would you spend it?

Three questions that help you understand yourself.

Take about two minutes (four at the most) jotting down your answers to each of those questions. Then spend another two minutes to review your responses and improve your goal statements. Again, if your statements conflict with your current life—if you're putting a disproportionate amount of effort into areas that do not reflect your life goals, if your five-year plan is a major departure from the present, and if the prospect of a six-month death sentence fills you with a longing for a better way of life—then some changes may be in order. And soon.

SELF-MANAGEMENT

Establishing clear goals is the first order on the agenda of self-management. Write them down. And review them every month or two reconfirm them or revise them (remember life is constantly changing and so, too, do our goals and priorities). Also, while it's natural to have more than one goal at any time, too many goals—or conflicting or competing goals—is certain to lead to frustration and distress. So be very selective and keep each goal in its proper perspective.

Too many goals lead to frustration and distress.

Some of your goals will no doubt be very concrete and specific: take a self-defense class, buy a new car, paint the kitchen. Others may be more vague and philosophical: be a better parent, expand your circle of friends, improve your feeling of self-worth. And then, of course, there are your long-term life goals: become financially independent, get in shape, achieve spiritual fulfillment.

Long-term life goals are top priority on everyone's scale. But with so many more immediate concerns, we often lose sight of them and as a result they may never become realized. That's why setting priorities and planning are essential to any stress management program.

Too often, our most important goals get lost among the rubble of busywork.

"Control starts with planning," says Alan Lakein in his book *How to Get Control of Your Time and Your Life* (Peter H. Wyden, Inc.). "Planning is bringing the future into the present so you can do something about it now."

Lakein begins and ends every workday with a plan. He makes a "To Do" list of everything he wants to accomplish

Make a "To Do" list every day.

that day. Then he reviews them in terms of his goals and determines the order of priority. The A tasks are those that are of highest priority—the important things that are absolute "musts" in order to achieve our goals, including our life goals. "I make it a point to do something every day toward my life goal," says Lakein.

B tasks are of secondary importance. "If I have time, I'll tackle them," says Lakein. "But not before all the As are taken care of first." And C tasks are those that when you really think about them, you realize that they're not significant at all. "If they don't get done, it's not a big deal," says Lakein.

On any "To Do" list, 80 percent of the items are unnecessary.

According to Lakein, 80 percent of the items on any To Do list are insignificant and unnecessary. It's in that 20 percent of significant tasks that 80 percent of the value lies.

"Concentrate your effort on these high priority items," he explains. "Don't get bogged down in C tasks no matter how quick and easy they are to do." And if you have trouble deciding which of your tasks deserve the C rating, Lakein says, ask yourself what would happen if you didn't do it. If you can live with the consequences, don't do it.

In his book, Lakein gives dozens of time- and energy-saving tips, several of which are included in Box 31. And

BOX 31: FINDING TIME TO ENJOY LIFE

So you say you're feeling overwhelmed because there just aren't enough hours in the day. You don't have time to do the things you really enjoy. You can't remember the last time you spent a weekend away from the obligations of home and work. And the harder you work, it seems the further behind you get.

Is that what's bothering you?

Well, wishing for more time won't help—and will even add to your level of frustration. What you need to do is take control of the time that you've got and

use it for those things that are most important to you.

"There's no such thing as a lack of time," says Alan Lakein, a Harvard M.B.A. and time management consultant for such firms as IBM and AT&T. "We all have plenty of time to do everything we really want to do. If, like so many people, you're 'too busy' to get things done, keep in mind that there are plenty of people who are even busier than you are who manage to get more done than you do. They don't have more time than

BOX 31 – *Continued*

you have. They just use their time to better advantage! Effective time use—like driving a car—is a skill that can be acquired."

Here, then, some suggestions from Lakein's best-selling book, *How to Get Control of Your Time and Your Life* (Peter H. Wyden, Inc.).

• Keep a *daily* "To Do" List.

• Consider that only two out of every ten items on that list are worth doing.

• Concentrate your effort on these high-priority items; don't get bogged down in insignificant tasks no matter how quick and easy they are to do.

• Determine your most productive time of the day and reserve it for prime projects. Don't squander prime time on routine tasks such as reading the newspaper, answering mail, making beds.

• Schedule routine tasks for non-prime-time hours, when your energy level is at a lull.

• Try to do some things at the same time every day. "This conserves energy by cutting down on indecision," says Lakein. "And it generates energy through habit—the habit of expecting to make phone calls, plan the meals, read the paper, attend a class, or go to a meeting—all at a particular time."

• Always reserve at least an hour of uncommitted time each day to accommodate crises and unexpected events.

• Arrange for time to relax and do nothing. "Nothing is a total waste of time, including doing nothing," says Lakein.

• Think of wait time—time spent waiting for a bus, in a doctor's office, while your child is having a music lesson, even during long drives and commute to work—as "found time," not lost time. Use it to do something you've been putting off for lack of time. Learn a language (on tape). Read a novel. Write a letter to an old friend. Plan a surprise birthday party for your spouse.

• Caught daydreaming? Get into it— completely. Just sit in a chair and do nothing for 15 to 20 minutes. Don't read a book. Don't shuffle papers. Don't knit. Don't watch TV. Just wallow in loafing. After 10 to 15 minutes of this, you'll be ready to dig into work.

• Just five or ten minutes to spare? Most of us would fritter away this time, or use it up on simple, insignificant tasks. But Lakein has a better idea: Get started on an important project. "Let's face it: Large blocks of uninterrupted time are comparative rarity," he says. If we wait for the "right moment," it may never come. But, by breaking down overwhelming high-priority projects into "instant tasks" that can be accomplished in five minutes or less, you can chisel away at something that's really significant.

• Don't waste time worrying about failures. "Think of each 'mistake' as bringing you closer to an eventual success," says Lakein. "Studies have shown that people who hoped (and strived) for success were happier and accomplished more than those who feared (and accepted) failure."

Time management controls pressures and helps manage the environment.

he's not the only one who's convinced of their importance. "Time management liberates," says Dr. Jaffe. "It is a way to control pressures and manage the environment."

As with most things, however, moderation is the key.

"If you think that trying to 'get control' of your time and your life means becoming super-organized, super-busy, or preoccupied with every moment as it slips by, let me assure you that this is not the case," Lakein explains. ". . . Too much organization is as ineffective as too little.

"The ideal is balance."

Balance: the word every stress manager lives by.

Balance. That's the word that every stress manager lives by. People who know how to balance work with play, wakefulness with sleep, stress with relaxation, activity with rest, giving with receiving, have discovered the key to health and happiness, they say. Balance blocks the road to burnout and opens the pathway to peak performance.

Bringing your life into balance requires self-control and time-management. Time to relax, to spend with family and friends, to play, even to do nothing doesn't just happen. You've got to plan for it just as you do work activities.

"One of the most difficult conflicts is finding enough time and energy to do everything we want. Work can eat up our time and energy, sometimes leaving us with little left over for our family," say Drs. Jaffe and Scott. "Tragically, working people too often make their family and personal relationships their lowest priority, giving them what, if anything, is left over. Yet people who are successful at managing stress and remaining healthy are often those who make their personal and family lives a priority and are able to say 'no' to some outside demands. Setting priorities to give importance to both work and family is a cornerstone of balanced life and self-renewal."

By developing contacts, support networks, you can free yourself to do what you enjoy.

Sometimes, says physician Rick Ingrasci, M.D., setting those priorities requires that you first develop new, more flexible attitudes toward yourself and your work. You've got to realize that you don't have to do everything yourself and, in fact, that you're more effective if you don't. By accepting that premise and developing contacts, networks, support groups—whatever you need to help you get your work done and problems solved—you can free yourself up to do more of the things that you enjoy doing and that you're good at.

BOX 32: THRIVING ON STRESS: WHAT DOES IT TAKE?

For every person who surrenders under the crushing weight of stress, there is another who triumphs—who sees stress as a worthy opponent and eagerly responds with a counterforce of creativity and energy. These are the peak performers, the people who thrive on stress. How do they do it?

Some say it requires a special ability. And, certainly, that can't hurt. But according to Dennis T. Jaffe, Ph.D., and Cynthia D. Scott, Ph.D., peak performance can be achieved through mastery of the same self-awareness, self-management, and self-renewal skills we use to beat burnout. As evidence of this, they cite the best studies on peak performers which point to people who are inner-directed (who know their feelings and understand their motivations), action-oriented (who take control of their time and life), and well-balanced (who know the importance of relaxation and renewal).

Some specific and distinguishing attributes of peak performers:

Inner-Directed

• Attuned to their own feelings and needs.
• Set their own goals.
• Feel that they are doing what they want.
• Set goals that are clear, concrete, and realistic.
• Have a deep inner sense of pur-pose, a *mission,* which sometimes carries them beyond their expectations.
• Are not afraid to do something they've never done before.
• Are not put off by limiting circumstances—what cannot be done, what the organization will not permit, the way things are done. Instead, they see everything as something to be questioned, tested, and transcended.
• Are more concerned with the personal fulfillment a task brings than how the performance will be perceived by others.

Action-Oriented

• Always look ahead to what they can learn or do next.
• Don't linger in the "comfort zone"; instead, seek out new challenges, take chances.
• Have little fear of failure.
• Know their priorities.
• Strive for excellence on high priority items but do not waste an undue amount of time or energy on low-priority tasks.
• Do not brood over mistakes.

Balanced

• Work hard but stop to play.
• Do not spend every waking hour in pursuit of their goals.
• Know how to relax.
• Rely on fulfilling personal relationships and time with family and friends for enrichment and renewal.

SELF-RENEWAL

Self-renewal is essential whether you're in burnout or peak performance.

Self-renewal is the ultimate exercise in balance. It is the process of continually renewing lost energy (physically and emotionally), something that is essential no matter in what performance state you are functioning.

"If you're in burnout and don't make some effort toward self-renewal, you'll break down," Dr. Jaffe reminds us. "And if you're in peak performance for too long—which requires a tremendous amount of energy to sustain—and lose sight of your need for self-renewal, you could eventually skid down the path to burnout. It's like running a marathon. That's a peak performance type of effort. Now you wouldn't just get up the next day and run another one. Common sense tells us that we've got to rest up and renew our energy. The same holds true with any high achievement activity."

How do we renew ourselves?

Meditation, close friends, and time off enrich and renew our lives.

Through meditation or other relaxation technique practiced on a regular basis (see Chapter 29, The Best of the Relaxation Techniques). By giving and receiving love and devoting time to people who energize you. Through physical pursuits—running and the like—which discharge tension and renew our energy (see Chapter 9, Head Strong: Emotional Conditioning through Aerobic Exercise). And by taking time off—if you can, perhaps even an extended leave of absense, a so-called job sabbatical.

"In corporations we usually have people who are dependent on external rewards, on recognition from their bosses," says Beverly Potter, Ph.D., author of *Beating Job Burnout* (Ace Publishers). "With a sabbatical, you can learn to find internal rewards."

People can use a sabbatical to get what they're not getting in their routine life.

"People can use a sabbatical to get what they're not getting in their routine life," adds Paula Jay, a New York City career development consultant. "If you've always wanted to play your guitar seriously but never had enough time for it, taking a sabbatical can be a real opportunity to satisfy that kind of need that's never been satisfied before. And some people want to travel. If their life is very routinized and sedentary, a traveling sabbatical fills a complementary need."

Even if you love your work, a sabbatical can be a good way to explore other sides of yourself. "No matter how exciting a job is, it won't provide everything for a person who is creative, who needs stimulation and knowledge," says Dr. Potter.

And, if you're less than 100 percent happy with your job, a sabbatical *could* be what you need. Time off can give you the perspective that helps you get over job burnout. "Taking time off can bring you back more motivated," says Dr. Potter. "A sabbatical is a nice alternative to quitting. People become so frustrated they just quit. A sabbatical is an opportunity to get a new start."

Time off can give you the perspective to help you through burnout.

31

In Pursuit of Tranquility: Comfort Zones and Special Mind/Body Treats

Each year, doctors write 50 million prescriptions for tranquilizers.

A warm cup of tea. A glass of wine. Maybe an evening spent vegetating. We've all got our own ways to unwind—some of them health-enhancing, but far too many of them health-depleting. Each year, for example, doctors write 50 million prescriptions for tranquilizers. Not only are these drugs potentially dangerous, they're ineffective for getting at the *cause* of anxiety. Tranquilizers, like alcohol, do not relieve stress. They merely blanket the mind, at least temporarily, from cold reality. But there are more effective and healthful alternatives that help release stress and renew our energy and enthusiasm. Try these:

SOOTHING SOUNDTRACKS

Chances are you've already got a favorite soundtrack—something you can switch on to tune out all the stress and pressures of the day. But whether your musical selection is capable of evoking a true relaxation response is another matter. According to composer and music researcher Steven Halpern, Ph.D., when it come to sounds that soothe, all is not what meets the ear.

Music stimulates a total body response.

"What most people don't realize is that our response to music is far more than an auditory response," Dr. Halpern says. "It is a total body response.

"If you were to have earplugs in your ears, you could still 'feel' the music," he explains. "That's because music is vibrations. And these vibrations affect your heartbeat, blood flow, brainwaves—your entire body chemistry."

Interestingly, researchers who have monitored these physiological responses say they occur independent of our musical preference. That is, you don't have to like a particular piece of music to benefit from its relaxation effect. They've also discovered that, often, the kind of music people think relaxes them doesn't—at least not significantly.

You don't have to like the music to benefit from it.

"I've had people tell me that classical music relaxes them," says Dr. Halpern. "And yet when these people are monitored for brainwave patterns, heart rate, blood flow, muscle response, and galvanic skin response—all standard stress indicators—there is no physiological evidence of relaxation.

"Generally, classical music doesn't induce deep relaxation. But that's not to say it can't," says Dr. Halpern. "The bottom line with any music is your personal response.

The bottom line is your personal response.

"Just watch your body and see how you feel. Allow the music to be your center of attention. Try to sit down or lie down, but even if you can't, do notice how you are feeling. If the music helps you to breathe slower and deeper, it is relaxing you."

ONE-BEAT-PER-SECOND

What Halpern and others have found is that sounds with a more natural rhythm—that reflect our own heartbeat and breathing—tend to be more relaxing to most people. "Parts of certain classical pieces do fall into this category," Dr. Halpern admits. "For example, the slow second movement of some Baroque pieces by such composers as Bach, Handel, and Telemann follows the natural one-beat-per-second rhythm of the heart.

Music that moves to the beat of the heart is relaxing.

"In contrast, the typical rhythm of rock music is exactly opposite to the heart's natural beat," he continues. "That's one reason why people find it irritating or exciting. It confuses our natural inclinations."

Charles Schmid, Ph.D., director of the LIND (Learning in New Dimensions) Institute in San Francisco, has also spent some time analyzing the human response to music—especially the effect relaxing music can have on our ability to learn (see Chapter 52, Super Learning). He too recommends the slower movements of certain Baroque works to relax and enhance learning potential. But because it was difficult for his students to isolate those sections from the faster movements on a soundtrack, he took the liberty of

50 minutes of relaxing Baroque movements.

doing it for them, assembling 50 minutes' worth of relaxing Baroque passages on a single tape. Some of the longer playing individual pieces for relaxation, he says, include Pachelbel's Canon in D, Mozart's Piano Concerto #21 (which became the theme song for the film "Elvira Madigen"), and Albinoni's Adagio in G.

But before you opt for Mozart in place of meditation, be aware that not all recordings are created equal. The type of instruments, how they are played and by whom—even the method of recording—can affect your response.

Electric piano, flute, and harp: instruments that soothe.

Dr. Halpern points out that, in studies, the best general relaxation response was evoked with the sound of electric piano (which, he says, sounds "like 88 tuning forks"), flute, harp, and piano. "A string ensemble playing sustained tones is also good for most people," he adds, "but the violin alone is too harsh."

Keep in mind too that the relaxation effect of any instrument hinges on the way it's played (a staccato flute is obviously less relaxing than a fluid one) and who's playing (musicians can radically differ in their interpretation of the same piece).

Sounds that echo relax us almost immediately.

Echo and reverberation are two other elements that can affect the relaxation potential of a recording, Dr. Halpern says. "Some of the most sacred ancient buildings, such as the Pyramids, the Taj Majhal, and gothic cathedrals, have extraordinarily long echo and reverb properties," he says. "The acoustic characteristics of these structures enhance the sound in a way that does something special to the brain. It apparently triggers the release of endorphins and relaxes you almost immediately."

ANALOG VERSUS DIGITAL

Apparently the method of recording—analog versus digital—can also make a difference in your total body's response to that music. Analog is a linear process that involves transferring continuous sound onto a magnetic tape. In digital recording, the sound is first broken down into small bits, then linked back together on laser-read compact discs.

You won't hear the difference in digital recordings. You'll feel it: Something's missing.

"If you listen to a digital recording, you probably won't detect any interruption in sound," says Dr. Halpern. "But the spaces are there and you can feel them. There's definitely something missing."

To its credit, however, digital recording lacks the hiss of tape recording. And it won't be long before this relatively new method is perfected. In the meantime, Dr. Halpern recommends that you look for the latest generation of compact discs and read the specs on the label. Those with a higher "sampling rate" have tighter gaps in the musical information.

There's also the element of familiarity to consider when evaluating your own response to a given piece of music. "If your parents forced you, as a child, to practice a particular piece on the piano each day, chances are listening to that music—no matter who's playing or how it's been recorded—won't relax you," says Dr. Halpern. "On the other hand, if you associate a piece of music with some comforting experience that's deeply ingrained in your memory, then whenever you hear it, it's likely to send you into a deep state of relaxation."

If you associate a melody with a comforting memory, it will most certainly soothe you.

DR. HALPERN'S RECORDINGS

Dr. Halpern, whose sound advice is well respected the world over and who has authored two books on the subject, *Tuning the Human Instrument* (Spectrum Research Institute) and *Sound Health* (Harper & Row), is perhaps best known for his own recordings. Based on a new form of music he calls an Anti-Frantic Alternative™, they are innovative compositions that combine the musical elements modern research has determined to be most soothing to the human body.

One striking feature of Dr. Halpern's music is that, no matter how many times you listen to it, you won't be able to hum the melody. That's because there isn't any. Nor is there a dominant harmony or rhythm. And that's precisely the point, says Dr. Halpern.

The Anti-Frantic Alternative™: no hummable melodies or constant rhythms.

"Western music tends to elicit a conditioned response," he expalins. "If I were to sing you the scale . . . Do-Re-Me-Fa-Sol-La-Ti . . . and stopped short of the last note, your mind would automatically sound the final 'Do' to complete the musical sequence. We're locked into certain progressions.

"What my music does is break through that anticipatory response so you can get to the true impact of the tone. Without a hummable melody or constant rhythm, the brain is at first confused. It can't analyze the music in the usual way. What happens then is that we respond to the sound as

We can respond to sound as sound, not as music to be analyzed.

sound as opposed to a piece of music that can be analyzed. In my experience, when the body is allowed to choose its own response—when it isn't forced to respond to rhythmic stimulus or melodic stimulus—it chooses a very natural, healthy, and relaxing modality."

Dr. Halpern calls his music "vitamins in airways." "Because we only use certain instruments, the music is very easy to listen to," he says. "It blends with the body. Also, we don't shift key centers as quickly as in traditional western classical music. This allows the body to resonate to certain frequencies in a more healthful manner."

No other music—including classical—relaxed people as deeply.

Studies confirm the relaxing effect of Dr. Halpern's music. No other type of music, including classical and easy listening, worked for as many people on as many different levels. For example, in the laboratory, 95 percent of all those listening to Dr. Halpern's tapes experienced an almost immediate change from beta to the more relaxed alpha brainwaves. Only 25 percent of those listening to classical music experienced alpha wave increases. "Classical music may be emotionally cathartic, and moderately relaxing," Dr. Halpern says. "But my music has the potential to bring you to a deeper state of relaxation, similar to meditation."

EDITOR'S NOTE: For more information on tapes, contact LIND Institute, P.O. Box 14487, San Francisco, CA 94114, (415) 864-3396 or Halpern Sounds, 1775 Old Country Road #9, Belmont, CA 94002, (415) 592-4900 or outside California, call toll free (800) 544-4444.

PEACEFUL WATERS

Lost to antiquity is the first person to discover that water hath the power to soothe tense, overwrought spirits. In all likelihood, this momentous event in human self-care history transpired when some perturbed cave dweller accidentally stumbled into a shallow and mildly warm hot spring after a harrowing day at the mastodon factory.

When the startled screams turned to soft sighs, the therapeutic bath was born.

Since then, all sorts of water-based therapies have been developed. Some depend on temperature, some on scent, while others use the particular quality of the water to create tranquility.

A warm or neutral bath (92°F) is most relaxing.

Bath water, for example, can be a natural sedative or stimulator, depending on the taps you turn. According to Richard Hansen, M.D., medical director of the Poland

Spring Health Institute in Poland Spring, Maine, a warm or neutral bath (about 92 degrees Fahrenheit) dilates the blood vessels and increases circulation to the extremities, which dissipates heat throughout the body to relax and induce sleep. The warmth of the water relaxes muscles, too. A cool bath (about 80 to 90 degrees Fahrenheit), on the other hand, stimulates the nerves and acts as a tonic.

TUB SOAKS FOR BODY AND SOUL

Botanicals and other bath additives can enhance the soothing quality of a warm bath. Many people find that baking soda, chamomile, lavender, and/or salt are particularly calming. Or try apple cider vinegar, Epsom salts, sage, and/or seaweed for their muscle relaxant properties. Baking soda, salt, Epsom salts, or apple cider vinegar may be added directly to the bath water. Loose herbs are best brewed first as tea and then strained into the bath. Or secure the loose ingredients in a small muslin or cheesecloth bag and dangle from the faucet as water pours from the spout. Use approximately a handful of herbs per bath—or a tablespoon of each if you're combining several botanicals.

THE MIND ADRIFT

If you really want to get away from it all, you might consider an hour in a "float tank," an isolation chamber developed by John Lilly, M.D., a California dolphin researcher interested in how the mind functions when deprived of all external stimuli.

Float tanks: deep relaxation through sensory deprivation.

In the inky silence of the tank, warm, very salty water supports your body in the nearest thing to a weightless state this side of the space shuttle. Many people report that their cares drift away like summer's stifling heat after a windy thunderstorm.

But the experience is not everyone's return to the proverbial peace of the womb, for some note that isolation is in itself tension producing. And the opportunity to try the tanks is very limited, as only a few cities have them.

A WARM CUP OF HERB TEA

The ritual of preparing tea can offer some psychological advantage, says California herbalist Nan Koehler. "In China and Japan they often drink plain hot water," she says.

Holding a warm cup in your hands and feeling the steam can be soothing.

"Heating the water, holding the warm cup in your hands, and feeling the steam rise up can be tremendously soothing and relaxing."

For added comfort, however, you may want to include some herbs in your tea. First choice: chamomile. Long recognized by traditional herbalism as a harmless sedative, chamomile was tested by Lawrence Gould, M.D., and colleagues, who reported their findings in the *Journal of Clinical Pharmacology.* Actually, the purpose of their test was to see if chamomile tea had any ill effects on cardiac patients who had undergone ventricular catheterization as part of their treatment. The tests showed that drinking chamomile tea had no significant cardiac effects. But there *was* a positive reaction of a different kind: "A striking hypnotic (sleep inducing) action of the tea was noted in 10 of 12 patients," the medical team reported. "It is most unusual for patients undergoing cardiac catheterizations to fall asleep. The anxiety produced by this procedure as well as the pain associated with cardiac catheterizations all but preclude sleep. Thus," their report continues, "the fact that 10 out of 12 patients fell into a deep slumber shortly after drinking chamomile tea is all the more striking."

Chamomile: the #1 natural tranquilizer.

It seems that if someone can fall asleep right after undergoing a painful medical procedure, the more garden-variety traumas of everyday life ought to be easy work for a nice warm cup of chamomile tea.

Other herbs valued for their soothing properties include basil, catnip, hops, jasmine, lemon verbena, passionflower, peppermint, and violet leaves. Used individually or in combination, these herbs can create delightful teas.

NATURE

Head for the hills, the ocean, or a sunny meadow when you need to unwind.

Nature. What is it there that draws us when the problems get too heavy to carry around? At times it seems almost elemental, some unconscious force that leads us to a natural place to collect and define ourselves. Who at one time or another hasn't had a secret place to escape to? Sitting by the ocean, in a sunny meadow, or deep in a forest, our minds can unhook and let go of the day's troubles.

It's hard to find two people who will describe being in nature in the same way. It's a deeply personal experience, and we all bring different feelings to it.

"Nature is always changing before our eyes," says Aaron Katcher, M.D., an associate professor of psychiatry at the University of Pennsylvania. "It holds our attention and keeps us stimulated, but it doesn't demand anything. Watching the surf on a beach or the clouds roll by is a form of meditation. When our thoughts are focused on the rhythm of things, they're not occupied with problems or worries. That's why being in a natural surrounding is so good for relieving stress."

Nature holds our attention but doesn't demand anything.

For Joan, a painter and illustrator in New York City, the country is a tonic to relieve the aches and pains of living and working in a high-pressure environment.

"When New York and my job get to be too much, I head for my parents' cabin in New Hampshire," she says. "Being up there is the greatest tranquilizer in the world for me. I get out my fly rod and walk miles up and down the river every day. When I get hungry, I sit down by the water and eat my lunch. Considering how hectic my life is back in the city, it just amazes me that I can get such a kick out of looking at frogs and turtles. I feel like I'm using my brain in a different way. I'm more aware of things."

"I feel like I'm using my brain in a different way."

Others find that nature is sweeter when it offers a challenge. They'd rather scale the mountain than sit on a log in the valley. Susan, a Boston social worker, spends nearly all of her free time in the summer rock climbing. "Most of my challenges are in dealing with people," she says. "Whenever I can, I like to test myself in a different way. Climbing up a mountain lets me use a whole different set of skills. The view from up there is so much nicer when you know you've risked something to see it."

THE CALL OF THE WILD

But we can get distraction from a television set and a challenge from just driving to the supermarket. Obviously, there's something else at work here, a force that lures us to the country. It could be simply that we sometimes need a break from civilization and all the clutter that it forces on our lives.

A break from civilization—and all the clutter it forces on our lives.

"We're finding that sending someone out into the park is just as effective as giving that person tranquilizers or biofeedback training," says Michael Smith, Ph.D., of the University of Wisconsin and formerly chief of the motiva-

Nature "therapy" can be as effective as tranquilizers or biofeedback.

tion and stress research section at the National Institute for Occupational Safety and Health. "Just getting her away from the source of stress and into a relaxing environment may be the most important factor."

Two years ago, for example, Jane, an Atlanta science teacher, had all the symptoms of job burnout. The boredom of yearly repetition and the strain of performing daily for her students left her exhausted. For a time she considered leaving her job. Then one day she ran across a brochure from Earthwatch, a Belmont, Massachusetts, foundation that recruits amateur volunteers to join scientific expeditions around the world. Although she'd taken up scuba diving only a few months before, Jane decided to join an underwater team in Hawaii studying a rare mollusk that lives on the coral reefs there.

"In a way, it was a logical extension of my work, which is science, but obviously it was entirely different from teaching. I felt really involved and close to the environment," she says. "There were other people there, but when you're underwater, it's like being totally alone with nature. There aren't any noises or distractions to come between you and the beauty of the place. It's a lot like meditating."

Creating Calm through Massage

When you bump or bruise a part of your body, it's natural to try to rub away the hurt.

For the physical and mental injuries that come with the stressful territory of daily living, massage is often an effective way to lift sagging spirits.

Precisely why it works so well is difficult to say. But regardless of whether there's something in the manipulation of battle-worn muscles or a special magic in the gentle touch of caring fingers, the end result is rest and relaxation.

"The goal is to open up channels of energy, remove blockages, and restore the sense of wholeness," says Nancy Post, massage therapist and teacher from Philadelphia.

Massage is a general term that refers to several different styles of treatment. But almost any type of massage does at least the following: dilates the blood vessels and promotes circulation, cleanses the body of toxins by promoting the flow of lymph, relieves muscle tension, and makes a person feel very good.

"Swedish massage" is the kind that most people are familiar with. Developed in the early nineteenth century, this technique emphasizes long smooth strokes that always go in the direction of the heart. That is, a massage therapist using the Swedish technique would take your arm and stroke it from the wrist to shoulder. The treatment is said to give the skin a finer texture and increase muscle tone.

"Neo-Reichian massage" is another form of muscle manipulation. This method emphasizes stroking away from

Massage is a way to rub away physical and emotional hurt.

The goal is to open channels of energy.

Swedish is the most familiar form of massage.

Stroking away from the heart drains the body of nervous energy.

the heart as a way to drain the body of nervous energy. It's often used as an adjunct to psychotherapy.

"Trigger point massage" is another variation. This school of thought takes advantage of key points in the muscles which, when manipulated, cause the muscles to relax automatically.

Shiatsu: acupuncture with fingers instead of needles.

For those interested in a more Eastern massage method, there's shiatsu. In Japanese, "shi" means finger and "atzu" means pressure. Put them together, and they form the name of a treatment that is very much like acupuncture, but with fingers instead of needles.

Shiatsu massage practitioners believe that the body is mapped from head to toe with invisible "pinstripes" called meridians. Along these meridians passes the life force, called "ki" or "prana" or "innate intelligence." According to shiatsu therapists, touching makes the ki flow more freely. The easier the flow, the better our emotional lives.

Headaches, tension, and fatigue can be relieved.

The promises of shiatsu are many. Headaches, tension, constipation, and fatigue are said to be relieved by it. Some say it preserves beauty and bestows serenity.

That may sound improbable, but it sounds fine to the New York state massage licensing board. The board, which requires professional shiatsu therapists to meet educational requirements and pass a test to be certified, recognizes that shiatsu can relieve psychological stress and speed healing.

A spokesperson at the Shiatsu Education Center of America in New York City says that a session works only if the ki is flowing freely through the practitioner's body into the receiver's body. (This aspect of shiatsu is sometimes compared to jump-starting a dead car battery.) In fact, if the ki is flowing, the treatment is energizing for both of them.

Foot massage yields whole-body benefits.

Reflexology—a form of foot massage—is very similar to shiatsu. Both depend on the existence of pressure points on the surface of the body which, if massaged, promotes better circulation to the organs corresponding to the pressure points, stimulates them to function, and eliminates waste efficiently, as well as draining tension from the body as a whole.

People who regularly receive these treatments describe them as "absolutely marvelous."

At first, it feels like nothing more than a massage. Then you begin to relax. The therapist may roll her thumb along the heel, and there's that feeling of mashed Grape Nuts. Those are the crystals which, reflexologists say, are waste deposits that build up in the nerve endings and the capillaries of the feet and hinder the free circulation of the blood. The treatment supposedly breaks up the crystals so they can be flushed out of the body.

But even without that reputed benefit, the foot therapy seems to be a deeply relaxing experience, something more than just an ordinary rubdown. It may very well stimulate better circulation in the outermost extremities of the body, as it promises. At the least the treatment feels very, very good.

Massage therapists often combine a number of Eastern and Western methods in their therapy of "integrating mind, body, and spirit." But Philadelphia therapist Nancy Post maintains that for the beginner, "technique is not that important. There's knowledge in your hands that is good."

Therapists combine Eastern and Western treatments.

Your job in giving a massage, she feels, is to learn to trust your innate skills.

"Stay balanced, use complete strokes, don't jar your partner, and, above all, learn to move into the sphere of the other person with a loving intent."

Stay balanced, use complete strokes.

"Loving intent," beyond the basic knowledge of body mechanics, may have a lot to do with the bliss of a good bodyrub. Indeed, Frederick Cornhill, Ph.D., of the Ohio State University College of Medicine at Columbus, found that ordinary "TLC"—petting laboratory rabbits—reduced the rabbits' incidence of arteriosclerosis, despite a high-cholesterol diet, by 50 percent over rabbits that never knew a caring touch *(Brain Mind Bulletin)*.

The TLC that flows back and forth between massage partners may well have a similar effect in reducing stress-related diseases.

The TLC that flows between massage partners may help release stress.

And it's hard to imagine anything more relaxing than this kind of giving and receiving.

So when that ache is saying, "Slow down!" listen to your body's message and put your stress in caring hands.

LEARNING THE ART

Giving a thorough and effective massage isn't only easy—it's fun. For you don't need any familiarity with formal anatomy to give a good massage. Nor do you need

All you need is a floor mat and vegetable oil.

the herculean hands of a burly Swedish masseur. And all that's needed in the way of equipment is some padding to lay on the floor and some vegetable oil.

Do you and a partner have a few idle moments and a warm and private room? Then you're ready to begin learning the soothing art of massage. Read on—and enjoy.

The first instruction is: Don't use your bed for massage. A bed is too soft to provide a firm enough support. So, instead of bouncing around on a Beautyrest®, take two or three blankets, fold them lengthwise on the floor, and cover them with a sheet. You can also use foam as a padding, or move a single mattress onto the floor. But whatever padding you use, make sure it's at least an inch or two thick, and it should be wide and long enough so that when your partner lies down, there's still room for you to sit or kneel to one side.

Dim the lights, warm the room.

Also, you might want to turn off the overhead light; both the atmosphere and your partner will be more relaxed. Bright light that falls directly on the face will cause your partner to tense his or her eye muscles.

Keep the room warm and free of drafts. George Downing, author of *The Massage Book* (Random House), cautions that "nothing destroys an otherwise good massage more quickly than physical coldness." If your partner begins to feel cold, use a spare sheet to cover the body parts that you're not working on at the moment.

Put the oil first in the palm of your hand.

Now prepare the oil. Why use oil at all? Without a lubricating agent, your hands can't really apply enough pressure and still move smoothly over the skin. When applying oil, put about a half teaspoon into your palm and then spread it smoothly on your partner's skin. Keep the oil near you during the massage; a shallow bowl makes a handy container. Cover the entire surface area you're about to massage—arm, leg, hand, or back—with a barely visible film. Massage experts recommend sesame and olive oil, which are the easiest to wash out of sheets and clothes. You can scent the oil, mixing a few drops of essences such as clove, cinnamon, lemon, rosemary, or chamomile.

"DOES THAT FEEL GOOD?"

Keep your hands relaxed; apply pressure.

Before you actually use specific strokes, here are a few general hints. Keep your hands relaxed. Also, apply pressure.

You'll probably discover that your partner wants quite a bit more pressure than you had expected. But use the weight of your whole body to apply pressure rather than just the muscles of your hands.

Experiment with all the different ways of moving your hands that you can think of. Move them in long strokes. Move them in circles. Explore the structure of the bone and muscle. Move slowly—then speed up your tempo. Or use only your fingertips, pressing them firmly against the muscles or brushing them lightly over the skin. Gently slap. Or tap. Ask your partner for feedback: Is that enough pressure? Does that feel good?

While you're taking care of your partner, don't forget to take care of yourself. Keep your back straight whenever possible. And don't worry about how much or how little you do. You'll be moving and positioning your body in many new ways; if you don't take care of yourself, you'll end up with sore muscles. For now, concentrate on one or two body parts at a time.

Giver, keep your back straight or you'll end up with sore muscles.

Although the massage is arranged in a particular order, you should start wherever you want and end wherever you what. If you decide to work on more than a single part, apply more oil each time you move to a new area.

Finally, try to minimize the amount of turning over that your partner has to do. (It's easiest to work on the arms, hands, feet, and neck while your partner is lying face up.)

BE KIND TO YOUR SPINE

Let's start with the back, for the back is the most important part of a massage. The spine is the stalk of the central nervous system, and often anxiety and nervous tension are caused by nothing more than tight, sore muscles around the spine. Loosening these muscles can, in the words of George Downing, bring a "deep sense of release."

Loosening the back muscles can bring a deep sense of release.

First, straddle your partner's thighs. It's the easiest way to work on the back.

Now put your hands on the lower back with the fingertips pointing toward the spine. Move your hands straight up the back. When you get to the top of the back, separate your hands and bring them over the shoulder blades to the floor, and then pull them back down along the sides. Do this stroke four to six times.

Use the balls of your thumbs and make short, rapid strokes.

Now work with your thumbs on the lower back. Use the balls of your thumbs, and make short, rapid strokes away from you toward the head. Work close to the spine just below the waistline, first on the left side and then on the right.

Now put both hands on one hip with your fingers pointing straight down. Pull each hand alternately straight up from the floor, working up to the armpit and then back again. With each stroke, begin pulling one hand just before the other is about to finish so that there is no break between strokes. Do both sides.

Knead the muscles that curve from the neck to the shoulders.

Now move to the upper back. Knead the muscles that curve from your partner's neck onto his or her shoulders. Work these muscles gently between the thumb and fingers.

Now use your thumbs on the upper back just as you did on the lower back.

Finally, take the heel of your hand and place it at the base of the spine. Gently press and release, moving little by little up the spine to the neck.

A NEW WAY TO TOUCH

The effleurage: long, flowing strokes with the heels of your hands.

Now that you've finished the back, ask your partner to turn over so that you can massage the arms. But first, we'll learn a new stroke: the effleurage.

Place your hands together, one hand on top of the other and thumbs interlinked. When you move your hands, make your strokes long, flowing, and unbroken, and put your weight on the heels of your hands rather than on the fingertips. This is an effleurage.

First, effleurage the entire arm, from the wrist to the shoulder, taking your hands up over the shoulder and down the side of the arm.

Now massage the inside of the wrist with the balls of your thumbs. Work your hands downward until you have covered all the muscles lying along the inside of the arm.

Return your partner's arm to his or her side.

Now explore and massage the shoulder joint with your fingers. And end with another effleurage of the entire arm.

SOOTHING STROKES FOR THE BROWBEATEN

Don't apply oil to the face.

Now let's go on to the head. Don't apply any oil to the face before you begin; just put a few drops on your fingertips.

Massage the forehead just below the hairline with the balls of your thumbs. Start from the center of the forehead and glide both thumbs at once in either direction. Continue to the temples; now move your thumbs in a small circle. Repeat this stroke until you have covered the whole forehead—your last stroke should run just above your partner's eyebrows.

Cover the forehead with the entire left hand, heel toward one temple, fingertips toward the other. Press down. Now using the right hand, slowly and evenly add more pressure until maximum pressure is reached (your partner will tell you if it's too much). Hold ten seconds, then release very slowly. Massage lore has it that this stroke can be used to cure a nagging headache.

Now that you've smoothed your partner's harried brow, move on to another area of tension on the face: the jaw. Lightly grasp the tip of the chin between the tips of the thumb and forefinger of each hand. Follow the edges of the jaw until you have almost reached the ears, and then glide the forefingers into a small circle on the temples. Do this stroke three times.

Easing tension in the jaw.

Most of us have neck and shoulder muscles that are habitually tense—so much so that we don't even realize they're tight and bunched up. That's why loosening these muscles feels so very good.

Most of us have neck and shoulder muscles that are habitually tense.

First massage in egg-shaped circles just above the shoulder blades. Start the outer shoulders, work in toward the spine, then back along the shoulders. You might want to change the direction, speed, and width of your circles as you go. Now work between the shoulder blades and the spine. Move your fingertips in small circles. Then put your hands under the back of your partner's head, gently lift it a little and turn it slightly to the left until it rests easily in your left hand. Massage the neck with your free hand. Then turn the head and work on the other side.

33

The New Health Tapes: Relaxation Plus

Audio cassette tapes offer deep relaxation, home counseling, and more.

The prediction that our homes would someday become "electronic cottages" has come true. We can do our banking and bill paying by pushing buttons on a telephone. We can fight intergalactic video wars on our own television screens. Some of us can even choose to work at home on personal computers. We can also, with simple audio cassette tapes, relax to the soothing words of an eminent psychologist, or fall asleep to the chugging of bullfrogs down in the bayou—without leaving our armchairs.

The use of pocket-sized cassette tapes as a tool for better health and self-improvement has exploded in the last few years. With names like "Letting go of Stress," "Imagine Yourself Slim," and "Health and Wellness," there are hundreds of tapes on the market that are intended to help you get healthier—by giving you the guidance and incentive to relax, lose weight, stop smoking, recover from surgery, or improve your vision. The list is almost endless.

There's no better reinforcer of behavior change than tapes.

The physicians, psychologists, and others who produce these tapes claim that they are a more personal and effective teaching tool than books. They say the tapes blend relaxation techniques, mental imagery, and music in a way that reaches people who have a hard time sticking to book-oriented self-help plans. As one doctor says, "There's no better reinforcer of behavior change than tapes."

One highly regarded producer of tapes is Emmett Miller, M.D., of Menlo Park, California. In 1970, Dr. Miller began using hypnosis to relieve pain, and then transferred the technique to tapes. He has made tapes on all kinds of medical subjects and they're based, essentially, on the pleasure principle.

"My tapes work because they are incredibly enjoyable," says Dr. Miller. "They're much more than cold words on paper. We put together a tape with words and music that I composed, along with classical music and nature sounds. What we created was an auditory environment that seduces the person into really relaxing."

And unlike the old Hollywood image of the hypnotist having complete control over his subject, Dr. Miller's tapes teach self-hypnotic techniques to give the listener control over himself. The tapes can induce a peaceful state of mind and deep relaxation.

Teaching the listener how to relax is a key element of many of the mass-produced tapes. Typically, a voice on the tape asks you to close your eyes, breathe deeply and rhythmically, and imagine that your limbs feel warm and heavy . . . as tension ebbs from your body. Relaxation can be a goal in itself, or it can make the listener more receptive to the advice about quitting smoking or losing weight that comes later on the tape. "It's easier to learn when you're relaxed," one pyschologist says. "When you're anxious, you don't learn as well."

"It's sort of a sugar-coated pill," Dr. Miller says. "There's important information on the tape, but the listener doesn't feel bored or lectured at." Background music sweetens the pill even more.

"The right kind of music helps you relax," says C. Norman Shealy, M.D., director of the Shealy Pain and Health Rehabilitation Institute in Springfield, Missouri. Like most tape makers, he uses music.

But he has his own special theory about why music enhances the teaching power of tapes.

"My theory is that music helps occupy another channel in the mind," Dr. Shealy explains. "The brain is divided into a left hemisphere and a right hemisphere. My voice on the tape speaks to the left brain. But unless there is something to engage the right brain, it will jump around, lack focus, and try to reject the suggestions that I'm making. The music engages the right brain." In other words, the music helps his advice slip past our resistance to new ideas.

Dr. Shealy says that he began making tapes in the early

Soothing words and music create an auditory environment that seduces you into relaxing.

Relaxation can be the goal or the means to achieve a goal.

Voices speak to the left brain; music engages the right hemisphere.

seventies. He has made about 30 so far, with titles like "Sleep Harmony" and "Relaxation/Healing."

He thinks his tapes are perfect for someone who has trouble sticking to a book-oriented plan for self-improvement.

"PEOPLE NEED A GUIDE"

Pain markedly lessens when patients listen to tapes.

"We've found that many people need a guide," Dr. Shealy explains. "Very few people have the persistence to practice these mental exercises on their own. It's not an easy job. I look upon this as a retraining of the nervous system." He claims that 80 percent of his pain patients "wind up markedly improved" if they listen to the tapes every day.

Nature sounds are often combined with words and music, but they can have a dramatic effect when used alone. One one tape, called "Sailboat," you can turn your living room into an oceangoing sloop, complete with the cries of circling gulls, the splash of salt spray, the creaking of the mast, and the ringing of buoys. Another tape takes you to the Okefenokee Swamp in Georgia, where you can hear everything from the grumbling of alligators to the songs of bullfrogs and aquatic birds.

The list goes on: You can buy recordings of a summer rain on pine needles or even "melodious English songbirds, recorded at the site of a long-ruined monastery."

The most exciting element of self-help tapes is "guided imagery."

Music and nature sounds are soothing, but the really exciting element of the better self-help tapes is "guided imagery." Once it has you relaxed, the voice on the tape might ask you to form certain mental images. If you're listening to a weight-loss tape, the voice might ask you to "imagine yourself looking and feeling as you would like to look and feel in the body you'd like to develop." If you have a broken bone and are listening to a healing tape, the voice would suggest an image of the bones knitting together. If you are trying to control anger, an anti-anger tape might ask you to imagine yourself dealing calmly with anger-provoking situations. As Dr. Miller puts it, we can "rehearse new, more appropriate behavior in the mind."

Sometimes the tapes use metaphorical images with great power. On a tape called "Freedom from Worry," the listeners are asked to picture themselves "in a peaceful field, sitting in a hot-air balloon, which is tied down to the ground by long ropes." The ropes are intended to represent the worries that bind the listeners down, and they "set themselves free" by cutting the ropes with a "magical blue sword" in their minds.

A CUSTOM-MADE PROGRAM FOR PAIN RELIEF

At the Albert Einstein College of Medicine's Community Mental Health Center in New York, psychologist Stephen DeBerry, Ph.D., has taken the use of imagery one step further. Unlike the therapists mentioned above, who use standardized images for a mass audience, Dr. DeBerry custom makes anti-pain and anti-insomnia tapes for the elderly people he counsels in the New York area. Instead of using general images, like the beach or a forest, he tries to work into the tape those images that are meaningful to each person.

Custom tapes incorporate images from personal memories.

Dr. DeBerry made a tape for an 85-year-old woman of Swiss-German descent who had undergone painful bone surgery. He asked her to think of an image from the happiest time of her life. The image was of a château in Switzerland where she lived as a child. She said it looked like a castle, that it was made of yellow brick and had tall windows full of light. Dr. DeBerry put all of that into her tape and asked her to listen to it whenever she experienced pain.

After listening to the tape four or five times, the woman reported that she was almost pain-free for hours after hearing it and that she needed less pain medication. "You can go to Macy's and buy a suit, or you can have one made for you," says Dr. DeBerry. "They'll both serve the same purpose, but you'll feel more comfortable with the one made for you. Everyone is different, and how would a standardized tape know about that château in Switzerland?"

Dr. DeBerry's tapes are usually extensions of live counseling sessions with his patients. The tapes work, he says, because his voice on tape strongly reminds them of the good feelings they experienced with him in person. "Auditory memory is very vivid for many people . . . more vivid than a photograph," he says. "It's like the difference between listening to radio and watching TV. With radio you have to use your imagination more."

Auditory memory is more vivid than a photograph.

Convenience is something else that cassettes offer.

Once you have made the initial investment in a cassette player, they're as portable as books and you can use them in places where you can't read—such as in your car.

ANTIDOTE FOR TRAFFIC JAMS

A California cardiologist produced a relaxation tape for people stuck in traffic jams.

The idea of using self-improvement tapes while driving could only have come from California, and it did. Los Angeles cardiologist Gershon Lesser, M.D., has produced a relaxation tape for helping people with bad hearts stay calm when they're sitting in a traffic jam on the Santa Monica freeway.

"We spend a major portion of our time in automobiles," says Dr. Lesser. "Here in Los Angeles, people commonly drive two hours a day, to work and back, and sometimes get stuck in traffic. If they listen to music on the radio, it makes them even more frazzled. This is a good time to listen to my tape."

Imagine that your heart is "warm, safe, and understanding."

Dr. Lesser's voice on the tape reminds those with Type A, workaholic, heart-attack-prone personalities that it's all right for them to relax and not do three things at once. He also asks them to imagine that their hearts are "warm, safe, and understanding." Dr. Lesser designed the tape to help his heart patients prevent a second coronary, but now he also gives it to people who want to prevent their first coronary. He claims that before he started using the tape, half of his patients suffered a second heart attack in five years. Less than 1 in 100 patients has a relapse now, he says.

Take a relaxing walk with your cassette player.

The new miniature headset-type cassette players that people wear while walking make the tape even more convenient, Dr. Lesser says. "It's great for the noon hour," he says. "Instead of going out for a 3,000-calorie lunch, you can put the tape in one of those players and take a walk. You'll come back and find that you're relaxed and a pound or two lighter."

Tapes are effective, Dr. Lesser believes, because they establish a human, rather than a professional, connection between doctor and patient. Participation is another factor. "In order to learn better, you've got to participate. The tapes get you involved by meditating or exercising along with the tape," he says. "Reading is fine, but you can go a step further by working with a tape."

A tape can also make life more convenient for people

who are too shy to attend a live exercise class. Grace Hill, a dance and exercise instructor in Hanover, New Hampshire, conducted live classes for years before deciding to expand her audience by publishing a tape and workbook, *Fitness First* (Grace Hill).

"There are some people who say they can never find the time for a class, and then there are people who say, 'I wouldn't let anyone see me in tights.' And people have told me, 'I can't remember the exercises after I leave class,'" Hill says. "I made the tape partly for them.

Shy about attending an exercise class? Take a private tape lesson.

"One of the advantages of the tape is that you can take it with you anywhere. And it's better than a workbook alone, because on the tape I keep reminding them to relax their facial muscles, release the tension in their shoulders, and stay well balanced on their feet. A book alone can't do that," she says.

(Tapes, by the way, are perfect for those of us who get lazy from time to time. For example, it's much easier to plug in a relaxation tape than to recite a mantra [a word or sound that, when repeated in the mind, brings on a meditative state]. Dr. Shealy says, "When I'm tired I even listen to my own tapes—it's sort of a treat.")

It's easier to plug into a relaxation tape than recite a mantra.

You can make your own tapes too. Tom Ferguson, M.D., editor of the California-based magazine *Medical Self-Care,* says he has created a tape to help wake himself up in the morning. "On my wake-up tape, I say to myself, 'You don't have to get up right now. Just enjoy lying there for a few more minutes. Now you're becoming more alert. It's going to be a wonderful day . . . ' and so on," he says. "You can really tailor the tape to suit yourself. You can put on your favorite music or you can tape passages from your favorite books." He switches on his cassette player in the morning with a simple electric timer.

Tapes can also be sent to special friends in place of letters. "Maintaining close human relationships is essential to health," Dr. Ferguson says, "and taped messages can have more impact than letters." He gives one warning, however: If you tape your own voice, it will sound strangely high pitched. Ordinarily, internal resonances within your body make your voice sound lower to you than to others.

Make your own tape and send it to a friend.

If you decide to experiment with a relaxation tape, be patient with it. Peggy Taylor, formerly an editor with *New Age* magazine in Boston, Massachusetts, explains, "Your first impression when you listen to a tape is that it's making you more, not less, tense. That's because you're moving along at your usual high speed, and the tape forces you to slow down and listen to it. The tension can be unbearable at first. You think, 'It's not working,' but by the end of the tape, you find that you're settled down."

Tape quality varies considerably.

Taylor and others say that shopping for a good tape that suits your purpose can be difficult. There are hundreds of tapes on the market. Some use sophisticated music and guided imagery, others are simply the sound of a man or woman lecturing. Some tapes are good, others bad, and it can be difficult to tell which is which before you lay down the $8.98 or so.

EDITOR'S NOTE: You can find information on tapes in *Medical Self-Care* magazine, P.O. Box 1000, Point Reyes, CA 94956. The best source of all is probably the Yes! Bookshop, 1035 31st Street NW, Washington, DC 20007, which publishes a large catalog of tapes that have been screened for quality and effectiveness.

Expanding the Bounds
of Your Private Space

In a busy airport, a sail-
or sits down beside you. You move over to "make room."
Waiting in line for a bus, you and a dozen other people space
yourselves out like sparrows on a telephone wire. At a party,
a talkative bore keeps advancing on you, and you keep
moving back . . . until you find you've been pushed across
the room.

A sense of "personal space"—that invisible front lawn
we put between ourselves and the world out there—is
something we rarely even notice. But let some unwelcome
stranger violate our private domain, and suddenly we feel
on edge, uneasy, even hostile.

"When our personal space has been invaded, we are
likely to react with discomfort, anxiety, irritation . . . even
anger and aggression," says Paul Insel, Ph.D., a consultant
to a study of the human need for solitude and coauthor of
Core Concepts in Health (Mayfield Publishing Co.). Perhaps even more important, however, privacy is necessary
for "permitting us to carry out self-understanding and
self-identity," he adds.

But what happens to our health when there is just no
space left for private domains? What happens when the
elbow room runs out? With the earth's population expected
to double in our lifetime (to seven billion by 2006), the
effect of crowding on human health is something we can't
afford to ignore.

American social thought has held for centuries that
big, crowded cities are morally degrading and dangerous to

**Privacy helps you establish
your identity.**

**When our space is invaded,
we react with discomfort
and anxiety.**

your mental and physical health. And the idea that crowded living conditions breed emotional ill health seemed to be confirmed in 1962, when the results of a comprehensive mental health survey called the Midtown Manhattan Study were published. Conducted by a team from Cornell University, the study concluded that 23 percent of the residents of Manhattan's East Side, both rich and poor, showed psychiatric symptoms. It looked like nearly a quarter of the city's population was in emotional trouble!

At the same time, animal studies on the effects of overcrowding—particularly the rat studies of John B. Calhoun, Ph.D.—were adding scientific evidence to preconceived notions. And together they created a grim picture indeed.

A study of a rat paradise.

Dr. Calhoun, a research psychologist at the National Institute of Mental Health, began a now-classic crowding study by building a quarter-acre "paradise" for a population of rats. They had plenty of food, no worries about predators or disease, and were allowed to breed freely until, after 27 months, the little society had stopped growing at 150 adults. At that level of population density, Dr. Calhoun observed an unusually high rate of baby deaths and other signs of stress.

Next, he moved his experiment indoors and allowed the rats to breed to twice that density. And for the next 16 months, he and his associates watched as the rat society broke down into sickness, chaos, and death.

Crowding's effect on humans isn't so simple.

But the true picture of crowding's effect on humans may not be quite so simple, many scientists now believe. Dr. Calhoun's rat studies were just that—studies of rats and not humans, whose behavior is far more complex. And for every statistic showing that cities breed crime, violence, and disease, there's another to show it's just the same in the country . . . only more spread out.

Jonathan L. Freedman, Ph.D., in his book *Crowding and Behavior* (Viking Press), describes a study he and his colleagues conducted to explore the relationship between population density and crime in various metropolitan areas in the United States. Dr. Freedman was especially interested in crimes of aggression like murder, rape, and assault (rather than car theft or burglary) because, he explained, many earlier crowding studies were based on the assumption that crowding causes people to become more aggressive.

But strangely enough, his study showed that "those crimes most related to aggressive feelings, which should be the best indication of the effects of crowding, show absolutely no relation to population density." Crime rates *were* related to other things, particularly income and education, but not crowding.

In fact, when Dr. Freedman examined juvenile delinquency in several poor neighborhoods in New York City, he was surprised to find that population density had a *reverse* relation to crime rates: Crowded neighborhoods had a *lower* juvenile delinquency rate that uncrowded ones. Dr. Freedman points out that a noisy, bustling, crowded city street is actually much safer than a quiet, dark, deserted one. After summing up his own research and that of others, he concludes that "crowding does not have generally negative effects on humans."

A study of rural Nova Scotia indicates that city life is no more harmful to your health than life down on the farm. Done at about the same time as the Midtown Study, it found that about a third of the residents there suffered from emotional troubles of one kind or another.

City life is no worse than life on the farm.

Thus Nova Scotia, with a population density of about 20 residents per square mile, had a higher incidence of mental illness than Manhattan.

Could it be that "population density" isn't really the point? That "crowdedness" is just the name for a feeling that depends more on our sense of mental space than the nearness of our neighbors?

"A widowed person living alone in a large suburban house may have more than enough room. But two warring marital partners occupying a space similar in size may complain bitterly of a lack of room," observe Norman Ashcraft, Ph.D., and Albert Scheflen, M.D., in their book *People Space: The Making and Breaking of Human Boundaries* (Doubleday & Co.).

STAKING OUR CLAIM

Drs. Ashcraft and Scheflen maintain that people stake out a personal space or territory (usually unconsciously) in much the same way a songbird or a grizzly bear stakes out its hunting ground. But the size of the space we lay claim to depends on all sorts of things—our sex and mood, the nature of the occasion, even our cultural background.

Our personal territory may depend on our mood.

People with North European or British ancestry use about a square yard of space for conversation in uncrowded conditions, the scientists claim. But people from more tropical climates stake out a much smaller personal turf, and are much more likely to reach out and touch the occupant of a neighboring space.

Observing the way different cultures make use of space.

As part of their research, Drs. Ashcraft and Scheflen arranged to have videotape cameras left running in various households in New York City. And they observed some distinct differences in the way families of differing cultural backgrounds made use of space.

"It is not unusual to witness a Puerto Rican family of six or seven huddled closely together in one room for the duration of the evening hours," they noted.

Puerto Rican children tended to congregate together.

In one Puerto Rican home, they observed three small boys crowded together in a single rocking chair watching television, with the smallest one sprawled across the laps of the other two—even though there were other places to sit in the room. During commercial breaks one of the youngsters might get up, stretch, horse around, leave the room, and then come back to climb into the chair on top of his brothers. This went on for most of an afternoon.

But blacks, and whites of Anglo-Saxon heritage, they observed, tended to spread out through the apartment rather than congregate in one room, sat further apart when they did sit down together, and in other ways used space much differently. One person's warmheartedness may be another's violation of privacy.

People felt crowded in a messy room.

Trying to put their finger on exactly what crowding is, Drs. Ashcraft and Scheflen could only point to other studies that demonstrated how subjective it all is. Students in a test situation felt crowded if the room was messy, even though its only occupants were the student and a researcher. Yet they *didn't* feel crowded when the room was cleaned up, even when several other people were present. Some felt crowded when the heat and humidity were high. For others, it was the presence of strangers that made them feel boxed in.

The zones of intimacy: personal, social, public.

Some anthropologists point out that people follow quite firmly established rules in how far apart they stand, depending largely on their relationship to one another. According to one theory, friends, spouses, lovers, parents, and children

BOX 33: IS YOUR WORLD TOO CLOSE FOR COMFORT?

As any interior designer knows, illusions created with color, mirrors, and windows can make a room feel airy and spacious—or cramped and uncomfortable. In the same way, researchers believe, you may feel crowded because of all sorts of subjective things, although that doesn't make the feeling any less real. Your mood, cultural background, sex, status, and, of course, who you're crowded *with* can all make a difference.

This quiz helps you understand why you may feel "hemmed in" at home or at work.

1. Do you have any "dual-purpose" rooms in your home, like a kitchen/dining room or bathroom/utility room? (Any space seems more crowded if it's being used for more than one purpose.)

2. Are there rooms in your home you're using in a way for which they weren't designed? (That makes a space seem more crowded, too.)

3. Are a great many *different* things being done in your home? (Researchers say high "role density," or a large number of different activities going on at once, can make a home feel smaller.)

4. Can you get away from home as much as you'd like? (If not, your home may feel more cramped than it really is.)

5. Are you really unsure what to expect from your children, parents or other housemates? (A space seems smaller if the people in it are uncertain of each other's status.)

6. Do you have a big yard, or a park near your home? (How much indoor space you need depends on the amount of outdoor space you have access to.)

7. Does your home have large windows with a pleasant view? (Windows "borrow space" from outdoors.)

8. Are there rooms or parts of rooms in your home that you rarely use? (Having enough unoccupied space plays an important role in whether you feel crowded or not.)

9. Do you live or work with people of only your own sex? (Several studies have shown that women don't mind being crowded with other women as much as men mind being crowded with other men.)

10. Do you share your home or workplace with others who are very different from you in age or social class? (That, along with the presence of strangers, makes space "shrink.")

tend to stand inside a sort of "zone of intimacy," or within arm's reach. A "personal zone" (about four feet) is for conversation with acquaintances and strangers. There is a still-larger "social zone," and a "public zone" of 25 feet or more, reserved for public figures on formal occasions.

There is also some evidence that men and women have different space requirements. One researcher found that females tend to stand closer together than males at all ages, even as young children. Another researcher set up two model rooms, one large and one small, with a number of dolls in each room. Then the reactions of a group of men and women were tested. Men, the researcher found, saw the small room as smaller than the females saw it, and consistently rated rooms with a large number of dolls in them as more crowded than the women did. The study concluded that men are more sensitive than women to space restrictions (*Science Digest*).

Fifteen Healthy
Reasons to Take
a Vacation

"**I** need a vacation."

It's what you say when you're at the end—the very

At the end of your rope?

end—of your rope. But is a vacation really the answer to your problems? Won't they be just the same when you get back? Fortunately, no. Because you'll be different.

Whether you're taking off for the Alps or a mountain lake 30 miles from home, the pink beaches of some tropical island or the pink back porch of your cousin's cottage at the shore—your vacation is going to change you for the better. According to psychologists, getting away from it all—breaking free from routine—can bring new perspective to old dilemmas and put a positive charge in your mental outlook—even help to fan those waning embers of enthusiasm. You'll also get to know yourself a little better. And when you return home, you'll be happier, healthier, and much more effective in coping with stress.

Sounds like a tall order. But vacations can fill it. Here are 15 reasons why.

1. Relaxation.

"Just the act of getting away from your daily frustra-

**Vacations break your
day-to-day routine.**

tions will relax you," says Richard I. Curtis, author of *Taking Off* (Harmony Books). "Even if you come up against some new problems on your trip, you can treat these like a game. They're temporary. The important thing is, you are getting out of your day-to-day rut," continues Curtis.

Edward Heath, Ph.D., professor in the department of recreation and parks of Texas A&M University, agrees:

"When you take a vacation, you escape the humdrum

of daily life. You leave your troubles behind you. Even if all you do is sit on the edge of the river and watch the water move, it's a valuable change of pace. You're going to recharge your batteries. You'll return refreshed and renewed."

2. Stimulation of new sights.

Richard Curtis says, "Almost any travel is good. Staying at home for too long tends to crimp our awareness. We need the exposure to new sights and experiences. Think of the first time you saw mountains, or the sea, or the desert, or the Grand Canyon—I don't mean pictures. I mean actually being there, in a place which is totally different from anything you're used to."

New sights give us new insights.

New sights of things around us can give us new *insights*, too, according to Dr. Heath. "You can get a broader view, a new perspective on your own world, if you visit a different place. For example, if you live at the mouth of the Mississippi, or the Hudson, or some other great river, you may understand your own region better after visiting the headwaters of the river. You may learn something about yourself, too, namely, that you might like to move to that new area. Lots of people take advantage of their vacations to look over other regions they might like to move to someday."

3. Meeting new people.

"We're very social animals," Dr. Heath says.

Seeing how other people live broadens our perspective on our own lives.

"A vacation gives us the opportunity to form new friendships—or just to satisfy our curiosity about how other people live. This gives us a broader perspective on our own lives."

Richard Curtis agrees: "The more people you know, the more eyes you can borrow to look on the world. And the further those eyes are from your own world, the better."

4. Fellowship and camaraderie.

"Sharing an adventure with other people allows us to share their enthusiasm, too. That's good. It's positive reinforcement for our own enthusiasm about life," Dr. Heath says.

Shared hardships also form bonds of love and friendship.

"But it doesn't necessarily have to be easygoing. Shared *hardships* also form bonds of love and friendship and give us something to look back on with pride and pleasure.

"Every year thousands of people meet at one spot in Canada and form a caravan with their recreational vehicles and eat each other's dust all the way to Alaska. Then they're back again the next year.

"Twenty years from now, you'll remember and talk about the canoe trip where the weather suddenly changed and you spent two days huddled over a campfire, shivering.

"There's also a benefit in associating with like-minded people in some competitive event. People travel thousands of miles to cheer their team in the Super Bowl or the playoffs.

"Marathon runners travel halfway across the world to run in a race and be surrounded by thousands of other runners."

5. Education.

"You may need or want to learn new skills on your vacation," Dr. Heath says.

Learn a new language.

"You may decide to learn a new language before traveling to a foreign country. Or you may learn as you go along in order to communicate with people there. You may decide to learn snorkeling, or tennis, or golf, or skiing, or mountain climbing, or hang gliding, or any new skill."

6. Adventure.

"Travel returns a sense of adventure to your life," says Curtis. "Pulling yourself off your native turf is going to make demands on your resourcefulness—to find suitable lodging and food. But you're also allowed to *experiment* with your personality and lifestyle without having to live with the consequences. If you're usually too shy to say hello and smile at strangers, you may allow yourself the adventure of doing just that on your vacation in a new place. It may then become a habit you can bring home with you."

Improve your self-esteem by accepting challenges that don't exist in everyday life.

The element of *risk* is also a part of many vacation adventures, according to Dr. Heath. "Most travel involves accepting and meeting challenges. You test yourself against a new environment. You can improve your self-esteem by taking on challenges that everyday life doesn't offer. Of course, sometimes everyday life may involve greater risk. Waterskiing, mountain climbing, skydiving—all *seem* quite scary. But though they may be more thrilling, they actually are safer than driving on the freeway."

7. Surprise.

Learning from the unexpected.

"It is the unexpected in life that we learn from," says Curtis. "We gain the most when we put ourselves on the line and remain open to new experiences. On a trip you have to adapt very quickly. You bring much of that enhanced adaptability home with you." Not to mention the stories of all your surprises, which you'll remember for many years.

8. Beauty.

Open your eyes and tune into the majesty of nature.

"When you're standing in the middle of a beautiful environment, and you open your eyes to it, you start to feel in tune with it. You can actually begin to feel beautiful *yourself*. You share in some of the beauty and power," Dr. Heath says. "You may have such a peak experience in a natural setting, like the Grand Canyon—or your awe might be inspired by the beauty of some man-made edifice such as the Vatican, or a bridge, or a whole city.

"These experiences we never forget are very important to our enjoyment of life."

9. Anticipation.

The planning and preparation are also good for you.

Have we got you itchin' to hit the road for action and adventure and new people, places, and things? Are you so excited you can't wait to plan your vacation? Good, because that's part of the benefit of a vacation. "Your vacation," according to Dr. Heath, "is more than the actual time spent away from home. The planning and preparations are also good for you. Many vacations are actually year-long projects. A person may prepare for a fishing trip, for example, by tying flies. The anticipation is pleasurable. The trip is, too, because you reap the rewards of extensive preparation."

10. Memories.

"Your life is enriched before, during, and after a vacation," Dr. Heath says. "You'll always have the joy of reflecting on pleasant memories."

11. Freedom.

"A vacation gives us the freedom to do what we want to do," says Dr. Heath.

Even if you are generally satisfied, you may yearn for something more.

"Our bodies have the remarkable ability to recognize a deficiency and try to compensate for it," notes Curtis. "For instance, North American Indians who lived in northern regions where sources of vitamin C were rare compensated by eating pine needles. The mind seems to have a myriad of ways to deal with psychological problems, too, without necessarily consulting the brain's owner. Our desire for change occurs regularly. Even if you are generally satisfied with your life and work, you may still feel the need for something more. You may feel closed in. Take a vacation and you will realize your own freedom. You'll see that the mundane world can be transcended at will. It can be left behind. You're not a prisoner if you choose not to be."

12. Self-discovery.

"A vacation can be a great opportunity for sorting out life's experiences," Dr. Heath says. "You can shut off the sensory overload that may be your everyday life and get away to a deserted beach or a mountain stream.

"You can let your soul talk to itself. The dialogue you carry on with yourself is very important. You need it to develop your creativity and your inner peace and harmony."

Let your soul talk to itself.

13. Appreciation of things taken for granted.

"You'll be surprised at the things for which you become homesick," Curtis says. "You'll crave the simple pleasure of finding someone who speaks your language. I have felt almost sick for the sight of a lilac, for a maple tree, for ice cream sodas, for a long, hot shower and even—I hate to admit it—for American fast food. I once ran alongside an American's car for three blocks in Yugoslavia—just to hear an old Simon and Garfunkel song on his tape player.

"When you get home, you will get more from life. You'll see the miracles where you live."

Homecoming brings a rediscovery of the commonplace.

14. Time stands still.

"If you're really enjoying yourself," Dr. Heath says, "time does not progress in equal units. You stop thinking about everything else but what you're doing then and there.

"You get lost in the activity of the moment. You may be catching fish, or trying to keep dry while canoeing through the rapids, or looking for pretty shells along the beach.

"Time is standing still for you and that's good. There's evidence that happy people are those who can give full attention to what's going on at *that moment*."

The best part is when you get completely lost in the moment.

15. Happiness.

We saved the most important reason for last: "The major goal of a vacation is happiness," says Dr. Heath. "Your leisure time should make you happier. A vacation is not a necessary evil you endure to enable you to work harder when you get back. Your leisure makes up a large segment of your life, and it can and should be a valuable force for good. You should like your life a little better after a vacation."

36

Choosing a Counselor

If you found yourself bogged down in a legal dispute, you probably wouldn't hesitate to consult a lawyer. If you found the Dow-Jones average rising or falling at an alarming rate, you'd naturally pick up the phone and call your broker. And when you're in the backyard planting tomatoes, you aren't too proud to look over the fence and ask your neighbor for advice.

Why feel inhibited about seeking a health counselor?

Why is it, then, that like so many others, you feel inhibited about seeking expert counsel when it comes to problems concerning your physical or emotional welfare? Your personal life is obviously far more important than any stocks, bonds, or tomatoes.

There is certainly no shortage of professional guidance. Most communities offer, in addition to the usual selection of physicians, psychiatrists, and psychologists, a cornucopia of health educators, lifestyle counselors, family therapists, ministers, and others who are able and willing to help.

The good ones give you skills to cure yourself.

Even if you're a stickler for self-reliance and would prefer not to lean on a professional, you'll find that the best health counselors will not be out to treat or cure you. The good ones would rather give you the information and the skills that you will require to treat and hopefully cure yourself.

What follows is a survey of a few of the less usual and often overlooked sources of health-related advice and counseling. Not to be confused with self-help groups, these are categories of professionals who in most cases command fees comparable to those of M.D.'s and psychologists. For example:

FAMILY THERAPISTS

Suppose that several ticklish problems are confronting your family at the same time. Maybe you and your spouse are fighting a long, entrenched cold war. Maybe your daughter's asthma is getting worse. And maybe your son stays out late every night and is flunking biology.

One course of action would be to hire a marriage counselor for yourselves, send your daughter to an allergy specialist, and let the school guidance counselor take care of your son. But that strategy could turn out to be both expensive and ineffective. It overlooks the possibility that all three issues feed on one another, and that they should be treated as parts of a single, complex problem. And the right person to turn to for advice might be a family therapist.

Family issues are treated as parts of a single, complex problem.

"We try to get behind the scenes," says family therapist Joan Barth of Doylestown, Pennsylvania. "If the man of the house has had friction with his wife for the past few months, I ask some questions. I might find out that he's about to turn 50, and that his father and brothers all died at that age. Or I may talk to the daughter who has asthma. It may turn out that her wheezing attacks come on whenever her parents fight.

"We go beyond simple cause and effect and show that there are lots of causes and lots of effects when it comes to the problems in a family. And we try to get rid of the idea that there are good guys and bad guys. We don't blame anyone."

"We go beyond simple cause and effect."

Unlike a psychiatrist, a family therapist routinely sees more than one family member at once. Barth says that she might talk to the parents alone, or just the daughter, or just the father and son. Sometimes she'll have supper at home with the family, to study its dynamics up close. "Every member of the family has a contribution to make toward solving the problem," she says. "A three-year-old once said to me, 'Mommy and Daddy aren't talking to each other anymore.'"

Family therapists are often the counselors of choice when one member of the family suffers from a chronic illness such as heart disease or epilepsy, Barth says. Even when its symptoms are sporadic, as in epilepsy, an illness has the power to keep an entire family on edge for years. Their anxieties can become so entangled that only a professional can unknot them.

The counselors of choice during chronic illness.

Unlike psychologists or psychiatrists, family therapists generally do not treat their clients for more than a few months. And they emphasize teaching the family how to treat itself. "When I arrive, there's usually some kind of logjam," Barth says. "So I get the logjam unstuck, and then I get out of there."

MINISTERS, PRIESTS, AND RABBIS

Some family or personal crises seem to demand help from the clergy. At the death of a child, for instance, religious parents often turn to their pastor for help in dealing with their grief, their anger at God, and their guilt about feeling angry. Similarly, devout couples may feel that only a rabbi or minister can help when they feel angry or disappointed that their child married outside of the faith. But many people don't feel obligated to wait for a crisis before seeing their pastor. They feel free to ask for the pastor's advice at any time.

Someone familiar, someone to trust.

"When a person is in a crisis, he comes to someone who is familiar, whom he can trust," says Rabbi Jack D. Frank, leader of an orthodox synagogue in Chicago. "Today many of the clergy are trained to handle crisis, and most seminaries require a certain amount of psychological training for ordination."

Indeed, a growing number of pastors and ministers have chosen to be full-time counselors rather than leaders of congregations. The Institute for Religion and Health in New York, which was founded by author-clergyman Norman Vincent Peale and psychiatrist Smiley Blanton, M.D., has been offering advanced training in counseling to pastors for more than 50 years. The American Association of Pastoral Counselors, headquarters in Fairfax, Virginia, has 2,500 members and is growing. Large congregations sometimes employ several ministers, one of whom might specialize in counseling, and sometimes you'll find a counseling clinic attached to a church or hospital.

Open to those of any faith, or no faith.

For formal counseling sessions, pastoral counselors do charge fees, but they say that they don't turn anyone away for lack of funds. Their doors are always open, in most cases, to those of any faith or no faith at all.

"We draw on religious tradition and wisdom," says Tim Barett, a student at the Institute of Religion and Health, "but we don't tell people what to do with their lives.

And it's not like going to confession." Rev. William North, a full-time counselor at a clinic in St. Louis, adds, "We look upon the counseling process as one leading to spiritual growth, but we won't bring up the subject of spirituality unless it's important to that individual."

There's one caveat, however, to consulting your minister. **Not for long-term counseling.** Pastors sometimes discourage members of their congregation from coming to them with problems that will require more than four or five one-hour sessions to resolve. For a pastor who also has a church to run, intensive counseling can create conflicts of interest. If your minister is one who shies away from long-term counseling, he or she can probably refer you to a pastor who counsels full-time.

FRIENDS

"Almost any problem that will yield to professional counseling also will yield to counseling by a friend," says Paul Welter, Ed.D., a professor of counseling and educational psychology at Kearney State College in Nebraska. "Friends can even help in situations where there are no easy answers, such as depression or anxiety, or suicidal intentions."

A good friend can bring respect, loyalty, and an up-close **For people reluctant to reveal** awareness of the way you really feel to every counseling **secrets to a stranger.** session, Dr. Welter believes. And people who are reluctant to reveal secrets to a stranger, or who reject professional help as a sign of weakness, often feel more comfortable confiding in a close friend. In his book *How to Help a Friend* (Tyndale House), Dr. Welter offers some advice on how to tell which friends make the best counselors.

"Not all people can act as counselors," Dr. Welter says. "Look for someone who cares unconditionally about you, and has gotten past the stage of handing out easy answers and cheap advice."

And be on the lookout for "felons," he says. Ninety **Felons: people who steal the** percent of the people whom you confide in will commit a **conversation.** "felony." That is, they will immediately reply with a story about how the same thing happened to them two years ago at Aunt Clara's and so on and so forth. "These people steal the conversation from you. And once they've taken it, you probably won't get it back," Dr. Welter says.

Other would-be counselors to avoid, Dr. Welter says, are those who are merely curious about your problem and probably can't keep a secret, those who listen to you only because they are lonely and need company, those who would rather give you advice than hear you out, and those who rush in and try to solve our problems for you.

HEALTH EDUCATORS

A health professional who has the time.

Maybe you're in reasonably good health, but you want to lose some weight. Or perhaps you're curious about nutrition but you can't find a health professional who has the time or the patience to just sit down with you and talk about the finer points of developing a good diet or supplement regimen. Or maybe you have a condition that made your doctor throw up his hands and say there was nothing he could do to help you.

In any of those cases, you might try consulting a health educator. You can often find one on staff at wellness centers and health clinics that have sprung up in the past few years. They often work under the supervision of an M.D., and they may or may not have professional degrees after their names.

One such health educator is Susan Rutherford, whose private practice, Vitality Fair, is located in North Bend, Washington, a little town nestled in the foothills of the majestic Cascade range. Rutherford boasts a decade of experience as a family-planning counselor, a teacher of stress management, and a counselor of people with self-image problems. During those ten years, she also lost 30 pounds, and now feels qualified to show others how to lose weight on their own.

"I don't treat; I educate."

"I don't treat; I educate," Rutherford says. "I can't prescribe medication, but I can counsel people on changing their diet, getting more exercise, and relaxing more. I usually deal with people who are trying to manage chronic diseases like colitis or high blood pressure or diabetes. I have a lot of success with people who are trying to lose weight.

"One of my major successes was a woman who weighed 260 pounds and suffered from myasthenia gravis. Her muscles had lost all their tone and were virtually useless to her. Her doctor said he couldn't help her. I told her, 'Let's try to get to the root of this thing.'

"So we cut refined carbohydrates out of her diet. Then we discovered that she was allergic to about 40 different foods. We also found that for most of her life, she was the full-time nurturer of her family. Subconsciously, her illness was giving *her* a chance to be the nurtured one. Then we used biofeedback techniques to help her learn to relax and to get in touch with her feelings about the illness. Within a year she was down to 150 pounds and free from symptoms of myasthenia gravis.

"In California," Rutherford explains, "almost everyone knows what a health educator is. But up here in Washington, very few people have heard of us. We tell them that we just use commonsense health methods. We're not fanatics, we don't use a lot of jargon, and we don't have any books or products to promote."

"We don't have products to promote."

SOCIAL WORKERS

Suppose that your elderly parent or grandparent begins to behave strangely. She might suddenly decide to wander around the house in the wee hours. She might lose her temper for no apparent reason, or accuse you of stealing her favorite pair of scissors. If you take her to a psychiatrist, chances are that she'll be diagnosed as a victim of Alzheimer's disease, a poorly understood and untreatable form of dementia.

But if you're dissatisfied with that diagnosis and want a second opinion, where could you turn?

You might try consulting someone like Naomi Feil of Cleveland, Ohio. As a master of social work who conducts workshops throughout Canada and the United States, Feil uses counseling techniques similar to those of a psychologist. Like a psychologist, she focuses on her patients' choice of words, their body language, and the way they dress. Then she forms an opinion of their mental state. Her specialty is counseling "old, old" people (age 80+)—and their families— who, in her opinion, have been misdiagnosed as having Alzheimer's disease.

Counseling techniques similar to those of a psychologist.

The bizarre behavior that appears to be the symptom of Alzheimer's disease, she says, is often the awkward, desperate, but innocent attempt by older people to vent fears and angers that they've bottled up for decades.

A different interpretation of Alzheimer's disease.

"The adult children of these people and the staffs of nursing homes assume that the doctor is right when he says they have dementia or Alzheimer's disease. But in many cases, an older person is just trying to say, 'I can't take it anymore,'" says Feil.

"Older people's feelings become incontinent. Suddenly

the cork pops and everything that was bottled up for all those years comes flying out." But it doesn't have to be that way, Feil explains, if those feelings can be released in a healthy way.

"If a person learns how to grieve, and how to face problems as they come up, then he or she will probably not become confused or disoriented in old age," she says.

Fitness specialists. Those are, of course, only a handful of the kinds of counselors that you will find in most communities. There are many others worthy of mention. For example, most YMCAs employ fitness specialists who can put you on a stationary bicycle and measure your level of fitness and heart rate. Then they'll give you the advice you need to set up a custom-made exercise program.

Sex therapists. For people whose problems originate in the bedroom, the members of the American Association of Sex Educators, Counselors, and Therapists can help. There are about 1,300 certified therapists and they deal with physical as well as emotional barriers to healthy sex.

Clearly, there is no problem too large or small, too common or unusual, for which there are no trained counselors or advisors. And finding good advice may be as easy as riffling through the yellow pages, contacting a nearby university, or simply telephoning a close and trustworthy friend.

PART VII

Psychological First-Aid

Quick Relief
from High Anxiety:
An Energizing Five-Minute
Routine

You remember the feeling: You'd been out since nearly daybreak, ski touring through the silent, snowy woods—or hiking along the seaward cliffs, or swimming in the surf, or even cleaning out the garage—and by the time you got back to the house you were *beat*. But it felt so good! Your exhaustion was a strange kind of sensuous pleasure. It seemed to fill your whole body with a sleepy warmth, a sensation of really having lived.

For most of us, unfortunately, that "good tired" feeling is all too rare an experience. When we feel tired, it's just plain tired—worn out, dragged down, done in. That's because, of all the many causes of fatigue, physical exertion is the least common, says M. F. Graham, M.D., a Dallas physician.

"Exhaustion due to stress and tension, caused by mental and emotional pressures, is far more common in this day and age than physical fatigue," Dr. Graham says. "But the great thing is that tension fatigue responds very nicely to a simple antidote: exercise."

The reason for that, Dr. Graham says, goes way, way back. Long ago, our bodies began to develop a complex response to impending danger known as the "fight or flight" or "adrenergic" response. The crackle of twigs outside the cave door put the cave-owner's body on instant, emergency alert. He was ready to take on whatever was out there—or, if it was too big, to turn tail and run. Whichever he did, all that built-up tension would be completely drained out of his system by the time he was through.

Physical exhaustion is a "good tired" feeling; mental exhaustion just wears you out.

Tension fatigue responds to a simple antidote: exercise.

Stress is not new. What's different is our lifestyles: Cave people ran; twentieth-century people sit and stew.

But today the world is different. There's a genuine shortage of saber-toothed tigers, for one thing, and for another, most of us aren't as active as we ought to be. So the twentieth-century housewife or office worker has to make do with a chronically alerted "fight or flight" response. The physiological result is tension fatigue. And the physiological solution is just what the cave folks did: exercise.

BEST ANTIDOTE FOR TENSION

"It can be said without fear of contradiction that physical exercise . . . is the best means of combating tension available," says Dr. Graham. Adds University of Montana exercise physiologist Brian J. Sharkey, Ph.D., "The benefit of a short exercise break is probably as much psychological as it is physiological. It can rejuvenate by giving you a new perspective on things, just by breaking up your day. It helps you go back to work with gusto."

Take five to energize and renew your peace of mind.

So when you're running low on gusto and you just can't seem to get moving, here's an energizing, tension-draining routine for you to try. The ten movements are designed to give you an overall body stretch and get that blood pumping. They can be done anywhere, at any time, in just five minutes.

Breathe deeply, keep smiling.

If you're at home, you might want to try putting the whole routine to music. Most albums alternate between slower and faster songs; find a low-key song about three minutes long that's followed by a more upbeat tune, to pick up the pace as you go along. Remember: Breathe deeply, keep smiling, and try to make the movements flowing and graceful. You're sure to feel better when you're through!

1. Head Rolls

Start with your feet a little wider than shoulder width apart, feet turned out slightly. Drop your head forward, then left, then back, then right. Use a slow four count and really let your head fall like dead weight in each direction, letting your mouth open when your head falls back. Do two revolutions in each direction.

2. Shoulder Lifts

Do five shoulder shrugs.

Shrug your shoulder up to your ear and push it back down again. Do five with each shoulder.

3. Waist Stretches

Extend your arms straight out to the sides, at shoulder level. Bending from the waist, stretch to the left as far as you can, bringing your right arm up and over your head as you do so. Look straight up at your palm, count to four, and return to center. Now extend to the right side, counting to four again. Then do five quicker ones to each side without pausing to count.

4. Inner-Thigh Stretches

Stand with your feet spread, hands on hips. Now lean right, bending your right leg but keeping your left leg straight, while you reach up and cross your wrists over your head. Then return to center, bringing your hands back to your hips. Do five on each side.

Feet apart, lean right, bending your right leg.

5. Windmills

Bend forward from the waist and lace your fingers together near the floor. Now swing your whole upper body to the right, erect, and down on the left, making a full "windmill" circle. Rotate from the waist and keep your head between your arms for a complete upper-body stretch. Do five in each direction, but slowly, so you don't get dizzy.

6. Long Legs

As you complete the last windmill, stay bent over. Bend your knees and place your palms flat on the floor between and slightly in front of your feet. Look up and in front of you. Now lower your head and straighten your legs, but don't worry if they don't straighten all the way. (Flexibility comes with time—exercise time!) Do ten, then bend your knees slightly and curl up slowly to your beginning standing position.

Bend your knees with palms on the floor. Now, gently straighten your legs.

7. Reach Outs

Now, with your feet spread, turn your body toward your left leg. Your left foot should be pointing left, your right foot perpendicular to your left heel. Extend your arms in front of you and reach out as though you were accepting a gift, making an easy stretching lunge forward and then back. Your left leg bends, your right stays straight. Do ten in each direction.

8. Jazz Stretch

After each set of ten Reach Outs, bring your feet

Clasp your ankles or calves and pull your head toward your knees.

together and slowly lower your head toward your knees. Grab your ankles or calves and gently pull your head toward your knees. Don't force the stretch, and don't bounce! Relax and hold for a four count as you breathe deeply. Now curl up slowly, returning to a standing position one vertebra at a time.

9. Jog in Place

Pick your heels up high in back, and move those arms! Think of yourself as a young filly let loose in a field. Jog for a count of 50.

10. Forward Kicks

Keep jogging as you kick your right foot forward with a small kick and push forward with your left arm. Then kick with your left, push with your right. Make it flow, and keep it up for a 50 count. Done!

Nineteen Ways to
Wake Up Refreshed

You can love your job, your family, your breakfast cereal, and "Good Morning, America"—but still hate to get up in the morning. What is it about having to rise and shine that is such a consistently humbling experience?

A number of things.

First of all, it's not natural. Or at least not the way most of us in the modern-day world do it, it's not. Throughout our evolution we awoke because our bodies, not our clock radios, told us to. We functioned on what sleep specialists call *circadian* rhythms, cycles of sleep and wakefulness dictated *naturally* by the rising and setting of the sun. (An understandable reaction to being roused by an alarm clock 50,000 years ago might have been to silence it with a stick.)

Then, too, the process of sleep itself has taken a turn for the worse since the good old days. Prehistoric man no doubt went to bed physically exhausted, relatively worry free, and sober. We cuddle up with restless legs, bad debts, kids flunking out of school, and a couple of stiff drinks under our belts. No wonder we wake up feeling ready for bed.

But even for those of us who live wisely and sleep well, getting the old engines going can be tough.

"Difficulty in getting up is a widespread problem," says sleep specialist Jerrold S. Maxmen, M.D., author of *A Good Night's Sleep* (W. W. Norton & Co.). In a recent survey of 600 people, for example, fewer than one-third said they awoke feeling refreshed, and 17 percent confessed

As you might have suspected, waking up is not natural.

If you cuddle up with stress, you may wake up feeling ready for bed.

it took them a full hour or more to feel alert. Many people, as you may know, take even longer than that.

Is there anything we can do about minimizing our A.M. plights?

Yes, but it's not apt to be easy because making it more pleasant to get up in the morning is something that may have to be approached, Dr. Maxmen says, from both ends of the candle—not only by doing what we can to improve the quality of the sleep that we're waking up *from,* but also by improving the desirability of the days that we're waking up *to.* And that can be difficult because the two, unfortunately, are usually intertwined. Indeed, before you can stop fouling up your sleep with alcohol or sleeping pills, it would certainly help to straighten out the aspects of your life that may be turning you to these aids in the first place.

"Chemicals, whether drugs or alcohol . . . make getting up more difficult because they disrupt natural sleep . . . and exert a direct influence on the brain's arousal apparatus," reports Dr. Maxmen. Sleep is not the inert pastime many people think. It is an intricate and psychologically active process that likes all the sobriety it can get. Five distinct stages must be gotten through in proper order and style, and if those stages are disrupted for any reason, daytime inefficiency and grogginess can be the result. So here are 19 tips for making it easier to get up in the morning.

1. Go easy on alcohol.

"You don't have to be pie-eyed for alcohol to disrupt your sleep," Dr. Maxmen notes. Even an innocent nightcap can suppress the all-important dream stage of sleep and also disrupt delta sleep—physiologically the deepest stage of sleep. What's more, alcohol is a strong enough diuretic to have you visiting the bathroom with more than restful frequency. So even though a drink before retiring may help you get to sleep initially, it's a detriment in the long run. "Let the drink you have with dinner, therefore, be your last for the evening," Dr. Maxmen suggests.

2. Reduce excessive noise.

That may seem obvious, but "even if you are not *awakened* by loud noises, the quality and depth of your sleep may be disturbed," Dr. Maxmen says. "If you are in deep

To wake up refreshed, you've got to improve the quality of tonight's sleep and tomorrow's agenda.

For sound sleep, drink only nonalcoholic nightcaps.

sleep, noise may lighten your sleep without actually awakening you. Air conditioners and fans are a good way to mask potential disruptions, as are earplugs, Dr. Maxmen says.

3. Maintain a moderate room temperature.

"The old wives' tale that cold air improves sleep is quaint but wrong," Dr. Maxmen says. Somewhere between 60 and 65 degrees Fahrenheit is best.

Don't sleep with the window open unless it's a perfect spring day.

4. Get a reasonable amount of daily exercise.

We say "reasonable" because the aches and pains that may follow overexertion can keep you awake. Studies have shown that *judicious* amounts of regular exercise, however, can extend the amount of time spent in delta (deep, physical) sleep.

Exercise any time is good, but to help get a better night's sleep, the best time seems to be shortly before or after dinner, and not too close to bedtime. For most people, the ideal is a 30-minute walk before or after dinner. Scientists say this gives you a more restful, deeply refreshing sleep.

A 30-minute walk before dinner is optimal for a deeply refreshing sleep.

5. Have sex before sleep.

But only if it's physically and emotionally rewarding, Dr. Maxmen counsels. "Whether sex will enhance or inhibit sleep . . . depends on whether it occurs in the context of a supportive, trusting, and long relationship. If sexual problems interfere with your sleep, it is valuable to discuss these matters honestly yet sensitively with your partner. By doing so, you will not only obtain a better night's sleep but also enrich your relationship."

6. Eliminate evening caffeine.

"The stimulating effects of caffeine peak between two to four hours, linger for seven hours, and may persist for as long as *twenty* hours" in some people, Dr. Maxmen warns. So caffeine, in any form, should be avoided at least six hours before bedtime.

The effects of caffeine can persist for 20 hours.

7. Stop smoking.

Nicotine is a central nervous system stimulant. Hence, despite the inherent discomforts, heavy smokers who quit find themselves sleeping dramatically better within just three days.

8. Have a snack.

A snack, not a feast. Whereas something relatively light and satisfying (such as a glass of milk, some yogurt, or a *small* sandwich) can aid sleep, an entire pizza with anchovies can disturb it. You might also want to avoid anything with monosodium glutamate (MSG). It's a flavor enhancer that in some people can cause symptoms akin to those produced by coffee.

9. Relax before bed.

Contemplation and problem solving: Two anti-sleep activities.

Ambition, paradoxically, can make it as difficult to get up in the morning as sloth. If you're scheming right up until bedtime—and even after—you're going to pay for it in the morning. "Any pre-bedtime activity that stimulates the mind is bound to keep you awake," warns Dr. Maxmen. So if you've got a problem to solve, try to tackle it at least an hour before lights-out.

10. Establish a regular schedule.

Variety may be the spice of life, but routine forms the foundation for sleep. It all goes back, remember, to those circadian rhythms that we used to heed in the old days.

11. Wake up slowly like a cat.

Start out by wiggling your fingers and toes.

Dogs and cats do a slow, luxurious, full-body stretch every time they get up from a nap. *Your* body tells you that's the right way to start the day, too—body and soul need a little time to cross the threshold of this world from another. The easiest way to begin is simply to wiggle your fingers and toes while under the covers, until you're ready for more serious undertakings. A more involved routine was developed by the Kripalu Center for Yoga and Health in Lenox, Massachusetts. The great thing about it is you don't even have to get out of bed (though you may have to lie across it diagonally).

Lying on your back, slowly raise your arms straight up in the air. Rotate your wrists in each direction and gently lower.

Ease into motion with slow stretches and deep breathing.

Clasp your hands on your stomach. Invert your palms so they face your feet and *stretch* downward. Now slowly lift them in the air, breathing deeply and slowly, until they're fully stretched above your head (or flat on the floor behind you, if you've ventured out of bed). Exhaling, stretch and arch your back, loosening your spine.

While inhaling, stretch your right arm and right leg in opposite directions so they form a straight line, making the right side of your body longer than the left, while lifting your right hip. Relax and exhale. Repeat on the left side. Exhale, then stretch your arms to the side at shoulder level. Relax, breathing deeply.

Inhaling, slowly draw your right foot up until it reaches the back of your left knee. Exhaling, slowly and gently twist your body by dropping your right knee over toward your left while turning your head to the right. Don't push or strain. Relax, then repeat on the other side.

Gently get out of bed and complete the routine on the floor (preferably on a thick, soft carpet). Simply sit with your hands clasped around your knees, your head bent forward to form a kind of ball. Now rock back on your shoulders with your spine curved and your head tucked in. Rock a dozen times or so, then get up and start your day.

Complete the stretching routine out of bed.

If that's not enough to get your blood running, there are a number of brief, invigorating exercise routines you can try, such as the Royal Canadian Air Force program. Basically calisthenics, it's graduated so it steadily increases in difficulty and number of repetitions, but the total time required is only about 12 minutes. Or try checking the TV listings for morning exercise or yoga classes in your area. You may be surprised how many exercise evangelists have taken to the airwaves these days. Even a ten-minute workout will help point your day in the right direction, and you don't even have to get dressed.

12. Step outside.

Quite a few people report that just stepping outside into the "real world" helps them wake up. The morning air outside your window may not be "all awash with angels," as one poet was moved to report, but even if it's only awash with the sound of clattering garbage cans it can sometimes galvanize you into action.

Poke your head—or better yet, your whole body—outside in the crisp morning air.

13. Let the sunshine in.

One variation on the outdoorsy theme: Sleep near a window with the shade rolled up. As one fan of this method commented, "I hate waking up to an angry buzz, or a noisy radio DJ, whereas sunshine is, well, shucks, sweet and gentle."

14. Arise to words of inspiration.

Imagine Tolstoy or Dickens whispering softly in your ear.

Some people can't seem to get going without reading the morning paper. But instead of all that death, disaster, and politics, why not try something a little more inspirational? Tom Ferguson, M.D., editor of the California-based magazine *Medical Self-Care,* has created a series of inspirational wake-up tapes for himself. A simple electric timer switches on the tape in his cassette player in the morning and he's greeted by philosophical or spiritual quotations from Tolstoy, Rilke, Dickens, and other residents of *Bartlett's Familiar Quotations.* On other tapes, he simply tells himself, "You don't have to get up right now. Just enjoy lying there for a few more minutes. Now you're becoming more alert. It's going to be a wonderful day . . . "

"Getting up in the morning is a very individual matter," Dr. Ferguson says, "so it would be hard to make wake-up tapes that would suit everyone. I'd encourage people to find their own individual way of waking up, and if you make your own tapes, you can."

15. Give yourself a loofah rub *before* showering.

Mariane Kohler and Jean Chapelle, in their little book *101 Recipes for Sound Sleep* (Walker), have an interesting suggestion: "Give yourself a dry friction rub with a loofah, or nylon scourer, or a good brush. Rub your arms, from the hands to the armpits, and your legs, from the feet to the hips and stomach, with a circular movement. Take a shower and rub yourself with a light oil to soften your skin. Now you are completely awake and ready to start a new day." A rough washcloth or an abrasive facial scrub may also work to get your skin tingling.

16. Eat a "power" breakfast.

Eating breakfast: a link to longevity.

Researchers in California followed a group of nearly 7,000 people from 1965 through 1974 in an effort to find out what sort of habits the healthiest ones had in common. It turned out that seven "health rules" strongly correlated with a longer, healthier life—and eating breakfast was one of them. One of the researchers, James Enstrom, Ph.D., associate research professor in the school of public health at UCLA, told us that the study didn't indicate that any particular *kind* of breakfast was best (that wasn't its purpose), simply that the longest-lived subjects ate breakfast regularly.

In fact, death rates were 40 percent higher for men and 28 percent higher for women who "rarely or sometimes" ate breakfast, compared with those who ate breakfast "almost every day" *(Preventive Medicine).*

Other studies have indicated that a nutritious, high-protein breakfast—one that includes dairy products, eggs, or meats, for example—will keep your blood sugar at a consistently high level through the morning, increasing your productivity, energy, and sense of well-being.

17. Personalize the music you wake up to.

The mind and soul seem particularly sensitive to sounds during the period when you're just waking up. At that hour, music can be doubly soothing (or doubly irritating) and set the tone for your entire day. Clock radios have been around a long time, but now there are devices that can activate a stereo or tape system at whatever time you set them for to help you engineer your own musical awakening. Morning music seems to be a highly personal matter, from the range of suggestions we heard: Bach piano concertos, mellow jazz, Emmylou Harris, even the rip-roaring "Muleskinner Blues" by Dolly Parton, or brassy Sousa marches.

Clock radios put your morning mood in the hands of a disc jockey.

18. Beat stiffness and headaches.

If you're one of those people who wake up, take one look at the day, then retreat under the covers for another dozen winks . . . and then wake up with an aching head, you might be suffering from what doctors call "turtle headache." It's caused by breathing too much carbon dioxide and too little oxygen while you're buried under the covers. The solution is simple: Don't go back to sleep once you wake up, or if you do, don't crawl under the covers.

If you tend to wake up with backaches, try sleeping on your side with your legs curled up, or else sleep on your back with a big, fluffy pillow under your knees. That flattens the part of your back that tends to stay in toward your stomach and takes the strain off the muscles. One simple movement may also help: Bring your knees up to your chest, lock your arms around your shins, hold a few seconds, and then release. Repeat this several times. If you have arthritis and are bothered by morning stiffness, spending the night in a sleeping bag or wearing thermal underwear can help.

Sleep with your knees bent for a pain-free back.

Motivate yourself by scheduling fun on every day's agenda.

19. Try the old carrot-and-a-stick trick.

If you've really got problems getting out of bed in the morning, maybe you're not giving yourself enough to look forward to. As one person commented, "I have no trouble at all getting up at six . . . when I'm going skiing." You can't go skiing every day, of course. But you *could* deliberately arrange your day so that some nice little thing would be waiting for you shortly after you got up. It might only be some favorite piece of clothing, pressed and laid out the night before, all ready to wear. Or a big jug of freshly squeezed orange juice sitting in the fridge. Or some small, pleasant task that was *first* on the day's list.

How to Beat
the Afternoon Slump

It's 3:00 P.M. But it feels like 5:00. Your eyelids are heavy. Your mind is in a fog. What do you do?

Probably you reach for a cup of coffee. Or a candy bar. Or a soda. Or if you're a smoker, you light up. And by 4:15 you feel even worse than you did at 3:00.

The afternoon blahs. It can strike any time between one and four—usually after lunch. And few people are immune to its effects.

Few people escape the 3 P.M. energy letdown.

It may make you restless or lethargic, depressed or dullwitted—or some perplexing mosaic of them all. And it isn't only a psychological phenomenon.

"We scientists call it the *postprandial* [after-eating] dip," says John D. Palmer, Ph.D., of the University of Massachusetts in Amherst. "It is characterized by a drop in body temperature, blood sugar, work efficiency, and mood."

After eating, body temperature and blood sugar drop along with efficiency.

But it doesn't have to get you down. One good way to see that it doesn't is by taking a good look at some other things that go down—down the hatch, that is.

Eat substantial amounts of protein for breakfast. That means eggs, meat, cottage cheese, a whole-grain natural cereal, milk, or yogurt instead of a sweet roll, pancakes and syrup, or no breakfast at all (see Chapter 3, Energy Balancing: Diet Strategies for Peak Performance and Sound Sleep).

Then go light on the lunch. That's the advice of Timothy H. Monk, Ph.D., research psychologist with the department of neurology at Montefiore Hospital in New York City. Dr. Monk began his research in Sussex, England;

The light lunch: your best bet for a heavy P.M. production schedule.

he says that a study conducted by a colleague there found that "people who had eaten a heavy lunch suffered impaired judgment and were less able to detect signals. They could not differentiate as well between varying sizes and intensities of light."

"An excellent antidote for the afternoon slump is to eat a 100 percent raw lunch," says Ray C. Wunderlich, M.D., of St. Petersburg, Florida. He agrees with Dr. Monk, saying that "overeating at lunchtime is one of the biggest causes of fatigue in the afternoon. A heavy meal will drag you down, making you feel tired and heavy afterward.

Not every "health food" is an energy booster.

"Even if your lunch isn't totally raw, many people should get rid of refined foods, sugars, including honey, and high carbohydrate fruits such as dates, figs, and bananas," Dr. Wunderlich says. "Eat a salad for lunch, one containing such things as watercress, sprouts, chick-peas, tofu, tuna, sardines, seeds, and nuts. Or have a chick-pea spread (hummus) and sprout sandwich on whole-grain bread."

FRUIT JUICE AND CANDY BARS

Look for an afternoon "pick-me-up" that won't let you down.

And when you head for the refrigerator or snack bar looking for an afternoon pick-me-up, watch out for that sugar-laden "quick fix." Candy bars—and even orange juice (one glass may actually have more sugar in it than the chocolate candy bar)—can short-circuit your energy systems at the most critical time.

Eat something very sweet, and your blood sugar goes up quickly, reaching a peak in about one hour. You may feel nicely re-energized at that time, particularly if what you ate was a between-meal snack. But for the next hour or so, it's all downhill. In response to the sugar surge, the pancreas secretes insulin, often enough to drive the blood sugar level *below* where it was before you ate anything. From that low point, it climbs to "normal" at a slow rate. For most of us, this may not cause any particular trouble. But for those who are sensitive to the ups and downs of blood sugar, snacking on sweet food or drinks may mean the periodic and sudden onset of fatigue or lightheadedness.

The tricky part is that you can bring on sugar-related fatigue even if candy, cake, or soda never touch your lips. That's because natural sugars in sweet fruits and juices (as well as honey) can send your blood sugar level bouncing around just as easily as the sucrose added to manufactured sweets (or your coffee).

What's even trickier is that the effect these sugars have on the body and your energy levels is influenced in large measure by the *form* in which they're consumed. The more they are separated from the bulk or fiber of the food in which they occur, the quicker and harder they hit your system. British scientists have found that if you eat an apple on an empty stomach, your blood sugar rises quickly, then falls to a level just slightly lower than the starting point. No big deal. When the same amount of apple is pureed into applesauce before being eaten—breaking up the fiber into small bits—your blood sugar drops lower. But when only the *juice* of the apple is swallowed, blood sugar drops *much* lower.

Why an apple is better than apple juice.

The snacks in the experiment demonstrating these differences were each engineered by scientists to contain exactly the same amount of carbohydrates, so that the effect of changing the fiber in the apple would be clearly revealed. Yet the sheer *amount* of carbohydrates you consume will obviously contribute to the net effect on your blood sugar and energy levels, with larger amounts intensifying the violence of the ups and downs. Now, you might not suppose that a glass of juice is a particularly potent source of carbohydrates. But a quick look at Table 11, which shows the carbohydrate contents of different drinks, may surprise you. Note that one glass (8 ounces) of apple juice contains the sugar equivalent of more than 5 teaspoons of plain table sugar. That's more sugar per ounce than cola. In fact, it's 40 percent more sugar than there is in a chocolate candy bar!

One glass of apple juice contains more sugar per ounce than cola.

Keep in mind we're just talking about the sugar content of beverages. Drinks have other stories to tell, too. Milk, for instance, offers lots of protein, calcium, and B vitamins. Orange juice has lots of vitamin C and is certainly a "healthful" beverage despite its high content of fruit sugar. But if energy is your problem, you can't afford to ignore these natural sugars.

If you *are* worried about fluctuating energy levels, you don't necessarily have to stop drinking fruit juices. But you may have to use a little strategy. Try to combine your juice with a solid protein or starch food, like cheese, nuts, crackers, or bread.

TABLE 10: Why Fiber Is the High-Energy Food Factor

The three lines of the chart show the course of the average blood sugar level in nine normal people after eating 60 grams of carbohydrates in the form of whole apples, pureed apples, or apple juice. Breaking down the natural fiber in apples by pureeing them causes a greater drop in blood sugar following the initial rise. When all fiber is removed, as in apple juice, the drop in blood sugar is even greater, particularly from one to two hours following consumption.

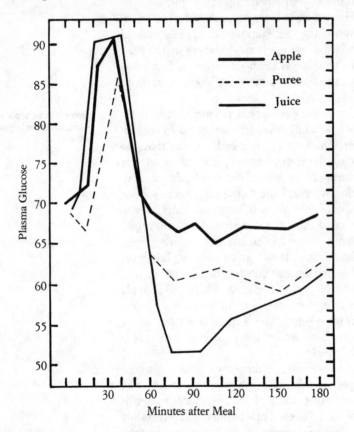

Adapted from: G. B. Haber et al., "Depletion and Disruption of Dietary Fiber: Effects on Satiety, Plasma-Glucose, and Serum-Insulin," *Lancet,* October 1, 1977, pp. 679-82.

An alternative is simply to eat whole fruits instead of juices, so there is less effect on your blood sugar level.

TABLE 11: Sugar Content of Beverages

The juices and drinks with *lower* sugar content may provide more of a pick-me-up—they keep blood sugar steady instead of causing it to bounce from a high to a fatigue-laden low.

Beverage	Grams of Carbohydrates per 8-oz. Glass
Vegetable juice cocktail	11.0
Milk	11.4
Cola	24.6
Orange juice	25.8
Apple juice	29.0

Note: 1 teaspoon of sugar contains 4 grams of carbohydrates; a 1-ounce milk chocolate bar, 16 grams.

Adapted from

Catherine F. Adams, *Nutritive Value of American Foods in Common Units,* Agriculture Handbook No. 456 (Washington, D.C.: Agricultural Research Service, U.S. Department of Agriculture, 1975).

Consumer and Food Economics Institute, *Composition of Foods: Dairy and Egg Products,* Agriculture Handbook No. 8-1 (Washington, D.C.: Agricultural Research Service, U.S. Department of Agriculture, 1976).

Consumer Nutrition Center, *Composition of Foods: Fruits and Fruit Juices,* Agriculture Handbook No. 8-9 (Washington, D.C.: Human Nutrition Information Service, U.S. Department of Agriculture, 1982).

Nutrition Monitoring Division, *Composition of Foods: Vegetables and Vegetable Products,* Agriculture Handbook No. 8-11 (Washington, D.C.: Human Nutrition Information Service, U.S. Department of Agriculture, 1984).

Another alternative is to drink water, vegetable juice cocktail, or milk instead.

Washing down a few vitamin and mineral supplements with this midday drink might not be a bad idea, either.

"Many times, the afternoon slump occurs because the supplements people took with breakfast are all used up by midafternoon," Dr. Wunderlich says. "If these vitamins and minerals are not restored at the midday meal, a person may 'run out of gas' by midafternoon." The most susceptible nutrients are magnesium, calcium, zinc, chromium, copper, vitamin B complex, and vitamin C, he says.

Supplements taken with breakfast are often depleted by midday.

SI, SI, SIESTA

An after-lunch catnap may better suit our body rhythms.

"Another reason we feel sleepy in the afternoon is that we naturally operate with a 12-hour cycle superimposed on a 24-hour day," explains Dr. Timothy Monk. "It's a hold-over from when we were babies, and many scientists think that our bodies actually expect to take a rest at that time of day."

In many parts of the world, people do. "In Mediterranean and Latin American countries, for example, the afternoon siesta is the rule rather than the exception. People go home at lunchtime and sleep up to four hours in the afternoon, then return for an evening's work. But in our culture, the thing to do is sleep at night," Dr. Monk says. People who indulge in siestas, however, can get by with less than eight hours at night. That means they can wake up earlier because, according to Dr. Wunderlich, it is not a good idea to go to bed too late.

The most important hours for sleep are between 10 P.M. and midnight.

"The most important hours for sleep are between 10:00 P.M. and midnight," Dr. Wunderlich says. "The way our bodies' rhythmic cycles work, those are the hours of sleep that pay off during the afternoon of the next day." If you don't feel like sleeping then, you will surely feel it 12 to 16 hours later.

Or maybe what you need is not more sleep but more exercise.

The best is a short, easy burst of exercise.

But you're *already* tired, you say.

No you're not. You're groggy. And there's a difference. If you were physically exhausted, you'd be sweating. What you *are* is half asleep.

"College kids have the right idea," Dr. John Palmer muses. "I see them playing Frisbee on the lawns after lunch." You don't have to be quite so energetic, however. Any light exercise is good.

Sometimes we confuse physical exhaustion with mental grogginess Grogginess can be dispelled with exercise.

Dr. Wunderlich recommends taking a brisk ten-minute walk. "And breathe deeply. Overlooked factors in afternoon fatigue may include being sedentary and breathing stale air all day. Get some fresh air—and sunshine."

Exercise gives the cells in your body a fresh supply of oxygen. And it's oxygen that you need to get cooking. You don't think so? Then try this:

If you've been sitting, stand up. If you've been standing, give yourself some room. Then simply do 25 jump-ing jacks.

One minute of jumping jacks will double your body's intake of oxygen.

It may sound silly, but don't laugh until you've tried it. Because what that minute or so of jumping up and down like a ten-year-old will do for you is:

- force your body to nearly double its intake of oxygen.
- pump about twice as much blood through your veins.
- convert blood fats into blood sugar (the same stuff that candy bar tried to give you).
- raise your metabolic rate (idling speed) by anywhere from 25 to 75 percent.

What all this adds up to is renewed energy. Because what you've done is call upon your body's supply of reserve fuel (which it has plenty of) instead of adding fuel in the form of calories from outside.

If jumping jacks aren't your style, find something that is. A short walk. Or a quick dash out to look at your car. *What* you do doesn't matter. Just so long as it gets you breathing. You'll be amazed at how much faster five o'clock will roll around.

40

Read This and
Fall Asleep Fast

**This is a potion on paper,
an insomniac's dream.**

More than any-
thing you've ever read, the following has designs on you.
It's neither tale nor treatise nor tract, but a kind of spell, a
potion on paper that pulls you toward that realm that all
insomniacs yearn for: sleep.

No, don't look for the secret to this sleight of hand, for
looking can only keep you awake. Don't expect elaborate
explanations of how the words reach into your brain's sleep
center and flip the switch to "snooze." There won't be any.
The following sentences are psychotechniques in motion,
calibrated to the rules of autogenic training, self-hypnosis,
systemic desensitization, and progressive muscle relaxation.
And that's all you need to know. Nothing else matters if you
really want sleep to come. There will be time tomorrow
morning to try to figure out how these few words on paper
helped you slip toward slumber.

**Let your body—not the
clock—whisper that it's
bedtime.**

So prepare yourself. Before you read the next paragraph,
let evening set in. Let your body—not the clock—whisper
that it's bedtime. Take the phone off the hook, set the house
thermostat to 64 degrees, soothe yourself in a hot bath,
drink a warm glass of milk (just as you did when you were a
child), dim the lights (you need barely enough light to read
by), make that last trip to the bathroom and go to bed as you
always do. Lie in a comfortable position and use a pillow to
prop this book in front of you.

Now, just read, read as you would a novel or a poem
without looking for information or advice or an answer to
anything, watching the words lumber past your mind from

left to right. Your eyes descend on every word in slower and slower time, for it matters little whether you ever get to the last sentence, for every line is a concluding remark.

Slower. Every period of each sentence you pass signals your mind to reduce your reading pace. There's this period. And this one. And this one. And there's no place you have to be, no problems you have to solve now. Tomorrow will wait for tomorrow, and you'll meet it better after this good night's rest.

There's no place you have to go, no problems to solve.

Just say yes. Ever so softly whisper it now: yes. Say it when you're tempted to analyze what you're reading. Say it when you start to wonder if this spell will work. Say it and give up your last ounce of resistance to these words and the sleep lurking between the lines. Say it without trying to make anything happen, without expecting to doze off, without caring whether sleep comes or not. Just say it: yes.

And breathe deeper, letting your chest rise and fall slowly in even rhythm. Beneath the surface of these words should flow the currents of your breaths, long and steady, air easing in, air easing out. And if you listen to them long enough, you'll see how discrete each one is, each one with a slightly different depth or duration or strength. When you come to the end of this paragraph, close your eyes and listen to them until you start to distinguish one from another. It may take you ten seconds or ten minutes. And when you open your eyes, that slow current of respiration will seem steadier than before, and you'll hear it more as you continue reading, and it will flow on its way with the words that flow from left to right.

Let your chest rise and fall with the currents of your breaths.

You're lying on the white sands of a beach that stretches to meet a clear sky. There is only sand the color of snow, and sky the color of robins' eggs. Your eyes are closed, and you feel the rays of a sun that warms but does not burn, and a breeze that brings along salty sea air. In the distance you hear the cry of a lone gull, and the sound mixes with the cadence of your slow breathing.

You're lying on a beach; feel the warmth.

Place your right arm at your side and clench your fist. Right now. Tense every muscle as hard as you can—your wrist, forearm, upper arm. Feel the tension build as the muscles strain and burn. Feel it. Now, listen to your breathing in the background. Wait for one of those slow exhalations. Wait. Now let your arm go limp as you exhale. Feel the muscles loosen up, feel the heaviness, enjoy it. Your arm

**Tense each muscle,
then relax.**

hasn't been this relaxed all day, and you know that the feeling is the calling card of sleep.

Now, do the same thing with your left arm: Tense, hold the tension, then relax as you exhale. It feels so good you want to close your eyes to savor it. And you will close them, but not yet.

Tense your scalp, face, neck, and shoulders. Tighten your scalp as if someone were giving your head a vigorous shampoo. Push your tongue against the roof of your mouth, wrinkle your nose, purse your lips, clench your back teeth. Freeze your neck muscles and thrust your shoulders toward your ears. Now you're holding your breath, and your taut muscles are just starting to ache. Hold the tension. Just a little longer. Now go limp and exhale. Let your mouth fall open, your head droop slightly as gravity wills. Feel the heaviness in the muscles, the spreading warmth. Listen to the slow, slow march of your breaths toward long rest.

As you lie on the long, white shore you hear only the muffled rasp of ocean waves far away, and from the sun that doesn't burn comes warm yellow light that bathes you, down to every cell. The rays melt tension, calm your thoughts, until you glow yellow with warmth and peace.

Slowly arch your back as you take in a breath and hold it. Now, stiffen your spine and push your chest forward, letting tension course through the muscles. Wait for a count of five. Now release tension and exhale. Feel the wave of relaxation wash over your muscles as you let your breathing even out again. Your body has never seemed so heavy, so warm. You can hardly move. It takes great effort just to turn the page.

Think now of the muscles in your abdomen, your stomach, your buttocks, your hips. Wait for a languid exhalation. There. Stop breathing and squeeze the muscles in your stomach and abdomen, contract every sinew in your buttocks and hips, make your midsection harden to stone. Tense every fiber as hard as you can. Let the tension build. And build. Now release the strain and exhale. The muscles loosen and loosen and now you can't feel them, just the heaviness of stone, the warmth of ease, the slow rising and falling of your chest.

Listen for one of those inhalations. Listen. And hold it. Hold it and tense your legs and feet. Straighten your legs and bend your ankles, pointing your toes upward toward your knees. All these muscles are now as stiff and hard as wood. Keep them rigid. Rigid. Now exhale and let them go limp, letting the tension seep away. Let them relax until they can't relax any further. Then relax them some more, and hear the muffled rasp of your steady breathing.

You feel warm all over, your whole body is lead, every muscle is now cousin to sleep. And yes, at the end of this paragraph you can close your eyes. And only if you open them again before morning should you keep reading these words that crawl from left to right.

Your body is lead, every muscle is cousin to sleep.

The waves are tolling louder now, swelling in the yellow light, then splashing on the warming sands. You lie still, listening to the surf as it draws back then washes in, like the sound of air easing out of your chest, then flowing in again.

There's something here that tranquilizes the brain, nudges it toward natural sleep . . . Deepen your breathing, slowly pulling in all the air you can, gently pushing out all that's possible. There. Now do it again. And again: Take in a roomful of air, a houseful . . . now expel, emptying out every trace of breath. Stop. Hold till your chest strains for air. Now release.

Take in a roomful of air, a houseful.

This gorging and clearing your lungs then holding your breath is the opiate for slumber, and when you come to the end of this paragraph, you'll indulge. You'll close your eyes and repeat the pattern until your body's desire for normal breathing overwhelms the long breaths. All the while you'll have your eyes turned upward, as though watching a scene at the back of your head. You'll imagine each of those grand breaths drawing in warm and yellow air, air that enters through your right foot, seeps up your leg into your chest and neck, down through your left leg and out your foot. Chances are you won't open your eyes again before morning, and if you do you'll hear only the muffled rasp of your regular breathing.

On the white sand you lie leaden, basking in the thick yellow warmth, hearing the splash and roar of the talking sea. In rhythmic rounds of swaying water, it says something, something you can't quite make out . . .

The rhythmic sounds of the ocean say something you can't quite make out.

Say it: I'm a breath away from sleep. Yes, whisper it now: I'm a breath away from sleep. Exhale: I'm a breath

**Close your eyes now . . .
and sleep.**

away from sleep. Exhale: sleep. Exhale: sleep. Exhale: sleep. Say it when this paragraph is done and your eyes are closed. As the air washes out of your lungs, whisper it. As the waves crest and fall on those white sands in your mind, think it. As the sea exhales its saline air, think it. As you lie there in the drowsy warmth of the sand, as the scene curls up to a soft yellow glow, think it: sleep.

PART VII

PART VIII

Taking the Reins

From Compulsion to Free Choice: Getting To the Root of "Soft" Addictions

Jacquelyn Small knows the anatomy of an addiction. A psychotherapist and consultant from Austin, Texas, she has worked with nearly all the major alcoholism and addiction schools in the country. And what she's discovered about the hard addictions, she says, holds true for the soft ones—you know, all those "minor" obsessions that can become major hurdles in our pursuit of happiness. Workaholism. Perfectionism. Procrastination. Sugar, coffee, and cigarette addictions. Even addictions to unhealthy relationships.

"These are all symptoms of the same basic problem," says Small. "The only difference is, people with soft addictions can get away with them longer. The softer addictions don't break down the body as fast. They don't cause hospitalization and bouts with the law like alcohol or drugs."

But there's still a lot of pain and unhappiness on the soft side. Workaholics typically suffer from anxiety reactions and heart, circulation, and stomach ailments. Perfectionists and procrastinators report the same. And no one has to remind us of the long-term consequences of cigarette smoking.

Oh, that we could quit, our problems would be solved. Or so we think. But Jacquelyn Small—whose two books, *Becoming Naturally Therapeutic* (The Eupsychian Press) and *Transformers: The Therapists of the Future* (DeVorss), have drawn wide acclaim in addiction-counseling circles— disagrees.

"Certainly eliminating the addictive element, particu-

What's true for the hard addictions holds for the soft ones.

There's still pain and unhappiness on the soft side.

Kicking the habit is a prerequisite to treatment.

larly if it's a chemical, is the first step," she says. "But I almost see that as a prerequisite to treatment. Treatment should be directed at the underlying cause. And, in my mind, the addictive food, or drug, or situation—while it undeniably contributes to the problem—is never the cause of it.

"I know this because I spend a lot of time with recovering alcoholics. They stop drinking because they have learned methods for doing that. What I see instead is a lot of really heavy cigarette smoking. I see people who practically live on coffee and sugar. They haven't changed their behavior: They are as compulsive as ever. They've just shifted their attention."

Dual addictions suggest that there's more involved than a bad habit gone overboard.

Dual addictions also suggest that there's more involved here than a bad habit gone overboard. Think about it: the workaholic who chain smokes, the perfectionist who consumes coffee by the potful, the person who clings neurotically to a one-sided relationship and relies on tranquilizers to cope.

WHAT'S THE UNDERLYING CAUSE?

Small is convinced that addiction is a problem of imbalance or "unease" within the body/mind. It's the result of losing touch with ourselves, of always reaching outside for stimulation and satisfaction because we no longer find gratification within.

Characteristics of the addiction-prone: high anxiety and outer-directed.

We asked Small if she could characterize the addiction-prone personality. "That's very interesting," she replied, "because research says it doesn't exist, but my experience tells me it does—definitely. The traits include extreme anxiety, restlessness, insecurity, and an orientation that's outer-directed (always reaching outside for satisfaction).

"The trouble is, we're living in a society that stresses outside stimulation. We set up dissatisfactions within ourselves all the time. We go by what society says is the right way to be gratified. More prestige. More status symbols. More ways to talk about ourselves through which we can be accepted.

To counter this, then, we must tune out external expectations and reconnect with ourselves. Overcoming any compulsions, as Small explains, is a process of self-discovery—of tuning in to our thoughts and feelings and coming to terms with our inner self. From that standpoint,

she says, this is not a process of *re*forming—of rejecting
who we are and trying to be someone else; it's one of
*trans*forming—of accepting ourselves for who we are while
learning to "operate on a higher octave" where we feel more
relaxed, self-confident, content, and complete.

"The quickest way to get someone on the path toward
self-discovery is to introduce him to the concept that he has
a wise self within," Small says. "Sometimes, as I'm speaking to a client, I'll notice that he changes before my very
eyes. One minute he'll act extremely balanced and speak
from a very true place. The next minute, he'll just wilt and
get into self-pity or grief, acting very unbalanced. He might
even speak in a different voice. Usually he's not even aware
of the changeover.

**Beating addictions: a
process of *transforming*,
not *reforming*.**

BOX 34: A NEW VIEW ON ADDICTION

Addiction = non-growth. It is a
way of staying stuck in the past, repeating like a robot the same outworn modes
of operation that do not work. . . . One
cannot maintain an addiction consciously.
We have to put ourselves to sleep in
order to act out an addiction. Conscious
awareness, moment by moment, fully in
the here and now, transforms addiction.

Addiction = attachment. When
we are attached to something (or someone), we have forgotten who we are. We
feel we cannot be whole without this
something. We experience pain and suffering whenever our attachment threatens to leave us . . . like losing an arm
or a leg. Attachment is the cause of
suffering. *Addiction* is the cause of
suffering. Non-attachment does not mean
non-caring; it is non-*needing* . . . non-
obsessing. It is removing emotional investment so that one can truly see clearly
and therefore care appropriately for the
other's sake. Paradoxically, *attachment*
is non-loving.

Addiction = postponement. Repetition is hypnosis. You did it yesterday,
you are doing it today. Tomorrow will be
the same. Repeating, repeating. And this
is how addictions grow. The more you
repeat, the deeper you carve the groove
of that particular tape loop . . . the more
the affliction is worked into the fiber of
your being. You know you want to do
something else with your life, but always
you feel . . . tomorrow! Then I'll be
ready. Tomorrow I will be stronger. Tomorrow I will have gained more knowledge;
I will have more energy. I will be out of
the current crisis. *But tomorrow never
comes!* And transformation happens
NOW! It is *this* moment. . . .

Reprinted by permission of the publisher from *Transformers: The Therapists of the Future,* Jacquelyn
Small (Marina del Rey, Calif.: DeVorss & Company, 1982), p. 69.

People with addictions know only the voice of their unbalanced side.

"Most people who have addictions—who are hurting and suffering from low self-esteem—know only the voice of their unbalanced side," she contends. "They don't recognize that there is a part of them that's really healthy, a part that 'knows,' a part that can observe their actions and suggest very quietly that they make one move instead of another or remind them of their successes when their self-esteem suffers a blow. But we all have that part—that wise self within. Knowing that can serve as an anchor when we begin to explore our feelings."

Small uses guided imagery and breathing techniques to help people relax and release pent-up tensions that have been blocking their true feelings.

People are afraid to look at their true feelings.

"This is a very scary process for many people because they are afraid to face up to their feelings," she explains. "Certainly the experience can be a painful one but it's always positive. Always a revelation. I've had people say to me, 'I never knew I felt this way about that experience. It happened so long ago, I forgot all about it. I can't believe I've been harboring such powerful feelings ever since.'"

GETTING IN TOUCH

How do we get there on our own?

Meditation or another relaxation technique is an essential tool. Once you feel deeply relaxed, your mind clear of unnecessary clutter, you can spend some time in silent reflection—listening to your inner voice, or as Small calls it, "the wise self within."

Relaxation techniques are essential to the process.

Another technique that Jacquelyn Small says is particularly useful to reach the depths of your feelings and relieve the pain associated with withdrawal is to focus on the pain you're feeling. If you are a compulsive eater, for example, focus on a hunger pang. If you're a coffee-drinker, concentrate on your withdrawal headache. If you finally walked away from a bad relationship and are feeling depressed, use that depression as a point of focus. Really get into it. Focus on it. Ask it to speak to you. And listen carefully to what it has to say.

The pain dissolves and feelings surface.

"In time, the pain or hunger or depression will dissolve," says Small. "And, in its place, you'll discover a lot of repressed emotions. It can be a real eye-opening experience."

Of course, there are many other techniques to use to

get in touch with our feelings, relax, and build self-esteem
(see Part III, Tuning In to Optimism, Part IV, Shedding
Negative Emotions, and Part VI, Healthful Living in a
Stressful World).

Remember, too, the prerequisite for treatment is kicking
the habit—whatever it is. In the following chapters, then,
some info and advice on some of our worst compulsions.

42

Get Ready, Get Set, Get Motivated

Y ou may have been telling yourself for years that you want to lose weight and get in shape or quit smoking or get a new job. But getting out and doing something about it depends on just how bad the excess pounds, the flabby muscles, the smoke in your lungs, or the current job problems make you feel.

"How people are feeling is what usually gets them to overcome their inertia," contends Jerry Vandel, M.D., who operates his "Health by Design" practice in San Antonio, Texas. "They might be feeling older or lousy. They realize they can't do things the way they used to and they want to try to get back to those activities. So, they'll seek a diet and exercise program."

"People have to acknowledge that they really want to do something and why," notes Cindy Casterella, a yoga instructor and stress-management consultant at Jefferson Community College in Watertown, New York. "You have to decide that changing something in your life (like your diet or exercise program) would be good for you *right now*. Then find someone you can trust who can help you achieve that change."

GETTING RESULTS

The object of an improvement program, obviously, is to get the desired results, either for self-satisfaction or to meet social expectations. What's needed to reach the goal is motivation. You must *get* motivated and *stay* motivated. We polled the experts, and their five-point plan should really get you rolling.

1. Set easy, short-term goals and list the steps it will take to achieve them.

What is it you need? Is it a diet, exercise program, new career? Whatever, know exactly what it is and how to go about doing it—the right way. If you don't know anything about achieving your goal, the library or a bookstore can help you out. Read and follow the suggested plan.

Be realistic. An aspect of maintaining motivation is to rework your lifestyle gradually, with patience and a positive frame of mind. After all, caterpillars don't become beautiful butterflies overnight.

"When a woman comes in with headaches, aching muscles, and a weight problem, I don't get very far suggesting that she stop all red meat, eat more grains, exercise, take vitamins, and meditate all at once," says Christiane Northrup, M.D., a gynecologist/obstetrician from South Portland, Maine. "You've got to start small, with a specific plan for tackling one problem at a time. Then the rest falls into place."

Nora Irvine, of South Berwick, Maine, spent seven years developing a lifestyle that best suits her needs.

"When I went off to college, I gained 20 pounds in three months. I came rolling in the door at Thanksgiving," she recalls, laughing. "I'd offset the junk food with a diet cola. Somehow I managed to lose some of the weight before I graduated, but I still wasn't eating very good food. When I got a job in a health-food store, people would ask me questions, so I read everything I could find about nutrition so that I could answer them. That got me going to do something about my own diet.

"My social consciousness made me cut out meat when I realized how much meat Americans eat. A meatless diet made it easier to keep my weight down and then I started feeling so much better, keener.

"When I got a job at a newspaper in Maine a few years later, I started running with a 53-year-old secretary who ran circles around me. A number of years later, when my husband, David, and I decided we would eventually have a baby, I buckled down even more during a training program

Find out exactly how to achieve your goal.

Start small with a specific plan of attack.

"Vanity kept me going."

for women who get pregnant after 30," continues Irvine, the mother of an eight-month-old daughter. "Vanity and wanting to have a superior baby kept me going."

2. Find a person or group of people who can help you keep going.

"Support is essential in keeping a lot of people going," says Susan Smith Jones, Ph.D., an instructor in health sciences at UCLA.

"Even if it's just one partner or a whole group, people are a great way to encourage motivation," says Dr. Jerry Vandel. "People like company and they can set goals together. Say you're going out running. If someone else is counting on you, you're more likely to be there."

Minister and health educator Leo R. Van Dolson, of Washington, D.C., adds, "When everyone in the group is striving for the same thing, they can offer each other support. Maybe everyone in the class was supposed to lose 2 pounds one week and someone comes to the next class and says she couldn't do it. Someone else might speak up and say, 'Me, too,' and then other people will make supportive suggestions.

"The group situation is a way of rejuvenating motivation on a regular basis," Rev. Van Dolson concludes.

Some people don't necessarily need a whole group of people but just one other person in whom they can confide and from whom they can get information and support.

"People need to find someone who won't lay a heavy trip on them," Dr. Northrup notes. "They're usually grateful for that. Finding a doctor or someone they can bounce ideas off of is important. Finding someone with a degree, like an M.D., makes some people feel more at ease. If I tell a woman to get a massage to help her reduce some of her stress, it's like I've given her a doctor's prescription to go and feel good, as if she needed permission to do something good."

3. Experiment for a month or two until you find the program that most appropriately suits you. Give yourself time to adjust.

"Behavioral scientists say that it takes the body 21 days to accept new behavior," says Dr. Jones. "If you give up sugar, for instance, you must keep at it for at least 21 days before your body accepts the change as natural. Set goals

If someone else is counting on you, you're more likely to be there.

Groups regenerate motivation on a regular basis.

The body takes 21 days to accept new behavior.

that are so realistic and easy to achieve that you won't fail. Take it one day at a time."

Also, remember that the first group, doctor, or program that you find may not be what you want or what you need. But don't be discouraged and stop. Keep on looking.

Lauro Bustamante, a young lawyer from San Antonio, Texas, is an example that trial and error need not be a setback. Bustamante went to see Dr. Vandel after he repeatedly encountered injuries and fatigue from the running and weight-lifting program he created for himself.

"I needed someone to tell me how to do it right, how much to do," Bustamante remembers. "He gave me a stress and physical analysis and dietary plan. I did more research on my own before I came up with a nutritional program I liked, but I followed his exercise program and found it a scientific approach to conditioning. I was just getting in such good shape that I didn't want to go back to my old habits."

Feeling good—and good about yourself—prevents you from taking up old habits.

4. Be flexible—leave a little room for error. No exercise or diet program should be so rigid that it doesn't leave room for a little diversion.

Rigid programs are just simply too difficult to follow. A day off from exercise or an occasional dip of ice cream are all part of handling a practical, long-term program.

"Once you have less of something you don't need, the less you want of it," says Nora Irvine of her fondness for ice cream. "After a while it just doesn't appeal to you as much."

By cutting back—instead of cutting out—you reduce the desire.

Cindy Casterella agrees, adding, "I give myself permission to fail. If I do, it's not such a big deal.

"You've got to have a trusting, positive attitude about yourself," says Casterella. "I stopped smoking by betting myself to see how long I could hold out. When I got to 13 years, I figured I had it licked!"

Casterella arrived at her philosophical attitude through help from Jeffrey Migdow, M.D., at the Kripalu Center for Yoga and Health in Lenox, Massachusetts. "I wanted to refine what I already knew about yoga," she explains. She gradually lost 13 pounds, but that became secondary to the healthy feeling she gained by developing and following a good diet to complement her yoga program. To overcome the temptation to return to old eating habits, she says, "Look at it as simply an experiment. Say, 'It's nothing that I

Say, "It's nothing that I must do forever."

must do forever. I can change it if it doesn't suit me.' This makes things easier to follow."

5. Visualize how good the "new you" will look and feel.

Mentally rehearse a positive result; imagine the new you.

"Cut out pictures from magazines that remind you of how you want to look and feel and pin them in noticeable spots around your home," advises Dr. Jones. It may sound old hat, but it really does help you achieve your goal.

Actually seeing the physical results is the best way to keep your motivation in high gear.

"As long as I'm in shape, I don't get depressed like I used to. And I don't feel run down or get the same colds or injuries," notes Lauro Bustamante.

Another effect of his perseverance has been a 10-pound weight loss. "I was originally on a six-month program with Dr. Vandel. It's hard to do it on your own. With someone looking over your shoulder, you push yourself to stick with it. I asked him a lot of questions and he answered them all. I really got my money's worth—I saw the results."

43

Curb Your Sugar Craving

If the mere mention of a savory, sweet snack brings a lip-smacking smile to your mouth, chances are there's a sweet tooth anchored somewhere in that grin. And it's a good bet it's got you hooked on sugar.

"People can get hooked on anything—sugar, honey, alcohol, even corn or milk," says Lendon Smith, M.D., author of *Feed Yourself Right* (McGraw-Hill). "Any food has the potential for being addictive. Sugar is high on the list."

Of course, no one knows better than the true-blue sugar hounds just how troublesome this problem can be. They're reminded of it every day when the nagging craving forces them to stick their hand in the cookie jar—or anywhere else something gooey, sugary, and sweet just happens to be. And the sugar addicts probably don't need to be told how bad the stuff is for them, either. They know it causes tooth decay. And they know it aggravates a weight problem, diabetes, and gout. Yet, they go after it anyway. Like the junkie hooked on heroin, they have to get their daily fix.

Ah, but there is hope. You can kick the sweet habit. Authorities in the field say that it is possible to adjust your palate to desire less sugar, even no sugar at all! To find out how to go about it, we sought out the trade secrets of the medical people who deal with the problem every day. The nicest thing we found is that yanking a sweet tooth requires little pain. Here's a baker's dozen's worth of steps leading to a new life without sweets.

If you panic when there's nothing sweet in the house, you're addicted.

If thoughts of false teeth, obesity, and diabetes can't dissuade you, you're hooked.

KEEP A SUGAR DIARY

Kicking the habit requires,
first and foremost, a lot of
consciousness raising.

"Kicking the sugar habit requires, first and foremost, a lot of consciousness raising," says Allen McDaniels, M.D., of San Pedro, California. You have to want to get off the stuff. The surest way to convince yourself that you're overloading on sugar is to keep a diary of everything you eat and drink for a week. Check off all the items containing sugar, either added by the processor or by yourself. The second week start eliminating. Cold turkey is the best way to go about it. If you find this absolutely impossible, start by gradually cutting down.

Teenagers get 50 percent of
their calories from sugar.

Just keep in mind that you don't have to breakfast on cola and a cupcake (yes, such people do exist) to be tagged a sugar junkie. Even a teaspoon of sugar in your morning coffee is a sign that you're hooked. The plain truth of the matter is that far too many Americans eat too much sugar. Statistics show that sugar added to food contributes about 25 percent of adult calorie intake. For teenagers, the percentage is closer to 50 percent! The researchers at Georgetown University in Washington, D.C., who came up with these figures say they indicate "a potential widespread health problem." So, just being average puts you at risk. Where do you fall in these statistics? Your weekly sugar diary can give you a good idea.

BANISH ALL SUGARS AND SWEETS FROM THE HOUSE

This may sound like the cure-all for the problem. But unfortunately for sugar lovers, out of sight doesn't also mean out of mind. But it is a start. "Keep no sugar in the house—including white, brown, and corn sugar, maple syrup, and molasses," advises Dr. Smith, "though one small jar of pure raw honey is OK to keep around."

The average person eats 143
pounds of sugars and
sweeteners a year.

Feeding a sugar craving simply is a lot more difficult to do when the goodies are out of reach. And it's not just white sugar you must avoid. Even though white sugar consumption is down, Americans still eat way too much of it. Statistics show that we each eat an average of 88 pounds of white sugar a year, down from the peak of 103 pounds per person in 1972. But the story changes dramatically when you add together all things sweet. In 1980, the use of all sugars and sweeteners was at a record high, up 50 percent from 91 pounds a year per person at the turn of the century to 143 pounds a year for each and every one of us in 1980. The popularity of corn syrup alone has skyrocketed from two pounds per person in 1972 to 26 pounds per person in 1980.

TAKE TIME OUT TO NIBBLE

Sugar craving is a vicious cycle. A quick dose of it causes blood sugar to rise rapidly. To compensate for the overdose, the body rapidly releases insulin, forcing the blood sugar level to plummet. The end result? Another sugar attack. Some people suffer such common side effects as nervousness, crankiness, headaches, and bad dreams. "The trick to avoiding sugar pangs is to keep the blood sugar fairly even," Dr. Smith says. "Nibbling on good food in between your regular meals is a way to achieve this." Nuts, seeds, raw vegetables, fruits, cheese, and hard-cooked eggs are all good anti-sugar snack foods. "If you nibble every two to three hours you'll find out you crave less. You'll eat less at regular meals, and be more cheerful in the morning," he says.

Nuts, seeds, raw vegetables, and cheese are good anti-sugar snacks.

Former cravers told us that nuts are particularly helpful in fending off a sugar urge. "I can remember staring at this candy bar in a store and really wanting it," one woman says. "It was one of those gooey chocolate bars with lots of nuts and caramel. But I resisted and when I got back to the office I bought a bag of nuts. They tasted great and it occurred to me that that's probably what I was really craving all along." Now she nibbles on nuts when the urge gets strong.

INCREASE YOUR INTAKE OF COMPLEX CARBOHYDRATES

We all know that whole grains and fresh vegetables are packed with nutrition. But unfortunately these same foods are most likely to be at the bottom of the sugar addict's list of foods they like to eat. "Overloading on sweets is a bad diet and a bad diet leads to vitamin deficiency," says Dr. McDaniels. "The result is craving more sweets. It's a vicious cycle. The straight nutritional approach is the easiest way to get around a sweet tooth. You'll find that eating a good, well-balanced diet helps eliminate the sugar craving."

The straight nutritional approach is the easiest way around a sweet tooth.

Ray C. Wunderlich, M.D., of St. Petersburg, Florida, adds another bit of advice. "Make sure you have adequate protein in your diet every day," he says. "I don't mean excessive protein, just adequate." He also touts nuts and seeds as a great substitute for sugar. "They can take the edge off a sweet craving," he says, "but don't just eat peanuts. Try almonds, sesame seeds, and sunflower seeds. Be versatile."

BEAT BINGES WITH EXERCISE

Instead of sugar, push-ups.

Putting the body in high gear, even for just a few minutes, is a great sugar stabilizer, says Dr. Wunderlich. "If the blood sugar is high, exercise will bring it down. If it's low, it will bring it up." In his own practice, Dr. Wunderlich found that a few minutes spent bouncing on a mini-trampoline can do wonders for a sugar urge. But any kind of exercise will do—calisthenics, jumping jacks, a brisk walk, and of course jogging. "If you want sugar, get down on the floor and do a couple of push-ups. It'll put you in a whole new frame of mind," he says.

But don't just exercise when you get the sugar urge. Regular day-after-day exercise enables your body to handle glucose more efficiently. When you exercise daily, less insulin is needed to control sugar swings.

GET A DAILY DOSE OF B VITAMINS

The B vitamins are essential to glucose metabolism.

When it comes to sugar-fighting vitamins, the B complex gets an A. The B vitamins are all-important to sugar addicts because of their ability to keep blood sugar working at an optimal level, says Dr. Smith. In his own practice, he's found that B vitamins, particularly niacinamide, help assuage the sugar hunger in hypoglycemic patients—those whose sugar allergy causes sickness and even pyschological problems. And, the Bs help sour a sweet tooth, too. What foods contain B vitamins? You guessed it—complex carbohydrates. Whole grains, fresh vegetables, wheat germ— all the foods you've already been encouraged to eat.

GET YOUR FAIR SHARE OF CHROMIUM, MANGANESE, AND ZINC

Like the B vitamins, this trio of trace minerals is important in keeping the blood sugar on an even keel. And, according to Dr. Wunderlich, they are the minerals most commonly found to be in short supply in sugar lovers. Chromium helps insulin do its job efficiently. Zinc and manganese help stabilize blood sugar, particularly when it is at an ebb.

But the major role of zinc in nutrition is to enhance taste acuity. And most recently, it has been found to actually help control the sweet tooth. This was discovered when ten healthy people were fed zinc supplements for 15 weeks to see how it would affect their sense of sweet, sour, salty, and bitter. Most dramatic was their sensitivity of the taste of sweet. They found they could get by on less sugar *(Biological Trace Element Research)*.

Zinc sharpens taste buds so it takes less to satisfy your cravings.

AVOID RED MEATS

This is strictly anecdotal, but there are people who claim it helps. One such person is William Dufty, whose personal successful war in fighting sugar addiction resulted in the book *Sugar Blues* (Warner). "In kicking sugar, the most helpful extra hint I can give you is the one that worked for me," writes Dufty. "Kick red meat. Just switching from red meat to fish or fowl reduces your desire for a sweet concoction at the end of a meal. It makes it easier to settle for something natural, like fruit, or even no dessert at all."

Red meat appears to increase sugar cravings.

Dr. Smith says he also heard similar positive reports from his own patients. "There's definitely something to it," he says, "especially for those who have an allergy to beef. When vegetable protein is used in place of animal protein, it's somehow easier for a person to pass up sweets."

READ PACKAGE LABELS VERY CAREFULLY

Sugar can end up in the most unlikely items—even some toothpastes contain it—which is why it's important to follow this tip. If some kind of sugar, such as corn syrup, fructose, dextrose, or honey, is listed as one of the first two or three ingredients, then you can bet the product contains a lot of sugar. And you'd be best off avoiding it. Some things you'd never think of adding sugar to at home—like soups— often list it as an ingredient when you find them on the supermarket shelf. So get in the habit—read all labels!

Fructose, dextrose, and corn syrup are just different names for sugar.

AVOID ARTIFICIAL SWEETENERS

Trying to trick your taste buds into thinking you're eating sugar when you're not just isn't going to do you any good. "Saccharin and cyclamates taste sweet, but they are chemicals and the liver has to detoxify them," says Dr. Smith. "Besides, anything that tastes sweet promotes the idea that everything *must* taste sweet." The bottom line is forget sweeteners. You can live without them.

WARD OFF VENDING MACHINES

A real downfall to many sugar addicts is vending machines, those handy little fixtures that can send you to sugar land at the drop of a coin and a flick of the wrist.

Don't run on empty. Snack on healthy foods so you can resist junk food.

Just how bad an influence a vending machine can be was demonstrated on the campus of the University of Illinois, where the snack habits of the students were monitored. Thirty-five percent of the students skipped at least one meal a day, opting for sustenance instead from the vendor. And it was the soft-drink lever that got the biggest work-out. Candy and chewing gum came in second and third. Next came coffee, popcorn, potato chips, pretzels, pies, yogurt, fresh fruit, hot chocolate, crackers, and milk *(Illinois Research)*.

One way to snub the vending machine is to carry your own nourishing snacks to work, says Dr. Smith. But he has an even better idea. Ask your employer to have them removed. Sugar overloading can lead to job dissatisfaction, he says, even in offices that are relatively stress-free. "If the boss wants the best from the workers, he or she would do well to ban the junk machines."

REACH FOR FRUIT, YOUR NATURAL SWEET

The perfect snack: fruit. It picks you up, quenches your thirst, and satisfies your craving.

Keep an assortment of fresh fruit in the house at all times. It's a great thing to grab during a sugar attack. Take it with you in the car, too, if you have the habit of munching candy bits or other sugary tidbits when you're driving. Not only is fruit high in vitamins, it makes you feel full and satisfied much longer. It's also a natural thirst quencher, helping to fight the urge to feed coins to the soda pop machine.

And, yes, we can't forget those with a six-pack-a-day habit—six-pack of soda, that is. What's a poor addict to do? The answer's simple: Give it up altogether. And it really is simple to do. "Switch to fruit juices—only the unsweetened varieties," says Dr. Wunderlich. "Before long you'll wonder how you could stand drinking all that sweet soda all day long." And if it's the feeling of the bubbly carbonation sliding down your throat that you really long for, switch to club soda or mineral water with a wedge of lemon or lime.

THE FINAL REWARD

This one's optional and you can try it only if you've given the other 12 your best. Take a day every month or so and have a sugar splurge. "Total deprivation just doesn't work," says Dr. McDaniels. "You have to be good to yourself. A day of overdosing on sugar isn't harmful, if your problem is a psychological one. For the hypoglycemic person, it's a different story. But I've found it's fun and a nice reward for living a healthy life to set aside a day on a rare occasion to have a sugar-loading or junk-food day."

So go ahead. If all goes well, you may be surprised to find how quickly you can be turned off by sugar!

Occasionally splurge on a junk-food day. It's a healthy reward.

44

Smoke No More

Wanting to quit is the first step.

If you are a smoker who really would like to quit, congratulations. You've just completed step one, and you may already be on your way to successfully kicking the habit.

You have to *want* to quit smoking before you can really do it, says Jerome Schwartz, Dr. P.H., a health care research consultant in Davis, California. Dr. Schwartz has evaluated a variety of smoking control programs and written numerous articles on how to quit.

"Smoking can be a difficult habit to break. When you smoke cigarettes, you may do it more than anything else you do in your life—more than tying your shoelaces, more than eating. If you are lighting up a cigarette 20 or 30 times a day, it has become a habit entwined in your very lifestyle."

If the desire is strong, quitting is possible no matter how long you've smoked.

If the desire to stop smoking is strong enough, quitting may be accomplished no matter how long you've smoked. Clemmie Fishback had smoked nearly a pack and half a day for 30 years before she quit.

"I really liked smoking. I like the taste of cigarettes," she says. Then a lung tumor appeared on an x-ray during her annual physical exam. "I figured it was probably cancer since I'd smoked so long. But I made a vow that if it wasn't cancer, I'd never smoke again." A subsequent operation revealed that the tumor had started to grow around her aorta at a very rapid rate—but it was not malignant.

In retrospect, quitting isn't that difficult.

It has been ten years since Clemmie Fishback quit smoking. "If you really make up your mind to do it, you can do it," she says. "When I first quit, I used to *dream* about smoking a cigarette. The dreams were so real that I'd wake up the next morning thinking I probably had. But it wasn't all that difficult to quit. Every time I wanted to smoke, I'd think about something else. A year after I quit, I didn't have any real desire to smoke, even when I was around other smokers."

Health reasons can provide strong incentives to quit for some smokers, yet not for others. Any motivation will suffice. "Basically, I just got sick of running out of cigarettes and having to go out and find a place that was open so I could buy a pack," says Joanne Lannin, a freelance writer in Manchester, New Hampshire. "I also had some friends who had quit. I have always been a competitive person. I figured if they could do it, so could I."

FOUR TYPES OF SMOKERS

Once you are motivated to quit, you might start thinking about how you're going to do it. The methods you use may depend on the type of smoker you are.

How you quit depends on how you smoke.

"There are basically four major identifiable types of smokers," says Dr. Schwartz. The *habit smoker* is the one who automatically lights up. He may smoke after an evening meal, when he's on the phone, having a coffee break, or sipping a cocktail.

"You have to do things to constantly remind that person to quit. Tie up his cigarettes with cellophane and rubber bands so he will consciously realize he is reaching for another cigarette. He might change brands, use his opposite hand to smoke, or put the cigarettes in different pockets. He must be made very aware that he is smoking and that he wants to quit."

The *positive affect smoker* finds smoking pleasurable and smokes for enjoyment or concentration. That person can substitute something like jogging or walking for cigarettes while going through the toughest stage of quitting, says Dr. Schwartz. The substitute always should be something that fits appropriately into the person's lifestyle.

If you smoke for enjoyment, substitute something you enjoy even more.

Negative affect smokers smoke when they are nervous or feel under pressure. "This person often has a very difficult time quitting and may need professional help to do it," says Dr. Schwartz.

Those smokers with a *psychological or physical addic-*

tion are the ones who can't wait for the concert's intermission so they can rush out to the lobby for a fix.

For some, "cold turkey" may be the only way to go.

"People with a psychological or physical addiction cannot quit smoking by trying to cut down. They may cut down to five cigarettes a day, then go to a party and start all over again. They have to quit cold turkey," says Dr. Schwartz.

FEWER WITHDRAWAL SYMPTOMS

The words may strike terror in the hearts of many a nicotine addict, but "cold turkey" actually may be the best way for any smoker to quit. A study done by Saul Shiffman and Murray E. Jarvik, M.D., Ph.D., at the University of California at Los Angeles indicates that withdrawal symptoms disappear more quickly when smokers quit abruptly.

The physical symptoms of withdrawal are predictable.

"People experience all sorts of distress when they first quit smoking," Shiffman says. "They have a craving for cigarettes. They also may experience psychological discomfort in which they become short-tempered or anxious. Physical problems like nausea or dizziness may be encountered, and the person may feel either very hyper or very tired and sleepy at first."

In their research, Shiffman and Dr. Jarvik found that people quitting cold turkey experienced fairly rapid relief of their withdrawal symptoms after one week. Those who only cut down their cigarette smoking by 60 percent experienced the same level of stress throughout the two-week period. "Cutting down just seemed to prolong their withdrawal symptoms," says Shiffman.

Set a definite quit date—not too soon, not too far away.

If someone becomes motivated to quit and decides to quit cold turkey, the next question is, when? A number of professionals suggest that a smoker set a very definite quit date. "It should not be too soon, and it should not be too far away," says Shiffman.

During deadlines or on a Reno gambling vacation may not be the time or place.

Timing is important. "If you are under a lot of pressure to draw up a company contract, that's no time to think about quitting. Two weeks after it's finished, you might be ready to try it," explains Dr. Schwartz. "A vacation can be a good or a bad time to quit. If you are going to Reno to gamble, I wouldn't advise quitting then. A vacation hiking in clear mountain air might be a more conducive setting."

Joanne Lannin had smoked more than a pack a day for eight years when she decided to quit prior to a trip with some nonsmokers. "I knew I was going to Michigan for a week with friends who didn't smoke, and I would have to cut down my smoking anyway. So I decided I would quit that week. The day before we left, I bought a pack of cigarettes, and I stayed up until 3 A.M. until I had finished the pack. The next morning I didn't want a cigarette.

"I did drive my friends nuts during the first part of the trip though. Finally one of them told me if I mentioned smoking again he was going to throw me out of the car, and I'd have to *walk* back to New Hampshire. That was a challenge. I didn't talk about it for the rest of the week. I decided I'd suffer through it alone. By the end of the week, I had nearly forgotton about smoking."

She kept a journal about her experience, and every time she felt like having a cigarette, she would write about it.

Keep a journal to record your feelings while quitting.

"I SET SMALL GOALS"

"I also never said to myself that I was never going to smoke again. I think, at the time, it would have loomed too large over me," says Lannin. "I set small goals for myself instead. I said, 'I'm not going to smoke for a week,' and I didn't. Then I said, 'All right, Now I'm not going to smoke for a month, and I'll re-evaluate things at that time.' That provided me an incentive and a motivation to discontinue cigarettes for three months, then six. . . .

Lannin adds that her friends provided a lot of emotional support. She might not have consciously planned it that way, but enlisting the support of family members and friends seems to be an important factor in quitting.

Friends and family provide emotional support.

"Some people won't even tell their co-workers that they are trying to quit, but they should," says Shiffman. "Even your friends who still smoke may choose not to smoke when they're around you and may provide a lot of encouragement as you go through the difficult stages of quitting."

Some people actively seek out stop-smoking clinics for the added comfort of commiserating with others who are trying to quit, too.

Stop-smoking clinics can provide the support of a buddy system.

"I knew what I needed was for somebody else to quit with me," says Judy Webster of Crofton, Maryland, who attended a stop-smoking clinic sponsored by the American Cancer Society. Webster had smoked 1½ packs a day for 20 years. She attended one session a week for six weeks and walked away an ex-smoker. "I had tried to quit on my own but never succeeded. I know some people can quit without a 'buddy system,' but I couldn't do it alone."

Neither could Lois Sylva, who took part in the same clinic. She also told all of her friends she was going to quit, but not necessarily for their support. "In order to save face with them, I knew I couldn't let myself slip back. I was afraid my friends who still smoked would say, 'Oh, you're smoking again, eh?' "

The clinic advised participants to cut down and to set a quit date, says Judy Webster. Weekly presentations included a film, guest speakers, and a variety of techniques demonstrated as possible aids to help the smokers quit.

Orange juice and cigarettes don't mix.

"I took all of the advice the class had to offer," says Lois Sylva. "I drank lots of water to flush out my system and drank more fruit juices." There's something about orange juice and a cigarette that just doesn't go.

Sylva also kept a lot of fresh fruit handy—especially grapes. When she felt like having a cigarette, she'd pop a grape into her mouth and feel satisfied.

TAKING THE FINAL STEP

She wrote down her smoking habits and the times she felt most like having a cigarette. When she did smoke, she waited ten minutes before lighting the cigarette and only smoked it half the way through. After two weeks of gradually cutting down, Sylva decided to go cold turkey.

"It was a Wednesday. I had had no cigarettes the night before, and I had gone all day without one. When dinnertime came that night, I got ready to make the spaghetti sauce I had been making every Wednesday night for the past 20 years. Suddenly I could *not* remember how to do it. My brain just wouldn't think. It was as if somebody had knocked me over the head and I'd lost my memory. It was really scary. I wondered if I was going to keep blanking out like that, but it only happened once. I ended up using a canned spaghetti sauce or something. My family told me it was one of the worst meals I had ever prepared."

The dilemma of withdrawal: Your mind says no; your body says yes.

That was the beginning of intense withdrawal symptoms that lasted about one week. "I had the most problem with a terrible feeling of anxiety—that something was awfully wrong and I wasn't able to fix it," Lois Sylva says.

"Of course, I knew that if I picked up a cigarette, I'd fix it right away. I also felt very lightheaded and was short-tempered and cranky. It was as if I wanted to get off the habit, but my body was saying, 'It's not worth it, pick up a cigarette.'"

Sylva says friends and family members were called upon to be "saints" when she was trying to quit. "My poor husband really got it at times, but he never once told me, 'I'd rather have you smoking and a happy woman.' He just bore it until I was a human being again."

Since she has quit, Sylva says she has more energy and ambition. "It is a good feeling. I feel well, happy, and interested in things around me.

Quitting meant more energy and ambition.

"I'm a joiner. I like groups and being in one was the simplest way for me to kick the habit. When I tried quitting on my own, I just got discouraged. It was always easy to quit, but going back was easy, too. The first little thing that came up, I would say, 'Aw, the heck with it,' and light up."

AVOID BACKSLIDING

Shiffman says that once you do quit, you must think about how you will *remain* an ex-smoker. What can you do to keep from falling back into the old habit?

Think about how you're going to remain an ex-smoker.

"Sit down with someone and brainstorm. What situations might arise in the future that will tempt you to reach for a cigarette?" says Shiffman. "Plan ahead for those situations so you'll know what to do.

"Find out what works for you. If you have always needed to smoke at parties, avoid parties for the first month or so after quitting. Or maybe you can attend a party and avoid smoking by avoiding alcohol.

"People may be there who will kid you about not smoking. Practice assertive, positive ways of refusing offers of cigarettes. Some ex-smokers repeat 'I'm not going to smoke' like a mantra, but it has to be practiced ahead of time or it won't be an automatic response when you are challenged.

Practice assertive ways to refuse a cigarette.

"It also helps to know that urges pass very quickly. If you are at a party and get the urge to smoke, go out and walk for five minutes." Shiffman assures us that those urges become less frequent and much less intense.

Some people think they can just quit without thinking about it. They may quit, but their chances of quitting for good may be less.

YOU MUST PREPARE

"Someone may think, 'I'm not going to use any of that pop psych stuff. I just won't smoke,' " says Shiffman. "Well, the fact is, you *do* have to prepare. I think that is something that is absolutely critical if you want to succeed. A number of studies show that, of those who quit smoking, possibly three-fourths of them will be smoking again in six months."

Let's review the battle plan. First there must be the determination to quit. Then you decide how you might do it. Perhaps you decide to quit cold turkey. You set up a good quit date, enlist the support of others, and proceed to try any reasonable techniques you think will help *you* to quit. Once off cigarettes, you may experience withdrawal symptoms, but they eventually will subside. In the meantime, you sit down with someone and think of how you will remain off cigarettes.

You can slip and still not fail.

There is one last step. An ex-smoker must realize that it is possible to slip and still not fall. "Even those people who are successful often slip and have one cigarette at one point or another. They may think that's the end of the road and they're failures. But they can use that slip as an education. The ex-smoker should examine the situation and ask himself what occurred to make him take that cigarette," says Shiffman. "By closely reviewing the action, you can learn how to handle things better the next time you're confronted with a similar situation.

"Instead of using the slip as a learning experience, ex-smokers have tended to use it as a justification to go back to cigarettes. They say, 'See? I can't do it. I don't have the willpower.' They think if they have one they have ruined everything and go back to smoking whole packs again."

Some ex-smokers are loath to even touch a cigarette. They don't want to have to go through the battle of quitting again. "I think if I had smoked again, I would have been like an alcoholic—I would have been hooked. But I haven't smoked a cigarette in ten years, and I haven't had the desire to smoke for a long, long time," says Clemmie Fishback.

Low-calorie food substitutes.

Some smokers express a fear of gaining weight if they quit. Some of the people we interviewed gained weight. Others remained stable in their weight, and some actually lost weight. If a food substitute is needed at the beginning, fresh fruits and vegetables offer nutritious and low-calorie choices.

Other smokers believe that it's too late for them to quit. According to research in Israel, men who give up smoking as late as their 60s and 70s still live longer than men who continue to smoke.

At the Hebrew University-Hadassah Medical School in Jerusalem, men between the ages of 65 and 74 who continued smoking were found to have a 24 percent higher death rate than those who quit. Men between 75 and 84 had a 12 percent higher death rate when they continued to smoke *(American Journal of Medical Sciences)*. More recent research indicates that older smokers actually may be more successful than younger ones at quitting.

Quitting at 70—and living longer as a result.

The fact, is if you're a smoker, you're running out of excuses. If you really want to quit, chances are you can. And you don't necessarily need any magical, fairy-dusted, money-back-guaranteed gewgaws to do it. It is estimated that 95 percent of the 29 million smokers who have quit since 1964 have done so on their own. You may already know that. You also may already know that *you're* going to quit, too—someday.

Join a club of 29 million.

"Quitting is something that really has to be done. For most of us, we're running out of time to fail," says James Billings, Ph.D., a clinical psychologist in Berkeley, California. "I work with people who are essentially going to kill themselves if they don't quit smoking.

"Someday has to be now."

Are You a Coffee-Holic?

Abook on emotional health would not be complete without some mention of the effect caffeine can have on your nerves.

Compulsive coffee drinking is a type of drug addiction.

According to Sanford Bolton, Ph.D., of St. John's University in New York City, "Caffeine is a potent drug, affecting the central nervous system, cardiovascular system, gastrointestinal tract, adrenaline release, and muscle contraction. . . . Because of the ubiquitous use of tea, coffee, and cola beverages, caffeine is probably the most widely used drug. As such it is subject to overindulgence and abuse" *(Journal of Applied Nutrition)*.

For some people, the immediate effects of caffeine are "coffee nerves." Symptoms, such as shaky hands and an overall jittery feeling, become apparent within an hour of drinking as little as one cup of coffee (about 100 to 150 milligrams [mg] of caffeine). The effects last several hours. Then you crash.

Energy letdown: the aftermath to the coffee "high."

Coffee initially raises blood sugar (one reason you get a lift). But soon the body's insulin overrides that and you're left with a letdown feeling.

PERMANENT ANXIETY

For those who can't stop at one cup, the adverse effects are multiplied, too. A syndrome known as caffeinism occurs in people who drink five or more cups of coffee a day (about 500 mg of caffeine). The syndrome is very much like anxiety neurosis, and the people afflicted suffer from nervousness, irritability, agitation, headache, muscle twitching, and rapid heartbeat.

If you're starting to get worried, that's good. Because in order to kick the caffeine habit, you've got to have the incentive. Once you have that, you're ready to go.

Worried? Good. You need incentive to quit.

QUIT COLD TURKEY

Sounds easy. One day you're a coffee drinker and the next day you're not. But look out. Caffeine can be, after all, physiologically addictive. That means when your body is deprived of its usual "fix" it may rebel. The most common symptom is a headache that begins about 18 hours after your last cup of coffee, says John F. Greden, M.D., of the University of Michigan Medical Center in Ann Arbor. It begins with a feeling of cerebral fullness (as if your brain were too big for your head) and rapidly progresses to a painful and throbbing headache. It peaks about three to six hours after onset, explains Dr. Greden, but it's not unusual for the pain to last a day or more *(New England Journal of Medicine)*.

A person desperate for relief may reach for an aspirin, but again, beware. Many over-the-counter pain remedies contain—what else?—caffeine. Sure your headache will go away, but then you're hooked again and have to start all over.

Beware of caffeine-containing pain medications.

Besides the headache, you may also feel extreme irritability, lethargy, or anxiety. In fact, the same kind of anxiety associated with heavy caffeine consumption is experienced during withdrawal as well.

Still, if you persevere, it won't be long before you see some positive results—only about three days. However, it may take two to three weeks before the full benefits are felt. Then you'll notice that you are sleeping more soundly, feel more relaxed and less tense during the day, and are better able to handle everyday stresses in stride.

In just three days, you'll feel better.

TRY TAPERING OFF

Some people find tapering off less painful than cold turkey because they spread out the final event over several weeks. But that doesn't mean you get off scotfree. Depending on how addicted you are, your symptoms may be severe just from cutting down. One man who was accustomed to 15 cups of coffee a day had severe headaches on weekends

Cutting back a cup a week is one feasible plan.

when he drank much less. How you cut back is really up to you. Just do whatever feels most comfortable. You may choose to reduce your intake by one cup per week or one cup per day. Remember, each reduction in caffeine is a plus for you.

REWARD YOURSELF

A group of "coffee addicts" entered a program at the University of Maryland, Baltimore County, which was based on a reward system of behavior modification. The goal was to decrease their caffeine intake from over 1,000 mg per day to 600 mg per day (less than five cups of coffee). While that's still a rather large amount of caffeine, there's no reason that this program could not be adapted to eliminate caffeine completely from your diet.

One study paid people to quit.

Each of the three people in the study were required to deposit $20, half of which was to be returned to them in four equal steps during the treatment and the other half at the three-month follow-up.

During each of those four equal steps, the volunteers were to reduce their coffee intake by 100 mg or more. If they succeeded, they received $2.50 for each phase plus a $1 bonus, and remained eligible to receive another $10 at the end of treatment. If they goofed and drank more coffee, they forfeited the money.

Two out of three did better than expected.

Two of the three volunteers in the study not only succeeded in every phase, they managed to reduce their caffeine intake to below 300 mg, much better than originally expected. The third person slipped up slightly, but by the end of the ten-month follow-up he did manage to average below 600 mg per day.

"All subjects reported positive physiological and behavioral side effects at the end of treatment," say the researchers. "Subject one said she felt 'healthier.' Subject two reported that he noticed he was less tense and 'hyper' at work and in his relations with others, and that he felt better physically. Subject three reported that he felt less irritable" (*Journal of Applied Behavior Analysis*).

Devise your own reward system: a dinner out, a new dress.

You can devise a reward program that's special to you. Perhaps you can buy a new dress as your reward or go out to a fancy restaurant. Whatever gives you the incentive to succeed can be used as your own personal prize.

CHANGE YOUR RITUALS

Do you know how many cups of coffee you drink each day? Do you know when you like your coffee the most? Do you need coffee to wake up? Do you always crave a cup after meals? With friends? At work?

It's important for you to answer these questions so you'll know when you're most susceptible to that caffeine habit. For some people, the ritual of making a fresh pot of coffee in the morning is as much a joy as drinking the brew. Opening the container, smelling the fresh ground coffee, the crunchy sound the scoop makes when you dig into the beans, and the gurgling of the percolator may all contribute to the pleasing and familiar patterns that you associate with coffee drinking.

Recognizing your own vulnerability to coffee can help you break out. If morning is your roughest time, get up later and don't leave enough time for coffee.

Recognize your vulnerability and create safeguards.

If you crave a cup after dinner, get right up to do the dishes. Then get away from the kitchen as quickly as possible.

Visiting friends? Let them know you're kicking the habit. In fact, let everyone know. It makes you want to succeed even more if you have to answer to inquisitive friends or family members. Besides, they'll probably offer their support by not tempting you with the stuff you're trying to avoid.

Ask for support from your friends.

Meanwhile, you can be creating a new set of rituals and habits to replace the ones you're giving up. That's where caffeine-free or low-caffeine beverages come in.

DISCOVER ALTERNATE BEVERAGES

Anyone who's recently given up caffeine will be delighted by the new influx of herb teas to hit the market. Not just in health food stores, either. Herb teas can be found in almost any grocery store right alongside the regular caffeinated varieties.

Herb teas are naturally caffeine-free. What's more, some have nutritional benefits not found in ordinary tea. For example, rose hip tea is high in vitamin C and dandelion tea is loaded with vitamin A.

Almost all herb teas are blends of several ingredients, such as alfalfa and hibiscus flowers, cinnamon, lime, orange peel, and mint.

You can choose something with peppermint to wake you up in the morning or an herb tea of chamomile to soothe and relax you.

You can even grow the herbs yourself and create your own special brew. Spring is the perfect time to start an herb garden to supply you with lots of leaves for brewing hot drinks.

If you still favor the flavor of real tea, even that's still a possibility. Some companies have developed a decaffeinated black tea, which is not 100 percent caffeine-free, but close enough.

No substitute for the real thing? Try the new fancy decaf beans.

Of course if it's coffee you crave, you can prepare the decaffeinated kind, either instant or ground roast.

Another possibility is to try a coffee substitute: roots, grains, or seeds that have been dried, roasted, and ground. After all, real coffee is made from a well-roasted seed, too.

Chicory is a very popular coffee substitute, but you can do the same with carrot, parsnip, corn, barley, wheat, rye, chestnut, and others.

LEARN TO RELAX

What better counter to the high-anxiety brew? Of course, relaxation.

Relaxation techniques helped reduce caffeine intake for one overtaxed graduate student who was badly hooked. She practiced a meditation technique in a quiet environment in a comfortable position twice a day for 20 minutes each.

Before the technique was started, the student had been consuming between 600 and 1,000 mg of caffeine per day.

After starting relaxation therapy, her caffeine intake dropped to about 200 mg per day *(Psychological Reports)*.

Beating Procrastination . . . Now

Procrastination — what one wag called "the art of keeping up with yesterday" — is something we all have in common. Everybody puts things off, especially things that are bound to be unpleasant or difficult. In our more charitable moments, we think of this as a rather charming little flaw, a small and harmless human weakness. But when procrastination starts getting in the way of all the things we'd like to get out of life, it's no longer quite so charming or harmless.

Procrastinators often see their problem as a harmless human weakness.

"There are a lot of people out there — even bright, successful people — who live with a sense of fraudulence and anxiety because they can't seem to get hold of their procrastination," says Lenora M. Yuen, Ph.D., who with her colleague Jane B. Burka, Ph.D., devised a system to help chronic procrastinators lick the habit.

"Time lost in procrastinating can take years out of a person's life," adds William J. Knaus, Ed.D., executive director of the Fort Lee (New Jersey) Consultation Center, psychologist, and author of the book *Do It Now: How to Stop Procrastinating* (Prentice-Hall). "It saps enormous amounts of energy, emotion, and time. But worse yet, the fears, self-doubts, and low tolerance for the unpleasant that are part of the procrastination pattern can lead to alcoholism, depression, and anxiety."

On the tail of procrastination: depression, anxiety, alcoholism.

Dr. Yuen maintains that procrastination "is a complex psychological problem that rarely yields to simple remedies." Few of the participants in her seminars succeeded in beating the habit of putting things off until they came to understand "the function that procrastination was serving in their lives," she says.

So the first step on the road to beating procrastination is learning how to observe yourself—becoming your own closed-circuit TV monitor, restlessly scanning your own activities and thoughts to figure out how and why you keep putting things off . . . and putting them off . . . and putting them off . . .

Why are you putting things off . . . and off . . . and off?

"STEWERS" AND "DOERS"

To really become conscious of the little ways we procrastinate may be difficult at first. After all, your reasons for postponing that basement clean-up project seem perfectly logical. But if you take a hard look at the excuses you're handing yourself—what Dr. Knaus calls your "self-cons"—you may discover they're not so awfully rational after all. They're just . . . excuses.

Those little lies we tell ourselves are really expressions of inner turmoil of two basic types, Dr. Knaus believes: self-doubt and "discomfort dodging," a low tolerance for tension and frustration.

Two types of inner turmoil: self-doubt and discomfort dodging.

"Self-doubt is a crippler of action," Dr. Knaus says. "And people who habitually put things off are almost always self-doubters, always asking themselves, 'Should I or shouldn't I do this or that?'" They are "stewers," rather than "doers." They blame and criticize themselves. They are preoccupied with their own faults. And the sense of inadequacy and shaky self-confidence all this brings about leads to a paralyzing fear of failure. Rather than start a project that they fear may come off badly, they put it off. And put it off.

Self-doubt reaches its highest pitch in perfectionists, who have set such high standards for themselves that they fear doing anything at all. Nothing could measure up to their own expectations . . . so instead of trying but falling short, they procrastinate. Drs. Yuen and Burka described a hypothetical young lawyer who feared he wouldn't be able to measure up to his brilliant student record, so he developed a habit of preparing legal briefs only at the last possible moment. That way, if the brief was not first rate, he could always say, "I could have done better if I'd had another week." The self-con strikes again. (And the young lawyer's illusion of perfection goes untested.)

It's not that there's anything wrong with striving for excellence, Dr. Knaus explains. It's just that procrastinators of this kind "mistake doing the best they can for doing the best there is." And since nobody can do the best there is, every time, they end up doing everything late—or never.

"Discomfort dodgers," Dr. Knaus explains, procrastinate because they're afraid of the anxious or uncomfortable feelings they associate with beginning a task. Their goal in putting things off is to avoid feeling bad. "Discomfort dodging is like a mental pollutant that colors inconveniences and makes them seem more weighty and difficult than they actually are," he says. But because nearly everything you try to do in life is bound to produce its tensions and frustrations, discomfort dodgers are chronic avoiders, shrinking from anticipated pain.

And the task is put off. And put off, again and again.

Procrastinators very often have an unrealistic sense of time, consistently underestimating the amount of time it will take to complete a given task, Dr. Yuen adds.

One of her students, for example, was always late for his nine o'clock class—and astonished when he finally realized that he'd been allowing himself 15 minutes to get up, shower, dress, and make it to the class. He really thought 15 minutes would be enough time.

Procrastinators are often "magical thinkers" as well, she says: They hope to be seized by inspiration before they do anything, or they think the problem will simply go away.

BECOMING AWARE OF THE "SELF-CON"

Those are some of the basic patterns the "self-con" tends to take. We're fooling ourselves, but we get away with it because we're not really conscious of the way it's being done. How do you go about shedding some light on these self-deceptions?

Dr. Yuen says that at the first session of the procrastination seminars and classes she and Dr. Burka conduct, participants are asked to draw up a list of excuses they use for putting things off. "I've been working so hard I deserve a break," some say. Or, "I'll wait until I'm inspired to start working." Or, probably the oldest excuse of all, "I'll have plenty of time tomorrow." The students are then asked to

Procrastinators often mistake doing their best for THE best.

They consistently underestimate the amount of time it takes to do something.

Draw up a list of excuses.

monitor their own thoughts, and pay attention to these
excuses as they occur.

Another helpful way of teaching yourself to observe
yourself is to buy a notebook and begin keeping a daily log of
your "antiprocrastination campaign," Dr. Knaus says. What
types of things do you tend to put off? Does there seem to be
a pattern? Are the things you avoid really important to you
after all? Are they taking you closer to your goals? What *are*
your goals? And so on.

Verbalize your excuses as a way of weakening them.

A more immediate way of reflecting on your own
experience, he suggests, is to use a small tape recorder. If
you're trying to lose weight, for example, start the recorder
on your way to the refrigerator and simply tell yourself why
you want to eat that double-fudge sundae. "Your desire may
have been making so much noise in your head you could
hardly hear anything else," he says. "But once you verbalize
something, it's not quite to powerful anymore. Excuses for
not doing something are the same way."

On the other hand, becoming aware of the ways you
procrastinate is only half the battle. "Some of my patients
have all kinds of insights about their problems—they understand them better than I do," Dr. Knaus observes. "Yet
they're still at square one." It's one of procrastination's
saddest ironies that its victims often can tell you what they
ought to do, but can't seem to get around to doing it.
Self-awareness, by itself, isn't enough. There comes a time
when you have to *act.*

THE "UNSCHEDULE" AND THE "FIVE-MINUTE PLAN"

But how do you get across the chasm that separates
thinking about doing something and actually *doing* it?

Wait until you have enough time to finish a project and you may never get started.

Drs. Yuen and Burka say many procrastinators fail to
start a project unless they have enough time to finish the
whole thing; they value only the completed task, and not
the many steps that lead to its completion. As a way of
breaking through that impasse, they suggest trying the
"Swiss cheese" approach, described by management consultant Alan Lakein in his book *How to Get Control of
Your Time and Your Life* (Peter H. Wyden, Inc.). Instead of
taking on the entire project at once, Lakein advises "poking
holes" in the work by taking whatever time you have to do

one small part of the overall task. That way, it's easier to get started, you learn to consider each half-hour's work an accomplishment, and you may eventually even complete the job.

Dr. Knaus suggests something similar in his "five-minute plan." Instead of committing yourself to completing a task that seems overwhelming, commit yourself only to starting the task and working on it for five minutes. At the end of five minutes, decide if you'll continue working for another five minutes. And so on. (There's nothing sacred about five minutes; you could make it half an hour, or an hour.) This method helps make that frightening first step easier, and as you become involved, the work is likely to gain momentum and seem easier.

Other ways of getting yourself started:

• Procrastinators, says Dr. Yuen, tend to think in "global terms" about work; instead of aiming to put the storm windows in by November 15, they vow to "save money on energy." Make your goals specific and observable, and divide the steps needed to get there into small, do-able parts.

Set specific and observable goals.

• Whenever possible, Dr. Knaus suggests, develop the habit of doing it *now*, as soon as you think of it, rather than simply adding it to your list of things to be done (which takes time and energy).

• Once you have your work momentum going—say, by reorganizing your kitchen cupboards—transfer that energy to another project, like writing a long-neglected letter. You'll probably find it's easier than starting later from zero.

Once your momentum is going, don't stop. Go on to another project.

• Reward yourself by scheduling a pleasant task after you've completed a boring or unpleasant one.

• Use what Dr. Yuen's colleague Neil Fiore calls an "unschedule." First, determine how much time you've already committed to your regular responsibilities; what remains is unscheduled time that can be thought of as the maximum amount of time you can afford to devote to other projects. As a way of rewarding yourself for steps taken along the road to completion of those projects, note each half hour of work on your unschedule only *after* it has been completed.

ATTACKING THE ATTITUDE

Whatever you find works for you, the very act of *doing it now* instead of putting it off will tend to carry over into

Don't expect Instant results.

the rest of your life. "Every time you tolerate a frustrating circumstance, every time you act instead of hesitate, every time you deal with one of the things that's causing you to procrastinate, you're mounting a concerted attack on the attitude . . . and *that's* the problem," says Dr. Knaus.

But in your personal war against putting things off, don't expect instant results, he warns. Procrastination isn't an isolated habit but part of a whole "psychological mosaic" of behavior, and these things don't change quickly. By its very nature, he adds, procrastination is resistant to change because procrastinators tend to put off the very things they know can help them. So "play for small percentage gains," reward yourself for your progress, and think about those long-awaited, long-term goals your small gains are bringing closer.

In the process of altering your behavior, your attitudes will change three times.

Procrastinators who have originally gotten around to working on their problem tend to go through three distinct changes of attitude, Drs. Yuen and Burka have observed. Students in their seminars start out full of optimism, expecting that their procrastination will be put to death quickly, painlessly, and forever. After a few sessions, when they discover lifelong habits don't change quite so easily, they despair of ever changing at all. But by the time the workshop ends, most have gained some insight into the psychological roots of their problem—such as their perfectionist tendencies—and have more realistic expectations about how long it will take to change their habits.

As you demand less perfection, you'll get more done.

"Ironically," says Dr. Yuen, "as the students demand less perfection of themselves, they find they can do more."

Tony and Robbie Fanning, in their delightful little book about personal time management called *Get It All Done and Still Be Human* (Ballantine Books), point out something else that should be remembered. Some "time experts," the Fannings observe, tell people to start the day by making a list of all the things they want to accomplish. "If this approach really works for you and you feel good about your use of time without feeling harried and frazzled, then by all means use it," they write. "But this kind of nonstop scheduling is what drove most of us nuts in the first place." The real aim in time management is to *feel good,* not necessarily to do more.

There's More to Life Than Work

"**T**he workaholics I see are not happy people," says Jay B. Rohrlich, M.D., assistant professor of psychiatry at Cornell University Medical College and author of *Work and Love: The Crucial Balance* (Summit Books). "They are using work to block out emotional disorders or to fulfill neurotic needs.

"There is no typical work addict because each finds something different about work that he or she finds gratifying. Some like the aggressiveness they can display in the work environment. Others crave the security and order their work provides. Some enjoy the competitive aspects of work. There are even some who become addicted to the comforts of being in a subservient role in the workplace."

"Workaholics are people who just don't know when to stop working," says John M. Rhoads, M.D., professor of psychiatry at Duke University Medical Center. "Some people seem to lack an inner monitoring device for regulating the work-rest-recreation balance. Plagued by a compulsive need to work, they deny the existence of fatigue and push themselves beyond reason."

That people in high-pressure, high-powered executive jobs are often workaholics is well known. Not so well known is that anyone—from schoolkids to housewives and elderly people—can be workaholics, too.

"Everyone is susceptible," says Dr. Rhoads, who has conducted two ground-breaking studies on workaholism.

In Dr. Rhoads's first study of workaholics, he presented a typical case: a 39-year-old woman who finally sought

There is no typical workaholic: Each finds gratification in different ways.

Anyone—not just the high-powered executive—can be a workaholic.

psychiatric help when she came down with excruciating headaches, chronic fatigue, crying spells, weight loss, and constipation. When the results of physical and laboratory tests showed that she was not suffering from any disease, Dr. Rhoads questioned her about her work habits.

A FANATICAL HOUSEKEEPER

Perfectionism often goes hand in hand with workaholism.

He discovered that she was known to all her friends as a fantatical housekeeper. Rather than make her daughter iron her own clothes and clean up her own room, the housewife felt compelled to do it herself. "I know she's taking advantage of me," Dr. Rhoads's patient told him, "but I just can't stand to pass the room and see the mess." The woman was also unable to keep a maid—even with her two jobs—because she couldn't tolerate tasks that weren't done perfectly. Her family insisted that the house was clean enough, but that couldn't dissuade the woman from her compulsive cleaning *(Journal of the American Medical Association).*

Workaholics are often striving to meet unrealistic expectations.

That woman may have been too lenient with her daughter. But in other cases unrealistic expectations in young people can turn *them* into little workaholics. "Students . . . frequently suffer similar difficulties as they attempt to 'do their best' without having a realistic definition of just what their 'best' should be," wrote James C. Sams, M.D., associate professor of psychiatry at the University of Virginia, Charlottesville, in response to Dr. Rhoads's study. The misconception of the schoolchild "and especially the college student as one who has limitless energy and abundant rest and recreation may cause the unwary physician to fail to consider the possibility of overwork as a cause for vague symptoms in this age group and may result in a spurious [false] diagnosis of mononucleosis" *(Journal of the American Medical Association).*

When workaholism is habitual, work patterns must be re-evaluated.

When workaholism is habitual and shows the more severe symptoms, its victims need to be reoriented to be made aware of their physical and emotional requirements and attend to them. That involves helping them understand the origins of their work compulsion and counseling with respect to future work patterns.

The "work ethic" is probably the culprit.

"The 'work ethic' is probably the culprit here," says Dr. Rhoads. "It's striking that in my field there are few articles dealing specifically with problems of overwork, but by contrast a large number dealing with the inability or unwillingness to work. Apparently we are all so agreed on the inherent sinfulness of laziness that we overlook even the obsessive causes of overwork."

That attitude is well illustrated in remarks by some of the workaholics in Dr. Rhoads's study. One man, a 55-year-old attorney who never worked less than 65 hours a week and had not taken a vacation for five years, felt guilty if he felt tired. If he left work early or didn't go in early, he also suffered from a guilty conscience. "I feel sinful if I'm not working," he told Dr. Rhoads. When advised to relax and take a holiday, another workaholic said: "Fun is something you have to learn to do by working hard at it."

"Workaholics are commonly attempting to solve life's problems by excessive, distracting work," explains Dr. Rhoads. "Overwork may represent an effort to maintain a clear conscience by saying to the world: 'See, I am blameless. I have done all that I could, even working to the edge of total exhaustion.'"

Overwork may be a way of maintaining a clear conscience.

"I have found it useful to compare their overwork and decreased efficiency to a finely tuned automobile spinning its wheels in the snow: The need is not to burn more fuel, race the engine faster, and dig in deeper, but to let up on the gas so that normal progress can resume," says Dr. Sams.

LETTING UP ON THE GAS

But letting up on the gas is not the same as letting the car idle. A hard worker, who enjoys his job and is dedicated to it, is not the same as a workaholic. "Long hours of work are not what make one ill," says Dr. Rhoads. "If the work is enjoyed and provides a reasonable amount of freedom, there is no good reason for an individual to become ill. But the crucial factor is certain personality features that enable the individual to cope.

A hard worker, who enjoys his job and is dedicated to it, is not a workaholic.

"The most striking personality feature of the healthy, hard workers in contrast to the workaholics is that they know when to stop. They could spot fatigue and respond to it promptly. Most respond by quitting work early or taking time off. They schedule and enjoy vacations, spend time with their families, keep up with their friendships, and exercise regularly. In short, they have other outlets for their drive besides work."

Hard workers know when to stop and take time off.

"LEISURE NEUROTICS"

Workaholics feel trapped by free time.

By contrast, one psychiatrist has described workaholics as "leisure neurotics." "It may sound silly, but some people don't like time away from the work routine," explains Richard Kraus, Ed.D., professor at Temple University's department of recreation and leisure studies. "They can't adjust to having free time and using it properly. On weekends, they virtually break down. In very extreme cases, they may take trips, but after a day or two—even a day or two in Europe—they fly back. Leisure implies a kind of personal freedom and they can't deal with that. They can't leave the security of their job's routine. Work for them is a structured, organized, socially approved activity with a clear outcome."

In a work-obsessed society, even "leisure" time is structured.

The prospect of unfilled, unscheduled time can be scary. "A good instance of how scary the freedom of leisure time can be is that in a work-obsessed society such as ours we tend to organize even our leisure," Dr. Kraus says. "We schedule ourselves for leisure time: We take classes and learn 'leisure skills,' we compete, and we gain status through our play. Obligation is an important factor—we have commitments to the community band, the bowling league, and the Girl Scout troop.

"The original meaning of leisure, on the other hand, implied that it was time for freedom, contemplation, choice, and was not necessarily structured, purposeful, or even constructive. Leisure is more ambiguous than work, with a wider range of choices and outcomes. It's very hard for someone who has the kind of rigid personality one observes in workaholics to accept the freedom."

Free time is time to discover yourself.

Though leisure time may be truly "free time" only when it remains unscheduled, it is not the same as mere resting or idleness. "That is the idea of free time that a work-ethic society develops," says Dr. Kraus. "If you're not working, then either you're idle or resting up to work more. But leisure is something positive. It's time when you can discover yourself, when you can make your biggest commitment to life and get your greatest enjoyment and satisfaction.

PART **IX**

Heightening Self-Awareness

48. Dream It: New Techniques for High Awareness
49. A Journal Workshop: Learning to Capture Feelings on Paper
50. Body/Mind Work: A First-Hand Account of Four "Hands-On" Experiences
51. Biorhythms and You: Finding Your Best Time for High Performance

Dream It:
New Techniques
for High Awareness

Freud called them "the royal road of the unconscious"—a well-marked path for exploring the inner workings of the troubled mind. Patricia Garfield, Ph.D., a dream expert and author of *Creative Dreaming* and *Your Child's Dreams* (both published by Ballantine Books), agrees that these fantastical nocturnal wanderings are a rich source of information on who we are and what we feel. But, she says, a dream is really more than a road map of our mental and emotional state. It's a vehicle for personal growth. And you don't have to be deeply troubled or in analysis to benefit.

More than a road map of our emotional state.

"Dreams help us whether or not we pay attention to them," says Dr. Garfield, citing studies in which people who are systematically deprived of dreaming (who are awakened whenever they slip into a dream state) quickly become disturbed and disoriented. "But I believe that by becoming more aware of our dreams and, further, by getting involved with them on a 'conscious' level, we can add a vitally important dimension to our lives."

Dr. Garfield, who's been recording her dreams for nearly four decades and has studied dreamers all over the world, has discovered how to harness the power of dreams and put it to use. Through a process she calls "creative dreaming," she maintains that we can gain fresh insight into our feelings and personality, increase our self-confidence, cope more effectively with stress, find solutions to troublesome problems, and tap our well of creativity.

Creative dreaming: a process for personal growth.

To find out how, we spoke with Dr. Patricia Garfield in San Francisco, where she lives.

**Dreaming is a body rhythm,
its function still unknown.**

Question: Why do we dream? Does dreaming serve some psychological or physiological function?

Patricia Garfield, Ph.D.: That's a question that continues to be the source of much speculation and research. On a physiological level, I think dreaming is as much a part of our body rhythms as the fluctuations in body temperature we experience over the course of the day. We're not absolutely sure what the function of it is. Some people think that dreaming is necessary for the brain to retain information. There are many other theories. But no one really knows.

In any case, overlaid into the physical dream rhythm— which, incidentally, goes on and off about four or five times in an average night— is the whole psychological experience that is related to what happened to us during the day and all the days past. All of our feelings, expectations, and hopes for the future contribute in some way to the shape of a dream.

**If the room temperature falls,
your dream may take you to
the Antarctic.**

It's even more complex than that. The dream may also incorporate sensations you may be experiencing during the night. Some say it's an attempt by your subconscious to explain what's happening. If, for example, you get a twitch in your big toe while you're in a dream state, you might interpret it as having just stumbled over a rock. Or if the room temperature suddenly falls, you might dream that you're in the Antarctic or making love in a chilly hotel room.

So the dream combines many things: the environment, our physical state, and, of course, our psychological state and emotional feelings—which is why they've become such a popular tool in psychoanalysis.

FOR PERSONAL USE

Question: What led you to suspect that dreams might be an invaluable resource—not just for the professional therapist, but for the rest of us, too?

Dr. Garfield: Ever since I was 14 and my mother introduced me to the theories of Freud and Jung, I kept a dream journal. I'd always been a vivid dreamer so I began writing down my dreams and working with them, making associations and so forth. It didn't take long before I became absorbed in the process. It did something for me.

When I got to college and graduate school I began to realize that I was on to something unique. At that time there wasn't much interest in dreams. You only paid attention to dreams if you were deeply troubled and you had a professional therapist who would analyze them for you.

Then, in 1972, I hit on to something really exciting. At the suggestion of Dr. Joe Kamiya of San Francisco, I spent time in Malaysia studying the dream practices of the Senoi, a primitive tribe of people (at least by our standards) who live so far out in the jungle you can get to them only by riverboat or helicopter. I was only able to talk with a few Senoi at a hospital at the fringe of the jungle.

Psychologically, the Senoi are extremely civilized. They are described by researchers who have lived with and studied them for years as peaceful, cooperative, and happy. They don't suffer from emotional disturbances or stress-related mental disorders. Of course, what sparked my interest was the importance they attach to dreams: They consider dreams the focal point of their life. They plan their day, make decisions, get their creative inspiration, even determine when to move their compound based on their dreams. And what I found especially intriguing was the way they were able to relate to their dreams at a higher level of consciousness. They learn from the time they are very young how to become an active participant rather than a passive observer in their dreams. And everybody is said to practice this, from the smallest child to the oldest tribe member.

Used to be, you only paid attention to dreams if you were in analysis.

On being an active participant instead of a passive observer in dreams.

BECOMING A DREAM PARTICIPANT

Question: Can you give us an example?

Dr. Garfield: Suppose a Senoi child has a nightmare in which, he says, he was frightened half to death because a tiger chased him. His parents would tell him that the next time he sees a tiger in his dreams he should face it and fight back. This is a key principle: *confront and conquer* fear-producing images. Indeed, the next time the child sees a tiger in a dream, he doesn't run. He stands his ground and fights to the finish, or he calls on other dream figures to help him combat the tiger. He makes a conscious effort and is successful in altering his dream behavior. And, as a result, he overcomes his nightmare.

Question: But how is it possible to consciously control something that is an unconscious event?

The conscious mind can control involuntary actions.

Dr. Garfield: It's true, dreaming is considered an involuntary action. It happens without any conscious intervention in the same way our heart beats, our blood flows, our stomach secretes acids to aid digestion. And yet, today we're beginning to realize what the Yogis have known for centuries, that the conscious mind has the power to control many "involuntary" actions. Using biofeedback techniques, people in the lab have learned how to lower their blood pressure, regulate their body temperature, control the amount of acid secreted in their stomachs, or increase the alpha wave frequency in their brains. It's not so different for someone to alter their dreams. Have you ever been aware that you were dreaming while you were in a dream state? Perhaps you were in the middle of a nightmare and you said to yourself, "Don't get excited, it's only a dream." Then you know what it's like to be momentarily "conscious" while you are dreaming. And you have some notion of how it's possible to control the action and outcome of a dream. That moment of awareness can be expanded to an entire dream.

Question: But somehow—maybe because it involves psychological factors—the idea of tampering with a dream sounds, well, unnatural. Are there any risks?

We can shape our dreams to our benefit.

Dr. Garfield: No. There's nothing unnatural about it. The fact is, your thoughts are already "tampering" with your dreams without you knowing it. As I mentioned earlier, anything that passes through your mind—people, sights, sound, experiences, expectations—shapes your dream. What the Senoi system involves—and what I propose in "creative dreaming"—is that we can deliberately shape our dreams in a way that is certain to be beneficial to us.

SCIENTIFIC SUPPORT

Question: Do you have any scientific evidence to support your theory?

"Wet dreams" have rarely been observed in the dream lab.

Dr. Garfield: Hard scientific data? There's not a lot yet. But it is interesting to note that "wet dreams" (a common and natural occurrence in which the male ejaculates semen during a dream) have rarely been observed in a dream lab. This suggests that some type of control is involved. It's as if the subject, though in a dream state, is "conscious" of the fact that he is being observed and actively prevents an otherwise involuntary action from taking place.

We do have evidence that the Senois *confront and conquer* principle may be on the right track in dealing with fear-producing dream images. In a study, a group of children with terrifying nightmares were exposed to three types of therapy. One involved reassuring them that it was only a dream. "Don't worry about it," they were told. "It's not real. It's just a dream." The second group were told to think about something pleasant before falling asleep. "What would you really like to do?" they were asked. "Go to the playground with your favorite friend? Visit your grandmother? Eat a big ice cream cone? Whatever it is, close your eyes and pretend it's happening." The children in the third group were taken to do things that were specifically relevant to the problem they were facing in their dreams. For example, one boy was having nightmares about fire and fire engines. So the therapist took him to visit a fire house, to climb on board a fire engine and to talk to all the firemen there.

This last group, who actively participated in something related to their dreams—who confronted and conquered their fears in real life—on the average, improved much more rapidly than either of the other two groups. These children stopped having nightmares.

Confronting fear-producing images in real life reduced nightmares.

Otherwise, most of the evidence we have is clinical. One well-known case involves a little boy who was having recurrent nightmares about a monster. Psychologist Leonard Handler told the child to close his eyes and picture the monster. After a few minutes, Dr. Handler pounded his fist on the desk and shouted, "Get out of here, you lousy monster. Go away and leave my friend alone!" He repeated this over and over again. Then he encouraged the child to join in and together they pounded the desk, demanding that the monster go away. This action continued for about 15 minutes, after which the child promised to use this technique to chase the "real" monster during their next dream encounter. The following week, the child reported that, indeed, he was successful in scaring off the monster: After just a few minutes of yelling and screaming at it, the monster disappeared—never to return.

After just a few minutes of yelling at the monster, it disappeared—never to return.

BAD DREAM, GOOD EXPERIENCE

Question: Essentially, what you're saying is that a bad dream can become a good experience if we know how to control our behavior in it. But what if we don't affect its outcome? Do bad dreams have a detrimental effect on our psychological well-being?

Dr. Garfield: Not necessarily. Usually the anxiety that's produced in a dream is actually anxiety that already exists in us, although we may not be aware of it. The dream is the body's way of helping us come to terms with it.

Recently, for example, a study of the relationship between dreams and childbirth showed that the more a woman had anxious dreams during pregnancy, the more likely she was to have a shorter and easier delivery. The researchers believe that through acting out their fears in their dreams, these women were better able to cope with the real-life childbirth experience. They were, in effect, "psychologically immunizing" themselves in their dreams. On the other hand, the women who reported having few anxious dreams during pregnancy [and longer, more difficult deliveries] were probably so fearful they were psychologically blocked from even symbolic dream expression.

So, it's possible that bad dreams serve a psychological function. But by becoming an active participant in that dream and by changing the outcome to a more positive one, you increase the effectiveness of that dream several hundred times.

WHAT IS "CREATIVE DREAMING"?

Question: Is this then the basis for "Creative Dreaming"?

Dr. Garfield: The whole concept that eventually became creative dreaming is that it's important to take action, to become an active participant in your dream state. When we allow ourselves to remain passive victims—when we just let the dream happen—we continue to feel victimized and hurt. But, by fighting back against the monster, or robber, or would-be rapist—or even befriending it—we bring on a process of emotional healing.

I believe that by practicing within a dream—by changing the dream—you not only deal with the difficult situation in the dream, you carry over to the waking state an attitude that allows you to cope more effectively. You have more confidence. It teaches you the message, "Hey, you can do something about your life." You don't just have to let

Sidebar notes:

Sometimes, the anxiety "produced" by a bad dream is anxiety that already exists.

By changing the outcome, you increase the dream's effectiveness.

The message: "Hey, you can do something about your life."

things happen to you. You can do something to make life better. And in this way, the dream is a kind of rehearsal.

Question: How difficult is it to learn this technique?

Dr. Garfield: With children it tends to be easier because they don't have to do so much *un*learning. If their parents say, "You don't have to let that tiger or monster chase you in your dream," they believe it almost immediately. To adults, especially here in the Western world, it's contrary to their experience. To have a dream and work with it later is the usual therapeutic technique, but to do something to prepare for a dream, to change the dream during the dream— these are concepts that are strange to them. So, understandably, developing creative dreaming takes time and practice. A lot of it has to do with developing necessary attitudes.

> **Developing creative dreaming takes time and practice.**

I tell my students that creative dreaming is a lot like believing in the possibility of love. If you've never experienced it, you may have a difficult time believing it can exist for you. But, once you've loved someone, there's not a person in the world who could convince you that it doesn't exist. The expectation is very powerful.

I'm not saying that you have to believe 100 percent in the idea of dream control in order to be successful. But if you're at least open to giving it a try—if you can say, "Well, maybe . . . let's go through the steps and see what happens," or "That's an interesting idea . . . I'm going to give it a try,"—and you persevere, you will eventually succeed.

> **If you're willing to give it a try, it can work for you.**

STARTING POINT

Question: How do we begin?

Dr. Garfield: Developing dream consciousness is an advanced exercise in dream work. It's the ultimate goal of creative dreaming. The more aware you become in your dream state while you're in it, the more you can use dreams to your benefit.

But delightful things can happen to you without total dream consciousness yet with a certain amount of dream awareness. You can see a beautiful design that may become an inspiration for a painting or a dress. You may get a brilliant idea for an ad campaign at work. You can read the symbols and find hidden meaning that could lead you down a path of self-discovery—maybe to a career change or new pursuit.

> **Delightful things can happen to you even without dream consciousness.**

By tuning in to these messages, questioning dream images, and using them, you'll soon come to regard dreams as important and meaningful aspects of your life. This is the first step—a prerequisite, if you will—to creative dreaming.

How can we interpret our own dreams?

Question: Deciphering symbols and looking for hidden meaning sounds like a job for a professional therapist. How can we, without formal training, interpret our own dreams?

Unless a therapist knows you as well as you do, he's just guessing.

Dr. Garfield: If you're deeply troubled, it may help to discuss your dreams with a professional. But, generally, my feeling is that dreams are a very personal form of expression and no one is better qualified to interpret them than you. Dreams are an amalgamation of your thoughts, your experiences, your beliefs, your fears. They draw material from every nook and cranny of your personality and your past. Unless a therapist knows you as well as you know yourself, he's making an educated guess. Also, his own experiences, thoughts, and feelings—not to mention his professional training—influence his interpretation. Chances are, if you went to three different therapists you'd come away with three different interpretations of the same dream. That's not to say that all or any of them isn't valid. It's just that dream interpretation, like the dream itself, is very personal. What's important is that *you* can find meaning in it.

DREAM JOURNALS

Question: How, then, should we go about interpreting our own dreams so that we can learn more about ourselves?

Dr. Garfield: You can start by keeping a dream journal. When you have collected a set of your own dreams, you will be in a better position to examine and learn from them than if you only have a few isolated dreams. That way, you can look for recurrent themes and symbols. Sometimes, too, later dreams may add insight to previous ones.

When dream images recur, pay attention.

When similar dream images appear in recurrent dreams, it's a sign to pay attention; your subconscious may be trying to get a message across to you.

Idiosyncratic images—a person with some whimsical or bizarre characteristic, a strange-looking animal—are thought to represent other sides to your personality. Draw these symbols and ask yourself questions about them. If we ignore these images, we may miss an opportunity for personal growth. But if we reflect on them, explore their hidden meanings, perhaps even start up a dialogue with them, we may discover things about ourselves—a side to our personality—that we never knew existed.

Question: How can we use dreams to heighten our creativity?

Dr. Garfield: I believe we are at our most creative during the dream state. If we never stop to recall our dreams, all that creativity is lost. But by simply being in touch with our dreams—remembering, recording, and working with them, using the images that come to us in our artistic endeavors—we can ascend to a higher level of creativity.

We are most creative during dreaming.

The title of my book *Your Child's Dreams* was from a dream. I had originally titled the book *Dream Child,* which I thought was much more poetic. But as we got closer to the deadline, my editor insisted that we change the title to something less ambiguous. Then I remembered that the night after I decided on the title *Dream Child* I had a dream in which a woman said to me, "Well, I would have called it *Your Child's Dreams.*" I went right home and looked up the entry in my dream journal. And there it was, sure enough: *Your Child's Dreams.*

Well, at my next meeting with the editor, I submitted a list of possible titles, including *Your Child's Dreams.* She read down the list and when she came to that one she said, "That's perfect. It's clear. And it's much better than *Children's Dreams* [which is the title she proposed] because anything with 'Your' in it sells really well." I never heard that before, that the word "your" helps sell books. But some level of my mind knew that. Call it intuition if you like. But dreaming helped me tune in to it.

Tune in to your intuition.

Of course, the more you experience in life—the more you read, the more films, museums, and concerts you go to, the more you travel to different places and meet interesting people—the more you have to draw on for your dreams. And, consequently, the more you are able to draw from them for ideas and solutions to problems.

STAGING THE DREAM

Question: Suppose you'd like to dream about a certain subject—to direct your creative ideas or solutions in a given area. Can you explain a creative dreaming technique to use?

If you want to dream about something, immerse yourself in it.

Dr. Garfield: The first thing you need to do is fill your mind with it. Really get into it—think about it, read about it, take part in relevant activities. The more you think about what you want to do in your dreams, the easier the same thoughts will come in your dream.

I also find it helpful to put your intention into a short phrase such as "Tonight I'm flying" if you want to experience that in your dreams, or "Tonight I hear music" if you're looking for musical inspiration. Always put the phrase in the present tense. Repeat this phrase to yourself throughout the day and especially in that period just before you doze off to sleep when the mind is more susceptible to suggestions.

Relaxation improves creative dreaming.

It helps to be really relaxed while you're doing this. If you meditate or practice yoga, do that right before you go to sleep. Otherwise try progressive relaxation or listen to a stress-reduction tape. Then, when you feel relaxed, lie still with your eyes closed and repeat the phrase over and over again in a rhythmic way as if you were repeating a mantra. At the same time, visualize how the scene will appear in your dreams so that you are not only programming your mind with words but with related images.

Question: Suppose in your dream you are confronted with a problem that defies resolution. How can creative dreaming help?

Dr. Garfield: To execute rule number one of creative dreaming—to *confront and conquer* a problem in your dream—you may have to explore your real life for solutions. Think about the dream during your waking hours and formulate your mode of attack. Expose yourself to the positive thing you wish to dream of. Sometimes this involves acting it out in the flesh. Remember the little boy who pounded on the desk for 15 minutes in practice for chasing a monster in his dreams? Let me give you another example. In his autobiography, Italian author Giovanni Guareschi describes his efforts to help his wife resolve a problem in a recurrent dream. In her dream she walks the street all night by herself and wakes up feeling very depressed, isolated, and exhausted. Guareschi suggests that she ride her bike instead. Several days later his wife reports that she got a bicycle in her dreams and was feeling much less exhausted, thank you.

A week later, however, she became depressed again. She told Guareschi that she had gone back to walking in her dreams because her bike had a flat tire. Why don't you just fix it, he suggested. His wife's reply: She didn't know how. Guareschi did an unusual thing at that point. He taught his wife skills in her waking life to use in solving her dream problems. First, he led her by the hand to his garage workshop, where he took his own bicycle from the wall and showed her how to change a tire. After several attempts, she finally managed to change the tire herself. He repeated the process again a few days later, instructing her in how to change the bicycle tire over and over again. He even had her change the tire blindfolded. Several days later, she reported that she had successfully changed her bicycle tire in her dreams.

Develop skills in waking life to solve dream problems.

It is also helpful to try rule number two: *Call on your dream friends* to help. Build friendly figures into your dream and call on them whenever you need help or support.

Find friends in your dreams to help you and lend support.

The goal in all this, of course, is to achieve dream consciousness, to be aware and fully participating in the dream as you are experiencing it.

SPECIAL EVENTS

Question: What are some of the most remarkable results people have reported with creative dreaming?

Dr. Garfield: I've had people who swore that after they played tennis in their dreams, they were better at the game in real life. This makes sense because after all, mental practice is almost as effective as physical practice. People have demonstrated that using visualization techniques. And dreaming is similar to visualization except it's stronger.

Playing tennis in your dreams can improve your game.

One man that I know makes drums and in the process of pulling the skin tight over the top of the drum securing it, he often injures himself. He uses creative dreaming to speed the healing of his hands. He tells me that if he has a lucid dream [a dream in which he knows he's dreaming], he watches his hands heal before his very eyes. The next day he notices that his hands are healing much more rapidly in real life. I don't know how that can be verified. But I think it is worth further investigation.

Question: What advice do you have for people who say they don't dream?

Dr. Garfield: Everyone dreams, unless they are taking certain drugs (most barbiturates, sleeping pills of any sort) or drinking a lot of alcohol—either of which can temporarily suppress the dream state. When people say they don't dream, what they really mean is that they don't *remember* their dreams.

Dream recall is a very delicate type of skill.

As children, we remember our dreams quite well. But for whatever reason—perhaps because our dream disclosures were met with disinterest from our parents—we got into the habit of forgetting. Dreams require a very delicate type of recall. It's a special skill. But it can be relearned and developed. I've trained myself to the point where I can recall almost every dream I have (see Box 35).

BOX 35: TIPS TO SHARPEN YOUR DREAM RECALL

1. Remind yourself before you go to sleep that you will remember your dream.

According to Patricia Garfield, Ph.D., the power of suggestion can be a mighty tool in dream recall, a way of preprogramming the brain. Repeat "Tonight I will remember my dreams" quietly to yourself several times before dozing off.

2. Arrange a time when you can spontaneously awaken.

The best time to start developing the skill of dream recall is in the morning after a natural awakening, says Dr. Garfield. That's because, when you wake up naturally—without any bells, buzzers, or voices to jar you—you are coming directly out of a dream state. And if you can maintain the serenity of the moment, you have a much better chance of catching the dream.

3. Lie still with your eyes closed and let images flow into your mind.

Don't start thinking about what you have to do today or what you forgot to do yesterday. And, whatever you do, don't open your eyes, as visual stimuli will chase away the more delicate images still remaining in your mind. When you get a glimmer of a dream—even if it's just a fragment or a vague feeling without an image—explore it. Review any action. Feel the emotion. Let the scene unfold, gently and without any pressure.

4. If you hit a block, let your mind wander over images of people close to you, your family, your intimate friends.

It may trigger associations to your dream. Notice what you were thinking about when you awoke; it's usually connected to the recent dream.

5. Then roll over.

For some as yet unknown reason, Dr. Garfield explains, additional dream recall often comes when you move gently from one position and settle into another.

BOX 35—*Continued*

One theory is that the dream is best remembered when it is recalled in the position in which it was dreamed.

6. Record your dreams while they are fresh in your memory.

According to research, you've got less than ten minutes to catch a dream. After that time only vague snatches remain—unless, of course, you've had a nightmare. If you've ever awakened in the middle of the night, a dream vivid in your memory, then fallen back to sleep only to awake the next morning with absolutely no memory of that dream, you know the frustration of letting a dream get away. Dr. Garfield's solution: Capture it in writing.

"When I self-awaken from a dream, during the night or in the morning, I pick up the 5"×8" pad on my night table with the pen that lies on top of it

and record the dream," she explains. "I write a complete description of the dream—not just phrases. When a dream is impossible to describe, I state what I can of it and add 'complex' or 'many-layered,' as the case may be. I make these notes with my eyes shut, using my fingers as a guide."

7. Tell a dream to a friend.

"The very act of putting the dream into words and trying to explain or express it seems to stimulate both recall of the dream and insight into aspects of it," says Dr. Garfield. It's tempting, however, to tell a dream as an alternative to recording it in a journal. That's not the point. Share a dream experience with a friend whenever possible, but be sure to record it as well. You'll have a treasure for years to come—a book of knowledge about yourself.

A Journal Workshop: Learning to Capture Feelings on Paper*

New York psychologist Ira Progoff has introduced thousands of people to themselves.

L ast year, thousands of Americans with no literary pretensions whatsoever started producing stories of surpassing interest that will probably never be published, or even read by their best friends. They were writing their own often eye-popping, tear-evoking journals, under the direction of a tieless, tireless New York psychologist named Ira Progoff.

They wrote these journals in 392 workshops sponsored by colleges and universities across the land, by branches of the armed forces, by army hospitals and women's prisons, by groups of artists, priests, poets, business people, and engineers (and combinations of all of the above); they didn't enroll in them (for an average tuition of $70 each) because they felt they needed therapy, but because they wanted to put their lives in perspective and find in them some deeper meaning.

There's an underground stream of images and recollections within each of us.

For those who want to plumb the sources of meaning, Progoff likes to use a metaphor that many find helpful. He says that there's an underground stream of images and recollections within each of us. The stream is nothing more or less than our interior life. When we enter it, we ride it to a place where *it* wants to go. He says this is not a discursive method, not analytic. "There's no neat wrap-up;

you don't end up with 'insight.' It's *an event,* and when it's happened, your life is different."

All of this may sound rather mystical. But then the mysticism gets terribly concrete, because everyone at a Journal workshop ends up with a workbook weighing several pounds, full of stories and recollection and often surprising new insights about the most fascinating mystery of all: themselves and their relation to the world around them. To produce a Journal, however, Progoff is quick to point out, "You don't need to be a mystic. All you need is a life. Almost anyone can do it."

But how? I didn't quite understand until I had gone to a Journal workshop myself. I spent a weekend with a disparate group of artists, teachers, housewives, and some college students at the Terros Center in Warwick, New York. Father Lewis Cox, a tall, placid New York Jesuit who is one of 95 consultants trained by Progoff and authorized to give the workshops, got us started at 8:00 P.M. on a Friday by passing out loose-leaf notebooks filled with blank, lined paper and a series of 21 colored dividers. He invited us to enter the interior worlds of our own memories and imaginations, opening our "exploration" by helping create some preliminary moments of meditative silence. Then he invited us to answer the question for ourselves, "Where are you now in your life?"

Where are you now in your life?

Father Cox said the answer might not, probably would not, come in the form of a judgment or as an answer in a college quiz. We might have an image—see a picture of ourselves on a bumpy plane ride or hear the strains of a favorite symphony. Whatever it was, the point was not to merely *think* about it. We were to write it down in a section of the Journal called the "Period Log" and were to refrain from making any judgments about whether the images we recorded were good or bad. It was all right, Father Cox said, soothingly and assuringly. We would return to it later.

After perhaps half an hour of work on the Period Log, Father Cox asked us to turn to some red sections in the middle of our books, first to the "Life History Log," subtitled "Recapitulations and Rememberings." He invited us to submerge ourselves in our own underground stream of recollection, but not to begin writing anything like an autobiography—just quick, significant *scenes* in our lives. Again, no judgment. Just get into that underground stream.

Don't write an autobiography—just quick, significant scenes.

CHAPTER HEADINGS OF YOUR LIFE

Soon we were into the next section of the Journal workbook, called "Steppingstones." Here, Father Cox asked us to set down what could be chapter headings in an autobiography—not only an objective sequence of events, epitomized in a word or two or an image, but also a subjective perception of meaning and value. My Steppingstones turned out to be people. I wrote down a few dozen names— people I'd loved, people I had a hard time loving. Next, I wrote down the titles of the four books I'd published, the significant jobs I'd had.

And then it was time to retire until the next morning. So far, there had been hardly any conversation, hardly any noise. At one point, I had looked around the room and seen a few dozen heads bobbing over a few dozen notebooks, a few dozen ball-point pens gliding away. A lot of intensity and then, when the evening ended, a collective exhaling of breath and blinking of eyes. I thought I noticed tears streaming down the cheeks of an elderly man with a gray beard.

For some of the next day we amplified our Steppingstones section, going deeper into any period that seemed to draw our special interest. We made the same meditative trip in another section of the workbook called "Intersections," subtitled "Roads Taken and Not Taken." I thought of my own spiritual intersections: I'd studied to be a priest for ten years, then took another path. I thought of my emotional intersections: marriages, other loves. I thought of my career intersections: I'd worked for *Time,* then went free-lance and lived in a paradise in the High Sierra, then opted for a richer life of the mind by taking a job in New York with the *Times.*

And then Father Cox asked us to move to another section of the workbook, the "Twilight Imagery Log." "We turn our attention inward, and we wait in stillness," he said, "and let ourselves observe the various forms of imagery that present themselves. We let them come of themselves. As they take shape, we perceive them. We observe them as though they were dreams. We describe them in the same neutral noninterpretive, nonjudgmental way that we record our dreams."

Unbidden, the image of a roller coaster came to mind, and I recorded the roller coaster of my life. I didn't dwell

A lot of intensity and then, a collective exhaling of breath.

Looking for symbolism in daydreams.

much on it there and then, but later I realized that that was what Progoff meant when he wrote that, frequently enough, images deep inside us "enable our life to disclose to us what its goals and its meanings are." For me, the image of the roller coaster was fun—and depressing: How can I ever manage to get *off* the roller coaster without breaking up in little pieces?

CREATING DIALOGUES

For many of us, the most creative time was spent in the "Dialogue Dimension," part of an entire system of "Journal Feedback" where, after laying out our life, we could not only step back and look at it but also explore its meanings. We did this, in part, by engaging in imaginary conversations with some of the significant people we'd already listed in the Steppingstones section.

Engaging in imaginary conversations with significant people.

To help make sure that the conversation wasn't one-sided and that we didn't give ourselves all the good lines, Father Cox suggested that we go through a short Steppingstones exercise for "the other." (I recalled an old Indian proverb I'd heard in my Arizona boyhood: "Judge no man until you've walked a mile in his moccasins." Father Cox's suggestion made sense.)

I did the Steppingstones for my daughter Polly, in England, who has been visiting me only in the summers since she was a tot, except for last summer, when she didn't come to the United States at all. I got into her moccasins, and this dialogue ensued:

Polly: You going to ignore me again?

Me: Ignore you?

Polly: You did last time.

Me: I was in a different place last time. That was two years ago. I was broke, alone, insecure.

Polly: And now?

Me: I've got some money in my pocket, I've got friends, I'm secure. And I'm so happy you're coming this summer.

Polly: You'll spend some time with me?

Me: I'll have to—or lose you.

Polly: No. Not for that reason. Because you want to, because I am someone, too. I don't want you to love me because you have to. I want you to love me because you want to. I am a person, too, flesh of your flesh, but my own person, too. Look at me, listen to me, understand what I want.

Me: That's very hard. I get a lump in my throat.

Polly: You feel . . . ?

Me: I don't know. Guilty, maybe. Afraid that I won't come through for you?

Polly: I don't want anything from you. Just your undivided attention for a time.

Me: Polly, you have to let me be me, too. I enjoy the roller coaster. If you want to be with me, you've got to get on the roller coaster, too.

Polly: Okay. But don't forget I'm here, next to you.

"I knew this all the time, but I wasn't paying attention."

At the end of this exercise, Father Cox suggested we might start to reread what we had written, then write down how we felt. I wrote: "Sense of shame: I knew this all the time, but I wasn't paying attention. Enlightening. Shocking."

There were other dialogues: with society, with events, with the body, with works. The most productive dialogue was with the book I'd been doing on and off, mostly off, for two years.

Book: Help!

Me: Hello.

Book: Don't you recognize me?

Me: Oh, yes, you're my memoir.

Book: You're not paying me enough attention.

Me: Strange, that's what the women in my life keep telling me.

Book: You can't do everything.

Me: I try.

Book: At what cost?

Me: Everything suffers, I suffer.

Book: So?

Me: So, I guess I'd better set some priorities.

Book: That sounds very old and very . . . Jesuitical. What do you really want?

Me: I want it all.

Book: You've got to conserve your energies for the most important things first.

Me: The old "necessary, useful, agreeable" rule, huh?

Book: That's too puritanical. Have you ever thought about going with your feelings?

Me: Sometimes it gets me in trouble.

Book: Some people call that living.

Me: Say, whose side are you on, anyway? I thought you were complaining that I wasn't giving you enough attention.

Book: I was, but if you're harried when you come to me, what good are you? You're only going to be writing down stuff you end up throwing away.

Me: So how do I arrange to come to you unharried?

Book: Don't be taking on so many things, so many people.

Me: Some call it living.

Book: Touché! But can't you strike a happy balance? Get a rhythm going?

Me: I got rhythm, I got music.

Book: Buffoon. You're avoiding something by being a buffoon. What is it?

Me: I don't know.

Book: You afraid of something?

Me: Maybe. Some of this stuff is pretty intimate.

Are you avoiding something? Afraid?

Book: That's what makes a good memoir. I *love* that.

Me: But I just don't want to look like a fool.

Book: You want to write an honest memoir?

Me: Yes.

Book: Then maybe sometimes you have to risk looking like a fool—*if* you want to be honest.

Me: An honest fool, huh? Some people may laugh at me.

Book: Who?

Me: Stupid people.

Book: Good people?

Me: No. They'll applaud me for taking chances.

Book: Then why don't you?

Me: Loosen up, huh?

Book: You don't want me to sound staid and stuffy and boring, do you?

Me: Nope.

Book: Then let go.

Me: Okay.

For the record, although I did not make any "resolutions" at the Journal workshop, that dialogue helped point a way for me: I started working on my memoir, something I had been postponing for ten years, and finished it just before Christmas. The book took about nine months to "emerge." I must have a dialogue with it soon.

That dialogue helped point a way for me.

At the Journal weekend, there was hardly any interplay among the members of the workshop. We'd chat a bit at coffee breaks or at lunch, and that was it. There was none of the social pressures I'd experienced in any number of encounter groups, and therefore, no playacting was necessary. Furthermore, since I knew no one was going to see or hear what I was writing, I felt a sense of perfect freedom. Several times Father Cox drew a session to a close by issuing an open invitation to the group: Would anyone care to read what he or she had just written? Some accepted his invitation, some didn't. It didn't seem to matter. Father Cox said that reading aloud was for the reader's benefit, not the group's. Even so, I couldn't help feeling good about the feelings, often of joy, that were evident in the notebooks of others.

One woman kept a diary for 50 years, never listing a feeling or awareness—just events.

One woman reported that she had kept a diary for 50 years and had "never listed a feeling or an awareness—just events as they happened." Now, under guidance, she said she had been able to write down her own feelings and felt exhilarated in the process. Moreover, she found new direction in her life: Recently widowed, she simply didn't know what she'd do next. But in the Journal chapter called Intersections, she remembered a road she had very much wanted to take at one time—but had taken another that led to marriage and a family. Now, she realized, there was nothing stopping her from going back and taking the other road.

After my own Journal workshop, I was all too aware that I'd only just begun to scratch the surface of the Journal process. There were a good many sections of the Journal that Father Cox hadn't even told us about. I found that I was in the first of three stages: a Life Context Workshop. I could go on to a Depth Feedback Workshop and then, finally, to a Process Meditation Workshop; in these, I would get a chance to work with, among other things, my own dreams.

I thought I might attend further workshops. However, I also realized that I could work on alone and at my own pace, using Progoff's two major guides in the Journal method: *At a Journal Workshop* [Dialogue House], a basic introduction that would help me take my life in my own hands and draw it together, and *The Practice of Process Meditation* [Dialogue House], which would help me open up a whole new spiritual dimension.

Journals help people toward intimacy—with themselves and others.

Anaïs Nin, a diarist who logged an estimated 150,000 pages before her death in 1977, reviewed *At a Journal Workshop* in 1975 and noted that Progoff had found a way to help people toward intimacy: intimacy with themselves, intimacy with others. She then remarked:

"The lack of intimacy with one's self, and consequently with others, is what created the loneliest and most alienated people in the world. Progoff ultimately proves that the process of growth in a human being, the process out of which a person emerges, is essentially an inward process."

50

Body/Mind Work:
A First-Hand Account of Four
"Hands-On" Experiences*

**From Acu-Yoga to
Zen Shiatsu.**

In California, everybody falls into one of two categories: getting bodywork or giving it (or sometimes both). The Bay Area is awash in a veritable alphabet soup of body therapies—from Acu-Yoga to Zen Shiatsu. Now that once-esoteric new-age buzzwords like "holistic" and "wellness" have wended their way into mainstream phraseology, the bodyworkers know no bounds. Rolfers regularly get referrals from physicians (and vice versa); nurses earn extra credit studying Feldenkrais.

As our knowledge of the body has grown, so has our body of knowledge. And although we may be the wiser and healthier for all this hands-on activity, the entire bodywork field has become so overrun with alternatives, derivatives, and derivatives of derivatives that even the relatively well-informed health-care consumer needs a scorecard to tell one from the next.

**The point of these
therapies is to restore
smooth functioning to
the "bodymind."**

For starters, the very term bodywork is problematic—and entirely inappropriate, say some, since it sounds too much like the human equivalent of straightening out bent fenders. Others might argue that the right rubric would be something like "bodymindwork," since the whole point of the exercise is to restore that essential synthesis to smooth functioning. By current definition, bodywork is a huge umbrella sheltering every conceivable therapy that seeks to put the participant back in touch with his or her body.

"*Anything* that takes you out of your normal patterns of muscular or sensory activity can be considered valid bodywork," says Ken Dychtwald, author of the influential 1977 bestseller *Bodymind* [Pantheon Books]. As he told *Medical Self-Care* magazine, "For some people, it may mean sports or massage; for others, sitting quietly in a peaceful place. The fact that there's no 'right way' is what makes this field so exciting. Instead of some set of rules to follow, there's real freedom to explore."

Dychtwald became a bodywork aficionado as an Esalen rookie in 1970 when a workshop leader, after studying his naked body, rattled off his entire life story like a laser-vision psychic. The uncanny character analyst was Dr. John Pierrakos, a student of [renowned psychotherapist] Wilhelm Reich and a founder—with fellow disciple Dr. Alexander Lowen—of the bodywork school known as bioenergetics. In fact, the much-misunderstood Reich—himself a protégé of Freud—was the progenitor of *all* the emotion-focused styles of bodywork currently in vogue, from Rolfing to Radix. It was he who first thought to look above and beyond the psychoanalytic couch to see what patient's bodies had to say.

What Reich discovered was that psychoemotional conflicts and blocks tend to house themselves in the muscular tissue, forming what he logically called "body armor." When he began working to break down that armor with breathing exercises and physical manipulation—quite a radical move at a time when psychotherapy was strictly "talking heads"—he found it much easier to treat the attendant neuroses. Essentially, he rediscovered what Oriental medicine had known for millennia: that mind and body are one and can be approached as a continuum—with mental well-being redounding to the physical, or the other way around.

Psychoemotional conflicts tend to house themselves in the muscular tissue.

When the current bodywork craze first got rolling, I must admit, I was a bit suspicious. It's all very well for people with real *problems,* I thought—chronic pain sufferers who truly need it—but a bit self-indulgent for anyone not so hard-pressed. It took a winter of persistent heartache, professional burnout, and seemingly impenetrable writer's block for me even to consider giving it a try. It would be hard to imagine anyone more "stuck" than I was at this juncture. My longest walk—metaphorically and otherwise—was from

It's not just for people with "problems."

bed to typewriter. Writing and obsessing, and obsessing *about* writing—all of which, I discovered, feed off the same mental loop—had left me very much up in my head and out-of-body (not in the celestial sense). So I took the plunge: I decided to put my body on the line, for the purposes of both scientific research and personal gratification. In one short winter, I sampled no less than a dozen brands of bodywork—*not* the best way to go about it, as any practitioner will tell you, but a great way to get a feel for the terrain. [Here, then, four in-depth reviews:]

ROLFING: UNCOVERING PHYSICAL AND EMOTIONAL PAIN

To live in California and not get Rolfed is like visiting Coney Island and passing up the Cyclone coaster. Unfortunately, both experiences tend to elicit equal parts terror and delight.

That Rolfing can be painful is common knowledge.

That Rolfing can be painful is common knowledge. The way Ken Dychtwald's Rolfers explained it to him, "they are not creating pain when they work but rather uncovering the pain that chronically lives within the bodymind." That reassurance did not prevent him from perceiving one therapist's hands, deep within his adbomen, as a pair of "searing blowtorches."

The session was undoubtedly salubrious (he came away, after a paroxysm of sobs, feeling "relieved of a hundred pounds of dead emotional weight"). Still it was with considerable dread that I approached the Sacramento Street Center office of Rolfer Neil Powers.

Rolfing is based on the premise that your body structure determines your behavior.

A dark, angular, blue-jeaned man, he put me at ease immediately by addressing the pain issue head-on (if tongue-in-cheek): "You're only allowed three screams in ten sessions." His humor dissipated my anticipatory tension; it's hard to keep your muscles tightly clenched as you laugh. Next on the agenda was an assessment of the way I stood and walked, how my weight was distributed, what position I slept in, whether I participated in any sports. (Evidently these "leanings" are significant; Rolfing is based on the premise that structure determines behavior, rather than the reverse.) Next came a photo session—front, back, and side views for an eventual "before and after" comparison—and a brief explication of the method.

Ida Rolf, Ph.D. (who died in 1979), developed the technique she called Structural Integration during the course of fifty years working as a biochemist at, among other institutions, the Rockefeller Institute. The origins of Rolfing, as it became known, are a bit vague. Dr. Rolf herself has said that she suffered from curvature of the spine and was prediabetic as a youngster. After treatment by an osteopath, she was inspired to develop her own school of manipulative therapy—a method "for aligning the random body into an orderly, balanced energy system that can operate in the field of gravity," as she described it in the 1978 anthology *Wholistic Dimensions in Healing* [Doubleday & Co.].

Rolfing's familiar trademark depicts the idea pretty well: One stack of brick-like body segments looks as if a two-year-old plopped them on top of one another; the other has a nice, neat vertical axis transecting ears, shoulders, hips, knees, ankles. Dr. Rolf's central thesis was that the body is a "plastic medium": Although years of conforming to a "badly organized" structure may leave a body with fasciae (connective tissues) hardened into all the wrong patterns, it is possible to manipulate these tissues back into their proper places. "Gravity is the therapist," wrote Dr. Rolf. "The Rolfer (through manipulation, verbal direction, and understanding) merely helps Rolfees use their bodies in a way that allows gravity to contribute energy." Moreover, she added, "the body, unless too severely traumatized, reponds quickly and 'gladly' to this demand for normalization."

It's possible to manipulate the body back into alignment.

All very well, but those little quotation marks made me nervous. How would *my* body respond in the moment of truth?

Not too badly, as it turned out. Powers reassured me some more as he went matter-of-factly to work. "Some people are Rototillers," he said. "I'm a sculptor." I had to believe him: As he pressed and pushed his powerful fingers against my ribs, I felt sections of my chest shifting like lumps of clay. His advice also helped: "Don't try to avoid the pain; you'll only get in the way of the process. If it hurts, remember it will pass." Between especially deep strokes, he would walk around the room pruning his plants to give the sting time to subside. By the end of the session (and for a couple of days afterward) I did feel a slight soreness under my armpits, but I also distinctively felt my weight redistributing itself into a better alignment—longer neck,

"Some people are Rototillers," he said. "I'm a sculptor."

more expansive chest. I'd swear I could even breathe easier. The normal course of treatment is ten one-hour sessions: the first seven spent focusing on specific areas (in a predetermined sequence), the last three on the reintegration of the entire body along its new lines. Rolfees have been known to return for a "refresher course" from time to time.

A UCLA study showed an improvement in muscle function.

How effective is the method? A study commissioned by the Rolf Institute and carried out by two doctors at UCLA showed a definite improvement in muscular functioning. However, some critics fault the method for being too "passive" and—ironically—too rigid to accommodate individual differences.

Rolfers fail to address the negative mind-set that formed the body in the first place.

Dychtwald considers Rolfing "partly deficient" in that it's a purely physical process and fails to address "the emotional and attitudinal sets that formed the body in the first place," he writes in *Bodymind*. Without such attention, he feels, no lasting change is possible. "What would you do if you were given a brand-new body right now? Chances are, you would hold yourself within you new body exactly as you had within the old." In his extensive experience (he witnessed over a hundred Rolfings), he found that people "whose bodies are tight, unused, unappreciated, and poorly cared for seem to reap the greatest and quickest rewards"; those already fit and healthy tend to experience little change.

Access: There are some four hundred certified Rolfers in the world who have completed up to two years of training under the Rolf Institute and have agreed to five years of continuing education. Only graduates in good standing may identify themselves as Rolfers. A list of certified Rolfers in available from The Rolf Institute, P.O. Box 1868, Boulder, CO 80306. A one-hour session costs approximately $70 (depending on location and the practitioner's experience).

FELDENKRAIS: MOVEMENT EDUCATION

The least painful, least stressful mode of bodywork.

Feldenkrais has a reputation for being the *least* painful, least stressful mode of bodywork. Actually, those schooled in Feldenkrais are quick to point out that it's not "bodywork" at all. "We don't like the term," Oakland practitioner Elizabeth Beringer told me somewhat touchily over the phone. "We do *movement education.*"

"I am not a therapist, and my touching a person with my hands has no therapeutic or healing value—though people improve with it," insisted Moshe Feldenkrais in his book *The Elusive Obvious* (Meta Publications), published 2½ years before his death in July 1983. "I think what happens to them is *learning:* I bring about a state in which they learn to do something without my teaching them."

Feldenkrais himself was remarkably elusive—and illusive—when it came to explaining his work, especially for a man trained as a hard-nosed scientist. "The first principle of my work is that there isn't any principle," he was fond of saying—yet he wrote four rather impenetrable books to describe it. A Russian-born Israeli who worked as an engineer and physicist (he did atomic research under Joliot-Curie), Feldenkrais was also a judo black belt fond of soccer. When a sports injury damaged his knee, he turned his mind to the mechanics of the body. This investigation turned into a lifelong study and ultimately into a quest to reprogram the brain to allow the entire bodymind to work more efficiently—"movement integrity" is this movement's Holy Grail.

In essence, Feldenkrais's goal was to unlock human potential by helping people to explore all the possibilities that get shunted aside as we learn how to do things "right." As we grow up, Feldenkrais believed, the way we move is conditioned and altered by every bodily encounter, good or bad. A barefoot boy who scrapes his toe running may run differently from that day forward. And the "successes" are even worse: Once we've mastered a movement, Feldenkrais observed, the function "clicks in" the nervous system and development stops right there.

Exploring the possibilities that get shunted aside as we learn how to do things "right."

The reeducation he recommended consists of two components. One is Functional Integration, "tablework" sessions in which the practitioner gently bends, pushes, rolls, turns, and twists the various parts of your body so that you begin to become aware of the minutest dynamics of how you move—how you rotate, where the pain is, where your limits lie. (These manipulations, Feldenkrais specified, are to be done "as slowly and as pleasantly as possible, with no strain or pain whatsoever.") The other part of the method, Awareness Through Movement (ATM), comprises a series of simple exercises that can be self-directed (with written or taped instruction) or done with a practitioner, either alone or in a group.

In the final years of his life, Feldenkrais used to oversee three hundred people at a time—whole gymnasiums full—in

Not just pushing muscles around but changing things in the brain itself.

Amherst, Massachusetts during the course of his annual U.S. visit. These trainings drew pupils (never "patients") of every stripe, from children with cerebral palsy to celebrities such as Julius Erving ("Dr. J" of basketball fame). Other admirers included anthropologist Margaret Mead, violinist Yehudi Menuhin, director Peter Brook, and neurophysiologist Karl Pribram of Stanford University, who raved: "He's not just pushing muscles around, he's changing things in the brain itself."

Pretty heady stuff, for something that *looks* like mere bodywork. But "it's not pretentious," protested Beringer at the outset of our lesson. "I deal only with what I can feel or touch or see." At that moment she felt, touched, and saw the unmistakable stiffness in my scrunched neck and shoulders. Yet she went straight to work on my feet. (Feldenkrais practitioners, I later found out, often prefer to work on a problem area indirectly, so as not to exacerbate the very patterns causing the pain.) "I push through your feet down here," she said from the bottom of the table, "to see how movement travels through your skeleton up to your head." I looked puzzled, so she explained: "I'm looking for how you, Perry, uniquely organize yourself as you move."

These are not positions you would find yourself in during an ordinary day—or lifetime.

Since I usually organize myself like a gargoyle hunched over a hapless manuscript, I had little trouble with the ATM segment that came next. The ATM movements are designed to reproduce and reinforce the manipulative, hands-on work. These are not positions you would necessarily find yourself in during the course of an ordinary day—or lifetime, as I was to learn. How often, for instance, do you notice yourself sitting on the floor, leaning on your right arm, left arm bent at the elbow and suspended straight in front of your eyes? I could not disguise my fatigue and discomfort as we practiced these moves for what seemed like an eon.

"Some people learn faster than others," Beringer said sympathetically. Feldenkrais advised a course of one lesson per year of age, but Beringer prefers to adjust that curriculum to students' wants and needs. I figured that I'd need my weight in lessons, rather than my age, to achieve the Feldenkraisian ideal of one who "feels that his body is hanging light from his head, his feet do not stomp the ground, his body glides when moving." And yet I did find after even one lesson, that I could definitely turn further in both directions, with less pain and effort. Better still, this progress held the exponential power of suggestion: I could really see and feel that my body—the same body I had thought was dead set on disobeying me—was a built-in learning device for corrective change.

Not surprisingly, Feldenkrais work has few detractors (no pain, no blame?). It appeals especially to people who move for a living—athletes, actors, musicians—as well as to just plain busy people who value fitness and versatility. It's hard to resist a teacher who insists that "learning must be fun and it must be easy." Feldenkrais's theories may be a bit hard to follow but is it so farfetched to posit that movement—inextricably involved as it is in every aspect of our daily lives—can have a profound effect on the deepest levels of psyche and soma?

It appeals to people who move for a living.

Feldenkrais wouldn't take the obvious at face value: He approached every motion, he once said, like someone trying to explain swallowing to a Martian. "We do much without knowing consciously how," he observed. "'Correct' remains forever correct; 'better' can be bettered."

Access: Practitioners authorized by the Feldenkrais guild (there are some 300 worldwide) have completed a four-year course of training. For a referral, contact the Feldenkrais Guild at Box 11145, San Francisco, CA 94101. Fees for Functional Integration generally run about $30 to $60 per hour; Awareness Through Movement classes cost $5 to $8.

HEAD FIRST WITH ALEXANDER

"We don't consider ourselves bodyworkers," began Eleanor Rosenthal of San Francisco, western regional president of the American Center for the Alexander Technique. Here we go again, I thought, as she led me to a table and proceeded to demonstrate a variety of hands-on techniques remarkably similar to the other "bodyworks" I'd already been through.

To be sure, there were differences. The Alexander Technique is ever-so-subtle, more like somatic suggestion than actual manipulation. And the tablework, with its mantralike guided imagery ("neck, back and free . . . head, forward and up . . . let the torso lengthen and widen"), is just preparation for the more important, individualized lessons in posture and balanced body mechanics that take place as the subject is studied in the act of sitting or

The Alexander technique: more suggestion than actual manipulation.

walking. The instruction continually comes back to the head and neck area, locus of what Alexandrians call the "primary control." When the relationship between head and spine is aligned, goes the theory, the spine lengthens, thereby relieving abnormal curves and pressures; consequently, the musculature supporting the skeletal frame falls into line as well.

The technique was developed by F. Matthias Alexander (1869-1955), an Australian actor whose recurrent attacks of laryngitis threatened curtains for his career. Suspecting that his vocal difficulties were caused by something he was doing while performing, Alexander shut himself up with a three-way mirror to see what that might be. After several months of scrutiny, he ascertained that every time he was about to speak, he would take a deep gulp of air, tense his neck and throat muscles, and pull his head back and down so that it pressed on his larynx. He also noted that the problem was not localized: His entire organism suffered from similar patterns of misuse. What "comes naturally," he realized, is often totally *unnatural,* the result of lifelong bad habits.

"A general heightening of consciousness on all levels."

Alexander spent ten years reconditioning himself, then returned to the stage, where he attracted widespread acclaim for his extraordinary powers of projection. Other actors and public speakers came to him seeking instruction in how to put their instruments to better use; among his satisfied students were George Bernard Shaw and [English novelist] Aldous Huxley, who credited the method with engendering "a general heightening of consciousness on all levels."

Just what the "primary control" is, let alone how it works, is a matter of some mystery. "Scientific explanations in neuromuscular terms haven't satisfied me," admitted Rosenthal, a former attorney. "What I do know is that if one takes Alexander seriously and works on the assumption that there *is* a primary control which can be activated by improving the relationship between the head, neck, and torso, one will get results which are reassuringly similar to those Alexander got. I can explain it better with my hands." And so she did.

She stood behind my head, slowly rolling it, with a touch that was pure velvet.

As I lay on a table, she stood behind my head, slowly rolling it from side to side, with a touch that was pure velvet. She moved to my shoulders and arms, stroking so softly it seemed she was just straightening the wrinkle out of my shirt. There was a definite effect, though; the top of my back and neck seemed flatter on the table, and a general sense of relaxation moved from the top to the bottom of my spine. Standing at my feet, Rosenthal placed her hands on my legs and, pulling ever so gently, suggested that I imagine my legs first hanging over the table, then wandering down the hall, out the front door, up the street, and all the way out to the Pacific. "Can I stop at Hawaii?" I inquired.

Then she had me stand and, with her hands, balanced my head so that it felt tilted forward. She smoothed my back, hinting manually at a change in alignment. At that point I felt certain I resembled some anthropoid just learning to walk without the aid of front limbs. But she turned me toward the mirror and, lo and behold, it reflected a perfectly postured hominid. Next, she directed me toward the long hall of her apartment and, after readjusting the balance of my head and neck, propelled me forward with a gentle push, like a mother giving her teetering toddler his walking papers. I walked stiffly, self-consciously, certain that a hanger inserted in my shirt would have felt more comfortable. And yet despite the awkwardness of readjusting to this bizarre new stance, I also felt lighter, taller, centered, almost as though I were gliding along a conveyor belt. This sensation, in turn, affected my mental attitude: I felt right on course; I knew where I was going and that I was going to get there.

> **I felt lighter, taller, almost as though I were gliding on a conveyor belt.**

Several repetitions later, I felt I really had the hang of it, though I wondered how I would ever walk again without her aid. As weeks went by, however, I discovered a little bell in my mind, like a backstage cue, reminding me time and again to resume that right "wrong" position.

Access: Certified instructors have a minimum of 2½ years' training; there are approximately 200 fully qualified instructors in the U.S., listed with the American Center for the Alexander Technique (ACAT) at 142 West End Avenue 1P, New York, NY 10023. The course of treatment is open-ended; it can run anywhere from weeks to years. Private lessons vary in length from half an hour to an hour, and range in fee from $25 to $50 on the average.

TRAGER WORK: UNLOCKING THE UNCONSCIOUS MIND

The Trager Work technique has been compared, altogether aptly, to fluffing up a pillow. Trager Psycho physical

Integration (TPI) and Mentastics, as it's officially called, was founded by Milton Trager, M.D., but to hear him describe it, it found him—"pure accident," he says. In the late twenties, as an 18-year-old pro fighter, he stunned his manager with a knockout session of bodywork. "You've got great hands, kid," raved the trainer. Trager went on to cure his father of sciatica and, during the next 50 years, continued to concentrate on people with neuromuscular disorders. Along the way he picked up a medical degree (in his 40s) and set up a private practice in Waikiki.

Though he'd been initiated into Transcendental Meditation in 1958, for the next two decades Trager worked at somewhat of a distance from what would come to be called the human potential movement. Eventually, news of his therapy traveled to California, and he was invited over to demonstrate the technique at a remote coastal retreat. That was Esalen, circa 1975.

The workshop participants were extraordinarily receptive, and none more so than Betty Fuller, who at that time was a Feldenkrais practitioner. She has since become Trager's number one disciple, and director of the international Trager Institute.

Luckily for me, she was in town long enough to give me the master-class version of the Trager technique.

"First we hook up," she said, standing at my head as I lay faceup on the table. "Hooking up" is Trager lingo for establishing a climate of enhanced sensitivity and noncoercion; it's short for hooking up the "universal life force." As Dr. Trager explains it, "It's a feeling of oneness, of connectedness, of quiet—the same kind of feeling I experience in meditation or by the ocean."

Step one is to elicit a feeling of oneness, connectedness, and quiet.

With all systems go on the transpersonal plane, Fuller set to work. For the next hour and a half, she proceeded to rock and roll me, stretch and shake me, jiggle and wiggle me from head to foot. Sometimes she "talked" to my body, as she put it; sometimes she breathed with me, sighed with me, laughed with me, all the while continuing a regular, rhythmic, rocking motion. "Dr. Trager says that for every physical nonyielding condition there is a psychic counterpart," she explained when we finally wound down to a stop. "So my every move, every touch, every thought is directed to unlocking your unconscious mind."

By now I was feeling thoroughly unlocked—relaxed and invigorated, and rather like a human vibrator. It was time to try Mentastics, a deceptively simple five-minute exercise sequence similar to the shake-out dear to dancers and athletes. The idea here, as in other bodywork lessons, is "to show the mind that the body can move in another way, and to allow the nervous system to learn another, preferable behavior pattern," Fuller explained. Echoing the wisdom of many a manipulator, she said, "Hurts and pains in the body are registered not in muscles but in the mind, which rules the nervous system. We assume protective, restricting modes, and these compensations become part of who we are."

The idea is to allow the nervous system to learn a preferable behavior pattern.

Trager practitioners usually recommend a series of sessions since the benefits are considered to be cumulative. The theory behind TPI seems as sound as any other, and yet the approach is especially appealing because it feels more intuitive than intellectual—like Dr. Trager himself. I would gladly go another few rounds the next time my all-too-conscious mind is too much with me. Meanwhile, my body seems to be enjoying some kind of permanent private joke—an unshakable psychic giggle.

Access: Trager practitioners train for between 12 and 22 months. The Trager Institute is located at 10 Old Mill Street, Mill Valley, CA 94941. Fees average $35 to $40 per visit.

COMING SOON, TO A CLINIC NEAR YOU . . .

To list all the bodywork methods worth checking out would require a tome the size of a telephone book—and in fact there are several of these which can give you good background and leads. *The Alternative Health Guide* by Brian Inglis and Ruth West (Knopf), Shane Watson's *Massage and Bodywork Resource Guide* (Orenda/Unity), *Medical Self-Care* by Tom Ferguson, M.D. (Summit Books), and two classics, *The Holistic Health Handbook* compiled by the Berkeley Holistic Health Center (And/Or Press) and Leslie Kaslof's *Wholistic Dimensions in Healing* (Doubleday & Co.). Meanwhile, here's a sampler of some additional methods to help you get started.

Other books that can give you leads.

Aston Patterning: A Rolf protégé, dancer Judith Aston devised her own three-pronged approach, encompassing tablework (of a softer sort), movement reeducation, and "environmental design." Aston Patterning Institute, P.O. Box 544, Mill Valley, CA 94941.

Hellerworkers ask probing questions as they probe your muscles.

Hellerwork: Joseph Heller, another student of Rolf's and a former aeronautical engineer, introduced two new elements to the technique: movement education (e.g., how to sit—it's not simple!) and an emphasis on emotions and attitudes as an avenue to permanent change. Hellerworkers ask probing questions as they probe your muscles—which you may find a welcome diversion or a distraction. 147 Lomita Drive, Suite H, Mill Valley, CA 94941. The average cost is $75 for 11 sessions.

Lomi: The Lomi School was founded in 1970 by four people with eclectic backgrounds spanning Gestalt, yoga, aikido, vipassana meditation, psychology, psychiatry, breath awareness, polarity therapy, Rolfing, Neo-Reichian techniques, and Tibetan Buddhism. Cofounder Richard Heckler, Ph.D., describes the method as a way to work *on* the body (with chronic and acute disorders); *with* the body (connecting emotion to body armor); and *through* the body ("using the body as feedback to attain more refined states of awareness"). Lomi's most salient characteristic is mindfulness. 1211 Lattie Lane, Mill Valley, CA 94941.

BOX 36: BEFORE YOU BOOK AN APPOINTMENT, READ THIS

The benefits of bodywork, especially when experienced firsthand, are hard to refute. But they're also hard to substantiate, notes Kenneth Pelletier, Ph.D., assistant professor at the University of California–San Francisco School of Medicine and author of numerous books on holistic health and self-care. "Clinically, I've seen benefits, but my longstanding concern is that when I'm hard-pressed by colleagues to prove the efficacy of body-oriented therapies, very few have been empirically evaluated in controlled studies. At this point, the burden of proof is on the practitioners."

Of course, as researchers Brian Inglis and Ruth West note in *The Alternative Health Guide* (Knopf), "It would be extremely difficult to set up a fully controlled trial with one group of patients having manipulative therapy, and the other group getting only 'pretend' manipulative therapy." Still, M.D.'s like Dr. Dorothy Waddell, director of the Alternative Therapies unit at San Francisco General Hospital, are sufficiently satisfied that body therapies such as shiatsu, acupressure, and yoga can prove useful in cases of migraine, hypertension, stress, and chronic pain. "I'm most impressed with practices like Feldenkrais, Alexander, and Aston Patterning, which are theoretically based on how the nervous system develops," she says. "They're powerfully effective—far more than traditional physical therapy. You can feel a quick change."

BOX 36—*Continued*

With the rapid proliferation of schools and offshoots, even old hands are having trouble assessing the efficacy of the newer approaches. For example, Edward G. Stiles, D.O., a prominent Oklahoma osteopath, has no doubt that properly performed bodywork can complement quality medical and surgical care. Yet he's concerned that "there are lots of people doing lots of things, and some not even aware of what others are doing." Dr. Pelletier is equally alarmed by what he perceives as the increasing "fragmentation" in the field: "Subtle modifications in basic systems don't merit a new name," he protests. "It just adds to the confusion." He sees the move toward specialization as "a misguided attempt to become quasi-medical."

David Teegarden, M.D. [formerly] clinical director of the Berkely Holistic Health Center, brings up another important caveat: "People put things on cards that are misleading," he warns. "For instance, when they say they've studied such-and-such, that doesn't necessarily mean they've completed the training and are certified. They can get very nonspecific. They could have attended a weekend workshop. It's a subtle kind of fraud." In selecting a course of bodywork, he advises, it's best to "judge by the practitioner and not just the practice. They all have *some* value as general therapy, if only to fulfill the need to be nurtured and touched."

Many physicians—and indeed many practitioners—would agree that . . .

most manipulative therapies are intended not for patients per se, but for people who want to avoid becoming patients in the first place, by treating somatic disorders at the source. If you are suffering from an illness or injury, it goes without saying, you owe it both to yourself and to your prospective therapist to disclose all; a good practitioner takes a detailed medical history in any event.

What else should you look for in a bodyworker? It's trite, to be sure, but sheer interpersonal "vibes" count for a lot here, and there's no way to quantify that dimension—or teach it, either. You can learn awareness through movement, through meditation, through studying the body or the mind, but you cannot train a person how to "be" with another. Those who do bodywork or get bodywork, and even physicians who recommend it, agree that no matter how much you and your bodyworker know, the ultimate criterion is how you feel about the practitioner.

So shop around. Visit practitioners where they work; ask questions, study diplomas, talk to regulars. Then, if the spirit moves you, try a session—or two, or three. In fact, the more variations you explore, the easier it will be to perceive the underlying universals: the fact that *no* body is perfect, for instance, but that easing physical tension can relieve mental tension, and a better body posture might just foster a healthier psychological stance.

51

Biorhythms and You: Finding Your Best Time for High Performance

"To every thing there is a season," sang the poet of *Ecclesiastes.* And nobody appreciates the truth of that more than someone who's tried doing something out of its season. Like planting a carrot in January. Or eating a big meal when you're not hungry. Or darning a sock when you're too tired to keep your eyes open.

Timing is everything.

The proper timing of things, you might say, is as crucial to science as it is to art: Just ask a farmer or a nightclub comic. But have you ever stopped to consider that knowing the proper "time to every purpose under the heaven" may have a real effect on your health? That eating, sleeping, working, or exercising may have an ideal natural location in your day?

If you have, you're not alone. The study of time's relation to living systems, or chronobiology, has become a regular boom town on the frontiers of science during the past decade or so, and a great deal of information has been unearthed about the mysterious rhythms that govern us.

The human body swings through a whole series of cycles every 24 hours.

It is known that over the course of a day the human body swings through a whole series of cycles of roughly 24 hours in length, with fairly predictable peaks and troughs. Blood pressure, body temperature, blood sugar levels, hormonal tides, heart rate—even subjective things such as moods and sensitivity to pain—all have an internal rhythm, an ebb and flow, a rise and descent.

In practical terms, what that means is that there are a few precious hours each day when all systems are go, your energy is at its peak, and your mind functions at its most alert. It also means there are times each day when your body is a few steps off the beat, and certain things (like important decisions or delicate manual work) shouldn't even be attempted. Learning how these internal cycles operate—"telling your own time"—can help fit your life to your body's schedules, and make more of the time you do have. Because there really *is* a "best time" to do just about anything.

ARE "BIORHYTHMS" BUNK?

The notion that we're not precisely the same person from one hour or day to the next isn't really so awfully farfetched. Everybody experiences their "up" days, when they feel wide awake and full of energy, and other days when life is just a laundry list of dull, menial chores. The idea that there might be some predictable pattern to these ups and downs, which could be mapped out like a tidal chart, has intrigued humans for centuries.

Mapping your ups and downs.

One recent attempt to do just that, the theory of "biorhythms," enjoyed a great surge of popularity a few years back. The theory held that at the moment of birth, three great internal cycles of varying lengths were set in motion inside every human being: a 23-day "physical" cycle; a 28-day "emotional" cycle; and a 33-day "intellectual" cycle. Throughout life, these three cycles were supposed to fluctuate between a positive phase—imparting vitality and alertness—and a negative phase, when thoughts, feelings and energy were low.

The day any of the curves crossed the zero line into a new phase was considered a critical day, when the system was in transition and therefore unstable, and the risk of illness or accident was particularly high. Since these critical days occurred at regular intervals, computed from the date of birth, it was easy to predict when they were coming, and therefore when a person should use extra caution to guard against error.

Is it possible to predict accident- and illness-prone periods?

It was also easy to test the truth of the theory. In one study, for example, data from 205 carefully investigated highway crashes in which the drivers were clearly at fault were compared with the driver's biorhythm charts for that terrible day. According to the theory, the accidents should have occurred more frequently during critical days, or negative phases in the cycle. But as it turned out, the crashes had occurred during those days no more frequently than they had during up phases of the cycle.

Data from the investigation, the researchers concluded, "provide no support whatsoever for any aspect of biorhythm theory." Still, admitted two of the scientists, the whole thing had a "certain wistful appeal" *(Archives of General Psychiatry)*.

FINDING YOUR ENERGY PEAK

Does that mean that science has turned up its nose at the whole notion of inner rhythms in man? Not at all. It's just that biorhythms are too simplistic to account for them all.

For one thing, there is a bewildering array of cycles in progress inside us at any moment, like the arrivals and departures of trains in a busy station. And for another, each person's physiological train is on its own private schedule.

Each person's physiological train is on a different schedule.

There really *are* "larks" and "owls," for example— people who roll out of bed with the sun, fresh and sharp, but who fade early in the evening; and those who drag fuzzily through the morning, only reaching their peak late in the day. There are also people who are neither one. For each of them, the best time to do something may very well be different.

On the other hand, we all have things in common because many basic human cycles are roughly the same for everyone. The body temperature cycle, for instance. Despite what you may think, your body doesn't maintain a steady 98.6 degree temperature throughout the day—it swings through a 24-hour roller coaster ride of about 1.5 degrees in range. It's at its lowest during the wee small hours of the morning and at its highest in the late afternoon to early evening.

When body temperature reaches its daily peak, so does your energy, alertness, and physical performance.

When your body temperature reaches its peak, so do a number of other things: energy and alertness, physical performance, dexterity, and overall mental acuity. It's a sort of mental and physical Mount Everest, with the best view you'll see all day. You may be very well aware of when you reach this peak each day. But many people, "befuddled into thinking they should be the same smiling, efficient functionaries at all hours," don't pay attention to their body's ups and downs, says Gay Gaer Luce, Ph.D., in *Body Time*

(Pantheon Books/Random House).But the simple fact is, she says, "we are not the same at all hours."

An easy (though not terribly precise) way to locate your daily performance peak is to take your temperature at various times throughout the day until you've pinpointed those hours when your body is hovering at its hottest. A better way, Dr. Luce suggests, is to learn to pay attention to yourself: "We do not need to wait until there has been enough research to construct a time map of the body, for each person with a little introspection can begin to sense his own inner timing—one can listen to one's own daily round of changes without opening up the body to look."

A little introspection, and the following advice, may help you find your own best times:

Learn to pay attention to yourself.

EATING

For several reasons, *when* you eat can be as important as *what* you eat. In general, modern research supports the time-honored advice, "Eat breakfast like a king, lunch like a prince, and dinner like a pauper."

Why? Because the digestion of a meal doesn't reach its peak until about seven hours after dessert. If you eat a heavy, fat-laden meal at 6:00 P.M. or later (an old American custom), you're probably asleep—with your metabolism at its lowest, slowest ebb—when most of that digested food hits your bloodstream.

With all those saturated fats making their leisurely way through your arteries, you've got a situation "highly conducive to the production of arteriosclerotic lesions in the arteries of the heart and brain," says Paul B. Roen, M.D., a retired California doctor who has spent more than 30 years studying atherosclerosis. Eating too heavily, too late is "ideal for clot formation, possibly resulting in a stroke, a heart attack, or sudden death."

So how should you schedule your meals? Dr. Roen advises: "A substantial breakfast, a good noon dinner, and a light supper in the evening should promote a situation in which less blood fat will be circulating in the arteries during the relaxed sleeping hours. . . . " *(Journal of the American Geriatrics Society).*

Another advantage of scaling down your meals as the day wears on: It helps keep the weight off. In one study,

When you eat can be as important as *what* you eat.

The benefits of eating a substantial breakfast and light dinner.

seven volunteers ate 2,000 calories a day at breakfast, and all seven lost weight. But when they ate the same 2,000 calories as an evening meal, they lost less weight—or even *gained* weight. Dieters, the researchers suggested, should consider "the importance of timing apart from the amount of caloric intake" *(Chronobiologia)*.

MAKING LOVE

For women, sexual desire rises sharply at the onset of menses.

You wait for the full moon, right? Well, the moon *does* seem to affect sexual desire, at least among women. In one study, 30 women were (tactfully) asked about their desire for sex almost daily over many menstrual cycles, which are closely linked to lunar cycles. The women's responses showed that sexual desire rose sharply at the onset of menses, remained high through the 15th day (about the time of ovulation), then dropped off, reaching a second peak just before the onset of the next menses.

Another study showed that love-making reached a peak among 40 married women right around the 15th day after the onset of menses.

This pinnacle of sexual activity is apparently a result of monthly fluctuations in women's sex hormones, which also peak around the time of ovulation. Researchers have reached this conclusion because women taking oral contraceptives, which suppress these hormones, do not report a peak in sexual activity around the 15th day.

Is sexual desire in men also linked to monthly hormonal changes? There *does* seem to be a link, says Domeena Renshaw, M.D., a psychiatry professor at Loyola University in Maywood, Illinois. But so far the studies have been too limited to suggest the perfect night to greet your mate with champagne and roses.

EXERCISING

Competitive swimmers did significantly better in the evening.

Physical performance has been linked to the daily peak in body temperature in numerous studies. The speed and accuracy with which subjects could deal cards, for example, matched the temperature peak in one study; in another, it was shown that competitive swimmers did significantly better in the evening than in the morning, when their temperature was likely to be lower. Conclusion? Attempts to achieve new records should preferably take place in the evening.

But what if you're not interested in breaking records? For Betsy Bates, a yoga and exercise instructor from Brattleboro, Vermont, four o'clock in the afternoon is the best time of day for breathing, stretching, yoga, or meditative exercise. It's best to do those on an empty stomach, for one thing, and you're also more limber in the afternoon, she says.

On the other hand, says William Zuti, Ph.D., former national director of health-enhancement programs for the YMCA, "It's been my personal experience that people do best when they exercise at whatever time feels best to them." Just one thing to remember, he cautions: If you work out too close to your bedtime, you may get yourself so charged up you can't sleep.

To which we might add: For the weight conscious, one advantage of working out at lunchtime or before dinner is that it may suppress your appetite. And for the work conscious, a lunchtime workout may help you overcome something known as the postprandial dip, a decline in efficiency that occurs in many people for a couple of hours after lunch. Oddly enough, it's not that you feel slow and drowsy because you've just eaten—the "dip" occurs even if you skip lunch. It's just one of those dependable biological trains and you have to learn its schedule.

Working out before dinner can curb your appetite.

AVOIDING PAIN

A person's tolerance to pain, at least pain in the teeth and on the skin, also fluctuates with a regular rhythm over the course of a day. In one study, a group of courageous volunteers had their teeth zapped with a painful instrument at various times of the day and night. The pain, they reported, varied noticeably depending on the time of the zap.

Unfortunately, it hurt the least from midnight to 2:00 A.M., and steadily increased in agony between 8:00 A.M. and 6:00 P.M.—dentist's usual business hours. One researcher suggested that the fainthearted might seek out a moonlighting dental student to fill their cavities at night.

Pain perception is lowest from midnight to 2 A.M.

MAKING A DECISION

Because body temperature is linked to efficiency and alertness, by locating your "heat peak" you can figure out the best time to schedule important decisions—and when to avoid them. "Many people find that it's relatively easy to identify their own prime time once they know that such a thing exists," comments science writer Flora Davis in *Living Alive!* (Doubleday & Co.).

DRINKING

Drinking after midnight will produce a more lasting rise in blood alcohol.

Alcohol works its well-known effects on the brain only as long as it is circulating in the blood. But the length of time it circulates varies, depending on the time of day. Practically speaking, this means that a glass of wine will not affect you as much between noon and midnight as it will between midnight and 8:00 A.M. In short, notes John Palmer, Ph.D., of the zoology department of the University of Massachusetts, "the last drink of the party—'the one for the road' after the bewitching hour—is metabolized relatively more slowly than the preceding ones and will produce a more lasting rise in blood alcohol. . . ." *(Bioscience).*

DOING SOMETHING CREATIVE

During normal sleep, you go through a dreaming cycle every 90 minutes or so all night long. But what's only recently become known is that these cycles continue through the day, with periods of alertness and practical thinking alternating with periods of daydreaming, also in cycles of roughly 90 minutes.

If you're feeling alert, keep working.

In a series of studies, people sitting alone in a room who were asked to record their thoughts every five minutes showed that they passed through these alternating modes of thought on a remarkably regular basis. Just knowing these cycles exist can be handy: If you feel your down-to-earth alertness cycle is in full swing, avoid taking a break from work just then. But if your daydreaming cycle takes over and creative fancies well up inside, *that* may be the time to follow the Muse wherever she may lead.

TAKING MEDICATIONS

The time of day or night you take a medication can make a tremendous difference in what it does to your body. In the treatment of mice with leukemia, for example, the mortality rate can be changed up to 80 percent, depending on the time a drug is administered. Unfortunately, there are so many drugs, and so much has yet to be learned about "chronotherapeutics," as the study of drug timing is called, that there is no simple advice to give. Just be aware: When you take a medication makes a difference, and your doctor's advice is the best.

LEARNING OR MEMORIZING

Although students are famous for burning the midnight oil, research indicates that's just about the worst time to try committing anything to memory. This was vividly demonstrated in a study with two groups of nurses. Each group was shown a training film, one at 8:30 in the evening and the other at 4:00 in the morning. Both groups were tested on the film's content immediately.

Late-night studying may give you the edge on tomorrow's test, but not on long-term recall.

Strangely enough, the 4:00 A.M. group had a slightly better recollection of the film than the 8:30 P.M. group (though the difference in scores wasn't considered statistically significant). But the real test came a month later, when both groups were again tested on their memory of the movie. By then, the 4:00 A.M. "midnight oilers" had forgotten over twice as much as the group who'd seen it at an earlier hour.

But if 4:00 A.M. is the worst time to learn something, what's the best? A now-classic study of California college students, conducted in 1916, showed that there are two "learning peaks" during the daylight hours (8:00 A.M. to 5:00 P.M. were the only hours tested). One hundred and sixty-five students, quizzed on memory tasks over a period of three days, showed virtually identical learning curves: They were at their best between 9:00 and 11:00 in the morning (peaking at about 10:00), and again between 3:00 and 4:00 in the afternoon. These results showed that the students' subjective judgment about when they *thought* they were at their best was not at all accurate.

Learning peaks: 10:00 A.M. and 3:30 P.M.

They were right about the best time to take a break—during the "postprandial dip" after lunch, when the learning curve took a dramatic dive. Their bodies seemed to know it was not time for memorizing a sonnet.

PART X

Getting Better at Everything You Do

52

Super Learning

What if you could use only 10 percent of your fingers—one finger? Everything would be a chore, from picking up a pen to changing the channel, and you'd probably feel inadequate and frustrated. In fact, you'd probably give up trying to do much of anything. Well, you may already be using as little as 10 percent of a part of your body—your brain.

That's right: Scientists say the average person uses only a small part of the brain. The rest is available, but untapped. And because of that, most people give up trying—to study, to memorize, to learn. But learning doesn't have to be drudgery. It can be fun—an easy, joyful process of opening your life to new interests and expertise—if you get your entire brain in on the act.

And the first step is to use both sides of your brain.

Over the last 20 years, scientific research has shown that the brain has two sides, or hemispheres, and that they function very differently.

"Most classroom teaching only makes use of the left hemisphere," says Owen Caskey, Ed.D., a psychologist with the El Paso Independent School District. The left hemisphere, he explains, works with facts—logical, point-by-point thinking. But the right hemisphere works with feeling—fantasy, imagination, mental imagery, and intuition.

"When both hemispheres of the brain are involved in learning," says Don Schuster, Ph.D., professor of psychology at Iowa State University, "learning is easier, faster, and

If we used our hands like we use our brains, we'd have to make do with one finger.

Optimal learning utilizes the brain's two hemispheres.

much more fun." And here's where we may do well to take a few lessons from our youngest generation.

Ease of learning relates to *how* the information is presented.

Of course, it's true: A young, developing brain absorbs information at a much faster rate. But now there is evidence that the ease of learning is related in part to how the information is presented and assimilated by the learning center of the brain.

The way children actually learn their mother tongue is very different from the way most of us learn a foreign language in school, and it's a good thing, or we'd all still be saying "goo-goo" at age 50. As a young child feels heat radiating from a stove, he hears, "Careful, that's hot!" The word "milk" is accompanied by the taste of milk in the child's mouth. And, in response to the world of language and sensation, children use their bodies to get the hang of new words: crouching and clasping their hands together to say "little," throwing their arms wide for "big," making circles with their arms as they say "around and around." At age two or three, learning words is not only a mental activity but also a physical experience.

Let your mind and body make beautiful music together.

But what does this mean for the 30-year-old beginner of French or Portuguese, the flute or the tuba? It means: Let your body and mind make beautiful music together; make a new language a total experience.

That is, roughly, the advice of James J. Asher, Ph.D., a psychologist concerned with Americans' seeming inability to master foreign languages. Traditional methods of language study, which involve memorizing big chunks of vocabulary and grammar, and the mental manipulation of foreign words with no "feel" of real experience to reinforce them, are difficult for all but the most gifted students.

To make a second language possible for anyone to learn, Dr. Asher has come up with an approach he calls Total Physical Response (TPR), which relies on listening to and experiencing the spoken language rather than concentrating on the written word.

TOTAL PHYSICAL RESPONSE

Ordinary students learn as well as gifted students.

The idea behind TPR is to use a big part of your mind that, according to Dr. Asher, most educators neglect—the right hemisphere of the brain. It is Dr. Asher's opinion that "right-brain learning" is so much more effective that ordinary language students can learn as well as "gifted" students now do by traditional methods. But how, exactly, can we get the right brain working for us?

"If adults want to acquire a second language without stress, they should construct a reality in the new language." Only by acting out the new vocabulary can learners really convince themselves that Fido is also un chien, ein Hund, or un cane.

Thus, a teacher of the Asher method might enliven a lesson in Japanese by saying, "Give me your wristwatch, walk around the table, and scream." Or "Run to Maria, take her purse, and throw it out the window." For certain excitable souls, these orders might have the effect of a match in a munitions dump, but, despite the possible loss of your timepiece, your handbag, and your inhibitions, Dr. Asher's method has much to recommend it. Study after study has shown that material learned this way sticks in the mind like a burr.

"Long-term retention is the bright, bright feature of the right-brain strategy that we're offering," says Dr. Asher. "Suppose you learn to ice skate on Lake Michigan as a child and later move to California. Even if you don't put on ice skates in 25 years, when you do, you'll perform roughly at the same level as 25 years before. Ice skating is a motor skill, and the fact that it stays with you after 25 years seems to be characteristic of anything learned through the body. We acquired our first language by interacting physically. If we stimulate that infant experience at a speeded-up pace we get three beautiful features: accelerated comprehension, stress-free learning, and very long-term retention. Not only language but any skill or discipline is easier to learn with an approach that incorporates right-brain learning."

And if you can't coax your body to "construct a reality" in which the learning process can take place, call on your mind to conjure up a convincing illusion.

Body moves make a lasting impression.

PICTURES INSTEAD OF WORDS

Another effective way to perk up the right hemisphere is to think in pictures, says Dr. Owen Caskey. "People are taught to think only in words—to hear words in their head, but not to make picture," he explains. "But you learn much more effectively if you make a picture in your head about

Mental imagery helps you achieve any skill.

the material you're dealing with. Think of it as constructive daydreaming."

Dr. Don Schuster agrees. "I tell students, 'Picture yourself in the book. Feel that it's happening to you. Make up a story about the material and see it. Get the right half of the brain involved."

The professors believe that mental imagery isn't only for book-learning. It helps you achieve any skill.

Daydreams of the good life.

"If you want to improve your life," says Dr. Caskey, "make a picture in your head—of getting along with your husband or wife or of communicating with your boss. If you don't make pictures in your head, there's not going to be very much in life that's easy for you."

Dr. Schuster calls this approach to learning "success goal imagery." He explains that mental imagery—right brain thinking—sparks the powerful subconscious mind into action. "The subconscious mind responds to success goal imagery and works to make the goal image a reality in your life."

If you expect that learning is easy, it will be.

Dr. Schuster "trains" students by having them use success goal imagery to overcome a major block to learning—the fear of difficulty and failure. "A person who expects that learning can be easy will learn easily, and enjoy it in the process," he says. "I instruct people to picture themselves mastering material and having fun doing it. For instance, a student will picture himself sitting at a desk with a book and a smile on his face."

Dr. Schuster believes most people develop the idea that they can't learn easily when they're very young.

Fear of failure can block real learning ability.

"Most people have accepted other people's evaluation of their learning ability," he says. "When you were young, it's likely that someone called you 'stupid' or 'dumb' or yelled at you with words like, 'Didn't I tell you . . . '— implying that you were a failure at learning something. At home and at school, a young person's learning ability is often criticized and belittled, but the criticism has nothing to do with his real learning ability."

Carl Schleicher, Ph.D., the director of Mankind Research Unlimited, a Silver Springs, Maryland, organization that offers classes to "develop the full range of left-right hemisphere learning," says that fears of all kinds inhibit learning.

The mind is unlimited in its capacity to learn.

"There is the fear that comes from remembering a previous painful and difficult learning experience," he says.

"There is the fear of failure. In older people, there is the fear that the mind can't remember as well as it used to. But there is no need for stress and mental pain while learning. People have been brainwashed to accept limitations. The mind is unlimited in its capacity to learn—the only limitations are those that have been imposed on us or that we impose on ourselves."

And to free the mind of fear and anxiety, Dr. Schleicher—and many other education experts—emphasizes the necessity of a relaxation technique.

"A relaxation skill is the most crucial element to improve learning ability," says Dr. Caskey. "Anxiety interferes with learning. Any kind of anxiety, not just that type associated with the learning process itself. If you can rid an individual of anxiety, he is more likely to learn."

Relaxation: the most crucial element in super learning.

"Yoga or TM [Transcendental Meditation] is very helpful in calming the mind and making a person more receptive to what he has to learn," says Dr. Schuster, whose statement is backed up by two studies on a relaxation technique.

In the first study, the memory of people who had practiced TM for an average of over two years was compared to people who had never meditated. Both groups learned a list of words and were tested a week later to see how many of the words they could remember. The meditators recalled almost twice as many words as the nonmeditators.

Recall was twice as good in meditators as nonmeditators.

In the second study, college students who practiced TM and students who didn't were asked to figure out the path through a maze puzzle. The meditators only needed an average of 10 tries to discover the path, while the non-meditators needed an average of 22 tries. "The superior learning ability displayed by the meditators could be explained by decreased anxiety," wrote the researcher who conducted the study (*Scientific Research on the Transcendental Meditation Program*, Maharishi European Research University Press).

MUSIC FOR STUDYING

While yoga and relaxation techniques are used before studying, listening to music while studying is also very calming, says Dr. Schuster.

"Reviewing material while listening to Baroque music—

Bach, Handel, and Vivaldi make great study partners.

music that has approximately one beat per second, such as quite a bit of music by Bach, Handel, and Vivaldi—helps keep you in a relaxed state of mind."

Dr. Caskey thinks that any soothing music will do. "Unhurried, stately music makes a wonderful background for studying," he says. "We use both classical music and the type of music you hear on 'easy listening' FM radio."

Choose music that suits you personally.

Easy listening music—also called Musak or Moosak—isn't for everyone, however. Steven Halpern, Ph.D., author of *Tuning The Human Instrument* (Spectrum Research Institute) and *Sound Health* (Harper & Row), finds that it irritates more than relaxes. But, he admits, musical taste is a personal thing, which is why it's important to choose music that works for *you*.

Dr. Halpern, who's an acknowledged pioneer in music composition, has created a new brand of relaxation music, which he calls an Anti-Frantic Alternative™. Carefully arranged and orchestrated, this music purposely lacks the dominant melody, harmony, and rhythm of Western music; this, says Dr. Halpern, "allows the body to find its own modality while activating both hemispheres of the brain."

The type of music that relaxes like meditation.

Apparently, too, it works. According to studies, more people respond favorably and reach deeper levels of relaxation while listening to Dr. Halpern's "Anti-Frantic" tapes than to any other kind of music, including classical and "easy listening."

Learning potential also seems to be improved with this type of music. School children achieved higher grade-point averages when Dr. Halpern's tapes "Spectrum Suite" or "Comfort Zone" were played as background music in the classroom.

Achieving a balanced brain state for heightened creativity.

"The music brings you to a balanced brain state so you're able to absorb, retain, and recall information much more easily," Dr. Halpern explains. "It also improves your creativity. For example, when I was working on my book, I found there were days when I just couldn't get into it. I didn't feel like writing or being creative. So I listened to tapes like "Comfort Zone," and I found that I could write much better.

A tape that specifically accesses the brain's learning centers.

Taking this effect even one step further, Dr. Halpern produced a tape that's designed specifically to access those areas of the brain involved in learning. Entitled "The Joy of Learning," it combines "Anti-Frantic" music—some of it to the Baroque beat—with what Dr. Halpern calls "AudioActive affirmations." These affirmations, which include such statements as, "You can remember all that you have studied at any time," "Studying comes easily to you; you enjoy it," and "The music makes it easy to understand all that you read," are woven into the fabric of the music in such a way that they are practically inaudible to the consicous ear.

TV AND JUNK FOOD

Jane Bancroft, Ph.D., associate professor of French at the Scarborough campus of the University of Toronto, was one of the first people to conduct studies on music and learning.

"I first became interested in methods to enhance memory and concentration when I realized that year by year my students were becoming poorer in their ability to learn French. After thorough research, I attribute this trend to two main factors": the influence of television, which trains

TV lulls the mind's attention into passivity.

BOX 37: CAN'T THINK STRAIGHT? SIT UP STRAIGHT

Ever feel like you just can't think straight? Check to see if your posture is putting a crimp on the blood supply to your brain, says E. Fritz Schmerl, M.D., teacher of gerontology at Chabot College, Hayward, California.

"The brain needs up to 30 times more blood than other organs," Dr. Schmerl says. "But allowing your upper body to sag—with rounded shoulders, head hung over, and chin jutting outward—can create kinks in the spine that squeeze the two arteries passing through the spinal column to the brain, causing an inadequate blood supply." The result? "Fuzzy thinking and forgetfulness, especially as we age," says Dr. Schmerl.

Hunched-over posture can contribute to strokelike symptoms, known as transient ischemic attacks, which are brief blackout periods. Worse yet, disturbances in the blood flow of the pinched artery might cause a buildup of fatty deposits that can cause partial blockage, according to Dr. Schmerl.

"It's important to get a head start on proper alignment while you're young," Dr. Schmerl says. "Poor posture is a hard habit to break when you're older. Be consciously on guard to prevent this process by holding yourself straight, with your head back and your chin in," he says.

attention to be passive and dull, and the increase of junk food and additives in the diet.

"Right diet is one of the basics of good memory," Dr. Bancroft continues. "If you don't eat properly, you don't nourish the brain. A colleague of mine came to the U.S. and stayed in a typical chain hotel, eating most of her meals in the restaurant there. After a few days, she remarked that her mind wasn't as sharp as usual. I think it was because the food served in such restaurants is often processed and loaded with additives."

Deep, rhythmic breathing relaxes and clears the mind.

But, says Dr. Bancroft, the brain isn't nourished only by food. "If a person sits in a cramped position in a windowless room with no fresh air, he's not going to be able to concentrate or memorize well because his brain isn't getting enough oxygen. Deep, rhythmic breathing during a study session is very helpful to maintain an alert, relaxed state of mind."

And if you use one or many of these learning techniques—mental imagery, relaxation, restful music, good diet, and deep breathing—you may find that not only your learning ability, but your life ability improves, too.

"People are most able to accept and learn from the challenges of life when they use more of their brain," says Barbara McNeill, a wellness educator practicing in the San Francisco Bay area.

"Life is learning," she told us, "you can't separate the two. A person who is healthy and happy is someone who knows how to learn from life."

BOX 38: STRATEGIES FOR REMEMBERING

If you have trouble remembering where you last laid your watch, keys, or whatever, try associating it with pictures, gestures, or a physical experience. Suppose, for example, that you have misplaced your winning Irish Sweepstakes ticket. Recreate the experience of holding the ticket: I was holding it (you make a grasping motion), and you asked me for my pen to sign the card we sent to Aunt Lil (you pat your pockets and realize), and *that's* when I put it down.

If you wish to avoid the trauma of forgetting in the first place, make a habit of associating the mental image you wish to recall with something more concrete. For example, if you are putting an important document in a bottom

BOX 38— *Continued*

drawer, be conscious of the muscles in your back as you bend. Think of the document, look at the drawer, and place your hand on the drawer for a moment to fix it in your mind.

If you have to make a presentation, do as the ancient Greeks used to do when delivering a flawless three-hour oration, and associate the speech with your own house. Think of the opening paragraphs as the front door and entry hall, and your main arguments as kitchen, dining room, bedroom, bath, in the natural order you'd walk through them. End up by associating your conclusion with your back porch.

If you have to remember a number, first look at it, hard. It might be enough to "see" it in a color—salmon pink or aquamarine. If not, imagine the number clearly in some unusual setting: in gold on a fluted column; spelled out in white boulders on the side of a hill.

If you want to burn into your memory important information you just read, picture the page. Too often we try to memorize things abstractly, ignoring the physical reality of a bit of data. Think how often you remember "it was on the bottom of the left hand page" or "it was toward the end of the book." Your mind wants to present you with a picture—so help it along, and think of necessary facts *as they appear* on the page.

If you have a number of errands to run, but realize as you pedal your bike toward the center of town that you've forgotten your list of tasks, don't despair. In the first place, they'll be easier to keep track of if you know how many there are. Let's say there are six: take your watch in for cleaning; look up a zip code at the P.O.; go to the library; meet a friend for lunch; pick up some wine for dinner; and buy an 8-inch pot for the fern in your kitchen. The odds are slim that you'll remember such a jumble of data, so associate the forgettable items with something there's no chance you'll forget: the alphabet. With a little verbal legerdemain you can remember the zip code as "address" and going to the library as "books". Your watch can wedge itself into your consciousness as "clean the clock," the bottle of wine as "dinner drink" and lunch as "eat with Allen" (or whoever). The last item quite easily becomes "fern pot." Address, Books, Clean the Clock, Dinner Drink, Eat with Allen, Fern pot. ABCDEF—there you have it, as long as concentrating on your errands hasn't caused you to run your Motobecane into a ditch, necessitating one more errand: G, for "Get bike fixed."

BOX 39: THINK YOU CAN

Telling yourself you just weren't born smart, that you can never remember things, or that you're too old to learn are good ways to sabotage your true intellectual potential, say David Lewis, Ph.D., and James Greene, authors of *Thinking Better* (Rawson, Wade Publishers). Such negative thoughts "put your brain behind bars." They keep you from pursuing knowledge and learning better ways to remember. They can push you into a mental rut as you age.

Feeling good about your ability to learn is important to intellectual functioning, and it's one of the first things to be tackled at Mankind Research Unlimited, a Silver Spring, Maryland, "superlearning" center that has turned highschool dropouts into gifted learners and blind people into computer programmers.

"We tell people who don't think they can learn that they really have a lot more brain than they think, and that they can learn to use more of it than they ever thought possible," says director Carl Schleicher, Ph.D.

His learning program uses a number of different techniques—listening to stately Baroque music, visualizing a quiet, private getaway place for thinking, and breathing deeply to create an aura of relaxed awareness. Then, the student receives suggestions—that he *will* do better, that he *can* learn. He begins to picture himself doing that successfully, and his successes in real life are praised. He may also use creative imagery to bolster a sagging self-image. An insecure scientist might practice imagining himself in the role of a successful professional in his own field—Albert Einstein, let's say, or if he prefers a neater-looking appearance, Robert Oppenheimer.

"Limits on learning are self-imposed," Dr. Schleicher says. Make the sky your limit by keeping your thinking powers fit.

Problem Solving Simplified: Three New Mind and Body Techniques

Try pulling six feet of molding off a wall with your fingertips and you know why someone invented the crowbar. Try unparking your loaded van from a really tight spot and you appreciate power steering. Try getting someone's attention in a crowded room and you know at least one reason why they invented the smile. Leverage, in one form or another, is used by people every day, in almost every conceivable kind of task. Except one. Thinking.

Leverage is used in all tasks except one. Thinking.

Sure, we live in the age of computers, but we're not talking about mere calculating; we're talking about real, honest-to-goodness, 100-percent-natural-fiber *thinking*. The stuff you have to do lots of when your job is beginning to drive you crazy, when your relationship is turning into a nonrelationship, when you can't handle your kids or find time to relax, when you're in a rut—and out of ideas. When what you need is a brainstorm and all you get is intellectual humidity.

It's a place we've all been before, and where we'll all be again. As long as there is life, there will be lulls. But, with the following techniques for creative problem solving, you can quickly work through them and get your life back in motion. What they do, in effect, is toss some cinders under your spinning wheels.

CREATIVE DAYDREAMING

Most of us grew up believing that daydreaming is a royal waste of time. "Don't just sit there, do something!"

Daydreaming is no longer considered a social sin.

commanded our parents, who believed that inactivity was some sort of social sin.

"How wrong we have been," says Jerome L. Singer, Ph.D., professor of psychology at Yale University. And he should know. He's devoted a major portion of his career to the study of daydreams and their mostly unappreciated values.

Imagination: a powerful tool in problem solving.

"In all of our research, we have found that daydreams not only enrich life, but can lead to more creative thought and better physical and emotional health," Dr. Singer reports. "Your imaginative life—your directed fantasying—can give you tremendous power to work out your most troublesome problems," he says.

Eric Klinger, Ph.D., a psychologist at the University of Minnesota in Morris and Minneapolis, agrees. "People are walking around with a whole bunch of current concerns." They may want to ask the boss for a raise, or they're worried about the in-law's planned visit next month. Commonly, they'll take the analytical approach to solving the problem—systematically weighing the pros and cons.

FANTASY BECOMES REALITY

Unfortunately, this approach often serves to highlight two equally arguable sides to the issue but offers no one solution. But by taking those points and rehearsing them in your mind—playing out the best and worst consequences with all the detail of reality—you put yourself in a better position to deal with the actual situation. Mistakes are eliminated. And realistic expectations can be separated out from those that are wildly optimistic or unnecessarily pessimistic.

Dr. Singer offers an exemplary scenario.

To clarify the process, Dr. Singer offers the following scenario:

"Let's suppose that your problem is whether or not to change jobs. An old friend approaches you with an exciting and challenging job opportunity. It sounds almost too good to turn down but, that night, as you mull things over, you realize that there are a lot of unknowns. The company is new—it could fold tomorrow. You don't know the boss—he could be a real ogre. The responsibilities are quite different from your current position—you may find that you're unsuited for it. What seems on the surface like the opportunity of a lifetime could become the disaster of all times. On the other hand, your current job is no longer challenging or fulfilling and you've been quietly thinking about leaving anyway. But it does pay well and, heaven knows, it's secure.

"So there you are. You've made a case for both sides. But in the process, your mind becomes a jumble of fears and anxieties leaving you tense, frantic, and without a decision.

Analyzing the pros and cons creates a mental jumble of fears and anxieties.

"Now, let's utilize the power of our imagination. Close your eyes and envision the worst possible scenario. Day one: Imagine yourself arriving at the office. Your desk is already stacked high with paperwork. Your boss is tense and irritable, impatient with your questions and unable to define your job responsibilities. Your secretary is downright malicious. You go back to your desk but can't make heads or tails out of the work, fumble around till quitting time and get nothing accomplished. Day two: You arrive at the office to find a pink dismissal slip on your desk.

"After you have mentally rehearsed this depressing scene (and any others you can think of), ask yourself whether any of these worst fears are actual risks. How realistic are they?"

How realistic are your fears?

THE BENEIT OF 3-D

"Often, by imagining our worst fears—by deliberately letting ourself dream them in vivid detail—we can see them in context. And in this way we can alleviate much of our anxiety.

"You can fantasize further on the negative side. Imagine yourself in your current job ten years from now. If it's challenging and unfulfilling now, how will it feel then? Which is worse: your fear of insecurity in your new job or the lack of excitement in the old job?

What's worse: your present situation or the future unknown?

"Now let your daydreams take you to the positive side. Imagine the best possible new job experience: Job responsibilities that are even more exciting than your friend described, a boss who's bright and creative and immediately takes you under his wing, associates who appreciate and admire your work.

"You might also want to try this approach with your current job. Imagine that some unexpected opportunity presents itself and immediately catapults you into a new and exciting position in the old firm.

Imagine your wildest dreams coming true.

"Which of these scenarios makes you happier?

"Of course, all these positive and negative fantasies

are extremely unrealistic. So now play through a new scenario that draws on the most realistic elements from the earlier fantasies. Combine your fears and anxieties with your hopes and expectations. If you can do this, you will feel freer and less anxious about coming to a final decision" *(Executive Health)*.

Using this technique to get in touch with yourself.

"Daydreaming," adds James Morgan, Ed.D., a counseling psychologist at the University of Florida, "is actually rehearsing behaviors to try out at another time. I've used it for years in group counseling as an unlocking technique. It allows people to get in touch with themselves and to deal with their future plans and goals."

Suppose, for example, you're trying to lose weight. Imagine how you would look if you were thin. Picture your new wardrobe and all the admiring glances and words of praise from friends and family. Now think how comfortable you'll feel. No more bulging seams, no more waistbands cutting deeply and painfully into your stomach. Try to have a positive image fully developed and ready to use *before* you reach for the pie or ice cream. It will help you resist those temptations.

FROZEN IN ACTION

When fears prevent us from making decisions.

According to Dr. Jerome Singer, mild, irrational fears commonly obstruct our goals, blocking us from taking the actions necessary to move ourselves forward. To unlock ourselves, he recommends a variation on the creative daydreaming technique described above. He calls it "vicarious modeling."

"Suppose you are afraid of using the telephone," says Dr. Singer. "A surprising number of otherwise reasonably well-adjusted individuals find themselves becoming very tense if they have to call up a doctor or speak to a potential employer about job opportunities, or even to reconnect with an old friend.

Envision someone you admire.

"If there is someone you admire—a person who's poised or who handles phone conversations easily—imagine him or her having to make a series of such calls. . . . Picture this person walking to the phone, picking up the receiver, dialing, and then calmly and assuredly saying: 'Hello there. is this Dr. Smith? This is Mr. Simmons. I've been troubled by a bad cough . . . .'

"Once you've run through the sequence a few times,"

continues Dr. Singer, "you might begin to picture yourself in each of these situations. It might even be helpful to talk the conversation out loud, in private. It's a good idea to have a speech prepared in advance; some people get stymied on just whether to say 'Hello,' 'Hi,' 'Who's this?' or other pat phrases. You may feel phony at first working from a prepared script for your phone calls, but soon it will become quite natural and you'll find the telephone a friend and not a foe."

EPS—EFFECTIVE PROBLEM SOLVING

Liz Forrest, the dynamic 36-year-old owner of Innovation Labs Inc. in Stamford, Connecticut, spends most of her time running Idea Labs for leading companies, from the Fortune 500 to philanthropic organizations. But the same techniques that have helped companies develop new products, new marketing strategies, and new ideas for growth can do at least as much for you. She calls it simply EPS (which stands for Effective Problem Solving).

An idea-generating technique used by leading corporations can help you, too.

WHAT DO YOU WANT?

Brenda, 29, was a junior sales executive working in the office of a small textile company. She enjoyed her work but worried about her future. Chances for promotion to a senior sales position seemed slim. In fact, the company she worked for wasn't doing well. To complicate things, Brenda very much wanted to get more involved in the design part of the industry, but had no real background in design. She'd thought of moving to a different company, but that would probably entail moving out of state, and she rejected that because of her husband's job. She'd even thought of quitting and striking out on her own, but she rejected that possibility too, because without her steady income, the family would not be able to meet its mortgage payments.

"Sounds like a soap opera, I guess," Brenda laughed when she met Liz Forrest. Which is part of the problem, Forrest explains. "Most problems start as one big mess. The first step is to sort out what is happening and come up with a simple statement of the major problem. The key to knowing your real problem is to identify the thing you most want in the situation and to isolate what keeps you from getting it." And that begins with the words I WANT.

First, come up with a simple statement of the major problem.

Write those words down on a piece of paper and complete the sentence with exactly what it is you want to happen. Brenda had to stop and ponder for a moment. What was the real payoff she was looking for? The *one* important goal? After a few minutes, she wrote, "*I want* to advance myself by getting involved with the design aspects of the apparel field."

Next, identify the major stumbling block.

Forrest then instructed Brenda to write another phrase under the first sentence: BUT I. Here's where you express the *one* major stumbling block that seems to be keeping you from achieving your *I want* statement. Don't write down every last pebble in your path, just one big boulder.

Brenda wrote: "*But I* am currently in a sales position, which does not involve me in design."

The *But I* statement focuses on *you* (in this particular case, Brenda). Don't write down, "But Harry won't let me," because you have no control over Harry. All you can control are *your* actions. At this point, you have the heart of your problem right in front of you. It's also the point where EPS starts to be fun.

Take your pencil and cross out the phrase *But I.* Over it write AND I.

To get moving, you have to temporarily gag the "but" part of your brain.

Why do that? Because, Liz Forrest explains, to proceed further, you have to temporarily knock out of commission the "but" part of your mind. The part that's forever analyzing and criticizing, smothering new ideas in the cradle. So what you're left with is not so much a problem as a kind of paradox, or odd state of affairs. In Brenda's case: "I want to advance myself by getting involved with the design aspects of the apparel field . . . *and I* am currently in a sales position, which does not involve me in design."

Notice how different the problem statement rings in the mind without that big clunky "but" in there—even though it's as true as the first statement.

TRY WISHFUL THINKING

Now the fun begins. Be playful. Give yourself magical powers.

Now it's time to go wild—almost literally. The next step in Forrest's technique is called, simply, *wishing.* Glance over your problem statement again. Then begin writing down absolutely outrageous, absurdly impossible solutions in the form of wishes. Don't censor yourself—whatever wish pops into your brain, write it down. "Be playful,"

Forrest advises. "Give yourself magical powers. Use fantasy and free association. Keep the wishes coming!"

Do your wishing for as long as you like, but be sure to come up with at least 5. With any luck, you ought to get 10 or 15 real doozies.

Here are some that Brenda wrote down:

1. "*I wish* I could hypnotize Calvin Klein into giving me a job."

2. "*I wish* I could clone myself, send one of me to my job and the other of me to the Parsons School of Design in New York."

3. "*I wish* my husband would get a new job in a town where there were 500 textile mills."

4. "*I wish* my husband would win the lottery and buy me my own factory."

5. "*I wish* everyone I met thought I was a genius."

Give yourself magical powers, Forrest urges:

6. "*I wish* I could fly anywhere in the world on my lunch hour, buy all the best fabrics and clothing, and sell them from my garage on Saturday afternoons."

Think big, Forrest urges. Really *big:*

7. "*I wish* my eyes could see all over the world, and my arms were so long I could reach out and be the first to grab up the exciting new designs to sell."

Wonderful! Now think *small.* I mean, *really* small:

8. "*I wish* I had 20,000 little designers and weavers working in my attic and I could choose what I wanted, make it big and sell it."

At this point, Brenda felt she was just about through, but in glancing over her list of wishes, she free-associated two more wishes from the first eight.

9. "*I wish* I could fly to New York City on my lunch hour and get orders for the clothes the elves in my attic were making."

10. "*I wish* my next-door neighbor was a fantastic designer and I could get orders for her on my lunch hours in New York City."

What are you supposed to do with all those crazy wishes, you ask?

Let each wish bounce around in your head. Listen for interesting reverberations.

Well, begin by reading them, Forrest suggests. Let each one bounce around in your head for a moment. Listen for any interesting reverberations. Then pick the one that appeals to you most, no matter how wild it may be.

Brenda chose her last wish: "I wish my next-door neighbor was a fantastic designer and I could get orders for her on my lunch hours in New York City." It had a kind of cozy feeling to it and while it was pure dream-stuff, it *sounded* like something she'd actually enjoy doing.

"Once you've selected your favorite wish," says Forrest, "ask yourself: *'What's the real point of this wish, and how could I translate it into a reality that I could actually work on?'*"

After a moment or two, Brenda decided that the point of her wish was that she didn't have to be a designer herself to get involved in design. She could use her sales ability in working closely with a designer.

MAKING YOUR DREAMS COME TRUE

Out of wild fantasy come fresh ideas.

But *how?* That takes us to the real climax of the EPS technique, transforming wishes into ideas. "An idea," Forrest explains, "is simply a more practical way of doing what the wish implies." Again we invoke a facilitating phrase. In this case, it's HOW ABOUT.

Back to pencil and paper. Here's what Brenda wrote:

1. "*How about* teaming up with a first-rate designer and representing her work to the industry."

2. "*How about* advertising for designers who want representation, and asking my boss to let me work late four nights a week so I can go to New York the fifth day."

3. "*How about* finding new designers and asking my boss to let our regular salespeople try to sell their work."

The next step continues to bring us closer to reality. "In the *idea evaluation* stage," Forrest explains, "you study the action possibilities you've written down and choose your favorite. List the strong points or advantages of that idea. Any possibility that has at least three strong points means you may have found a viable new direction, something worth pursuing."

Brenda liked her second idea best, but modified it somewhat, so that she'd ask her boss to allow her to work only four days a week, with a proportionate cut in salary. As an added incentive, she'd tell him that she would give exclusive manufacturing contracts to the company for any orders she got.

LOOKING FOR NEW DIRECTIONS

Brenda quickly found four strong points to this approach: It permitted her to become involved in choosing designs without actually creating them (which she felt unqualified to do); New York City was only a two-hour drive from her New England home; her boss—because business was not good at the company—would probably welcome the chance to cut his payroll a little while creating an opportunity for new business; and finally, she'd be able to earn more money without endangering her present job.

Considering the feasibility of your new idea.

What about negatives? Any real roadblocks left in the path you've charted? Brenda could see only two: It might be difficult to find good designers (but certainly not impossible), and her boss might refuse to cooperate. Neither negative seemed overwhelming.

So. You, like Brenda, are now ready to write down your plan of action. That includes a strategy for overcoming what Liz Forrest calls "the troublesome parts in the idea."

Ready to write down your plan of action.

Brenda's plan fell together quickly. First she would discuss the idea with her husband and get his support. Then she'd "trial balloon" the idea with her boss. If he was agreeable, she'd ask for the plan to go into effect only when and if she were able to line up some good designers and exciting samples.

What happens next is strictly up to Brenda (or you), and fate. EPS does not guarantee success stories—only new directions, new opportunities. And, eventually, new problems. "Each action you carry out will create a new situation, which may, in turn, lead you to want something new," says Forrest. "It's a never-ending process."

For all the muscle in EPS, it has a hidden strength that lies not so much in what it *does*, as in what it *doesn't* do. It does not offer a solution to all your problems all at once. Just one problem at a time.

EPS has a hidden strength in what it doesn't do.

Second, it must be a problem that you personally have

control over. There is nothing you can do, for instance, to lower mortgage rates. All *you* can do—and all EPS can help you do—is create ideas for alternative financing, housing choices, ways to increase your income, and so on.

Finally, the opportunity for action that EPS helps you formulate does not presume to be the absolute *best* possible answer to your problem. All it is, really, is a way to get you moving in the direction you want.

Maureen, 33, did not see Liz Forrest professionally. They met socially, and Forrest introduced her to EPS. Maureen decided to use the technique on a personal problem. The problem, she felt, was her boyfriend. "No" said Forrest. "The problem is *you*—how you choose to handle your boyfriend's behavior." "Ah, so," said Maureen, who then wrote:

"*I want* to have a good and lasting relationship with my friend *and* I am very concerned about his instability and drinking problem, enough to think of ending the relationship."

After making a number of wishes, Maureen chose this one as the most appealing: "*I wish* I were a great psychologist so I could counsel my boyfriend every day and lead him to overcome his self-defeating behavior."

A way of moving you in the direction you want to go.

The underlying point of that wish, she decided, was that her friend needed psychological help and that she would somehow encourage him to seek it.

In the *How about* step, Maureen came up with an idea that needed little further work. She would, she decided, give her friend the name of two good therapists she knew of, and tell him that if he did not see one of them, she didn't think the relationship could go on.

Maureen saw a rather intimidating "negative" to this approach: What if her boyfriend flatly refused? In that case she would know that their relationship was not that important to her boyfriend, and certainly not worth pursuing.

How this plan turned out we don't know . . . but suppose it didn't? Suppose Maureen chickened out?

"No catastrophe," Forrest says. "She could go back to the drawing board—literally—and write '*I want* to give my boyfriend an ultimatum . . . *and* I am afraid of the consequences.' Then she could work on a new approach that wouldn't seem like a dreadful ultimatum, but more like a strong suggestion, leaving an escape route for herself. Even that might not work, but it's probably better than to just go on worrying, feeling that you may be wasting your life, and not doing *anything.*"

FOCUSING*

And if mind-power isn't enough to get you on track, you might want to engage your body—not for hard physical labor but deeper, at the sensory level—through a method called "Focusing." First, let's see how it works.

A problem-solving technique that relies on the body more than the mind.

FEELING THE PROBLEM

Fred's day began badly. The boss didn't like his plan for reorganizing the company's sales force, and the two of them got into a fight. The emotional residue settled in Fred's stomach and stayed there.

The knot was still there as he drove home from work. He tried lecturing himself. He went over the argument word by word, thinking of all the things he should have said. He tried pretending the problem didn't exist. He tried analyzing it. None of it worked. He decided to stop at a bar and have a few drinks, but the alcohol only dulled his pain.

Denying it, analyzing it drowning it in alcohol won't help.

Later, when the drinks had worn off, he decided to try focusing, a psychological self-help method he had learned from a psychologist a few weeks earlier. Here is Fred's account of what happened:

I made myself shut up inside, turned off all the lecturing and intellectualizing and other noises that had been thundering in my skull. I let my attention go down, not just to the argument, but to all my concerns about my job and my future and what I was going to do with my life.

Turn off the intellectualizing and turn in to your innermost feelings.

I asked myself what was the worst of it? Where did it hurt the most? What was the quality of the feeling?

The answer came at once—it was the feeling of something being out of place, the kind of feeling you might get from seeing a picture hanging crooked on the wall or a book placed upside-down in a bookcase, the feeling that something was not quite right.

I waited for words to describe the feeling and got "out of place" and "off." They were close, but not quite right.

What one word best describes that feeling?

*Reprinted with permission by the publisher from "Focusing" by Mary Howell, M.D., Ph.D., and Tom Ferguson, M.D., in *Medical Self-Care,* Summer 1983, pp. 57-59.

Then I got it: inappropriate. *That was my word. The tight place in my stomach started to come loose.*

I understood why I'd been so upset that my plan had been turned down: I'd been hoping it would be some kind of magic solution that would somehow make everything in my life all right. I'd had so much tied up in it I couldn't help but act stupid.

It won't solve your problem but it will give you insight.

Fred had not solved his problem by any means, but he had gained some real insight into what was going on, and had relieved a good deal of tension he had been experiencing. The insight led to a new degree of freedom in thinking about his work.

"SOMETHING THE CLIENT WAS DOING"

Attaining many goals of psychotherapy without professional help.

Focusing provides a way to be in closer contact with our inner states, a way to let go of patterns and habits that block our full experience of who and what we want, a way to release our full creative energies. Focusing is a tool we can use to attain many of the goals of psychotherapy without the need of professional supervision.

The focusing method grew out of the work of psychologist Eugene Gendlin [Ph.D., a professor of psychology at the University of Chicago and author of *Focusing* (Everest House)]. Dr. Gendlin started out looking at differences between people who did well in therapy and those who did not. He set out to discover which therapeutic skills worked the best, but what he found was something very different indeed.

Success in therapy depended on something the client was doing.

He expected that success or failure would depend on the techniques used by the therapist. He found just the opposite—the success of therapy depended on *something the client was doing.* Successful clients exhibited a different approach to their problems during the very first therapy session: *They spoke of what was happening in terms of physical feelings.*

The successful clients had learned to *sit* with a problem, not rushing to label or analyze it, but allowing themselves to become aware of it as a total *felt-sense,* a unique bodily experience. Dr. Gendlin called this skill *focusing.* He concluded that the most important thing a therapist could do was to encourage the client to go through the focusing process. Once he had uncovered and described this process, Dr. Gendlin worked out a method for teaching people to use it.

THINK OF A PERSON

Here's an exercise to give you a feeling of what this body-based *felt-sense* is like: First, pick two people who are very much involved with your life. Say the first person's name to yourself, and allow yourself to experience "everything about" that person. Close your eyes and allow a felt-sense of the person to arise. Now do the same thing for the second person. Unless you have chosen two very similar people, you will notice that the "felt-sense" of the first is entirely different from that of the second.

This felt-sense is more than just an assemblage of data or memories. It doesn't come to you in words or thoughts or other separate units, but as a complex (and sometimes puzzling) bodily feeling, an unfamiliar but unmistakable gut-level sensation. In thinking of Alice you don't think, "Oh, yes, Alice: She's 5'4", has red hair, has a birthmark on her right forearm, works as a hospital nurse, puts up her own pickles, drives a 1979 Toyota, likes country music, has two children, ages 11 and 8, and has a mad crush on Paul Newman." Instead a sense of "all about Alice" comes to you all at once.

A felt-sense is not an emotion, though it may have emotional undertones. It is bigger and more complex than any emotion—and much more difficult to describe. In Dr. Gendlin's words:

The body is a biological computer, generating enormous collections of data and delivering them instantaneously. Your thinking isn't capable of holding all these items of knowledge you know about your friend and your relationship to her. . . . Your body, however, delivers "all about your friend" in one great, rich, complex experience of recognition, one felt-sense.

HOW TO USE FOCUSING

Prepare for a focusing session by making yourself comfortable and eliminating all possible outside intrusions.

Experience "everything about" someone you know.

The "felt-sense" is more than an assemblage of data. It's a gut-level sensation.

The body is a biological computer delivering enormous collections of information in one rich experience.

You need to be able to give your total attention to the focusing process.

For teaching purposes, Dr. Gendlin breaks the act of focusing into six parts:

Establish the atmosphere of a "friendly hearing."

1. Clear a Space. Begin by pushing all your problems to one side, creating a space where you can sit and be comfortable without being overwhelmed by them. Establish the atmosphere of a *friendly hearing*—you are going to listen to your body in a way you may never have listened before.

Let your awareness go to what you're feeling within you body—inside your chest, stomach, and abdomen. What do you feel there when you ask yourself, "How's my life going? What's the main thing for me right now? What's going on that's keeping me from feeling wonderful?"

If something isn't right, you'll get a distinct body-sense.

Or you might try saying, "Everything is perfectly all right. There is no problem whatsoever. What's happening doesn't bother me at all." Then pay close attention. If something is *not* right, you would get a distinct body-sense.

When a body-sense comes up, examine it, but don't let it overwhelm you. Put it to one side and ask yourself what *else* is going on. You will usually be aware of several responses.

Become fully aware of your sense of the problem.

2. The Felt-Sense. From those responses, choose the problem that seems most pressing: Let one worry or concern push itself into the foreground. Again, do not go inside it, do not let yourself be swept away by it, simply stand back from it and be fully aware of your sense of the problem as a whole. Where in your body do you feel it, and how does it feel? The problem may still be fairly unclear, but you should feel a distinct feeling-sense of your primary concern.

3. A Handle for the Problem. Now let a word, an image, or a phrase rise up out of the problem itself. It might be a word like *sticky, tight, scary, jealous, heavy, uneasy*. It might be a phrase like *pushing too hard, just fine, out of luck, messing up again,* or *not letting myself win*. It may be an image, a sound, a strain of music, or the words of a song. Don't hurry things. Take all the time you need for the right handle to come up.

4. Resonating. Now take the word or image you've come up with and check it against the felt-sense of your present situation. If they fit, you should experience a deep feeling of release. If it's not quite right, wait again for a more precise word or image to come up from the feeling. When you get a good match, stay with it for a few moments to let your body get all the release it wants from the satisfying feeling of having found the right handle.

Finding the right word to describe that felt-sense should release you from the feeling.

5. Asking. By this stage you may already have experienced a noticeable feeling of bodily release, perhaps even one that has significantly changed your sense of the situation. If so, go on to stage six. If not, use your handle to take you back to the felt-sense, and ask what makes it the way it is. If, for example, your handle is *wary,* ask yourself, "What is there about this situation that makes me so wary?"

What is it about this situation that makes you feel this way?

You may at first find your mind full of quick answers that spark no special bodily response. Let them go by—these are what Dr. Gendlin calls "merely mental" answers, your mind rushing in with quick, superficial responses that leave no space for you to contact your felt-sense directly.

Reestablish your inner wordless space, reconnect with the felt-sense, and ask again. When you get an authentic answer, you will feel the felt-sense stir, and from that stirring an answer will emerge. Two additional questions it sometimes helps to ask at this stage are, "What is the worst thing about this?" and "What would it take to make it OK?"

6. Receiving. You need not necessarily believe, agree with, or act on the message you've received. Just sit with it and let it develop. Immerse yourself in the message as you might soak yourself in a tub of hot water. Resist the temptation to criticize or dismiss the answer. Let the questions wait. You are not committing yourself to anything. You may receive a subsequent message that takes you in a very different direction, but at this stage it is important to protect the shift that just came from negative voices. As Dr. Gendlin says, "They may be right, but they have to wait. Don't let them dump a truckload of cement on this new green shoot that just came up."

Immerse yourself in the message as you might soak in a tub of water.

Finally, decide whether you want to continue the focusing process by returning to steps one and two, or bring this session of focusing to a close. . . .

Keep in mind that although at times focusing can produce seemingly miraculous results, it does not always go smoothly. Dr. Gendlin's book, experienced focusers, and focusing teachers can offer tips on getting past stuck places. (One favorite technique is to turn your attention to the stuckness, and ask, "What is *that* like?").

There is a great need, in our fragmented civilization, for methods to put mind and body back together and encourage intuition, creativity, and immediacy. Focusing is a tool that is holistic in the best sense of the word. As Dr. Gendlin says, "A felt-sense is body *and* mind before they are split apart."

"A felt-sense is body and mind before they are split apart."

How to Say What You Really Mean

If you've ever backed down unassertively from someone who mistreated you or lashed out uncontrollably against someone who meant you no harm, you know: Talk isn't cheap. The price you pay for not saying what you mean or saying something you *didn't* mean can be dear indeed: guilt, anger, loss of self esteem. And that doesn't include the hurt feelings and other emotional "claims" of the guy who falls casualty to your unruly tongue.

Linda Adams understands all about that. As director of the program Effectiveness Training for Women at Effectiveness Training, Inc., in Solano Beach, California, she sees the results of inappropriately expressed emotions every day.

The results of inappropriately expressed emotions.

"Women enroll in our program because they are afraid to speak up for their needs at all," Adams reports. "But you can tell something is gnawing away at them. They frequently complain of headaches or of feeling depressed, bored, or anxious. Sometimes they ridicule others or make sarcastic remarks.

"The other type of person who comes to us is the one who is *too* aggressive. She has the opposite problem. Her needs are expressed, all right, but they come out in angry, accusatory, judgmental bursts.

"Stating what they want too strongly, by screaming and being pushy, puts people off," Adams says. "They stop listening and you wind up with one-way communication—which is as good as no communication.

Screaming puts people off. They stop listening.

"The courage and ability to translate feelings, thoughts, and needs into language so others can know you, and you can know yourself, is a powerful, exciting way of communicating," Adams continues. "Unfortunately, clear and honest communication with others is unusual for most of us. Women, in particular, have been taught to be coy, subtle, and vague.

How to state your wishes in a nonhostile way.

"Our program shows women that it's OK to have their own needs met, too. Then we teach them how to state their wishes in a nonhostile way."

Of course, learning how to say what you really mean isn't just for women. It's for everyone.

FIRST, TRY LISTENING

Fortunately, the experts pretty much agree on how to go about improving your communication skills. Oddly enough, they begin with listening.

"The biggest mistake you can make in trying to talk convincingly is to put your highest priority on expressing your ideas and feelings," says David D. Burns, M.D., associate professor of psychiatry at the University of Pennsylvania School of Medicine in Philadelphia.

Express your understanding of the other person's point of view.

"What most people really want is to be *listened* to, *respected,* and *understood.* The moment people see that they are being understood, they become more motivated to understand *your* point of view. That's half the battle won, right there," says Dr. Burns, who is the author of *Feeling Good: The New Mood Therapy* (New American Library).

"Once you have correctly summarized the other person's *thinking,* acknowledge the *feelings* he might have," advises Dr. Burns. "Ask questions to be sure you haven't misread his emotions."

Try to find a grain of truth in what the other person is saying.

Of course, your natural impulse all the while may very well be to lash out and try to prove how wrong your opponent is. "Resist," says Dr. Burns, "with all your might. Instead find some grain of truth in what he or she is saying and agree with that. Yes, it's difficult to do but it's worthwhile, especially when you feel attacked. That's because when you agree with what the other person is saying and feeling, you paradoxically take the wind out of his sails, and you end up the winner. He'll usually feel like a winner, too, and will then be much more open to your point of view."

Here's an example of how it works: Your boss says,

"This proposal stinks. Did you write it while you were daydreaming?" Actually you put a great deal of time and effort into the proposal and you feel it contains a lot of good points. You'd like to strangle him. In spite of this, you can disarm him by responding, "It sounds like I really missed the boat on the proposal. Would you tell me what there is about it that you don't like?" Your response will calm him and he'll communicate in a more tactful manner.

Disarm an outraged person by responding in a calm, tactful manner.

But what happens when it's finally your turn to do the talking? Well, if you've been listening, you should be in a good position to state your side of the issue.

INFORMING WITHOUT HURTING

The object is to make your point without being accusatory, threatening, or judgmental—without hurting the other person's feelings or putting them down.

First of all, don't overlook your partner's good points. They're there. Nobody wants to hear continuously what's wrong with them.

"Compliments especially work wonders in the heat of battle," adds Dr. Burns. "Expressing a positive regard for someone during a conflict makes it much easier for that person to open up to your ideas. They automatically feel less threatened and less defensive."

Compliments actually work wonders in the heat of an argument.

You can soften the blow even more by delivering your thoughts in the form of I-messages instead of you-messages, says Linda Adams. Apparently this technique is practiced frequently among those skilled in the art of communication. And with good reason—it works. Here's an example:

Instead of saying, "You *never* take me to dinner on our anniversary," better to say: "I'd really enjoy celebrating our anniversary at a restaurant this year instead of having dinner at home."

"By switching from the accusatory *you* to the non-threatening *I*, you raise the chances that your partner (or whoever) will hear you without becoming defensive and combative," Dr. Burns explains.

Switch from an accusatory *you* to a nonthreatening *I*.

"You-messages (regardless of how they're intended) come through as aggressive and accusatory," says Linda Adams, "because they say, in effect: 'It's your fault' or 'You're to blame!' They risk damaging a relationship by diminishing the other's self-esteem and by producing feelings of guilt."

Once you turn off the other person, he or she will fail to hear what you're saying—no matter how effectively you think you're coming across.

"Sometimes it helps to make a written dialogue when you're not getting your point across," suggests Dr. Burns. "Describe the whole interaction on paper and then show it to a friend. It could be that your blind spot is just the thing he's good at. Or ask someone skilled in communication for advice on handling the situation."

Sometimes a written dialogue can help you handle the situation.

BODY SIGNALS: THE SILENT LANGUAGE

Of course, words are not the only tools for communicating our needs to others. Yawning, sending penetrating looks, nudging, and checking the watch—all of those acts are examples of nonverbal communication, a silent language that often speaks louder than words. Even when we aren't consciously sending, the message is often "written all over our faces." Sometimes we can't help it; we fidget, blush, laugh, or get goose bumps—silent signals come pouring forth all the time.

Nonverbal statements can clue us in to unconscious feelings.

It's very possible, psychologists say, that we can learn a lot about ourselves and the people around us if we become more sensitive to such nonverbal statements. They can clue us in to unconscious feelings, they can help us nip problems in the bud, and they can help prevent us from getting our "signals crossed" with our fellow men and women.

In *The Silent Language* (Anchor Books), anthropologist Edward T. Hall, Ph.D., describes how a simple gesture can make a strong nonverbal statement: "When a husband comes home from the office, takes off his hat, hangs up his coat, and says 'hi' to his wife, the way in which he says 'hi,' reinforced by the manner in which he shed his overcoat, summarizes his feelings about the way things went at the office. If his wife wants the details, she may have to listen for a while, yet she grasps in an instant the significant message for her; namely, what kind of evening they are going to spend and how she is going to cope with it."

Hugging, kissing, and facial expressions are spouse-to-spouse signals.

Hugging, kissing, and emotionally charged facial expressions are other spouse-to-spouse signals. A knowledge of them might help you prevent family quarrels. In a similar way, awareness of the expression on your face might alert you that you're having the same old disagreement with your spouse.

Tuning in to our own facial expressions might help us understand our emotions better. One California psychologist, Paul Ekman, Ph.D., has made a specialty of teaching himself and others to sense the expressions on their faces. He proposes, for instance, that a tightening and narrowing of the lips is a sign of anger. "When my lips tighten," he says, "I know immediately that something's making me angry."

Sometimes you can learn a lot from your own hands, says Randall Harrison, Ph.D., of the University of California in San Francisco. For example, you might be talking to a friend about yourself, your spouse, and your children. As you speak, you may be making a short chopping motion with your hand, which Dr. Harrison calls a "baton." If you insert the baton between the words "I" and "my husband," Dr. Harrison says, you may be revealing an emotional barrier between you. In the same way, you might indicate a barrier between yourself and your children, or between your husband and your children, and so on.

Sometimes you can learn a lot from your own hands.

You may also find yourself fidgeting. Finding out when you fidget can show what makes you—unconsciously—anxious. In one case, according to Dr. Harrison, a young husband was talking about his apparently unexplainable anxiety. He spoke at length about his love for his wife and his happiness with her, but every time he mentioned her he nervously pulled his wedding ring on and off. Further talks uncovered repressed conflicts in the marriage, which were later resolved.

TALKING IN YOUR SLEEP

The way you sleep also tells your spouse something about your feelings. In fact, recognizing changes in sleep behavior might help you nip marital problems in the bud. Samuel Dunkell, M.D., in his book *Sleep Positions: The Night Language of the Body* (Signet), says that, "Even in sleep we use our bodies to communicate with or express our feelings about our partners."

Changes in sleep behavior can be early signs of marital problems.

If you sleep in positions that Dr. Dunkell calls the "spoon" and the "hug," then you may be expressing your love to the fullest. In the spoon, the man and woman lie on their sides, facing in the same direction and "nestling against

How you sleep may reflect how you act.

one another like two spoons in a drawer." In the hug, the sleepers lie on their sides, facing and embracing each other.

On the other hand, Dr. Dunkell proposes, if you sleep with your arms spread wide dominating the bed, you might be saying that you want to dominate the marriage. And if you sleep on your back you might be telling your spouse—unintentionally—that you feel superior.

"Couples who have been together for some time can make use of their knowledge of sleep positions to keep their fingers on the pulse of their emotional union," Dr. Dunkell writes. "Changes in the sleep position of a partner can . . . indicate what is currently happening in the partner's life. . . . Being aware of the significance of such changes can sometimes make it possible for a couple to focus and deal with a conflict before it becomes too disruptive."

If you're physically attractive, people often assume you're outstanding in other ways.

Your appearance and personal grooming also have a big impact, whether or not you are aware of it, on the judgments that some people may make of you (and *their* appearance might partly color your opinion of them). According to studies at the University of Minnesota, if you are considered physically attractive, many people will jump to the conclusion that you are outstanding in other ways. In one survey, attractive people were rated more warm, poised, sensitive, kind, sincere, and more likely to succeed in marriage or career than others. Asked to predict the personalities of people depicted in head-and-shoulder photographs, students in another study assumed that the attractive people were more interesting, strong, modest, outgoing, exciting, and responsive.

WHAT CLOTHES TELL US

Clothes communicate in a universal tongue.

The clothes you wear, of course, tell people a lot about you. In her book *The Language of Clothes* (Random House), author Alison Lurie tells it like this: "Long before I am near enough to talk to you on the street, in a meeting, or at a party, you announce your sex, age, and class to me through what you are wearing—and very possibly give me important information (or misinformation) as to your occupation, origin, personality, opinions, tastes, sexual desires, and current mood. . . . By the time we meet and converse, we have already spoken to each other in an older and more universal tongue."

Sometimes our clothes reveal more than we suspect. Lurie, a professor at Cornell University, says that when we wear the popular "layered" look, the color and style of the inner layer may tell people what's *really* going on inside us. For instance, a woman who wears a frilly pink blouse under a sensible gray suit announces that under her businesslike exterior lives a lively, feminine spirit. Conversely, the woman who wears a curvey silk suit over a mouse-gray sweater might be telling us that on that day she may look charming but underneath she is preoccupied or depressed. Among men, an architect wearing a tan cord suit, but a business shirt and tie underneath, is reassuring his clients "that their buildings will not run over the cost estimate or fall down."

Clothes, says Dr. Randall Harrison, start by being merely functional, but later we use them to make statements about ourselves. Sometimes clothes become what he calls "tie-signs," or signs of loyalty and allegiance.

Whether we know it or not, we use clothes as statements about ourselves.

High schoolers tend to wear the school colors after their team wins a big game, and couples often wear matching jackets or sweaters or rings as tie-signs.

One cautionary note on the use of nonverbal language: It can be very ambiguous. Even if you express yourself accurately, the person on the receiving end still might misunderstand you. Studies have shown that the other person's mood and prejudices can distort the signals you send. In one study, people were asked to listen to a man reciting the alphabet and to identify the emotion expressed in his tone. One listener felt it to be sad, another thought it sounded fearful, and a third called it loving.

Ultimately, by becoming fluent in nonverbal language and using it more, you may be helping yourself physically as well as socially. One psychologist at the University of Connecticut has found that people who consistently express themselves visually—by being animated or direct or by responding to happy or sad events with appropriate facial expressions—are apparently under less physiological tension than other people, and may put their bodies under less stress over the course of their entire lifetimes.

55

The Psychology of Successful Weight Loss

Imagine your life without the pressure of dieting.

I f you have friends who diet all the time but never get slim, ask them how they imagine their lives might be when the years of salads and cravings and premeasured meals are finally over and they attain a stable, comfortable, close-to-ideal weight.

Chances are they will tell you that on such a day their lives will become totally positive. They will be able to wear designer swim wear and tapered shirts. They will be their own best friends. In short, life will be as it should be.

But current wisdom on weight loss—as it applies to those who tend to overeat—is that people are more successful at shedding weight and keeping it shed if they start thinking positively about themselves right now, while the pounds are still in place.

Start positive thinking now, while the pounds are still in place.

Easier said than done, of course. But many psychologists say (and psychology now plays a major role in the weight-loss world) that effective weight loss is easier when people banish negative thought patterns from their minds and replace them with positive ones. Kelly Brownell, Ph.D., of the University of Pennsylvania's Obesity Research Clinic, has studied these negative thoughts. He divides them into four categories.

"Light bulb thinking": You're either "on" or "off" a diet.

The first category he calls "Dichotomous Thinking." "Overweight people," Dr. Brownell says, "tend to split their lives into two separate compartments. They are either 'on' or 'off' their diets—never in between. We also call this 'light-bulb thinking' because a light bulb is either on or off.

"For instance," he continues, "I asked one of the women

at the clinic how her diet was going. She said it was terrible. It turned out the last week she stayed on her 1200-calorie-a-day diet for six days out of seven. But all she could think about was that she had gone 'off' the diet once. She didn't think positively about the six days she was on it."

He calls the second category of negative thinking "The Impossible Dream." Dieters apparently set unrealistic goals for themselves and then feel guilty about not reaching them. "One woman told me that she was going to lose 50 pounds in time for her daughter's wedding," Dr. Brownell said. "The wedding was only a month away and she obviously couldn't have done it. She may actually have lost 20 pounds, but she would still feel as if she failed."

"The Impossible Dream": setting unrealistic goals.

"The Awful Imperative" is the third category. Dieters, it seems, establish strict rules for themselves which, because of normal human nature, they will inevitably break. "They tell themselves, 'I will *never* eat chocolate cake again,' or 'I will *never* stop for fries and a milkshake on the way home,' or 'I will *never* buy a doughnut when the cart comes around at the office,' " Dr. Brownell says. "And when they fail, they can't forgive themselves."

Then there's number four: "Dead-End Thinking." It's based on envy. Overweight people fall into it when they focus on the unchangeable fact that some people seem to "eat like horses and still look like models." This form of thinking goes nowhere.

"Dead-End Thinking": dwelling on what you think you can't have.

Why establish these four categories? To provide dieters with mental first-aid, Dr. Brownell says. Whenever they feel anxious or guilty, they can stop and ask themselves whether their racing thoughts belong in one of the categories. Thoughts that do fit one of the four descriptions can be dismissed as irrational.

THINK THIN

Sometimes, however, positive thought patterns aren't enough—it takes positive imagery to reinforce them and make them more effective. Hypertensives lower their blood pressure with thoughts of Hawaii and cancer patients envision their white blood cells destroying tumor cells. In a similar way, overweight people can, to some extent, get thin by thinking thin.

Reinforce your positive thinking with positive imagery.

"We ask them to imagine themselves lighter," says

First, build confidence. Then, lose the weight.

psychologist Peter Miller, Ph.D., founder of the Sea Pines Behavioral Institute, a weight loss spa at Hilton Head, South Carolina. He believes that building confidence and self-esteem is more important, at first, than losing pounds.

"Instead of asking them to pretend that they are already at their ideal weight—that could be discouraging—we tell them to imagine that they are about 20 pounds lighter. Then we tell them to close their eyes and see themselves standing in front of a mirror with a bathing suit on, looking the way they'd like to look," Dr. Miller says.

Visualize yourself shopping for flattering clothes. How does it feel?

"Then we ask them to imagine how it would feel to be shopping for flattering clothes, or to be working in an office, or to be in certain family situations. It's important for them to visualize themselves behaving differently rather than just appearing different."

Images as mental tools are also important to Suki Rappaport, Ph.D., director of the Transformations Institute in Mill Valley, California. She believes that people with a positive attitude can make over their lives against great odds. To help her overweight clients she has created two images. For lack of formal names, call one "the nourishment pie" and the other, "the human tape deck."

Is food your only source of physical and emotional nourishment?

If you're serious about controlling your weight, she says, draw a circle and prepare to divide it up as if it were a pie. Pretend that it represents all of the various ways in which you can give yourself physical or emotional nourishment. If you are someone who can't lose weight, that pie may, at the moment, be filled with nothing but food.

Dr. Rappaport asks her clients to identify every potential source of nourishment and tells them to give each one a proportionate slice of the pie. If they like swimming, they should give swimming a slice that reflects its importance to them. If they like films, theatergoing should get a slice. Using this image, Dr. Rappaport shows people, in a very positive way, that food isn't their only source of pleasure.

Is bingeing your response to life?

She also asks her clients to imagine that their bodies are cassette tape recorders and that each of their customary ways of responding to the world is represented by a different tape. She says that overweight people too often reach for the "binge" tape when they become anxious. Ideally, in her opinion, overweight people should get rid of their eating tape and come up with a tape that is more constructive.

"We try to say 'yes' to positive, life-affirming things,

rather than 'no, no, no' to negative things," Dr. Rappaport says. "Then people realize, 'I could have gotten a great massage with the time and money I spent eating.' This approach gives people new options."

CLOTHES MAKE THE PERSON

Clothing, interestingly, can have symbolic value for someone who is trying to lose weight. Max Rosenbaum, Ph.D., a New York psychologist, has found that men and women who have been losing and gaining for many years often accumulate a closet full of clothes of many different sizes. A man may have shirts with necks of 15, 16, and 17 inches, and a woman might have dresses from size 7 to 13 and from "junior" to "misses."

Clothing can have symbolic value for someone trying to lose weight.

"One woman we know spent her adolescence swinging back and forth, gaining weight and losing it," says Dr. Rosenbaum, who runs an obesity treatment program at the American Short-Term Therapy Center in New York, which he and a colleague founded. "As a result, she never gained a clear image of herself. Her closet was full of clothes of different sizes, depending on her measurements at the moment, and these clothes prevented her from gaining a stable self-image. 'If I am fat today and skinny tomorrow,' she would think, 'then who am I? Which is the real me?' "

Dr. Peter Miller's patients have run into the same sort of problem. He deals with it this way. "We tell people to throw away their bigger sizes," he says. "They've got to cut down to one size of clothes. We say, if they intend to keep their weight down, why keep those clothes? We know that as long as those clothes are in the closet, they will have doubts about their ability to change, and they'll be more likely to slip." In this way, clothes change from being a negative incentive into a positive incentive.

Yet another way to develop a positive self-image is simply to start reaching out to other people. "I tell my overweight women patients to start saying nice things to their husbands and children and start thinking positively about their friends," says Aileen B. Ludington, M.D., of Los Angeles, who once battled a weight problem of her own. "People find that if they can make other people happy, then their own self-image improves. I ask them to make a list of the things they like about their spouses and children.

If you can make others happy, your own self-image improves.

If you write things down, it's easier to visualize a problem. And it works for them. They come back with stories about how much their families are responding to them."

FAT INSULATES THE PSYCHE

Within the field of psychotherapy, there is an approach to solving weight problems significantly different from the ones mentioned so far. Many psychiatrists, for example, believe that overeating is self-destructive behavior and they treat it as a symptom of self-hate. Overeaters use food to comfort themselves when they are unhappy, the theory goes. They do so because it is less painful to raid the refrigerator than to unearth the emotional roots of their unhappiness.

"Food is a basic form of oral gratification, an immature method of finding security. And when people are agitated, eating helps them feel better," says Dr. Rosenbaum. "People use their weight as a defense against upsetting problems. Their fat acts as insulation against hurt."

"Staying fat can become very comfortable. The idea of losing weight and actually becoming thin would present a whole new set of problems," says Mildred Klingman, a New York psychotherapist and author of the book *The Secret Lives of Fat People* (Houghton-Mifflin).

"People who are overweight are very sensitive people," adds Dr. Rappaport. "They can sense dishonesty, and when they do, they retreat into a system that they have control over. They can control the size of their bodies. And their fat gives them a buffer zone."

Overweight young women often have mothers who habitually criticize their appearance, psychiatrists say. In many cases, the same mother once urged her daughter to "eat, eat, eat" for good health. This situation makes the girl angry with herself and with her mother. Overeating supplies an outlet for the anger.

"One young woman we know got even with her mother by overeating," says Milton Berger, M.D., who co-founded the American Short-Term Therapy center with Dr. Rosenbaum. "She knew how upset her mother would get. There's a certain satisfaction to that, a vindictive satisfaction in triumphing over others. At the same time she is really only hurting herself."

Dr. Kelly Brownell takes issue with the emphasis of this approach. He believes that some professionals err in suggesting that the majority of overweight people have emotional problems and that they need to resolve their repressed conflicts before they can solve their eating problems.

"Some professionals tell people that they are maladjusted," he says. "So many overweight people fall prey to the idea that they hate themselves and that they are stuck in an immature stage of development. This is counterproductive."

Hating yourself is counterproductive.

Which technique, then, works best: learning not to fall into one of Dr. Brownell's four negative thought patterns, or remembering not to plug a "binge" cassette into your metaphorical tape deck, or searching your childhood for the source of the problem? The answer can only be that different therapies work for different people. But it's clear that change can't take place until the overweight person upgrades his or her self-image.

Indeed, self-love is apparently the only way out. "Overweight people must learn to respect their bodies," Dr. Max Rosenbaum says. "That's very basic to successful weight loss. Overeating is closely related to poor self-concept. And when they begin to go through withdrawal, as all overweight people do, they have to say to themselves, 'I respect my body. I respect my body. I want to live.'"

The key to effective weight loss: Love yourself and love your body.

56

How to Become a Sports Whiz— By Using Your Head

Athletic success is more than physical skill and strength.

The experience of watching—or being—an underdog coming from behind against impossible odds to win, or of an inferior team suddenly finding some spark as they knock off a much better team, indicates that athletic success is more than physical skill and strength. What else does it take?

The Eastern Europeans asked the same question almost 20 years ago, and came up with some fascinating answers. They decided that superlative, repeatable, consistent performance contains two components—a physical one, to be sure, but just as importantly, a mental one. They started seriously investigating psychological training, and since that time, have routinely used a larger number of techniques with their athletes. To Eastern Europeans, psychological training is no gimmick; it is considered especially important in individual sports which require extreme levels of concentration, attention, motivation, and general psychological preparation. In these sports the proof is undeniable that psychological training has worked: The East Germans and Russians are now dominant in cycling, fencing, weight lifting, gymnastics, and pistol-shooting, for example.

The United States Olympic teams have just recently begun to apply psychological principles. You, too, can profit from some of these techniques whether you want to get the edge on an upcoming marathon or just improve your weekend tennis game. All it takes is a few minutes a day and the belief that psychological training can help you improve. Read on; here are some things you can start doing today.

ALTERNATE CONSCIOUSNESS TRAINING

We all operate during part of our day in a state of hyperconsciousness—basically describable as a logical, decision-oriented, rational, verbal mode—a state in which we force our minds to attend. Examples of this mode are studying, the careful, logical mental activity we experience during business meetings, and report writing. At other times, however, we relax a bit, shift modes, and operate in an altered state of consciousness. It occurs when we daydream, or when we are completely immersed in some pleasurable activity, or when we've driven a long way, and suddenly realize that many miles have gone by without our conscious awareness. In other words, our "automatic pilot" is in effect.

Part of our day is spent in a state of hyperconsciousness and part on "automatic pilot."

The difference in attentional modes makes intuitive sense, for although there's been a lot written about the difference between left and right brain activity, we don't have to be researchers to know that our consciousness operates on a very different level in different situations.

Certainly elite athletes know what altered consciousness feels like.

When bicyclist Ted Waterbury won his Junior National Road Championship, he remembers, "We were all there at the end. It could have been anybody. But I knew it was going to be me . . . when the sprint started I shifted into another kind of space, and suddenly I was flying." Whether the feeling is of being poised ten feet above your bike, looking down and watching yourself cruise along, or whether it's a feeling of your body and your bicycle being one unified machine, we all can make use of the mind's ability to shift states of consciousness.

Shift consciousness while bicycling; suddenly you're *flying*.

All this goes back to a well-established theory that most of what we are capable of is determined by part of our mind of which we can never be aware—the unconscious. W. Timothy Gallwey—well-known author of *The Inner Game of Tennis*, *The Inner Game of Golf*, and *The Inner Game of Running*—has a name for these different parts of our mind. He calls them Self 1 and Self 2.

Self 1 is the conscious, demanding, competitive, ordering, list-compiling self; Self 2 is the noncompetitive, reasonable, undemanding self. Self 1 insists that we finish

Self 1: competitive. Self 2: undemanding.

first every time, that we hit the ball a certain way and also creates tremendous anxiety when we don't; Self 2 only experiences what we do, just as we experienced the many ways of running or cycling we did so effortlessly when we were kids.

Gallwey points out forcefully that for superb performance, you have to be in touch with both parts. He has a saying: "Let it happen . . ." He means the same thing we've been saying, but we believe it takes more than just wanting to use both parts to be able to do it. So do the Eastern Europeans; so does the U.S. Olympic Committee.

Thus we're passing along some kinds of psychological training that have been found successful in working with athletes. These are relaxation techniques and mental rehearsal. Here's a short "how-to" for each.

RELAXATION TECHNIQUES

Muscle tenseness works against peak performance.

Gallwey's "let it happen" is another way of saying, "During physical performance, don't make it hard on yourself by carrying tense muscles." Tenseness in muscles works against peak performance. Tenseness wastes energy; tenseness causes anxiety. The best performances come when the mind and body are floating, enjoying the activity just as we did when we were young children, completely absorbed in the experience and unaware of any consequences of the actions. This is true relaxation. Each of us is capable of it since each of us, during some 24-hour period, experiences complete relaxation by giving in to sleep. But relaxation during exercise doesn't make one sleepy; on the contrary, it causes an exhilaration that is almost beyond description.

THE FIRST STEP: ALTERED STATE TRAINING

By now we hope you're convinced that altered states are nothing out of the ordinary, but are essential when you want to achieve important mental "workout" conditions; heightened awareness of inner processes; suspension of interest in outside events; increased concentration; an increase in the strength of any suggestion you might offer yourself during mental workouts.

Close your eyes and count back from 900.

Here's one easy way to do it that has been developed in training work with athletes; it takes only a few minutes. (Transcendental Meditation [TM], self-hypnosis, and progressive relaxation are other ways.) Find a private place, either lie down or sit in a comfortable chair, and pick out any object you can fixate on. Then, as you breathe normally and rhythmically, on each breath count down, out loud, starting at 900. As you do this, attend to your eyelids, which will begin to feel heavy. Resist closing them until you get down to 840. During the counting, let yourself enjoy the relaxed pleasurable feeling that rhythmic breathing brings about.

At 840 (or when they get too heavy to hold open), let your eyelids close, and stop counting. Remember, this is not work—don't force this part. Likewise, remember that you're in complete control—if you need to count to 800, that's okay, or if you need to interrupt the procedure, you can do so easily, then go back to it later.

Most importantly, enjoy the relaxed, pleasurable feeling that comes with the exercise. When this exercise is done with athletes, they often say, "When it was time to open my eyes, I went, 'No, not yet, can't I stay here just a little longer?'" Then it's clear the exercise is having a maximum effect.

Enjoy the feeling of deep relaxation.

When your eyelids close, you've blocked out about 95 percent of all external stimuli, and are in a state of heightened awareness and concentration, much as elite athletes are during peak performances. Now, with your eyelids closed, practice recalling some familiar object, such as your bicycle, running shoes or tennis racket. Use all your senses to re-create how it felt to use that object (ride it, wear them, or hold it in your hand) in your mind.

When you become good at this, then move to an image of one place that is, for you, private, relaxing, and safe. It may be your room or the mountains; it doesn't really matter so long as you can imagine it fairly vividly, using as many senses as possible. For the next few minutes, relax, then open your eyes. This basic relaxation exercise can be used any time you feel tense or anxious.

Visualize a mountain hideaway or private beachfront setting where you feel relaxed and safe.

THREE MORE EXERCISES

You're now ready to use some other skill-strengthening exercises. Here are three you can try and then invent your own variations. Once you have a goal in mind, the possibilities are endless. Let's take a sample goal here: the ability to bike ride a 25-mile trial in 60 minutes.

Visualize yourself performing your athletic pursuit—perfectly.

Identification: While in your altered state, create, then watch, a mental movie (in full Dolby sound and color) of someone you have seen ride effortlessly and gracefully. Perhaps you know a specific person well, perhaps you have seen a race or time trial and remember the impression you came away with. Perhaps you only have pictures in a magazine. It really makes no difference. You're doing something you've done many times, both as a child, consciously, and as an adult, daydreaming. You're calling up images—pictures, sounds, colors, smells, feelings—of how a performance looks when it's done perfectly, then putting yourself in place of the imaginary performer.

We all model performances based on an imaginary ideal anyway, so let this technique work for you.

Concentrated mental rehearsal is as important as actual practice.

Mental Rehearsal: Do you have a specific weakness in your sport that needs work? A bicyclist, for example, might have troubles with hill climbing, riding into the wind, riding through traffic, riding in large groups, sprinting, keeping a steady pace, cornering, or spinning. Once you relax yourself into an altered state, try this exercise. Put on a movie again, this time of yourself performing the skill as ideally as possible. Do this a number of times, say 10 or 15, until you can really "see" or "feel" yourself performing that skill. The secret here is that if you can't image it, you can't do it well. So practice mentally until your own moving image becomes crystal clear. You may have to flip your mental projector into "slow motion" to isolate a part of the skill, or even put it in reverse if you're making mistakes in your movie. Remember, research shows that concentrated mental rehearsal is as important as actual practice—so practice mentally and watch your improvement.

How does it feel to accomplish your goal?

Future Time Technique: Are you starting to get a feel for the power of these simple exercises? Here's a very effective technique used by the San Diego State University soccer team. It's based on the idea that to be successful, you have to feel successful.

Here's how this one goes: After altering your consciousness by counting backward, create a vivid image in your mind of some time in the future when you have accomplished the goal you have set.

Again, make a color movie, scripting in a location, conversation, movements, etc., which could actually occur after the skill is mastered. For the time trial example, your

BOX 40: HOW TO IMPROVE YOUR TENNIS WITHOUT EVEN TRYING: AN INNER TENNIS WORKSHOP WITH TIM GALLWEY

by Emrika Padus

When tennis pro and author of the best-seller *The Inner Game of Tennis* [Random House] Tim Gallwey stepped onto the Princeton University tennis courts to serve his notions of "yoga tennis," of "Self one vs. Self two," of "effortless effort," I took a step—backward. Having played tennis for a number of years and taken lessons from what I considered very competent instructors, I thought I knew what "good" tennis was all about. True, my form and win/loss record do not always reflect it. Nevertheless, I know the correct grip for each stroke. I am aware of proper body positioning. I understand court strategy. And I play to win. What more is there?

Unlike the tennis newcomer seated next to me whose long nods and wide eyes reflected a blind faith and unquestioning approval, I was a little less receptive to Gallwey's initial remarks: "Don't concern yourself with form. Don't concentrate on hitting the ball. Abandon those competitive thoughts." What was he telling us?

If we try less, we may win more? . . . Exactly!

During those introductory statements, Gallwey casually tossed tennis balls into our group. "I can't even catch a ball," one young woman squealed frantically as she grappled for the ball. Gallwey invited her out onto the court for a quick game of catch. Told to concentrate on catching the tennis ball, she put her whole body to task. With outstretched arms and open mouth, she charged every ball as if it were a fallen piece of fine china. She was all over the court even though the balls were tossed directly to her.

Then Gallwey introduced another point of concentration. "Count the number of times the seam of the tennis ball rotates as it comes toward you," he instructed. Apparently relieved that the ball-catching ordeal was over, she calmly but intently watched the seam of the ball. Oddly enough, during this seam-counting exercise, she caught the ball each time without the least bit of trouble. She had improved her ability to catch a ball without even trying. Even for a skeptic, the demonstration was convincing.

" 'I can't even catch a ball' leads to trying hard to catch it," explained Gallwey. "But no one 'tries' to sit down or 'tries' to turn on the lights." We carry out those activities almost unconsciously by relying on our kinetic sense. Gallwey suggests that we approach tennis in much the same way. It's only when we are convinced of the difficulty of a certain activity that we become preoccupied with it. The activity becomes a threat. We perceive the worst possible result and anticipate it by tightening our muscles.

For example, suppose you're convinced you've got a weak backhand and your opponent serves you a strong shot in that direction. Gallwey refers to this as the "Oh-Oh Experience," because you

(continued next page)

BOX 40 – *Continued*

immediately perceive that serve as a point lost. Your muscles grow increasingly tense as the ball crosses the net. Your arm takes the racket back in a tight, jerky motion, not a smooth, continuous movement. Consequently, you'll probably hit the ball off-center and miss whatever target you may have set.

As your worst fears are confirmed, your dissatisfaction with your backhand is reinforced. So, the next time a ball is directed toward your backhand, the threat will reappear in the form of that previous experience. It becomes a cycle of distorted images. Again your muscles grow tense. Again you miss.

And not only can this tension interfere with your accuracy but also your power. To prove this point, Gallwey mystified us with another demonstration. This time he chose a middle-aged gentleman who looked as though he could overpower Gallwey with little difficulty. Gallwey outstretched his right arm, clenched his fist and through gritted teeth challenged the gentleman to try to bend his tightened elbow. Within a few seconds the challenge was met.

Then, while Gallwey almost effortlessly held out his arm, he calmly asked the gentleman to test his strength once more. Judging from the first encounter, this hardly seemed like a formidable feat! But as the gentleman huffed and puffed and gritted his teeth, the obvious became less apparent. He eventually bent Gallwey's arm, but it took more strength and more time to do so. To assure us that this was not tennis trickery, Gallwey invited all of us out on the court to select a

partner and try this experiment for ourselves. I must admit, it did work.

The explanation made sense too. "When we 'try' to keep our arm straight we tighten every muscle—our arms, our hands, our cheeks, our other cheeks. That's wasted effort," said Gallwey. In addition, tensing the biceps helps to draw up the forearm, and "that's sabotage," he exclaimed. In tennis, "trying" hard will not only waste power, but lose it.

How do you train yourself to play with "effortless effort"? According to Gallwey, it's simply a matter of tuning out that little voice that keeps reminding you that your timing is off, that you didn't get the racket back fast enough, that your shot missed by a mile. By redirecting these outer attentions, you can relax and let your body's innate sense of motion take over and play for you.

Begin by practicing the "bounce-hit" exercise. Every time the ball touches the court (on either side of the net), say aloud "bounce." When the ball makes contact with a racket (either yours or your opponent's), say "hit." Your verbal description should occur at *precisely* the same moment that contact is made. Don't cheat by drawing out your words such as h-i-i-i-i-t. Then you surely can't miss. "It's got to be staccato," says Gallwey. "It's got to be precise." This takes concentration, which of course is the point of the exercise. Concentrating on bounce-hit will divert your attention from the game itself. It will give your little voice something else to talk about other than the quality of your strokes. If you come out of this state of concentration

BOX 40—*Continued*

long enough, you'll immediately realize how smooth and fluid your strokes have become.

Another way to relax on the court is by concentrating on the ball's movements through space. If you're a modern art lover, envision the ball's course as a paint brush creating undulating shapes on a canvas of air. If geometry is your thing, make note of the intersecting lines and planes created by the ball's flight and the top of the net. Be creative.

Part two of Gallwey's approach involves body awareness. "Raise your arm," he commands. "Now experience your arm rising—it's different, isn't it?" In tennis, becoming aware of an otherwise unconscious body movement can draw your attention away from the tennis problem you've been trying hard to correct. This will allow your body a chance to correct it for you. Hitting the ball too close to your body? Become aware of your arm holding the racket. How far back is it when your swing changes direction? Where is it when the ball crosses the net?

Got a pain in your shoulder or elbow when you serve? Concentrate on it. That's right, focus your attention on the discomfort and rate the degree of pain (on a scale of 1 to 10) each time you serve. Eventually your body should correct itself. It will alter your stance or grip or whatever it takes to alleviate the discomfort without conscious intervention.

Don't be frightened by your body's capabilities. You may be sacrificing awareness and conscious control, but you'll be increasing your net value!

For many people, "inner tennis" offers an effective method for improving their power, accuracy, and consistency on the court. For others, it interferes with their competitive urge and intrudes on their judgmental sense. As one lawyer commented to Gallwey after rejecting inner tennis—even though it had improved his serve three-fold—"*My* serve may not have the power. It may not have the accuracy. But at least I know what I'm doing!"

Which, unfortunately for his game, was true.

movie might be of the period an hour or so after the time trial, as you talk over the ride with a friend or spouse. How do you feel? What are you saying? What is the conversation like?

It's your personal movie, so make it as rewarding as possible for yourself. Imagine the club newsletter with the announcement of your time in it; imagine a friend calling you on the phone to congratulate you on your time. Really indulge yourself; imagine a letter arriving in the mail with the Presidential seal on it. You open it. It says, "The President of the United States would be honored by your presence at dinner to celebrate your outstanding achievement in the field of cycling . . . " Your boss finds out you're going to see the President and offers you a big promotion. That "special person" who never has enough time for you suddenly wants to see you every day . . .

Don't be afraid to push the limits of reality.

All thoughts are legal, so don't be afraid to really push the limits of reality if you want to—it's between you and your imagination.

As you do these exercises, keep in mind the few simple guidelines: Don't work at these; don't treat them like something you have to do; don't try to browbeat your conscious mind into accepting and meeting objectives it has a thousand logical reasons for not achieving.

Use the concept of altered state processing to get past your consciousness, into the part of your mind that knows no limits. Then spend a few minutes every day doing these exercises, or making up one of your own, and watch your performance improve. In addition to improved performance, you will also teach your body to recognize the relaxation response more readily; as you learn how it feels to use breathing to flood yourself with a relaxed, floating feeling, you can put this training to work in other stressful situations.

Calculated Risk Taking:
The Key to Exhilaration

A dozen rapidly wilting yellow roses, an expensive, creased tie and a half-empty bottle of champagne sat on the dining room table. Outside, on the porch, Earl cleared his throat dramatically.

"Suzie . . . ?" he began.

"Yes, Earl?" Suzie said, looking up into his eyes.

Then the terror seized Earl's vocal cords. She'd be nice about it, but she'd turn him down cold. Or she'd ask if she could think about it and *then* turn him down cold. Meanwhile, the word would get around: Earl proposed to Suzie and she turned him down! He felt himself sinking into his shoes. What was the use? She'd *never* say yes! Besides, bachelorhood wasn't so bad. He could make a better tuna casserole than she could anyway . . .

The terror of getting turned down.

Later that night, on his way home, Earl asked a maple tree to marry him.

To us, Earl's longing for a better life, his fear of rejection, his desire to be loved, and his humiliating retreat into the safe and familiar seem slightly humorous. But how many of us, out of plain fear, have failed to reach for something we longed for in just the same inglorious way? "Playing it safe" has its advantages. But the fear of taking risks, when risking is called for, can hold us back from life itself.

Not risking is the surest way of losing.

"Not risking is the surest way of losing," says California psychiatrist David Viscott, M.D., author of *Risking* (Simon & Schuster). "It eventually destroys your life. You never learn who you are, never test your potential, never

You never learn who you are, never test your potential.

stretch or reach. You become comfortable with fewer and fewer experiences. Your world shrinks and you become rigid. You become a victim."

Earl feared rejection, so he stepped back from the brink; others may fear being disappointed or embarrassed, losing money or love, losing control, getting hurt. There are even those who *invent* things to be afraid of in order to keep from risking.

Scary? Dangerous? Uncertain? Of course.

It's a timid, hesitant way to live—and ironically not without its risks. The greatest risk is that you will fail to grow at all. "If your life is ever going to get better, you must take risks," Dr. Viscott says. "There is simply no way to grow without taking chances." Scary? Dangerous? Uncertain? Of course. But in order to take a step forward, you have to leave someplace known and secure behind. In every risk there is some unavoidable loss. If that doesn't frighten you a little, Dr. Viscott says, "the risk is probably not worthy of you. . . . No risk worth taking can ever be completely secure."

DON'T BE A "RISK ADDICT"

Calculated risks: different from being rash.

General George S. Patton, the daring tank commander and military strategist of World War II, once advised a relative in a letter, "Take calculated risks. That is quite different from being rash."

The difference is a crucial one. In a "calculated risk," your potential gain is greater than your potential loss, and you stand a reasonable chance of coming out on the plus side. It's worth the try. A "rash" risk is not. But those who cannot distinguish between the two—or who are "addicted" to the death-defying risk, the foolish and unnecessary gamble— are as bad off as those whose fear paralyzes them completely.

Who are these "risk addicts"?

Accident-prone people: Who are they?

A U.S. Navy study of "accident-prone" pilots provides some intriguing clues. In an effort to identify personality traits common to 12 fliers who were killed in plane crashes caused by their own error, the Navy conducted interviews with family, friends, and peers of the dead men.

A composite profile based on the interviews, described in an article by Robert Alkov, Ph.D., of the U.S. Naval Safety Center in Norfolk, Virginia, revealed a man who was aggressive, impulsive, and immature, "an egocentric perfectionist with a high opinion of himself . . . resentful of authority . . . 'ladies' man' . . . drinks too much . . . feels he is above ordinary mortals and lives (and dies) by his own rules" (*Approach*, The Naval Aviation Safety Review). Ironically, Dr. Alkov observes, that's not a bad description of some of the Navy's very best pilots.

But the difference between those who lived and those who died was judgment. "The good naval aviator knows his capabilities and his limits. He knows his aircraft's capabilities, and he flies it to its limits—but not beyond." Triggered by setbacks in his personal life, an "accident-prone" flier dares beyond his abilities; bloated with false confidence, he miscalculates a risk. And he loses it all.

Know your capabilities and limitations.

ENRICHING, NOT ENDANGERING

You'll probably never find yourself sliding into the cockpit of an F-14 jet fighter, so that's not a risk worth worrying about. But knowing your own limits, and having the courage and good sense to take risks within those limits, can enrich your life without endangering it. As a matter of fact, a sensible, courageous attitude toward risk may even be good for your health.

Reasonable risks may be good for your health.

That conclusion is clearly suggested by the frequently cited research psychologists Suzanne Ouellette Kobasa, Ph.D., and Salvatore R. Maddi, Ph.D.

After examining the life stresses and physical health of hundreds of business executives, lawyers, and army officers, Drs. Kobasa and Maddi concluded that one reason some people are more stress resistant is that they are open to change. In other words, they maintain a positive view of life's unending risks.

"The whole concept is that in dealing with events in your life, you transform them into something more meaningful and worthwhile," Dr. Maddi says. "Constructive risk taking, you might say. Excessive risk taking is just the opposite: an avoidance of those things in your life. Taking up skydiving as a way of avoiding troubles at work, for example."

Constructive versus destructive risks: making the distinction.

In one study, Drs. Kobasa and Maddi collected information on 259 business executives at three different times over a period of two years. The doctors began by analyzing the men's personalities to determine their attitudes. To rate them on attitudes toward change, for example, the men were asked to what extent they agreed with statements like,

"Boredom is fatal," or "I would be willing to give up some financial security to be able to change from one job to another if something interesting came along." People who agreed strongly rated high on the hardiness scale; they understood the dangers of stagnation and weren't afraid of taking a chance to change things.

Then, over the two-year period, the executives were asked for information about their physical health, with each illness they mentioned given a numerical value. A cold, for example, rated 20 points; an ulcer, 500 points; a heart attack, 855 points.

The hardy group had an illness rating of 510, compared to 1,080 for their fainthearted counterparts.

At the end of the study period, the results were clear: The men whose attitudes were rated high in hardiness remained in much better health. In fact, despite high levels of stress in their personal and professional lives, the "hardy" group had an average illness rating of only 510 in two years, while their fainthearted counterparts averaged 1,080 during the same period.

Stress can be good— leading to real growth.

The stress itself doesn't make the difference, Dr. Maddi maintains. Your attitude toward it is what counts. In fact, he says, "stressful events can be a good thing for some people, leading to real growth." Of course, anybody accustomed to the rewards and uncertainties of risk could have told you that.

If a bold and bright-eyed approach to life can be good for your health, it stands to reason that the riskless rut, where nothing is ventured or gained, can be equally bad. And that seems to be precisely the case, according to a series of studies conducted at the University of Michigan's Institute for Social Research.

"BOREDOM IS FATAL"

Hard-driving executives feel the most stress, right? Wrong.

In one of the studies, 2,010 men in 23 different kinds of jobs were surveyed, in an effort to pinpoint key sources of occupational stress. The hard-driving professionals, strapped with long hours and heavy responsibilities, were under the greatest job-related stress . . . right? Wrong. Workers performing dull, unchallenging, repetitive jobs reported the greatest stress—and the greatest boredom, job dissatisfaction, and physical and emotional ill health. Family doctors, working an average of 55 hours a week, reported fewer physical complaints and emotional strain.

"One of the key factors in job satisfaction is self-utilization—the opportunity to fully utilize your abilities on the job, to be challenged, to develop yourself," John R. P. French, Jr., Ph.D., director of the study, explained in an interview. "Frustration and anxiety over *not* being challenged can have physically debilitating effects." Is all this beginning to sound familiar?

HOW TO RISK

OK, so you've decided to take these messages from science to heart. You've decided the rut is more dangerous than the risk, and you want to change. But how? Do you just take a wild leap and hope for the best?

The rut can be more dangerous than the risk.

Actually, Dr. David Viscott explains, any calculated risk can be compared to passing in an automobile, probably the most dangerous maneuver in driving. Whether the obstacle you're trying to get around is a car, another person, a social convention, or your own fear, "the act of passing symbolizes the moment of truth, leaving the position you've grown accustomed to, forging ahead, and confronting the unknown." Any risk, he says, can be thought of in three parts: preparing, committing, and completing.

First, you have to recognize your need to risk, and that's always threatening because you're forced to admit your present situation must change. Stuck behind an unpredictable or drunk driver, you may decide to pass because staying where you are is more dangerous than taking that risk. And, because the decision to risk means leaving something behind, "you've got to figure out what things you're going to lose, and accept that, so it doesn't become a negative force later on."

The decision to risk means leaving something behind.

Then you must think out a course of action, wait for the right moment to act and, if you're smart, come up with a "backup" plan, in case Plan One runs into trouble. What if he hits the gas? Shall I brake or accelerate?

Step two is putting your plan into action, committing to the risk. "Take your time getting ready, but when you go for it, don't let up until you're sure everything is in place," Dr. Viscott advises. The time is right. The road is clear. You step on the gas, pull out, and go. Once you've committed yourself, hesitation can be fatal.

Once you've committed yourself, hesitation can be fatal.

And finally, the third step, completion: You swing

back into your own lane, exhilarated and a little shaken, mission accomplished. Was it worth it? Sometimes you know immediately, sometimes you don't really know for years. But one thing's certain: No single risk is going to solve all your problems, and don't expect it to. Up ahead are other challenges, other risks, other glories.

Living victoriously, Dr. Viscott says, "requires a dedicated belief in a higher life—a higher life that is right here in this world, where your job is to give the best of yourself."

PART XI

Using Emotions to Heal

58

Beyond Physical Well-Being: The New Health Perspective

Naomi Remen, M.D., has high hopes for the future direction of medicine— and it has nothing to do with the artificial hearts and technological hardware that many of today's medical researchers dream of. The true medical frontier, she says, lies within the individual—you and me.

A Cornell-trained physician, former faculty member of Stanford Medical Center, and author of *The Human Patient* (Anchor Press/Doubleday), she presents a convincing case:

"Take a look at today's so-called medical breakthroughs. A man without a heart is hooked up to a machine the size of a filing cabinet. Doesn't that strike you as being crude?" she asks. "On the other hand, if we can, with our own consciousness, gain greater mastery over our bodies and mobilize our natural healing processes, then we've really achieved something. And, one day, when we've perfected this art, it will make taking a pill look like hitting an egg with a sledgehammer."

Not surprisingly, Dr. Remen believes the field of psychoneuroimmunology holds the most promise for our medical future. But, she says, it's going to take more than scientific data to drastically alter our course. What's also necessary is a change of perspective. Without that, we'll never fully realize the mind/body potential.

From her office in Sausalito, California, Dr. Remen elaborated on this new perspective—an alternative way of

The true medical frontier lies within.

Once we learn to consciously mobilize our healing process, taking pills will become obsolete.

Realizing the mind/body potential depends on a radical shift in perspective.

looking at health, illness, and healing that may revolutionize medical thought.

Question: Today's growing health consciousness places great emphasis on the body. The result has been very positive: people working out, eating healthier foods, etc. But by concentrating our effort on the physical, is it possible that we may be missing another—perhaps even more important—dimension of health?

Naomi Remen, M.D.: Yes, definitely. We tend to equate the body with the person. That's a mistake. We are as much our thoughts, feelings, and insights as we are our flesh and bones.

When we focus on the body, we begin to think of health as an end in itself. We spend all our time eating the right foods, taking the right vitamins, doing the right exercises. We become obsessed with our bodies and narrow our focus to physical goals. A most important question never gets asked: How can I use a healthy body to accomplish my life goals?

It's like having a car and spending all your time repairing and polishing it, but never driving it. At some point you have to stop and ask yourself: What's this car for? What is possible now that I have this car? Where can I go? What can I see? What can I learn?

The healthy body is a vehicle that takes us to a destination. Health is a means, not an end. It is something we can use to live in a meaningful, rich way.

THE HEALTHY LIFE

Question: Could you describe someone who, according to your definition, is living a healthy life?

Dr. Remen: It's interesting that you should ask that because, when I taught at Stanford, I used to pose the same question to my medical students. They would invariably respond with examples of people who met all the medical criteria for optimal physical function. Then I'd bring up the case of Tony Suditch.

Tony was totally paralyzed below the neck. He lived his life in an iron lung. His physical function was limited to talking and moving a finger. And yet, Tony led a life of meaning, purpose, achievement, and accomplishment. He was a psychologist who founded the Association of Trans-

We tend to think of the body as the person. It's not.

At some point you've got to ask yourself: How can a healthy body enrich life?

The healthiest people aren't necessarily the most physically fit.

personal Psychology and developed the prototype for the Journal of Transpersonal Psychology, which the association now publishes. His vision was instrumental in opening the doorway between psychology and consciousness studies.

Was this a healthy man? In my mind, yes.

In defining health, I ask whether people are using whatever physical capacity they have to accomplish their purpose and to live meaningfully. There are people who are very healthy physically who are not living what I would call a healthy life. For them, life has no value, direction, or purpose. There are also people who are quite ill who lead a very rich life in terms of those parameters. I would call them healthier than the people who simply have physical health and no reason to live.

Defining health in terms of quality of life.

Question: But isn't it true that some people are more susceptible to physical illness and less capable of recovering as a result of having lost that direction or purpose—the so-called will to live?

Dr. Remen: Perhaps. There are a great many people who are sick and have lost their life's purpose. But there are also many people who are sick and have found greater meaning in life—as a result of their illness.

Rediscovering meaning and purpose through illness.

Question: Are you suggesting that, in some cases, illness can be a positive experience?

Dr. Remen: Eventually it often has some positive outcomes. I think we can learn an invaluable lesson by looking at the way Eastern cultures view illness. To them, an illness is not necessarily a disaster or crisis, but rather a happening that can represent the beginning of a whole new way of seeing or experiencing life.

Illness isn't necessarily a disaster. It's a happening.

RESERVING JUDGMENT

In Eastern philosophy, an event is not judged to be good or bad. It is just an event. How it influences your life over time will determine whether it was a good or bad event. Something may strike you at the moment as very fortunate but, five years down the road, you may wish it never happened—look at what it led to! On the other hand, something may strike you at the moment as a total disaster, such as contracting a chronic illness or losing the function of some part of your anatomy, but, in the long run, you may find that the event somehow enriched your life. In

Physical losses can result in important gains—mentally, spiritually, emotionally.

other words, the body may be less but the total person may be more.

The point I'm trying to make is this: There's more to having an illness than returning to your pre-illness state. That's a low goal. Human nature moves forward with every experience—positive or negative. And something as important as a major illness can really catapult you ahead—mentally, spiritually, and emotionally.

Question: Can you explain the process by which an illness becomes a positive force in our life?

Dr. Remen: There's a line in a song: "You don't know what you've got til it's gone." Well, a lot of us seem to believe that we're going to live forever. We take our relationships for granted. We take for granted the fact that we're going to wake up tomorrow and not hurt. When illness strikes, it's like hitting a wall at 90 miles per hour. We're stopped cold. We put everything on hold for a period of time. And then, often spontaneously, we begin to recognize the value of things that we've long taken for granted.

The classic example is the high-powered business executive stricken with a heart attack. His values prior to his heart attack centered on achievement, productivity, visibility, power, and influence. Suddenly he finds himself lying in a hospital intensive care unit and realizes that there are some important things in life that he's been missing. He doesn't know his children very well. He can barely recall the last time he took a day off to go sailing or walk a nature trail.

People come out of an experience like this saying, "I don't want to work 80 hours a week anymore—there's more to life than this." There is often a spontaneous refocusing of their values.

I'll give you another example. When I first went into practice, I had a patient with uterine cancer. Fortunately, she recovered—but only after a long and frightening ordeal. In interviewing her at the end of her therapy, I asked if she'd learned anything from the experience. Her response was that she'd never go back to being the way she was before she got sick.

"I was 'crazy clean,' " she told me. "If my house wasn't perfect, I couldn't enjoy the beauty of it. If I'd see one dandelion in my yard, I couldn't appreciate all the other flowers. When I got so sick, I didn't have the energy to do that. And I realized I was driving my family crazy. Now

When illness strikes, it's like hitting a wall at 90 m.p.h.

The I.C.U.: a place to refocus our values.

"If I'd see one dandelion in my yard, I couldn't appreciate all the other flowers."

we have three new kittens and a lot of dirty, happy kids. There's more important things in life than keeping a kitchen floor clean."

A TIME FOR REFLECTION

It's too bad we have to get stopped. But it does offer us a "time-out" to reflect—something that's very rare in our society. Eastern society has a tendency to recognize the need for reflection, for periods of withdrawal, for periods of assessment.

Most of us are still living by the values that served us 20 years ago, and we haven't taken the time to update them. We haven't asked ourselves: Do we still have the same beliefs? Is this still worth living for? What's new that is important? Is there something that needs to be let go of? Yet an illness often forces us to do exactly that. It puts us in a room with a white wall and we lie there in bed and we just look at that wall. It's like a Western form of meditation.

It's like a Western form of meditation.

Question: Do you think if we'd take the time for reflection while we're healthy, we wouldn't need to get sick?

Dr. Remen: Isn't that the question! I think it would be tough to prove that connection. But to me it almost doesn't matter. As long as we're aware that when we're ill it is important to use that time in a constructive way so that, when we regain our physical health, we live at a higher level.

That potential—to be better *after* an illness than *before*—is not yet medically recognized. We're so focused on getting back to the way we were. We focus on preventing loss—no loss of function, no loss of economic stability, no loss of anything. While this is unquestionably important, we overlook the fact that sometimes, when something's lost, something bigger replaces it. The gentle art of learning to let go of things is what allows us to meet with the new—to meet with the future.

Sometimes when something is lost, something bigger replaces it.

Question: That sounds very rational. But, when we're faced with a serious illness, the fear of the unknown can give rise to some rather irrational emotions. We panic and worry, anticipating the worst possible outcome. How can we free ourselves from negativity so that we're open to the positive changes you've just mentioned?

Dr. Remen: By using the same energy that goes into

worrying and redirecting it into positive healing images. The process is called imagery.

Negative imagery is called worrying.

Interestingly, most people who come to me for the first time—many of them overwrought with worry—insist that they cannot imagine. The fact is, everyone imagines. It's one of the major ways we think. And when we conjure up negative images, it's called worrying.

To the body, imagination and reality are the same.

If I were to say to you, "You have a suspicious lump in your breast. We'll have to do a biopsy next Tuesday," you immediately start a train of negative images. And, of course, the body does not always differentiate between an image and a reality. So, as you begin to play out these negative images in your mind, your body reacts. Your heart pounds. Your breathing quickens. You literally work yourself into a sweat.

TAKING CONTROL OF YOUR IMAGINATION

The points I'd like to emphasize here are first of all, everybody imagines; secondly, freewheeling imagination is usually negative; and thirdly, taking control of your imagination can be constructive, positive, and very empowering.

Question: In what way can imagery be an empowering experience?

People come through an experience with greater self-respect and trust.

Dr. Remen: By taking yourself out of the victim role and recasting yourself as a survivor. Every victim is a survivor who doesn't know it yet. In the process of imaging, people often refocus their attention on their strengths rather than their weaknesses. They come through their experience with greater self-respect and trust.

I can't survive . . . it's unfair . . . why me?

Let me give you an example. I had a patient who has Crohn's disease—a very significant disease of the intestinal tract that frequently requires multiple surgeries. At the time the woman came to me, she was quite victimized and essentially housebound although she had the physical capacity to live a much fuller life. After a year of therapy she took a part-time job and began to engage more fully with her life. I didn't hear from her for two years. Then her husband called to ask if I could see her. Apparently her dentist had discovered a small abscess on her tooth that required minor surgery. Negative feelings suddenly well up inside her. She acted very much the victim, complaining bitterly: I can't survive it. It's unfair. After all I've been through, now this. Why me!? I can't do it.

So I led her through a very simple imagery exercise. I had her close her eyes and imagine that I was holding up a mirror to her. "What does this mirror look like?" I asked.

"It's round and it it has an oak rim," she answered.

"Fine," I said. "Now look into the mirror and you will see something that will help you deal with your problem."

Her medical history immediately began to pass before her and she began to describe it to me. She saw herself going through surgery after surgery and relapse after relapse—13 in all. With each surgery came more complications. She saw all the hope and the disappointment over and over again.

While she was doing this, my rational mind kept asking, "How is this going to help her? Isn't this going to make her even more the victim?"

FROM VICTIM TO SURVIVOR

Then as she got to 1972 and what was probably her ninth or tenth surgery, she suddenly opened her eyes and burst out laughing. "Are you kidding me?" she said. "I can do this tooth thing with one hand tied behind my back. Where is the telephone? I want to talk to that dentist."

I *can* do that.
I survived much worse.

Now, what accounts for this dramatic transformation? As she looked at the whole picture, she experienced the common thread that ran through the experience! Something she could trust. Her own courage and strength—and her ability to heal herself again and again. She was a survivor.

Hers is not a unique case. We all have a tendency to cast our strengths as weaknesses. Patients will tell me stories of their ordeals, totally oblivious to the strength and courage that's right there. When I ask how they managed to survive against the odds, they respond with such negative statements as, "I'm just plain stubborn," or "I'm such a fool, I never give up hope."

We all tend to think of our strengths as weaknesses.

That's where imagery can help. It redirects our attention away from our pain and toward our strengths. It lessens the fear and anxiety. That allows us to move forward as survivors.

Question: It's easy to see how imagery can help ease our anxieties. But can we also use imagery to consciously stimulate the healing process?

Any injury—no matter how small—immediately activates the healing process.

Dr. Remen: To answer that question I should first explain, as I do to all my patients, that healing is not something you have to make happen. It happens naturally without any intervention on your part. If I were to stick you with a pin right now you would start to heal immediately. Just by a little pin stick, your healing mechanism becomes activated. That affords a new perspective on injury or illness—people who are in a healing state are healing more intensely than the rest of us.

PATIENCE, PLEASE

You can't force a bud to bloom by hitting it with a hammer.

The trouble is, we're too impatient. Healing is slow and certain in the same way a bud opens into a flower. You can't force a bud to bloom by hitting it with a hammer. Yet, we have a tendency to hit our diseases with hammers. This is an instant culture. We expect instant results. So, when we don't see noticeable signs of improvement—and very often we can't because healing takes place so slowly and at the cellular level—we doubt our own ability to heal and look for ways to speed the process.

I remember wondering: How will this ever heal?

Let me just tell you about an experience I had. About two years ago I developed complications following abdominal surgery. My surgeon had to reopen the wound—a large 14-inch incision—and was unable to suture it closed because of a severe infection I developed. For some reason, however, he neglected to tell me that he had to leave my wound open. So you can imagine my shock, when, a few days later, a nurse came to change the dressing and I looked down at this enormous gaping wound. I have never seen anything like that except in the operating room when I used to hold retractors as a medical student. I remember wondering: Oh my God, what will happen? How will this ever heal? I felt utter despair. I don't even recall what the nurse was saying to me. I just shut everything out.

After that, every time the nurse can to change the dressing, I turned my head away. Finally, about a week to ten days later, when I felt brave enough to look, I was flabbergasted at what I saw. The wound had begun to grow together.

The wisdom of the body: Every cell knows exactly how to heal.

Very slowly and inevitably—the same way that most natural processes occur—the gaping hole in my abdomen turned into a hairline scar. It made me realize that, although I have no idea in my mind how to bring about this healing, every cell of my body knows exactly how. There is such a thing as the wisdom of the body. Of course, not everything heals fully. Yet there is a natural tendency toward healing which can be promoted and trusted.

To illustrate this point to my patients, I'll ask them to tell me about a personal experience involving serious injury or major surgery. Then I'll have them focus on their scar for a moment before closing their eyes. Our dialogue would go something like this.

Physician: What did the injury initially look like?

Patient: Oh, it was horrible. It was swollen, the bone was sticking through the skin.

Physician: What was your first thought?

Patient: I was scared to death.

Physician: And what was your worst fear?

Patient: What's going to happen if it never heals?

At that point, I take the patient in imagery through their entire healing process: imagining the scar with the stitches in it, the stiches coming out, etc. Then I ask two important questions: One, do you remember the moment your injury healed? The answer to that is always "no." And secondly, what did you do to make it heal? To that, the patients may reply that they ate good food or rested or took their medication.

But eating the right food or taking medicines is like watering a plant. You don't make the roses *happen*. You nurture the rose bush, which has the know-how to produce a rose. By the same token, you don't make the healing happen. You nurture the body, which knows how to heal.

Question: Why do some people resist that sort of nurturing and, in fact, seem bent on self-destruction, judging from the careless way they treat their sick bodies?

Dr. Remen: Some people who come to my office with a broken leg or diabetes or whatever are very angry with their bodies. They don't realize that the body is part of the solution. It's not part of the problem. The broken leg or diabetes is the problem. But the body is what's going to enable that to become whole. Imagery can help put people in touch with their bodies. After all, it's hard to take care of something you're so angry with. People may forget their medication. Or not eat right, not give the body every chance it needs to heal. The body at a time of sickness may seem like an obstacle rather than a friend.

Opening old scars to ease their anxiety over new injuries.

Do you remember the exact moment your wound healed?

The body is not the problem. It's part of the solution.

UNSPOKEN EXPECTATIONS

Question: Of course, no one goes through life alone. And our interactions with people—husbands, wives, doctors, friends, etc.—help shape the way we perceive experiences. In your view, what's the most important way we can act as a positive influence on each other's health?

If I believe you are strong, you will be.

Dr. Remen: By believing in each other's tremendous potential. How I view you, the beliefs I have about you, how I relate to you—can be more powerful than any technique. If I believe in you, I empower you. If I believe that you have untapped strength and resiliency—even though you may appear very weak at the moment—then you've been encouraged to find a way to overcome the adversity you face. How that happens, I don't know. It may be conveyed through my tone of voice or choice of words. But somehow those beliefs and unspoken expectations are transferred and received.

This can work both ways—for better or worse. For example, when I was about 13 years old, my aunt decided I was awkward. That was the year I grew seven inches. I didn't know where my feet were. And once, in her presence, I tripped over them and fell full length in the street. She never forgot that. To her, I am still an awkward and clumsy person. Indeed, when I'm with her, even now, I become the part. I've spilled water on the table in restaurants. I've walked into closed glass doors. I've dropped things. It's as if I'm fulfilling her unspoken expectations. It's very irritating!

I see an acorn as the seed of an oak tree.

That's why I'm very careful how I think of other people. I like to view them with the same respect I hold for an acorn. Some people see an acorn as a little round piece of woody stuff. I see an acorn as a seed of an oak tree. Somewhere inside every acorn is a mechanism, waiting to unfold—a part that knows precisely how to become an oak tree. The potential is there. To see ourselves and others as acorns, then, is to recognize our tremendous potential to grow, to change, to heal. And that alone can be empowering.

59

First, Heal the Mind

Ask anyone in the know—from immunologist to new-age therapist—who's who in mind/body healing and the name Gerald Jampolsky, M.D., invariably is mentioned. Trained in all the usual traditions of Western medicine and psychiatry, Dr. Jampolsky now practices a rather unconventional form of therapy called "Attitudinal Healing." He's convinced that thoughts can affect the course of an illness and that, by retraining the mind to avoid negative thought traps, we can open ourselves up to the healing process.

Dr. Jampolsky has authored several books related to attitudinal healing, among them the bestseller *Love Is Letting Go of Fear; Teach Only Love;* and *Goodbye to Guilt* (all published by Bantam) and *To Give Is to Receive* (Minicourte). But the ultimate expression of his work can be experienced at The Center for Attitudinal Healing in Tiburon, California, a remarkably happy place where children and adults with catastrophic illness come to open their minds to healing.

We visited Dr. Jampolsky there.

His office, in a small wooden structure on the edge of a pier, sharply contrasts the modern professional building just a few yards away where several physicians have their names emblazoned in brass. The friendly, hand-painted name plaque that adorns his front door says something about the M.D. you're about to meet.

A caring, mild-mannered physician who shuns the handshake in favor of a hug and insists that his patients call

By avoiding negative thought traps, we can open ourselves to healing.

The friendly, hand-painted name plaque says something about this doctor.

**No surgery here. Jerry
Jampolsky helps heal the
person within the ailing body.**

him Jerry, he takes a more "personal" approach to healing.
You see, Jerry has devoted his practice to healing the *person*
within the ailing body—or, more precisely, to helping his
patients help themselves and each other. "People heal with
their own minds," he says. "I'm really here to listen and
lend support."

When we arrived, Jerry and co-counselor Diane V.
Cirincione were just concluding a support session with a
young woman. Then Jerry and Diane sat down with us to
explain the process of "Attitudinal Healing": what it is;
why it can have a dramatic effect on our physical health;
and how we can put it into effect in our own lives.

Question: How do you define "Attitudinal Healing"?

**Health is inner peace; healing
is letting go of fear.**

Jerry Jampolsky, M.D.: We define health as inner
peace and healing as letting go of fear. Attitudinal Healing is letting go of negative thoughts and replacing them
with love.

Question: Are you saying that if we become more
loving and less fearful we can physically heal ourselves?

Dr. Jampolsky: Yes. Physical healing is sometimes
the end result of Attitudinal Healing, but we really look at
that as almost an offshoot of the process. It's not the
primary goal. Inner peace is really the core goal of attitudinal
healing.

Question: It's difficult to imagine that someone faced
with a life-threatening illness is concerned first and foremost with finding peace of mind. Isn't survival and healing
the main reason people come to you for help?

**With inner peace, the
outcome doesn't matter.**

Dr. Jampolsky: Yes, but it is fear that is at the
top of their list—fear of death, fear of the future, fear
of pain. Inner peace can be your goal, regardless of the
physical outcome; you can learn to accept anything that
comes along.

Question: But isn't there any value in hope or power
in positive thinking?

**To believe that nothing is
impossible is powerful
medicine.**

Dr. Jampolsky: Oh yes, I think it is important to
believe that nothing in this world is impossible; that your
potential to get well is limitless; that healing the mind is a
natural process when we let go of our grievances through
forgiveness. There's a big difference between being "attached
to healing" and believing in your power to overcome illness.

TAKING CONTROL

Diane Cirincione: I keep thinking here of the word "control." When people are consumed with fear—when they're running scared from illness or whatever—they lose control over their perception of what's occurring. On the other hand, if we're able to find peace of mind in the midst of that chaos—if we learn to love instead of fear—we can learn that we don't have to be sick. We can learn to be responsible for anything we see and experience.

Dr. Jampolsky: I know this from personal experience. When I was younger, I had a lot of colds and flu. It was in my genes, I thought. My parents had about 20 colds a season. My two older brothers were frequently sick. Then, as I got involved in the principles of Attitudinal Healing, I began to realize that if I change my belief structure I could live a much more healthy life and not be subject to colds. Something in me said I don't need to be sick anymore. And that came from a really internal place. Now it is quite rare that I subject myself to a cold.

"Something in me said I don't need to be sick anymore."

Question: How do we change a deeply ingrained belief structure and open ourselves up to the healing powers within?

Dr. Jampolsky: By shifting your focus. Away from the fear of past preconceptions, or future unknowns. Away from the anger toward yourself, or your parents, or your doctor, or God, or whoever for "getting you into this predicament." Away from the guilt that comes from placing the blame on other people or yourself.

Shifting your focus to the present brings you peace.

You see, by shifting your focus to the present and using this time to love rather than cast judgment and to offer help rather than seeking help from others, you'll begin to find peace. And that's where things begin to happen. Because when there's an attitude shift, oftentimes the body shifts, too.

Health shifts often follow attitude shifts.

Question: Do you think that perhaps one reason this is so is that worry, guilt, fear, and all those negative emotions drain us of energy that could be used to nourish and heal us?

Dr. Jampolsky: There's no question that negativity can be incapacitating. If you spend your whole life determining what is impossible, it limits you as to what is possible. If

Dwelling on the impossible limits your possibilities.

you spend your whole life worrying and feeling guilty, you will never know what it feels like to be truly happy and at peace. And that makes it pretty tough to tap in on our healing energies.

Cirincione: In terms of health, the thoughts we put into our minds are as valuable—if not more so—than the food and vitamins we put into our bodies. A steady diet of anger, fear, resentment can have devastating consequences. But love is the antidote.

ATTITUDINAL HEALING AT ITS BEST

Question: Can you recall a situation that demonstrates Attitudinal Healing at its best?

Dr. Jampolsky: The first person that comes to mind is a young woman who came to The Center with her Seeing Eye dog. She was blind and she asked me if I thought it was possible for her to regain her sight. I told her that if she would have come to me a few years ago, I may have said no. But knowing what I do now, I must say there is no disease known to humankind that doesn't have the potential to be cured. Than I proceeded to set her straight about our goals: We're not here to change bodies, I said, we're here to change attitudes.

In reviewing her medical history, I learned that the disease that led to her blindness was caused by a once-common medical procedure in which premature infants were put into oxygen tents. Not surprisingly, she was still resentful of her doctors and even of her parents. It's common for blind people to have a lot of anger and unforgiving thoughts. But once this young woman got involved in the principles we practice at The Center—especially those that deal with forgiveness—and learned to let go of the grievances she was holding on to, she began to change psychologically and physically. Everyone commented on how different she looked. Her face lit up and her blind mannerisms such as constant head-shaking began to disappear.

About seven months later we got a call from her ophthalmologist who said that, although she was still legally blind at night, her vision had improved to the extent that she is now sighted by day. After that, she moved away and we lost track of her for awhile. But, then, a year later, we received a letter from her in which she told us she had

There is no disease that doesn't have the potential to be cured.

retired her Seeing Eye dog, Natasha, and that she was now taking driving lessons!

That seemed like a miracle. But the important point here, as Diane and I see it, is that if for any reason this woman loses her sight again, she'll be better able to accept it because of the attitudinal shift that took place. She's a much happier person today than she was when we first met her and that's not just because she can see. By going through our program she found that her purpose in life was to help others and that's what brings her joy. Remember, regaining her sight wasn't the goal. Peace of mind through healing her mind of negative thoughts was the only goal.

Her purpose in life was to help others.

FROM CATASTROPHE TO CONVICTION

Question: Why is it that so often we've got to hit rock bottom or face catastrophic illness to get motivated to become more loving, caring human beings—something that seems so natural?

Dr. Jampolsky: I think it really takes a feeling that your whole belief structure is working. You have to believe with your soul that it's possible for you to achieve peace of mind. And you've got to want it so badly you can taste it. Unfortunately, most of us come to that conviction only through trying times.

It takes a total conviction to really achieve peace of mind.

Question: What would you say is the one experience or event that had the most impact in changing your perspective?

Dr. Jampolsky: The turning point was in 1975, at a time in my life when I was extremely depressed and had very severe personal problems. I had just gone through a painful divorce, was suffering with tremendous back problems, and had an alcohol problem. It was at that time that I came across a book series called *A Course in Miracles* [Foundation for Inner Peace], which is about spiritual transformation.

A Course in Miracles: the turning point.

I wasn't looking for God. In fact, at that time, I was an agnostic. Religion was the last thing I wanted to hear about. But there was something in that book that struck a very deep chord. It taught me that there is another way to look at the world—through a spiritual lens. I no longer thought of myself as a victim, blaming the whole world for my unhappiness. I began to change from a rather angry person to a person who began to find peace and happiness through helping others. The teachings in *A Course in Miracles* became the basis for Attitudinal Healing.

Question: Is it necessary to embrace God to benefit fully from the process of Attitudinal Healing?

Dr. Jampolsky: Absolutely not. The principles of Attitudinal Healing are universal. It doesn't matter whether you're a Christian, Hindu, Buddist, Jew, or subscribe to your own brand of spirituality.

Spirituality: the link between mind and body.

Cirincione: Attitudinal Healing is involved with spiritual principles. *Spirituality* is the key word here. It's the link between mind and body.

LOVE WITH A CAPITAL L

Dr. Jampolsky: What we're talking about is love—with a capital L. That's where the power is. Once you tap into it, you have joined up with a universal energy force. And with that power, nothing is impossible.

Question: Do you believe in miracles, then?

A boy in a wheelchair; of course he'd like to fly.

Dr. Jampolsky: You bet I do. Let me tell you a story, and I'll try to make it as brief as possible. Last spring, Diane and I visited Belfast, Northern Ireland, where we met a lovely little boy with muscular dystrophy. His parents expected him to die within the year and understandably he was very depressed. We were only there for a day but I asked him, if something could happen this day that could really make him feel differently—give him a zest for life—what would it be? He thought for a moment then said, "Well, flying in a helicopter." Here's a boy with no muscles, sitting in a wheelchair. Of course he'd like to be like a bird—free, high.

Finding a helicopter in Belfast—impossible?

It seemed like a reasonable request. But where were we to find a helicopter in Belfast in one day! I mean, this wasn't California! In Northern Ireland, the only helicopters you're likely to find are those with soldiers and guns. My old rational mind would have said "give up," but something inside me kept me going, looking.

I phoned a small private airport and although they rarely have helicopters there, that day one was expected in from Nottingham, England. Well, to make a long story short, after several calls—including one to the chairman of the board of a mining company that had reserved the helicopter—we got what we wanted.

It was incredible. When the word got out about what

we were doing, the whole community became alive. When we got to the airport, which is normally a very depressed place, it too became electric. Even the security guards were interested. But, what was really incredible, was to see the shift in Martin, the young boy whose wish was to ride that helicopter. He was transformed from a pale and depressed youngster to an energetic and vibrant boy.

A transformation: from a pale and depressed youngster to a vibrant and energetic boy.

Now that whole street in Belfast is not going to think that anything is impossible, I'm sure. What we all need is an occasional miracle like that to help us realize that anything is possible. With the power of love, nothing is impossible. There are no limitations.

What we need is an occasional miracle.

THE KEY TO HAPPINESS

Question: If you had only a few moments to get across the essence of Attitudinal Healing, what would be your message?

Cirincione: Forgiveness. Forgiveness is the key to happiness, the key to peace of mind. Unfortunately, most people miss the real point of forgiveness. It's not enough to forgive someone for having done something you disagreed with. You have to go much deeper than that. You've got to forgive yourself for your misconception of that person—for judging that person and not seeing them as a loving human being. And that relieves guilt.

It's not enough to forgive someone else. You've got to forgive yourself.

Dr. Jampolsky: Letting go of judgment really takes a shift in perspective. There are 360 degrees of everything that exists on this planet. So whether you're looking at a flower or a human being, there are 360 different ways to view it. Unless you've explored every angle, there's no way you can totally know that object or person. And without knowing everything about someone, you can't possibly understand the reasons for his actions. So why not be open to that fact? Why waste your energy judging?

There are 360 degrees of everything—360 different points of view.

In my experience, when people let go of their judgment— which, as Diane just pointed out, is in reality letting go of their guilt about having those judgments—a shift in their state of health often follows.

Question: Fear is another crippling emotion that we all face. What's your prescription for healing this attitudinal malady?

Dr. Jampolsky: Limit your thoughts to the present. Don't worry about the awful things that have happened in

Limit your thoughts to the present.

the past or could happen in the future. Too many of us have lived for too long with the belief that the past predicts the future. The truth is, the past has no relevance to your future. The present is where it's at. And once you learn to live in the present, and think of the future as an extension of that moment, then you've opened yourself to healing.

ON STATISTICS AND PROGNOSES

Question: It seems ironic that physicians, who are in the business of healing, constantly remind us of the past and project into the future when they cite statistics or present prognoses. Don't they, in effect, superimpose fear onto our life and, as a consequence, reduce our ability to heal?

Dr. Jampolsky: I think that there are times that we physicians, including myself, have unwittingly created fear and taken away hope from our patients. I don't care what the statistics say. They're absolutely meaningless when you're talking about an individual.

Doctors can't predict the course of disease.

I think we need to tell the facts as we know them. But we need to remind ourselves that all we know about the future are probability curves. We really cannot predict with absolute accuracy the course of disease in any individual.

Question: Thinking peaceful, forgiving thoughts at a time of heightened emotional turmoil is never easy. Can you recommend a technique that we can use at the moment we're feeling uptight and uneasy to jolt us out of negativity and set us on a course of contructive thinking?

Three questions determine the source of internal unrest.

Cirincione: Whenever I'm feeling unpeaceful I ask myself three simple questions: What is upsetting me? Why am I holding on to it? What do I really want?

What is upsetting me? This question helps determine the importance of the problem. Is it something that is happening right this second? Or is it something that has already happened or something that I'm afraid is going to happen? That narrows it down quite a bit. Usually the moment is just fine but it's where the mind takes us—into the past and future—that creates the disturbance. The key then is bringing the mind back to the present and really getting into the moment.

Everything is a choice— including your feelings.

Why am I holding on to this negative feeling? We feel that everything is a choice. Everything you feel is a choice.

So if you're feeling confined, restrained, unloved, there must be some value in it for me to hold on to it. I used to be attached to depression, thriving on being the victim. Now I know that I can really let go of that feeling if I want to. Or, if I need to hold on to that feeling for awhile, that's okay too.

What do I really want? This is an easy one to answer because everyone should have a singular goal: peace of mind. Not peace at any price, but I want to be peaceful by reshifting my perceptions. So whenever I seem to get out of focus, I pull back and say, I want peace.

If I'm angry at someone, I realize that anger is just my desire to make myself feel guilty. And I know that love and guilt can't coexist. I have to choose. And then I choose love.

Love and guilt can't coexist.

GOODBYE AND GOODNIGHT

Dr. Jampolsky: There's another very simple thing you can do as a sort of check to ensure that you don't carry over your negative feelings to the following day. While you're lying in bed at night, with your eyes closed, imagine a great big garbage can and put into it anything that you're fearful or guilty about—any negative thoughts you've had during the course of the day. Now close the lid tightly and visualize a large helium balloon taking the garbage can with all your negative thoughts up into the sky. Watch it getting smaller and smaller and finally disappearing.

The way you start the day can also be important to your well-being. Remind yourself that your goal for the day is peace of mind, that in order to achieve that you're going to have to give of yourself to others. Approaching the day with that attitude can have a tremendous effect.

Your goal for the day: peace of mind.

Question: Is that why The Center for Attitudinal Healing is so special and has achieved such remarkable results with catastrophically ill people—that it is a place for giving?

Dr. Jampolsky: Yes. I think we're living in a world where it's difficult to find a place where it's truly OK to give—where you can find unconditional love. But if you come into our center you'll find an aura of that. Everyone, whether staff or participant, is here to create a positive healing environment. They're not here to judge. They're not even here to counsel. They're here to give unconditional love, which means listening and seeing each person

No judging, no counseling. Just listening and unconditional love.

as a loving individual or an individual who's giving a call of help for love.

Anyone who visits The Center comes away with a "wow" kind of feeling. At a meeting, you may encounter children who have lost limbs and hair to cancer therapies. You might anticipate a rather depressing sight, but instead you see these kids laughing and having fun. They're experiencing joy by helping each other. And when you're truly giving your love and joy away, you can only end up feeling joyful yourself. We do our best to make alive the following concepts:

1. Choose peace instead of conflict.
2. Choose love rather than fear.

BOX 41: THE SEVEN PRINCIPLES OF ATTITUDINAL HEALING

1. Health is inner peace. Therefore, healing is letting go of fear. To make changing the body our goal is to fail to recognize that our single goal is peace of mind.

2. The essence of our being is love. Love cannot be hindered by what is merely physical. Therefore, we believe the mind has no limits; nothing is impossible; and all disease is potentially reversible. And because love is eternal, death need not be viewed fearfully.

3. Giving is receiving. When our attention is on giving and joining with others, fear is removed and we accept healing for ourselves.

4. All minds are joined. Therefore, all healing is self-healing. Our inner peace will of itself pass to others once we accept it for ourselves.

5. Now is the only time there is. Pain, grief, depression, guilt, and other forms of fear disappear when the mind is focused on loving peace of this instant.

6. Decisions are made by learning to listen to the preference for peace within us. There is no right or wrong behavior. The only meaningful choice is between fear and love.

7. Forgiveness is the way to true health and happiness. By not judging, we release the past and let go of our fears of the future. In so doing, we come to see that everyone is our teacher and that every circumstance is an opportunity for growth in happiness, peace, and love.

Reprinted by permission of the publisher from *Teach Only Love,* Gerald G. Jampolsky, M.D. (New York: Bantam Books, Inc., 1983), p.34.

BOX 42: A PLACE FOR GIVING, SHARING, AND HEALING

No one can relate to another's fears, hurts, and ordeals like someone who's going through a similar experience. That's why so much of the program's success at The Center for Attitudinal Healing in Tiburon, California, is the result, not of therapists helping patients, but of people helping each other.

Group sessions—which are attended by those with catastrophic illness, parents, siblings, and facilitators—usually begin and end with a joining of hands and a brief moment of silence to experience the feeling of unity. Then participants are encouraged to share their feelings and experiences and offer their insight to others who may be wrestling with the same problems, such as:

I'm embarrassed to leave the house because I lost all my hair.

I feel all alone.

I'm afraid my child is going to die.

I feel people around me withdrawing and I'm angry about that.

I'm jealous because my sick brother is getting all the attention.

The Center also offers a Pen Pal/Phone Pal program, a matchmaking service of sorts to put seriously ill people in touch by long distance to others who share like experiences. For example, a nine-year-old boy in Wisconsin who has leukemia can get mutual support and encouragement from another nine-year-old in Texas who's going through the same treatments. The Center, a privately funded, non-profit organization, picks up the tab for all long-distance calls. All services are free.

Another program called Person-to-Person, which is open to everyone whether or not they're seriously ill, is designed to teach us how to form therapeutic partnerships. Two people are introduced and given some time alone together to get to know each other. Their only instruction is to be nonjudgmental and forgiving. Jerry Jampolsky, M.D., explains the process:

"When two people meet they often behave like insects bumping into each other. Their 'antennae' begin flapping and they try to sense what about the other person is different from them. They make comparisons and form quick judgments about each other's traits and appearance.

"In the Person-to-Person program, it is suggested that we begin the encounter with an entirely different mind set. We resolve beforehand that we will scan the other person for signs of love, gentleness, and peace, and that the only information we will retain in our mind is that which will permit us to continue looking upon this person kindly. In other words, we seek only their innocence, not their guilt. We look at them with our heart, not with our preconceived notions."

This, as Jerry points out, is an approach we can all use every day in our relationships with others.

For more information on The Center, write: The Center for Attitudinal Healing, 19 Main Street, Tiburon, CA 94920, or call: (415) 435-5022.

There are other centers throughout the U.S. that offer similar programs. None of them are directly affiliated with The Center in Tiburon, although many do follow the same principles of Attitudinal Healing.

60

Mind Over Cancer

*S*pontaneous remission. It's medicine's explanation for the inexplicable—when cancer or another serious disease apparently improves or disappears "by itself." We tend to think of it as a favorable accident of fate—a modern-day miracle of sorts.

Or is it? Bernard S. Siegel, M.D., doesn't think so. "Patients who get well when they're not supposed to are not having accidents or miracles or spontaneous remissions," he says. "They're having self-induced healing."

That someone with Dr. Siegel's credentials would speak of *self-induced healing* may strike many as something of a miracle, however. Attending surgeon at Yale-New Haven Hospital and Hospital of St. Raphael and assistant clinical professor of surgery at Yale Medical School, he not only is affiliated with one of the nation's leading medical schools, he practices in a field that's regarded as perhaps the most mechanistic and least humanistic of all medical specialties.

But Dr. Siegel is about as unconventional a surgeon as you are likely to find—anywhere. He hugs his patients and insists that they call him Bernie. His diagnostic tools include a box of crayons with which he asks patients to draw pictures of their illnesses. And he fills the O.R. with soothing music, playing preselections of the anesthetized patient or personal favorites such as an oboe solo of "Amazing Grace."

Beneath these practices lies a natural healing philosophy,

Spontaneous remission: a modern day miracle?

A surgeon speaks of "self-induced healing."

free of the confines of conventional medicine. Dr. Siegel believes, for example, that the best medical treatment is only as effective as the patient's unconscious mind allows and that a combination of stress reduction, conflict resolution, and positive reinforcement (in the form of visualizations and positive emotions such as hope and love) can stimulate the immune system and allow healing to take place. His extensive work with cancer patients bears this out.

We first caught up with Bernie Siegel at a workshop he was giving called "The Psychology of Illness and the Art of Healing in Exceptional Patients" at the Omega Institute for Holistic Studies in Rhinebeck, New York. Later, we talked with him about his clinical experience in treating cancer—what psychological and emotional factors affect our vulnerability and how we can dramatically improve our chances for recovery.

Question: When did you first come to recognize the power of the mind in healing cancer?

Bernard Siegel, M.D.: My awakening grew out of pain I was feeling in my own life. I had become disturbed and unhappy in my role as a surgeon. My problem was in dealing with my feelings while being told that doctors don't behave like that. They don't touch people. They don't hug people. They don't get involved with their patients' personal problems. So, in an attempt to make myself happier as a doctor, I went to workshops—the first one, given by Carl and Stephanie Simonton of the Simonton Cancer Counseling Center, then in Dallas, Texas. There I met some of my own patients. They said to me, "Look, you're a good doctor. You listen to us and support us. But what are we supposed to do *between* office visits? We need help in learning how to live with our illnesses."

So I set up a group therapy type of situation to help them do that. But, what happened was, as I saw people learning how to live with their illnesses, I saw them having incredible control over their wellness. I saw people dealing with conflict in their lives and then, suddenly, having their cancer shrink or disappear.

These were things I had never seen before. I was astonished. And, as a physician, I felt uncomfortable with it. They were getting better and I didn't lift a finger.

The best medical treatment is only as good as the unconscious mind allows.

Cancer patients need help learning how to live with their illness.

"My patients were getting better and I didn't lift a finger."

But, they said to me, "Be patient, you're a doctor. You'll learn. You've given us hope. You've given us control. We do feel better. We are getting better."

Question: Why did you have so much difficulty accepting this?

Dr. Siegel: You have to remember that medicine is failure-oriented. We deal only with patients who *don't* get well. Those who get well when they're not supposed to are told not to return. These are patients we really ought to be studying.

Once, when I was giving a speech, a man came up to me and handed me a card. On it he had written, "Ten years ago, your partner operated on my father. He told me he had cancer of the pancreas and would die in six months. I was to go home and prepare the family for his death. I didn't. I didn't tell anyone. My father just had his 85th birthday. My mother was beaming at his side."

Well, I went back to the office and pulled this man's records from our files. My first reaction was that maybe there was some error in diagnosis. But, no, by all statistics, he should have died ten years ago. I said to everyone in the office, "Look at this. Isn't this wonderful! Mr. Jones is alive. We all assumed he died because he never came back to the office." Now, no one in the office would think to go over to Mr. Jones's house, knock on his door, and say to him, "Mr. Jones, you were supposed to die ten years ago. Why didn't you? What did you do to heal yourself of cancer?" That's just not done.

WHEN CANCER DISAPPEARS

Question: How then does the medical profession explain these cases?

Dr. Siegel: They treat them as medical anomalies. I got a note from an oncologist the other day. It said, "Roz is doing *amazingly* well. Her cancer is gone."

I know Roz. I know why her cancer disappeared. Roz was sent to a nursing home to die. She hated it there. They weren't attending to her needs. So, instead of passively accepting her situation, she stood up and led a revolution in the nursing home. She returned home and her cancer went away.

I'll give you another example: I know a woman who had extensive abdominal cancer. She underwent every kind

---

Sidebar notes:

Doctors only deal with people who *don't* get well.

Assumed *dead* because he didn't return to the doctor's office.

Roz stood up and said, "I'm leaving." Then her cancer disappeared.

of therapy—chemotherapy, radiation therapy, surgery—but the cancer could not be arrested. She left the hospital and went to her daughter's house—again, presumably to die. Several months later she returned to our office for a checkup. A partner of mine examined her and found that the cancer was gone. He called me in. He said, "Hey, you're interested in this stuff." So I went in and I said, "Irene, tell him what you did." And Irene said, "I went home, decided to live to be 100 and leave my troubles to God."

Question: It's that easy?

Dr. Siegel: It's not easy at all. If I said to patients, you have two choices if you want to get well—you can change your lifestyle or have an operation—the majority would say, "Operate. It hurts less."

Operate. It hurts less.

When I first started group therapy sessions, I sent out 100 letters to cancer patients, inviting them to the meetings and offering to teach them how to get better and live longer. I fully expected a crowd. Only 12 people showed up. Only 12 out of 100 people were willing to participate in their own recovery. That really tells you how difficult it is.

THE EXCEPTIONAL PATIENT

Question: Are these the people you refer to as "exceptional patients"?

Dr. Siegel: Yes. Generally, I find that about 15 to 20 percent of all people with chronic or catastrophic illness are truly exceptional patients or survivors. They are people who, when confronted with illness, are willing to take responsibility for it and redirect their lives accordingly. They are also willing to participate in their own recovery— to join with the doctor and become a healing team, and to seek out all available resources (medical, psychological, spiritual, etc.) to give themselves the best chance for getting well. These are people who are really willing to fight for their lives.

Only 15 to 20 percent of cancer patients are willing to fight for their lives.

The majority of people—50 to 60 percent—are content to sit back and let their doctors direct their treatment. Their attitude is: "You're the doctor. You're the mechanic. You take care of me."

Then there's another 20 percent who are happy to die because their lives are in shambles. For them, the cancer is a very easy way out. Of course, they're not going to admit

Another 20 percent are happy to die.

that to friends or relatives. If you ask them how they're doing, they're not going to say, "Trying hard to die, thank you." But I'll confront them and ask point blank, "Are you trying to die?" And many of them will answer honestly because they know that I know the truth. The reason I know is that they've been avoiding treatment or withdrawing from people who are offering them help.

Question: Are you saying that surviving cancer has as much to do with our mental attitude as it does with the extent of the disease?

Why did you need the illness?

Dr. Siegel: Yes, absolutely. I can usually determine where a person stands in regard to his illness by asking four simple questions: Do you want to live to be 100? What does your disease mean to you? Why did you need the illness? What happened in the year or two before you got sick?

The first question, *Do you want to live to be 100?* gives me an idea whether he or she feels in control of his or her life and looks forward to the future. The second question, *What does your disease mean to you?* tells me if the person sees the disease as a challenge to overcome or as an overwhelming obstacle—a death sentence.

Your sister gets a cold, you'll get it; your sister gets chicken-pox, you'll get it; your sister gets cancer . . .

Sometimes, too, I can find out whether the disease holds some significance in the person's past. For example, I had a patient who developed cancer at the age of 60, just several months after his sister died of cancer. During my conversation with him, he confessed that he knew he was going to get sick. Apparently, as a child, his mother told him that whatever his sister gets, he will get. He said that because his sister, who was two years older than he was, repeatedly infected him with colds and childhood diseases she picked up at school. But his mother's words, "Whatever your sister gets, you will get" registered in his unconscious and stayed with him into his adult life.

The unconscious mind meets its needs by creating illness.

The third question, *Why do you need this illness?* tells me whether the disease serves some psychological or emotional purpose. Is it a cry for love and nurturing? Or is it a signal from the body that you need some time off—from a job or from responsibilities? You know that we give people "sick days" and in so doing we train them to get sick. The unconscious quickly learns that it can meet its needs by creating illness.

My final question, *What happened in the year or two*

before you got sick? lets the patient know how he may have participated in his own illness. In about 90 percent of the cancer patients I see, I can ascertain in their histories that they experienced some significant change in their lives within the previous year or two. It may be a very devastating kind of thing, like the death of a child or spouse—something the new field of psychoneuroimmunology is showing has a depressive effect on the immune system. But it can also be a positive change, such as moving to a new house, having a baby, or changing jobs—the kind of changes about which you might say, "Isn't it wonderful," or "It's terrific."

What happened in the year or two before you got sick?

LIFE CHANGES AND CANCER

Question: That sounds very much like the popular Holmes-Rahe Stress Rating Scale in which various life changes (both positive and negative) are assigned significance ratings in terms of their likelihood to precede illness. Do you feel that scale is valid?

Dr. Siegel: Absolutely. Not only do I feel it, I know it from personal experience. Shortly after I started my practice and moved into a new home, I wound up in the hospital with a severe infection. While I lay there in isolation, I began to wonder whether there was any correlation between these changes in my life and my immune system's inability to fight off this infection.

"I started my practice and moved to a new home. Then I wound up in the hospital."

When I went back to the office, I decided to play some games. Patients would come in with a problem and I would say, "Okay, did you get a new job?" or "Did you move into a new house?" and they would look at me and say, "How did you know?" They thought I was a genius.

Question: But there are many people who change jobs and move to new homes and don't get sick. What do these people do differently that protects them from disease?

Not everyone who changes jobs gets sick.

Dr. Siegel: Generally, it has a lot to do with meeting your own needs, expressing your feelings, learning to say "no" without guilt. If you worry a lot about your new role and let yourself get worn out, you'll get sick. I think this is particularly true for illnesses—such as cancer—which are related to the immune system.

Question: Is it possible, however, that by suggesting that a person brought on his own disease, we risk depressing him further and thereby jeopardize his recovery?

Don't blame yourself. See illness as a message to redirect your life.

Dr. Siegel: I didn't blame myself for getting an infection. I learned from it. I think the cancer patient should look at this the same way—not to say, "Oh my goodness, this is awful. What did I do to myself?" but rather to see the illness as a message to redirect his or her life accordingly—to resolve conflicts with other people, express anger and resentment and other negative emotions they've been bottling up inside, to begin looking out for their own needs. And, in so doing, the immune system becomes stimulated and healing takes place.

STIMULATING "LIVE" MECHANISMS

Question: Can you explain further how these changes promote healing?

Dr. Siegel: Learning to let go of negative emotions is key. The person who smiles on the outside and is hurting on the inside is killing himself. He's not dealing with himself or his life. And all his "live" mechanisms are told to stop working. By "live" mechanisms I mean endorphins, immune globulins, white blood cells, etc.

Feeling fine? Look out. Feeling lousy? That's wonderful.

Doctors see examples of this every day. You are making rounds at the hospital and you ask a patient how she's doing and she says, "Fine." But you know she's not doing fine. Her husband ran off with another woman. Her kid is a drug addict. Her house just burned down. And she has cancer. But still she says, "Fine."

When I find a person who answers, "Lousy," I say, "That's wonderful! You want to get better so you're dealing with the truth. If your mind and body are feeling lousy and you're relating to that, you'll ask for help. Your 'live' mechanisms will work for you."

If you feel hate toward someone, they don't suffer. You do.

The inability to express anger is a characteristic of cancer patients. If you don't display anger, it goes on to resentment and hate. If you feel hate toward someone, they don't suffer in the physical sense because of it. You do.

Expressing negative feelings is an enormous part of the healing process.

And so I tell my patients, express your anger, fear, and guilt. That I see as an enormous part of the healing process. In our group therapy sessions we get people to vocalize their emotions, to work out their conflicts, in order to achieve peace of mind or clear conscience or whatever you want to call it. Ninety percent of them have to yell and scream and cry in order to find peace. I say do whatever it takes. Get those emotions out.

MIND/BODY COMMUNICATION

Question: What other steps can we take to help our "live" mechanisms work for us?

Dr. Siegel: Essentially, we must learn to open the lines of mind/body communication—to send "live" messages to the body. There are two ways to communicate these "live" messages. One is through emotions. I tell patients, "If you want to die, stay depressed; if you want to live, then love and laugh." Positive emotions like love, acceptance, and forgiveness stimulate the immune system. Mental health, if you want to call it that, is the greatest stimulus to physical health—the greatest survival characteristic.

Positive emotions stimulate the immune system.

The second way to send "live" messages is through images—by visualizing the healing process taking place in your body. Guided imagery tapes are available for this purpose. But if you don't have a tape, you can do it on your own. First select symbols to represent your cancer cells and your white blood cells. You can visualize many things. But if you have difficulty choosing your symbols, I suggest that you think of your cancer cells as morsels of food and your white blood cells as birds, kittens, or Pac-Man—any food-eating image you feel comfortable with. Then close your eyes, quiet your mind, and play out the action in your mind. Imagine your white blood cells gobbling up the cancer cells. The more they eat, the stronger you become. In this way, the disease becomes a source of personal strength and psychological growth.

Imagine your white blood cells gobbling up the cancer.

Question: How often should one repeat this visualization exercise to maximize the healing benefits?

Dr. Siegel: I suggest at least a half dozen times a day. Just sit back, close your eyes, and reprogram your mind.

PEACE, NOT WAR

Question: Is this the same visualization technique used by the Simontons?

Dr. Siegel: It's based on their technique. They introduced me to guided imagery. But there is one aspect of their technique that I disagree with—that is, the use of aggressive

You can't ask people to *kill* something inside of them.

symbolism. They suggest that cancer patients visualize aggressive white blood cells *attacking* or *killing* the cancer cells in their bodies. I think the majority of people have difficulty reconciling attack images in a healing context. You cannot ask people to kill something inside of them, to make the body a battleground. It doesn't work. They reject it at the subconscious and unconscious levels.

Question: But isn't that the general perception of cancer—that it is an enemy that has somehow invaded the body? And don't physicians perpetuate this concept by presenting their treatments as methods to "eradicate" and "wipe out" the cancer cells?

"Fighting the war against cancer" may be counter to healing.

Dr. Siegel: Yes, And I think that's a problem, too. This notion of "killing" or "fighting" cancer is pervasive in our society. Have you ever been asked to donate to heal a disease? You've probably been asked to help "fight the war against cancer." Medicine uses words like this all the time— assault, insult, poison, blast, and kill. The unconscious hears this and says, "Get me out of here! This is no place for healing."

The ultimate example is a Quaker who refused treatment because his oncologist said, "Take this and it will kill your cancer." The patient said, "I don't kill anything," and walked out.

The rejection takes place at the subconscious level.

For most people, however, the rejection takes place at the subconscious or unconscious level. Their body simply refuses to respond to treatment. I can give you many examples of this.

I have a child patient who was first brought to me because she wasn't responding to chemotherapy. I asked her to draw a picture of herself receiving the treatment. In her picture, she's got a spear in her hand, supposedly to kill the cancer, but it's pointed in the wrong direction. Her cancer cells are crying, "Help me."

A doctor administering chemotherapy is perceived as the devil giving poison.

In another case, a woman came into my office complaining of severe side effects from her chemotherapy— side effects that aren't even associated with her treatment. Again, I gave her some crayons and asked her to draw me a picture. She drew a picture of the devil giving her poison.

To me, the problem is obvious. In each of these cases, the patient's *perception* of her treatment hampered her body's ability to respond favorably to it.

CHEMOTHERAPY WITHOUT SIDE EFFECTS

Question: How can we shift our perspective from an attack mode to a healing mode?

Dr. Siegel: One effective method is to program yourself for a positive outcome using a type of visualization technique that athletes use in training. Close your eyes and picture yourself sitting comfortably in a chair and having the chemotherapy or other treatment. Feel the cancer shrinking and your strength returning. After the treatment you feel good—even energized—and leave the hospital to go shopping.

Rehearse your treatment with a positive outcome.

If you do this maybe 100 times before starting the therapy, your body will respond quite favorably to the actual treatment. By living the event in your mind, your body will get the message as to how it should respond in real life.

Of course, the best way to insure the effectiveness—and minimize the side effects—of any treatment is to know that the decision to have that treatment is yours. The key is to evaluate all your options and to make a responsible choice—something you can accept and feel comfortable with. Know that it's what *you* want.

Evaluate all your treatment options and make a responsible choice.

What's so discouraging is that people have denied traditional therapy because the doctor presented it as a sort of ultimatum. If you agree to a treatment because you are afraid what might happen if you don't, I doubt that any healing will take place. You've got to do it out of positive motivation.

I had a patient, a young woman, who was very health conscious. She wouldn't eat anything that contained chemicals or preservatives. When she developed cancer, she rejected chemotherapy and radiation therapy because she saw them as potent chemicals that were potentially more threatening to her than the cancer itself. I didn't argue with her. I said, "Fine. If that's the way you feel, it probably wouldn't do you much good anyway." A few weeks later she returned and said, "You know, I've been thinking about radiation therapy. I can see it as a kind of healing energy. I think it can help me." So she had the treatment and it was very successful. So, you see, one person's poison is another person's gift.

One person's poison is another person's gift.

My advice is, find a physician who's willing to talk

People who choose their cancer therapy have one-fourth the side effects of those who silently submit.

with you and lend support. Explore all your options together. Then choose the course of treatment you want. People who share and talk with their physicians—and who choose their therapies for positive reasons—have maybe a fourth to a tenth the side effects of people who just silently submit to treatment because their doctors or spouses told them they *had* to have it. Those are really don't die messages, not live messages or love messages.

TEAM HEALING

Question: Do you think that most physicians are ready for this kind of team-effort approach to healing?

Dr. Siegel: There's no question that many doctors prefer submissive, nonquestioning patients who either live or die according to their choices. I know doctors who have shouted obscenities at patients when asked a question and have heard of one doctor who has a sign on his desk that says "Compromise means doing it my way." This is absurd. We're talking about people's lives here.

Pesty patients live longer.

My advice is, don't worry if your doctor thinks you're being too assertive or inquisitive. In fact, consider it a healthy sign. Studies have shown that the patients physicians say are the biggest pests are the ones whose immune systems are the most active. They are the long-term survivors. The patients physicians say are wonderful—submissive and unquestioning—are the ones who are dying. So I tell people, develop a poor relationship with your doctor.

Question: But isn't it true that having faith in your doctor's ability to heal you can also contribute to a positive outcome?

Develop a poor relationship with your doctor.

Dr. Siegel: Yes, of course. Faith and confidence in your doctor is a powerful healing factor. When I say develop a "poor" relationship, I am basing that on the *doctor's* definition of a poor relationship. "Poor" or "bad" by his standards is "good" by yours.

Question: Can you give us some tips on how to be "bad" patients?

Dr. Siegel: Be assertive. Ask questions. Try calling your doctor by his or her first name. Give him a hug. The goal is, get to be a person—not just a disease—to that doctor. By approaching him on a more human level, it

BOX 43: THE CANCER PATIENT'S BILL OF RIGHTS

Bernard Siegel, M.D., the founder of ECAP (Exceptional Cancer Patients, Inc.), a support group for people willing to fight for their lives in the face of *any* major illness, has compiled the following "Bill of Rights."

Dear Doctor:

Please don't tell me what I don't have. We both know I came to you to learn if I have cancer. If I know what I have, I know what I am fighting, and there is less to fear. If you hide the name and the facts, you deprive me of the chance to help myself.

Doctor, when you are questioning whether I should be told if I have cancer, I already know. You may feel better if you don't tell me, but your deception hurts me.

Do not tell me how long I have to live. I alone can decide how long I will live. It is my desires, my goals, my values, my strengths, and my will to live that will make the decision.

Teach me and my family about how and why it happened to me. Help me and my family to live now. Tell me about nutrition and my body's needs. Tell me how to handle the knowledge and how my mind and body can work together. Healing comes from within, but I want to combine my strength with yours. If you and I are a team I will live a longer and better life.

Doctor, don't let your negative beliefs, your fears, and your prejudices affect my health. Don't stand in the way of my getting well and exceeding your expectations. Give me the chance to be the exception to your statistics.

Teach me about your beliefs and therapies and help me to incorporate them into mine. However, remember that my beliefs are the most important; what I don't believe in won't help me.

You must learn what cancer means to me—death, pain, or fear of the unknown. If my belief system accepts alternative therapy and not recognized therapy, do not desert me. Please try to convert my beliefs and be patient and await my conversion. It may only come at a time when I am desperately ill and in great need of your therapy.

Doctor, teach me and my family to live with my problem when I am not with you. Take time for our questions and give us your attention when we need it. It is important that I feel free to talk with you and question you. I will live a longer and more meaningful life if you and I can develop a significant relationship. I need you in my life to achieve my new goals.

Reprinted by permission of the author from the cancer patient's "Bill of Rights" by Bernard S. Siegel, M.D.

causes him to confront you in a different way—to treat you like a person with feelings and concerns.

Tape record all conversations with your physician.

I have another list I give to patients who are going into the hospital. We call it "The Good Patient/Bad Patient List." It suggests such things as tape record all conversations with physicians and take a tape recorder and your favorite tape along into the operating room so you can tune in to relaxing music during the surgery. Even if you're under general anesthesia, the unconscious mind benefits and I believe this can have a positive healing effect.

CONTROL AND HOPE

Question: What's the most important contribution a doctor can make to the recovery of a patient?

Dr. Siegel: I think there are two contributions a doctor can make. The first, as I just mentioned, is to give the patient control over his or her own treatment. The second is to offer hope.

There's no such thing as false hope.

If there's one thing I learned from my years of working with cancer patients, it's that there is no such thing as false hope. Hope is real and physiological. It's something I feel perfectly comfortable giving people—no matter what their situation. I know people are alive today because I said to them, "You don't have to die."

The doctor's dilemma is statistics. If statistics say that nine out of ten people die from this disease, most physicians will tell their patients, "The odds are against you. Prepare to die." I tell my patients, "You can be the one who gets well. Let's teach you how." I'm not guaranteeing immortality. I'm asking them if they want to learn how to live.

People aren't statistics; they're individuals.

People aren't statistics. They are individuals. And they should be treated as individuals. If a doctor told me that everybody with my illness dies in six months, I would say to myself, "That's impossible. No two cases are alike. What he's talking about is the *average*. Maybe one person lived for five years and someone else dropped dead in three days."

To me, the worst thing a doctor can do is tell a person he's going to die. For one thing, it's a deception. There's no way anyone can predict with any certainty the course a disease will take in an individual. Secondly, it's the quickest way to make that patient another statistic.

Hope acts as a placebo. And there is no question that

placebos can affect the immune system. In one study, for example, published in the literature in 1957, a patient was given an experimental drug called Krebiozen. He believed it to be a powerful anti-cancer drug that would save him. His cancer disappeared. Then an article appeared in the newspaper saying that Krebiozen was an ineffective anti-cancer drug. His cancer recurred. His doctors then told him that they were giving him a super-refined version of Krebiozen, which *is* effective against cancer. In fact, he was given weekly injections of water. Nevertheless, his cancer went into remission for a second time. Then the newpapers carried another article, stating that the FDA was removing the drug from trials because it didn't work. He died in three days.

So, I don't care how seriously ill a patient is, I will offer him hope.

Hope acts as a placebo.

BOX 44: TWO SOURCES OF TAPES FOR HEALING

Tapes by Bernard Siegel, M.D., for relaxation and healing are available through:

> Exceptional Cancer Patients, Inc.
> 2 Church Street South
> New Haven, CT 06519
> (817) 444-4073

Carl and Stephanie Simonton also offer relaxation and guided imagery tapes, which are available through:

> The Simonton Cancer Counseling Center
> 875 Zia de la Paz
> Pacific Palisades, CA 90272
> (213) 454-7755

Tapes from either source run about $10 to $15 each plus postage and handling. Call or write for additional information.

Question: What's the best piece of advice you can give a cancer patient?

Dr. Siegel: The best piece of advice I give to anybody is *live each day as if it were your last.* That's not to say go rob a bank or spend your family savings. I'm talking from a spiritual standpoint. Make yourself happy. Resolve your conflicts. Get things off your chest. Find that peace of mind, that clear conscience. I guarantee, you'll wake up the next morning feeling so good, you won't want to die.

I say to my patients, "If you were going to be killed on the way home from the office today, would you need to use my telephone to call anybody." If they answer no, then they are leading the right life. If they jump up and say, "Oh my God, give me that telephone. I have to call my brother-in-law and tell him off, I have to call my wife and say 'I love you' because we had an argument this morning," and so on, then you're not living right. It's learning how to live that's everything.

Live each day as if it were your last.

Make a Life Wish

The "will to live" is an undeniably powerful force for survival—probably *the* most important factor in health and healing. But what are the emotions, attitudes, and behavior that feed this flame of inner strength? How do we keep it burning bright or rekindle it once it begins to flicker and die?

To find out, we spoke with a longevity expert whose roots run deep in the field of mind/body health: Kenneth R. Pelletier, Ph.D. An assistant clinical professor of medicine at the University of California School of Medicine in San Francisco, he has authored numerous books, including the international bestseller *Mind as Healer, Mind as Slayer; Longevity; Holistic Medicine;* and *Healthy People in Unhealthy Places* (all published by Delacorte). Dr. Pelletier's ongoing study of longevity has taken him all over the world, including the U.S.S.R.

We interviewed him near his home in Berkeley, California. There, we discussed the healing mind and how we might program it for a longer life.

Question: When you go to a doctor with a complaint, and he says, "It's all in your head," what does that mean?

Kenneth R. Pelletier, Ph.D.: Traditionally, calling something psychosomatic, saying it's all in the head, is dismissing it. As if something that's "all in the head" is not really there, or anywhere at all.

However, more and more we're coming to see that *all* states of health and illness are in some way psychosomatic.

> What attitudes feed the flame of inner strength?

> "Psychosomatic" doesn't mean "it's all in your head."

Not in the sense that they're imaginary, either, but in the sense that they all involve mental and physical factors.

Question: How can the mind make someone ill?

Dr. Pelletier: Well, at any given time there are many, many forces influencing the state of our health. Among those factors are nutrition, exercise, stress, genetic predisposition, psychosocial factors, purely medical factors like injury or infection. The question is, do some of those become disproportionate influences that result in illness, or do they all maintain an optimal balance which results in health?

What I believe happens is that you begin with a certain level of stress which most of us are under all the time. Long-term, unabated stress. Then along comes a "life stress event." You suddenly get an accumulation of stress that precipitates the original condition into a real illness. For example, you might have a family history of hypertension and you're under a constant level of stress at your job. So your blood pressure is slightly elevated. Suddenly, one or more stressful life events take place and your blood pressure might zoom up to an alarmingly high point, resulting in dizziness, headaches, or worse.

Then, you can have a certain type of personality or psychological makeup that predisposes you to developing a specific kind of disorder. Again, it's not *the* cause, but it is an influence. One of many. And in order to treat a person, we've got to unravel all these influences and go all the way back and untangle the whole skein.

Question: How about an example of this process?

Dr. Pelletier: Sure. Remember, what I'm saying is that at some point a psychological difficulty actually begins to affect the physical system in the body. A stress becomes an excess secretion of hydrochloric acid and predisposes a person toward ulcers. Another form of worry may elevate the blood pressure. At some point, physical symptoms arise.

In one very graphic case, a 72-year-old lady came in with a condition known as spasmodic torticollis—wryneck—where her head was turned over her shoulder to the right. It's extremely disorienting, very painful, and she could hardly walk. She had been through everything: chiropractic, cortisone injections, traction, a collar. When she came in we started doing biofeedback. We placed the electrodes on her left sternomastoid, which is the muscle that contracts

Many factors influence health, from genetic predisposition to mental attitude.

Psychological makeup may *predispose* you to illness.

Four weeks of biofeedback. Then progress stops cold.

when you turn your head to the right. I told her to relax that muscle. When she did, her head began to turn back to straight ahead. After about four weeks of progress, it just stopped cold. We made no more progress.

I noticed there was a little spike on the machine recording her nerve impulses, indicating some excess muscle activity. I told her that when that spike occurred to openly express what went on in her mind. She did, and said she felt uneasy. I asked her what kind of unease it was. She said she felt guilty. What kind of guilt? "I feel ashamed," she said. Ashamed of what?

She said her symptoms had been going on for five years, since she had had an affair with a younger, married man. In describing the affair, she said that if her neighbors ever found out about it, she could never look them straight in the face. As soon as she said those words, the instrument activity went normal. That wasn't a cure, but from that point on, she made progress under the biofeedback therapy and psychotherapy. Finally, she regained complete lateral movement of her head. There are other cases like this that demonstrate the same principle of how a particular mind set can influence the body.

Talking about the "unmentionable" unlocked a physical block.

You find many heart patients who have unconsciously formulated their disorder as a form of a death wish. They don't necessarily wish for extinction, but for *release from responsibility.* One example is a 53-year-old man whose father and brother had both died of heart attacks at age 54. This man came into our clinic experiencing severe angina pain, approaching *his* 54th birthday. He had a perfectly normal electrocardiogram and perfectly normal blood pressure. There appeared to be no physical reason why he should be developing those symptoms. Nevertheless, the pain persisted.

Heart patients sometimes look for release from responsibility.

What we found in measuring his stress levels was that his whole left arm and hand had a circulatory constriction. In worrying about his potential heart attack, he had involuntarily closed down the circulatory system in his left arm, thereby producing the angina.

Worrying about a heart attack can bring on angina.

PROGRAMMED TO DIE

What he had done was program himself that at age 54 he was going to die. And the way he was going—restricting his exercise, becoming increasingly less active, depressed, removed—he probably would have been right on schedule. He *was* acting like someone who was about to die.

Question: You can program yourself for failure?

Dr. Pelletier: No question. And success. There is a reality that exists out there. How you see and perceive that reality makes all the difference in the world in whether you attain a state of health or illness.

Question: Let's talk about programming yourself for success, for health.

Dr. Pelletier: There is no specific recipe. There are some people who can drink, smoke, carry on, eat bad food, live in the worst possible toxic environment—and live to be 100. And there are people who stringently adhere to every single thing I'm going to talk about—and they die at 30 of ill health. Of course, those people are exceptions.

For most of us, the physical parameters that seem to influence longevity and health are diet, exercise, some method of stress alleviation or management (which a person can use to break the course of cumulative stress), and the psychosocial environment (liking what you do, remaining active and involved in your life). If I had to choose the single most important one, the one major predictor of longevity and health, it would have to be the last one, perhaps because it so deeply involves the consciousness of the individual. It's important to stay involved and curious about life, your own life and the life around you. You have to feel fulfilled, that your life has meaning, that it's important for you to be alive. You need the *life wish*.

Question: What about diet and exercise?

Dr. Pelletier: We've kept track now for three years of people in our clinic who seem to move toward optimal health. They tend to markedly reduce the amount of refined carbohydrates and white sugar they eat; they increase the amount of roughage, fresh fruits, and vegetables, they switch from more processed to less processed foods; they reduce their intake of red meat and turn to poultry, fish, whole grains, and legumes for protein; they reduce the amount of caffeine they get and they increase their liquid intake.

As for exercise, it's clear that the body is made for physical exertion. You don't have to achieve competitive levels of fitness. In fact, most of the literature you find on professional athletes tends to show they have a higher mortality rate and higher incidence of what we call stress-related or psychosomatic disorders. So we're talking about

How you perceive the "reality" of your illness determines how you feel.

The single most important predictor of longevity is enthusiasm for life.

Professional athletes have more stress-related problems.

a moderate level of exercise that is regular, three times a week or so, that taxes the cardiorespiratory system. It should also be something that's fun for you to do. It makes a world of difference, exercising or not exercising. The most convincing argument of all is that when you've been following an exercise program for a while, then stop, *you feel awful.* That's when you realize how valuable it's been.

Question: How can people cultivate the life wish?

Dr. Pelletier: You can start by making a habit of simply quieting your mind to the point where you can stand back from your life to see if it's in fact the way you wish it was. Just because your answer to that question might be "no" doesn't mean you're necessarily courting ill health. It may just mean you haven't attained a certain goal yet. As a matter of fact, it seems to be psychologically valuable to have a goal greater than you can immediately fulfill. You often see instances of spontaneous remission from terminal diseases among people working toward a goal or waiting for something fulfilling to occur, something specific like the completion of a book, the birth of a relative's child.

Make a habit of quieting your mind.

The will to live is a real desire to remain an active participant in life, whether at work or play. Another component shows up in the willingness to experiment, to try new things and not be bogged down in one particular activity. Another factor is the realization that there's something bigger than the self: a belief in the spiritual. This is not necessarily in the form of religious dogma. In fact, very seldom does it take that form. It's simply a sense of something greater than the individual self. This can really be a factor promoting health. When people get a sense of that, during therapy, for example, they change markedly.

The will to live is a real desire to remain an active participant in life.

SLOW DOWN AND LIVE

Question: Is there any value to just lying back and doing *nothing* every now and then—for instance, by a pool or under a tree?

Dr. Pelletier: It's fantastic! I learned that from personal experience. Several years ago I was doing research on the neurophysiological stress profile, and I happened to hook *myself* up to the instruments one morning. I was a wreck! I knew what pathological profiles looked like and there I was! It was an enlightening experience. All kinds of things about my life just flashed before me: how I was living, how I was treating people, how I was relating to myself.

Play may be the most vital thing you do.

So I began taking small meditative breaks during the day, telling myself it's OK to work in the morning and then go lie in the sun for a few hours. We tend to look at free time as something we're not supposed to have. As if it were a *waste,* somehow. What I realized, though, is that this rest is an absolute necessity for adequate functioning on a mental and physical level. The body requires exertion; it also requires rest. Your play may be the most vital thing you do for your life.

Question: How can people free themselves from feeling that rest is a waste of time?

Don't feel that rest is a waste of time.

Dr. Pelletier: I tell people to assume a meditative posture, and as they lie in the sun a little voice will come up and say, "What are you doing here? You're supposed to be *working*." Our normal way is to grab onto that and start worrying about it, to let it get us. But what you do instead is just see it as a *thing,* as a *thought*. It could be about anything, this thought. In this case, it happens to be about lying in the sun. So you just look at this thing and . . . let it go. Then another thought will come up. Your foot is itchy, don't you want to get up and scratch it? You say wait a minute, that's just *another* thing that floated in front of my mind. Let it go.

Don't let the internal critic run your life.

You treat all those thoughts as if they were objects, which is what they are. And there are a finite number of them. I've yet to find any person who can sit down and try to have more than 15 ruminations come up. There are about 15 themes that consistently come up. After a while, you can number them. Oh yes, I know that one. It's number 12: foot itches. There's number 14: mother saying her son will grow up to be a bum. Pretty soon you get bored with listening to that little voice, bored with letting that part of your mind run your life. You literally let go of it, so it just isn't there anymore, or so that when it comes, it leaves very quickly.

Be sensitive. The ultimate measure is how these things make you feel. When you make changes—in your diet or in your exercise habits, for example—ask yourself how they make you feel. How is it affecting your health?

You are your own recipe. What do you do after you put together all the ingredients of a recipe? You taste it! If it tastes bad, who cares that you followed it perfectly? On the other hand, it might taste terrific.

The Painkiller
in Your Mind

John, a 52 - year - old cardiologist, lived with constant, agonizing low back pain following treatment for rectal cancer. The pain, he said, was "unbearable," and had reduced his options to three: successful treatment, somewhere; voluntary commitment to a mental institution; or suicide. He could not go on living without relief. In desperation, he sought the help of a psychologist at the pain control unit of a local hospital.

In reviewing John's records, the psychologist noticed that during an earlier psychiatric workup, John had described his pain with terrible vividness: It was like "a dog chewing on my spine," he had said. Believing that this image was more than merely picturesque—that it was, in fact, a sort of nightmarish picture postcard for the source of his pain—the psychologist tried to convince John to make contact with the dog, to talk to it, to find out why it was chewing his spine and, somehow, to make it stop.

Talk to your pain and make it stop.

With his training in traditional medicine, John at first considered the idea absurd, but his pain was so intense that he decided to give it a try. Over a series of sessions, the psychologist taught John to relax physically and mentally, and open his mind to the image of the dog. Then John started talking to it—and the dog talked back.

The dog said John never really wanted to be a doctor in the first place; he'd wanted to be an architect, but his mother had pressured him into medical school. As a result, his glowering resentment was directed at his mother, his colleagues, and his patients. It was also directed inward, the

The pain talked back.

dog said, and had contributed to the development of his cancer and his low back pain, too.

The dog told John he was a good doctor. "It may not be the career you wanted, but it's time you recognized how good you are at what you do. When you stop being so resentful and start accepting yourself, I'll stop chewing on your spine." These insights were accompanied by an immediate easing of the pain, and during the following weeks it slowly subsided.

THE "LAND OF IMAGERY"

It may sound like an unorthodox—not to say just plain nutty—approach to the problem of chronic pain. "After all, what would be your initial reaction to a doctor who encouraged you to talk to little animals in your head?" asks David E. Bresler, Ph.D., director of the Bresler Center for Allied Therapeutics in Los Angeles, and author of *Free Yourself from Pain* (Simon & Schuster).

Pain-control imagery techniques could provide relief.

But Dr. Bresler, who describes in his book how he helped John using pain-control imagery techniques, says the method is "basically just a way of talking to ourselves, which is hardly a new concept." Yet for the many Americans who suffer from chronic pain—pain that persists after the solutions offered by traditional medicine and psychiatry have been exhausted—it could provide blessed relief.

"The divorce rate among chronic pain sufferers is horrendous," says Neal H. Olshan, Ph.D., a private practitioner in Scotsdale, Arizona, and author of *Power Over Your Pain without Drugs* (Rawson, Wade Publishers). "Typically, they've been on a kind of merry-go-round of drugs and surgery, seeing specialist after specialist, with only limited relief."

Pain is a friendly warning.

Dr. Bresler frowns on modern medicine's widespread use of painkilling drugs as a means of suppression. "Pain," he says, "is a symptom that tells you something is wrong. Symptoms are the way the body tries to heal itself. Pain is a friendly warning and not an enemy to be suppressed."

But, Drs. Bresler and Olshan agree, pain control imagery is the key to coping with the suffering until the cause of the pain can be resolved.

How does imagery work?

How does imagery work? By triggering the release of the body's natural painkillers. Called endorphins—literally, "morphine within"—these complex substances affect the body very much like a narcotic. By "talking" to our bodies, we can learn to control endorphin release, easing pain without the side effects of powerful human-made drugs. Dr. Bresler explains that this inner dialogue also contacts the autonomic nervous system, which controls such involuntary functions as heart rate and digestion and plays a critical role in the relief of chronic pain.

Because the autonomic nervous system is linked to the unconscious part of our minds—the part that processes information in an abstract, symbolic way—the only language it understands is that of symbolism and imagery. We can reach parts of our bodies controlled by the conscious mind with verbal commands: "Arm, reach for the sky!" or, "Tongue, stick out!" But to the unconscious mind, these commands are a foreign language. To talk to it, Dr. Bresler says, we need a new language, though "the land of imagery is largely neglected, and its language is often as unfamiliar as one spoke in a faraway country."

The only language our unconscious understands is symbolism and imagery.

For example, try telling your mouth to "produce and secrete saliva" (an involuntary function). Any luck? Then try—as clearly and vividly as possible—imagining a fresh, juicy, yellow lemon . . . imagine the spray of bright, tart juice as you slice it open with a knife . . . then take a wet slice and slip it in your mouth, tasting its incredible sourness, its sharpness, its wetness. Did that work any better?

With practice and guidance, the power of this kind of mental image making can often be harnessed to ease pain caused by everything from arthritis to angina. And in pain-control centers around the country, the use of imagery techniques has become increasingly common.

Dr. Olshan warns, however, that imagery's effectiveness could be dangerous if improperly used: "Since pain is the body's warning signal," he says, "It wouldn't be appropriate to use these techniques for an undiagnosed pain because they could mask the symptoms. You should see a doctor first."

See a doctor first.

In essence, imagery techniques are a way of reestablishing contact between mind and body. How Western medicine ever got them separated in the first place is a long story, but what is now becoming abundantly clear is that they've had a marvelously complex and intimate affair going all along, like two lovers conversing with winks and signals across a crowded room. Each one, it's now known, has an astonishing degree of control over the other.

A REMARKABLE PHENOMENON

The so-called "placebo effect," for example, has been described as "one of the most remarkable of all medical phenomena," yet it's so common that it's a factor in every medical experiment. Give a group of patients some utterly worthless treatment, such as a sugar pill or saltwater injection, tell them it's powerful medicine, and a certain percentage of them (usually about a third) will actually get better. What's important, apparently, is not the treatment itself but the patient's belief that it will work—an image of healing that becomes *real* (that is, physical) through a mysterious transformation we are only beginning to understand.

The mind is so powerful it can reverse the effects of strong drugs.

The mind's ability to trigger the body's self-cure, given the proper suggestions, is so powerful that in some cases it has been known to *reverse* the effects of strong drugs. In one case, a pregnant woman complaining of nausea was given ipecac—one of the most widely used emetics (vomitting-inducing agents) known—and was told it would soothe her discomfort. Within minutes, her nausea disappeared! It's a phenomenon that led Irving Oyle, M.D., to declare in his book *The Healing Mind* (Celestial Arts), "Whatever you put your trust in can be the precipitating agent for your cure."

Why we can't cure ourselves at will.

Of course, most of us can't just "take" the placebo effect any time we want, like a pill—otherwise there wouldn't be any doctors, drugs, or hospitals. We'd just cure ourselves at will. But the power is still there, whether we know how to use it or not; refining the technique of calling it up when it's needed is what the new pain-control therapies are all about.

With new research into the actual mechanism behind the placebo effect, it now appears that endorphins play a key role. In one study at the University of California at San Francisco, 23 dental patients who had teeth pulled a few hours earlier were injected with a placebo. Over a third reported that their pain eased up as a result. But when they were injected with a second substance that blocks the action of endorphins, pain returned to all of them. Apparently, their belief that the placebo was working triggered the release of those natural painkillers, which really do provide "fast, safe relief."

Are pain-control imagery techniques really effective in doing the same thing? C. Norman Shealy, M.D., founder of the Pain and Health Rehabilitation Center in La Crosse, Wisconsin, says he has found relaxation and visualization techniques to be "the single most important therapy which we can offer to chronically ill individuals with a wide variety of problems."

Visualization: "The most important therapy for the chronically ill."

Dr. Bresler says drugs and surgery are often the *least* effective methods of dealing with chronic pain.

And Dr. Olshan reports that his rate of success—that is, the number of people who learn to reduce and control their pain to the point they're able to resume a productive lifestyle—is roughly 60 percent, with many more achieving "at least significant relief." Do any of them relieve their pain completely? "Those people are in the minority, although there are some who do," he says. "But most people, by their own subjective rating, learn to reduce their pain by 60 to 80 percent.

60 percent reduce and control their pain.

A REAL "PAIN IN THE NECK"

Deep relaxation is the foundation of all the pain imagery techniques, Dr. Olshan explains. The reason is that when the mind and the body are relaxed, many physiological changes occur, including an increase in the body's ability to produce endorphins. "You're putting your body in the best posture to work toward healing itself," he says. "I like to look at the body as a self-righting sailboat: If you just relax and leave it alone, it will right itself."

If you relax, the body will heal itself.

Then, in a state of deep relaxation, the patient is guided through various exercises designed to focus relief on the source of the pain. All these exercises are actually a form of self-hypnosis, Dr. Olshan explains: a way of putting the conscious mind "to sleep," so that all messages will be funneled to the subconscious mind and the involuntary nervous system.

Dr. Bresler uses one exercise called "glove anesthesia," in which the patient is first taught to make his hand numb, then is told to transfer the numbness to the body part that's in pain. In another, patients are instructed to seek an "inner advisor," usually an animal (like John's dog), who can

Seek an "inner advisor."

provide advice on how to reduce stress and pain and also
help the sufferer discover "the message behind the pain."
Sometimes the message is one of repressed anger and
frustration, as in John's case. Other times, the pain may
have its source in an anxiety-producing lifestyle or an unpleasant relationship.

In fact, there may be people in your life who are quite
literally "a real pain in the neck," "a constant headache," or
just "too much to stomach," according to Rene Cailliet,
M.D., medical director of the physical medicine and rehabilitation department of the Santa Monica Hospital and author
of nine textbooks on pain syndromes. Dr. Cailliet says that
Americans may be spending billions of dollars and subjecting
themselves to unnecessary surgery for chronic pain caused
by relationships that hurt—and show up as low back pain,
migraines, peptic ulcers, or even heart attacks.

Most people aren't aware that the cause of pain is emotional.

"Most people aren't aware that the cause is emotional,"
Dr. Cailliet says. "But with back pain now one of the most
common of all patient complaints in the nation, back surgery isn't being done as often without a psychological
evaluation first."

Helping Others
Heal Themselves

Most of us will have to nurse someone we love through an ailment from time to time, even if it's only the flu or a sprained ankle. So as health amateurs, what's the best thing we can do for our partners? Different experts use different names for it, but they all prescribe the same thing: love and compassion.

Patients need "unconditional positive regard," says Harry Krop, Ph.D., a psychologist at the Veterans Administration (VA) Medical Center in Gainesville, Florida. Krop is a specialist in helping cardiac patients recover from the emotional stress of their illness.

"The important thing is unconditional positive regard," he says. "A spouse must show that he or she really cares, regardless of what the illness may mean. The spouse must show that it doesn't matter if the other person can't work or socialize. And the way a person recovers can depend on this kind of encouragement."

Elizabeth Daubert, R.N., uses another word: closeness. In her work with the Connecticut Association for Home Care, she visits people who are recovering from illnesses at home, and she knows what helps them most.

"A good close relationship will get you through almost anything," she says. "If you have a good, strong relationship, your chances of recovery are much better. That's not to say there won't be stress, but if you don't have closeness you're in for a lot of problems."

Communication sometimes breaks down when a hus-

People on the mend need "unconditional positive regard."

A good, close relationship will get you through almost anything.

band is reluctant to talk about his health. Many men in their 50s and 60s, Daubert says, grew up believing that men should "tough things out" and present a calm exterior, even if they're anxious about their health. Men believe that women may be able to talk about their health problems, but that men shouldn't.

ROLES ARE REVERSED

An illness in the family requires that the whole family adjust.

In fact, sticking to a certain stereotyped behavior can cause two people a lot of trouble during an illness, and Elizabeth Daubert isn't alone in thinking so. Alice Cooper, a mental-health consultant to the Visiting Nurses Association of New York, has found that people experience a lot of stress if their spouses' illnesses force them to do things they're not used to doing.

"Role change is really a very big issue among the people I see," Cooper says. "Very often, the wife has always been the chief caretaker of the home. She does all the cooking and cleaning and she may have waited on her husband for years. But if she is ill and can't do those chores, her husband may suddenly feel helpless.

"On the other hand," Cooper adds, "the husband may have always handled the family's financial matters. If he gets sick, his wife might have to take on that job. It's strange, but what sometimes happens is that the woman will enjoy her new duties and not want to give them up when her husband gets well."

However, for those who truly enjoy the role of caring for their spouses when they are ill, Cooper has this warning: Make sure you don't accidentally prolong their illness. That's something to look out for when a couple's home turns into an "empty nest."

Sometimes a spouse's illness fills a psychological need.

"There can be a hidden incentive to keep a spouse ill," she says. "Sometimes the spouse's illness fills a need. A woman might be through raising her children and might be suffering from the 'empty nest' syndrome. Her husband's illness might give her an opportunity to care for someone again.

"Unconsciously, the two of them might perpetuate the illness. For example, the husband might also be a traveling salesman, and if the illness keeps him at home, his wife might like having him at home."

Indeed, the idea that couples might have something to

gain from an illness—or that they might pretend to be sick—has been looked into by many doctors. One of them is Edward Waring, M.D., a psychiatrist at the University of Western Ontario in London, Canada.

Dr. Waring studied 13 married couples. In each case, one of the partners suffered mysteriously from chronic pain—a headache, backache, or stomach pain—that they couldn't cure. X-rays didn't reveal any logical source of the pain, and no medication could relieve it.

In 13 cases of chronic pain, no physical cause could be found...

FOCUSING ON AN ACHE

Using an "intimacy questionnaire" that he invented, Dr. Waring decided to evaluate the couples emotionally. They were asked 90 questions on their feelings about sex, marriage, relations with other people, and other personal areas. When he compared their answers to the answers of 30 healthy couples, a distinct pattern appeared.

Unlike the healthy couples, the ill couples said they had difficulty sharing their emotions and ideas, felt isolated from other couples, expressed very little affection, and lacked sexual satisfaction. Unable to talk about important things, they talked instead about one partner's pain. "The symptom became a major topic of conversation and the focal point of how the couple organized their lives," Dr. Waring says.

. . . but marital difficulties were more prevalent than among healthy controls.

"Some people say that it's easier for them to complain about a bad back than try to talk about the relationship," he says. But after openly confronting the problem, most of the couples were able to give up the psychosomatic pain they'd been hanging onto.

Clinging to an illness as a way of avoiding intimacy also occurs among men who have recovered from heart attacks. According to VA psychologist Dr. Harry Krop, some cardiac patients who have had sexual difficulties in the past use their condition as an excuse to avoid intimate contact.

Clinging to an illness can be a way of avoiding intimacy.

But it is more likely, says Dr. Krop, that a man will refrain from sex because of unfounded fears about overtaxing his heart.

"I'm working with a couple right now where the husband was a workaholic," says Dr. Krop. "He enjoyed the stress in his life, and he had always put his work ahead of his family. But when he had his heart attack, the family suddenly became important.

"Six months after the heart attack, though, he and his wife still hadn't resumed relations. His wife came to see me, and told me that he seemed to be avoiding the issue. She was afraid she was no longer attractive to him. When we explored the situation, it turned out he was still anxious about his heart."

Wives should know if the heart attack really rules out sex. Finding out can be difficult, however, since wives are often not included in conversations between husbands and their cardiologists. And the husband himself may not be sure, since some physicians are as embarrassed to bring up the subject of sex as their patients are.

In most cases, a heart attack does not prevent sexual relations.

In the majority of cases, a heart attack does not prevent normal sexual relations, Dr. Krop says. The exertion of sex—which raises the pulse to 115 or 120 beats per minute—is usually within the capacity of someone who has recovered from a heart attack.

Readjustment after a heart attack is a serious issue, but cooperation and understanding between the marriage partners can be equally important in less serious situations. In changing routine habits, for example, Elizabeth Daubert points out that a woman won't be able to talk her husband out of an unhealthy habit unless she uses tact.

"For instance," she says, "a woman might want her husband to stop smoking. If she says, 'Smoking is a dirty habit and I can't stand having you do it anymore,' she won't get anywhere.

"I love you and I don't want you to smoke."

"But if she says to him, 'I love you and I don't want you to smoke because I want you to be with me for as long as possible,' then her husband will take the message to heart. It might be enough to motivate him to change."

Doctors have also found that often they can't change a patient's eating habit unless the spouse cooperates. Elmer Cranton, M.D., of Trout Dale, Virginia, says that it's difficult for his patients to stick to a wholesome, natural diet if the spouse won't prepare healthful foods.

"I try to talk to both people in my office at once, and tell them both what needs to be done," he says.

"But it happens sometimes that one of them thinks the natural approach is crazy.

A hostile spouse can stand in the way of recovery.

"Sometimes a spouse is openly hostile, and that can be the thing that prevents recovery. On the other hand, a supportive spouse can really prevent backsliding. A person might have a tendency, for instance, to start eating salty foods again. But a gentle nagger might prevent that."

OPPORTUNITY FOR GROWTH

Although nursing your spouse through an illness can be very stressful, it can also be an opportunity for a husband and wife's relationship to grow.

Dr. Harry Krop's patient, for example, felt that his heart attack was a turning point in his marriage.

"The heart attack made that couple aware of how vulnerable they were," Dr. Krop said. "They realized that they had kept putting off the things they had always wanted to do, like travel. And they realized that those plans were meaningless unless they could be together. Instead of putting things off, they decided to take advantage of the time they did have."

Alice Cooper also thinks that an illness might offer a chance to grow. "Every time you have a crisis, you have an opportunity to move to a higher level," she says. "Some people are able to take advantage of it. It all depends on how each person copes with the strain.

"People also adjust to illnesses differently. If one person copes by denial, by sweeping the problem under the rug, and the other copes by talking things over, then you'll just have conflict. But if the man and woman both cope with problems by discussing them rationally, or if both cope by saying, 'We'll enjoy each day as it comes,' then they have a chance to grow together."

One woman who cared for her husband at home for many years, and later wrote a book on the subject, also talks about squeezing good feelings out of a bad situation. She is Evelyn Baulch, a Redwood City, California, woman, and since publishing her book, *Home Care* (Celestial Arts), she has talked to many other spouses with similar experiences.

"Over and over, people tell me that it was an experience that was very important for them," Baulch says. "They say they wouldn't want to have missed it. They look back years later and say that it was a turning point in their lives. Something very positive came out of it.

"Nothing in life is absolutely negative," she says. "It all depends on how you look at it. You can look at things as a problem or as a challenge. You get stronger by pushing up against things."

Squeezing good feelings out of bad experiences.

PART XII

The Mind/Body Connection

64. A Practical Guide to Self-Healing

A Practical Guide to Self-Healing

It is estimated that 90 percent of all physical problems have psychological roots. That may sound like a gross exaggeration. In fact, it's probably a conservative estimate. A growing body of evidence indicates that virtually every ill that can befall the body—from acne to arthritis, headaches to heart disease, cold sores to cancer—is influenced, for better or worse, by our emotions.

From acne to arthritis, emotions are involved.

That's not to say that we can prevent or cure every disease through mind power; disease states are incredibly complex and involve a myriad of contributing factors. But, based on the latest research, it's clear that the mind is a healing tool like no other. Through such techniques as guided imagery, self-hypnosis, biofeedback, and acupressure, for example, we can literally send healing messages to the brain where they are translated into biochemistry, the language of the body.

What follows is mind/body research as it relates to a wide variety of physical ills—with practical suggestions on how to put your mind to healing.

ACCIDENTS

Accidents are the fourth biggest cause of death in America. Only heart disease, cancer, and strokes kill more people than accidents.

To get a handle on why people have accidents, safety researchers used to try to understand the "accident-prone" personality—someone who not only gets out on the wrong

Everyone is "accident prone"—sometimes.

side of bed, but *falls* out. However, researchers have realized that anyone can go through a period of life when they're more likely to have accidents. And they've found the reason—stress.

ODDS STACKED AGAINST YOU

"During stressful periods in life, your odds of being in an accident increase," says Abraham Bergman, M.D., a researcher at the University of Washington in Seattle.

One group of boys had over twice as many accidents—why?

Dr. Bergman came to that conclusion after conducting a study of 103 junior-high-school boys. For five months, the boys reported their accidents and also reported any "life changes," such as moving to a new school or a serious illness in the family. After the five months were up, Dr. Bergman and his two colleagues tallied the life changes and the number of accidents. The boys under little stress from change had a total of 395 accidents; the boys under high levels of stress had 946.

In a similar study, two researchers from the University of Michigan gave a questionnaire to over 500 men, asking about the stress in their lives over the preceding year and also about the number of car accidents they had had. The researchers then compared the amount of stress to the number of accidents to see if they matched up. They did.

The four types of stress that "predict" accidents.

Life changes and stress, they write, "are significantly related to traffic accidents." The events most likely to "predict" accidents were physical stress responses (smoking, insomnia, headaches, ulcers); problems with parents or in-laws; problems or pressure in school or on the job; and financial troubles *(American Journal of Psychiatry)*.

In another study to see if excess stress had something to do with everyday accidents and errors, researchers tested 31 nurses by tallying all their positive and negative "challenging events" (ranging from illness or injury to the birth of a grandchild). From the data collected, they were able to successfully predict which nurses were the most likely to suffer from a rash of physical accidents (dropping things, auto mishaps) and job-related errors (mistakes in judgment) in the following weeks *(Science News)*.

Stress causes accidents. But why?

"People who are under a lot of stress are likely candidates for accidents—big and small—because they can't think, act, and react in a normal, relaxed manner," says a former supervisor of safety management programs for Pennsylvania State University's Institute of Public Safety.

Instead of paying close attention to the task at hand, the stressed person is preoccupied.

Stress is very significant, because should a person be having problems at home, with marriage, children, finances, or whatever, that person definitely won't be able to pay 100 percent attention to what they're doing. When the individual is preoccupied with problems, when they're tense and worried, that's when accidents often occur.

ALLERGIES AND ASTHMA

It's difficult to fathom how emotions can trigger allergies—those itching, wheezing reactions that result from close encounters with dust, ragweed, tomatoes, and a whole host of other environmental irritants. But within the last 20 years, researchers have uncovered a definite link.

In one study, guinea pigs subjected to stress and exposed to a chemical irritant showed greater skin sensitivity than another group of non-stressed animals exposed to the same irritant. Studies on people have yielded similar findings. Researchers have discovered, for example, that stress and personality factors contribute to contact dermatitis and that the psychological state described as "suppressed weeping" can give rise to hives.

Bronchial asthma has also been tied to emotional factors. Psychological studies suggest that people with asthma may have "unconscious dependency wishes" and that feelings of frustration or conflict related to those unconscious desires can trigger an attack.

The psychology behind an asthma attack.

The crux of this mind/body link is the immune system. In many allergic people, white blood cells, the body's key defenders against infection and disease, mistake a perfectly normal and harmless substance like wheat or dust or pollen for an enemy antigen. Inappropriately, they jump into action to initiate plasma production of antibodies—usually of the type known as IgE (shorthand for Immunoglobulin E)—against the "enemy" antigen. These antibodies then latch onto cells in the nose, throat, and lungs; stomach and intestines; or skin. And, boom, you've got a full-blown allergy.

Not surprisingly, people suffering with allergies or asthma tend to have elevated blood levels of IgE. But George Solomon, M.D., professor of psychiatry at UCLA and adjunct professor of psychiatry at the University of California at San Francisco—the man who's known as the "father of psychoneuroimmunology"—has demonstrated that stress may increase IgE levels in animals.

Although this has yet to be confirmed in people, the link between stress, emotions, and allergy is now widely accepted.

"Any period of stress may weaken the immune system, so that you react more easily to foods or chemicals," says Iris R. Bell, M.D., Ph.D., a San Francisco psychiatrist. Managing stress, therefore, can help you weather allergic encounters.

Imagery creates a stronger biological state.

"An important approach I use to alleviate stress is some form of relaxation therapy," says Dr. Bell. "There are a variety of approaches. One is imagery, in which I tell people to imagine themselves in a safe environment whenever they find themselves exposed to a threatening food or chemical. That takes advantage of what the mind can do for the body; a message is sent from the brain to the rest of the body, putting you in a stronger biological state.

"The relaxation method you choose is not all that important, as long as it works for the individual," she adds. "All achieve the same basic goal—reducing stress" (see Chapter 29, The Best of the Relaxation Techniques).

WILLING AWAY THE ALLERGY

Take the case of a young man who has been highly allergic to many things from early childhood on. He has learned to suppress allergic reactions at the first inkling of symptoms by concentrating very, very, hard and saying to himself, "I will not react." He calls it "willing the allergy away." And it works! There's nothing magical about it, either. Robert W. Boxer, M.D., an allergist in Skokie, Illinois, says, "It's well established that, just as the body can affect the mind, the mind can affect the body. You can actually lower your body's levels of chemical mediators [histamine and other allergy-provoking substances] by your mental attitude—how you look at things and how you handle stress."

"It comes down to a matter of how much control you have," says Dr. Bell. "Some people are extremely good at using their minds to control their bodies. For them these techniques are ideal. Most of us fall into a range—we can be at our best if we're relaxing in some way, *plus* watching our diet and perhaps doing one or two other things."

Regular exercise may be an additional way to diffuse stress in your life—and reduce your allergy symptoms at the same time. "Just minor, nonvigorous exercise like walking a block can produce measurable, beneficial psychological changes," says psychologist-neurologist Ronald Lawrence, M.D., Ph.D.

Exercise reduces allergy symptoms.

MORE HELP FOR ASTHMA SUFFERERS

When an asthma attack strikes, a reaction of panic, and a fear of not being able to draw in enough air, may be overwhelming and can cause the attack to worsen. Bronchodilators and drugs can be livesaving tools at such times. Ideally, though, the asthmatic should strive to avoid the panic, or at least to short-circuit it. And there's lots of evidence that some easy-to-learn techniques of progressive relaxation can help avert an asthma assault.

How to short-circuit an asthma attack.

Self-hypnosis is another worthwhile approach. When doctors in San Antonio set out to train eight young asthma sufferers in self-hypnosis, they found gratifying results. The six who completed the study reduced the severity of their symptoms in just two months, and in three months reduced the frequency of their attacks, plus had fewer visits to the emergency room compared to the previous year. They also seemed to need less medication *(Journal of Allergy and Clinical Immunology)*.

One of the more amazing aspects of the use of hypnosis in this area is the way asthma sufferers literally can be turned on or off. A simple suggestion to a hypnotized asthmatic that he or she has just come into contact with something that normally causes a sensitivity reaction causes that reaction to occur, simply because the person believes it to be so. The other side of the coin—the beneficial side—allows an asthmatic to click into a hypnotic state in order to shut down an attack. So far, though, self-hypnosis hasn't proved to be nearly as effective in stemming hay-fever episodes.

ANGINA

"Excessive stress can trigger an angina attack," says James L. Levenson, M.D., assistant professor of psychiatry at the Medical College of Virginia in Richmond. "In some forms of stress the adrenal glands secrete epinephrine—the hormone associated with the 'fight or flight' response. This in turn increases heart rate and blood pressure and hence the workload on the heart. Also, some patients may be more vulnerable to artery spasms at these times," Dr. Levenson says. "Any of these occurrences has the potential of closing down the arteries, bringing on angina pain." (See Part VI, Healthful Living in a Stressful World, for tips on relaxation.)

POSITIVE THINKING

Denying your angina is serious may reduce the pain.

Believing you will lick your problem, even denying that it's terribly serious, can actually work in your favor, according to Dr. Levenson. At least it did in a group of patients with unstable angina. "We divided these patients into two groups—deniers and nondeniers—based on their score on a specialized set of questions," Dr. Levenson explains.

Despite similar treatment regimens, it took the nondeniers about twice as long to become medically stabilized— pain-free for 36 hours *(Psychosomatic Medicine)*.

Are you a denier?

Are you a denier or nondenier? "It's not hard to tell," says Dr. Levenson. "Deniers are people who are less flustered and less frightened by the news of their illness. They'll be lying there in the intensive-care unit, smiling. Ideally, they are able to follow all the recommended advice, but still deny the danger they're in. In other words, they're not incapacitated by fear.

"Deniers are people who may flirt with danger; you know, the daredevil types. On a more positive note, they also have a more carefree, jovial attitude toward life.

"Of course, denial can be taken too far, and we watch out for that," says Dr. Levenson. "Continuing to smoke, for example, is downright reckless. On the other hand, when a patient is scared to death, we try to play down their illness a bit, to help them deny it.

"There used to be a tendency by some doctors to try to break through the denial, to make patients own up to their illness. But that is unwarranted when the patient is acutely ill. If denial is protective for the patient, then it's a bad idea to intervene."

ARTHRITIS

People with rheumatoid arthritis are full of inner turmoil, likely to be excessively conscientious, fearful of criticism, frequently depressed, and have a poor self-image, says Robert Fathman, Ph.D., a Dublin, Ohio, clinical psychologist. Dr. Fathman and Norman Rothermich, M.D., professor emeritus, Ohio State University, Columbus, conducted a study that evaluates the personality traits of rheumatoid arthritis sufferers.

The five common personality traits of people with rheumatoid arthritis.

"We found they have a personality that leads them to try overly hard to be nice to other people, to not lean on others for emotional support, and to stow things away down inside, especially anger," Dr. Fathman says. "They were remarkably conforming to these traits, which seem to precede the disease, not result from it."

Many rheumatoid arthritis sufferers also had a situation of long-term tension or anger in their lives, Dr. Fathman says. But these are people who will say everything's just fine when that couldn't be further from the truth.

They say, "Everything's fine"—but it's not.

"One woman first said that her husband was marvelous," Dr. Fathman recalls. "And as I started questioning her further, tears came to her eyes and it turned out that before they would go out in the evening she had to stand inspection. Her husband would take a brush and do something to her hair, or tell her what she needed to do better for herself before they went out. Her husband was very controlling and she permitted him to be that way."

The end result, Dr. Fathman says, is that these people have so much repressed anger that it "eats them up." "The anger gets turned against the person herself," Dr. Fathman says. And in this case it might literally. Rheumatoid arthritis is thought to be an autoimmune disease, in which the immune system mutinies against the body.

PHYSIOLOGICAL EVIDENCE OF A PSYCHOLOGICAL LINK

In what is already considered a classic study in the new field of psychoneuroimmunology, California psychiatrist Dr. George Solomon and Rudolf H. Moos, Ph.D., both then at the Stanford University School of Medicine, discovered that people who are genetically predisposed to arthritis but are emotionally healthy avert the disease.

Drs. Solomon and Moos focused their attention on a blood factor present in most rheumatoid arthritis sufferers—and in about 20 percent of their healthy relatives. This "rheumatoid factor," as it is called, is an autoantibody—an antibody which, through some quirk of the immune system, reacts against the body's own protective antibodies.

A genetic time bomb that's defused by emotional health.

The question is this: Why do some people remain perfectly healthy despite the presence of this menacing autoantibody in their blood? The answer, say Drs. Solomon and Moos, lies in their psychological profile. Physically healthy relatives of arthritis sufferers who tested positive for the rheumatoid factor were, *without exception,* emotionally healthy. By comparison, those relatives who were free of the autoantibody represented a psychological cross section of the general population—ranging from emotionally healthy to significantly disturbed.

"We assume from this that if you have the rheumatoid factor in your blood but stay in good condition psychologically, you won't get arthritis," Dr. Solomon says. "On the other hand, if you're genetically predisposed, and endure long periods of anxiety and/or depression or suffer some major emotional upset, you are at a high risk for arthritis."

With 5 percent of the general population silent carriers of this arthritis-related autoantibody, his words sound a warning to all of us. And his theory linking rheumatoid arthritis with emotional stress is gaining wide support among physicians and researchers alike.

STRESS AS A TRIGGER

First a divorce, then juvenile rheumatoid arthritis.

For example, John Baum, M.D., at the University of Rochester, examined the medical records of 88 children who had been treated for juvenile rheumatoid arthritis at a Rochester hospital. He found that 28 percent of them—many more than in the general population—came from broken homes. And for half of these, the divorce or death of a parent had taken place within two years of the onset of the disease.

"Quite possibly, stress is a trigger for juvenile arthritis," Dr. Baum says. "It probably doesn't cause it, but it may set it off."

The same thing applies to adults, says George Ehrlich, M.D., director of the division of rheumatology at the Hahnemann Medical School and Hospital in Philadelphia. Emotional stress can initiate rheumatoid arthritis in a susceptible person, and once the disease has established itself, stress can make it worse.

"Acute stress—losing your job, a death in the family, a divorce—can make arthritis flare up. It makes you vulnerable. When you're under stress, your body's defenses can be breached." Small, constant irritations are less dramatic but can be just as harmful.

"There's such a thing as wholesome stress," Dr. Ehrlich says. "A challenging job, for instance—that's exercise for the mind. It's unwholesome stress, frustration, that lays you open to the disease."

There are social implications as well. "Women have rheumatoid arthritis up to four times more frequently than men," explains Dr. Robert Fathman, "and I think it's because of what we do to little girls in our society. We teach them that it's wrong to get angry."

Why women have four times more arthritis than men.

Assertiveness training, relaxation techniques, and traditional group therapy help his rheumatoid arthritis patients function better, Dr. Fathman says. "They reported feeling less pain and were able to function better. They could identify stress with intensification of their pain very clearly."

At the arthritis center at Philadelphia's Albert Einstein Medical Center, Dr. Ehrlich says, psychologists and psychiatrists work with patients, teaching them how to deal with frustration and stress. Other clinics have used relaxation training to reduce pain.

Sexual activity can also help relieve pain. When doctors at the sexual dysfunction clinic of Chicago's Cook County Hospital questioned 55 arthritics about their sexual activity, 24—nearly half—reported that sex not only made them feel better, but actually relieved pain.

Sex can relieve pain.

These patients ranged in age from the 20s to the late 60s. Most were in the older range. "The reports were often striking," says Wanda Sadoughi, Ph.D., director of the clinic. "Not just 'the pain was reduced,' but 'I was free of pain for several hours.'"

How does sex relieve arthritic pain? "It could be any number of things," Dr. Sadoughi says, "something biochemical or hormonal, perhaps. And the emotional aspect is obviously important. Possibly, it involves both. Stress, after all, is both psychological and physiological, and sex can alleviate stress."

Many arthritics allow their disease to slow them down sexually more than they have to, Dr. Sadoughi says, and this is unfortunate. "Sex is a wonderful source of self-esteem— the feeling 'I'm still wanted, I'm still worthwhile.' A good sexual adjustment can improve your whole outlook toward life. These patients in the study didn't allow the disease to disable them."

"You can't give up."

Just such a positive attitude, in fact, could be the most powerful weapon you can bring to the struggle against arthritis. "You can't give up," says Dr. Baum. "You have to fight the disease."

"We have patients with severe arthritis, severe deformity, who refuse to give up, and they do as well as patients with milder cases but less determination. Your desire to keep on going is the most important thing. If you aren't determined to make the best of your illness, doctors can pour in drugs, pour in everything, and it won't do any good."

IN REMISSION

And don't lose hope. The medical literature is laced with cases of arthritis remission—many of them related to the resolution of emotional conflicts.

Feelings expressed, disease cured.

In one case, for example, a woman who exhibited many of the psychological traits discussed earlier developed arthritis at the age of 12. She never complained, wouldn't ask for help, and considered herself independent although she did admit that she had difficulty standing up for herself. She married at the age of 18 but was unhappy. When she finally resolved on divorce, she discovered she was pregnant. Her disease markably worsened. After the baby was born, she and her husband reconciled. He became more responsible and she became substantially more expressive of her feelings. The arthritis went into remission.

In another case, a woman with severe *lupus erythematosus,* an inflammatory skin condition that appears to be triggered by the same immunological mechanisms as arthritis, is said to have "cured herself" by spending a year "unloading all her deep-seated and concealed hostility toward her father on [her doctor]." At last report she had been off cortisone treatment for six years and without recurrence.

In a paper entitled "Emotions, Immunity, and Disease" (published in the *Archives of General Psychiatry* back in 1964), Drs. George Solomon and Rudolf Moos relate some of the stirring observations of the late, well-regarded rheumatologist, Loring T. Swaim, M.D.—which take on added significance in view of today's increased knowledge of psychoneuroimmunology. In his book, *Arthritis, Medicine and Spiritual Laws: Power Beyond Science* (Chilton), Dr. Swaim "came to the conclusion from many years of practice that emotional factors are crucial in the [cause] of rheumatoid arthritis and attributed a number of remarkable remissions and 'cures' to Divine intervention as a result of faith. His case material lends itself to the interpretation that God serves as a powerful forgiving, protective transference figure to the patient leading to the abandonment of [emotionally triggered] symptoms. Dr. Swaim found that the first attack of arthritis was almost always preceded by unhappy events and long periods of sustained emotional strain. The feelings and emotions found most frequently were chronic bitterness and resentment (evidently unexpressed and guilt provoking). Patients were encouraged to admit their resentment, sincerely ask forgiveness . . . and then ask God for help and sustenance. Rheumatoid arthritis 'definitely improved in those who went the whole way.' "

BACK PAIN

While back pain can result from pulled muscles, slipped discs, and other mechanical problems, it is estimated that as high as 95 percent of all backaches are triggered by the mind.

Most backaches start in the mind.

Commonly, back muscles tense up in response to emotional stress. And, as Hans Kraus, M.D., a New York physiatrist, and author of the book *Backache, Stress and Tension* (Pocket Books), explains, "If muscles are tense for too long, it gets painful, as in a tension headache."

Consider, too, that the back is more susceptible to injury when the muscles are tense—and that accidents, in which back injuries occur, are more likely to happen when you're under stress.

Backaches also can result from the unconscious mind responding to internal conflict. When you think to yourself, "I wish he'd get off my back," or "she's really a pain in the neck," the unconscious mind can sometimes take your

"A pain in the neck"—literally.

musings literally, creating real pain. Also, with backaches responsible for more "sick days" than the common cold, doctors suggest that they, again, may be masterminded by the unconscious fulfilling an urgent need for time off.

"An individual develops pain in his back as a defense mechanism in a situation in which he finds he can no longer cope with emotional difficulties," says Leon Root, M.D., of the Hospital of Special Surgery in New York City. "But the pain he feels is still real and must be treated."

Biofeedback for back pain.

Biofeedback is one effective therapy for relieving back pain, according to an article in the *Back Pain Monitor,* a newsletter for back-pain sufferers and professional back-care specialists. Though not a panacea, biofeedback can help patients ease the anxiety and muscle tension that accompany most chronic back problems.

Biofeedback therapy can help people recognize when they are tensing muscles. Once the tension is recognized, back-pain sufferers can learn to relax stiff, sore muscles and thus ease the pain. It's especially helpful for people who are out of touch with their bodies and not even aware of being tense.

The electromyograph—a machine that turns pain into sound.

One popular method used for back-pain sufferers is to monitor electrical impulses in the back muscles, with the help of a special biofeedback machine called an electromyographic device, says the *Back Pain Monitor.*

When a back-pain sufferer is tensing, or contracting, a muscle, the machine will emit a tone. The sufferer then learns how to make that tone disappear by relaxing, or releasing back muscles.

Biofeedback gives back-pain sufferers a way to take control of their pain problem, reports the newsletter. That's especially crucial for people who want to avoid taking too much medication.

STIMULATING ENDORPHINS

Like morphine, but 200 times more powerful.

Acupuncture has also been used with much success. This Eastern therapy, which involves the insertion and stimulation of needles along points of the body, is still a mystery to the Western world. There's no doubt that it can produce an analgesic effect. But how? Interestingly enough, one explanation is that acupuncture somehow stimulates the body's production of endorphins, a natural painkiller similar to—but 200 times more powerful than—morphine.

A do-it-yourself alternative to acupuncture, which is said to produce similar results, is acupressure. Instead of needles, you use your fingers. For best results with acupressure, you'll eventually have to get used to pressing hard with your fingers on your skin, sometimes as hard as you can. But when you first start, you have to accustom yourself to finding and pressing the points. So don't jab yourself too hard in the beginning. Needles are used in acupuncture because the points for treatment lie a little below the skin, sometimes as deep as an inch and a half. With acupressure, you're not substituting your fingers for needles; you're substituting pressure for direct stimulation, and that pressure travels down to the treatment points.

A good acupressure point for backache relief is located on the top of the thigh. To locate the point on your left leg, sit down, then cross your legs by placing your left ankle on your right knee; your right foot should be flat on the floor. Now lean forward and place the palm of your right hand as flat as you can over your left knee. With your palm on your kneecap, put your thumb at a right angle to your hand and bend it so that the joint forms a right angle. The point is underneath your thumb. To be sure you have located this point, apply thumb pressure around your thigh in the area we just described until you feel a sensation radiating out from the pressure. Some low-back-pain sufferers will also experience a certain amount of pain and tenderness at this point. That's a good sign. The tenderness means that the point is related to your problem and, when treated, may help alleviate a lot of your pain.

Pressure points for backache relief.

Another backache treatment point is also located on the thigh but is along the outside. To find it, sit with your feet flat on the floor. Next, extend one of your legs out straight and lay one of your thumbs alongside the top border of your kneecap. Then place your other thumb along that one, on the side not touching the knee. Next to this second thumb, on a line with the outside border of the kneecap, is this point.

Once you've located a point, use the meaty section of your fingertip (away from your fingernail) and make a steady circular motion in and around the point for about 15 to 30 seconds. You can do this any time you feel the pain. One man who uses acupressure for his backaches often has pain while shopping in supermarkets; shopping involves standing for a long time and pushing a heavy cart. The man simply finds a relatively untraveled aisle, bends over and pretends to scratch his knees—all the while applying pressure to these points.

BURNS

Faster healing with hypnosis.

"Although the use of hypnosis in burn patients can result in pain relief, promotion of healing, and improvement of self-image, the therapy is often under-rated and underused," writes Beverly Merz in the *Journal of the American Medical Association.* She tells of an experiment at the Alta Bates Hospital in Berkeley, California, which profited from the knowledge that blood flow can be increased by hypnotic suggestion. By planting a suggestion into the minds of hypnotized burn victims to step up the flow of blood to only one of two affected limbs, the researchers noted not only a 4 degree Fahrenheit rise in limb temperature in the designated arm or leg, but faster healing there, too.

CANCER

Early studies depicted the typical cancer victim as passive and emotionless, someone with a loveless childhood who as an adult compensates by trying to build a better life for her family. She was portrayed as someone who works hard to please and to win love—all the while repressing anger, loneliness, and hopelessness.

When things go wrong in her life, the portrait continued, the cancer personality is engulfed in loneliness and depression. The cancer soon follows.

The pat answers of these early studies are flawed because they tend to look at people who already have cancer, says Joan Borysenko, Ph.D., of Harvard Medical School in Boston. "You are seeing their reaction to the diagnosis of a dread disease, which changes their personality. There is no way of knowing if the personality preceded the disease."

One possible cause of cancer: a poor relationship with your parents.

Dr. Borysenko, a psychologist and cell biologist, is among a group of doctors looking at the link between personality and cancer. There are two studies, she says, that have monitored the psychological and social factors prior to illness. One was started in 1946 by Caroline B. Thomas, M.D., professor emeritus, Johns Hopkins University School of Medicine. Dr. Thomas gave medical students a number of psychological tests and has been following them to see what kinds of illnesses they get. She found that a major difference between those who later developed cancer and the rest of the group was a poor relationship with their parents.

Thirty percent of those in the cancer group described themselves as "neither admiring nor comfortable" with their fathers or mothers, five times the rate in the healthy group.

Another large, ongoing study looking for behavioral precursors to cancer is being done by Richard B. Shekelle, Ph.D., professor of epidemiology, University of Texas School of Public Health in Houston.

Starting in 1957, it has followed about 2,000 men at a Western Electric plant in Chicago. The study has found that men who scored highest on depression went on to have more than twice the rate of cancer deaths as the rest of the group.

Depression doubles the cancer death rate.

"You might argue that depressed people simply smoke more and eat less well, but when the study was controlled for those factors, there was still a strong link between depression and cancer," Dr. Borysenko says.

In fact, several studies have shown that depression is associated with a weakened immune response.

Before the American Psychiatric Association, a psychiatrist disclosed the first clue to the process. He and his associates at the Mount Sinai School of Medicine in New York have been observing men whose wives have advanced breast cancer. As early as two weeks after the wives died, the men showed a striking drop in the white blood cell response to stimulants of the immune system (Medical World News).

In a similar study, Bernard S. Linn, M.D., professor of surgery at the University of Miami School of Medicine, and Margaret Linn, Ph.D., professor of psychiatry at the University of Miami, evaluated 49 men at risk for stress because of a recent death or severe illness of a family member. They found that the white blood cells that are the body's "cancer surveillance system" weren't working up to par.

Why the "cancer police" go off duty.

How people reacted to stress seemed to determine how badly their immune system was affected, Dr. Linn says. "Stress-hardy" people—those with less anxiety and fear— showed less impaired immune response than their more anxious counterparts.

LIVE YOUR OWN LIFE

Feeling hopeless and helpless under stress, and thinking you are responsible for the crisis, does seem to increase your chances of developing cancer, says Lawrence LeShan, Ph.D., author of *You Can Fight for Your Life* (M. Evans & Co.) and a specialist in psychotherapy for catastrophic illness.

"The big thing the majority of cancer victims have in common is that they have lost their major outlet for creative energy," Dr. LeShan says. "The death of a spouse, retirement, whatever, has closed off their channel of expression, their uniqueness."

Illness can remind us of our purpose in life.

Dr. LeShan views illness as a way to remind people of their purpose in life. "I don't ask you what's wrong with you and how you got that way. I ask you what's *right* with you. What's your special music for creating and relating, and what's blocking that expression?"

EXPRESS YOUR ANGER

Other physicians in the field believe that anger suppression—something that was linked to cancer in earlier studies—is a valid risk factor.

Learn self-defense.

"In the 1950s, two researchers looked at the life history patterns of about 400 cancer patients," says Marjorie Brooks, Ph.D., of Jefferson Medical College in Philadelphia. "They found the patients had some very interesting similarities. Many of them seemed unable to express anger or hostility in defense of themselves. The patients *could* get angry in the defense of others or in the defense of a cause. But when it came to self-defense, they didn't follow through.

"Suppressed hostility was another significant factor appearing in some of the other patients. They seemed to lack the discharge mechanism needed to allow anger to surface, so they kept all of their anger inside."

Other research, which focused on English women undergoing breast biopsies, "indicated that women who were very, very seldom angry and women who were highly volatile were more likely to have malignant tumors than women who had an appropriate expression of anger," says Dr. Brooks.

Her own research seems to confirm previous findings. She surveyed 1,100 women who did not have breast cancer and compared the results to those of 15 women with benign tumors and 15 women with malignancies.

"A significantly higher proportion of both benign and malignant patients stated they had experienced much more anger during the previous year than the 1,100 respondents who did not have disease," Dr. Brooks says. "A larger percentage of women having malignancies had felt angry more often than the women having benign tumors. And a larger percentage of women with benign tumors had felt angrier the previous year than women in normal health."

The *ways* in which the women expressed anger also were different. Women with malignant breast cancer were more likely to apologize for their anger, even when they were right, says Dr. Brooks. So whenever they *did* express their hostility, they often took it back.

Three styles of anger—one of which may prevent cancer.

Women with benign tumors tended to get angry and stay angry. Their anger often became an unresolved internal conflict.

Women in normal health were more likely to blow up and then forget about it, says Dr. Brooks. They redirected their attention and energies to more pleasant things.

Dr. Brooks's research suggests ties between anger and progression of disease. "Often, people feel angry over being dependent and helpless in a treatment situation," she says. "But if that angry energy can be redirected, they feel less stress, and quite likely their physical condition will be positively affected."

ACCEPTANCE VS. DENIAL

In a major study of breast cancer patients in England, researchers classified the women according to the way they responded to the diagnosis of breast cancer. They found four distinct approaches to the disease among the women they interviewed.

Some women reacted with complete denial that any of the signs of their disease were serious. The denial was so complete that some patients told the researchers after mastectomies that their breasts had been removed only "as a precaution." Other women took the attitude that they could personally fight and defeat the disease. They tried to find out everything they could about breast cancer in order to conquer it. A third group acknowledged that they had

Who survives cancer and who doesn't—and why.

cancer, accepted the diagnosis stoically, and made no effort to find out anything more about the disease. The last group reacted by simply giving up. They felt totally powerless to improve their conditions and resigned themselves to an early death.

There were dramatic differences in the survival rates of the four groups. Three-quarters of the patients who responded to their diagnosis with either denial of the existence of the disease or a firm fighting spirit were alive and well five years later. Only 35 percent of the other women, those who either accepted their fate stoically or gave up completely, were still alive at that time. The patients in those two groups accounted for 88 percent of the women who had died five years later *(Lancet)*.

"IMAGING" AWAY CANCER

"Visual" improvement.

Findings about the importance of the mind's role in disease have led O. Carl Simonton, M.D., a Pacific Palisades, California, physician, and his wife, Stephanie Matthews-Simonton, to set up a program for terminal cancer patients. At the Simonton Cancer Counseling Center, patients practice a kind of meditation called *imagery,* in conjunction with traditional cancer treatments. They visualize the cancer cells in their bodies being overwhelmed by their treatment and flushed out of their bodies. Then they "image" good cells—healthy cells—taking over and, in their mind's eye, picture themselves as healthy and free of disease.

In their book *Getting Well Again* (J. P. Tarcher, Inc.) the Simontons report that over a four-year period they worked with 159 patients with diagnoses of incurable cancer. At the end of that period, 63 were still alive, having survived an average of 24.4 months after their diagnosis. That was more than twice the national norm for similar cancer patients. Even the patients who had died lived 1½ times longer than ordinary patients. Of the patients who were alive, some 40 percent were either improving or had no evidence of the disease whatsoever.

The state of mind is more important than the seriousness of the disease in predicting longevity.

When you consider that 100 percent of those patients had been told they had incurable cancer, you get some idea of the importance of the mind in healing. A study of the Simontons' patients has found that their performance on psychological tests is a better indicator of their chances for survival than even the seriousness of the disease at the time of the tests. Their state of mind seems to be more important for survival than their physical condition.

For some time now, too, hypnosis has been a device that could be used with cancer patients to help them through depression, the side effects of radiation and chemotherapy, and their pain. Hypnosis can defuse the perception of pain entirely, and so eliminate or reduce the need for medication. The process also utilizes a technique very similar to the imagery suggested by the Simontons. In hypnosis, however, the concept is called "creative suggestion." Hypnotized patients are asked to visualize their white blood cells swarming over and gobbling up their cancer cells. And, not surprisingly, their conditions improve. A study at Pennsylvania State University showed that healthy self-hypnotized people could raise their per-minute white-blood-cell count as much as 40 percent. Explained one researcher: "The mind can influence the body by changing the biochemistry of the blood."

Reducing the need for pain pills.

A NEW KIND OF CANCER TREATMENT CENTER

All this has led to an increased acceptance of the mind/body approach to cancer management—and a growing number of treatment centers offering these therapies.

Cancer patients at a new treatment center in Pennsylvania, for example, are learning how to marshall *all* their capacities to fight their disease. At the Institute for Adjunctive Cancer Therapy (IACT) in Radnor, patients receive psychological and nutritional support in addition to the surgery, radiation, or chemotherapy provided by their own doctors.

By focusing on the mental and spiritual needs of its patients, IACT hopes to reduce the three "d's" of cancer— despondency, despair, and depression. "We include standard psychological counseling, but in addition we go into a lot of stress reduction and coping skills work," says Steven Levy, M.D., the Institute's medical director. "In additon to the direct benefits, I think this approach also has a beneficial effect on the immune system. Patients with adjunctive therapy feel better and respond better to treatment."

A treatment for despondency, depression, despair.

"In a sense, we're not really pioneering," IACT President Aaron Goldstein, D.P.M., says. "We're just putting together the two components (treating mind and body) and making them work better together than either has been able to work all by itself."

Doctors treating cancer are often too busy to deal with the psychological problems that arise for the patient and family after the illness is diagnosed. But that's not the case at IACT.

"We use several types of imagery techniques with patients," says Dr. Levy, "not only to induce a more relaxed state but also as a problem-solving tactic—such as to help a patient stop smoking or get out and do things with his family.

Positive thoughts help.

"We don't ask the patients to focus their mental imagery on the disease itself, however. Many cancer patients are already overly concerned about their bodies. We try to get their minds on a higher plane, a plane that involves spiritual ideas, positive thoughts, and concern for others."

Nutrition is also very important. "We provide dietary guidelines for our patients," Dr. Levy says. "We stress diets higher in fresh fruits and vegetables, with more whole grains and decreased fat and animal protein. Vitamins and minerals may also be used to correct deficiencies and help restore immune function."

How is the total approach working? "By now, we've managed more than a dozen cases," Dr. Levy reports, "and each one has benefited to some extent. Some more than others. It depends on the individual's capacity to use these tools. Frequently, we've found that people with cancer have some deep underlying problems, such as family conflicts, that have been going on for years. We can offer help in those areas."

"We are getting some pleasant results," adds Dr. Goldstein. "I never thought I'd be saying that about cancer, but now I can.

Reestablishing goals.

"These patients (I hesitate to use the word terminal) are grasping and desperate because they've been given what amounts to a death sentence. We help them to reestablish goals in life. For instance, one of our patients came in the other day with a sunburned face. I asked him where he got that. He said, 'I finally broke 100!' He'd been out on the golf course—something he didn't think he'd be doing anymore."

Small victories like that lead IACT adviser Patricia Norris, Ph.D., of the Menninger Foundation, to conclude, "One thing I think I can say unequivocally is that the adjunctive treatments have much to add to a cancer patient's quality of life and chances for recovery."

CHILD HEALTH PROBLEMS

The strains of the boardroom may not be so different from the tensions of the playpen when stress-related disease is considered. As many as half of all children in the United States suffer from some type of stress-inspired psychosomatic illness, estimates Harold Jackson, M.D., of the pediatrics department, Greenville Hospital System, South Carolina.

Colicky babies, bed-wetting three-year-olds, and kindergartners with stomachaches and sore throats are often responding to major sources of stress in their environments, Dr. Jackson told the annual meeting of the South Carolina Academy of Family Physicians. Ten percent of school-age children develop chronic recurring abdominal pain after being forced into the competitive, stressful school world for the first time, he says. Other sources of illness-inducing stress, according to Dr. Jackson, may include parental fighting and alcoholism, relocation, and a death in the family.

A list of stress-induced illnesses.

Certain mind/body treatments have also been used successfully with children. One example is the use of hypnosis to control bed-wetting.

Karen Olness, M.D., of the Children's Health Center in Minneapolis, decided to try teaching self-hypnosis to a group of 40 children as a means to overcome this particular problem. The children, 20 girls and 20 boys, ranged in age from 4½ to 16 years. Only 2 of the group were teenagers. These 2 were taught a standard self-hypnosis technique. The rest of the children were shown a special method adapted to their age.

Hypnosis cures 31 of 40—no more bed-wetting.

The 40 children had been followed for periods ranging from 6 to 28 months at the time Dr. Olness reported on her study. Thirty-one appeared to have been cured completely of bed-wetting, 28 in the first month of treatment. Six others improved.

Some of the parents reported that as their children gained bladder control they also improved in their school work and in general behavior—an instance in which overcoming one undesirable habit leads to benefits all around.

COLD AND CANKER SORES

Two of the most common, and most annoying, diseases of the mouth—cold sores and canker sores—puzzle scientists.

Scientists know that cold sores (also known as fever blisters) are caused by the herpes simplex virus, which is transmitted by direct contact. In most people, most of the time, herpes remains latent, living peaceably among healthy tissues. But occasionally it can flare up. Stress—such as overwork, emotional upset, or illness—appears to be a key triggering factor. The sensitive mouth registers stress early on.

Canker sores, ulcers that usually occur *inside* the mouth, have also been associated with emotional stress.

Stress reduction to control canker sores.

Is stress reduction as effective as drugs in controlling recurrent canker sores? A study under way at the University of Nebraska Medical School is intended to find out.

Preliminary results are encouraging, says Donald Cohen, D.M.D. Patients who received stress-management training seemed to fare about as well as those receiving steroid drugs.

"It's usually low-level, chronic stress that is associated with canker sores," says Dr. Cohen. Uncovering the roots of that stress and teaching patients to avoid or cope more effectively with stress-provoking situations "seems to really help reduce the incidence of outbreaks," he says.

DENTAL CAVITIES

Stressful thoughts may actually contribute to dental cavities, while inner serenity could help protect our teeth. At least that's the intriguing possibility raised by a team of investigators at the Temple University School of Dentistry in Philadelphia.

Relaxation puts mouth bacteria to sleep.

The researchers analyzed the saliva of a group of 12 dental students both before and after a 20-minute meditation session. Visually, the saliva, which had been opaque prior to meditation, became more watery and translucent after the volunteers were deeply relaxed. And bacteria levels decreased *(Journal of Human Stress)*.

"Considering the salivary changes that occur during stress, it could be hypothesized that chronic stress would be an etiological [causative] factor in the development of dental caries," the researchers conclude.

EPILEPSY

More and more, doctors are experimenting with holistic therapies to help epileptic patients. One doctor with a unique approach is M. B. Sterman, Ph.D., chief of neuropsychology research at the Veterans Administration Medical Center in Sepulveda, California, who treats patients with grand mal epilepsy (major epilepsy) whose seizures persist despite drug therapy. He trains his patients to increase or suppress brain rhythms at different frequencies, thereby exerting control over their own conditions.

"The biofeedback method we use," says Dr. Sterman, "rewards the patients for producing rhythmic middle-frequency brain waves. We monitor our patients' electroencephalograms in the laboratory, and when they produce the right rhythms, a bell rings. Telling them to relax and to think about pleasant experiences helps them increase those rhythms.

"The results are encouraging," says Dr. Sterman. "In six out of eight patients, the rate of seizures decreased an average of 74 percent, and the improvements continued after training was stopped.

"Studies such as these demonstrate that biological disorders are susceptible to behavioral modification. And behavioral methods must certainly be considered safer and more desirable than current treatments with drugs" *(Human Nature)*.

Francis M. Forster, M.D., retired director of the Francis M. Forster Epilepsy Center at the Veterans Administration Hospital in Madison, Wisconsin, uses another type of behavioral approach, called Pavlovian conditioning, as a way to counteract seizures.

He treats patients with reflex epilepsy, a type of seizure disorder in which attacks are brought on by such everyday activities as eating, reading, or listening to music.

"About 6 to 7 percent of all epilepsies are of this type," Dr. Forster says. "We condition the patient so that the thing that triggers his attacks becomes innocuous.

"For example, if a certain piece of music causes a seizure in our patient, we will reproduce that seizure in the lab. Then we keep playing that same melody over and over as the patient returns to consciousness. We will play it for one hour twice a day until it no longer evokes the negative response. It takes about two weeks to condition most patients,"

A treatment that's safer than drugs.

Pavlov II.

Dr. Forster says. "Then each time we locate something which triggers a seizure, we repeat the conditioning program. Often we are able to reduce the amount of drugs the patient takes."

Ultimately, researchers hope to find a cure for epilepsy. Meanwhile, seizure control with less dependence on drugs is a promising substitute and a step in the right direction.

GUM DISEASE

Gum problems also may be linked to the emotions. Trench mouth, a particularly acute form of gingivitis—or gum inflammation with pain, bleeding, and ulceration—gets its name from its widespread occurrence among soldiers in battle. Bacteria alone don't seem to explain it.

A University of Alabama study indicates that trench mouth victims have higher levels of a hormone called cortisol in their urine. Changes in cortisol secretion can affect immune response. And emotional disorders and stress may influence cortisol levels.

The investigators found that the gum-disease patients had experienced more negative, unsettling life events in the preceding year than other people. And they also demonstrated higher levels of anxiety, depression, and emotional disturbance *(Journal of the American Medical Association)*.

HAIR AND SCALP PROBLEMS

Is there any truth to the notion that stress can cause gray hair or, worse, hair loss?

Stress is a gray area.

"It can be a factor," Irwin Lubowe, M.D., a dermatologist and author of numerous skin and hair care books, says. Hair turns gray—or white, actually—due to a lack of pigment (melanin) produced by the cortex of the hair shaft. That is most directly related to aging, but environmental factors—stress and diet—also can come into play.

"There have been extreme cases in wartime situations, for example," Dr. Lubowe says, "where melanin secretions have stopped in direct response to extreme emotional duress." (That, of course, would not cause hair to whiten at the moment, but the effects would begin to show as the new, colorless hairs grew out.)

Nutrition is another potential contributor. "Laboratory tests with black rats have shown that feeding them a diet deficient in the B vitamins turned their hair white," reports Philip Kingsley in his *The Complete Hair Book* (Grove Press). "On reintroducing vitamin B, the hair regained its color."

"What's so fascinating about all this" says Kingsley, "is that personal stress demands more B vitamins because the body used more of them up. In fact, the B vitamins have become known as the 'nerve vitamins.' So, it wouldn't seem unreasonable to conclude from that that stress could be the underlying cause."

Dr. Lubowe says he has had some success in both preventing and treating whitened hair by prescribing pantothenate and PABA (para-aminobenzoic acid). Kingsley has had luck with B vitamins, particularly in the form of brewer's yeast and defatted liver extract. Of course, it wouldn't hurt to learn how to relax.

Kingsley also notes that he can tell when a client who is predisposed to dandruff is under a lot of tension. His dandruff acts up. And, as Kingsley explains, dandruff is usually a symptom of *overproduction* of sebum or oil. So any oily scalp or hair condition can signal a need for relaxation.

The link between dandruff and tension.

Researchers in Italy believe that stress can cause another scalp problem: *alopecia areata.*

Alopecia areata is a condition in which the scalp or face becomes inflamed at a microscopic level. The inflammation causes patchy hair or beard loss.

Giulia Perini, M.D., and a team of doctors from the University of Padua, Italy, studied 48 alopecia areata patients and found that 87.5 percent of them had experienced some sort of stressful "life event" within the six months before the disease appeared, and that 66.6 percent of them had suffered a serious depressing setback, such as the death or departure of a friend or family members.

To find out if stress could also affect other kinds of baldness, the doctors examined 30 people who were losing their hair due to common inherited baldness and 30 people who had lost hair due to a fungal infection. Just over 50 percent of those with common baldness had experienced a recent stressful life event and only 33.3 percent had experienced a serious event. Among those with fungal infections, 40 percent had had stressful life events and only 16.6 percent had suffered a serious event.

Clearly, stress promotes alopecia areata more than it

**Are bald men mentally
"pulling their hair out"?**

promotes common baldness and fungal infections. Dr. Perini
told a meeting of the American Psychosomatic Society, in
Denver, she believes that stress lowered the alopecia patients' white blood cell levels (an indicator of resistance to
disease) and left them vulnerable to the disorder *(Skin and
Allergy News).*

HEADACHES

Few people are unfamiliar with the aching or squeezing discomfort, as if the head were wrapped with a tight
band or clamped in a vise. Tension headache may last for a
few hours, a few days or—rarely—even years.

**How tension headache
takes hold.**

Although some researchers disagree, the source of
discomfort in a tension headache most probably lies in
muscles of the neck or scalp that automatically knot up
with tension when we're anxious, upset, or worried. We're
not talking about fleeting tension, the kind we feel when we
recoil from a loud noise, but tension without letup, like the
kind caused by stewing over a stack of bills or waitressing in
a crowded restaurant. Or tension may build up in muscles
according to the way we sit, stand, crane our necks, and so
on. Either way, it doesn't take long before prolonged muscle
contraction—and, consequently, tightening around blood
vessels—results in dull, steady pain on both sides of the
head. Indeed, many tension headache sufferers can actually
feel the tightening in the head or neck.

Stress-caused tension headaches often strike when we
can't vent our anxiety or anger. But they can strike even
when we *anticipate* an unpleasant event. Or they can catch
us totally off guard. They may be conspicuously absent
during a period of actual anxiety or stress, only to hit later,
when we think all our troubles are over. What happens in
that case is that muscles accumulate tension during the
period of stress but hold off with pain for a grand finale.
You may even wake up with tension headache first thing in
the morning.

While the tension headache isn't a twentieth-century
invention, it's surely one of the hallmarks of modern life. If
a videotape of just one night of prime-time television survives for a thousand years, thirtieth-century archaeologists
will probably conclude that we all ran madly about in search
of headache relief and found it in little white pills and "tiny
time capsules."

Although you wouldn't know it from the ads, there *are* ways to relieve a tension headache other than running for the nearest aspirin bottle. Essentially, all of them involve relaxing those tightened-up muscles.

The key to relief: relaxing those tightened muscles.

One good one is to soak in a warm bath with your shoulders and neck submerged. Or stand under a warm shower. Warmth gets the blood flowing again and loosens muscle contractions. A good facial and neck massage can also do wonders—as can a session of progressive relaxation that zeros in on the muscles of the shoulders, neck, and head.

AN ANTIHEADACHE TECHNIQUE

The basic principle of progressive relaxation is this: By deliberately relaxing all of our muscles, group by group, we can shed accumulated tension from our bodies. Because tension buildup in our facial, neck, and head muscles is behind many headaches, the progressive relaxation principle, with special focus on those muscles, may be adapted as a useful and effective antiheadache technique for some people.

Take a comfortable position, either sitting in a chair with both hands resting in your lap and feet flat on the floor, or lying down on your back with your feet against a wall or heavy piece of furniture. Close your eyes. Beginning with your hands, wrists, then forearms, tense each set of muscles for a few seconds, then let them go limp.

Lie down and close your eyes.

While you continue to relax both forearms and both hands, tense your upper arms and shoulders. Feel the tension, the tightness, and now, relax. Just allow those muscles to go, the muscles in your arms and your shoulders. Let the tension roll down your arms and out through your hands and fingertips. Allow the tension to roll off your shoulders and release the muscle tightness as everything feels more comfortable and more relaxed. Your forearms are relaxed, your hands are relaxed, your shoulders are becoming much more relaxed, your upper arms are relaxed. Your whole upper body starts to feel more relaxed and more comfortable. Continue to relax your shoulders, your arms, your forearms, your hands, your fingers, as your whole upper body begins to feel more relaxed and more comfortable.

Now tense up your neck muscles. Feel the tension in your neck . . . it's probably the tensest part of your entire body. And now, relax those muscles. Allow those muscles

Let the tension drain out of your body.

to go. Concentrate on the muscles in the back of your neck. Let the tension drain down through your shoulders, your arms . . . out through your hands and your fingertips. Let the muscles in the front of your neck go. Let that tension drain. Those tight muscles are now giving up tension and stress as your entire body feels more relaxed. Your shoulders feel more relaxed, your arms, your hands, even your fingers. Just allow that tension to drain from your neck. Concentrate on allowing your neck to relax. If you're sitting and you feel as if your head wants to tip forward to take some of the weight off the neck, that's quite all right, because it may, as you allow some of the tension, stress, and tightness to drain from those muscles. Allow your head to tip forward a bit as gravity seems to pull you down, as it seems to tug at you and make you feel very comfortable and very relaxed. Your neck is more relaxed, your shoulders, your arms, your hands, and your fingers. Keep on relaxing. Your whole upper body feels more relaxed and more comfortable. Allow the tension to drain from your neck as you sink into a more relaxed state, a more relaxed feeling throughout your upper body. Your shoulders are more relaxed, your upper arms, your forearms, your hands, and your fingers. Continue to relax . . . keep relaxing your upper body.

Tighten . . . relax . . . relax.

Now make a frown with your forehead. Tighten those muscles around your forehead . . . and now, relax. Allow your forehead and facial muscles to relax. Allow your face to relax . . . it doesn't have to do any work, just relax . . . let those muscles go. Allow your forehead to relax, your eyes, your cheeks, your lips. Allow all the facial muscles to go, to relax. As they do, you'll feel a sense of well-being throughout. Your neck is more relaxed, your shoulders, your arms, your hands, and your fingers. Allow your entire body to become more relaxed and more comfortable. Continue to relax your facial muscles, your eyes, your forehead, your cheeks, your lips, your entire face. Allow those muscles to relax, plus your neck, your shoulders, your arms, your hands, and the rest of your body.

To conclude the exercise, slowly count to four.

Yet another way of getting at your head is through your feet. According to the art of foot reflexology, there are points on the foot that correspond to other areas of the body. Massaging the lower part of the big toe and the area on the foot beneath all the toes will release tension in the neck, which is often related to headache. Also, massaging a point below the middle toe relieves pain at the back of the neck. The authors of *The Woman's Holistic Headache Relief Book* (J. P. Tarcher)—which, incidentally, isn't just for women—also suggest that you "press each toe between the fingers until you locate the sore or tender places and massage these until the tenderness is gone."

THE MIGRAINE PERSONALITY

Migraine headaches are another problem altogether. In fact, some doctors are convinced that there is actually a migraine personality. While there is no scientific proof—no controlled experiments—years of seeing migraine sufferers come and go have led many doctors to the conclusion that people damned with migraines are generally ambitious, hard-working, hard-driving, demanding of themselves and others, eager to please, and sensitive to criticism. (In short, your basic workaholic.)

Six typical characteristics of the migraine sufferer.

The same goes for cluster headache sufferers. Doctors' general impressions, psychological tests, and a detailed study of patients demonstrated that cluster sufferers tend to be highly conscientious—to a fault, you might say—and share many of the traits of the migraine personality, with the addition of heavy goal orientation. That all adds up to what is sometimes known as the Type A personality—a mix of traits that, incidentally, can land you in the cardiac ward, even if you don't get headaches.

It's generally agreed that migraine headaches of either type are caused by constriction of the blood vessels in the head during the preheadache phase, and swelling (dilation) of those same blood vessels during the headache phase. The result: intense, debilitating pain. The constriction and swelling have something to do with changing levels of certain chemicals in the body—serotonin and prostaglandins—that act on blood vessels.

Why migraines hurt.

As with tension headache, migraine is more likely to attack when you are tired or under stress. And also like its less-brutal cousin, migraine may not hit until Friday evening or Saturday morning, when you're about to relax.

One way to get rid of them: Think warm. Researchers at a Texas university taught five migraine patients to

**Think "warm" for
migraine relief.**

consciously raise their skin temperature—an antimigraine technique—by thinking the word "warm." Once they mastered the technique, two of the patients were able to stop headaches that were just getting started, and the other three achieved shorter, less painful, or less frequent headaches.

To try this technique, sit down or lie down, close your eyes and gently quiet your mind. Now, imagine that it is summertime at the beach. An ocean breeze cools your face, while your hands and arms grow warmer and warmer in the hot sun. Your hands are really soaking up the sun now. They're hot to the touch. Minutes have passed in your "reverie of warmth." When you open your eyes, you're left with very warm hands . . . and *no* headache. The act of *thinking warmth* into your hands redirects the blood flow to outer extremities, away from the head.

This same concept of warming the extremities to avert a migraine is also used in conjunction with self-hypnosis. While in a hypnotic trance, the suggestion of "warm hands" is made. This is a very effective treatment for migraine, says Kathryn A. Hynes, a clinical psychologist from Media, Pennsylvania. One reason migraine sufferers respond so well to self-hypnosis, she says, is "because migraines are frequently a stress-related disorder. And stress disorders respond favorably to trances."

If you suffer from chronic headaches, you might want to look into some biofeedback training, says Seymour Diamond, M.D., director of the Diamond Headache Clinic in Chicago. The training, which includes muscle relaxation exercises and a form of self-hypnosis, allows many of Dr. Diamond's patients to reduce the amount of drugs they take. They also suffer from fewer headaches than before *(Internal Medicine News)*.

PRESS FOR PAIN RELIEF

One final suggestion: Tension headaches, migraines, and sinus headaches can all be relieved with acupressure. As we mentioned earlier in this chapter in our discussion of back pain, it is thought that this Eastern method of pain relief works by increasing the body's production of endorphins, a natural painkiller.

Eyebrow massage—it works.

In our experience, the most effective point to use for headache relief lies in the center of the eyebrows (all acupuncture/acupressure points come in pairs, in mirrored locations on both sides of the body). If you run your finger along your eyebrow, you'll notice a dip in the surface that feels as though two bones are joining under the skin. This is the point. It is where the supraorbital nerve comes closest to the surface of your head. This point, in the middle of your eyebrow, is right over the pupil.

Use the knuckles of your thumbs to press on this point. In a seated position, place the knuckles against both points in the eyebrows and slowly turn them back and forth, increasing the pressure until you feel pain. If pressing with your knuckles doesn't produce a good deal of pain, then you probably are pressing in the wrong place. This point, so close to a nerve, should be very tender when you apply sufficient force.

Another tip: Press both sides simultaneously for best results and hold for about 15 to 30 seconds. According to Howard Kurland, M.D., author of *Quick Headache Relief without Drugs* (William Morrow & Co.), this point is particularly good for relieving sinus headaches. We have found that it can clear up other kinds of headaches as well.

HEART DISEASE

Ever since San Francisco cardiologist Meyer Friedman, M.D., and associate Ray H. Rosenman, M.D., published their landmark book *Type A Behavior and Your Heart* (Knopf), the link has been firmly established: Hard-driving, fast-paced people face a higher risk of heart disease.

Typical Type A people are impatient, aggressive, fast-talking workaholics—people who can't play a game of Scrabble with a couple of kids without trying to beat the pants off them, people who gnash their teeth when caught in a traffic jam. They are ambitious and self-driven, always trying to squeeze more and more activities into less and less time. Type A is "individualism gone haywire," as one researcher puts it. And it is a continuum. You can be mildly to extremely Type A.

"Individualism gone haywire."

But even if you're the worst, don't worry yourself sick over it. Type A, after all, is not an inherent personality flaw; it's a pattern of behavior which can be modified, changed, or countered (see Chapter 28, You, Your Own Worst Enemy; Chapter 30, Mastering Stress; and Chapter 47, There's More to Life Than Work).

In fact, Dr. Friedman and his associates at the Harold

Anger, impatience, and your heart.

Brunn Institute, Mt. Zion Medical Center, are in the midst of a five-year study to determine if changing Type A behavior can help lessen the risk of having additional heart attacks.

"Type A behavior boils down to two things—easily aroused anger and easily aroused impatience, either of which is mistakenly considered by many as a propeller for corporate advancement," Dr. Friedman says. These are the two components of Type A that lead to hormonal disturbances, which accelerate development of coronary heart disease.

Dr. Friedman's program helps people ease themselves out of the fast lane—to rearrange their schedules and their lives so they're not so rushed. The homework he gives them includes eating more slowly, lingering over a meal, deliberately waiting in lines, and talking more slowly and really listening to the person they're talking with.

The program also attempts to make changes in people's belief systems. Type As in the program receive a quotation to ponder each week. "The ones that seem to work best link impatience with inferiority, like 'There are two creatures in nature that exhibit impatience: men and puppies,'" Dr. Friedman says.

Don't be a "rock" or an "arrow."

"We try to get these people to cease being rocks or arrows," he says. "We want them to look at and to really be interested in other human beings, animals, and plants. Our main thrust is to get these people out of their ego-centric shells."

But there's good news for all you hardworking, fast-paced, yet basically happy people. The results of three independent studies now have experts agreeing that it's not so much *high job involvement* or *a sense of time urgency* that leads certain people toward heart disease. The key factor is *hostility*, the third trait in that troika of typical Type A characteristics.

For you folks who have problems with hostility, the news isn't good.

Besides heart-disease risk, two of the studies showed, a hostile attitude is associated with a risk of death from many other causes, too.

What does it really mean to be hostile? Most of us know people who fly off in rages or convey hostility in more subtle, yet equally powerful ways. But that's just the expression of hostility.

A lack of trust can be deadly.

What the researchers in all three studies looked for was

an attitude toward people in general. "It is a basic lack of trust in human nature, in human motives," according to Redford B. Williams, Jr., M.D., a Duke University associate professor of medicine and professor of psychiatry who was involved in two of the three studies. "It's a belief that people are more bad than good, and that they will mistreat you."

To measure that kind of hostile attitude, all three studies used the same 50-item hostility scale. The scale is part of a reliable personality test that scientists employ frequently.

The first study, authored by Dr. Williams and others at Duke, evaluated over 400 patients for Type A behavior and, separately, for hostility. The people were then examined for clogged arteries, a sure sign of heart disease. The researchers discovered that their patients' hostility levels were much more accurate predictors of disease than their general Type A behavior patterns.

Only half of the patients with low hostility scores had at least one clogged artery, compared with 70 percent of the patients with high hostility scores.

Hostility correlates with clogged arteries.

In the second study, authored by John C. Barefoot, Ph.D., of the University of North Carolina in Chapel Hill (with participation from Dr. Williams), 255 male medical students were followed for 25 years. At the beginning of the study, the students had completed the same hostility test.

The researchers found that high hostility scores were associated with a sixfold higher incidence of coronary disease in the doctors who were alive after 25 years. Of the doctors who had died from all causes, high hostility scores figured in over three-fourths of the cases.

A third research project, this one carried out on almost 2,000 men as a part of a large Western Electric coronary-heart-disease study, was performed by Dr. Richard B. Shekelle of the University of Texas School of Public Health in Houston.

The men were employed, middle-aged, and free of coronary heart disease when they were enrolled in the study and tested for hostility during the late 1950s. But those who had high hostility scores were later linked with a much higher risk of heart attack and sudden cardiac death. High hostility also left these men vulnerable to increased risk of death from all causes, including cancer.

Dr. Williams says that he and his colleagues aren't sure

yet whether the way a person deals with hostility (by either suppressing or expressing it) affects his risk of developing heart disease.

But the psychiatrist says it is possible to have a high level of hostility and not other Type A characteristics.

So whether you're a quiet brooder or a screamer, tone down the hostility. And learn to relax—for the sake of your heart.

STRESS AND THE HEART

The mood that dooms.

Who among us has not felt the sharp talons of stress pinch the heart? However painful, such episodes probably pose little danger to the heart that is not already ill. The truly sinister side of stress seems rather to express itself when tension or anger or grief or hostility graduates from being an event to become a recurring mood. While the body (and soul) seems well-equipped to bounce back from bad news and narrow escapes, these recuperative mechanisms never get a chance to work when you literally take stress "to heart."

Muscular tension squeezes off blood circulation, and chronic shallow breathing reduces the amount of oxygen reaching the heart.

In addition, unrelieved tension changes the hormonal biochemistry of your body, encouraging the process of atherosclerosis.

As further evidence of this, researchers at the University of Southern California School of Medicine divided 14 rabbits into two groups on the basis of their response to minor stresses, such as opening their cage doors and handling them. Passive rabbits were classified as low stress, aggressive rabbits as high stress. When all were fed a high-cholesterol diet, it was found that the high-stress group showed more signs of wear: higher systolic blood pressures and more evidence of atherosclerosis *(Clinical Research)*.

TENSION TRIGGERS CHOLESTEROL

But you don't have to be a rabbit or necessarily eat a high-cholesterol diet to suffer. If you're serious about keeping your cholesterol under control, you probably know all the tricks when it comes to restricting dietary fat intake— tactics like peeling the skin off chicken because much of the fat is found in and just under the skin. But perhaps you ought to be paying just as much attention to what may be getting under *your* skin—in the form of daily aggravations and tensions.

New findings indicate that nervous distress can send blood cholesterol in the same direction as a helping of bacon-and-Cheddar-cheese quiche—upward!

The people in question were a group of several hundred coronary-prone middle-aged men. At the time they were recruited for the study, all showed risk factors such as elevated cholesterol levels or blood pressure, an overweight condition, or a cigarette habit. The men were followed for at least five years, and were regularly asked to rate their perceived level of tension. The investigators, affiliated with the department of community health and preventive medicine at Northwestern University Medical School in Chicago, also measured cholesterol levels.

Periods of nervous upset were found to correlate with small but significant jumps in cholesterol, and the rise was independent of other variables, such as changes in weight *(Journal of Human Stress)*.

COUNTERPOINT TO STRESS

Research—again on rabbits—suggests that there may be a way to avoid this effect—with TLC, or tender loving care.

Some years ago, researcher Frederick Cornhill, Ph.D., was working in his laboratory at Ohio State University College of Medicine at Columbus when he inadvertently discovered this. Dr. Cornhill had been feeding rabbits high-cholesterol diets as part of an experiment designed to test the effects of a new cholesterol-lowering drug. But the results he got seemed to make no sense until he found out that a new factor had crept into the experiment. It seems that his associate had gotten into the habit of petting the subjects. Not all of them, just some. But those rabbits lucky enough to receive this daily affection turned out to have fully 50 percent less plaque buildup in their arteries than their unpetted lab mates. "Tender loving care dramatically reduced arteriosclerosis," Cornhill declared after a series of follow-up studies corroborated these first accidental results.

People, too, need their tender strokes. A life cut off from love, laughter, and affection is likely to be a short life.

The anti-cholesterol caress.

Being cut off from people cuts off circulation, too.

In one study, social isolation levels—measured by marital status, church attendance, and group affiliation—were used to rank some 4,000 middle-aged men. And the highest incidence of coronary heart disease was found among the most isolated, the lowest among the most social.

In other research, James J. Lynch, Ph.D., of the Center for the Study of Human Psychophysiology at the University of Maryland School of Medicine in Baltimore, has found that people who live alone have higher incidences of disease and premature death. And in an Australian study, researchers found that 26 people who had recently lost their spouses had a significant reduction in their bodies' immune function, a condition that was linked with an increased susceptibility to coronary artery disease and other diseases.

A simple touch soothes the heart.

In his book *The Broken Heart: The Medical Consequences of Loneliness* (Basic Books), Dr. Lynch reports a number of cases in which striking changes in the heartbeats of cardiac patients were apparently caused by the simplest touch. In one instance, Dr. Lynch and his colleagues observed a 54-year-old man with heart disease. The man died after 14 days of intense medical care and a period in a deep coma. As he lay dying, a nurse came to his bedside and briefly held his hand. His heart, despite the coma, reacted immediately. The heart rate decreased and the rhythm of the heartbeat stabilized, and both remained improved after the nurse left.

Stimulated by cases like this, Dr. Lynch decided to examine the effects of touching on a larger scale. Because pulse taking was a simple kind of touching that all patients regularly experienced, Dr. Lynch decided to observe its effects on arrhythmia, irregular heartbeat, in a group of over 300 cardiac patients. "After examining these patients," he wrote, "it was clear that even the routine event of pulse taking had the power to completely suppress arrhythmias that had been occurring."

PSYCHOLOGICAL AID FOR THE SMITTEN

Don't panic.

Should a heart attack strike despite your valiant efforts to stay calm and enjoy life, don't let up with the psychological tactics. They could give you the edge on recovery. As Norman Cousins explains in his book *The Healing Heart* (W. W. Norton & Co.), staying calm and maintaining a sense of humor helped him overcome the panic that began to well up inside him during his own heart attack. And panic, he says, can deliver a deadly blow to a troubled heart. It constricts blood vessels and destabilizes an already unstable condition.

Coping styles can also affect your recovery. Heart-disease patients who deny the seriousness of their illness may actually recover faster than those who face up to cold reality.

In a study of 26 patients with unstable angina, 14 were categorized as deniers and 12 as nondeniers. Both groups received nitroglycerin and other medication, but the non-deniers took more time to become pain-free, says Dr. James Levenson of the Medical College of Virginia in Richmond.

Dr. Levenson told an annual meeting of the American Psychosomatic Society that, while denial seems to lead to rapid medical stabilization, its effects on long-term recovery still aren't known.

HEMOPHILIA

Hemophiliacs usually have their life-threatening spontaneous-bleeding episodes when they are tense or even under what to us would seem like very minor stresses. By using self-hypnosis to calm themselves when they feel tension coming on, hemophiliacs are able to do with fewer blood products and transfusions, and reduced periods of hospitalization.

HIGH BLOOD PRESSURE

Cases of hypertension due to specific disease states are actually quite rare. So, if you've got high blood pressure, chances are it's related to your behavior. You either eat too much (or too much salt) or don't exercise enough, or subject yourself to too much stress.

Emotional tension releases adrenaline, which is known both to speed heart rate and cause blood vessels to narrow—the result of which, obviously, is increased pressure. Studies have shown, for example, that people with high blood pressure have higher levels of adrenaline circulating in their blood than people with normal blood pressure *(Journal of Clinical Pharmacology)*.

Chain reaction: tension, adrenaline, high blood pressure.

That's where relaxation techniques come in.

According to Herbert Benson, M.D., associate professor of medicine at Harvard Medical School, patients with high blood pressure should be instructed to practice relaxation techniques for 10 to 20 minutes, once or twice a day. They should sit in a comfortable position, close their eyes, concentrate on relaxing each muscle group individually, and repeat a word or phrase of their choosing each time they exhale. Patients who practice this type of meditation, which is simple to learn, may significantly decrease their blood pressure *(Lancet)*.

The relaxation response helps medication work.

As a specialist in hypertension, Dr. Benson is naturally most interested in what that relaxation response can do for people with high blood pressure. He warns that hypertensives must not suddenly give up their medication in hopes that the relaxation response is going to take care of everything. In fact, all the patients Dr. Benson worked with were on their regular blood pressure medicine throughout the study. What the meditation did was to improve upon the benefit conferred by the medication, and it proved to be a very significant improvement indeed.

In one series of experiments, Dr. Benson selected 36 volunteers, all of whom remained with their original medication throughout the study. Prior to practicing the relaxation response, they had an average systolic blood pressure (the higher figure) of 146. The average diastolic blood pressure was 93.5. On the average, then, the 36 subjects had a blood pressure that could be expressed as 146/93.5.

After several weeks of regularly practicing the relaxation response, as we've described here, the average blood pressure fell to 137/88.9.

From high to normal.

What that means is that the average blood pressure went from borderline high down to the normal range. The measurements were taken *before* each meditation, so the residual effect was being checked, not just momentary improvement.

You have to keep meditating.

In no sense, however, were these people "cured" of their high blood pressure. Their readings remained low only as long as they practiced their relaxation response regularly. When several subjects stopped meditating, their blood pressures returned to their initial hypertensive levels within a month.

Here's how Dr. Benson, in his book *The Relaxation Response* (William Morrow & Co.), puts meditation in perspective: "Standard medical therapy means taking antihypertensive drugs, which often act by interrupting the activity of the sympathetic nervous system, thus lowering blood pressure. The pharmacologic method of lowering blood pressure is very effective and extremely important, since . . . lowered blood pressure leads to lower risk of developing atherosclerosis and its related diseases such as heart attacks and strokes. The regular practice of the relaxation response is yet another way to lower blood pressure. Indications are that this response affects the same mechanisms and lowers blood pressure by the same means as some antihypertensive drugs. Both counteract the activity in the sympathetic nervous system. It is unlikely that the regular elicitation of the relaxation response by itself will prove to be adequate therapy for severe or moderate high blood pressure. Probably it would act to enhance the lowering of the blood pressure along with antihypertensive drugs, and thus lead to the use of fewer drugs or a lesser dosage."

BIOFEEDBACK, MEDITATION, AND YOUR BLOOD PRESSURE

One study, however, did show that in mild cases, meditation combined with biofeedback could eliminate the need for drugs.

Eliminating the need for drugs with meditation *and* biofeedback.

This combination approch was used by Chandra Patel, M.D., and two other researchers in a study they reported in the *British Medical Journal.* They worked with over 200 employees of a large industry who had blood pressures of 140/90 or greater, assigning them at random to a biofeedback-relaxation group and a control group. Both groups received a short educational talk on risk factors for coronary disease. The biofeedback group also attended special one-hour sessions once a week in which they practiced deep-muscle relaxation, breathing exercises, and meditation (instructions were on cassette tapes), and they learned about stress and hypertension. Biofeedback was used to reinforce their relaxation techniques.

After eight weeks, the biofeedback group had significantly lower systolic and diastolic blood pressure readings than the group not trained in relaxation—and those measurements remained lower eight months later, when the researchers went back to follow up on results. Interestingly, of the employees whose blood pressures were initially higher than 140/90, the biofeedback group averaged a total drop of over 22 points systolic and over 11 points diastolic, but the untreated people dropped only 11 points systolic and less than 3 points diastolic. The drop in the diastolic measurement, the second figure, is extremely significant in the biofeedback-relaxation group.

Results so good they're revolutionary.

As none of the people in the study took antihypertensive drugs, the results here are not just encouraging, they're positively revolutionary. Revolutionary because they suggest the "relaxation-based behavioral methods might be offered as a first-line treatment to patients with mild hypertension," thus avoiding the hazards and costs of long-term medication.

EXPECT THE BEST

Remember, too, your expectations here may be at least as important to the drop in blood pressure as the exercise itself. If you doubt this, then consider a study carried out at the Standford University Medical Center in California.

Believe the technique won't work—and it won't.

Thirty patients under medical treatment for high blood pressure were recruited for a relaxation program designed to bring their pressure down. But before beginning, the people were divided into two groups. The first group was told that the muscle-relaxation exercises they were about to do would produce immediate effects that would persist and increase with continued practice. But those in the second group were informed that the good effects would be delayed, and that they might even experience a slight *rise* in blood pressure at first.

After three 20-minute relaxation sessions, the physicians conducting the trial reported "a dramatic finding." The expectant group achieved a 17-point mean drop in systolic blood pressure. But the delayed group showed only a 2.4 unit drop *(Psychosomatic Medicine)*.

According to the doctors, "those findings suggest that training in progressive muscular relaxation does not automatically lead to blood pressure lowering." Instead, the mind "can interfere with or promote the effect."

The study also has relevance for doctors as well as patients. "The powerful effects of the expectancy manipulation once more show the therapeutic importance of enhancing positive expectancy . . . ," they add. "The time taken to do this obviously has profound therapeutic advantages, and again the procedure used in this study may be useful in the clinic."

Beyond a relaxation technique—and a positive attitude—here are three more suggestions to help bring your blood pressure back to near-normal.

THE NOT-SO-SILENT KILLER

Reduce the stress produced by nerve-jangling noise. We mean everyday noises, like alarm clocks jangling, loud work-place noises, car engines, even televisions blaring. Noises like those can cause blood pressure to soar. It did in an experiment with monkeys. Researchers had the monkeys listen to the ordinary sounds of a worker's life for nine months. During that time blood pressure went up an average of 27 percent. When the experiment was over and the noises stopped, the raised pressure persisted at least a month *(Science)*.

Muffle noises for sound health.

SLOW DOWN, YOU TALK TOO FAST

Next step: Learn to talk more slowly. It's true. People who have high blood pressure are usually very fast talkers. "Some hypertensives [the name given to people who have high blood pressure] don't put commas in their sentences," says Dr. James Lynch. "And they don't breathe properly, either—not while they're speaking, anyway. The result is a rapid elevation of their blood pressure."

Add a few commas to your sentences.

Dr. Lynch has been able to demonstrate blood pressure response to rapid talking through the use of new computer-controlled equipment. "Traditionally, blood pressure has always been taken with a cuff and a stethoscope," says Dr. Lynch. "This method requires silence from both the patient and the doctor. The new automated blood pressure monitor allows the doctor to record the rises in blood pressure during conversation and other routine social interactions, because a stethoscope is not used.

"For the first time we were able to see blood pressure as a dynamic and interactive system. We found that virtually everyone's blood pressure goes up (anywhere from 10 to 50 percent) within 30 seconds after speaking begins. But hypertensives are the most reactive. The higher a person's blood pressure when quiet, the more it goes up when speaking. We examined almost 2,000 people—from newborn babies to the elderly, normotensives [people with normal blood pressure], hypertensives—and it happened virtually every time.

Everyone's blood pressure rises when they speak.

"Now we are able to use this information to treat hypertension patients without drugs. And some of those who are on drugs have been weaned off of them.

"Basically, what we do is teach patients how to speak more slowly," explains Dr. Lynch. "And we teach them how to breathe while they speak. They learn to put the commas back into their speech—commas being the pause for a breath of air."

Talking yourself out of high blood pressure.

Apparently, the method works. Dr. Lynch and his associates have successfully treated 30 patients so far and have followed some of them for as long as three years. "And some of these were the so-called 'last resort' patients . . . the ones whose medications were no longer doing the job and their hypertension was out of control," adds Dr. Lynch. "Within five months we got them down to normotensive levels—with *no drugs*. The results have held, too, through two to three years of follow-up. It takes a good deal of work and determination from the patients, but as they start feeling better, it motivates them to continue.

"This is not a quick cure or a gimmick," Dr. Lynch points out. "It's a gradual resetting of the body, downward. And it's a workable alternative to drugs."

DON'T GET PEEVED, GET A PET

A final suggestion: Get a pet. A dog, a cat, even a tankful of fish can have beneficial effects on your blood pressure, according to Aaron Katcher, M.D., associate professor of psychiatry at the University of Pennsylvania.

"Pets exert a calming influence."

"Companion animals, in particular, provide an access to intimacy," Dr. Katcher says. "You talk to your pet more slowly, you smile a great deal, voice tones become gentle, the cadence of speech changes. It's a much more relaxed dialogue, characterized by a combination of touching and talking. Pets exert a calming influence throughout the day, which probably has a lot to do with the blood pressure-lowering effects. In the patients we've studied so far, a 12 to 15 percent drop in blood pressure has been recorded in the presence of pets.

"In fact, anything that turns your attention outward to the natural environment around you is a powerful way of controlling tension, thereby lowering blood pressure," continues Dr. Katcher. That's because it interrupts your pattern of silent worrying—the kind of internal dialogue that you have with yourself about everything that's wrong with your life. Just looking at a tank of tropical fish, gazing into an open fire, or watching waves on a beach, all have a kind of stress-reducing effect. They have extremely hypnotic qualities because they are phenomena which are always different yet always the same.

"By considering the interactions of the nonhuman world around us, we can build a more complete therapeutic program for our patients who have high blood pressure or other illnesses."

INSOMNIA

"Better than sleeping pills." That's what researchers are saying about such relaxation techniques as progressive relaxation, deep breathing, imagery, autogenic training, and self-hypnosis (see Chapter 29, The Best of the Relaxation Techniques).

They work because your tossing and turning body is probably in a state of biological turbulence—a state that doesn't share a border with dreamland. "Many poor sleepers are more aroused than good sleepers," wrote sleep specialist Richard R. Bootzin, Ph.D., of Northwestern University, in a survey of sleep research. "Poor sleepers [have] higher rectal temperatures, higher skin resistance, more vasoconstrictions [narrowing of blood vessels] per minute, and more body movements per hour than good sleepers." All of those symptoms mean that the insomniac's autonomic nervous system, which controls involuntary body functions, is preparing him perfectly for dodging rush-hour traffic—but not for sleep. If the insomniac can put his autonomic nervous system to sleep, the theory goes, the rest of him should follow *(Progress in Behavior Modification)*.

Progressive relaxation is a particular form of muscle relaxation that helps quiet the nervous system, too. A variation of progressive relaxation has been evaluated by Thomas D. Borkovec, Ph.D., a psychologist and sleep researcher at Pennsylvania State University.

"We have the person start with the muscles of one hand, making a fist, holding it for seven seconds, and then relaxing it," says Dr. Borkovec.

"We ask the individual to learn to identify what both tension and relaxation feel like, so that he will be able to detect tension when trying to fall asleep. After sufficient

The four problems of a poor sleeper.

Learn what relaxation feels like.

practice, most people are able to deeply relax themselves within five minutes."

His students gradually learn to relax 16 of the body's muscle groups, Dr. Borkovec says. They also inhale when they tense their muscles, then exhale and relax very slowly (for about 45 seconds). That is good therapy for people whose main problem is falling asleep, and its effect improves with practice, Dr. Borkovec says.

Proper breathing is a lullaby.

Proper breathing, just by itself, is another way to reassure the autonomic nervous system that it can tone down for the night. In one experiment, volunteers were asked to "focus passively on the physical sensations associated with their breathing and to repeat the words 'in' and 'out' silently." Results indicated that this technique is as effective as progressive relaxation.

The fine points of breathing have been described by psychologist Beata Jencks, Ph.D., in her book *Your Body: Biofeedback at Its Best* (Nelson-Hall).

"Imagine inhaling through your fingertips," Dr. Jencks writes, "up the arms, into the shoulders, and then exhaling down the trunk into the abdomen and legs, and leisurely out at the toes. Repeat, and feel how this slow, deep breathing affects the whole body, the abdomen, the flanks, and the chest. Do not move the shoulders."

Imagery can accompany breathing exercises, and your choice of images doesn't have to be limited to the traditional sheep leaping over a split-rail fence. Any image that you personally associate with feelings of peace and contentment will work well.

A "number" of solutions.

One sleep researcher, Quentin Regestein, M.D., director of the sleep clinic at Brigham and Women's Hospital in Boston, says that one of his patients imagines a huge sculpture of the numeral one, hewn out of marble, with ivy growing over it, surrounded by a pleasant rural landscape. Then she goes on to the numeral two, and adds further embellishment, such as cherubs hovering above the numeral. "She tells me that she usually falls asleep before she reaches 50," Dr. Regestein says.

"Insomniacs come here from all over the world," he continues, "and ask me to prescribe a sleep cure for them. They are sometimes surprised to find that careful scientific investigation substantiates that commonsense remedies really work."

HEAVINESS AND WARMTH

Autogenic training is another natural and potent sleep aid. This technique acts on the premise that your mind can compel your body to relax by concentrating on feelings of heaviness and warmth. Through mental suggestion, the "heavy" muscles actually do relax, and the "warm" flesh receives better circulation, resulting in "a state of low physiological arousal," says Dr. Bootzin.

In an experiment, researchers taught 16 college-student insomniacs to focus their attention on warmth and heaviness. At the end of the experiment, the students had cut their average time needed to fall asleep down from 52 to 22 minutes. These results matched the findings of Dr. Bootzin in the Chicago area: "Daily practice of either progressive relaxation or autogenic training produced 50 percent improvement in time to fall asleep by the end of the one-month treatment period."

Awake time: cut from 52 to 22 minutes.

A Raggedy Ann doll, says Dr. Jencks, is one image that can facilitate autogenic training. To feel heavy, she says, "make yourself comfortable and allow your eyes to close. Then lift one arm a little and let it drop. Let it drop heavily, as if it were the arm of one of those floppy dolls or animals. Choose one in your imagination. Choose a doll, an old, beloved, soft teddy bear." Once the mind fixes on the doll's image, Dr. Jencks says, lifting and dropping the arm in your imagination works as well as really letting it drop.

Turn yourself into a living doll—a Raggedy Ann doll.

To invoke feelings of warmth, Dr. Jencks adds, "Imagine that you put your rag doll into the sun. Let it be warmed by the sun. . . . You are the giant rag doll, and you are lying in the sun; all your limbs are nice and warm, but your head is lying in the shade and is comfortably cool."

SUGGESTIONS YOU GIVE YOURSELF

Self-hypnosis, though it may require some practice in advance, has also been shown to help people fall asleep. Researchers in England compared the sleep-inducing ability of four various techniques—sleeping pills, hypnosis, self-hypnosis, and a placebo—on 18 volunteer insomniacs. Some of the volunteers learned to put themselves into a trance by picturing themselves in a "warm, safe place—possibly on a holiday someplace pleasant."

When they had put themselves into a trance, the

"You are getting sleepy . . . "

researchers told them, they would be able to give themselves the suggestions "that this would pass into a deep,
refreshing sleep, waking up at the usual time in the morning,
feeling wide awake."

The results showed that the subjects fell asleep faster
by hypnotizing themselves than by using either the drug or
the placebo. None of the self-hypnotized sleepers needed an
hour to fall asleep, while three in the placebo group and
four in the drug group did. Twelve in the self-hypnotized
group fell asleep in less than 30 minutes, while only seven
and ten, respectively, in the other groups did *(Journal of the
Royal Society of Medicine)*.

Perform a ritual.

Rituals also play a role in falling asleep. Dr. Regestein
says that when dogs go to sleep, they always sniff around
for a warm comfortable spot, circle it, and finally coil up
in their favorite sleeping position. People are a bit like this,
he says. They fall asleep most easily when they proceed
through a nightly ritual—flossing their teeth, for example
and then curling into their favorite sleeping position. In
support of that theory, researchers in 1930 found that
children who assumed a particular posture when going to
bed fell asleep faster.

Sex is foreplay for sleep.

The last but not the least effective route to immediate
relaxation is sexual activity. Psychologist Alice Kuhn
Schwartz, Ph.D., author of *Somniquest* (Harmony Books),
a book dealing with sleep disturbances, says that sex "alleviates
tension. It is a powerful soporific. And what is more, it's
fun. . . . The road to sleep branches into other byways.
Explore all of them."

IMPOTENCE AND SEXUAL DYSFUNCTION

No. Anxiety, frustration, and boredom are not forms
of pent-up passion. They're symptoms of stress, and you
would do well to reduce the amount of turmoil in your life
before expecting to be at your amorous best. In addition to
leading to chronic fatigue and adverse hormonal changes,
stress also can encourage the bad habits (poor diet, lack of
exercise, and heavy drinking) that make for bad sex in the
first place.

**Loss of desire—a symptom
of stress.**

"Even people with normal sexual appetites can psychologically turn themselves off with overwhelming problems,"
says Dr. Wanda Sadoughi, director of the sexual dysfunc-

tion clinic at Cook County Hospital in Chicago. "By the time some patients come to the clinic, they are having major dysfunctional problems—such as impotence or lack of orgasm. But before all that occurred the first symptom some of these people had was a loss of desire. And desire is crucial to sexuality," says Dr. Sadoughi.

"Depression, stress, and fatigue can damage sexuality profoundly," adds Helen Singer Kaplan, M.D., Ph.D., head of the sex therapy and education program at Payne Whitney Clinic of the New York Hospital. "When a patient is severely depressed, sex is the furthest thing from his mind. Even moderately depressed patients lose interest in pursuing sexual activity and are very difficult to seduce and arouse," says Dr. Kaplan, author of *The New Sex Therapy* (Brunner/Mazel).

Good marriages aren't immune either. A survey of 100 happily married couples showed that when it came to sex, 50 percent of the men and 77 percent of the women reported a lack of interest or an inability to relax *(New England Journal of Medicine)*.

Sometimes blind acceptance of cultural myths can dampen desire to the point of extinction. That's especially true of sex and the aged. "In the geriatric field, one of the last bastions of culturally enforced ignorance persists in the area of sex and sexuality," says William H. Masters, M.D., renowned sex therapist and author. "The widely accepted cultural dogma that sexual interaction between older persons is not only socially unacceptable, but may be physically harmful, results in thousands of men and woman withdrawing from active sexual expression every year" *(Journal of the American Geriatrics Society)*.

Sex isn't only for the young.

"It's true you can't do at 60 what you did at 20," adds John P. Wincze, Ph.D., professor of psychiatry at Brown University School of Medicine and chief of psychology at Providence VA Medical Center. "Many of my elderly patients get worried because they don't respond as quickly as they did when they were younger," Dr. Wincze says. "They'll see a pretty girl and it's not the turn-on it used to be. That's a normal part of aging. Desire may diminish, but just being old doesn't make it disappear. Mostly it's how you perceive yourself," explains Dr. Wincze. "If you think of yourself as too old for 'all that stuff,' then you *will* lose your desires."

Usually, when people say they're too old for sex, they really mean they're too *anxious* about their current level of

Anxiety—the prime inhibitor.

sexual peformance as compared to what they used to be able to do, Dr. Masters points out. In fact, anxiety and, more specifically, anxiety about sexual performance is the prime inhibitor of sexual response.

Sex is safe after a heart attack . . .

Those fears are particularly evident in people recovering from a heart attack. What's more, heart patients often avoid sex because they are afraid the stress may bring on another attack. With that thought hanging over them, it's no wonder the desire for sex is shot.

Yet research has demonstrated time and again that the actual amount of physical energy expended by an individual during sexual intercourse is equivalent to such everyday household activities as scrubbing a floor or climbing several flights of stairs, and is well below the energy demands of most jobs.

Nevertheless, the myth persists. In one study of 100 heart attack patients, 90 returned to work, but only 40 resumed normal sexual activity *(British Medical Journal)*.

Another study showed that of 48 similar patients, 17 had a change in sexual desire, a fear of intercourse, or were depressed *(Annals of Internal Medicine)*.

"In most instances," says Dr. Sadoughi, "when a person goes home from the hosptial, the danger level has passed."

"Sex in your familiar home surroundings with your partner of long standing will usually not cause excessive stress," comments Dr. Wincze.

. . . as long as it's with your spouse.

But having an extramarital encounter might. In fact, on the rare occasions when sex did coincide with a heart attack, it was under those circumstances and was usually combined with overeating and excessive alcohol.

Yet to a patient not properly informed, it may seem logical that *any* sexual activity would strain the heart beyond its capacity. That's why adequate sex counseling is clearly needed for a patient recovering from a heart attack. And it's just as important for the patient's spouse to be in on the sessions, too, because she (or he) can be plagued with the same doubts and fears as the patient.

DECREASED HORMONE LEVELS

Nobody really knows for sure why severe emotional states impair our natural desires for sex. Some experts think it's purely in the head. On the other hand, the physiological and hormonal changes that accompany stress and depression may also contribute to a lowered sexual appetite by affecting the central nervous system and by creating a decrease in the body's testosterone supply. (Testosterone, a hormone produced in both men and women, is needed for sexual desire.)

Leon Zussman, M.D., who served as director and therapist at the human sexuality center of the Long Island Jewish-Hillside Medical Center, talked with us about how stress and the chemical changes it causes in the body may lessen sexual desire.

Adrenaline isn't sexy.

"In Vietnam, when GIs were being prepared to go to the front for combat, their adrenaline levels increased and their testosterone levels decreased. They were not interested in sex. But after they returned from battle, testosterone increased and adrenaline decreased. They were again interested in sex."

Several recent studies confirm that men who are under stress show a significant and consistent depression of their blood testosterone level. After the stress has been mastered, this level rapidly returns to normal.

Exercise can help better your sex life in several ways. First, it helps by improving appearance. Second, it aids by improving circulation and reducing stress. Self-image may be one of the most important sex components of all, psychologists say, and exercise serves it royally. And third, by improving yourself physically, you improve your self-confidence, your energy levels, your outlook on life *and,* of course, your ability to perform.

How exercise makes you fit for sex.

It's also interesting to note that, in some cases where organic causes of impotence have been ruled out, a mix of hypnotherapy and sex counseling can do the rejuvenation trick *(Medical World News).* In one study at the University of Texas Health Science Center at Dallas, a doctor's use of the suggestive state in 100 impotent men returned 87 of them to full function, and the therapy remained successful during a one-year follow-up—far better than the 60 percent success rate he had before using hypnosis with the patients.

IRRITABLE BOWEL SYNDROME

We've all had "gut reactions"—a churning, uneasy stomach that says something just isn't right. The fact *is,* the gastrointestinal tract is particularly susceptible to emotional stress, says William E. Whitehead, Ph.D., associate professor of behavioral biology at Johns Hopkins Medical School in Baltimore.

"The GI tract very readily comes under the influence of external factors and events," Dr. Whitehead says.

Irritable bowel syndrome, or spastic colon, is the most common GI disorder influenced by psychological factors, Dr. Whitehead says. He estimates that about 8 percent of the adult population suffers from this ailment, which causes abdominal pain and alternate diarrhea and constipation.

Overreaction to everyday worries.

Irritable bowel syndrome (IBS) tends to occur in people who overreact to everyday worries, Dr. Whitehead says. "They are more anxious and depressed than the general population. They may be more concerned about work, finances, or family problems."

Overreaction to bodily symptoms.

Many of these sufferers also seem to be preoccupied with their health and have a number of other stress-related health problems, like headaches or insomnia. "And there's some evidence that they may have *learned* to be especially attentive to things going on in their bodies and to perhaps overreact to bodily symptoms," he says. In comparing irritable bowel victims with people with peptic ulcers, Dr. Whitehead found that those with irritable bowel were more likely to say that when they had a cold or the flu as a child their parents gave them toys, gifts, or "treat" foods like ice cream, which, he says, may have reinforced them for this type of health complaint.

As adults, having IBS may mean getting attention and having an excuse not to do certain things, Dr. Whitehead says. "But it's important to remember that most people with this disorder are simply responding to stress, and that their response is *not* intentional."

TREATING THE CAUSE

For years, doctors have recognized this psychological link, but treatment of this painful condition has nevertheless focused on drugs and diet, with often unsatisfying results.

Now researchers at the University of Göteborg in Sweden believe they have found a better way: a holistic approach that combines medical treatment and psychological therapy.

Psychotherapy vs. medicine: therapy wins.

In their study, 101 IBS patients were randomly assigned to two groups. One group received bulk-forming agents, antacids, and other drugs; members of the other group received a series of hour-long psychotherapy sessions in addition to medication. The latter patients learned to identify emotional problems in their lives and develop ways to cope.

When symptoms such as pain, diarrhea, and constipation were rated 3 months later, and again at 15 months, there were important differences. Patients receiving psychological therapy showed greater improvement than those in the drugs-only group. And their improvement tended to grow over time, while the conventionally treated group actually deteriorated *(Lancet)*.

Why the difference? "The likely explanation for this change," say the researchers, "is that patients who had received psychotherapy had acquired a new knowledge of themselves and had learned more effective ways of coping with their symptoms and with life in general."

"More effective ways of coping."

By combining the medical and the mental approach to IBS, they conclude, "the outcome can be essentially improved, not only in the short term but also in the long run."

For sufferers of IBS who do not respond to drug treatment, dietary changes, or psychiatric counseling, hypnosis could be the answer. Fifteen IBS sufferers all experienced substantial to complete relief following seven hypnosis sessions spread out over a three-month period. Once-a-month sessions were then sufficient for maintaining intestinal harmony *(Lancet)*.

PELVIC PAIN

Stress in your life may turn into pain in your pelvis. A Canadian gynecologist says that few women—or doctors—recognize that there can be a psychological basis for this very real pain. Pelvic pain of unknown origin leads to a lot of unnecessary hysterectomies, which might be avoided if doctors would point such patients toward counseling rather than surgery.

Avoiding an unnecessary hysterectomy.

Robert A. Kinch, M.D., of McGill University's faculty of medicine, says that reassurance, relaxation training, and sexual therapy can bring relief from pain in the pelvic area for many women. And a doctor willing to listen to his or her patient may be able to help her far more than a surgeon could *(Ob. Gyn. News)*.

PREGNANCY PROBLEMS

Major setbacks in a woman's life during pregnancy can produce an even bigger setback for her baby: premature delivery and low birth weight.

That's the conclusion of investigators at St. Mercy's Hospital in Manchester, England. More than 200 women were interviewed three times during pregnancy and again shortly after delivery. Major life events, such as job loss, reduced income, and illness among family members, were recorded.

"Low birth weight and prematurity were significantly associated with major life events but not . . . anxiety," the researchers conclude. In other words, the events that actually befell the women were more important than how they subjectively *perceived* those events. And events in the last three months of pregnancy seemed to be the most harmful *(British Medical Journal)*.

The more stress, the lower the birth weight.

"The data also suggest that the effects of stress may be additive—that is, the more objective major life events encountered during pregnancy, the lower the birth weight is likely to be. . . . " say the investigators.

The study also found that cigarette smoking was an even bigger predictor of low birth weight, possibly because those women who smoked may have smoked even more while under stress.

SKIN PROBLEMS

No stress is no sweat.

When you're nervous, you sweat. It's a common reaction and few would stop to contemplate the mechanism involved. But sweating in response to stress is a clear example of mind affecting body and, more specifically, of emotions manifesting through the skin.

Psychologists and psychologically minded dermatologists have known for some time that emotional problems can trigger skin problems. Robert Griesemer, M.D., a Boston dermatologist, finally confirmed it. Dr. Griesemer interviewed 4,576 patients to determine whether they had experienced a particularly stressful event—a serious argument with someone they cared about, job or school pressure, etc. —within the usual incubation period for their particular skin disorder.

His results were remarkable. He found that 94 percent

of the people with acne-like symptoms and 95 percent of the wart cases were set off by emotional factors. Some of the other ailments that ranked high on his "emotionally triggered" list include: psoriasis, 62 percent; hives, 68 percent; various types of eczema, 56 to 70 percent; pruritus, or itching, 86 percent; and *severe* itching, 98 percent.

Mind/body techniques including biofeedback, hypnosis, and progressive relaxation have been used to treat many of these problems with varying degrees of success. The use of hypnosis in the treatment of warts is perhaps the most documented.

HYPNOSIS CURES WARTS

The patient, a disabled Boston police officer, suffered from painful recurring common and plantar warts. Nothing seemed to help, until he entered an unusual treatment program in Massachusetts General Hospital's psychosomatic medicine unit. There he was placed under hypnosis and given suggestions that his warts would soon be disappearing. And sure enough, his problem was solved. When told that his health-insurance plan would not cover this type of therapeutic intervention, the officer requested a hearing and successfully challenged the ruling.

"Treatment of warts with hypnosis is a generally acknowledged if mystifying phenomenon," says Owen S. Surman, M.D. Although recent studies of the subject have been scarce, he points out that there is evidence the hypnotic suggestions must be "believed in" to be effective. The police officer's case, reported by Dr. Surman in the Institute for the Advancement of Health's journal *Advances,* is hardly unique.

An earlier study by Dr. Surman and several colleagues in Boston involved two groups of wart patients. Seventeen people were hypnotized weekly for five sessions and told their warts would disappear on one side only. Seven patients in a second (control) group received no treatment. After three months, 53 percent of the hypnotized patients showed "significant improvement," in most cases on *both* sides of their bodies. Four people reported sudden and complete disappearance of their warts. None of the untreated patients showed any improvements.

According to the researchers, all the people who improved "were capable of imaging the sensation of tin-

94 percent of acne cases were set off by emotional factors.

Sudden and complete disappearance of warts.

gling in their warts through hypnotic suggestion, and three were able to experience vivid sensory imagery as well." After the initial trial ended, four of the control patients also received hypnotherapy and three showed significant improvement.

How does hypnotic suggestion accomplish such results? In the police officer's case, further studies revealed a greater activation of cerebral blood flow in the left frontal temporal areas of his brain when the wart-vanquishing suggestions were repeated. "There are great limitations in deriving meaning from a single case," says Dr. Surman, "but it is tempting to think of a cure for warts stored somewhere in the frontal lobes."

Ted A. Grossbart, Ph.D., a clinical psychologist in the department of psychiatry at Harvard Medical School and clinical supervisor at Beth Israel Hospital in Boston, believes that psychological treatment holds the key for a wide variety of skin problems—many of which resist traditional treatment.

Eczema cleared up.

Of 15 patients with particularly difficult cases of warts, eczema, hives, and compulsive scratching who were referred to Dr. Grossbart for psychological treatment, "eight experienced total or near-total skin improvement," he wrote in *Psychology Today.* "For six, the improvement was partial but significant."

Dr. Grossbart's treatment program included a combination of progressive relaxation, visualization, hypnosis, and psychotherapy directed at five goals.

PSYCHOLOGICAL GOALS IN SKIN TREATMENT

Don't avoid painful feelings.

1. Relaxation. "Relaxation techniques should be learned with an awareness that the source of stress is not necessarily a painful situation; it is just as likely to be a struggle to *avoid* the situation and the feelings it arouses," says Dr. Grossbart.

Don't dwell on the pain.

2. Altering the perception of the problem. Dr. Grossbart points out that pain and itching is greater when we let our minds dwell on it. The key is to divert our attention away from these physical irritations. In so doing, we perceive less discomfort.

See yourself as getting better.

3. Altering the physical condition of the body. "If you visualize yourself sitting with your feet propped up in

front of a cozy fire, a thermometer between your toes actually rises," says Dr. Grossbart. "Some skin disorders are sensitive to temperature and moisture changes and may disappear if a patient visualizes alterations in bodily states."

4. Understanding the psychological meaning of the symptom. The skin is a barometer of our feelings. When we are hurt, it cries. When we are angry, it rages. When we blame ourselves for some real or imagined sin, it takes the punishment. "Symptoms seem to have very eloquent, personal symbolic meaning," says Dr. Grossbart. "Experiencing these meanings is a central part of treatment."

The skin "cries out."

5. Learning to let go. For some, the difficulty is in overriding an unconscious or subconscious need to hold on to the problem. "Painful as the disease is, it carries some advantages with it," Dr. Grossbart explains. "It can be an attempt to resolve overwhelming dilemmas, a respectable way to avoid work or ask for love, or a distraction from emotional pain. Improvement can rock the boat. For that reason, even the patients who suffer most at times sabotage treatment."

Is your disease helping you in some way?

TWO CASE STUDIES*

Dr. Grossbart gives an example of a patient whose skin condition responded to such psychological treatment:

Sal was a nice-looking 20-year-old, but his right hand was a mess, with layer upon layer of red, raw warts. He painfully told me about his warts and his life. Each of his buddies had gone off—one to the service, one to get married, one to take a job with the telephone company. Sal, unemployed, spent his days in front of the TV set. . . .

A year earlier, Sal had been working at a factory job that he liked pretty much. . . . Then, after six months, he was abruptly shifted to another line. . . . Warts began to appear. Quitting the job had not helped to cure the warts. Nor had any medical treatment.

To help Sal, I first had him imagine a feeling of relaxation as a thick, soothing, liquid, flowing down through his body. Then I had him concentrate, withdrawing attention from everyday distractions. Third, I suggested that he let himself feel a floating, drifting, or gliding sensation. This was the beginning of teaching Sal to alter perception. He was, of course, not floating or drifting, yet he was able to imagine himself floating in a way that felt real to him. Sal's right hand felt better when it was cool, so he now imagined that he was floating on a cloud up in cool, crisp air.

Having taught Sal self-hypnosis, I suggested that he repeat the sequence two or three times a day. By the second week, his warts were disappearing—but new ones were forming!

Might Sal, in a less than conscious way, have had a need to hold on to the warts? Were they giving him some benefit, as well as making his life miserable? . . .

Sal gained something from being stuck at home with an immobilized hand: He did not have to grow up. A second, subtler advantage centered on his anger over the shift in his job, the breakup of his gang . . . and the failure of doctors to cure his warts. Not that he felt consciously angry; in fact, that was the trouble. . . .

As Sal began to feel his sadness and anger more directly, new warts stopped forming, and by the ninth and final week of treatment, his hand showed only small discolored spots.

Dr. Grossbart presents another case:

Susan, a 50-year-old music teacher, told me about the early stages of a skin disorder that her doctors had labeled "neurodermatitis." It had appeared more than two decades before, not long after the difficult delivery of her eldest child, a son. His first year of life was a constant torment to him and to his mother. Colic had him crying nearly nonstop, day and night. The effect of the unusual demands from her son was heightened by her husband's withdrawal. . . . Unable to get emotional support from anyone or to confront her husband's passivity, Susan called on her skin to bring about symbolically what she wished for unconsciously. She developed a rash on her hand so severe that she had to have her wedding ring cut off. At that time the meaning of the event was far from her awareness. Only ten years later, and after several months of therapy, did Susan recognize that to be out of marriage and motherhood had been her secret wish.

If you don't call for help, your skin will.

Clearly, the relationship between skin problems and emotions is complex. But, in his years of experience as a psychotherapist, Dr. Grossbart has seen convincing evidence that healthy skin and a healthy expression of emotions go hand in hand. "It seemed that when people allowed themselves to experience the full emotional impact of a critical life situation, physical symptoms were much less likely to arise," he says. "By contrast, people who did not fully experience the pain of a difficult event were much more prone to physical symptoms. If they did not cry, rage, call for help, or remember painful events, their bodies seemed to do those things for them."

ULCERS

Like irritable bowel syndrome, peptic ulcers are also made worse by psychological stress. But rather than having a difficult time dealing with small things, those with this ailment tend to have been exposed to extraordinary stress. "They are police officers and air-traffic controllers, people in occupations that are either dangerous or involve a lot of time pressure," says Dr. William E. Whitehead, associate professor of behavioral biology at Johns Hopkins Medical School in Baltimore. "These people are reacting to the sorts of pressure that would affect anyone."

Ulcers and extra-ordinary stress.

But, due to the nature of their jobs, stress management techniques are essential to long-term health management (see Chapter 29, The Best of the Relaxation Techniques and Chapter 30, Mastering Stress). Hypnosis and guided imagery, in which you visualize the ulcer healing, are also used to speed recovery.

PART **XIII**

Stocking Your Mental Medicine Chest

65

Color and Light

A little girl is losing her sight. Blood tumors growing in back of her eye relentlessly push the eye forward. Surgery has been tried three times without success. All the standard treatments have failed. Then her doctor prescribes something extra: a holistic approach including better nutrition, healing visualizations, and an odd request. The child is to spend several hours a day outside in natural sunlight. And her bedroom walls, drapes—even her clothes—must be relaxing shades of green and blue. In a few months her tumors are gone and her vision is normal.

A prescription that includes sunlight.

A troubled teenager at a youth detention center is so hostile and aggressive he must frequently be placed in an isolation room. Each time he flings curses at the walls for hours, pounding them with his fists. But then the room is painted a particular shade of pink. The next time, he again enters in a state of rage, but within six minutes he is quietly sitting on the floor, weeping.

Room color: the difference between aggression and submission.

It's no coincidence that the above examples seem to suggest a long-overlooked possibility—that the subtle vibratory energies of color and light can have far-reaching effects on our physical and mental health.

Today, many psychiatrists and endocrinologists recognize that light can have a very complex effect on the body. It does much more than enable our eyes to see.

Although the process isn't entirely understood, it's believed that light enters the eyes, travels to the brain, and stimulates the pineal gland. Depending on whether light is

Light affects hormone production and may boost immunity.

coming in or not, the pineal gland either suppresses or releases a hormone called melatonin. This hormone induces sleep, raises the level of serotonin (a neurotransmitter that carries messages through the nervous system) and determines the release of still more body-regulating hormones. It is also believed that light may increase the body's protective immune system. In short, light seems to have tremendous impact on our health and behavior.

Two researchers in particular have made great contributions to our knowledge of light and health. One is Richard Wurtman, Ph.D., of the Massachusetts Institute of Technology. He has maintained for years that most of us do not receive enough of the right kind of light for optimal health. The artificial lights that we typically use indoors provide only about one-tenth of the light available outside under a shade tree on a sunny day, he says. And at best, artificial light isn't as beneficial as sunlight. Dr. Wurtman has shown that light, among other things, helps determine female ovulation, affects the ability of older people to absorb calcium, and can be used to treat jaundice among newborns.

Artificial light is like white bread, deficient in certain "nutrients."

Another leader in light research has been John Ott, who learned about the effects of light on plants while doing time-lapse photography for Walt Disney. A non-scientist, he has written two influential books on light (*Health and Light* and *Light, Radiation and You,* both published by Devin-Adair) and believes that most artificial light lacks essential wavelengths in much the same way that refined flour lacks certain vitamins and minerals. He claims that certain cells in the body can't function without those parts of the spectrum, and that most indoor lighting promotes illness, including cancer.

Other researchers have been building on the work of Ott and Dr. Wurtman. Some of the most promising breakthroughs have been made in the treatment of depression.

BEATING THE BLUES

Daylight Savings Time and the winter funk.

Light specialists now know that certain types of depression arrive in the winter and vanish in the spring. A surprisingly large number of people lapse into a wintertime funk when Daylight Savings Time ends. As one researcher put it, "Hibernation is not unknown among the human species."

"Most people say that they slow down a little in the winter," says Thomas Wehr, M.D., of the National Institute of Mental Health. "They sleep more, they gain a little weight. The number of people who have an extreme problem is larger than we thought at first. These are people who know that something is wrong, but they've never known what to call it."

In some cases, a mild funk turns into a serious mental illness. "The people we're seeing right now have severe symptoms," Dr. Wehr says. "They're almost incapacitated by it. They stop cooking meals, they don't see their friends. They are experiencing a great deal of stress and they may even become suicidal."

Patterns of darkness: fatigue, anxiety, depression.

Dr. Wehr and colleague Norman Rosenthal, M.D., recently treated a 63-year-old manic-depressive man whose depressive periods almost always began in midsummer and peaked around year's end. While depressed, he withdrew and became self-critical and anxious. He complained of fatigue and was afraid to go to work. Attempts to treat him with drugs were abandoned due to side effects.

With this pattern in mind, the researchers decided to bring the man out of his depression by doing something remarkably simple. They created the conditions of a spring day. During the first week of December, several weeks before the patient's depression was scheduled to end, the doctors woke him out of bed at 6:00 A.M. and exposed him to very bright artificial light—about ten times as bright as customary indoor light—for three hours. Then at 4:00 P.M. they exposed him to the same type of light for another three hours. In effect, they were lengthening his days. The treatment lasted ten days.

Within about four days, the man began to emerge from his depressive cocoon. In his own opinion, he felt much better. And the nurses who observed him thought so, too. The researchers came away from the experiment believing that humans, like bears and migratory birds and most of what used to be called the animal kingdom, have seasonal rhythms. Although the beneficial effect ended four days after the treatment ended, the researchers had established that strong artificial light can have as great an effect on mental health as does natural sunlight *(American Journal of Psychiatry)*.

Day-lengthening treatment reversed the depression.

Strong artificial light can also have an effect on people

Strong artificial light benefits mental health.

who suffer from depression all year round. Daniel Kripke, M.D., of the University of California, San Diego, believes that depression may occur when the body's circadian rhythm goes awry and the body's inner clock runs too fast or slow.

He thinks that waking a patient and exposing him or her to very bright light at a critical moment in the early morning hours might jolt the internal clock and relieve the depression.

MORNING LIGHT

In Dr. Kripke's study, 12 depressed patients agreed to be awakened at odd hours of the night for one hour at a time on three consecutive nights. On one of the nights, the researchers woke them between one and two hours before their usual time of arising and exposed them to a very bright white fluorescent light. On a second night, the procedure was the same, but this time the patients were exposed to a dim red light. On the third night they were awakened two to three hours *after retiring* and were exposed to a dim red light. Based on follow-up testing, the bright fluorescent light, used in the early morning, "significantly lowered their depression scores" temporarily *(Psychopharmacology Bulletin)*.

Light research is still in its infancy.

Whether these findings can be translated into information that health-minded people can use on their own remains to be seen. "It's all very interesting, it's promising, and I'm excited by it from a scientific point of view," says Dr. Kripke. "But we are in the early stages of this and we aren't sure what the practical applications may be."

In the foregoing experiments, light was used to rouse and activate depressed persons. In other cases, certain parts of the light spectrum have been used to calm down hyperactive children. John Ott has long maintained that the cool-white fluorescent lights customarily used in elementary school classrooms contribute to hyperactivity and restlessness among the children. Part of the problem, he thinks, is the fact that the tubes emit x-rays and harmful radio frequencies but do not emit the ultraviolet wavelengths that are found in sunlight. (Ott adds that fixtures have been developed that can remedy this problem.)

Can ultraviolet light relieve headaches and fatigue?

The wisdom of increasing our exposure to ultraviolet light has been hotly debated. According to Wendon Henton, Ph.D., of the National Center for Devices and Radiological

Health, there have been claims that ultraviolet light can increase calcium absorption in the elderly and relieve headaches and fatigue.

Dr. Henton and researcher Stephen Sykes, encouraged by Ott, conducted an experiment to compare the activity levels of mice living under ordinary incandescent light to their activity levels under the same light "supplemented" with ultraviolet light. Very simply, they put mice in cages with running wheels and measured how much they exercised under several lighting conditions.

As predicted by Ott, the mice logged the fewest wheel revolutions under the ultraviolet light. The researchers concluded that the blend of wavelengths in a given source of light can indeed influence the behavior of mice and possibly of humans. But whether or not the fact that the mice ran less under ultraviolet light was a positive change in behavior, they didn't know *(Physiology and Behavior)*.

Blending wavelengths for optimal health.

LIGHT: A CANCER FACTOR

Researchers have also investigated the possibility that certain components of light can affect our ability to mate and produce children, and to raise or lower our susceptibility to cancer. In 1964, Ott ran an experiment showing that mice living under pink fluorescent lights were more prone to cancer and to reproductive problems.

A group of researchers at the National Institute of Environmental Health Sciences (NIEHS) in North Carolina decided to find out whether Ott's theory held water. It did.

Colin Chignell, Ph.D., and his colleagues at NIEHS used a number of mice that belonged to a strain bred to develop tumors as they matured. They divided the mice into three groups and assigned them to three different habitats, each one lit by a different kind of fluorescent lamp. One lamp was pink; the second, "cool-white"; and the third, "daylight-simulating."

Theory confirmed: Full-spectrum lighting increases cancer resistance.

After the 573 days of the experiment, the mice living under the daylight-simulating lamp seemed to have the greatest resistance to cancer. The mice who lived under pink and cool-white lamps developed breast tumors after only 42 and 47 weeks, respectively, but those raised in full-spectrum light did not develop tumors until they were 51 weeks old. Light has been found to activate the pituitary gland, and

Dr. Chignell suspected that prolactin, a hormone secreted by the pituitary gland, might have somehow accounted for the difference *(Photochemistry and Photobiology)*.

More research needs to be done.

So far, the scientific world is just waking up to the effects of light on human health. The amount of research dedicated to light has been small. No one knows for sure how a given quantity or quality of light influences our body functions for better or worse.

Some important facts have been established, however. We now know that the eye, as one researcher put it, "isn't only for seeing." Light reaches the brain through the eye and stimulates the release or suppression of critical hormones. Sunlight seems to be healthier than artificial light, but full-spectrum artificial light can mimic the sun's powers.

IN THE PINK

As we've already seen, various fractions of light— colors—can have additional effects. The particular shade of pink mentioned earlier, for example, generated a strong physical response in Alexander G. Schauss, director of the American Institute for Biosocial Research in Tacoma, Washington. It also generated a remarkably useful idea.

Color exposure—at least to a certain shade—can lower blood pressure.

Using an 18 by 24-inch cardboard sheet of what has now come to be known as Baker-Miller Pink, Schauss recalls that "I experimented on myself and noted that my blood pressure, pulse, and heart rate *lowered* more rapidly upon exposure to the shade . . . after a period of intentional hyperexcitement than when viewing any other color. . . . If my heartbeat, blood pressure, and pulse could be brought down by an environmental variable like color, what effect might this phenomenon have on aggression?" *(Biosocial: The Journal of Behavioral Ecology)*.

The same color calmed violent aggressive prisoners.

When specially painted pink holding cells were tested at jails and other correctional centers, the results were consistent and amazing. Violently aggressive inmates were calmed within minutes and could be transferred to their regular place of confinement.

"It is important to understand," says Schauss, "that the effect of Baker-Miller Pink is *physical*, not psychological or cultural." Even people who are color-blind respond to its calming influence!

Creativity

It's no accident that Norman Cousins, in his book *Anatomy of an Illness* (W. W. Norton & Co.), included a chapter entitled "Creativity and Longevity." Cousins discusses the link betwen creativity and the evident vitality of both cellist Pablo Casals and Dr. Albert Schweitzer when they were in their 80s.

Norman Cousins links creativity with longevity.

Cousins noticed that when Casals laid hands on the cello, all of his symptoms of arthritis and emphysema disappeared. "Creativity for Pablo Casals was the source of his own cortisone," Cousins writes. "He was caught up in his own creativity, in his own desire to accomplish a specific purpose, and the effect was both genuine and observable."

When Casals laid hands on his cello, his arthritis disappeared.

About Dr. Schweitzer, who lived to be 95, Cousins writes, "The essence of Dr. Schweitzer was purpose and creativity." For Cousins, creativity—pursuing definite goals and expressing oneself through music or medicine or some other medium—is a necessary ingredient of a long and vital life.

What is creativity, exactly? How can we develop more of it? And what kinds of benefits can we hope to reap from it?

Social scientist E. Paul Torrance, Ph.D., a professor emeritus in the department of educational psychology at the University of Georgia, has been trying to identify and measure creativity, especially in children, for more than 20 years. In 1977 and 1978, he was involved in testing 200 men and women between the ages of 65 and 85 to find out how art classes would affect their lives. The study grew out of the Art for Older Americans Program, which

Measuring tangible health benefits of creative activities.

was administered in a nine-county area in rural north-eastern Georgia.

After a year of painting and drawing classes, 90 of the elderly students filled out a prepared questionnaire. Their answers showed some of the tangible health benefits of creative activity. Ninety-six percent reported feeling "more alive and fresh" after their art class, and 82 percent said they felt "more alive" than when the classes first began.

Seventy-one percent said they were more active than before; 93 percent said time passed faster for them; 59 percent said they were not sick as often as they were the year before.

More at peace within myself.

Eighty-eight percent said they were not as lonely as they once were; 93 percent thought they understood other people better; 94 percent felt "more at peace within myself."

While Dr. Torrance and his colleagues admit that "the claims these elderly citizens make may seem a bit extravagant," they also note that a study in Nebraska produced similar findings. In that study, a group of 35 elderly people received 18 weeks of instruction in oil painting in 1960. Eleven years later, in 1971, a follow-up survey was made with remarkable results. Sixty-seven percent of the art students were still living, compared to 38 percent of a matched control group. And while all of the remaining students were alert and active, only 62 percent of the controls still living were rated as mentally alert, and 38 percent were bedridden.

Creativity triggers optimal function of the endocrine system.

The healthy effects of drawing might be attributed, Dr. Torrance said, to the fact that the students were "using more of their powers." He also speculated that creativity could trigger a more optimal functioning of the endo-crine system.

"Creativity," as Dr. Torrance defines it, "is a process of becoming sensitive to problems, deficiencies, gaps in knowl-edge, missing elements, disharmonies, and so on; identi-fying the difficulty; searching for solutions, making guesses, or formulating hypotheses and possibly modifying and re-testing them; and finally, communicating the results.

Everyone has a creative person inside.

"It's a universal phenomenon," he says, "which all moderately functioning persons, including the mentally retarded and the handicapped, have. The important thing is to learn how to manage it, learn how to keep it alive."

DOING WHAT WE WANT

Teaching people how to keep their creativity alive is what Michell Cassou, an artist, tries to do at her Painting Experience Studio in San Francisco. For her, the secret is breaking free of external and internal criticism.

"To be creative is really just to do what we want," Cassou says in a French accent. "But this is very hard. We find that we don't know what we want to do. Most of the time people don't realize how many judgments they have about what they do. They don't give themselves the permission to do what they want.

"I tell them they cannot fail, because creativity is inside," she says. "I make them feel all right with whatever they paint. They're afraid to paint ugly, afraid that their painting won't have enough meaning. I tell them, 'What's ugly?' That's irrelevant. It's just conditioning."

Boredom and the fear of entering uncharted imaginative waters both tend to inhibit creativity, Cassou says. "People are bored most of the time," she says. "They're so used to it that they accept it." They might not be so bored, she believes, if they had the courage to let the unexpected happen.

Creativity depends very much on an individual's courage in forging ahead in the face of criticism, according to Erwin DiCyan, Ph.D., the New York author of *Creativity: Road to Self-Discovery* (Jove Publishing, Inc.)

"People stop when they are ridiculed," Dr. DiCyan says. "People don't seem to have the courage to say, 'So what?' Those who accept themselves, and have the courage of their own convictions, will find their own level."

A mixture of intuitive feelings and hard work provides the ideal spawning ground for creation. "Surrender yourself to the muse," Dr. DiCyan says. "You have to let your mind go. You don't start fermenting creativity. You just don't suppress it."

WINDY CITY WORKSHOPS

One place where creativity really seems to be blossoming is in Chicago. There, some of the most creative, funny, and talented figures in American show business—people like Alan Alda, Ed Asner, Alan Arkin, Barbara Harris, Mike

The secret is in breaking free of external and internal criticism.

Courage relieves boredom.

Intuition and hard work: the ideal spawning ground for creation.

Nichols, Shelley Berman, Anne Meara, David Steinberg, Valerie Harper, Robert Klein, and Paul Mazursky, to name a few—launched their careers. But why Chicago? Simple: Chicago is home to improvisational theatre. And when we're talking improvisation, we're talking about a powerful creative force.

Fun and games, practiced masterfully.

What exactly is improvisation? As practiced by the masters in Chicago, it's games, make-believe, an art, a sport.

Most people think of improvisation as training for actors—and they're right—but it can be much more. Lawyers, secretaries, writers, musicians, people of all professions and ages learn to play improvisational games. Why? To become more creative.

Webster's defines "creative" this way: to bring into existence; to bring about by a course of action or behavior; to produce through imaginative skills.

Tapping directly into the "right brain."

That defines improvisation, too: actions and skills that help people find newness in themselves—new ideas, new words, new movements, new characters. A good improvisational game helps people bypass their self-censoring instincts and tap directly into their emotions, their imaginations, their "right brain," the source of human creativity. It's an exhilarating feeling, that feeling of surprising yourself with your own creation.

And there are other benefits, too. Want to be less self-conscious? The games improvisers play are so enthralling that they're virtually guaranteed to ward off the worst cases of stage fright.

Want to think fast, feel more confident in your decisions? Improvisation is practice in quick decision making, performance under pressure.

Think fast, feel confident, make close friends.

Want to have fun? Guaranteed. Improvisation is dealing with people in a positive, affirming way. It turns a collection of individuals into a tightly knit group that cares about each other's feelings and actions, that helps each other over the rough spots and exults together in the good spots.

Interested? The gurus of improvisation—teachers like Paul Sills, Jo Forsberg, and Second City's Del Close and Don DePollo—who taught many of those celebrities, are still teaching their art to professionals and amateurs alike in the Windy City.

The father of Chicago improvisation is Paul Sills; he

inherited it from his mother. His mother is Viola Spolin, the woman who developed the games improvisers play. She discovered that games—each presenting a problem or an objective—make people less self-conscious. "Skills are developed at the very moment a person is having all the fun and excitement playing a game has to offer," she wrote in her classic book, *Improvisation for the Theatre* (Northwestern University Press). By demanding instant responses, games help people overcome inhibitions to reach the intuitive level, says Spolin. "All of us have known moments when we did exactly the right thing without thinking, usually precipitated by a crisis," she says. The games create a "crisis," and "ingenuity and inventiveness appear" to meet the challenge. "It is a time of discovery. Games free people to enter into an exciting, creative adventure."

> **By demanding instant responses, games force us to use our intuitive sense.**

Spolin now lives in California; her son, who founded the legendary Compass Players, which later became Second City, is still teaching the game-playing art in Chicago. He has his own theater, The Story Theatre; he's long since left Second City and teaches classes in "serious" improvisation.

GAMES CREATIVE PEOPLE PLAY

A class with Paul Sills is like a class in creative brainstorming—brainstorming with your mind and your body. But if you can't get to Chicago, try these improvisational games developed by Viola Spolin, which can be found in her book *Improvisation for the Theatre.*

> **Brainstorming with your mind and body.**

Trapped (single player). The player chooses a "where" from which he or she is trying to escape. (Examples: caught in a bear trap, tree trunk, elevator.)

> **The Great Houdini Make-Believe.**

Changing Intensity of Inner Action. Two or more players choose a "where, who, and what" (where they are, who they are, and what they're doing). They also choose an emotion. The emotion must become progressively stronger in the scene. For instance, the sequence may run from affection to love to adoration; from suspicion to fear to terror.

Poetry Building. On different slips of paper, each person in the group writes an adjective, a noun, a pronoun, a verb, and an adverb. The slips are placed in separate piles according to their classification, and each pile is jumbled up. Each player must then pick up five slips and construct a

> **Creative poetry like a chain letter.**

poem from the five words chosen, adding prepositions and other parts of speech if necessary.

Story Building (four or more players). The first player starts a story about anything he or she wishes. As the game progresses, the leader points to various players, who must immediately step in and continue the story from the point where the last player left off.

Gibberish. One player is to sell or demonstrate something to the audience in gibberish (nonsense words). Concentrate on communication—showing—to the audience. (And make sure there's variety in the gibberish!)

OTHER TECHNIQUES

Of course, improvisation isn't the only way to tap your creativity. Here are a few other suggestions from the experts.

Start a journal. Psychologist Richard Kirby of New York City suggests this as a daily or weekly routine for two people who can share their progress and make each other stick to it. ("Doing things alone is a pre-1980s syndrome," Kirby says.) Rather than an orderly account of the day's or week's events, the journal should be an exercise in jotting down thoughts as they appear uncensored in the mind "Nothing can equal or replace the personal journal as the sphere of action for . . . the continuing quest of the self," writes John A. B. McLeish in his book about creativity in later life called *The Ulyssean Adult* (McGraw-Hill Ryerson, Ltd., Canada).

Relax: Even if you aren't into Transcendental Meditation, this is a must. Drs. DiCyan and Torrance each recommend letting the mind indulge in fantasies and daydreams. "Without some element of the nonsensical in our lives, the drying-up process begins," writes McLeish. "When you create," says Cassou, "you don't have the feeling that you are working."

Learn from young people. Dr. Torrance has been working with children for years, and he thinks they have a special spark to pass on to their elders. "Teach them what you know," he tells adults, "but realize that you can learn something from them, too. This seems to be quite powerful."

Try something new. Join an environment action group or learn to play a musical instrument. Do whatever it takes to disrupt that sense of "total expectedness," to use McLeish's term.

Speak your mind—but don't say what you mean.

Writing for a captive audience: yourself.

Watching a child with your own wide-eyed wonder.

Find out what you really want. "What subjects keep us really interested? What are those on which we talk most easily, and with the greatest pleasure, to ourselves and others?" wrote Ernest Dimnet 50 years ago in *The Art of Thinking* (Simon & Schuster). Kirby recommends writing down 100 life goals for personal creativity, picking out the most important and most plausible ones, then doing them.

If you put some of these ideas into practice, you'll probably find yourself becoming more creative. But there's an additional benefit. Like the elderly art students in Dr. Torrance's study, you may notice yourself feeling better, both mentally and physically.

"There's a very strong relationship between emotional health and the free flow of creativity," says Kirby. He thinks creative concentration endows us with an "intrinsic orientation toward the good, the beautiful, and the healthy."

Write down 100 life goals for personal creativity.

67

Family Reunions

Therapeutic family reunions
can stimulate recovery from
serious diseases.

Harold Wise, M.D., has always found himself intrigued by the influence of the family on individual health. He believes that a great potential for healing exists in the family. Through what he calls the "therapeutic family reunion," he has mobilized that power to bolster the family in times of illness. The reunions have been followed in some cases, he says, by recovery from diseases as serious as cancer.

TRIBE AS HEALER

"When I was studying the roots of the healing process in tribal medicine, the clan was always involved," says Dr. Wise. "What I'm saying doesn't click in most people's heads in twentieth-century America.

For a million years people
lived in extended families.

"But as I began to work more and more in this area, I realized how much we underestimate the power of the family. For a million years people have lived in families, and only in the last hundred or so years have people split up. But the influence of the family is still there, the patterning is still there.

"The oldest healing form, in tribal medicine, involved bringing the whole clan together and working things through for 24 hours, or 72 hours. That was the way they did it. When anyone was ill among the old Hawaiian healers, they would regard it as a problem not only of the person, but of the whole system. They would ask, 'What's going on in the family that makes one of its branches sick?'

"They would bring everyone together, and everyone

had to confess any negative feelings they had toward the person or each other, and forgive each other, before the healer would work with the sick person.

Bringing the family together to confess negative feelings and forgive.

"Among the Kung Bushmen of the Lakahari Desert of Africa, families would meet weekly. When anyone was ill, they would dance all night. They would speak to their ancestors as well as to each other, and have a catharsis of whatever tensions had built up over the week."

Dr. Wise has organized many such "healing" reunions, but makes a point of emphasizing that they are exceptional occurrences in what is otherwise basically a traditional practice. Sometimes, however, circumstances dictate a departure from tradition.

"It's hard to say exactly what goes on at a reunion," says Ross Speck, M.D., a Philadelphia psychiatrist who uses similar techniques in his work with schizophrenic patients. "When you have that many people together, things are happening all over." Dr. Speck participated with Dr. Wise in the reunion of a cancer patient's family. "We met on a Friday evening and worked long into the early morning, then assembled again the next day. We were together all day Saturday and Saturday evening. Usually it's nice to meet in the home, but in this case we met at a hotel at the seashore, with 35 members of the patient's family.

When many people get together, things happen all over.

"We worked as a team, eight or nine specialists from different fields. An encounter group specialist would work to break down resistances. If the people became restless, we would do exercises. When we left, there were huge flow sheets tacked up on the wall, and the kids were sitting around while the older people made kinship maps, explaining where an uncle came from in Germany, and so on. They were retribalizing their heritage."

REUNITING THE MINDS

"One of the useful things is to off the usual schedule," Dr. Wise says. "Things seem to break open when you get off the usual schedule. It doesn't happen until about 12 hours have passed, in some cases 24 hours. You go into what I call the family level. It's a level where you're so tuned in to each other, one person seems able to speak for everybody. It's a very primal feeling, a sense that you have stepped out of time. And once the family is into that level, no one will leave."

After 12 to 24 hours of reuniting, you enter the "family level."

"It's a very moving event. And to my astonishment, there have been some remissions of the disease in the dying person." In fact, Dr. Wise has experienced only one case in which the family reunion has not been followed by an improvement in the patient's condition.

Dr. Wise generally organizes reunions around people suffering serious illnesses like cancer or heart disease, but he has worked with patients with other complaints, too. He tells of one patient suffering from Münchausen's syndrome, a psychological condition in which the patient repeatedly checks into the hospital with detailed physical complaints, all of which are false. Dr. Wise's patient would make 150 visits to her doctor in one year.

Reunions are generally organized for people with cancer or heart disease.

"I found that this person was the negative focus of her family. She was totally isolated, by her children, her ex-husband, her sisters, her friends. No one would come near her, and when you were around her you knew why. She emanated negativity. That's how she related to everybody, from the bus driver to the doorman. She was on many medications.

"We brought the family together for two six-hour reunions. She's now down to just one medication and has had only three visits to her doctor in the last year."

Exactly how the reunions combat disease is mystery to Dr. Wise, but he does have some ideas about what's going on. "A person who is cut, heals. There's a healing force within. There is likely a similar healing force within the family.

How reunions combat disease remains a mystery.

"I saw pictures of an elephant dying and what the elephant herd did to keep it alive. The families where the healings have happened go through a similar movement in that the sick person is taken into the center and surrounded with a spiral.

"It's almost as if you take your wounded hand and hold it here," Dr. Wise says, clutching his hand protectively to his chest. "I have a lot of notions about what's happening, but I don't have a theory that satisfies me. All I know is that the reunions are very healthful for the family. And as the ill person is a part of the family, it's also critical to that person.

MAKING WAY FOR LOVE

"You can clear out everything that prevents families from getting together, the unresolved grief, the unexpressed

Family support and love helps people heal better.

anger, and get to what lies underneath—a tremendous amount of love. If people feel supported and loved, they seem to heal better. The immune system seems to work better. But whether there's a remission of the disease or not, I know that this work is important for the healing of the family itself.

"I believe families can do this on their own," Dr. Wise adds. "And it's not a one-time thing. You don't work it out in one meeting.

"In my family, reunions have become part of what we do. The first one we had, in fact the whole idea of therapeutic reunion, was initiated by my brother David. Every time there's a wedding, we meet afterward. I'm going next week to a cousin's wedding and then the following month to another cousin's engagement party, and every time I go we feel more connected. Our baby girl connects with a huge clan now, and they're always coming to New York. In terms of her life, she knows she has family practically anywhere she goes, whether it's California or Canada.

Planning family reunions in times of health.

"Not everyone is going to go around meeting as whole families like that, for a weekend, but they can meet for shorter periods. Even a five-minute change can be a big change. If I can get a couple to sit down in a relaxed way, not so they're feeling any obligation, give each other a little massage for five minutes each day, I can show them that their blood pressure drops.

"It's the little things you can do that make a difference."

68

Humor

Former *Saturday Review* editor Norman Cousins, suffering from a physician-diagnosed "incurable disease," unreeled "Candid Camera" episodes and Marx Brothers films and, in part, belly-laughed himself into the pink. His anecdotal account of his self-styled healing became the best-selling book *Anatomy of an Illness* (W. W. Norton & Co.) and many people have looked upon that successful personal experiment as the throwing out of the first ball in the game of humor-as-Hippocrates.

But for years before then, white-coated scientists with very impressive credentials and very serious expressions had been exploring the many benefits of laughter. Research studies—thick with sticky technical jargon and topped off with nap-inducing titles like "Mirth and Oxygen Saturation Levels of Peripheral Blood" (yawn)—picked apart humor and clinically poked around inside the magical 17-jewel movement that makes it tick.

Humor, they found, has "a profound connection with physiological states of the body," writes Raymond A. Moody, Jr., M.D., in *Laugh after Laugh: The Healing Power of Humor* (Headwaters Press). He goes on to say that "over the years I have encountered a surprising number of instances in which, to all appearances, patients have laughed themselves back to health, or at least have used their sense of humor as a very positive and adaptive response to their illnesses."

There is a link between sense of humor and longevity, Dr. Moody reports, and there is also a definite anesthetic effect of laughter, an "inverse relationship between humor and pain." He speculates that because laughter causes a loss in muscle tone (try holding on to something tightly—try merely supporting yourself on your own two legs—when a series of belly laughs hits), muscle-related pains may vanish in the wake of a good guffaw. This is his scenario: "Unconsciously produced tension in the muscles increases, or causes, a headache. The person is presented with a humorous stimulus. He laughs, the tension of his muscles in the affected area decreases, and the pain is relieved." Dr. Moody reports that a physician friend of his was able to cure his patients' tension headaches simply by getting them to laugh.

There is also some evidence that laughter triggers the brain to release catecholamine hormones, which in turn cause the release of endorphins, the body's natural painkillers. Then, too, it may be that laughter's anesthetic effect rests largely on its ability to draw attention away from our pain.

"So much of pain is emotional," says Alan D. Russakov, M.D., Medical Director of Lourdes Regional Rehabilitation Center in Camden, New Jersey. "If you wallow in self-pity, the pain gets worse. But, through joy and laughter, you can ease the anxiety and depression that are so often associated with chronic pain and thereby eliminate the suffering."

Self-pity makes pain worse.

LAUGH AWAY STRESS

The stress-relieving power of humor is well established. Laughter, we are told, relieves tension, breaks negative "holding patterns," and helps put our problems in perspective. In fact, a study of midlife wellness factors by Harvard's eminent George Vaillant, M.D., singled out humor as a major stress-coping mechanism among healthy men.

No small wonder then that humor has been credited with reducing the coronary risk of a high-stress lifestyle. Not only does it help diffuse anxiety and anger but, as Norman Cousins, himself a heart attack victim, points out, it acts as a blocking agent against the ravages of panic. The panic produced by a heart attack can be just as dangerous as the heart attack. It constricts blood vessels and destabilizes the heart. But through humor, reassurance, and positive thinking you can control the panic and thereby enhance your prospects for recovery. Laughter creates an environment for healing, according to Cousins.

Humor blocks panic.

Laughter strengthens the immune system.

And that goes for all illnesses—not only coronary artery disease. The burgeoning field of psychoneuroimmunology has provided proof positive that negative emotions such as depression weaken the immune system, making us more susceptible to a whole host of illnesses ranging from colds to cancer. It stands to reason, then, that positive emotions such as humor and laughter may have the opposite effect, helping us to keep our immune system strong and defending us against sickness.

"Sick people, especially ones who are depressed, take themselves much too seriously," says psychologist Harry A. Olson, Ph.D., of Reisterstown, Maryland. That's just what doctors are discovering now. Even though controlled scientific studies measuring the chemistry of laughter are rare, what there is supports the theory that good humor breeds good health.

Demonstrating the measurable physiological effects of laughter.

In fact, just to prove that laughter was having a measurable physiological effect on his health, Norman Cousins' doctors took sedimentation rate readings just before as well as several hours after this laughter episodes. This test measures signs of inflammation in the body, a major characteristic of the illness Cousins was suffering from at the time. "Each time, there was a drop of at least five points. The drop by itself was not substantial," says Cousins, "but it held and was cumulative" *(New England Journal of Medicine)*.

Other doctors have proven scientifically that laughter enhances respiration and combats carbon dioxide levels in the blood *(Psychotherapy and Psychosomatics)*.

Actually, doctors in the business of dispensing humor along with or in place of prescription drugs have known for some time that there is such a thing as laughing yourself back to health.

A MASSAGE FOR THE INTERAL ORGANS

Furthermore, some researchers have suggested that by laughing, we provide a healthful massage for our internal organs (sort of like Magic Fingers, but without the motel room coin box), and that perhaps it is, in part, some sort of compensation for the natural inner rubbing we lost when early humans attained an erect posture.

And laughing is good exercise, too. Norman Cousins

called it "internal jogging," and he was pretty much on the mark. "Mirth—in contrast to many other emotions—entails physical exercise," writes William Fry, Jr., M.D., one of the world's leading physiology of laughter researchers, working at Stanford University. "Muscles are activated; heart rate is increased; respiration is amplified, with increase in oxygen exchange—all similar to the desirable effects of athletic exercise." Muscles in the face, arms, legs, and stomach get a mini-workout (remember how your stomach ached the last time you laughed really hard?) and so do the diaphragm, the thorax, and the circulatory and endocrine systems.

A mini-workout each time you laugh.

So, it's been well established that laughter and humor are good for you (but don't hold your breath waiting for Blue Cross to list a visit to a Woody Allen movie under "Outpatient Services"). What we need to know, then, is how to create those healthy ha-has and apply them to our everyday and work-a-day lives.

While there are a lot of situations that may make you laugh, not all of them have healing qualities, says Dr. Harry Olson. "Humor as a therapeutic tool must build instead of knock, and therefore excludes sarcasm and cynicism, which pump up the self at the expense of others," says Dr. Olson.

Cynicism and sarcasm don't heal.

Fact is, *why* you laugh is just as important as *how* you laugh.

"There are three levels of humor," explains Dr. Olson. "Sarcasm is one, but that's destructive. The second, a good pun that gives you a twist of expectancy, has positive qualities. And so does the third level, cosmic humor, which is an appreciation of the paradoxes and absurdities of life. The person who has this level of humor is more likely to be flexible and able to take in stride what life dishes out," says Dr. Olson. "I like level three the best for my patients."

The three levels of humor.

So does Dr. Raymond Moody, Jr. "A person with a cosmic sense of humor," says Dr. Moody, "is one who can see himself and others in the world in a somewhat distant and detached way. Such a person has the ability to perceive life comically without losing any love or respect for himself or for humanity in general."

FEIGNING FUN

Sounds like the easiest medicine in the world to swallow, doesn't it? But what if you just don't feel full of fun and laughter?

If you don't feel full of fun, pretend.

"Pretend." That's the suggestion of June Biermann and Barbara Toohey, authors of *The Diabetic's Total Health Book* (J. P. Tarcher, Inc.), but their advice can be applied to everyone, not just diabetics.

"You have to start somewhere," says Dr. Olson, "even if it means going through the motions at first. Because if you decide to be healthy, hopeful, and fun-loving, that's what you'll be.

Besides, everyone has the potential for a sense of humor, and we're all born with the capacity to laugh.

It's just that if some people were brought up without positive reinforcement of their funny bone, while others can find humor even in the most serious of situations.

Surround yourself with happy people.

"Eliminate the negative people," suggest Biermann and Toohey, "and surround yourself with the positive ones—people who fill you with joy and laughter, rather than gloom and doom."

"I find it draining to be around serious-minded people all the time," adds David Bresler, M.D., director of the UCLA Pain Control Unit. "Uplifting people uplift others."

Dr. Olson calls that "modeling," and it's one of the fastest ways to develop a positive sense of humor.

If modeling is what you're looking for—or a little humor training—you need go only as far as the Saratoga Institute, a nonprofit educational training and resource organization in Saratoga Springs, New York. And once there, to a friendly looking little office, inside of which can be heard the slightly Zen sound of one mouth laughing.

An inverse paranoid thinks the world is out to do them good.

If Joel Goodman, Ed.D., had his way, he'd wave his magic wand and turn the world's population into teeming communities of inverse paranoids. We hope he gets his way because, in Goodman parlance, inverse paranoids are people who think the world is out to do them good. They look at the world through rose-colored binoculars, arriving at this exalted level of happily flip-flopped reality by using their sense of humor—and by being on the receiving end of others'.

"I like to play around with words," says Dr. Goodman, director of the Humor Project and consulting services at Saratoga, "and one of the ways I do that with the word 'humor' is to break it down into 'you-more.' For me, humor is something that makes 'you' feel 'more' self-confident, more connected with other people, more relaxed, more part of a group. To me, it's a set of attitudes and skills that people can learn.

"It's suggested that the average American laughs 15 or more times a day. On some crazy level, I think that might be a fun yardstick for people to use. I actually challenge myself sometimes, to see what kind of week I've had. Have I gotten my 15 laughs a day?

"If I haven't, then that can be a key for me to suggest that I'm a little out of balance in what I call my 'serious: lightness ratio.' I'm a really serious, hardworking, dedicated, bust-my-tail, love-my-work kind of guy. And I also know that if I get too much into that and get too serious about it, then I'm not nearly as productive and effective. So, for me, the whole issue of the serious:lightness ratio is crucial."

Besides making you feel better, the use of humor can be a major tool for insight, what Dr. Goodman calls changing "ha-ha" to "aha!" It can show you a lot about your own idiosyncrasies and eccentricities, and can make you laugh at them, as well as laughing with others at their fun-worthy failings. Either way, it's a healthy technique for putting events and people in the proper perspective.

The positive relationship between good humor and good health can't be denied. Neither can the association between laughter and longevity. A doctor whose specialty is geriatric medicine has concluded that one thing which almost all his very healthy elderly patients seem to have in common is a good sense of humor.

Or as another doctor aptly puts it, "he who laughs, lasts."

Have you gotten your 15 laughs today?

BOX 45: HOW'S YOUR LAUGH LIFE?

That's the question Joel Goodman, Ed.D., poses to clients and readers of *Laughing Matters,* his quarterly magazine chock-full of tips to help people develop their humor skills and attitudes. Here are a few *Laughing Matters* suggestions for keeping that serious:lightness ratio of yours properly and healthfully on an even keel, and for becoming pals with the "elf" in yourself.

Put on your "Candid Camera" glasses. This is easy, fun, and loaded with "ha-ha" moments. Besides making you feel better, the use of humor can be a major tool for insight—what Dr. Goodman calls changing the "ha-ha" to "aha."

(continued next page)

BOX 45 — *Continued*

Take ten minutes or so out of your day, try to distance yourself from your office environment, and pretend that it's all a "Candid Camera" episode, and you're the camera. Look around you, and observe all the silly, goofy—and, therefore, very human—activities going on that just ten minutes before seemed so darn serious, earthshaking, and stomach churning. This can be a terrifically lightening and enlightening object lesson on the shaky foundation of "professional solemnity."

Humor meditation. For five or ten minutes, or whatever amount of time you can spare during the tensest part of your day, stop and take a humor meditation break. You don't have to sit on the floor cross-legged and say "Om." Sitting at your desk is just fine, and let your chortle be your mantra. During this "meditation," shut out the office and the outside world, and in silence read a funny passage from a jokebook or a novel or from a humor notebook/scrapbook you might keep for just such an occasion. Or turn on a cassette of your favorite comedian. Sit back and become one with the cosmic giggle. Then return to work relaxed, refreshed, happy—and, somehow, new.

Aikido. This is a form of Japanese self-defense which uses no aggressive moves, but rather turns aside the attacker by gently but effectively unbalancing his energy and momentum. In battles of wits, humor can be used as aikido to turn aside verbal aggressors. As in the real thing, practice makes perfect. What you have to do is prepare for "conflict" situations by creating scenarios (for example, you versus a particularly obnoxious co-worker about such-and-such a matter, you versus your mother-in-law about nearly everything). Work up great punchlines for each occasion, memorize those comebacks, and store them away. Observe good nightclub comics handling hecklers. Become "light on your feet"—"planned spontaneity," Dr. Goodman calls it. Doing all of these things can prepare you to act with grace under the pressure of a tense or embarrassing put-up-or-shut-up moment. The proper aikido zinger is like a masterful toreador: Both deflate the bull. It's far better to be prepared and never use your aikido (or tongue-fu) responses than to be driving home, haunted by all the great "I should have saids" you should have said . . . and could have said. Keeping yourself loose and alert is the key. For example, once while leaving a fancy Manhattan supper club, humorist Robert Benchley turned to the man in uniform at the door and said, "Would you get us a taxi, please?" The man stiffened, pompously. "I'm sorry," he replied icily, "but I happen to be a rear admiral in the United States Navy." "All right, then," said Benchley, "get us a battleship." That's black belt aikido.

Love

Love and health go hand in hand.

"**L**ove and health go hand in hand," says Peter Hansen, a therapist consultant who conducts workshops in getting people's affections in shape.

"Caring is biological," agrees James Lynch, Ph.D., author of *The Broken Heart: The Medical Consequences of Loneliness* (Basic Books). "The mandate to 'love your neighbor as you love yourself' is not just a moral mandate— it's a physiological one."

A nice idea, you might be saying to yourself. That love and longevity are partners. But where's the proof?

Researchers from the University of California at Berkeley found several years ago that socially isolated people were more susceptible to illness and had death rates about two to three times higher than people whose social lives were richer (See Chapter 8, Friends and Lovers: Guardians of Good Health.)

Scientists studying heart disease in Israel discovered that men suffering from angina (chest pain usually indicative of coronary blockage) were more likely than other men to answer no to the question "does your wife show you her love?"

But perhaps the most intriguing study was done by psychologists at Harvard. Measurements were made of a germ-fighting substance in the saliva of people before and after they watched various films: a Nazi war movie, a short film on gardening, and a documentary on Mother Teresa, the

Isolated people are more susceptible to illness.

Caring for others boosts your own immune system.

nun whose charitable works with orphans, lepers, and poor people earned her a Nobel prize.

Without a doubt, the film on Mother Teresa was kindest to the viewers' immune systems. Levels of IG-A (an immune agent especially effective in fighting colds and other viruses) rose sharply in response to the Mother Teresa film, while no changes occurred in response to the other movies.

Love sparks healthy biological reactions.

It seems something deep inside our cells responds positively when we feel love. Love appears capable of sparking healthy biological reactions in much the same way as good food and good fitness.

Why?

It stimulates other positive feelings of security, optimism, and hope.

Robert Taylor, M.D., a psychiatrist from California, thinks it may boil down to love's potential for being a great reducer of stress. "When people have close relationships, they feel less threatened, less alone, more confident, and more in control. Knowing you have people you can turn to in times of need can provide some very important feelings of security, optimism, and hope—all of which can be great antidotes to stress."

Dr. Taylor adds, however, that loving relationships also can be a source of stress if and when they go sour. "But that's the gamble you take. Nothing ventured, nothing gained."

You might want to keep that in mind this year if and when you're tempted to step on some toes as you run the rat race. When it comes to health, nice guys *can* finish first.

Music and Song

Patients at the Kaiser-Permanente Medical Center in Los Angeles have a choice. When in pain, they can either turn to prescriptions or turn on their portable tape player to 20 minutes of soothing harp music and guided relaxation. Some of the Center's doctors even "prescribe" the music tape instead of painkillers and tranquilizers. It is being used before cardiac surgery, during chemotherapy, and with patients with chronic back pain and crippling spinal injuries. In the hospital's outpatient stress-management center, the same music and relaxation training is used to treat many stress-related illnesses—including high blood pressure, migraine headaches, and ulcers.

"Difficulty in relaxing is a common problem in many illnesses," says David Walker, M.D., one of Kaiser-Permanente's psychiatrists specializing in behavioral medicine. "It's not unusual at all for people who are having surgery, or who have been told they have cancer, to stay awake late into the night, obsessed with what is happening to them. Relaxation is universally therapeutic, and people who can learn to relax deeply can create a better state of mind for getting well.

"Just knowing they have a way to reduce the anxiety helps. We tell them to use this any time they need it—just before they are wheeled into the operating room, or even as the doctors are talking to them. They can replay the tape in their minds, even if they can't listen to it, and get the same results."

Difficulty in relaxing is a common problem in many illnesses.

Using music to personalize the hospital environment.

Kaiser-Permanente is one of several facilities across the United States using music as a way to reduce stress, relieve pain, and personalize the often anxious, sterile hospital environment. Others include the University of Massachusetts Medical Center in Worcester, Beth Israel Hospital in Boston, and Hahnemann University Hospital in Philadelphia.

These hospitals are using music for everything from helping couples celebrate the birth of a baby to assisting a child prepare for heart catheterization, from enabling a stroke victim to learn to speak again to evoking the memories of a lifetime as someone prepares for death.

Music lowers blood pressure.

"Music is a marvelous and extremely powerful tool," says Nancy Hunt, a St. Louis music therapist who works in both a childbirth center and a hospice. "Music has a direct physiological effect on people. It increases blood volume, decreases and helps stabilize heart rate, and lowers blood pressure. And psychologically, it does a whole lot. It can make us relax, or remember, or have all sorts of feelings. It all depends on what we project onto the music."

Perhaps this is the biggest part of music's magic—that it can transform an environment by changing our own state of mind.

"We get a lot of patients here who have been through a number of different referrals," says Stephen Kibrick, Ph.D., the clinical psychologist who directs Kaiser-Permanente's stress-management program and who developed the tapes.

Cancer patients use music to relieve pain and calm their minds.

"We have cancer patients and other patients with chronic pain who are going through a lot of distressing treatments. We give them a tape and a little player and a set of headphones and they find that it not only relieves the intensity of the pain, it helps them calm their minds and relax their bodies."

Burn patients, in the hospital for weeks or months, have a difficult time because they are often in pain as their burns heal. "These people can't be kept on drugs all the time," Dr. Kibrick says. "This kind of music and relaxation instruction has proven very effective in helping them stay in a relatively calm, relaxed state while undergoing treatment."

A 57-minute-long University of Massachusetts Medical Center television program takes its viewers through what is called "mindfulness meditation," says Jon Kabat-Zinn, Ph. D., director of the hospital's stress-reduction and relaxation department. "The tape teaches people to pay attention to their body, the quality of their breathing, the sensations in their body, the music, and their thoughts as the thoughts move through their minds."

The end result, he says, is a state of detachment from, and relaxed observation of, the body—a state particularly useful if one is experiencing pain. He chose to have musical accompaniment for this tape, he says, because he theorizes that the meditation instructions would be more accessible to the patients within the flow established by the music. And he chose harp music, he says, because "the harp has traditionally been an instrument for healing and calming the mind."

Instructions are more accessible within the flow.

Dr. Kabat-Zinn's intent was to make available to all the hospital's patients (and its doctors) a relaxation program based on his eight-week outpatient training at the hospital's stress-reduction center. Of the 20 percent of the hospital's patients who have already used the relaxation tape, 80 percent have found it beneficial.

Dr. Kabat-Zinn has begun formal controlled studies of kidney-dialysis and cardiac-care patients to determine exact physical and psychological responses to the tape.

A LONG TRADITION

These contemporary uses of music may be new, but traditionally music has had a long and strong connection with medicine. The philosopher Pythagoras prescribed a daily regimen of music to wake up by, to work by, and to relax and sleep by. Ancient physicians used music to regulate the heartbeat, and from the Renaissance through the nineteenth century, music and singing were used as a cure for "melancholy" and to bring the body's mysterious "vapours" into balance.

Ancient physicians used music to regulate the heartbeat.

In the nineteenth and twentieth centuries, medical "progress" in anesthetics and painkillers left music far behind. It wasn't until the late 1950s that it started to be used again in the form of "dentist office music"—bland, mindless tunes that attempted to camouflage the nerve-racking whine of the dentist's drill and distract the distraught patient.

In the 1980s, however, the medical use of music has grown steadily, often in conjunction with other alternative medical practices like biofeedback and hypnosis.

Just how music works its wonders is something

**The physical and psycho-
logical responses involve
complex brain chemistry
changes.**

researchers are only beginning to understand. Both its physical and psychological responses involve complex brain chemistry changes, not only in the "thinking" part of our brain, but also in our "emotional" brain (the limbic system) and the "primitive" brain (the brain stem), which controls heartbeat, respiration, and muscle tension.

Therapists like Janalea Hoffman of Kansas City, Missouri, say you need to combine the music "with the mental awareness of what is going on in your body" and that most people must be trained to do that.

In her graduate study at the University of Kansas, she used visual imagery and music to teach 60 people to lower their blood pressure an average of 10 to 20 points. She uses the same techniques to help people with heart arrhythmias and migraine headaches, using music with a 60-beats-per-minute tempo, which is the ideal, or relaxed, heart rate.

How does music work to help reduce the perception of pain and to create a positive state of mind?

One theory is that some kinds of music can produce endorphins in the brain, the same "feel good" chemicals that running and meditation produce. But music therapists agree that more research must be done. Whatever the case, music does work, even if many of its effects have yet to be documented.

Georgia Kelly, whose lilting, free-flowing harp music has been used in several medical tapes, including those of the University of Massachusetts and Kaiser-Permanente says she didn't realize the potential of her music until people began to write to her that they were playing it during childbirth, in the operating room, and to relax and fall asleep.

"A PLACE WITHOUT PAIN"

"I feel my music takes the mind to another place," she says. "It helps you to move away from identifying with your body, and in doing that it is calming. It reduces your awareness of pain. It puts your mind someplace else for a while, in a place where there is no pain—psychic or physical."

At Hahnemann University Hospital in Philadelphia, Cynthia Briggs, director of music therapy, helps young patients to choose music that will be played for them while they undergo heart catheterization. "We use everything from Sesame Street to Neil Diamond," she says. "It's a way to personalize the experience, and hopefully, to make things more pleasant." Although the children's physical responses have not been monitored, Briggs says the surgeons performing the procedure have been extremely happy with the children's reactions.

At the Charing Cross Hospital in London, patients who opt for spinal rather than general anesthesia for certain kinds of surgery, like hip replacement, are given headphones and music to block out the noises of drilling and sawing.

Perhaps one of the more joyful ways music has been used in medicine is in childbirth and delivery. St. Louis music therapist Nancy Hunt uses musical cues as part of her program to teach couples relaxation methods during childbirth.

For a child's birth, she prepares an 8- to 12-hour tape that includes some of the songs the couple has learned to relax to, along with others of their choice. She says the theme from *Chariots of Fire* is particularly popular during the "pushing" stages of the delivery, and that for the celebration of the birth she has been asked to include everything from "Isn't She Lovely" by Stevie Wonder to "For Unto Us a Child Is Born" from Handel's *Messiah*.

Celebrating the joy of childbirth with music.

Hunt also works in a hospice, where she uses music to help terminally ill patients resolve their feelings toward death and talk with their family members. In what she calls "life review," she plays songs that were popular during the time the patient was most active—during courtship and early marriage, perhaps during a war.

"I use songs that are like mileposts in their lives," she says. Such music often evokes strong memories and facilitates heartfelt communication between loved ones. Many times, too, she will sit at someone's bedside and sing with them the old favorite church hymns they may have learned as children. "Amazing Grace," "The Old Rugged Cross," and "In the Garden" are songs requested over and over again, she says. "They give real comfort."

Heartfelt songs of the past can facilitate communication between loved ones.

SINGING AWAY THE BLUES

The mysterious ability of songs to tell the story of our lives—even if we don't really want to hear the story, and have buried it deep within ourselves—has led therapists to use singing to treat both emotionally and mentally damaged patients.

Singing is, in fact, one of the most effective mood lifting therapies available.

"I see the use of the voice as one of the ways of coping with the frustrations and traumas of life, helping us integrate experience on the feeling level, which can't be done with insight alone," says Connecticut psychiatrist John M. Bellis, M.D.

Using the body as a musical instrument.

Dr. Bellis, who is president of the Connecticut Society for Bioenergetic Analysis, makes extensive use of bioenergetic therapy in his practice. Bioenergetics, a therapy pioneered by Alexander Lowen, M.D., sees a crucial connection existing between a person's state of body and state of mind. Repressions of anxiety are believed to be reflected in the musculature of the body, and cannot be relieved until the muscular as well as the emotional tension is banished. Obviously, singing, the one form of music that uses the body itself as the instrument, is an invaluable tool in this kind of therapy.

When you're finished crying, sing.

"Sometimes," says Dr. Bellis "I find that people tell me, 'I've cried and I've cried and I've cried—what good does it do?' (I had told them to go ahead, let it out.) Sometimes now what I say is, 'Well, when you're through crying, start to sing some of the sadness, some of the loss, some of the appreciation of what you've lost.'

"And there they begin to find a sense of meaning, the beauty, where the heart was connected with what they've lost. It's a way that humans have of enriching, giving testimony to the enrichment of their lives. Music and song have that ability—to give expression to something that may be impossible to express any other way. You can hug somebody, but that really doesn't say it all."

VOCAL VIBRATIONS: INTERNAL MASSAGE

"The radiation of that vocal energy really starts right from the feet," Dr. Bellis says. "You can feel it vibrating up and down through your body, when you really are totally into sound."

Regain that childlike openness to song.

So what are you waiting for? You can't carry a tune? Nonsense. Some killjoy told you to move your lips at the age of eight because you didn't sound like Beverly Sills. You *really* can't carry a tune? Then honk with the other old honkers. There's no excuse not to, really; you've just got to

BOX 46: SOOTHING SOUNDTRACKS: A SOURCE GUIDE

Most music therapists recommend that people with medical problems, like high blood pressure, who want to use music to relax first train with a therapist. For information on music-based relaxation programs near you, contact the National Association for Music Therapy, 1001 Connecticut Avenue, N.W., Suite 800, Washington, DC 20036.

The University of Massachusetts Medical Center has an eight-week stress management program for patients referred by their doctor. Its videotape is for rent or sale to other hospitals. Contact the Center for Educational Resources, William Stickley, University of Massachusetts Medical Center, 55 Lake Avenue, N., Worcester, MA 01605.

If you're a health-plan member residing in Southern California, you can get tapes by Dr. Stephen Kibrick at Kaiser-Permanente Medical Center. Otherwise, write to: Self-Health Cassettes, 16661 Ventura Boulevard, Suite 822, Encino, CA 91436.

For more information on Georgia Kelly's music, write to: Heru Records, Box 954, Topanga, CA 90290.

For a catalog of Dr. Steven Halpern's music, write to: Halpern Sounds, 1775 Old County Road #9, Belmont, CA 94002.

Heaven on Earth, 803 Fourth Street, San Raphael, CA 94901, is a recording company for a number of West Coast artists involved in therapeutic music. Write for a free catalog and a sample tape (there's a fee for the tape).

The Institute for Consciousness and Music offers a Music Rx package of five cassettes. Their address is: ICM West, Box 173, Port Townsend, WA 98368.

Janalea Hoffman has put together a tape of 60-beats-per-minute Baroque piano music of her own composition. Her address is Mellow Minds, Box 6431, Shawnee Mission, KS 66206.

For information on Dr. Emmett Miller's behavioral changes, stress-management, and optimal-performance tapes, contact: Dr. Emmett Miller, c/o "Source," Post Office Box W, Stanford, CA 94305.

---

sing—sing in the shower, sing at work, sing at church, sing with your family, sing in the rain, but sing! You were singing songs before you had the slightest idea what the words meant, before you even knew what a word was. Probably the best thing that could happen to us would be to regain that childlike openness to song.

71

Pets

Having a dog as a running mate has its obvious fitness rewards. So when a University of Pennsylvania study revealed that heart attack patients with pets had one-third the death rate of pet-less patients, exercise seemed the logical explanation. But there was a hitch. According to the researchers, the pet owners prospered whether their "companions" had fins, feathers, or four furry feet. Evidently, psychological factors—more so than the much-touted daily walk—gave the people with pets an edge on survival.

"Having a pet did improve a patient's chances of surviving and did in some way help the patient to be healthier," researchers Alan Beck, Sc.D., and Aaron Katcher, M.D., write in their book *Between Pets and People* (Putnam). "For the patients in this study, severe heart disease increased the probability of dying by 20 percent. Having a pet could *decrease* the probability of dying by 3 percent. Three percent might seem to be a small amount of protection but [when you consider that] . . . there are over a million people who die of heart disease each year, a 3-percent effect could, in any one year, result in a saving of 30,000 lives."

Pretty impressive. But how can pets possibly evoke such a healthy response?

PETTING AND THE RELAXATION RESPONSE

The mere act of stroking an animal has its rewards. In a separate study, Dr. Katcher and psychologist James Lynch,

Ph.D., found that petting—along with all the usual sweet talk people shower on their pets—relaxed the petter as much as the pettee. In fact, people engaged in greeting and getting a friendly animal experienced a drop in blood pressure. By comparison, Dr. Lynch demonstrated in an earlier study that when people read aloud or spoke to other people their blood pressure rose above the resting level.

Greeting and petting a friendly animal can reduce your blood pressure.

Pets, they explain, are viewed as less threatening or judgmental than people, which makes them more relaxing company. Even watching the gentle undulations of tropical fish can have a calming effect, says Dr. Katcher. And anything that can help us relax is likely to have a positive effect on the heart, not to mention our general health.

Clark Brickel, Ph.D., a pet researcher at the University of Southern California and consultant to the Los Angeles Society for the Prevention of Cruelty to Animals, theorizes that the power of pets lies in their ability to attract attention like a magnet. Pets can shift our attention away from negative preoccupations that produce anxiety and threaten our emotional and physical well-being, he says. They give us a break from stress and a reason to smile. And, in the process, our state of mind improves so that when our attention returns to pressing concerns, we can put them in perspective and better cope with them.

Pets shift our attention away from negative preoccupations.

Actually, smiling and laughing in response to animal antics not only lifts our spirits, it may help boost our immunity to serious illness. Ever since Norman Cousins, former editor of *Saturday Review,* first elaborated on his personal experience in overcoming the pain and disability of an "incurable" illness through laughter in his book *Anatomy of an Illness* (W. W. Norton & Co.), psychologists and physicians are taking a more serious look at humor. Laughter, it seems, is good medicine (see Chapter 68, Humor, and Chapter 72, Play). And anyone who enjoys watching animals will tell you: Next to Bill Cosby, there's nothing more amusing than a cat trying to find its way out of a paper bag.

WHERE TRADITIONAL THERAPIES FAIL

Perhaps this is one reason many therapists find that pets are extremely useful in the treatment of depression and other emotional ills.

Pet therapy for depression and other emotional ills.

Two authorities in this area are a husband-and-wife team of scientists, Samuel A. Corson, Ph.D., and Elizabeth Corson, of Ohio State University. In 1967, the Corsons brought pets to the psychiatric hospital at Ohio State University. When they gave playful dogs to very depressed and withdrawn patients, the patients—who had previously resisted traditional treatments including electroshock, drugs, and psychotherapy—began to open up. The Corsons called their new technique "pet-facilitated therapy," or PFT, and it has been used successfully at many hospitals and nursing homes.

The Corsons maintain that pets arouse the attention and stimulate the interaction in persons who do not respond to human contact. They also emphasize that pets help facilitate—they don't replace—traditional therapy.

Pets offer love no matter what.

"The patients wouldn't communicate (with other people) because they thought no one would love or accept them," the Corsons say. "But pets offer love no matter what. They don't care if you're sad or happy, ugly or beautiful, old or young. They don't criticize you or try to change you. And they love to be loved, to be touched and held. When a person has this simple, relaxed outlet for emotional involvement, negative emotions fade into the background."

This concept was first demonstrated by the late Boris Levinson, Ph.D., the pioneer in pet therapy. In the fifties, Dr. Levinson found that his dog, Jingles, could succeed with disturbed patients where many a psychotherapist had failed. Dr. Levinson called Jingles his "co-therapist" and wrote two books on his experience.

Dr. Levinson, like the Corsons, observed that "a pet can provide, in boundless measure, love and unqualified approval" and that for many—particularly children, the elderly, and the lonely—pets satisfy vital emotional needs.

In children, pets help release the tensions of home and school and build trust in the child's abilities to accept responsibility. "Acceptance of responsibility in the care of a pet will eventually lead to an acceptance of responsibility for establishing meaningful, satisfying human relationships."

Loving and nurturing can provide a growth experience.

People who find themselves thrust into retirement and robbed of self-esteem can also benefit a lot from pets, Dr. Levinson believed. Their concepts of themselves as worthwhile persons can be restored, even enhanced, by the assurance that the pets they care for love them in return, he said. "Loving and nurturing can provide a growth experience. A lonely person who has a pet is no longer lonely."

Drs. Beck and Katcher agree. "When people face real adversity—disease, unemployment, or the disabilities of age—affection from a pet takes on new meaning. Then the pet's continuing affection is a sign that the essence of the person has not been damaged."

MEANINGFUL RELATIONSHIPS

Pets also benefit the aging person by giving purpose and meaning back to life. As we grow old, our former responsibilities dwindle. The children leave home and care for themselves. There is no job to go to. Friends are gone. Perhaps a spouse has passed away. Adjustments to these major changes can be devastating. For some, boredom, depression, and loneliness ensue. Life loses its meaning and the will to live withers.

Psychiatrists call this the helplessness/hopelessness syndrome, which is also common among the chronically and terminally ill. It's characterized by giving up. And the worst part, say Drs. Beck and Katcher, is that this attitude "can produce subtle pathological changes that disorganize the body chemistry, reducing resistance to infectious disease and accelerating the progress of chronic degenerative diseases such as coronary artery disease and cancer."

The constancy of pets helps counter life changes.

But here again, pets can come to the rescue.

"When people maintain patterns of caring . . . they are protecting themselves against despair, against giving up. They are rewarded by feeling needed," Drs. Beck and Katcher explain.

"The word 'care' has many meanings," they continue, "and one of them is 'worry,' as when someone is burdened with care. You do worry about the things you care for. Unfortunately, the association among care, effort, and worry leads us to conceive of old age as a period in which one should live a 'carefree' existence. After retirement, people are urged to give up their cares. It can be a lethal trade-off. The person who stops caring for something may have taken the first steps to the helplessness/hopelessness syndrome. And those who cope best with old age are those who continue the daily acts of caring, especially the most satisfying ones—care rendered to living things, such as pets."

Those who cope best with old age are those who continue the acts of caring.

BOX 47: WEIGHING THE PROS AND CONS OF PET OWNERSHIP

On the plus side, pets:

1. Offer unconditional love and steadfast companionship.

2. Cheer you when you're down and calm you when you're anxious.

3. Bring you back to play and laughter.

4. Take your mind off your troubles.

5. Satisfy your need for touching and close physical contact.

6. Improve your sociability. (Studies have shown that people are more inclined to strike up a conversation with someone who has a dog than someone who's alone. People with pets are seen as more attractive and valuable, which makes meeting people easier.)

7. Give purpose and meaning to life.

8. Increase your self-esteem.

9. Are a source of constancy in an ever-changing world.

10. Make you feel safe.

11. Get you out in the fresh air to exercise.

12. Restore communication with nature, something that is often lost in our plastic society.

On the minus side, pets:

1. Require daily care and feeding.

2. Can interfere with travel plans.

3. May display unacceptable behavior, such as hyperexcitability or poor housebreaking.

4. May damage furniture or other personal goods.

5. Can rack up annual vet and food bills totaling $250 to $350 for a medium-sized dog, and $150 to $200 for a cat. And that doesn't include adoption fees and the initial expenses for spaying or neutering, licensing, and all the toy-bed-bowl-collar-and-lease paraphernalia.

6. May provoke other household members and disrupt family harmony.

7. May cause worry and concern. Seventy percent of pet owners admit to fears that their pet may get hit by a car or kidnapped. Fortunately, these fears are rarely realized.

8. Eventually die, which can send owners into periods of bereavement.

Non-pet owners had more fears, headaches, and feelings of panic.

A recent study by Hiroko Akiyama, Ph.D., at the University of Oklahoma illustrates how pets help people adjust to one of life's greatest blows, the death of a spouse. In it, two groups of recent widows—those with and those without pets—were compared in terms of physical complaints, lifestyles, interaction with other people, and feelings toward self. The results support the theory that pets can help buffer the psychological and physical impact of bereavement. "There was a significant difference between pet owners and non-pet owners," Dr. Akiyama reports. "Non-pet owners,

BOX 48: CHOOSING YOUR PET PAL

Adopting a pet is like choosing a mate. Commit yourself to the first one you fall in love with and you could be lucky—or both of you could live to regret it. "That's why so many animals wind up in animal shelters and must be put to sleep," says Tim Donovan, a spokesperson for the American Veterinary Medical Association. "Too many people buy pets on impulse. They don't bother to investigate the types of breeds of animals that would best suit their personal needs and lifestyle."

In State College, Pennsylvania, elderly residents can take advantage of a pet/people match-making service called PACT (People and Animals Coming Together). PACT not only advises people in pet selection, they also offer pet-owner orientation and education programs, obedience training assistance, and a variety of follow-up aids including behavior-problem consultation and financial assistance with veterinary care and food costs.

If you don't live in the State College area or are under 55 years old (the minimum age for PACT participants), you can send a self-addressed stamped envelope to the Pets Are Wonderful Council at 500 N. Michigan Avenue, Suite 200, Chicago, IL 60611 for a free pamphlet on "How to Select Your Four-Footed Friend." They also offer two pamphlets for urban dwellers: one for tenants, which provides helpful advice on how to deal with such dilemmas as a no-pet clause in an apartment lease, and another for landlords with tips for screening pet-owning tenants.

The Delta Society at 212 Wells Avenue South, Suite C, Renton, WA 98055 distributes an excellent booklet on guidelines for animals in nursing homes. For $3.50, we found it an excellent aid for any potential pet owner, with lots of pointers on how to determine whether the animal you're contemplating will make a good pet.

for example, had more persistent fears, headaches, and feelings of panic. They also tended to take more drugs than the pet owners."

NOT FOR EVERYONE

Of course, not everyone benefits from a furry friend. The people who tend to gain the most from pets are those who truly love animals and who develop close attachments to their pets.

"Being a pet owner isn't enough to insure health benefits," warns gerontologist Daniel Lago, Ph.D., of Pennsylvania State University. "A national survey showed that

Pet owners who developed a strong attachment to their animals were more relaxed and outgoing.

40 percent of the dog owners we interviewed said they were worried or dissatisfied with their pets. So for them, having a pet had no effect—or perhaps even a negative effect—on emotional well-being."

Dr. Lago, who's been giving pets—dogs, for the most part—to elderly people for years and recording any changes in emotional and physical health, reports on his yet-to-be-published findings: "Pet ownership itself made no difference in mortality or level of health," he says. "But for those pet owners who developed a strong attachment to their animals, we found greater feelings of cheerfulness, a greater participation in social activities, and less muscle tension. Interestingly, too, even when these people were physically sicker than age-matched controls, they had higher morale scores."

72

Play

W hen was the last time you felt like doing something really silly just for the fun of it? Something like whipping your partner onto the dance floor and sashaying across the room clenched arm in arm—and back to back.

Or, do you think you'll ever have the urge, let alone the nerve, to stand on a table during a fun-filled party, cup your hands about your mouth, and come out with a raucous "I want a standing ovation!"—and have your friends and even strangers give you one to boot?

Outrageous? You bet. Not your style? Probably not. Unless, of course, you've crossed paths with Matt Weinstein, Ph.D., who has the uncanny ability to prod the most staid people into exhibiting their uninhibited, playful best. The method to Dr. Weinstein's madness is quite simple. He believes that good, honest, noncompetitive, let-down-your-hair fun is essential for total health—physical, emotional, and spiritual.

Behind Dr. Weinstein's youthful, devilish grin is a serious concern. "The problem with adults is that they lose the ability to play," he says. "We do most of our playing—using the right brain [the right hemisphere is the artistic/creative center]—in the first five years of life. Then we go to school and learn the power of the left brain [the analytical/learning center]. The problem is that we leave the right brain totally behind." That's when life also starts to get tough.

"People are not by nature depressed or bored, yet

The serious side of silly, outrageous behavior.

Play is essential to stress reduction.

Play means: things to enjoy for their own sake without trying to accomplish something.

everyone on this planet gets that way," says Dr. Weinstein. "To me, boredom is a form of slow death. But you never have to be bored in life. Too much stress and workaholism causes people to become ill. Play is really essential to stress reduction."

Stephen Polsky, Ph.D., a clincial psychologist in Walnut Creek, California, who describes play as "one of the most important things about children that adults tend to neglect," agrees. "By 'play' I mean doing things you enjoy for their own sake, without any particular goal in mind," he says. "Some adults never allow themselves that sort of non-goal-directed behavior; they're always trying to *accomplish* something. But there has to be a time when adults let up, when they're not out to achieve anything."

Dr. Weinstein and his Berkeley, California-based Playfair, Inc., group combat the seriousness of adulthood by discussing their "fun" philosophy and displaying their playful antics before colleges, conventions, and even nursing homes around the country. Within a two-hour workshop, Dr. Weinstein can transform a group of total strangers into jovial buddies simply by getting them to play a bunch of childhood games he has revised for noncompetitive fun. And, yes, he really can get them to dance back to back and demand standing ovations.

"Kids' games are based on competition, which is probably why most people stop playing," contends Dr. Weinstein, who claims to have once been shy.

Of course, the average Joe doesn't have around the dynamic Matt Weinstein and his comedic, let's-all-join-in-the-fun routine to propel him into a playful mood. But then, says Dr. Weinstein, play is something that can come naturally.

"Adult life is too stressful," he says. "You walk into a room of strangers and chances are you'll be intimidated by who these other people may be, if they're better than you, if they're going to like you. But if you get to talking about something mundane like your life before the age of 12, you'll find out everybody in the whole room had just about the same kinds of basic experiences. You get to know the people and find out they're just like you. The titles come later."

It's not important what you play—just that you play.

Play, says Dr. Weinstein, is a great leveler. "People need play in their lives," he says. "My method just gets them to remember how much fun it really is. It's not important what you play. It's just important that you play."

"There are tremendous benefits when people focus away from their routines and give themselves a little celebration," says Herbert Holt, M.D., a practicing psychiatrist in family and marriage counseling in New York City and author of the book *Free to Be Good or Bad* (M. Evans & Co.). "We don't use so much energy when we shift away to something more pleasant. We don't need tranquilizers or other drugs to feel better either. Our own bodies have magnificent mechanisms called endorphins (and enkephalins), which will go into action to uplift our spirits or soothe us."

Mark Tager, M.D., believes people often dwell too much on the routine aspects of their lives and overlook the importance of having fun. Dr. Tager says having fun is intrinsic to our well-being, "but when I ask my patients if they're having fun in their lives, they stare at me and say, 'Fun?'

People who are too pre-occupied with routine are overlooking something intrinsic to their well-being.

"I personally use any excuse I can to celebrate, including every Christian and Jewish holiday there is. What you do is get a big calendar that lists everybody's birthday from George Washington to Buddah. You'll even know when national flower day is and you can be prepared to celebrate it. By celebrating, I don't mean goofing off or wasting time but allowing a few good thoughts on a nice subject to pass through your mind."

The importance of play goes far beyond releasing the stress of daily life. Dr. Weinstein and other playful sorts like him will argue that play and laughter are also important in combating illness.

Play combats illness.

A REASON TO LIVE

One such person is O. Carl Simonton, M.D., a California physician who has witnessed the value of play in lifting the spirits of cancer patients with advanced malignancy.

"The first thing a person does when he finds out he's ill is stop playing," says Dr. Simonton. "It shouldn't be that way. Play is mandatory, not elective." It's an attitude he's successfully rubbed off on many of his patients.

The first thing a person does when he finds out he's ill is stop playing.

"Playing is an activity that tends to produce emotions of joy and the experience of having fun," says Dr. Simonton. "Feeling joyful and feeling like having fun increase our energy. Playing also mobilizes our desire to live because life becomes more meaningful."

But even more important is that play also promotes creativity, something most people, particularly ill people, don't think about very often.

"In play you suspend the rules, change the limits," says Dr. Simonton, who isn't at all shy about letting down his curly locks, even in Dr. Weinstein's wild workshops. An example he cites is the childhood game of cops and robbers. In just one afternoon of play, the good guys, the bad guys, and even the plot can change many times. "By doing so, playing forces us to practice creativity. Creativity is necessary for health. It is essential for overcoming incurable disease" (see Chapter 66, Creativity).

Play enhances the will to live. And the will to live can lengthen life.

The point is that the good feelings and the high energy that can be produced through play enhance the will to live, believes Dr. Simonton. And the will to live can lengthen life.

Think how often you come across a day when you can't think of anything fun to do. For a sick person it happens even more. Dr. Simonton solves this dilemma by getting his patients to draw up a list of 40 things that are fun to do. When the going gets dull, they have their list for inspiration.

Juggling as a type of play therapy.

One thing that's been a hit in increasing the playfulness of Dr. Simonton's patients is juggling. And he had to learn it to teach it. "You can juggle anything," he says, tossing a bean bag in the air, "balls, oranges, bean bags. It's easiest to start with scarves."

UNABASHED LOVE OF FUN

Childlike qualities worth maintaining as an adult.

The capacity for wonder, the ability to play, and the unabashed love of fun: These are childlike qualities worth maintaining throughout adulthood. And to that list some would add: a lack of concern about appearances, and the ability to set self-importance aside whenever a little plain old silliness is called for.

"Let's distinguish between childishness, which I take to be negative, and childlikeness, which is positive," Dr. Stephen Polsky says. "For example, it wouldn't be childish to play *when it's appropriate;* it would be childish to do so when it's not."

Delia Ephron, in her delightful little book *How to Eat*

Like a Child (Viking Press) provides some insights into the world of children that may serve to illustrate Dr. Polsky's point. In case you've forgotten, for example, here's how to eat mashed potatoes: "Pat mashed potatoes flat on top. Dig several little depressions. Think of them as pools or ponds. Fill with gravy. With your fork, sculp rivers between pools and watch the gravy flow between them. Decorate with peas. Do not eat."

Children's delight in creation, their fascination with colors and textures, and their steadfast refusal to do something against their will are qualities we'd admire in an adult—at the right time, in the right place, and for the right reason. But not at the dinner table. Real maturity may be knowing when and where certain kinds of behavior are appropriate . . . even acting like a kid.

Maturity: knowing when it's OK to act like a kid.

WHY WE PLAY

Why is play so important? Well, that's a question social scientists have been wrangling with for years—for the most part with a total lack of playfulness. Their somber theorizing has answered the question in dozens of different ways, but there's still little agreement even on what play *is*. Even though it's easy to recognize playful behavior in a dog, a dolphin, or a child, it can take so many different forms it's next to impossible to define.

Several things are known. First of all, you and I both know that we play because it's fun, and that's reason enough. Also, writes Mike Ellis, Ph.D., in his book *Why People Play* (Prentice-Hall), "research has been done showing clearly that the playful behavior indulged in by the young is critical for their development." Adds Dr. Polsky, "Kids *need* to play. If they haven't worked out the emotional issues appropriate to that stage, if they're not allowed to 'be kids,' there may be problems later in life."

Play helps kids work out emotional issues.

THE UNENDING SEARCH FOR STIMULATION

What's more, Dr. Ellis quotes an earlier researcher as observing, "In general play is more frequent, more variable, and occurs during a longer portion of the life span in higher animals than in lower. The play of fishes appears infrequent and stereotyped when compared with that of lower

Each bout of play is a voyage of discovery.

mammals, while the play of dogs is less diversified and prolonged than that of monkeys and apes."

What does it all mean? Desmond Morris, Ph.D., author of *The Human Zoo* (McGraw-Hill), suggests that play is part of our unending search for stimulation. Perhaps because our nervous systems are more advanced than those of lower animals, it takes longer and more intricate stimulation to satisfy us. And in the process, we discover and rediscover the world. "Each bout of playing is a voyage of discovery."

Perhaps the benefits of taking a childlike delight in life can best be described by considering what happens if we don't.

One of the most common casualties of adult life, it seems, is the emotional openness we had as children. If a five-year-old is unhappy, there's no mistaking it—even across a crowded room. Twenty years later, that child will have learned that a certain degree of control is a mark of maturity, and he will also have devised enough "adult" disguises to mask his unhappiness from other people and perhaps even himself.

"If you don't let those feelings out, you're likely to pay for it somewhere," Dr. Polsky says. "It may come out in a different form—for example, repressed anger may come out as depression or even physical disease."

It's a condition of adult life that can be thought of as "emotional constipation," says psychiatrist Hugh Riordan, M.D., director of the Olive W. Garvey Center for the Improvement of Human Functioning in Wichita, Kansas.

"Many organs of the body, for example, the heart, bladder, or bowels, are essentially fill/hold/release mechanisms," Dr. Riordan says. "Your bladder fills and holds, but if you don't release it, it bursts. Emotions work the same way. The trouble is that while kids have no trouble with their release mechanisms, many adults do.

But having as much fun as the proverbial barrel of monkeys just may not be as easy as you may think. For one thing, having fun often might bother your conscience.

The "I really-should-be-working" syndrome.

"How often are you having a fun time and saying, 'Gosh, I really should be working. I have a lot of work to do'?" says Dr. Simonton. Well, don't feel bad, you're not alone. The syndrome is quite common and should be ignored. Just be sure you don't play too hard. That can be just as bad as too little play.

"If we overwork and underplay we tend to feel depressed," says Dr. Simonton. "If we overplay and underwork, we feel fear. We feel we're ignoring our responsibilities."

Saving your playtime for vacation time won't necessarily do the trick, either. "Playing on a vacation is really hard," says Dr. Simonton. "Think of it. I can remember being on vacation and always having to be on schedule. Get the boat back by 4 to be out to dinner by 6 to get back early because you have to get up early. You spend a lot of money and have little fun."

Dr. Simonton admits that putting play into his own life isn't always easy because of his own tendency to work too hard. But he makes time for play on a regular basis.

He suggests people in the doldrums can give themselves a lift by instilling play in their lives on a routine basis. Start with a block of time every day or every week just for play. And *play*. Keep in mind that play is mandatory, not elective.

Overwork and underplay equals depression; overplay and underwork equals fear.

73

Poetry

A new breed of psychotherapist, the poetry therapist, is dispensing verses that may work better than Valium. Whether a person is mildly depressed by everyday cares, or traumatized by rape or cancer, help is available through the poetic prescription.

Nowadays, poetry is used in fields as diverse as mental health and dentistry. Poetry is helping the stressed to relax, the stricken to recover, and the psychotic to relate.

Hooked on Homer, not heroin.

Across the nation, in mental hospitals, drug-abuse clinics, and prisons, poetry is used as a tool to help the severely disturbed face reality. This application seems ironic, at least initially, because people tend to look at a poem as a thing apart from reality. "The truth is, poetry is one of the most effective 'grounding' mechanisms that exists," according to psychiatrist and author Jack J. Leedy, M.D., who has seen "addicts go from being hooked on heroin to being hooked on Hopkins, Herrick, and Homer."

In responding to the words of a poem, patients learn their problems are universal; that somebody—even a long-dead English poet—understands. Fear and rage no longer loom as monsters about to engulf them, but may be seen for what they are: all-too-human emotions.

"Poetry may be utilized in reflecting the inner turbulent mental state experienced by the patient. Thus the inner becomes the outer, or the conscious, making it tangible and workable," explains W. Douglas Hitchings, therapist and contributor to Dr. Leedy's books *Poetry Therapy* and *Poetry the Healer* (both published by Lippincott). When depressed patients are given poems to read, they will often "open up" and start talking about their own emotions while they are talking about a poem.

WARMING UP TO FROST

"Something there is that doesn't love a wall," wrote poet Robert Frost. And, says certified poetry therapist Joy Shieman, poetry is one such thing. "Poetry tears down walls, whether they exist between people, or within ourselves."

Shieman is director of the poetry therapy program at El Camino Hospital, 40 miles south of San Francisco in Mountain View, California. One of the most useful poems in her work is Robert Frost's classic "The Road Not Taken." It is a poem about indecision, an affliction that all of us have experienced at some point in our lives. One depressed woman, after reading it, was able to face the conflicting demands of her husband and job. Another poet prominent in Shieman's work is the late Loren Eiseley, Ph.D., who was also respected as an anthropologist. One of Dr. Eiseley's poems, "The Face of the Lion," has been especially useful.

"It is a poem about a stuffed toy that Dr. Eiseley held as a child, in the dark, when no help ever came," Shieman explains. "In the poem, he confesses how he, grown to be a great man of science, is humble enough to keep the toy, is human enough to still find comfort in its 'shoe-button eyes,' which stare at him from the bookshelf over his desk."

Reading this poem often leads into a discussion of strength, for which the lion provides an excellent metaphor. Shieman, whose list of clients has even included truck drivers, says, "Men respond to this poem because it builds their self-esteem and allows them to accept a part of themselves that may have made them feel embarrassed or guilty. But they learn that true strength is revealed in admitting one's weaknesses."

A poem that builds self-esteem.

Metaphor is unbeatable for projecting a holistic grasp of a situation, agrees Michael Shiryon, Ph.D., chief psychologist in the department of psychiatry at Kaiser Medical Center and Hospital in Oakland, California. In truckers' jargon, a name is a handle. A metaphor is a name that gives you something to hold on to. Metaphor also gives you the opportunity to hold your affliction at arm's length, and look at it from a more objective perspective.

THE ROAD NOT TAKEN*

Two roads diverged in a yellow wood,
And sorry I could not travel both
And be one traveler, long I stood
And looked down one as far as I could
To where it bent in the undergrowth;

Then took the other, as just as fair,
And having perhaps the better claim,
Because it was grassy and wanted wear;
Though as for that the passing there
Had worn them really about the same,

And both that morning equally lay
In leaves no step had trodden black.
Oh, I kept the first for another day!
Yet knowing how way leads on to way,
I doubted if I should ever come back.

I shall be telling this with a sigh
Somewhere ages and ages hence:
Two roads diverged in a wood, and I—
I took the one less traveled by,
And that has made all the difference.

—by Robert Frost

"It's a matter of distancing," Dr. Shiryon explains, "Art, the metaphor, takes your inner feelings and puts them outside so you can review them. Poetry enables us to take a second look, to reframe something in our experience."

Poetry helps foster the proverbial courage to change the things we can, strength to accept what we can't change, and wisdom to know the difference. One of Dr. Shiryon's patients was profoundly affected upon reading William Blake's poem "A Poison Tree."

The patient was moved to express the anger that was poisoning her relationship with her family. "She felt guilt over her feelings of anger, and so she was keeping it inside, breeding resentment and more guilt. The poem helped her to realize that while she had no control over her feelings, she did have control over what she did about them. And that is what counts," Dr. Shiryon says.

A Kentucky social worker learned a similar lesson when poetry helped her to battle breast cancer.

Margaret Massie Simpson discovered she had breast cancer in 1959. After two radical mastectomies, she was moved to chronicle her experience in a book, *Coping with Cancer* (Broadman). Poetry enabled her to cope.

In the hospital for her first operation, Simpson started reading poetry to take her mind off her pain. Within two years, she was writing verses of her own, dwelling heavily on images of water and the sea. She wrote a poem called "Devil Fish," and seemed fixated on a water-skiing trip she had taken shortly before surgery. Later, she told Dr. Leedy she understood the full meaning of her metaphor: She had been drowning in self-pity.

"A few months after surgery, I recognized that my main problem was emotional, not physical," she wrote to Dr. Leedy. "I had thought I was running from death and fear. My problem was that I was afraid of life."

In the meantime, she discovered that the physical benefits of poetry were also very real. "Under cobalt, linear acceleration, and during chemotherapy treatments, I have found that recitation of remembered poetry and the writing of my own poetry have been powerful anesthetizers," she wrote in 1974. "During each crisis or period of pain over the past fifteen years, I have found the writing of poetry a trancelike anesthesia, relieving me from fear and confusion. There was no fear of the operation. There was only anticipa-

Poetry enables us to take a second look.

Poetry helped her beat breast cancer.

A powerful anesthetizer.

A POISON TREE

I was angry with my friend:
I told my wrath, my wrath did end.
I was angry with my foe:
I told it not, my wrath did grow.

And I watered it in fears,
Night & morning with my tears;
And I sunned it with smiles,
And with soft deceitful wiles.

And it grew both day and night
Till it more an apple bright;
And my foe beheld it shine,
And he knew that it was mine.

And into my garden stole
When the night had veiled the pole:
In the morning glad I see
My foe outstretch'd beneath the tree.

—by William Blake

tion of removing the lump, one barrier between me and health. Without fear, I did not develop many of the side difficulties experienced by many other cancer patients, such as the nausea and the pain produced by fear."

Pain induced by the fear of pain is a factor in many types of surgery, not just mastectomies. In Brooklyn, an oral surgeon has found that "poetry could be considered a good substitute for tranquilizing drugs, narcotics, and sedatives in producing preoperative relaxation." Mort Malkin, D.D.S., has an assistant read poems to the patients in his waiting room. "My own judgment was that fear and anxiety were diminished noticeably during the poetry sessions," Dr. Malkin says. "Most patients felt that doctors who were concerned enough about their patients to present poetry in the waiting room would necessarily be more gentle and compassionate. This reduced apprehension even further.

A good substitute for tranquilizing drugs, narcotics, and sedatives.

"And poetry can also help members of the patient's family, who are often just as nervous as the patient."

Dr. Malkin's patients are partial to the poems of Emily Dickinson, Robert Frost, and William Carlos Williams.

BODY RHYTHMS AND RHYME

Poetry doesn't always rhyme, but it does have a rhythm structure that is sometimes unsophisticated, sometimes quite profound, according to Joost A. M. Meerloo, M.D. There is rhythm even in free verse. Verses tend to be clocked to a poet's body rhythms, Dr. Meerloo says, and the poets we like best tend to be those whose body rhythms match our own. Rhythm is what gives poetry its "balancing" effect. Poet Allan Ginsberg links poetry to measured breathing and meditation.

Some people retain their metaphoric capacity; others recover it in old age. Among the elderly, "everyone is a poet, didn't you know?" says Sylvia Baron, editor of *Expanding Horizons,* a literary magazine of poetry and prose that specializes in publishing the works of the elderly. She calls it a forum of "voices of the third age." Some of the most powerful verses of our day are being written by hands so stiff they can barely hold a pen. Older people have the experience and insight that gives them a lot to say, and they have a need to say it. Poetry gives them a way to say it; *Expanding Horizons* gives them a means to be heard.

Everybody is a poet.

BOX 51: A POETIC PRESCRIPTION

"Instead of one aspirin, take two poems," says psychiatrist Jack J. Leedy, M.D. When his patients have trouble getting to sleep, are anxious or depressed, he has found that the following poems work wonders:

For Insomnia:

Hymn to the Night, by Henry Wadsworth Longfellow
A Ballad of Dreamland, by Algernon Charles Swinburne
To Sleep, by William Wordsworth
Oft, in the Stilly Night, by Thomas Moore
Night, by John Whitaker
To Sleep, by John Keats
La Belle Dame Sans Merci, by John Keats
Annabel Lee, by Edgar Allan Poe
Tintern Abbey, by William Wordsworth

For Anxiety:

Anxiety, by Paul F. Whitaker
I'm Nobody! Who Are You? by Emily Dickinson
The Road Not Taken, by Robert Frost
Time, You Old Gypsy Man, by Ralph Hodgson
Ode on a Grecian Urn, by John Keats
The Day Is Done, by Henry Wadsworth Longfellow
Song of Myself, by Walt Whitman
She Dwelt Among the Untrodden Ways, by William Wordsworth
The Lake Isle of Innisfree, by William Butler Yeats

For Depression:

Today, by Thomas Carlyle
Light Shining Out of Darkness, by William Cowper
The Chambered Nautilus, by Oliver Wendell Holmes
The Day Is Done, by Henry Wadsworth Longfellow
On His Blindness, by John Milton
Ode to the West Wind, by Percy Bysshe Shelley
The Celestial Surgeon, by Robert Louis Stevenson
The Eternal Goodness, by John Greenleaf Whittier

"No one gets paid for writing or putting out this biannual magazine," says Baron. "It is a lot of hard work for a few people, and their interest is in improving the literary quality of older people's writing and providing an outlet for them." Baron is a retired schoolteacher living in the Forest Hills section of New York City. Although *Expanding Horizons* was launched in 1977 by an Elderhostel Program at the University of Massachusetts in Amherst, the magazine is now published out of Baron's living room. It's a completely nonprofit, volunteer operation with a subscription cost of $4 per year.

"Writing poetry helps fulfill the will to live on, to continue engaging in worthwhile and satisfying endeavors of an artistic nature or a service nature, and these factors should not be overlooked when we want to consider preventive 'medicine' as one of the goals in life," Baron says. "Writing poetry motivates us to go on living. There is also much pleasure in being published in a worthwhile literary magazine."

Dr. Jack Leedy agrees, adding that there is much pleasure to be gained by subscribing to one—or in keeping a collection of poetry in your medicine chest. Dr. Leedy quotes literary giant Robert Graves, who said that "a well-chosen anthology is a complete dispensary of medicine for the more common mental disorders and may be used as much for prevention as cure."

Writing poetry helps fulfill the will to live on.

74

Solacing Objects

Solacing objects offer us peace in a chaotic world.

W hat do teddy bears, security blankets, and memories have in common?

"They're all *solacing objects*," says Paul C. Horton, M.D., a psychiatrist from Meriden, Connecticut. "They're things that can give us comfort and peace—that can soothe us—in a world that doesn't always seem to offer much comfort or peace. They are, I think, the very essence of life itself."

Recapture that sense of comfort we felt when we were young.

Their power hinges on the fact that they recapture the essence of our childhood, that deep sense of soothing comfort we felt when we were young. Dr. Horton spells out all his ideas on the subject in his book *Solace: The Missing Dimension in Psychiatry* (University of Chicago Press), the result of five years of research, clinical observations, and case studies.

"As infants, we have a very close and emotionally satisfying relationship with our mothers," Dr. Horton writes. "Our needs are being met. We're fed and cared for by a special person who seems to belong to us alone. We learn to anticipate the voice, the look, the cuddling of our mother.

Trust in the world evolves from our special relationship with Mom.

"Because of this special relationship with our mother, we develop a basic trust in others and in the world around us. And this first relationship is so enormously satisfying that it actually becomes a permanent part of ourselves."

EVERYONE'S SECURITY BLANKET

And that's where teddy bears and security blankets come in. As we get a little older—between ages two and six—we're forced to give up the illusion of our mother as our sole possession, and, according to Dr. Horton, we often choose a colorful stuffed animal, a soft blanket, or some other similar object to soothe us and remind us of our all-important first relationship with her. Interestingly, sometimes we choose a "fierce" stuffed animal, like a lion or a tiger, as our special friend, or sometimes we have an imaginary friend we can talk to endlessly.

"But whatever objects we choose," says Dr. Horton, "they are thinly disguised representations of our early satisfying relationship. And they all help us make the transition from our mothers as our entire world to living in the world at large."

The teddy bear is a thinly disguised representation of mother love.

Somewhat older children may choose superhero dolls as their companions. And from about ages 7 through 13, collections of such things as airplane models, beer cans, soldiers, and dolls can be solacing objects. They may help us feel comfort when we're afraid or confused.

"The most difficult and stormy time emotionally is adolescence—the ages between 15 and 25," Dr. Horton says. "The main reason is that it's very hard to find dependable solacing objects. Kids can be depressed and anxious. They're trying to grow up and trying to turn away from their parents. But they're not mature enough to establish mature relationships.

Ages 15 to 25 is the roughest time—emotionally.

"In fact," says Dr. Horton, "adolescents are on a desperate search for solace. The objects they used when they were younger—dolls, stuffed animals—are frowned upon by themselves as just being kids' stuff. So they sometimes turn to dangerous things, such as drugs or alcohol, that can be self-destructive. They also turn to music.

"One of my young patients could hardly string his words together to make sentences. He was very inarticulate. But he could tell me story after story about his favorite rock groups."

IMPORTANT FOR ALL AGES

What does all this mean for adults? A lot. "Solacing objects are important at all stages of life—adulthood as well as childhood," says Dr. Horton. "The objects can be quite different, however. A young person's means of self-soothing are often prominently visible—the teddy bear, for example— and are not hard to identify. But later in life the solacing means are likely to be more subtle.

Objects of affection change from childhood to adulthood.

"Let me tell you about a 55-year-old woman whom I

hypnotized for pain relief. When I asked her to relate a happy event from childhood, she told a story about a train trip she took to meet her father. 'I can still smell the pungent smoke from the steam engine,' she said, 'and I can see and feel the old velvet curtains, mohair seats, and clean white linen; scrambled eggs and ice cream—the latter served in a silver dish—have never tasted so good; the train swaying gently, the clickety-clack, clickety-clack, the sudden clang, clang, clang and whistle and whoosh of a passing engine—all vividly soothing—live on in my memory.'

Vehicles for solace may relieve pain.

"This patient was able to use her childhood memory of a train to provide almost complete relief from pain that narcotic analgesics only partially and unsatisfactorily alleviated," says Dr. Horton. "Indeed, vehicles for solace may relieve all sorts of pains—physical as well as emotional and spiritual. For example, people who are depressed have often simply forgotten, at least temporarily, their means of self-soothing. And identifying a seriously depressed person's characteristic ways of self-soothing and sense of security, and discovering how he or she did it, or tried to do it, just prior to the onset of depression, is frequently as valuable as the prescription of an antidepressant drug."

Dr. Horton's patients come to him for help with a variety of problems: loneliness, unremitting anxiety, panic attacks, boredom, and just a general feeling that life is meaningless. He tries to help them in several different ways. First, he helps them understand that the need for solace is important. In many cases that means showing a patient that being too reality oriented—thinking that we have to be "grown-up" and "realistic" all the time—may make us think that it's somehow childish to need comfort every once in a while.

For some, rereading a favorite book may be soothing.

Second, Dr. Horton helps his patients see that what is solacing for each individual is a very personal matter. For one person, rereading a favorite book may be soothing, for another, a stuffed animal may do the trick, even if the person is an adult.

Dr. Horton also tries to show his patients that having a "safe harbor" in the home is crucial. That may mean simply making time at dinner for a family to talk together quietly rather than argue with each other, or finding time to read together or listen to music together. The point is to try to find an "island of solace" in our daily routines.

"These days, new ways of finding solace are necessary,"

says Dr. Horton. "Some of the solutions for providing comfort during the last two decades—alcohol, drugs, tranquilizers, technological advances, promiscuous sex, upward mobility, and the like—have proved ineffective.

Yesterday's solace—alcohol, drugs, promiscuous sex—have proven ineffective.

"I think we're going to see some interesting trends in seeking solace or comfort. There will be a return to greater intimacy: close and lasting love relationships, friendships, and a reinforcement of family ties. The birth rate may increase because babies are a powerful potential source of solace for some people.

"People will seek jobs that acknowledge family needs," continues Dr. Horton. "High salaries, bonuses, and stock-option plans will not be satisfying enough, and geographic relocation will be resisted. A return to religion will be possible. Music that's soothing and melodic, whether classical or modern, will again be in vogue, as will ballroom dancing. Pets will enjoy a resurgent popularity because they have always been a comfort. Similarly, stuffed animals, blankets, high-quality personalized pillows, and other warm and cuddly objects will be in great demand."

People will seek jobs that acknowledge family needs.

THE "BEAR" FACTS

One man—and about 7,000 other people—takes Dr. Horton's words very, very seriously. The man is Jim Ownby, and the 7,000 others are all members of the nonprofit organization that Ownby founded in 1973: Good Bears of the World.

An organization that takes teddy bear power very seriously.

"We're trying to promote love, friendship, and understanding by providing teddy bears to children and adults in hospitals, institutions, and just about anywhere we find people who need a teddy bear," says the ebullient Ownby. "We believe in teddy bear power!"

Ownby, a journalist, was inspired to begin Good Bears of the World by a story he read about a Lima, Ohio, man named Russell McClean. Confined to a lonely hospital bed during much of his childhood, McClean as an adult decided he would try to help other children in the same predicament. So he organized a program to give a teddy bear to each child admitted to Lima Children's Hospital.

Hospitalized children benefit from solacing objects.

"There's just something about a teddy bear that's impossible to explain," Ownby says. "When you hold one in your arms, you get a feeling of love, comfort, and security.

It's almost supernatural! Also, teddy bears never talk back and they're great listeners."

Good Bears of the World—or GBW, as Ownby likes to call the organization—has really gone international with "Good Bear Dens" not only in America but also in Canada, England, Scotland, Australia, and New Zealand. In the United States there are Good Bear Dens in California, Oregon, Washington, Missouri, Rhode Island, Michigan, New York City, West Virginia, Pennsylvania, and Texas. Hollywood stars such as Jean Simmons and Jane Withers are also supporters of GBW.

"The name for the teddy bear originated with President Theodore Roosevelt," explains Ownby. "On a hunting expedition in 1903, T. R. refused to shoot a cub bear, and *Washington Star* political cartoonist Clifford Berryman immortalized the event with a cartoon of Teddy and the bear cub captioned 'Teddy's Bear.' Well, a toy maker in Brooklyn, New York, designed a stuffed bear and got permission from Teddy Roosevelt to call it a teddy bear.

"So far, the governors of 11 states have proclaimed Teddy Roosevelt's birthday—October 27—as Good Bears Day," says Ownby. "Our main objective is to create a world where peace, love, and understanding play a more forceful role. We're just trying to extend the paw of love to everyone.

"You know, we've discovered that if you ask people, 'Do you have a teddy bear, or would you like to have one,' six out of ten will say yes," adds Ownby. "We'd like to get that number up to ten out of ten!"

For more information about Good Bears of the World, write to: GBW, P.O. Box 8236, Honolulu, HI 96815.

Touch

A fly scoots up and down the entire length of his leg without so much as a swish of interference. It doesn't tickle him. Nor does the grotesquely large ulcer developing on his heel cause him any pain. He is paralyzed from the waist down and sits motionless as he waits.

Suddenly, he recognizes a figure darting across a nearby clearing. It is a woman who is said to have "healing powers." He calls her by name. Within seconds she is at his side scanning his body with open hands. The hands come to rest in the vicinity of his left heel, apparently sensing the large open sore.

Despite the fact that the foot is thickly encased in boot and braces, she lays her hands directly over the area where the ulcer is developing. A few minutes later, the young man remarks of a strange sensation in his leg. He identifies it as a deep penetrating heat. Gradually, over the next few weeks, the ulcer begins to show signs of healing.

Paralyzed, the young man nevertheless feels deep heat where he was touched.

Sound like an Old Testament tale? It's not. It happened recently. And not on the banks of the River Jordan, but on the San Diego campus of the University of California.

The healing hands belong to Dolores Krieger, R.N., Ph.D., a professor of nursing at New York University, who has traveled coast to coast giving a series of workshops on the "therapeutic touch," which is derived from what is traditionally known as the laying on of hands.

The healing hands belong to Dolores Krieger, R.N., Ph.D.

"I have a great deal of confidence in the therapeutic touch, but to tell you the truth, I had my doubts whether I could evoke any sort of response through this young man's mass of braces and heavy shoes," Dr. Krieger explains. "But we had nothing to lose, so I put my mind to it and was able to locate the trouble immediately. Despite the heavy shoes, I could actually feel an energy change.

With no idea what to expect, he experienced the usual sensation.

"What amazed me most was the fact that as a paraplegic, this young man had no feeling in his legs. In addition, he had no idea what to expect from this strange method of treatment. Yet he felt what so many others have said they experienced—a deep sensation of heat. I guess that's why this particular experience stands out in my mind."

NYU TAKES THE LEAD

Dr. Dolores Krieger isn't the only one who's sold on the benefits of the therapeutic touch. New York University (NYU) now offers a fully accredited graduate course at the master's level, designed to formally teach the process of therapeutic touch and to investigate its underlying dynamics. "We call ourselves 'Krieger's Krazies,' because we are all a little bit 'touched,' " Dr. Krieger says.

A scientific evaluation of a well-known healer.

But there's nothing in the course or the mechanics behind the therapeutic touch to indicate that there's any sort of joke involved. Dolores Krieger is perfectly serious as she describes her first encounter with healing. It was a research assignment in which the well-known healer Oskar Estebany was scientifically evaluated.

"My particular job was concerned with taking case histories, vital signs, etc. But that gave me an excellent opportunity for observing Estabany and the patients during the treatments," Dr. Krieger explains. "I didn't see much happening. I didn't see anything dramatic. Estebany engaged in no extraordinary maneuvers or incantations as my imagination had led me to expect. Rather he sat quietly beside the person he was treating and simply laid his hands on the patient in some area he felt was important to the particular case. About 20 to 25 minutes later the treatment was ended, and the patient left, to come the next day if it was felt his condition warranted it.

A greater-than-chance number of people got well.

"This seemed to be a very straightforward, simple—almost casual—procedure and so you can imagine my surprise when follow-up reports showed that a greater-than-chance number of these patients got well."

Was the "power of suggestion" at play here? Maybe in

part, but there's definitely more to it than that, says Dr. Krieger. In the early sixties, Dr. Bernard Grad, a geriatrics researcher at McGill University's Allan Memorial Institute in Montreal, studied the effects of Estebany's touch on wounded laboratory mice and in experiments with flasks of barley seeds soaked in a salt solution to simulate a "sick" condition.

Animals and plants, he reasoned, cannot be persuaded by optimistic voice or a suggestive gesture. Yet in Dr. Grad's experiments, the animals healed more rapidly and the barley seeds sprouted more quickly and grew taller, greener plants with the help of Estebany's healing hands. The touch was clearly the crucial factor. But how does it work?

The touch was clearly the crucial factor.

FEELING FOR TEMPERATURE CHANGE

A review of the literature and of her own personal findings led Dr. Krieger to suspect that there may be some type of energy transfer involved. For one thing, temperature is key. Healers initially scan the entire body searching for an area of temperature change. This is a sure indication that something is amiss. Then, when the healer lays his or her hands over this "sick" area, the patient is the one to sense a change in temperature. Even those who do not know what to expect profess a feeling of deep heat in the area being touched.

Secondly, it isn't necessary for the healer to make skin contact in therapeutic touch in order for the patient to experience the feeling of heat. All that is necessary is for the hands to hover over the "sick" area while the healer is in a state of deep concentration known as "intentionality"—to make field contact.

It isn't necessary for the healer to make skin contact.

It was also noticed that healthy persons treated with laying on of hands feel nothing unusual. It's only those who are sick who seem to absorb whatever it is that radiates from the healer's hands.

From the above observations, Dr. Krieger and other researchers have theorized that all people probably radiate some energy. Healthy persons have an abundance of it, and sick persons, a deficit. In order to heal, a healthy person must be able to transfer his or her energy to the afflicted area of the other in order to effect a repatterning of energy.

All healthy people radiate energy. The trick is to direct it through the hands.

"To my way of thinking, the real role of the healer is relative to his potential to effectively direct energy," the NYU professor says. "All healthy people radiate some degree of energy, but much of it goes off randomly. The trick is to direct it through hands with intentionality."

Does this energy transfer evoke any measurable biological change? Dr. Dolores Krieger came up with the rather interesting theory that hemoglobin values may be altered. Hemoglobin is a part of the red blood cells responsible for oxygen uptake and distribution in the cells. Chlorophyll, the substance responsible for the green coloring in plants, works in a similar fashion, which would explain why Dr. Grad's "healed" barley seeds produced greener plants.

A pilot test confirmed Dr. Krieger's theory. She later repeated the study using 32 registered nurses and 64 patients of a hospital in the metropolitan New York area. The nurses were divided into two groups: The first group was taught the therapeutic touch, the second group wasn't. Group I practiced the therapeutic touch on their patients, while group II did not. Hemoglobin values for all patients were determined prior to the study and again while the study was in progress. To reduce possible bias, the lab technicians at the health facility were not informed of the study.

Hemoglobin levels rose in patients treated with the therapeutic touch.

Again, the theory was strongly supported. In all patients treated with the therapeutic touch, hemoglobin levels rose, while in those receiving only the standard nursing care, hemoglobin levels remained fairly stable.

Exactly how hemoglobin levels help to accelerate the healing process has yet to be determined. But at least we now have scientific proof that something very real is happening.

"Unfortunately, the legitimate reports get buried under mountains of sensational misnomers," says Lawrence LeShan, Ph.D., a psychologist who has spent years investigating psychic healing. "But after you discard the 95 percent of the claims which could have been due to hysterical change, suggestion, bad experimental design, poor memory, and plain chicanery, a solid residue remains."

LOVE—THE HEALING FORCE

Dr. LeShan assembled a group of serious healers from the "solid residue" and noted certain similarities among their healing techniques. In all instances he found healers went through certain behaviors inside their heads. This is typically characterized by an intense feeling of love and caring for the individual who is being touched.

The healer feels intense love and caring for the person being touched.

One very successful healer has said, "Only love can generate the healing fire." Another has explained: "We must care. We must care for others deeply and urgently, wholly and immediately; our minds, our spirits must reach out to them."

One's potential to heal, then, depends on the capacity to care. That explains why some people can direct their energy toward healing more effectively than others. And why some people have more success when they direct it toward someone they care for.

One's potential to heal depends on the capacity to care.

Mothers do it inherently. Lovers do it without a second thought.

Those who truly love know the secret of the therapeutic touch. And to the object of their affections, that tender loving care may be more than a luxury in life—it may be a necessity.

Anthropologist Ashley Montagu, Ph.D., believes that our survival depends in part on our being touched. In his book *Touching: The Human Significance of the Skin* (Harper & Row), Dr. Montagu writes: "During the nineteenth century more than half the infants in their first year of life regularly died from a disease called marasmus, a Greek word meaning 'wasting away.' . . . As late as the second decade of the twentieth century the death rate for infants under one year of age in various foundling institutions throughout the United States was nearly 100 percent.

Our survival depends on touch.

"It wasn't until after World War II, when studies were undertaken to discover the cause of marasmus, that it was found to occur quite often among babies in the 'best' homes, hospitals, and institutions. . . . Babies in the poorest homes, with a good mother, despite the lack of hygienic physical conditions, often overcame the physical handicaps and flourished. What was wanting in the sterilized environment of the first class and was generously supplied to babies of the second class was mother love. . . . What a child requires if it is to prosper, it was found, is to be handled, and carried, and caressed, and cuddled, and cooed to even if it isn't breastfed.

"Recognizing this in the late twenties, several hospital

pediatricians began to introduce a regular regimen of 'mothering' in their wards. . . . At Bellevue Hospital in New York, following the institution of 'mothering' in the pediatric wards, the mortality rates for infants under one year fell from 30 to 35 percent to less than 10 percent by 1938."

A husband's tender touch in the delivery room may be more than a psychological boost.

Judging from that evidence, the presence of a loving husband in the delivery room who touches, caresses, and comforts his wife during labor and delivery may in fact prove more than a psychological boost. Although there is no scientific data to substantiate the physiological benefits of a husband's tender touch during delivery, more and more hospitals are coming to realize the advantage of having a caring partner lend a hand.

Doris Haire, president of the American Foundation for Maternal and Child Health, explains that some hospitals actually *encourage* pregnant women to bring a close relative into the delivery room—if not a husband, then a sister or even a close friend. If a woman does not have a companion along when she enters Grady Memorial Hospital in Atlanta, says Haire, one of a group of caring volunteers will gladly come in and comfort her during labor.

AN INSTINCTIVE, EVERYDAY NEED

Caring, loving, and reaching out to touch other human beings should be part of our everyday existence. "It wells up from a basic and instinctive need to help," says Dr. Dolores Krieger.

Everything is experienced through touch.

Psychologist James Lynch, Ph.D., in studying the effects of human contact on health, has spent hours in coronary care units observing patients threatened with the possibility of sudden death. "I have been struck," he writes, "by the way that most people finally say good-bye. They will speak to each other, if the patient is physically able, usually in subdued tones; they will try to make every effort to appear confident, and sometimes they will even joke. But when they say good-bye, it is almost as if some deep, primitive, instinctive ritual takes over. . . . Just before leaving, they will stop speaking and silently hold the patient's hand or touch his body or even stand at the food of the bed and hold the patient's foot" (*The Broken Heart: The Medical Consequences of Loneliness,* Basic Books). Words somehow seem insufficient for the moment; everything is expressed in a touch.

John G. Bruhn, Ph.D., dean of the school of allied health sciences at the University of Texas Medical Branch in Galveston, thinks that human contact is exactly what's missing in modern doctor-patient relationships. Developments in medical technology and the introduction of new kinds of health professionals trained to examine patients have seriously reduced the amount of touching that goes on between doctor and patient, he believes.

Human contact is missing from most doctor-patient relationships.

In an article on this trend, Dr. Bruhn writes: "The quality of health care depends not only on how well physicians and other health professionals perform their tasks and the reliability of the technologies they use, but also on their ability to be human. To touch and be touched is part of the process of staying well or getting well" *(Southern Medical Journal)*.

To touch and be touched is part of the healing process.

"In folk medicine in many cultures, there is a lot of touching involved," Dr. Bruhn says, "and it humanizes the medical process."

Dr. Dolores Krieger couldn't agree more. "The need to help, I feel, is probably the most humane of human characteristics. It lies very close to the central motivations that bring most people into nursing. . . . In fact, therapeutic touch, I believe, is a tool frequently used by nurses in their care of patients either knowledgeably or unconsciously."

Index

sources of, 9
stress and, 15
Vitamin B$_{12}$
  acetylcholine and, 2
  benefits of, 6-8
  brain and, 43-44
  mania and, 53-55
  nervous system and, 54
  problems benefiting from, 8*b*
  psychosis and, 6
  sources of, 9
Vitamin B$_{12}$ deficiency, psychiatric
  manifestations of, 7, 54
Vitamin C
  brain function and, 43-44
  factors destroying, 15
  histamine and, 61
  problems benefiting from, 8
  schizophrenia and, 58-59
  sources of, 9
  stress and, 15-16
Vitamin dependency, 58
Vitamin E, problems benefiting from, 8
Vitamins
  alcohol and, 15
  coffee and, 15
  smoking and, 15
  stress and, 14
  sugar-fighting, 372
Vitamin supplements
  afternoon, benefits of, 347
  safety of, 13
Volunteer work
  elderly and, 123
  health and, 121, 123

W
Waking up, 335-42
  breakfast for, 340-41
  chemicals and, 336
  exercise and, 339
  loofah rub for, 340
  motivation for, 342

nature for, 339
stretching for, 338-39
tape recording for, 340
Warmth
  migraine headache and, 591-92
  role of, in autogenic training, 607
Warts
  emotional stress and, 615
  hypnosis and, 615-16
Water, therapeutic properties of, 290-92,
  589
Wealth, Hassle Factor and, 234
Weight gain
  food allergy and, 37
  as insulation against hurt, 486
Weight loss
  clothing and, 485-86
  exercising and, 443
  key to, 487
  mental first-aid for, 483
  nutritional needs for, 8*b*
  positive thinking and, 482
  psychology of successful, 482-87
  self-esteem and, 484
Well-being
  beyond physical, 507-16
  control over, 529
White hair, preventing and treating, 587
Will to live
  defining, 543
  play and, 666
Wish, life, 543-48
Wishful thinking
  problem solving and, 464-66
  unconscious fears and, 245
Withdrawal
  from smoking, symptoms of, 378-79
  stress and, 276
Women
  agoraphobia and, 172
  expression of anger by, 152, 579
  heart disease and, 210
  hormonal fluctuation in, 442

You'r